To Rex —
Thought you'd
enjoy these autobiographies —
With love,
Jane + Erskine
Christmas 1999

EDITED BY AMY MANDELKER

& ELIZABETH POWERS

*With an Introduction
by Madeleine L'Engle*

A TOUCHSTONE BOOK

PILGRIM SOULS

AN ANTHOLOGY OF
SPIRITUAL AUTOBIOGRAPHIES

PUBLISHED BY SIMON & SCHUSTER

TOUCHSTONE
Rockefeller Center
1230 Avenue of the Americas
New York, NY 10020

TOUCHSTONE and colophon are
registered trademarks of Simon & Schuster Inc.

Designed by Pei Loi Koay

Manufactured in the United States of America

10   9   8   7   6   5   4   3   2   1

Library of Congress Cataloging-in-Publication Data
Pilgrim souls : an anthology of spiritual autobiographies /
edited by Amy Mandelker and Elizabeth Powers ;
with an introduction by Madeleine L'Engle.
    p. cm.
  "A Touchstone book."
  1. Spiritual biography. 2. Christian
biography. I. Mandelker, Amy. II. Powers,
Elizabeth, date.
BL72.P55   1999
291.4'092'2—dc21   98-40813 CIP
[b]
ISBN 0-684-84311-0

The editors gratefully acknowledge permission from the following sources to reprint material in their control: Bibliotheca Persica for prayers by Rāb'a al'Adawīya, in Farid al-Din Attar, *Muslim Saints and Mystics*, tr. A. J. Arberry, University of Chicago Press, 1966. Chosen Books, Inc., a division of Baker Book House, for Charles W. Colson, *Born Again*, copyright © 1976, 1977, and 1995 by Charles Colson. Farrar, Straus & Giroux, Inc., for Madeleine L'Engle, *A Circle of Quiet*, copyright © 1972 by Crosswicks, Ltd. Farrar, Straus & Giroux, Inc., and Harold Matson, Inc., for excerpts from Flannery O'Connor "To Cecil Dawkins, 9 December 58," "To Louise Abbot, [undated] Sat. 1959," "To 'A,' 28 October 61," and "To Alfred Corn, 30 May 62" in *The Habit of Being: Letters*, ed. by Sally Fitzgerald, copyright © 1979 by Regina O'Connor. Harcourt Brace & Company for Thomas Merton, *The Seven Storey Mountain*, copyright 1948 by Harcourt Brace & Company and renewed 1976 by The Trustees of the Merton Legacy Trust. Harcourt Brace & Company and Faber and Faber for T. S. Eliot, "Ash Wednesday," in *Collected Poems, 1909–1962*, copyright 1930 and renewed 1958 by T. S. Eliot. HarperCollins Publishers, Inc., for Annie Dillard, *Holy*

CONTINUED ON PAGE 544

To my parents, both biological
and spiritual
—A.M.B.

To Richard Sussman, who sustains me
with solace, support, and joy in all
my endeavors
—E.P.

ACKNOWLEDGMENTS

We would like to acknowledge the invaluable assistance and encouragement of many friends and colleagues who shared their knowledge and time and generously made their libraries available to us: Professor Pamela Bleisch, Rev. and Mrs. Richard Burnett, Professor Clare Carroll, Charlotte Jones, Stephen O'Brien, John Pilsner, Rev. and Mrs. Tracy Troxel, and Micheline Watrous. Professor Caryl Emerson read through the entire manuscript in progress, taking time away from writing her own books to provide unflagging collegial support. Carole Sussman offered good-humored assistance to Elizabeth Powers in the preparation of headnotes. A special credit is due to Cyrus Moore for his new translation of the notoriously complex and intricate poetry of Sor Juana Inés de la Cruz. We are also grateful to research assistant Seth Young. Our deepest thanks are also due to the best of agents, Sheree Bykofsky, who has encouraged and nourished this project from its earliest stages. Caroline Sutton's patience and astute editorial guidance transformed a roughly conceived project into a finished book. The expert and thorough copyediting assistance of Ted Landry and Carole McCurdy of Simon & Schuster and of Janet Rosen of Sheree Bykofsky Associates is deeply appreciated. Amy Mandelker especially thanks her son, Nicholas, whose willingness to occupy himself with chess and artwork during long hours of manuscript production made possible her contribution to this book.

CONTENTS

INTRODUCTION BY MADELEINE L'ENGLE   13

EDITORS' PREFACE   15
Fashioning the Soul: The Shape of Spiritual Autobiography

PART ONE: WANDERERS & SEEKERS   21

KING DAVID, THE PSALMIST   25
From the Psalms

SAINT AUGUSTINE   38
From *The Confessions*

LEO TOLSTOY   48
From *A Confession*

EMILY DICKINSON   65
Selected Poems

JORIS-KARL HUYSMANS   70
From *En Route*

JOHANNES JØRGENSEN   85
From His Autobiography

SERGEI BULGAKOV   91
From His Autobiography

THOMAS MERTON   97
From *The Seven Storey Mountain*

MADELEINE L'ENGLE   117
From *A Circle of Quiet*

CHARLES W. COLSON   126
From *Born Again*

ELDRIDGE CLEAVER   138
From *Soul on Fire*

KATHLEEN NORRIS   141
From *Dakota: A Spiritual Geography*

PART TWO: PILGRIMS & MISSIONARIES   147

MOSES   151
  From Exodus and Deuteronomy
SAINT PAUL   161
  From His Letters
MARTIN LUTHER   166
  From His Writings
SAINT IGNATIUS OF LOYOLA   170
  From *Saint Ignatius's Own Story*
RABBI LEON MODENA   175
  From *The Life of Judah*
ANNE BRADSTREET   185
  A Letter to My Children
ARCHPRIEST AVVAKUM   190
  From *The Life of Archpriest Avvakum by Himself*
JOHN BUNYAN   201
  From *Grace Abounding*
JONATHAN EDWARDS   210
  Personal Narrative
JOHN WESLEY   221
  From *The Journal of John Wesley*
DAVID LIVINGSTONE   228
  From *Missionary Travels and Researches in South
  Africa*
ANONYMOUS RUSSIAN PILGRIM   230
  From *The Way of a Pilgrim*
CHRISTINA ROSSETTI   243
  From *Maude*
ALBERT SCHWEITZER   256
  From *Out of My Life and Thought: An Autobiography*
DAG HAMMARSKJÖLD   260
  From *Markings*

PART THREE: MYSTICS & VISIONARIES   263

RĀBI'A AL-'ADAWĪYA   267
  From Her Prayers
DANTE ALIGHIERI   269
  From *La vita nuova*

JULIAN OF NORWICH   279
  From *Showings*

SAINT TERESA OF AVILA   290
  From *The Book of Her Life*

SAINT JOHN OF THE CROSS   304
  From On a Dark Night

JOHN DONNE   313
  From *Devotions Upon Emergent Occasions, Dedication, First
  Meditation and Prayer, Number One*

BROTHER LAWRENCE   318
  From *The Practice of the Presence of God*

SAINT MARGARET MARY ALACOQUE   324
  From Her Letters

JEANE MARIE DE LA MOTTE-GUYON   332
  From Her Autobiography

FRANCIS THOMPSON   338
  The Hound of Heaven

HENRIETTA GANT   344
  Narrative of Her Baptism

SAINT THÉRÈSE DE LISIEUX   350
  From *The Story of a Soul*

ANNIE DILLARD   364
  From *Holy the Firm*

PART FOUR: PHILOSOPHERS & SCHOLARS   375

SOCRATES   379
  From *The Apology*

MARCUS AURELIUS   386
  From *Meditations*

ABŪ HĀMID MUHAMMAD GHAZĀLĪ (ALGAZALI)   393
  From *Deliverance from Error*

PETRARCH   399
  The Ascent of Mount Ventoux

SOR JUANA INÉS DE LA CRUZ   408
  First Dream

BLAISE PASCAL   421
  The Memorial

BENJAMIN FRANKLIN   423
  From *The Autobiography*

SAMUEL JOHNSON   432
  Prayers and Meditations

JOHN HENRY CARDINAL NEWMAN   439
  From *Apologia pro vita sua*

GERARD MANLEY HOPKINS   444
  Selected Poems

PAUL CLAUDEL   452
  My Conversion

T. S. ELIOT   458
  Ash-Wednesday

C. S. LEWIS   466
  From *Surprised by Joy*

VIKTOR E. FRANKL   487
  From Experiences in a Concentration Camp

SIMONE WEIL   498
  A Spiritual Autobiography

SHELDON VANAUKEN   513
  From *A Severe Mercy*

DENISE LEVERTOV   531
  Selected Poems

FLANNERY O'CONNOR   538
  From Her Letters

INTRODUCTION BY MADELEINE L'ENGLE

At this strange time in the century when we are hurtling towards a new millennium (with considerable trepidation), it is a comfort to read words from the heart of those who have gone before us and who have asked many of the questions we ask. Those who give the fewest answers seem the closest to us, brothers and sisters who share our concerns about God and the universe and flawed and faulty human beings. Flawed and faulty, yes, but fascinating!

In reading a spiritual autobiography like Tolstoy's, our own is widened and enlarged. We learn from each other what to hold on to and what to let go. Tolstoy said, "Live, seeking God, for there can be no life without God." Tolstoy's own search for God was often at the expense of his family. I was fascinated, when in Russia, to see the family line-up in Tolstoy's house, bedrooms plain and monastic for those of the children who agreed with Papa and bedrooms with French furniture and fancy bed- and window-dressings for those who agreed with Mama, giving the impression that it was a divided household and not a happy one. Our spirits develop in strange and unexpected ways, and it helps to know that we are not alone on the journey.

What a treasure is *Pilgrim Souls: An Anthology of Spiritual Autobiographies.* We start with David and the Psalms, amazing in their variety, their uninhibited love of God and equally uninhibited anger and angst. From "My God, my God, why have you forsaken me," to "The Lord is my Shepherd; I shall not want," our own autobiography responds . . . and continues to do so as we read Kathleen Norris and the strange beauty of *Dakota.*

We look back to that first amazing pilgrim, Moses, shy, stuttering, unable to believe that he can do all that God calls him to do and yet who is able to talk with God in the dark, to have a close friendship with the Lord, who helps us to understand the mystery of our spirits. Turning the pages, we move on to Dag Hammarskjöld, who managed to keep the United Nations on its pilgrimage, in a world as strange and secular as was that of Moses. It is a logical and musical journey from Rābi'a al-'Adawīya and her amazing prayers to Annie Dillard with her vision that is sometimes comic, sometimes tragic, and often a strange mixture of both.

From the great Socrates to Sheldon Vanauken, simply to list the men and women whose spiritual autobiographies are quoted is to tantalize. I may not agree with all the seekers, even some of those who are best known. Some are selfish, takers, rather than givers, though many, to our relief, are mixtures of both. I am more stirred by Hammarskjöld and Schweitzer than by Augustine and Newman, perhaps because I need to be taught that my own spiritual autobiography is thin unless it is part of a company much larger than my own.

This is indeed a marvelous anthology, not only massive in size but rich in depth. David, the sweet singer of the Psalms, says, "The Spirit of the Lord spake by me, and the word was on my tongue." This is true of most of the speakers who understand how to listen to God as well as to speak what they have heard. It is encouraging to listen to these seekers speak to us in their own voices. All our spiritual needs are addressed, and flipping through the pages is a joy. It is even better to start at the beginning and read slowly, for these spiritual autobiographies are nourishing and should not be gulped without thinking and deep appreciation.

This is a book to be kept on the bed table, close at hand. I am grateful indeed for the time Amy Mandelker and Elizabeth Powers have spent compiling it. It is a great and needed gift.

EDITORS' PREFACE

FASHIONING THE SOUL:

THE SHAPE OF SPIRITUAL

AUTOBIOGRAPHY

The idea for this book originated in a chance conversation between two literature professors lamenting the absence of a comprehensive anthology of spiritual autobiographies. We had both noticed that autobiography—the story of the formation of a self—is one of the most enduring genres of Western literature. Historically, writers view the self as a soul; for them the story of their life is a spiritual autobiography. Continuing this tradition, many contemporary authors write from a subjective framework: personal journalism and criticism, memoirs and family histories, spiritual journeys and geographies have all become popular. Yet where was the collection of spiritual autobiographies for interested readers, writers, students, and teachers? We felt they needed a volume that would be historically comprehensive, including the classics of the genre, and up-to-date, presenting the most recent writing of this kind.

In compiling this anthology, we began by asking: What is the source of personal writing about the inner life? When do stories about the self begin to be told? How did such writing develop historically? Unlike sister genres —travelogues, family memoirs—spiritual autobiographies focus on events and experiences that shape the inner person in relationship to God. The authors of spiritual autobiographies concentrate on examining their interior experiences in order to discover coherence, structure, and meaning in the shape of an individual life.

Most scholars locate the sources of spiritual autobiography in the personal histories of antiquity and in the Christian traditions of confession, profession of faith, and personal testimony. Early versions of these forms originate in the preclassical world, where the only individuals thought to be worth writing about were kings, pharaohs, or military heroes. These official histories and epics related public deeds as the justification for glory and honor; the individual's character or soul did not come under scrutiny.

When did attention begin to turn to examining one's inner life? Perhaps with the philosophical autobiographies of thinkers like Socrates or Marcus Aurelius. Their quest for truth and understanding involved self-examination and an active effort to resolve the moral and spiritual conflicts in the individual psyche, or soul.

The Wisdom books and histories of the Hebrew Bible bear a different emphasis, reflecting the development of monotheism. Solomon, the author of Ecclesiastes, rejects the idea that individuals can find meaning in life through their own efforts. Even the heroes and leaders of the Israelites, far from being glorified, are depicted in all their human frailty: Jacob was a deceiver, David an adulterer and murderer, Moses also a murderer who stammered and was afraid to appear in public. The source of wisdom for these figures is external; what shapes their lives and souls is the pursuit of God.

Although the foundations for the modern form of spiritual autobiography were established by Saint Paul in the New Testament, the most significant figure in its evolution is Saint Augustine, whose *Confessions* influenced many of the authors in this collection: Petrarch, Saint Teresa of Avila, John Bunyan, C. S. Lewis, and others. Most spiritual autobiographies adhere to the Augustinian formula, itself a revised and amplified version of Saint Paul's story. The basic plot structure contains four parts: (1) a description of the individual's life before spiritual awakening, (2) an account of the events leading up to the individual's encounter with God, (3) a description of the actual encounter with God and the impact of this event on the narrator, and (4) a celebration of the new life following this event. There are few surprises or changes in this basic story line, even in such modern revisitations as those by Paul Claudel, Leo Tolstoy, or Kathleen Norris.

Since most European and American spiritual autobiographies are crafted within the Judeo-Christian tradition, the reader should understand the supernatural terms of these texts and what was at stake for their writers. Although many of the authors refer to their works as "confessions," the meaning is not limited to the idea of penitence alone, nor is the question of guilt or criminality central to the genre. This form of spiritual autobiography is, more accurately, a type of testimonial intended to sway the reader to the author's way of belief, through what has been described as "first-person evangelization." The idea of providing witness reappears in the term *personal testimony*, introduced by the American Puritans.

Personal testimony conveys the almost legal idea of deposition or witness. Saint Paul's spiritual autobiographies were actually delivered in his own self-defense before Jewish and Roman tribunals. In a personal testimony, the confessor describes the radical changes that have taken place in himself and bears witness to the conversion that transformed his aimless life to a life dedicated to God. Yet the personal testimony is more than a conversion narrative, as it continues to relate the spiritual progress and growth of the confessor as a proof of God's power.

For writers of the medieval and Renaissance periods, moral struggle within the soul was described dramatically, with different characters taking on the roles of inner emotional states. In the courtly romance, spiritual goals were embodied in the form of an unattainable beloved. Personal accounts of spiritual struggles were often couched in terms of a dialogue between the individual and a spiritual confessor, as in Petrarch's confessional works, or between a troubador and his lady, as in Dante's *La vita nuova*.

During the Reformation, personal testimony of a spiritual conversion was crucial evidence of individual predestination, proving that one had been preselected by God for salvation. For the American Puritan communities, an individual's testimony was not only to be documented in prose, but was also to be verified by visible transformations of the individual's heart, mind, and actions. A convincing personal testimony was the requirement for church membership, and for inclusion among the community's "elect." The ultimate stakes, however, were even higher: eternal salvation or damnation. Many Christian writers stress that a godly life should supersede material pursuits, even to the point of apparent folly, as in the case of Saint Francis, who abandoned wealth and position to embrace poverty and service to a leper colony. Writers of spiritual autobiographies proclaim that what was previously of value is now of little reckoning in contrast to attaining the coveted "pearl of great price." The authors of spiritual autobiographies from Saint Paul to Albert Schweitzer sound this same note: after a spiritual rebirth, the absorptions and pleasures of their earlier lives appear empty and tasteless.

The Enlightenment transformed European and American life by eroding spiritual certainties, yet the formulaic structure of spiritual autobiography, where an enlightened narrator reviews a dismal past, continued in secular writing and fiction. Modern writers begin with a more skeptical attitude toward the possibility of obtaining a genuine understanding of themselves or their lives. The very process of writing about oneself is called into question. C. S. Lewis, for example, lamented that "even keeping a daily journal" was of little use, as events appear meaningful only in retrospect, so that unrecorded trivial occurrences might later prove to be of tantamount importance.

This uncertainty about knowing oneself or others pervades modern and postmodern thought and literature. Contemporary spiritual autobiographies have a secular starting point and are no longer based in a conventionally religious worldview. Curiously, this brings these works closer to their antecedents in antiquity, such as those by Saint Augustine and others who sought God while living in a pagan world. As Nietzsche wrote, the "shadow of God" persists, even in a faithless world; writers who reject organized religion, for instance, Simone Weil, continue to characterize their spiritual experiences in the very terms they seek to escape. Postmodern writers avoid any type of plotline that would suggest they subscribe to a discarded world view; their inner journeys are described quite differently, delighting in the uncertainties of time, space, and objects, as in Annie Dillard's free-form meditation on holiness.

In selecting works for this anthology, we have tried to identify and include the major classical works of Western spiritual autobiography. We have also searched for works that were written from an outsider's perspective, such as Jewish, colonial, or slave narratives. Whenever possible, we have presented complete or lightly edited texts. Each work is introduced by an informative head-note.

Four major types of spiritual quests and personal histories are presented here: wanderers and seekers, pilgrims and missionaries, mystics and visionaries, and philosophers and scholars. These designations do not necessarily indicate an author's occupation or identity; rather, they are meant to describe the writer's approach to the spiritual and supernatural.

The first type, wanderers and seekers, includes authors whose personal stories relate a sometimes feverish exploration of all available experiences and world views. Exhausting the enjoyment of "things under the sun" and perceiving the collapse of philosophies and ideologies, seekers cast themselves upon the spiritual truth that brings them to their authentic self. Typical of this group is the poet and Trappist monk Thomas Merton, who was attracted by communism, journalism, art, and philosophy before turning to the contemplative life.

The second, and perhaps most familiar, type of spiritual autobiography is written by pilgrims and missionaries. These stories describe individuals whose life goal has been the unwavering pursuit of God and holiness. Whatever sufferings or martyrdom they endure, these pilgrim souls, represented here by the writings of Saint Paul, Jonathan Edwards, Archpriest Avvakum, and others, remain unvanquished, even rejoicing in the opportunity to display their enduring faith despite trials and adversity.

Perhaps the most unworldly type of spiritual autobiography is written by mystics and visionaries, who focus on supernatural experiences and epiphanies. These writers' lives unfold not in actual events but in moments of ecstatic prayer and visionary meditation. Historically, many of these visionaries have been found in the Carmelite order of the Roman Catholic Church: Saint Teresa of Avila, Brother Lawrence, Saint John of the Cross, Saint Thérèse de Lisieux. But there have been other ecstatic responses, as in the poetry of John Donne or the slave narrative of Henrietta Gant.

Finally, the accounts of scholars and philosophers demonstrate a lifelong commitment to the discernment of truth through the exercise of the intellect. These writers, thinkers, and poets—such as Marcus Aurelius, Benjamin Franklin, C. S. Lewis, Gerard Manley Hopkins, and Denise Levertov—seek to anchor spiritual convictions in intellectual certainties and to claim the possibility of a rationally established faith.

The readings within each section span over two millennia and several continents. Although these authors are separated culturally, historically, and linguistically, they are connected in their efforts to respond to Socrates's challenge to "know thyself" and in their belief that "the unexamined life is not worth living." Saint Augustine's starting point, "I became a great question for myself," is the impetus for each of these authors as they pursue spiritual enlightenment in order to gain understanding of their lives. In looking backward, they try to pick out that connecting thread of significant events which Henry James called "the figure in the carpet." Modern skepticism may question whether such a thread exists in any sense other than that supplied by the recuperative powers of hindsight. But there are moments of self-assessment and reflection when a person may step outside the flow of experience to ascribe meaning and give shape to the past. The authors presented here have given expression to this activity in some of the greatest examples of introspective spiritual writing in the Western tradition. It is a tribute to the power of their writing and their passion to define the transcendent that we find their works still speak with power and immediacy.

Amy Mandelker and Elizabeth Powers

PART ONE

WANDERERS
& SEEKERS

THE AUTHORS IN THIS SECTION DESCRIBE A SEARCH FOR WHAT
T. S. Eliot called "the still point in the turning world." Many of these
writers begin with the intention of gaining understanding. The promise
of discovering the ultimate answers often leads them through a course of
engagements of a sexual or political nature. In the end, they are forced
to face the sterility of these pursuits. Despite the wide chronological
sweep of these selections, the narratives are remarkably similar in re-
counting journeys, both actual or imaginative, that lead to weariness and
spiritual dead-ends. Saint Augustine in the fourth century, for example,
explored divination and astrology as well as the major pagan philosophies,
only to become increasingly despairing before embracing faith in God.
Fifteen centuries later, Johannes Jørgensen traveled a similar path, likewise experiencing disillusionment in his espousal of utilitarianism, aes-
theticism, and nihilism.

These authors speak of a renewal that occurs only after the self seems
utterly depleted by its pursuit of systems that promised encompassing
solutions to life's vexing problems. The confessional nature of this writing provides examples of some of the most intense dissection of the
human soul. The contrast between the condition of the unredeemed self
on a path of despair and the attraction of a new life and spiritual maturity
lends dramatic power to some of the accounts, especially those that trace
the course of a prodigal life and a chastened return.

The tendency of authors writing in this confessional vein, exposing
the worst about themselves, accords with important changes in the as-
sessment of personality occurring in the West from the advent of Christianity. David the Psalmist was intensely aware of the presence of an
omniscient deity who saw into his heart and from whose wrath there
was no escape. Christianity sought to spread this awareness through its
emphasis on self-searching and cultivation of the soul, both of which
were essential for the attainment of individual salvation. Such self-

examination and therapeutic confession became, in turn, the starting point for the later development of secular autobiography.

The greatest work of self-scrutiny, of reflection on personal experience, was written at the end of antiquity: *The Confessions* of Saint Augustine. In this analysis of the soul's struggle for goodness—and for the first time in literary history—a ruthless and probing light was cast on the irrational and habitual forces of personality and human nature that conspire to keep us abject and to damage the soul's potential for growth and maturation. For the Greeks, the path to the Good was one that could be discovered through study, meditation, and training. Their philosophical writings, however, particularly those of the Stoics, testify to the frequent failure of reason and the intellect in this quest. The modern examples in this section convey the failure of worldly philosophies, despite the promise of these systems of thought to better man's material nature, to still a human craving for a purposeful ordering of life that is beyond rational calculation. The wanderers' and seekers' stories of despair and confusion end not because the mind has willed it, but because the heart says yes. These stories document the intensity of that dramatic turning to the quiet center and the powerful sensation of rescue from the point of no return, which Leo Tolstoy described so vividly as rowing against the current with his back to the waterfall and his face turned toward God.

[EP]

Attested author of seventy-seven of the 150 psalms in the Hebrew Old Testament, David was a shepherd and favored minstrel to King Saul until anointed as the next King of Israel by the prophet Samuel. Despite an intimate relationship with Saul's son, Jonathan, and his astonishing singlehanded victory over the Philistine giant Goliath, David was forced into exile to flee King Saul's wrath. Wandering from one hiding place to another, he was repeatedly pursued by Saul's men, who sought to destroy him. David's perseverance resulted in his coronation in 1010 B.C. Within seven years, he united the kingdom and became the first king to rule over all Israel.

The psalms presented here are those that Biblical scholars generally agree relate to specific events in David's life: his pursuit by Saul, betrayals by friends, praises to God for his deliverance, and his many victories in battle. Two psalms express his remorse over dispatching the husband of his concubine to certain death in battle; two others were probably composed on the occasions of bringing the ark of the covenant to Jerusalem and

KING DAVID, THE PSALMIST

[1 0 4 0 – 9 6 2 B . C .]

In the hidden part thou shalt make me to know wisdom.

dedicating the site of the future Temple. The history of David's life and reign can be found in the Biblical accounts given in I Samuel 16–II Samuel 24, I Kings 1–2, and I Chronicles 11–29.

David's psalms express his passionate loyalty to a personal God who he believed had lent him protection and numerous victories. The significant struggles for David were not so much political as spiritual: a fighting man yet a poet, his signal victories were over his own soul. His hymns of praise are equal in power to his laments of despair; both sound the refrain that spiritual solace can be found only by trusting in God. Capable of dancing naked in the streets in praise to the Almighty, David yielded himself to God's service in complete abandon. Renowned as a harpist, David's eloquence sings through translation in some of the greatest spiritual poetry ever written. The selection of psalms presented here is taken from the King James Version of the Bible, as are all other Biblical selections in this anthology.   [AM]

FROM THE PSALMS

Pursuit by Saul
PSALM 35

1 Plead *my cause*, O Lord, with them that strive with me: fight against them that fight against me.

2 Take hold of shield and buckler, and stand up for mine help.

3 Draw out also the spear, and stop *the way* against them that persecute me: say unto my soul, I *am* thy salvation.

4 Let them be confounded and put to shame that seek after my soul: let them be turned back and brought to confusion that devise my hurt.

5 Let them be as chaff before the wind: and let the angel of the Lord chase *them*.

6 Let their way be dark and slippery: and let the angel of the Lord persecute them.

7 For without cause have they hid for me their net *in* a pit, *which* without cause they have digged for my soul.

8 Let destruction come upon him at unawares; and let his net that he hath hid catch himself: into that very destruction let him fall.

9 And my soul shall be joyful in the Lord: it shall rejoice in his salvation.

10 All my bones shall say, Lord, who *is* like unto thee, which deliverest the poor from him that is too strong for him, yea, the poor and the needy from him that spoileth him?

11 False witnesses did rise up; they laid to my charge *things* that I knew not.

12 They rewarded me evil for good *to* the spoiling of my soul.

13 But as for me, when they were sick, my clothing *was* sackcloth: I humbled my soul with fasting; and my prayer returned into mine own bosom.

14 I behaved myself as though *he had been* my friend *or* brother: I bowed down heavily, as one that mourneth *for his* mother.

15 But in mine adversity they rejoiced, and gathered themselves together: *yea*, the abjects gathered themselves together against me, and I knew *it* not; they did tear *me*, and ceased not:

16 With hypocritical mockers in feasts, they gnashed upon me with their teeth.

17 Lord, how long wilt thou look on? Rescue my soul from their destructions, my darling from the lions.

18 I will give thee thanks in the great congregation: I will praise thee among much people.

19 Let not them that are mine enemies wrongfully rejoice over me: *neither* let them wink with the eye that hate me without a cause.

20 For they speak not peace: but they devise deceitful matters against *them that are* quiet in the land.

21 Yea, they opened their mouth wide against me, *and* said, Aha, aha, our eye hath seen *it*.

22 *This* thou hast seen, O Lord: keep not silence: O Lord, be not far from me.

23 Stir up thyself, and awake to my judgment, *even* unto my cause, my God and my Lord.

24 Judge me, O Lord my God, according to thy righteousness; and let them not rejoice over me.

25 Let them not say in their hearts, Ah, so would we have it: let them not say, We have swallowed him up.

26 Let them be ashamed and brought to confusion together that rejoice at mine hurt: let them be clothed with shame and dishonour that magnify *themselves* against me.

27 Let them shout for joy, and be glad, that favour my righteous cause: yea, let them say continually, Let the Lord be magnified, which hath pleasure in the prosperity of his servant.

28 And my tongue shall speak of thy righteousness *and* of thy praise all the day long.

Hiding in the Cave
PSALM 57

1 Be merciful unto me, O God, be merciful unto me: for my soul trusteth in thee: yea, in the shadow of thy wings will I make my refuge, until *these* calamities be overpast.

2 I will cry unto God most high; unto God that performeth *all things* for me.

· 3 He shall send from heaven, and save me *from* the reproach of him that would swallow me up. Selah. God shall send forth his mercy and his truth.

4 My soul *is* among lions: *and* I lie *even among* them that are set on fire, *even* the sons of men, whose teeth *are* spears and arrows, and their tongue a sharp sword.

5 Be thou exalted, O God, above the heavens; *let* thy glory *be* above all the earth.

6 They have prepared a net for my steps; my soul is bowed down: they have digged a pit before me, into the midst whereof they are fallen *themselves*. Selah.

7 My heart is fixed, O God, my heart is fixed: I will sing and give praise.

8 Awake up, my glory; awake, psaltery and harp: I *myself* will awake early.

9 I will praise thee, O Lord, among the people: I will sing unto thee among the nations.

10 For thy mercy *is* great unto the heavens, and thy truth unto the clouds.

11 Be thou exalted, O God, above the heavens: *let* thy glory *be* above all the earth.

PSALM 142

1 I cried unto the Lord with my voice; with my voice unto the Lord did I make my supplication.

2 I poured out my complaint before him; I shewed before him my trouble.

3 When my spirit was overwhelmed within me, then thou knewest my path. In the way wherein I walked have they privily laid a snare for me.

4 I looked on *my* right hand, and beheld, but *there was* no man that would know me: refuge failed me; no man cared for my soul.

5 I cried unto thee, O Lord: I said, Thou *art* my refuge *and* my portion in the land of the living.

6 Attend unto my cry; for I am brought very low: deliver me from my persecutors; for they are stronger than I.

7 Bring my soul out of prison, that I may praise thy name: the righteous shall compass me about; for thou shalt deal bountifully with me.

Hiding in the Wilderness
PSALM 63

1 O God, thou *art* my God; early will I seek thee: my soul thirsteth for thee, my flesh longeth for thee in a dry and thirsty land, where no water is;

2 To see thy power and thy glory, so *as* I have seen thee in the sanctuary.

3 Because thy lovingkindness *is* better than life, my lips shall praise thee.

4 Thus will I bless thee while I live: I will lift up my hands in thy name.

5 My soul shall be satisfied as *with* marrow and fatness; and my mouth shall praise *thee* with joyful lips:

6 When I remember thee upon my bed, *and* meditate on thee in the *night* watches.

7 Because thou hast been my help, therefore in the shadow of thy wings will I rejoice.

8 My soul followeth hard after thee: thy right hand upholdeth me.

9 But those *that* seek my soul, to destroy *it*, shall go into the lower parts of the earth.

10 They shall fall by the sword: they shall be a portion for foxes.

11 But the king shall rejoice in God; every one that sweareth by him shall glory: but the mouth of them that speak lies shall be stopped.

Betrayal to Saul
PSALM 59

1 Deliver me from mine enemies, O my God: defend me from them that rise up against me.

2 Deliver me from the workers of iniquity, and save me from bloody men.

3 For lo, they lie in wait for my soul: the mighty are gathered against me; not *for* my transgression, nor *for* my sin, O LORD.

4 They run and prepare themselves without *my* fault: awake to help me, and behold.

5 Thou therefore, O LORD God of hosts, the God of Israel, awake to visit all the heathen: be not merciful to any wicked transgressors. Selah.

6 They return at evening: they make a noise like a dog, and go round about the city.

7 Behold, they belch out with their mouth: swords *are* in their lips: for who, *say they*, doth hear?

8 But thou, O LORD, shalt laugh at them; thou shalt have all the heathen in derision.

9 *Because of* his strength will I wait upon thee: for God *is* my defence.

10 The God of my mercy shall prevent me: God shall let me see *my desire* upon mine enemies.

11 Slay them not, lest my people forget: scatter them by thy power; and bring them down, O Lord our shield.

12 *For* the sin of their mouth *and* the words of their lips let them even be taken in their pride: and for cursing and lying *which* they speak.

13 Consume *them* in wrath, consume *them*, that they *may* not *be:* and let them know that God ruleth in Jacob unto the ends of the earth. Selah.

14 And at evening let them return; *and* let them make a noise like a dog, and go round about the city.

15 Let them wander up and down for meat, and grudge if they be not satisfied.

16 But I will sing of thy power; yea, I will sing of thy power; yea, I will sing aloud of thy mercy in the monring: for thou hast been my defence and refuge in the day of my trouble.

17 Unto thee, O my strength, will I sing: for God *is* my defence, *and* the God of my mercy.

PSALM 54

1 Save me, O God, by thy name, and judge me by thy strength.

2 Hear my prayer, O God; give ear to the words of my mouth.

3 For strangers are risen up against me, and oppressors seek after my soul: they have not set God before them. Selah.

4 Behold, God *is* mine helper: the Lord *is* with them that uphold my soul.

5 He shall reward evil unto mine enemies: cut them off in thy truth.

6 I will freely sacrifice unto thee: I will praise thy name, O LORD; for *it is* good.

7 For he hath delivered me out of all trouble: and mine eye hath seen *his desire* upon mine enemies.

PSALM 55

1 Give ear to my prayer, O God; and hide not thyself from my supplication.

2 Attend unto me, and hear me: I mourn in my complaint, and make a noise;

3 Because of the voice of the enemy, because of the oppression of the wicked: for they cast iniquity upon me, and in wrath they hate me.

4 My heart is sore pained within me: and the terrors of death are fallen upon me.

5 Fearfulness and trembling are come upon me, and horror hath overwhelmed me.

6 And I said, Oh that I had wings like a dove! *For then* would I fly away, and be at rest.

7 Lo, *then*, would I wander far off, *and* remain in the wilderness. Selah.

8 I would hasten my escape from the windy storm *and* tempest.

9 Destroy, O Lord, *and* divide their tongues: for I have seen violence and strife in the city.

10 Day and night they go about it upon the walls thereof: mischief also and sorrow *are* in the midst of it.

11 Wickedness *is* in the midst thereof: deceit and guile depart not from her streets.

12 For *it was* not an enemy *that* reproached me; then I could have borne *it:*

neither *was it* he that hated me *that* did magnify *himself* against me; then I would have hid myself from him:

13 But *it was* thou, a man mine equal, my guide, and mine acquaintance.

14 We took sweet counsel together, *and* walked unto the house of God in company.

15 Let death seize upon them, *and* let them go down quick into hell: for wickedness *is* in their dwellings, *and* among them.

16 As for me, I will call upon God; and the Lord shall save me.

17 Evening, and morning, and at noon, will I pray, and cry aloud: and he shall hear my voice.

18 He hath delivered my soul in peace from the battle *that was* against me: for there were many with me.

19 God shall hear, and afflict them, even he that abideth of old. Selah. Because they have no changes, therefore they fear not God.

20 He hath put forth his hands against such as be at peace with him: he hath broken his covenant.

21 *The words* of his mouth were smoother than butter, but war *was* in his heart: his words were softer than oil, yet *were* they drawn swords.

22 Cast thy burden upon the Lord, and he shall sustain thee: he shall never suffer the righteous to be moved.

23 But thou, O God, shalt bring them down into the pit of destruction: bloody and deceitful men shall not live out half their days; but I will trust in thee.

Praise for Help from Abimelech, the Priest
PSALM 34

1 I will bless the Lord at all times: his praise *shall* continually *be* in my mouth.

2 My soul shall make her boast in the Lord: the humble shall hear *thereof*, and be glad.

3 O magnify the Lord with me, and let us exalt his name together.

4 I sought the Lord, and he heard me, and delivered me from all my fears.

5 They looked unto him, and were lightened: and their faces were not ashamed.

6 This poor man cried and the Lord heard *him*, and saved him out of all his troubles.

7 The angel of the Lord encampeth round about them that fear him, and delivereth them.

8 O taste and see that the Lord *is* good: blessed *is* the man *that* trusteth in him.

9 O fear the Lord, ye his saints: for *there is* no want to them that fear him.

10 The young lions do lack, and suffer hunger: but they that seek the Lord shall not want any good *thing*.

11 Come, ye children, hearken unto me: I will teach you the fear of the Lord.

12 What man *is he that* desireth life, *and* loveth *many* days, that he may see good?

13 Keep thy tongue from evil, and thy lips from speaking guile.

14 Depart from evil, and do good; seek peace, and pursue it.

15 The eyes of the LORD *are* upon the righteous, and his ears *are open* unto their cry.

16 The face of the LORD *is* against them that do evil, to cut off the remembrance of them from the earth.

17 *The righteous* cry, and the LORD heareth, and delivereth them out of all their troubles.

18 The LORD *is* nigh unto them that are of a broken heart; and saveth such as be of a contrite spirit.

19 Many *are* the afflictions of the righteous: but the LORD delivereth him out of them all.

20 He keepeth all his bones: not one of them is broken.

21 Evil shall slay the wicked: and they that hate the righteous shall be desolate.

22 The LORD redeemeth the soul of his servants: and none of them that trust in him shall be desolate.

Deliverance from Saul
PSALM 18

1 I will love thee, O LORD, my strength.

2 The LORD *is* my rock, and my fortress, and my deliverer; my God, my strength, in whom I will trust; my buckler, and the horn of my salvation, *and* my high tower.

3 I will call upon the LORD, *who is worthy* to be praised: so shall I be saved from mine enemies.

4 The sorrows of death compassed me, and the floods of ungodly men made me afraid.

5 The sorrows of hell compassed me about; the snares of death prevented me.

6 In my distress I called upon the LORD, and cried unto my God: he heard my voice out of his temple, and my cry came before him, *even* into his ears.

7 Then the earth shook and trembled; the foundations also of the hills moved and were shaken, because he was wroth.

8 There went up a smoke out of his nostrils, and fire out of his mouth devoured: coals were kindled by it.

9 He bowed the heavens also, and came down: and darkness *was* under his feet.

10 And he rode upon a cherub, and did fly: yea, he did fly upon the wings of the wind.

11 He made darkness his secret place; his pavilion round about him *were* dark waters *and* thick clouds of the skies.

12 At the brightness *that was* before him his thick clouds passed, hail *stones* and coals of fire.

13 The LORD also thundered in the heavens, and the Highest gave his voice; hail *stones* and coals of fire.

14 Yea, he sent out his arrows, and scattered them; and he shot out lightnings, and discomfited them.

15 Then the channels of waters were seen, and foundations of the world were discovered at thy rebuke, O LORD, at the blast of the breath of thy nostrils.

16 He sent from above, he took me, he drew me out of many waters.

17 He delivered me from my strong enemy, and from them which hated me: for they were too strong for me.

18 They prevented me in the day of my calamity: but the LORD was my stay.

19 He brought me forth also into a large place; he delivered me, because he delighted in me.

20 The LORD rewarded me according to my righteousness; according to the cleanness of my hands hath he recompensed me.

21 For I have kept the ways of the LORD, and have not wickedly departed from my God.

22 For all his judgments *were* before me, and I did not put away his statutes from me.

23 I was also upright before him, and I kept myself from mine iniquity.

24 Therefore hath the LORD recompensed me according to my righteousness, according to the cleanness of my hands in his eyesight.

25 With the merciful thou wilt shew thyself merciful; with an upright man thou wilt shew thyself upright;

26 With the pure thou wilt shew thyself pure; and with the froward thou wilt shew thyself froward.

27 For thou wilt save the afflicted people; but wilt bring down high looks.

28 For thou wilt light my candle: the LORD my God will enlighten my darkness.

29 For by thee I have run through a troop; and by my God have I leaped over a wall.

30 As *for* God, his way *is* perfect: the word of the LORD is tried: he *is* a buckler to all those that trust in him.

31 For who *is* God save the LORD? or who *is* a rock save our God?

32 *It is* God that girdeth me with strength, and maketh my way perfect.

33 He maketh my feet like hinds' *feet*, and setteth me upon my high places.

34 He teacheth my hands to war, so that a bow of steel is broken by mine arms.

35 Thou hast also given me the shield of thy salvation: and thy right hand hath holden me up, and thy gentleness hath made me great.

36 Thou hast enlarged my steps under me, that my feet did not slip.

37 I have pursued mine enemies, and overtaken them: neither did I turn again till they were consumed.

38 I have wounded them that they were not able to rise: they are fallen under my feet.

39 For thou hast girded me with strength unto the battle: thou hast subdued under me those that rose up against me.

40 Thou hast also given me the necks of mine enemies; that I might destroy them that hate me.

41 They cried, but *there was* none to save *them: even* unto the LORD, but he answered them not.

42 Then did I beat them small as the dust before the wind: I did cast them out as the dirt in the streets.

43 Thou hast delivered me from the strivings of the people; *and* thou hast made me the head of the heathen: a people *whom* I have not known shall serve me.

44 As soon as they hear of me, they shall obey me: the strangers shall submit themselves unto me.

45 The strangers shall fade away, and be afraid out of their close places.

46 The LORD liveth; and blessed *be* my rock; and let the God of my salvation be exalted.

47 *It is* God that avengeth me, and subdueth the people under me.

48 He delivereth me from mine enemies: yea, thou liftest me up above those that rise up against me: thou hast delivered me from the violent man.

49 Therefore will I give thanks unto thee, O LORD, among the heathen, and sing praises unto thy name.

50 Great deliverance giveth he to his king; and sheweth mercy to his anointed, to David, and to his seed for evermore.

Feigning Madness to Find Refuge with the Philistines
PSALM 56

1 Be merciful unto me, O God: for man would swallow me up; he fighting daily oppresseth me.

2 Mine enemies would daily swallow *me* up: for *they be* many that fight against me, O thou most High.

3 What time I am afraid, I will trust in thee.

4 In God I will praise his word, in God I have put my trust; I will not fear what flesh can do unto me.

5 Every day they wrest my words: all their thoughts *are* against me for evil.

6 They gather themselves together, they hide themselves, they mark my steps, when they wait for my soul.

7 Shall they escape by iniquity? in *thine* anger cast down the people, O God.

8 Thou tellest my wanderings: put thou my tears into thy bottle: *are they* not in thy book?

9 When I cry *unto thee*, then shall mine enemies turn back: this I know; for God *is* for me.

10 In God will I praise *his* word: in the LORD will I praise *his* word.

11 In God have I put my trust: I will not be afraid what man can do unto me.

12 Thy vows *are* upon me, O God: I will render praises unto thee.

13 For thou hast delivered my soul from death: *wilt* not *thou deliver* my feet from falling, that I may walk before God in the light of the living?

Confession of Guilt over Bathsheba
PSALM 51

1 Have mercy upon me, O God, according to thy lovingkindness: according unto the multitude of thy tender mercies blot out my transgressions.

2 Wash me throughly from mine iniquity, and cleanse me from my sin.

3 For I acknowledge my transgressions: and my sin *is* ever before me.

4 Against thee, thee only, have I sinned, and done *this* evil in thy sight: that thou mightest be justified when thou speakest, *and* be clear when thou judgest.

5 Behold, I was shapen in iniquity; and in sin did my mother conceive me.

6 Behold, thou desirest truth in the inward parts: and in the hidden *part* thou shalt make me to know wisdom.

7 Purge me with hyssop, and I shall be clean: wash me, and I shall be whiter than snow.

8 Make me to hear joy and gladness; *that* the bones *which* thou hast broken may rejoice.

9 Hide thy face from my sins, and blot out all mine iniquities.

10 Create in me a clean heart, O God; and renew a right spirit within me.

11 Cast me not away from thy presence; and take not thy holy spirit from me.

12 Restore unto me the joy of thy salvation; and uphold me *with thy* free spirit.

13 *Then* will I teach transgressors thy ways; and sinners shall be converted unto thee.

14 Deliver me from blood-guiltiness, O God, thou God of my salvation: *and* my tongue shall sing aloud of thy righteousness.

15 O Lord, open thou my lips; and my mouth shall shew forth thy praise.

16 For thou desirest not sacrifice; else would I give *it:* thou delightest not in burnt offering.

17 The sacrifices of God *are* a broken spirit: a broken and a contrite heart, O God, thou wilt not despise.

18 Do good in thy good pleasure unto Zion: build thou the walls of Jerusalem.

19 Then shalt thou be pleased with the sacrifices of righteousness, with burnt offering and whole burnt offering: then shall they offer bullocks upon thine altar.

Praise at Forgiveness of Sin with Bathsheba
PSALM 32

1 Blessed *is he whose* transgression *is* forgiven, *whose* sin *is* covered.

2 Blessed *is* the man unto whom the LORD imputeth not iniquity, and in whose spirit *there is* no guile.

3 When I kept silence, my bones waxed old through my roaring all the day long.

4 For day and night thy hand was heavy upon me: my moisture is turned into the drought of summer. Selah.

5 I acknowledged my sin unto thee, and mine iniquity have I not hid. I said, I will confess my transgressions unto the LORD; and thou forgavest the iniquity of my sin. Selah.

6 For this shall every one that is godly pray unto thee in a time when thou mayest be found: surely in the floods of great waters they shall not come nigh unto him.

7 Thou *art* my hiding place; thou shalt preserve me from trouble; thou shalt compass me about with songs of deliverance. Selah.

8 I will instruct thee and teach thee in the way which thou shalt go: I will guide thee with mine eye.

9 Be ye not as the horse, *or* as the mule, *which* have no understanding: whose mouth must be held in with bit and bridle, lest they come near unto thee.

10 Many sorrows *shall be* to the wicked: but he that trusteth in the LORD, mercy shall compass him about.

11 Be glad in the LORD, and rejoice, ye righteous: and shout for joy, all *ye that are* upright in heart.

Fleeing from His Son, Absalom,
PSALM 3

1 LORD, how are they increased that trouble me! many *are* they that rise up against me.

2 Many *there be* which say of my soul, *There is* no help for him in God. Selah.

3 But thou, O LORD, *art* a shield for me; my glory, and the lifter up of mine head.

4 I cried unto the LORD with my voice, and he heard me out of his holy hill. Selah.

5 I laid me down and slept; I awaked; for the LORD sustained me.

6 I will not be afraid of ten thousands of people, that have set *themselves* against me round about.

7 Arise, O LORD; save me, O my God: for thou hast smitten all mine enemies *upon* the cheek bone; thou hast broken the teeth of the ungodly.

8 Salvation *belongeth* unto the LORD: thy blessing *is* upon thy people. Selah.

Probably Composed on Occasion of
Bringing the Ark of the Covenant to Jerusalem
PSALM 68

1 Let God arise, let his enemies be scattered: let them also that hate him flee before him.

2 As smoke is driven away, *so* drive *them* away: as wax melteth before the fire, *so* let the wicked perish at the presence of God.

3 But let the righteous be glad; let them rejoice before God: yea, let them exceedingly rejoice.

4 Sing unto God, sing praises to his name: extol him that rideth upon the heavens by his name JAH, and rejoice before him.

5 A father of the fatherless, and a judge of the widows *is* God in his holy habitation.

6 God setteth the solitary in families: he bringeth out those which are bound with chains: but the rebellious dwell in a dry *land*.

7 O God, when thou wentest forth before thy people, when thou didst march through the wilderness; Selah:

8 The earth shook, the heavens also dropped at the presence of God: *even* Sinai itself *was moved* at the presence of God, the God of Israel.

9 Thou, O God, didst send a plentiful rain, whereby thou didst confirm thine inheritance, when it was weary.

10 Thy congregation hath dwelt therein: thou, O God, hast prepared of thy goodness for the poor. . . .

Dedication of the Temple Site
PSALM 30

1 I will extol thee, O Lord; for thou hast lifted me up, and hast not made my foes to rejoice over me.

2 O Lord my God, I cried unto thee, and thou hast healed me.

3 O Lord, thou hast brought up my soul from the grave: thou hast kept me alive, that I should not go down to the pit.

4 Sing unto the Lord, O ye saints of his, and give thanks at the remembrance of his holiness.

5 For his anger *endureth but* a moment; in his favour *is* life: weeping may endure for a night, but joy *cometh* in the morning.

6 And in my prosperity I said, I shall never be moved.

7 Lord, by thy favour thou hast made my mountain to stand strong: thou didst hide thy face, *and* I was troubled.

8 I cried to thee, O Lord; and unto the Lord I made supplication.

9 What profit *is there* in my blood, when I go down to the pit? Shall the dust praise thee? shall it declare thy truth?

10 Hear, O Lord, and have mercy upon me: Lord, be thou my helper.

11 Thou hast turned for me my mourning into dancing: thou hast put off my sackcloth, and girded me with gladness;

12 To the end that *my* glory may sing praise to thee, and not be silent. O Lord my God, I will give thanks unto thee for ever.

SAINT

AUGUSTINE

[3 5 4 – 4 3 0]

I became to myself a barren land.

The son of a Christian mother and a pagan father at the time of the dissolution of the Roman Empire, Augustine spent the first thirty years of his life in a tempestuous search for pleasure and an anguished quest for wisdom. Troubled by the problem of good and evil in human nature, Augustine felt an urgent need to discover the right philosophical explanation for the presence of evil in the world. He embraced, first, Manichaeanism, a philosophy based on a dualistic conception of the universe, then Neoplatonism, which held that the material world was only a shadow of truth and that pure spirituality required the complete rejection of material experience. By his own account, he suffered continually from depression and anxiety, despite his success as an orator and teacher of rhetoric. At his mother's urging, he sought advice from the Church, and at last accepted the Christian version of cosmology, that the world created by a good and loving God had been spoiled through human failures and redeemed through Christ.

In the selection of his *Confessions* given here, which follows the account of ·

his wandering period, Augustine relates his increasing yearning for spiritual resolution. Directed by a voice to "take up and read," he opened his Bible to a passage that brought about his immediate acceptance of God. The concluding chapters of his *Confessions* include meditations on the nature of creation, the material world, and the problem of good and evil in the soul.

Like Saint Paul and other early Christians, Augustine felt compelled to give an account of his conversion and life experience as a testimony to the power of Christ to renew his life. Following his baptism as a Christian, Augustine pursued holy orders, then became Bishop of Hippo, a Roman city in North Africa. His theological works, *The City of God, On Christian Doctrine,* and his essays on morality are among the most influential texts in Christian thought. His articulation of the struggle of good and evil in the soul and his designation of God's grace as the only recourse for individual victory profoundly influenced Christian doctrine and was seminal in the thought of Reformationists, in particular John Calvin and Martin Luther.

The structure of Saint Augustine's *Confessions* establishes the compositional principle for autobiographical writing in the Western European literary tradition. Most authors adhere to Augustine's form and consider their works to be confessional. In addition, the reading of his *Confessions* figures prominently in other works in this volume: for example, Petrarch, Saint Teresa of Avila, John Bunyan, and Saint Thérèse de Lisieux all cite the reading of Augustine's *Confessions* as the decisive turning point in their spiritual lives.

[AM]

FROM *THE CONFESSIONS*

I was displeased that I led a secular life; yea now that my desires no longer inflamed me, as of old, with hopes of honour and profit, a very grievous burden it was to undergo so heavy a bondage. For, in comparison of Thy sweetness, and the beauty of Thy house which I loved, those things delighted me no longer. But still I was enthralled with the love of woman; nor did the Apostle forbid me to marry, although he advised me to something better, chiefly wishing that all men were as himself was. But I being weak, chose the more indulgent place; and because of this alone, was tossed up and down in all beside, faint and wasted with withering cares, because in other matters I was constrained against my will to conform myself to a married life, to which I was given up and enthralled. I had heard from the mouth of the Truth, that there were some eunuchs which had made themselves eunuchs for the kingdom of heaven's sake: but, saith He, let him who can receive it, receive it. Surely vain are all men who are ignorant of God, and could not out of the good things which are seen, find out Him who is good. But I was no longer in that vanity; I had surmounted it; and by the common witness of all Thy creatures had found Thee our Creator, and Thy Word, God with Thee, and together with Thee one God, by whom Thou createdst all things. There is yet another kind of ungodly, who knowing God, glorified Him not as God, neither were thankful. Into this also had I fallen, but Thy right hand upheld me, and took me thence, and Thou placedst me where I might recover. For Thou hast said unto man, Behold, the fear of the Lord is wisdom, and, Desire not to seem wise; because they who affirmed themselves to be wise, became fools. But I had now found the goodly pearl, which, selling all that I had, I ought to have bought, and I hesitated.

To Simplicianus then I went, the father of Ambrose (a Bishop now) in receiving Thy grace, and whom Ambrose truly loved as a father. To him I related the mazes of my wanderings. But when I mentioned that I had read certain books of the Platonists, which Victorinus, sometime Rhetoric Professor of Rome (who had died a Christian, as I had heard), had translated into Latin, he testified his joy that I had not fallen upon the writings of other philosophers, full of fallacies and deceits, after the rudiments of this world, whereas the Platonists many ways led to the belief in God and His Word. . . .

Good God! what takes place in man, that he should more rejoice at the salvation of a soul despaired of, and freed from greater peril, than if there had always been hope of him, or the danger had been less? For so Thou also, merciful Father, dost more rejoice over one penitent than over ninety-nine just persons that need no repentance. And with much joyfulness do we hear, so often as we hear with what joy the sheep which had strayed is brought back upon the shepherd's shoulder, and the groat is restored to Thy treasury, the neighbours rejoicing with the woman who found it; and the joy of the solemn service of Thy house forceth to tears, when in Thy house it is read of Thy younger son, that he was dead, and liveth again; had been lost, and is found. For Thou rejoicest in us, and in Thy holy angels, holy through holy charity. For Thou art ever the same; for all things which abide not the same nor for ever, Thou for ever knowest in the same way.

What then takes place in the soul, when it is more delighted at finding or recovering the things it loves, than if it had ever had them? yea, and other things witness hereunto; and all things are full of witnesses, crying out, "So is it." The conquering commander triumpheth; yet had he not conquered unless he had fought; and the more peril there was in the battle, so much the more joy is there in the triumph. The storm tosses the sailors, threatens shipwreck; all wax pale at approaching death; sky and sea are calmed, and they are exceeding joyed, as having been exceeding afraid. A friend is sick, and his pulse threatens danger; all who long for his recovery are sick in mind with him. He is restored, though as yet he walks not with his former strength; yet there is such joy, as was not, when before he walked sound and strong. Yea, the very pleasures of human life men acquire by difficulties, not those only which fall upon us unlooked for, and against our wills, but even by self-chosen, and pleasure-seeking trouble. Eating and drinking have no pleasure, unless there precede the pinching of hunger and thirst. Men, given to drink, eat certain salt meats, to procure a troublesome heat, which the drink allaying, causes pleasure. It is also ordered that the affianced bride should not at once be given, lest as a husband he should hold cheap whom, as betrothed, he sighed not after.

This law holds in foul and accursed joy; this in permitted and lawful joy; this in the very purest perfection of friendship; this, in him who was dead, and lived again; had been lost and was found. Everywhere the greater joy is ushered in by the greater pain. What means this, O Lord my God, whereas Thou art everlastingly joy to Thyself, and some things around Thee evermore rejoice in Thee? What means this, that this portion of things thus ebbs and flows alternately displeased and reconciled? Is this their allotted measure? Is this all Thou hast assigned to them, whereas from the highest heavens to the lowest earth, from the beginning of the world to the end of ages, from the angel to the worm, from the first motion to the last, Thou settest each in its place, and realisest each in their season, every thing good after its kind? Woe is me! how high art Thou in the highest, and how deep in the deepest! and Thou never departest, and we scarcely return to Thee.

But when that man of Thine, Simplicianus, related to me this of Victorinus, I was on fire to imitate him; for for this very end had he related it. But when he had subjoined also, how in the days of the Emperor Julian a law was made, whereby Christians were forbidden to teach the liberal sciences or oratory; and how he, obeying this law, chose rather to give over the wordy school than Thy Word, by which Thou makest eloquent the tongues of the dumb; he seemed to me not more resolute than blessed, in having thus found opportunity to wait on Thee only. Which thing I was sighing for, bound as I was, not with another's irons, but by my own iron will. My will the enemy held, and thence had made a chain for me, and bound me. For of a froward will, was a lust made; and a lust served, became custom; and custom not resisted, became necessity. By which links, as it were, joined together (whence I called it a chain) a hard bondage held me enthralled. But that new will which had begun to be in me, freely to serve Thee, and to wish to enjoy Thee, O God, the only assured pleasantness, was not yet able to overcome my former wilfulness, strengthened by age. Thus did my two wills, one new, and the other old, one carnal, the other spiritual, struggle within me; and by their discord, undid my soul.

Thus, I understood, by my own experience, what I had read, how the flesh lusteth against the spirit and the spirit against the flesh. Myself verily either way; yet more myself, in that which I approved in myself, than in that which in myself I disapproved. For in this last, it was now for the more part not myself, because in much I rather endured against my will, than acted willingly. And yet it was through me that custom had obtained this power of warring against me, because I had come willingly, whither I willed not. And who has any right to speak against it, if just punishment follow the sinner? Nor had I now any longer my former plea, that I therefore as yet hesitated to be above the world and serve Thee, for that the truth was not altogether ascertained to me; for now it too was. But I still under service to the earth, refused to fight under Thy banner, and feared as much to be freed of all incumbrances, as we should fear to be encumbered with it. Thus with the baggage of this present world was I held down pleasantly, as in sleep: and the thoughts wherein I meditated on Thee were like the efforts of such as would awake, who yet overcome with a heavy drowsiness, are again drenched therein. And as no one would sleep for ever, and in all men's sober judgment waking is better, yet a man for the most part, feeling a heavy lethargy in all his limbs, defers to shake off sleep, and though half displeased, yet, even after it is time to rise, with pleasure yields to it, so was I assured that much better were it for me to give myself up to Thy charity, than to give myself over to mine own cupidity; but though the former course satisfied me and gained the mastery, the latter pleased me and held me mastered. Nor had I any thing to answer Thee calling to me, Awake, thou that sleepest, and arise from the dead, and Christ shall give thee light. And when Thou didst on all sides show me that what Thou saidst was true, I, convicted by the truth, had nothing at all to answer, but only those dull and drowsy words, "Anon, anon." ... I wretched, most wretched, in the very commencement of my early youth, had begged chastity of Thee, and said, "Give me chastity and continency, only not yet." For I feared lest Thou shouldest hear me soon, and soon cure me of the disease of concupiscence, which I wished to have satisfied, rather than extinguished. And I had wandered through crooked ways in a sacrilegious superstition, not indeed assured thereof, but as preferring it to the others which I did not seek religiously, but opposed maliciously.

And I had thought that I therefore deferred from day to day to reject the hopes of this world, and follow Thee only, because there did not appear aught certain, whither to direct my course. And now was the day come wherein I was to be laid bare to myself, and my conscience was to upbraid me. "Where art thou now, my tongue? Thou saidst that for an uncertain truth thou likedst not to cast off the baggage of vanity; now, it is certain, and yet that burden still oppresseth thee, while they who neither have so worn themselves out with seeking it, nor for ten years and more have been thinking thereon, have had their shoulders lightened, and received wings to fly away." Thus was I gnawed within, and exceedingly confounded with a horrible shame, while Pontitianus was so speaking. And he having brought to a close his tale and the business he came for, went his way; and I into myself. What said I not against myself? with what scourges of condemnation lashed I not my soul, that it might follow me, striving to go after Thee! Yet it drew back; refused, but excused not itself. All arguments were spent and confuted; there remained a mute shrinking; and she feared, as she would death, to be restrained from the flux of that custom, whereby she was wasting to death.

Then in this great contention of my inward dwelling, which I had strongly raised against my soul, in the chamber of my heart, troubled in mind and countenance, I turned upon Alypius. "What ails us?" I exclaim: "what is it? what heardest thou? The unlearned start up and take heaven by force, and we with our learning, and without heart, lo, where we wallow in flesh and blood! Are we ashamed to follow, because others are gone before, and not ashamed not even to follow?" Some such words I uttered, and my fever of mind tore me away from him, while he, gazing on me in astonishment, kept silence. For it was not my wonted tone; and my forehead, cheeks, eyes, colour, tone of voice, spake my mind more than the words I uttered. A little garden there was to our lodging, which we had the use of, as of the whole house; for the master of the house, our host, was not living there. Thither had the tumult of my breast hurried me, where no man might hinder the hot contention wherein I had engaged with myself, until it should end as Thou knewest, I knew not. Only I was healthfully distracted and dying, to live; knowing what evil thing I was, and not knowing what good thing I was shortly to become. I retired then into the garden, and Alypius, on my steps, For his presence did not lessen my privacy; or how could he forsake me so disturbed? We sate down as far removed as might be from the house. I was troubled in spirit, most vehemently indignant that I entered not into Thy will and covenant, O my God, which all my bones cried out unto me to enter, and praised it to the skies. And therein we enter not by ships, or chariots, or feet, no, move not so far as I had come from the house to that place where we were sitting. For, not to go only, but to go in thither was nothing else but to will to go, but to will resolutely and thoroughly; not to turn and toss, this way and that, a maimed and half-divided will, struggling, with one part sinking as another rose.

Lastly, in the very fever of my irresoluteness, I made with my body many such motions as men sometimes would, but cannot, if either they have not the limbs, or these be bound with bands, weakened with infirmity, or any other way hindered. Thus, if I tore my hair, beat my forehead, if locking my fingers I clasped my knee; I willed, I did it. But I might have willed, and not done it; if the power of motion in my limbs had not obeyed. So many things then I did, when "to will" was not in itself "to be able"; and I did not what both I longed incomparably more to do, and which soon after, when I should will, I should be able to do; because soon after, when I should will, I should will thoroughly. For in these things the ability was one with the will, and to will was to do; and yet was it not done: and more easily did my body obey the weakest willing of my soul, in moving its limbs at its nod, than the soul obeyed itself to accomplish in the will alone this its momentous will.

Whence is this monstrousness? and to what end? Let Thy mercy gleam that I may ask, if so be the secret penalties of men, and those darkest pangs of the sons of Adam, may perhaps answer me. Whence is this monstrousness? and to what end? The mind commands the body, and it obeys instantly; the mind commands itself, and is resisted. The mind commands the hand to be moved; and such readiness is there, that command is scarce distinct from obedience. Yet the mind is mind, the hand is body. The mind commands the mind, its own self, to will, and yet it doth not. Whence this monstrousness? and to what end? It commands itself, I say, to will, and would not command, unless it willed, and what it commands is not done. But it willeth not entirely: therefore doth it not command entirely. For so far forth it commandeth, as it willeth: and, so far forth is the thing commanded, not done, as it willeth not. For the will commandeth that there be a will; not another, but itself. But it doth not command entirely, therefore what it commandeth, is not. For were the will entire, it would not even command it to be, because it would already be. It is therefore no monstrousness partly to will, partly to nill, but a disease of the mind, that it doth not wholly rise, by truth upborne, borne down by custom. And therefore are there two wills, for that one of them is not entire: and what the one lacketh, the other hath. . . .

Thus soul-sick was I, and tormented, accusing myself much more severely than my wont, rolling and turning me in my chain, till that were wholly broken, whereby I now was but just, but still was, held. And Thou, O Lord, pressedst upon me in my inward parts by a severe mercy, redoubling the lashes of fear and shame, lest I should again give way, and not bursting that same slight remaining tie, it should recover strength, and bind me the faster. For I said with myself, "Be it done now, be it done now." And as I spake, I all but enacted it: I all but did it, and did it not: yet sunk not back to my former state, but kept my stand hard by, and took breath. And I essayed again, and wanted somewhat less of it, and somewhat less, and all but touched, and laid hold of it; and yet came not at it, nor touched nor laid hold of it; hesitating to die to death and to live to life: and the worse whereto I was inured, prevailed more with me than the better whereto I was unused: and the very moment wherein I was to become other than I was, the nearer it approached me, the greater horror did it strike into me; yet did it not strike me back, nor turned me away, but held me in suspense.

The very toys of toys, and vanities of vanities, my ancient mistresses, still held me; they plucked my fleshy garment, and whispered softly, "Dost thou cast us off? and from that moment shall we no more be with thee for ever? and from that moment shall not this or that be lawful for thee for ever?" And what was it which they suggested in that I said, "this or that," what did they suggest, O my God? Let Thy mercy turn it away from the soul of Thy servant. What defilements did they suggest! what shame! And now I much less than half heard them, and not openly showing themselves and contradicting me, but muttering as it were behind my back, and privily plucking me, as I was departing, but to look back on them. Yet they did retard me, so that I hesitated to burst and shake myself free from them, and to spring over whither I was called; a violent habit saying to me, "Thinkest thou, thou canst live without them?"

But now it spake very faintly. For on that side whither I had set my face, and whither I trembled to go, there appeared unto me the chaste dignity of Continency, serene, yet not relaxedly, gay, honestly alluring me to come and doubt not; and stretching forth to receive and embrace me, her holy hands full of multitudes of good examples: there were so many young men and maidens here, a multitude of youth and every age, grave widows and aged virgins; and Continence herself in all, not barren, but a fruitful mother of children of joys, by Thee her Husband, O Lord. And she smiled on me with a persuasive mockery, as would she say, "Canst not thou what these youths, what these maidens can? or can they either in themselves, and not rather in the Lord their God? The Lord their God gave me unto them. Why standest thou in thyself, and so standest not? cast thyself upon Him, fear not He will not withdraw Himself that thou shouldest fall; cast thyself fearlessly upon Him, He will receive, and will heal thee." And I blushed exceedingly, for that I yet heard the muttering of those toys, and hung in suspense. And she again seemed to say, "Stop thine ears against those thy unclean members on the earth, that they may be mortified. They tell thee of delights, but not as doth the law of the Lord thy God." This controversy in my heart was self against self only. But Alypius sitting close by my side, in silence waited the issue of my unwonted emotion.

But when a deep consideration had from the secret bottom of my soul drawn together and heaped up all my misery in the sight of my heart; there arose a mighty storm, bringing a mighty shower of tears. Which that I might pour forth wholly, in its natural expressions, I rose from Alypius: solitude was suggested to me as fitter for the business of weeping; so I retired so far that even his presence could not be a burden to me. Thus was it then with me, and he perceived something of it; for something I suppose I had spoken, wherein the tones of my voice appeared choked with weeping, and so had risen up. He then remained where we were sitting, most extremely astonished. I cast myself down I know not how, under a certain fig-tree, giving full vent to my tears; and the floods of mine eyes gushed out an acceptable sacrifice to Thee. And, not indeed in these words, yet to this purpose, spake I much unto Thee: and Thou, O Lord, how long? how long, Lord, wilt Thou be angry for ever? Remember not our former iniquities, for I felt that I was held by them. I sent up these sorrowful words: How long, how long, "to-morrow, and to-morrow?" Why not now? why not is there this hour an end to my uncleanness?

So was I speaking and weeping in the most bitter contrition of my heart, when, lo! I heard from a neighbouring house a voice, as of boy or girl, I know not, chanting, and oft repeating, "Take up and read; Take up and read." Instantly, my countenance altered, I began to think most intently whether children were wont in any kind of play to sing such words: nor could I remember ever to have heard the like. So checking the torrent of my tears, I arose; interpreting it to be no other than a command from God to open the book, and read the first chapter I should find. For I had heard of Antony, that coming in during the reading of the Gospel, he received the admonition, as if what was being read was spoken to him: Go, sell all that thou hast, and give to the poor, and thou shalt have treasure in heaven, and come and follow me: and by such oracle he was forthwith converted unto Thee. Eagerly then I returned to the place where Alypius was sitting; for there had I laid the volume of the Apostle when I arose thence. I seized, opened, and in silence read that section on which my eyes first fell: Not in rioting and drunkenness, not in chambering and wantonness, not in strife and envying; but put ye on the Lord Jesus Christ, and make not provision for the flesh, in concupiscence. No further would I read; nor needed I: for instantly at the end of this sentence, by a light as it were of serenity infused into my heart, all the darkness of doubt vanished away.

Then putting my finger between, or some other mark, I shut the volume, and with a calmed countenance made it known to Alypius. And what was wrought in him, which I knew not, he thus showed me. He asked to see what I had read: I showed him; and he looked even further than I had read, and I knew not what followed. This followed, him that is weak in the faith, receive; which he applied to himself, and disclosed to me. And by this admonition was he strengthened; and by a good resolution and purpose, and most corresponding to his character, wherein he did always very far differ from me, for the better, without any turbulent delay he joined me. Thence we go in to my mother; we tell her; she rejoiceth: we relate in order how it took place; she leaps for joy, and triumpheth, and blesseth Thee, Who are able to do above that which we ask or think; for she perceived that Thou hadst given her more for me, than she was wont to beg by her pitiful and most sorrowful groanings. For thou convertedst me unto Thyself, so that I sought neither wife, nor any hope of this world, standing in that rule of faith, where Thou hadst showed me unto her in a vision, so many years before. And Thou didst convert her mourning into joy, much more plentiful than she had desired, and in a much more precious and purer way than she erst required, by having grandchildren of my body.

LEO TOLSTOY

[1 8 2 8 – 1 9 1 0]

My life came to a standstill. . . .

Count Leo Tolstoy faced a grave psychological crisis at the time of completing his second masterpiece, *Anna Karenina.* A wealthy landowner of a large Russian estate, married to his one great love and the father of many children, acclaimed throughout the world as the author of *War and Peace,* Tolstoy suddenly found himself unable to be left alone with a weapon, for fear of committing suicide. While traveling to a distant province to conduct a real-estate transaction, he felt himself enclosed in the same room with death and was forced to flee homeward, overwhelmed by anxiety and despair.

In the selection that follows from his *Confession,* Tolstoy describes his tentative approach to the spiritual life and the revolution in his thinking and actions that resulted from his turn to faith in God. In the first part of his *Confession,* he outlines in great detail the self-indulgence of his early years and the negative effects on his health and psyche of a life of luxury and promiscuity.

Following his conversion to Christian faith, Tolstoy elaborated a unique pacifist Christian philosophy of nonviolent resistance to evil that became widely influential, winning followers from around the world and inspiring authors and thinkers as varied as D. H. Lawrence, Mohandas Gandhi, and Martin Luther King, Jr.

He produced his own version of the Gospels of the New Testament and engaged in a serious study of theology, composing several treatises, commentaries, and expositions of his faith. Although he never felt that he had reached a complete understanding of God—in answer to a friend's question near the end of his life, he acknowledged he was "still seeking the truth" —he imposed a harsh, ascetic lifestyle on himself, dressing as a peasant and working in the fields with his bare hands. Relinquishing his claims to wealth and property, he disclaimed the royalties on his earlier literary masterpieces, now rated by their author as so much "bad art."

In his later years, he turned to the composition of "stories for the people," fables that expressed Christian ideals in simple terms. He donated the proceeds from his last novel, the ideological *Resurrection*, to a Christian sect seeking to emigrate from Russia.

Fleeing an increasingly disturbed home environment made unendurable by the conflict between his family and his followers, Tolstoy died at the train station of Astapovo on his way to a monastery. His last words were said to have been, "The truth . . . I love much." [AM]

FROM A CONFESSION

I was baptized and educated in the Orthodox Christian faith. Even as a child and throughout my adolescence and youth I was schooled in the Orthodox beliefs. But when at the age of eighteen I left my second year of studies at the university, I had lost all belief in what I had been taught.

Judging from what I can remember, I never really had a serious belief. I simply trusted in what I had been taught and in the things my elders adhered to. But even this trust was very shaky. . . .

My break with faith occurred in me as it did and still does among people of our social and cultural type. As I see it, in most cases it happens like this:

people live as everyone lives, but they all live according to principles that not only have nothing to do with the teachings of faith but for the most part are contrary to them. The teachings of faith have no place in life and never come into play in the relations among people; they simply play no role in living life itself. The teachings of faith are left to some other realm, separated from life and independent of it. If one should encounter them, then it is only as some superficial phenomenon that has no connection with life.

Today, as in days past, there is no way to tell from a person's life, from his deeds, whether or not he is a believer. If there is indeed no difference between those who are clearly adherents of the Orthodox faith and those who deny it, then it is not to the benefit of the former. Then, as now, the open avowal and confession of the Orthodox faith occurred largely among narrow-minded, cruel, and immoral people wrapped up in their own self-importance. On the other hand, intellect, honor, straightforwardness, good naturedness, and morality were for the most part to be found among people claiming to be disbelievers.

They teach catechism in the schools and send pupils to church; functionaries must carry certificates showing they have taken holy communion. But now, and even more so in the past, a person of our class who is no longer in school and has not gone into public service can live dozens of years without once being reminded that he lives among Christians, while he himself is regarded as a follower of the Orthodox Christian faith.

Thus today, as in days past, the teachings of faith, accepted on trust and sustained by external pressure, gradually fade under the influence of the knowledge and experiences of life, which stand in opposition to those teachings. Quite often a man goes on for years imagining that the religious teaching that had been imparted to him since childhood is still intact, while all the time there is not a trace of it left in him.

A certain intelligent and honest man named S. once told me the story of how he ceased to be a believer. At the age of twenty-six, while taking shelter for the night during a hunting trip, he knelt to pray in the evening, as had been his custom since childhood. His older brother, who had accompanied him on the trip, was lying down on some straw and watching him. When S. had finished and was getting ready to lie down, his brother said to him, "So you still do that." And they said nothing more to each other. From that day S. gave up praying and going to church. And for thirty years he has not prayed, he has not taken holy communion, and he has not gone to church. Not because he shared his brother's convictions and went along with them; nor was it because he had decided on something or other in his own soul. It was simply that the remark his brother had made was like the nudge of a finger against a wall that was about to fall over from its own weight. His brother's remark showed him that the place where he thought faith to be had long since been empty; subsequently the words he spoke, the signs of the cross he made, and the bowing of his head in prayer were in essence completely meaningless actions. Once having admitted the meaninglessness of these gestures, he could no longer continue them.

Thus it has happened and continues to happen, I believe, with the great majority of people. I am referring to people of our social and cultural type, people who are honest with themselves, and not those who use faith as a means of obtaining some temporal goal or other. (These people are the most radical disbelievers, for if faith, in their view, is a means of obtaining some worldly end, then it is indeed no faith at all.) People of our type are in a position where the light of knowledge and of life has broken down the artificial structure, and they have either taken note of this and have left it behind them or they have remained unconscious of it.

The teachings of faith instilled in me since childhood left me, just as they have left others; the only difference is that since I began reading and thinking a great deal at an early age, I became aware of my renunciation of the teachings of faith very early in life. From the age of sixteen I gave up praying and on my own accord quit going to church and fasting. I ceased to believe in what had been instilled in me since childhood, yet I did believe in something, though I could not say what. I even believed in God—or rather I did not deny God—but what kind of God I could not say; nor did I deny Christ and his teachings, but I could not have said what those teachings consisted of.

As I now look back at that time I clearly see that apart from animal instincts, the faith that affected my life, the only real faith I had, was faith in perfection. But I could not have said what perfection consisted of or what its purpose might be. I tried to achieve intellectual perfection; I studied everything I could, everything that life gave me a chance to study. I tried to perfect my will and set up rules for myself that I endeavored to follow. I strove for physical perfection by doing all the exercises that develop strength and agility and by undergoing all the hardships that discipline the self in endurance and perseverance. I took all this to be perfection. The starting point of it all was, of course, moral perfection, but this was soon replaced by a belief in overall perfection, that is, a desire to be better not in my own eyes or in the eyes of God, but rather a desire to be better in the eyes of other people. And this effort to be better in the eyes of other people was very quickly displaced by a longing to be stronger than other people, that is, more renowned, more important, wealthier than others.

. . . .

SOMEDAY I SHALL RELATE THE STORY OF MY LIFE, INCLUDING BOTH the pathetic and the instructive aspects of those ten years of my youth. I think that many, very many, have had the same experiences. With all my soul I longed to be good; but I was young, I had passions, and I was alone, utterly alone, whenever I sought what was good. Every time I tried to express my most heartfelt desires to be morally good I met with contempt and ridicule; and as soon as I would give in to vile passions I was praised and encouraged. Ambition, love of power, self-interest, lechery, pride, anger, vengeance—all of it was highly esteemed. As I gave myself over to these passions I became like my elders, and I felt that they were pleased with me. A kindhearted aunt of mine with whom I lived, one of the finest of women, was forever telling me that her fondest desire was for me to have an affair with a married woman: *"Rien ne forme un jeune homme comme une liaison avec une femme comme il faut."* Another happiness she wished for me was that I become an adjutant, preferably to the emperor. And the greatest happiness of all would be for me to marry a very wealthy young lady who could bring me as many serfs as possible.

I cannot recall those years without horror, loathing, and heartrending pain. I killed people in war, challenged men to duels with the purpose of killing them, and lost at cards; I squandered the fruits of the peasants' toil and then had them executed; I was a fornicator and a cheat. Lying, stealing, promiscuity of every kind, drunkenness, violence, murder—there was not a crime I did not commit; yet in spite of it all I was praised, and my colleagues considered me and still do consider me a relatively moral man.

Thus I lived for ten years.

During this time I began to write out of vanity, self-interest, and pride. I did the same thing in my writing that I did in my life. In order to acquire the fame and the money I was writing for, it was necessary to conceal what was good and to flaunt what was bad. And that is what I did. Time after time I would scheme in my writings to conceal under the mask of indifference and even pleasantry those yearnings for something good which gave meaning to my life. And I succeeded in this and was praised.

At the age of twenty-six, when the war had ended, I came to St. Petersburg and got to know the writers there. They accepted me as one of their own, heaped flattery upon me. Before I could turn around, the views on life peculiar to the writers with whom I associated became my own, and before long all my previous efforts to become better were completely at an end. Having no discipline myself, I let these views justify my life.

The theory adopted by these people, my fellow writers, was that life proceeds according to a general development and that we, the thinkers, play the primary role in that development; moreover, we, the artists and the poets, have the greatest influence on the thinkers. Our mission is to educate people. In order to avoid the obvious question—"What do I know and what can I teach?"—the theory explained that it is not necessary to know anything and that the artist and the poet teach unconsciously. Since I was considered a remarkable artist and poet, it was quite natural for me to embrace this theory. As an artist and poet I wrote and taught without myself knowing what I was teaching. I received money for doing this; I enjoyed excellent food, lodgings, women, society; I was famous. Therefore whatever I was teaching must have been very good.

This faith in knowledge, poetry, and the evolution of life was indeed a faith, and I was one of its priests. Being one of its priests was very profitable and quite pleasant. I lived a rather long time in this faith without ever doubting its truth. But in the second and especially in the third year of such a way of life I began to doubt the infallibility of this faith and started to examine it more closely. The first thing that led me to doubt was that I began to notice that the priests of this faith did not agree among themselves. Some would say, "We are the best and the most useful of teachers, for we teach what is needful while others who teach are in error." Others would say, "No, we are the true teachers; it is you who are in error." They argued and quarreled among themselves and abused, deceived, and cheated one another. Moreover, there were many among us who were not even concerned about who was right and who was wrong; they simply pursued their own selfish ends and had the support of our activity. All this forced me to doubt the truth of our faith.

Furthermore, once I had come to doubt the faith of the writers, I began to observe its priests more closely and became convinced that nearly all the priests of this faith were immoral men, in most cases of a base and worthless character. Many of them were lower than those whom I had met earlier during my wanton military life, but they were complacent and self-satisfied to a degree that can only be found either among people who are complete saints or among those who do not know what holiness is. People became repugnant to me, and I became repugnant to myself. And I realized that this faith was a delusion.

But the strange thing is that even though I was quick to see the utter lie of this faith and renounced it, I did not renounce the rank bestowed upon me by these people, the rank of artist, poet, and teacher. I naïvely imagined that I was a poet and an artist, that I could teach all men without myself knowing what I was teaching. And so I went on.

As a result of my association with these people, I took up a new vice: I developed a pathological pride and the insane conviction that it was my mission to teach people without knowing what I was teaching them.

As I now look back at that period and recall my state of mind and the state of mind of those people (a state that, by the way, persists among thousands), it all seems pitiful, horrible, and ridiculous to me; it excites the same feelings one might experience in a madhouse.

At the time we were all convinced that we had to speak, write, and publish as quickly as possible and as much as possible and that this was necessary for the good of mankind. Thousands of us published and wrote in an effort to teach others, all the while disclaiming and abusing one another. Without taking note of the fact that we knew nothing, that we did not know the answer to the simplest question of life, the question of what is right and what is wrong, we all went on talking without listening to one another. At times we would indulge and praise each other on the condition that we be indulged and praised in return; at other times we would irritate and shout at each other exactly as in a madhouse.

Thousand of workers toiled day and night, to the limit of their strength, gathering and printing millions of words to be distributed by mail throughout all Russia. We continued to teach, teach, and teach some more, and there was no way we could ever teach it all; and then we would get angry because people paid us little heed.

Very strange indeed, but now I understand it. The real reason behind what we were doing was that we wanted to obtain as much money and praise as possible. Writing books and newspapers was the only thing we knew how to do in order to attain this end. And so that is what we did. But in order for us to engage in something so useless and at the same time maintain the conviction that we were very important people, we needed a rationale that would justify what we were doing. And so we came up with the following: everything that exists is rational. Further, everything that exists is evolving. And it is evolving by means of an enlightenment. The enlightenment in turn undergoes change through the distribution of books and periodicals. We are paid and respected for writing books and periodicals, and therefore we are the most useful and the best of people. This reasoning would have worked very well, had we all been in agreement; but since for every opinion expressed by one person there was always someone else whose opinion was diametrically opposed to it, we should have been led to reconsider. But we never noticed this. We received money, and people of our circle praised us; thus every one of us believed himself to be right.

It is now clear to me that there was no difference between ourselves and people living in a madhouse; at the time I only vaguely suspected this, and, like all madmen, I thought everyone except myself was mad.

THUS I LIVED, GIVING MYSELF OVER TO THIS INSANITY FOR ANOTHER six years, until my marriage. During this time I went abroad. Life in Europe and my acquaintance with eminent and learned Europeans confirmed me all the more in my belief in general perfectibility, for I found the very same belief among them. My belief assumed a form that it commonly assumes among the educated people of our time. This belief was expressed by the word "progress." At the time it seemed to me that this word had meaning. Like any living individual, I was tormented by questions of how to live better. I still had not understood that in answering that one must live according to progress, I was talking just like a person being carried along in a boat by the waves and the wind; without really answering, such a person replies to the only important question—"Where are we to steer?"—by saying, "We are being carried somewhere."

I did not notice this at the time. Only now and then would my feelings, and not my reason, revolt against this commonly held superstition of the age, by means of which people hide from themselves their own ignorance of life. Thus during my stay in Paris the sight of an execution revealed to me the feebleness of my superstitious belief in progress. When I saw how the head was severed from the body and heard the thud of each part as it fell into the box, I understood, not with my intellect but with my whole being, that no theories of the rationality of existence or of progress could justify such an act; I realized that even if all the people in the world from the day of creation found this to be necessary according to whatever theory, I knew that it was not necessary and that it was wrong. Therefore, my judgments must be based on what is right and necessary and not on what people say and do; I must judge not according to progress but according to my own heart. The death of my brother was another instance in which I realized the inadequacy of the superstition of progress in regard to life. A good, intelligent, serious man, he was still young when he fell ill. He suffered for over a year and died an agonizing death without ever understanding why he lived and understanding even less why he was dying. No theories could provide any answers to these questions, either for him or for me, during his slow and painful death.

But these were only rare instances of doubt; on the whole I continued to live, embracing only a faith in progress. "Everything is developing, and I am developing; the reason why I am developing in this way will come to light, along with everything else." Thus I was led to formulate my faith at the time.

When I returned from abroad I settled in the country and occupied myself with the peasant schools. This occupation was especially dear to my heart because it involved none of the lies that had become so apparent to me, the lies that had irritated me when I was a literary teacher. Here too I was acting in the name of progress, but I assumed a critical attitude toward that progress. I told myself that in many of its forms progress did not proceed as it should and that here it was necessary to leave a primitive people, the peasant children, completely free to choose the path of progress they wanted.

In essence I was still faced with the same insoluble problem of how to teach without knowing what I was teaching. In the higher spheres of literature it was clear to me that I could not teach without knowing what I was teaching; for I saw that everyone taught differently and that in the arguments they had they scarcely hid their ignorance from each other. But here, with the peasant children, I thought I could get around this difficulty by allowing the children to learn whatever they liked. It now seems ludicrous to me when I recall how I tried this and that in order to carry out this whim of mine to teach, all the while knowing full well in the depths of my soul that there was no way I could teach what was needful because I did not know what was needful. After a year of being occupied with school I went abroad once again in order to find out how this could be done without myself knowing how to teach.

I believed that I had found a solution abroad, and, armed with all this wisdom, I returned to Russia in the year of the emancipation of the serfs. I took up the office of arbitrator and began teaching the uneducated people in the schools and the educated people through the periodical that I had started publishing. Things seemed to be going well, but I felt that my mental health was not what it should be and that this could not go on for long. Perhaps even then I would have fallen into the despair that came over me at the age of fifty were it not for one more aspect of life which I had not yet experienced and which held the promise of salvation: family life.

For a year I was occupied with arbitration, with the schools, and with the magazine. But I was soon exhausted from being entangled in the whole thing. The struggle with arbitration became burdensome to me; my activity in the schools was a lot of trouble; and my shuffling around with the magazine became repugnant to me, since it was forever centered on the same thing—the desire to teach everyone while hiding the fact that I did not know what I was teaching. It finally reached a point where I fell ill, more spiritually than physically; I gave it all up and went to the steppes of the Bashkirs to breathe fresh air, drink *koumiss*, and live an animal life.

After I returned I got married. The new circumstances of a happy family life completely diverted me from any search for the overall meaning of life. At that time my whole life was focused on my family, my wife, my children, and thus on a concern for improving our way of life. My striving for personal perfection, which had already been replaced by a striving for perfection in general, a striving for progress, now became a striving for what was best for my family and me.

Thus another fifteen years went by.

In spite of the fact that during these fifteen years I regarded writing as a trivial endeavor, I continued to write. I had already tasted the temptations of authorship, the temptations of enormous monetary rewards and applause for worthless work, and I gave myself up to it as a means of improving my material situation and as a way of stifling any questions in my soul concerning the meaning of my life and of life in general.

As I wrote I taught what to me was the only truth: that we must live for whatever is best for ourselves and our family.

And so I lived. But five years ago something very strange began to happen to me. At first I began having moments of bewilderment, when my life would come to a halt, as if I did not know how to live or what to do; I would lose my presence of mind and fall into a state of depression. But this passed, and I continued to live as before. Then the moments of bewilderment recurred more frequently, and they always took the same form. Whenever my life came to a halt, the questions would arise: Why? And what next?

At first I thought these were pointless and irrelevant questions. I thought that the answers to them were well known and that if I should ever want to resolve them, it would not be too hard for me; it was just that I could not be bothered with it now, but if I should take it upon myself, then I would find the answers. But the questions began to come up more and more frequently, and their demands to be answered became more and more urgent. And like points concentrated into one spot, these questions without answers came together to form a single black stain.

It happened with me as it happens with everyone who contracts a fatal internal disease. At first there were the insignificant symptoms of an ailment, which the patient ignores; then these symptoms recur more and more frequently, until they merge into one continuous duration of suffering. The suffering increases, and before he can turn around the patient discovers what he already knew: the thing he had taken for a mere indisposition is in fact the most important thing on earth to him, is in fact death.

This is exactly what happened to me. I realized that this was not an incidental ailment but something very serious, and that if the same questions should continue to recur, I would have to answer them. And I tried to answer them. The questions seemed to be such foolish, simple, childish questions. But as soon as I laid my hands on them and tried to resolve them, I was immediately convinced, first of all, that they were not childish and foolish questions but the most vital and profound questions in life, and, secondly, that no matter how much I pondered them there was no way I could resolve them. Before I could be occupied with my Samara estate, with the education of my son, or with the writing of books, I had to know why I was doing these things. As long as I do not know the reason why, I cannot do anything. In the middle of my concern with the household, which at the time kept me quite busy, a question would suddenly come into my head: "Very well, you will have 6,000 desyatins in the Samara province, as well as 300 horses; what then?" And I was completely taken aback and did not know what else to think. As soon as I started to think about the education of my children, I would ask myself, "Why?" Or I would reflect on how the people might attain prosperity, and I would suddenly ask myself, "What concern is it of mine?" Or in the middle of thinking about the fame that my works were bringing me I would say to myself, "Very well, you will be more famous than Gogol, Pushkin, Shakespeare, Molière, more famous than all the writers in the world —so what?"

And I could find absolutely no reply.

MY LIFE CAME TO A STOP. I COULD BREATHE, EAT, DRINK, AND SLEEP; indeed, I could not help but breathe, eat, drink, and sleep. But there was no life in me because I had no desires whose satisfaction I would have found reasonable. If I wanted something, I knew beforehand that it did not matter whether or not I got it.

If a fairy had come and offered to fulfill my every wish, I would not have known what to wish for. If in moments of intoxication I should have not desires but the habits of old desires, in moments of sobriety I knew that it was all a delusion, that I really desired nothing. I did not even want to discover truth anymore because I had guessed what it was. The truth was that life is meaningless.

It was as though I had lived a little, wandered a little, until I came to the precipice, and I clearly saw that there was nothing ahead except ruin. And there was no stopping, no turning back, no closing my eyes so I would not see that there was nothing ahead except the deception of life and of happiness and the reality of suffering and death, of complete annihilation.

I grew sick of life; some irresistible force was leading me to somehow get rid of it. It was not that I wanted to kill myself. The force that was leading me away from life was more powerful, more absolute, more all-encompassing than any desire. With all my strength I struggled to get away from life. The thought of suicide came to me as naturally then as the thought of improving life had come to me before. This thought was such a temptation that I had to use cunning against myself in order not to go through with it too hastily. I did not want to be in a hurry only because I wanted to use all my strength to untangle my thoughts. If I could not get them untangled, I told myself, I could always go ahead with it. And there I was, a fortunate man, carrying a rope from my room, where I was alone every night as I undressed, so that I would not hang myself from the beam between the closets. And I quit going hunting with a gun, so that I would not be too easily tempted to rid myself of life. I myself did not know what I wanted. I was afraid of life, I struggled to get rid of it, and yet I hoped for something from it.

And this was happening to me at a time when, from all indications, I should have been considered a completely happy man; this was when I was not yet fifty years old. I had a good, loving, and beloved wife, fine children, and a large estate that was growing and expanding without any effort on my part. More than ever before I was respected by friends and acquaintances, praised by strangers, and I could claim a certain renown without really deluding myself. Moreover, I was not physically and mentally unhealthy; on the contrary, I enjoyed a physical and mental vigor such as I had rarely encountered among others my age. Physically, I could keep up with the peasants working in the fields; mentally, I could work eight and ten hours at a stretch without suffering any aftereffects from the strain. And in such a state of affairs I came to a point where I could not live; and even though I feared death, I had to employ ruses against myself to keep from committing suicide. . . . I was like a man lost in the forest who was terrified by the fact that he was lost, like a man who was rushing about, longing to find his way and knowing that every step was leading him into deeper confusion, and yet who could not help rushing about.

This was the horror. And in order to be delivered from this horror, I wanted to kill myself. I felt a horror of what awaited me; I knew that this horror was more terrible than my present situation, but I could not keep it away and I did not have the patience to wait for the end. No matter how convincing the argument was that a blood vessel in the heart would burst anyway or that something else would rupture and it would be all over, I could not patiently await the end. The horror of the darkness was too great, and I wanted to be free of it as quickly as possible by means of a rope or a bullet. It was this feeling, more powerful than any other, that was leading me toward suicide. . . . [Some passages, containing Tolstoy's sociopolitical observations, have been omitted here.]

My position was terrible. I knew that I could find nothing in the way of rational knowledge except a denial of life; and in faith I could find nothing except a denial of reason, and this was even more impossible than a denial of life. According to rational knowledge, it followed that life is evil, and people know it. They do not have to live, yet they have lived and they do live, just as I myself had lived, even though I had known for a long time that life is meaningless and evil. According to faith, it followed that in order to understand the meaning of life I would have to turn away from reason, the very thing for which meaning was necessary.

I RAN INTO A CONTRADICTION FROM WHICH THERE WERE ONLY TWO ways out: either the thing that I had referred to as reason was not as rational as I had thought, or the thing that I took to be irrational was not as irrational as I had thought. And I began to examine the course of the arguments that had come of my rational knowledge.

As I looked more closely at this course, I found it to be entirely correct. The conclusion that life is nothing was unavoidable; but I detected a mistake. The mistake was that my thinking did not correspond to the question I had raised. The question was: Why should I live? Or: Is there anything real and imperishable that will come of my illusory and perishable life? Or: What kind of meaning can my finite existence have in this infinite universe? In order to answer this question, I studied life.

It was obvious that the resolution of all the possible questions of life could not satisfy me because my question, no matter how simple it may seem at first glance, entails a demand to explain the finite by means of the infinite and the infinite by means of the finite.

I asked, "What is the meaning of my life beyond space, time, and causation?" And I answered, "What is the meaning of my life within space, time, and causation?" After a long time spent in the labor of thought, it followed that I could reply only that my life had no meaning at all. . . .

Thus in addition to rational knowledge, which before had seemed to be the only knowledge, I was inevitably led to recognize a different type of knowledge, an irrational type, which all of humanity had: faith, which provides us with the possibility of living. As far as I was concerned, faith was as irrational as ever, but I could not fail to recognize that it alone provides humanity with an answer to the question of life, thus making it possible to live.

Rational knowledge led me to the conclusion that life is meaningless; my life came to a halt, and I wanted to do away with myself. As I looked around at people, I saw that they were living, and I was convinced that they knew the meaning of life. Then I turned and looked at myself; as long as I knew the meaning of life, I lived. As it was with others, so it was with me: faith provided me with the meaning of life and the possibility of living.

Upon a further examination of the people in other countries, of my contemporaries, and of those who have passed away, I saw the same thing. Wherever there is life, there is faith; since the origin of mankind faith has made it possible for us to live, and the main characteristics of faith are everywhere and always the same.

No matter what answers a given faith might provide for us, every answer of faith gives infinite meaning to the finite existence of man, meaning that is not destroyed by suffering, deprivation, and death. Therefore, the meaning of life and the possibility of living may be found in faith alone. I realized that the essential significance of faith lies not only in the "manifestation of things unseen" and so on, or in revelation (this is simply a description of one of the signs of faith); nor is it simply the relation between man and God (faith must first be determined and then God, not the other way around), or agreeing with what one has been told, even though this is what it is most often understood to be. Faith is the knowledge of the meaning of human life, whereby the individual does not destroy himself but lives. Faith is the force of life. If a man lives, then he must have faith in something. If he did not believe that he had something he must live for, then he would not live. If he fails to see and understand the illusory nature of the finite, then he believes in the finite; if he understands the illusory nature of the finite, then he must believe in the infinite. Without faith it is impossible to live.

I looked back on the course of my internal life and I was horrified. It was now clear to me that in order for a man to live, he must either fail to see the infinite or he must have an explanation of the meaning of life by which the finite and the infinite would be equated. I had such an explanation, but I did not need it as long as I believed in the finite, and I began to use reason to test it out. And in the light of reason every bit of my former explanation crumbled into dust. But the time came when I no longer believed in the finite. And then, using the foundations of reason, I began to draw on what I knew to put together an explanation that would give life meaning; but nothing came of it. Along with the finest minds that mankind has produced, I came up with $0 = 0$, and I was utterly amazed at coming to such a resolution and at discovering that there could be no other.

And what did I do when I searched for an answer in the experimental sciences? I wanted to find out why I lived, and to do that I studied everything that was outside of myself. To be sure, I was able to learn a great deal, but nothing of what I needed.

And what did I do when I searched for an answer in the area of philosophy? I studied the thoughts of those who found themselves in the same situation as I, and they had no answer to the question of why I live. I was not able to learn anything here that I did not already know—namely, that it is impossible to know anything.

What am I? A part of the infinite. Indeed, in these words lies the whole problem. Is it possible that man has only now raised this question? And can it be that no one before me has put this question to himself, a question so simple that it rests on the tip of the tongue of every intelligent child?

No, this question has been asked ever since there have been people to ask it; since the beginning man has understood that to resolve the question by equating the finite with the finite is just as inadequate as equating the infinite with the infinite; since the beginning man has sought to articulate the relation between the finite and the infinite.

We subject to logical inquiry all the concepts that identify the finite with the infinite and through which we receive the meaning of life and the ideas of God, freedom, and good. And these concepts do not stand up to the critiques born of reason.

If it were not so terrible, it would be laughable to see the pride and complacency with which, like children, we take apart the watch, removing the spring and making a plaything of it, only to be surprised when the watch stops running.

A resolution of the contradiction between the finite and the infinite, an answer to the question of life that makes it possible to live, is necessary and dear to us. And the one resolution that we find everywhere, at all times and among all nations, is the resolution that has come down from a time in which all human life is lost to us. It is a resolution so difficult that we could come up with nothing like it, one that we thoughtlessly undo by again raising the question that occurs to everyone and for which we have no answer.

The concepts of an infinite God, moral good and evil, the immortality of the soul, and a relation between God and the affairs of man are ones that have been worked out historically through the life of a humanity that is hidden from our eyes. They are concepts without which there would be no life, without which I myself could not live, and yet, putting aside all the labor of humankind, I wanted to do it all over again by myself and in my own way.

I did not think so at the time, but even then the seeds of these thoughts had already been planted within me. I realized first of all that despite our wisdom, the position of Schopenhauer, Solomon, and myself was absurd: we considered life evil, and yet we lived. This is clearly absurd because if life is meaningless and if I love reason so much, then I must destroy life so there will be no one around to deny it. Secondly, I realized that all our arguments went round and round in a vicious circle, like a cog whose gears are out of sync. No matter how refined our reasoning, we could not come up with an answer; it would always turn out that $0 = 0$, and our method was therefore probably mistaken. Finally, I began to realize that the most profound wisdom of man was rooted in the answers given by faith and that I did not have the right to deny them on the grounds of reason; above all, I realized that these answers alone can form a reply to the question of life.

. . . I REMEMBER ONE DAY IN EARLY SPRING WHEN I WAS ALONE IN the forest listening to the sounds of the woods. I listened and thought about the one thing that had constantly occupied me for the last three years. Again I was searching for God.

"Very well," I said to myself. "So there is no God like the one I have imagined; the only reality is my life. There is no such God. And nothing, no miracle of any kind, can prove there is, because miracles exist only in my irrational imagination."

"But where does my notion of God, of the one whom I seek, come from?" I asked myself. And again with this thought there arose in me joyous waves of life. Everything around me came to life, full of meaning. But my joy did not last long. My mind continued its work. "The concept of God," I told myself, "is not God. A concept is something that occurs within me; the concept of God is something I can conjure up inside myself at will. This is not what I seek. I am seeking that without which there could be no life." Once again everything within me and around me began to die; again I felt the longing to kill myself.

But at that point I took a closer look at myself and at what had been happening within me; and I remembered the hundreds of times I had gone through these deaths and revivals. I remembered that I had lived only when I believed in God. Then, as now, I said to myself, "As long as I know God, I live; when I forget, when I do not believe in him, I die." What are these deaths and revivals? It is clear that I do not live whenever I lose my faith in the existence of God, and I would have killed myself long ago if I did not have some vague hope of finding God. I truly live only whenever I am conscious of him and seek him. "What, then, do I seek?" a voice cried out within me. "He is there, the one without whom there could be no life." To know God and to live come to one and the same thing. God is life.

"Live, seeking God, for there can be no life without God." And more powerfully than ever a light shone within me and all around me, and this light has not abandoned me since.

Thus I was saved from suicide. When and how this transformation within me was accomplished, I could not say. Just as the life force within me was gradually and imperceptibly destroyed, and I encountered the impossibility of life, the halting of life, and the need to murder myself, so too did this life force return to me gradually and imperceptibly. And the strange thing is that the life force which returned to me was not new but very old; it was the same force that had guided me during the early periods of my life. In essence I returned to the first things, to the things of childhood and youth. I returned to a faith in that will which gave birth to me and which asked something of me; I returned to the conviction that the single most important purpose in my life was to be better, to live according to this will. I returned to the conviction that I could find the expression of this will in something long hidden from me, something that all of humanity had worked out for its own guidance; in short, I returned to a belief in God, in moral perfection, and in a tradition that instills life with meaning. The only difference was that I had once accepted all this on an unconscious level, while now I knew that I could not live without it.

What happened to me was something like the following. Unable to recall how I got there, I found myself in a boat that had been launched from some unknown shore; the way to the other shore was pointed out to me, the oars were placed in my inexperienced hands, and I was left alone. I worked the oars as best I knew how and rowed on. But the further I paddled toward the center, the faster became the current that took me off-course, and I encountered more and more people who, like myself, were being carried away by the current. There were a few who continued to row; some had thrown away their oars. There were large boats, enormous ships, filled with people; some struggled against the current, others gave themselves up to it. And, looking downstream at everyone being carried along by the current, the further I rowed, the more I forgot the way that had been pointed out to me in the very center of the current. In the throng of boats and canoes, being carried downstream, I lost my way altogether and threw down my oars. All around me, in joy and triumph, people rushed downstream under sail and oar, assuring me and each other that there could be no other direction. And I believed them and moved along with them. And I was carried off a long way, so far that I heard the roar of the rapids in which I was bound to perish and saw boats being destroyed in them. Then I came to my senses. For a long time I could not understand what had happened to me. I saw before me the singular ruin toward which I was rushing headlong and which I feared, I could not see salvation anywhere, and I did not know what to do. But, looking back, I saw countless boats that were relentlessly struggling against the current, and I remembered the oars and the way to the shore and began to pull against the current and head back upstream toward it.

The shore was God, the stream was tradition, and the oars were the free will given to me to make it to the shore where I would be joined with God. Thus the force of life was renewed within me, and I began to live once again.

Amid a small circle of friends and relatives in Amherst, Massachusetts, Emily Dickinson spent a self-effacing life crafting a small body of poems that was only discovered after her death. "Quartz contentment," a lapidary phrase from one of her poems, might be a description of Dickinson's outward circumstances. Yet this contentment also represents the settlement the soul makes with life in the face of the unfathomable, be it despair or death.

Dickinson's poetry raises the profound questions of existence asked by the other authors included in this section. Although the scale of her world seems smaller than Augustine's or Tolstoy's, even the most homely and domestic objects in it direct one's attention to the same questions. The difficulty of her poems reflects her intimation of wonders beyond the ken of humans both to understand and to bear—as well as a rejection of easy answers.

In an 1876 letter, Dickinson wrote that "the unknown is the largest need of the intellect, though for it, no one thinks to thank God." Still, she was not pious in any conventional sense. She was proba-

EMILY DICKINSON

[1 8 3 0 – 1 8 8 6]

I dwell in Possibility.

bly an agnostic, but like Augustine she was obsessed with the condition of her inner life and with the power of God in relation to that inner life. God remains the great unknown, always pervasive, but always in the background.

[EP]

SELECTED POEMS

142

I saw no Way – The Heavens were stitched –
I felt the Columns close –
The Earth reversed her Hemispheres –
I touched the Universe –

And back it slid – and I alone –
A Speck upon a Ball –
Went out upon Circumference –
Beyond the Dip of Bell –

173

God made a little Gentian –
It tried – to be a Rose –
And failed – and all the Summer laughed –
But just before the Snows –

There rose a Purple Creature –
That ravished all the Hill –
And Summer hid her Forehead –
And Mockery – was still –

The Frosts were her condition –
The Tyrian would not come
Until the North – invoke it –
Creator – Shall I – bloom?

186

I am alive – I guess –
The Branches on my Hand
Are full of Morning Glory –
And at my finger's end –

The Carmine – tingles warm –
And if I hold a Glass
Across my Mouth – it blurs it –
Physician's – proof of Breath –

I am alive – because
I am not in a Room –
The Parlor – Commonly – it is –
So Visitors may come –

And lean – and view it sidewise –
And add "How cold – it grew" –
And "Was it conscious – when it stepped
In Immortality?"

I am alive – because
I do not own a House –
Entitled to myself – precise –
And fitting no one else –

And marked my Girlhood's name –
So Visitors may know
Which Door is mine – and not mistake –
And try another Key –

How good – to be alive!
How infinite – to be
Alive – two-fold – The Birth I had –
And this – besides, in – Thee!

231

My period had come for Prayer –
No other Art – would do –
My Tactics missed a rudiment –
Creator – Was it you?

God grows above – so those who pray
Horizons – must ascend –
And so I stepped upon the North
To see this Curious Friend –

His House was not – no sign had He –
By Chimney – nor by Door
Could I infer his Residence –
Vast Prairies of Air

Unbroken by a Settler –
Were all that I could see –
Infinitude – Had'st Thou no face
That I might look on Thee?

The Silence condescended –
Creation stopped – for Me –
But awed beyond my errand –
I worshipped – did not "pray" –

248

There is a pain – so utter –
It swallows substance up –
Then covers the Abyss with Trance –
So Memory can step
Around – across – upon it –
As one within a Swoon –
Goes safely – where an open eye –
Would drop Him – Bone by Bone.

270

I dwell in Possibility –
A fairer House than Prose –
More numerous of Windows –
Superior – for Doors –

Of Chambers as the Cedars –
Impregnable of Eye –
And for an Everlasting Roof
The Gambrels of the Sky –

Of Visitors – the fairest –
For Occupation – This –
The spreading wide my narrow Hands
To gather Paradise –

280

Each Life Converges to some Centre –
Expressed – or still –
Exists in every Human Nature
A Goal –

Embodied scarcely to itself – it may be –
Too fair

For Credibility's presumption
To mar –

Adored with caution – as a Brittle Heaven –
To reach
Were hopeless, as the Rainbow's Raiment
To touch –

Yet persevered toward – surer – for the Distance –
How high –
Unto the Saints' slow diligence –
The Sky –

Ungained – it may be – by a Life's low Venture –
But then –
Eternity enable the endeavoring
Again.

296

Behind Me – dips Eternity –
Before Me – Immortality –
Myself – the Term between –
Death but the Drift of Eastern Gray,
Dissolving into Dawn away,
Before the West begin –

'Tis Kingdoms – afterward – they say –
In perfect – pauseless Monarchy –
Whose Prince – is Son of None –
Himself – His Dateless Dynasty –
Himself – Himself diversify –
In Duplicate divine –

'Tis Miracle before Me – then –
'Tis Miracle behind – between –
A Crescent in the Sea –
With Midnight to the North of Her –
And Midnight to the South of Her –
And Maelstrom – in the Sky –

JORIS-KARL
HUYSMANS

[1 8 4 8 – 1 9 0 7]

I have led a shameful life.

n his novel of decadence *A rebours (Against the Grain,* 1884), the French writer Joris-Karl Huysmans is said to have invented the alienated and agonized modern antihero. In successive novels, Durtal, Huysmans's transparently autobiographical character, inhabits a world so disenchanted by modern science that man's spiritual longings have been replaced by an incessant pursuit of sensual and intellectual curiosities. In *Là-bas (Down There,* 1891), for instance, Durtal explores occultism, Satanism, and the outer reaches of blasphemy and impiety. *En route* (1895) is the last stage of Huysmans's journey of self-exploration: Durtal is portrayed as achieving moral purgation and cessation of his sensual obsessions through his acceptance of Roman Catholicism. Two further novels, *La Cathédrale* (1898) and *L'Oblat (The Oblate,* 1903), illustrate the attraction Catholicism exerted on many in the nineteenth century, especially those disillusioned by the prevalent belief that the secrets of human life and thought would one day be explained by the methods of experimental science. The following excerpt from *En route,* which portrays Durtal's conversion, is modeled on Huysmans's own conversion at the Trappist monastery d'Igny in 1892. Huysmans became a Benedictine oblate in 1901.   [EP]

FROM  *EN ROUTE*

He passed a most terrible night; it was so special, so dreadful, that he did not remember, in the whole of his existence, to have endured such anguish, undergone the like fears.

It was an uninterrupted succession of sudden wakings and of nightmares.

And these nightmares overpassed the limits of abomination that the most dangerous madness dreams. They developed themselves in the realm of lust; and they were so special, so new to him, that when he woke Durtal remained trembling, almost crying out.

It was not at all that involuntary and well known act, that vision which ceases just at the moment when the sleeper clasps an amorous form; it was as and more complete than in nature, long and accomplished, accompanied by all the preludes, all the details, all the sensations, and the orgasm took place with a singularly painful acuteness, an incredible spasm.

A strange fact, which seemed to point the difference between this state, and the unconscious uncleanness of night, was, beyond certain episodes and caresses which could only follow each other in reality, but were united at the same moment in the dream, the sensation clear and precise of a being, of a fluid form disappearing, with the sharp sound of a percussion cap, or the crack of a whip close by, on waking. This being was felt near him so distinctly, that the sheet, disarranged by the wind of the flight, was still in motion, and he looked at the empty place in terror.

"Ah," thought Durtal, when he had lighted his candle, "this carries me back to the time when I used to visit Madame Chantelouve, and reminds me of the stories of the Succubus."

He remained sitting up in bed, astonished, and looked with real uneasiness round the cell steeped in shadow. He looked at his watch, it was only eleven o'clock at night. "God," he said, "if the nights are always like this in monasteries!"

He had recourse to bathing with cold water in order to recover himself, opened his window to change the air, and lay down again, thoroughly chilled.

He hesitated to blow out his candle, uneasy at the darkness which seemed to him inhabited, full of ambushes and threats. He decided at last to extinguish it, and repeated the stanza he had already heard sung that evening in chapel:

Procul recedant somnia
Et noctium phantasmata,
Hostemque nostrum comprime,
Ne polluantur corpora.

He ended by falling asleep and dreamt again of impurity, but he came to himself in time to break the charm, experiencing again the impression of a shadow evaporating before he could seize it in the sheets. He looked at his watch; it was two o'clock.

"If this goes on, I shall be broken down to-morrow," he thought, but he succeeded somehow or other in dozing, and waking every ten minutes to wait for three o'clock.

"If I fall asleep again, I shall not be able to wake at the moment I wish," he thought, "suppose I get up."

He sprang out of bed, dressed, prayed, reduced his thoughts to order.

Real excesses would have exhausted him less than these sham freaks, but what seemed to him especially odious was the want of satisfaction left by the completed rape of these ghosts. Compared with their greedy tricks, the caresses of a woman only diffused a temperate pleasure, and ended in a feeble shock, but with this Succuba one remained in a fury at having clasped only the void, at having been the dupe of a lie, the plaything of an appearance, of which one could not remember the form or the features. It necessarily brought with it the desire of the flesh, the wish to clasp a real body, and Durtal began to think of Florence; she at least quenched his desires, and did not leave him thus, panting and feverish, in quest of he knew not what, in an atmosphere where he was surrounded, spied upon by an unknown whom he could not discern, by a phantom he could not escape.

Then Durtal shook himself, and would repulse the assault of these memories. "At any rate I will go and breathe the fresh air, and smoke a cigarette; we will see afterwards."

He descended the staircase, whose walls seemed not to keep their place, and danced in the light of his candle, threaded the corridors, blew out his light, placed the candlestick near the auditorium, and rushed out.

It was pitch dark; at the height of the first story a round window in the wall of the chapel cut a hole through the darkness like a red moon.

Durtal took a few whiffs of a cigarette, and then made his way to the chapel. He turned the latch of the door gently; the vestibule into which he entered was dark, but the apse, though it was empty, was lighted by numerous lamps.

He made a step, crossed himself, and fell back, for he had stumbled over a body; and he looked down at his feet.

He had come upon a battle-field.

On the ground human forms were lying, in the attitudes of combatants mowed down by grape shot, some flat on their faces, others on their knees, some leaning their hands on the ground as if stricken from behind, others extended with their fingers clenched on their breast, others again holding their heads or stretching out their arms.

And from this group in their agony rose no groan, no complaint.

Durtal was stupefied as he looked at this massacre of monks, and suddenly stopped with open mouth. A shaft of light fell from a lamp which the Father Sacristan had just placed in the apse, and crossing the porch, it showed a monk on his knees before the altar dedicated to the Virgin.

He was an old man of more than four-score years; motionless as a statue, his eyes fixed, leaning forward in such an access of adoration, that the faces in ecstasy in the Early Masters seemed, compared with his, forced and cold.

Yet his features were vulgar, his shaven skull, without a crown, tanned by many suns and rains, was brick-coloured, his eye was dim, covered with a film by age, his face was wrinkled, shrivelled, stained like an old log, hidden in a thicket of white hair, while his somewhat snub nose made the general effect of the face singularly common.

But there went out, not from his eyes, nor his mouth, but from everywhere and nowhere, a kind of angelic look which was diffused over his head, and enveloped all his poor body, bowed in its heap of rags.

In this old man the soul did not even give herself the trouble to reform and ennoble his features, she contented herself in annihilating them with her rays; it was, as it were, the nimbus of the old saints not now remaining round the head, but extending over all the features, pale and almost invisible, bathing his whole being.

He saw nothing and heard nothing; monks dragged themselves on their knees, came to warm themselves, and to take shelter near him, and he never moved, dumb and deaf, so rigid that you might have believed him dead, had not his lower lip stirred now and then, lifting in this movement his long beard.

The dawn whitened the windows, and as the darkness was gradually dissipated, the other brethren were visible in turn to Durtal; all these men, wounded by divine love, prayed ardently, flashed out beyond themselves noiselessly before the altar. Some were quite young, on their knees with their bodies upright; others, their eyeballs in ecstasy, were leaning back, and seated on their heels; others again were making the way of the cross, and were often placed each opposite another face to face, and they looked without seeing, as with the eyes of the blind.

And among these lay brethren, some fathers buried in their great white cowls lay prostrate and kissed the ground.

"Oh to pray, pray like these monks!" cried Durtal within himself.

He felt his unhappy soul grow slack within him; in this atmosphere of sanctity he unbent himself, and sank down on the pavement, humbly asking pardon from Christ, for having soiled by his presence the purity of this place.

He prayed long, unsealing himself for the first time, recognizing his unworthiness and vileness so that he could not imagine how, in spite of His mercy, the Lord could tolerate him in the little circle of His elect; he examined himself, saw clearly, and avowed that he was inferior to the least of these lay brothers who perhaps could not even spell out a book, understood that the culture of the mind was naught and the culture of the soul was all, and little by little, without perceiving it, thinking only of stammering forth acts of gratitude, he disappeared from the chapel, his soul borne up by the souls of others, away, away from the world, far from his charnel-house, far from his body.

In this chapel, the impulse had come at last, the going forth from self, till now refused, was at last permitted; he no longer strove with self as in the time when he escaped with so great difficulty from his prison-house, as at St. Severin or Notre Dame des Victoires.

Then he again realized this chapel, where his animal part had alone remained, and he looked round him with astonishment; the greater part of the brethren had gone, one father remained prostrate before our Lady's altar; he quitted it in his turn, and went back to the apse, as the other fathers entered it. . . .

The weather was warm that morning; the sun was filtered through the moving sieve of foliage, and the daylight, thus screened, was changed to rose colour as it touched the white. Durtal, who was about to read his prayer-book, saw the pages growing red, and by the law of complementary colours all the letters printed in black ink grew green.

He was amused by these details, and with his back to the warmth, he brightened up in this aromatic breeze, rested in this bath of sunshine from his fatigues of the night, when at the end of the walk he saw some of the brothers. They walked in silence, some carrying under their arms great round loaves, others holding milk cans, or baskets full of hay and eggs; they passed before him, and bowed respectfully.

All had a joyous and serious aspect. "Ah, good fellows," he thought, "for they helped me this morning, it is to them I owe it that I could keep silence no longer, and was able to pray, to have at last known the joy of supplication which at Paris was only a snare for me! to them, and above all to Our Lady de l'Atre, who had pity on my poor soul."

He sprang from his bench in an access of joy, went into the lateral walks, reached the piece of water he had partially seen the evening before; in front of it rose the huge cross he had seen at a distance from the carriage, in the wood, before he reached La Trappe.

It was placed opposite the monastery itself, and turned its back upon the pond; it bore an eighteenth-century Christ, of natural size, in white marble; the pond also took the form of a cross such as is shown on the greater part of the plans of churches.

This brown and liquid cross was spotted by duckweed, which the swan displaced as he swam.

He came towards Durtal, with extended beak, expecting, no doubt, a piece of bread.

Not a sound arose in this deserted spot, save the rustle of dry leaves which Durtal brushed as he walked. The clock struck seven.

He remembered that breakfast would be ready, and he walked quickly to the abbey. Father Etienne was waiting for him, shook hands, asked if he had slept well, then said:

"What would you like? I can only offer you milk and honey; I will send to-day to the nearest village and try to get you a little cheese, but you will have only a poor meal this morning."

Durtal proposed to exchange the milk for wine, declaring that he should then do very well, and said, "In any case I should do ill to complain, for you are fasting."

The monk smiled. "Just now," he said, "we are doing penance, on account of certain feasts of our order." And he explained that he only took food once a day, at two o'clock in the afternoon, after Nones.

"And you have not even wine and eggs to keep up your strength!"

Father Etienne smiled again. "One gets accustomed to it," he said. "What is this rule in comparison with that adopted by Saint Bernard and his companions, when they went to till the valley of Clairvaux? Their meal consisted of oak leaves, salted, cooked in muddy water."

And after a silence the Father continued: "No doubt the Trappist rule is hard, but it is mild if we carry our thoughts back to the rule of Saint Pacomius in the East. Only think; whoever wished to join that order had to remain ten days and nights at the door of the convent, and had to endure spitting and insults; if he still desired to enter, he fulfilled a three years' novitiate, inhabited a hut where he could not stand up, nor lie at full length, ate only olives and cabbage, prayed twelve times in the morning, twelve times in the afternoon, twelve times in the night; the silence was perpetual, and his mortifications never ceased. To prepare himself for this novitiate, and to learn to subdue his appetite, Saint Macarius thought of the plan of soaking his bread in a vessel with a very narrow neck, and only fed on the crumbs which he could take out with his fingers. When he was admitted into the monastery, he contented himself with gnawing leaves of raw cabbage on Sunday. Ah! they could stand more than we. We, alas! have no longer souls nor bodies stout enough to bear such fasts; but do not let that stop your meal; make as good an one as you can. Ah, by the way," said the monk, "be in the auditorium at ten precisely, where the Father Prior will hear your confession."

And he left the room.

If Durtal had received a blow on his head with a mallet, he could not have been more overwhelmed. All the scaffolding of his joys, so rapidly run up, fell. This strange fact had occurred, in the impulse of joy he had felt since daybreak he had wholly forgotten that he had to confess. He had a moment of aberration. "But I am forgiven," he thought; "the proof is that state of happiness, such as I have never known, that truly wonderful expansion of soul which I experienced in the chapel and in the wood."

The idea that nothing had begun, that all was still to do, terrified him; he had not the courage to swallow his bread, he drank a little wine, and rushed out of doors in a wind of panic.

He went, wildly, with great strides. Confession! The prior? Who was the prior? He sought in vain among the fathers whose faces he remembered the one who would hear him.

"My God!" he said, all at once, "but I do not even know how a confession is made."

He sought a deserted corner, where he could recollect himself a little. He was striding along without even knowing how he came there, along a walnut-tree walk with a wall on one side. There were some enormous trees, he hid himself behind the trunk of one of them, and sitting on the moss, turned over the leaves of his prayer-book, and read: "On arriving at the confessional, place yourself on your knees, make the sign of the cross, and ask the priest for his blessing, saying, 'Bless me, Father, for I have sinned'; then recite the Confiteor as far as *mea culpa* . . . and . . ."

He stopped, and without any need of probing it his life sprang out in jets of filth.

He shrank from it, there was so much, of every kind, that he was overwhelmed with despair.

Then by an effort of his will he pulled himself together, endeavoured to control and bank up these torrents, to separate them so as to understand them, but one affluent rolled back all the others, ended by overwhelming them, and became the river itself.

And this sin appeared at first ape-like and sly, at school where everyone tempted and corrupted others; then there was all his greedy youth, dragged through tap-rooms, rolled in swine troughs, wallowing in the sinks of prostitution, and then an ignoble manhood. To his regular tasks had succeeded toll paid to his senses, and shameful memories assailed him in a crowd; he recalled to mind how he had sought after monstrous iniquities, his pursuit of artifices aggravating the malice of the act, and the accomplices and agents of his sins passed in file before him.

Among all, at one time, there was a certain Madame Chantelouve, a demoniacal adulteress who had drawn him headlong into frightful excesses, who had linked him to nameless crimes, sins against holy things, to sacrileges.

"How can I tell all this to the monk?" thought Durtal, terrified by the remembrance; "how can I even express myself, so as to make him understand without defilement?"

Tears rushed from his eyes. "My God, my God!" he sighed, "this is indeed too much."

And in her turn Florence appeared with her little street-arab smile, and her childish haunches. "I can never tell the confessor all that was brewed in the perfumed shade of her vices," cried Durtal. "I can by no means make him face these torrents of pus.

"Yet they say this has to be done"; and he bowed under the weight of the foulness of this girl.

"How shameful to have been riveted to her, how disgusting to have satisfied the abominable demands of her desires!"

Behind this sewer extended others. He had traversed all the districts of sin which the prayer-book patiently enumerated. He had never confessed since his first communion, and with the piling up of years had come successive deposits of sins. He grew pale at the thought that he was about to detail to another man all his dirt, to acknowledge his most secret thoughts, to say to him what one dares not repeat to one's own self, lest one should despise oneself too much.

He sweated with anguish, then nausea at his being, remorse for his life solaced him, and he gave himself up; regret for having lived so long in this cesspool was a very crucifixion to him; he wept long, doubting pardon, not even daring to ask it, so vile did he feel himself.

At last he sprang up; the hour of expiation must be at hand, in fact his watch pointed to a quarter to ten. His agony as he thus wrought with himself had lasted more than two hours.

He hurriedly reached the main path which led to the monastery. He walked with his head down, forcing back his tears. . . .

HE WOKE WITH A BOUND AT ELEVEN O'CLOCK, WITH AN IMPRESSION of someone looking at him in his sleep. Lighting a match, he ascertained the time, and seeing no one, fell back in bed again, and slept at a stretch till four o'clock. Then he dressed himself in haste and ran to the church.

The vestibule, which had been dark on the previous evening, was lit up that morning, for an old monk was celebrating mass at the altar of St. Joseph.

He was bald and infirm, with a white beard waving from side to side in long threads with every gust of wind.

A lay brother was assisting him, a small man with black hair and a shaven head, like a ball painted blue; he looked like a bandit, with his beard in disorder and his worn-out robe of felt.

And the eyes of this bandit were gentle and startled like those of a little boy. He served the priest with an almost timid respect and a suppressed joy which was touching to see.

Others, kneeling on the flagstones, prayed with concentrated attention or read their mass. Durtal noticed the old man of eighty, immovable with outstretched face and closed eyes; and the youth whose look of pity had helped him near the pond, was following the office in his prayer-book with attentive meditation. He looked about twenty years old, tall and strong; his face, with an air of fatigue, was at once masculine and tender, with emaciated features, and a light beard which fell over his habit in a point.

Durtal gave way to his emotions in this chapel, where everyone did a little to help him, and thinking of the confession he was about to make, he implored the Saviour to help him, and prayed that the monk would completely explore his soul.

And he felt himself less dismayed, more master of himself, and firmer. He collected and pulled himself together, feeling a melancholy confusion, but he had no longer the sense of desolation which had overcome him the evening before. He set his mind on the idea that he would not abandon himself, that he would help himself with all his might, and that in any case he could not collect himself better.

These reflections were interrupted by the departure of the old Trappist, who had finished offering the sacrifice, and by the entry of the prior, who went up in the rotunda between two white fathers to say mass at the high altar.

Durtal was absorbed in his prayer-book, but he ceased reading when the priest had consumed the Species, for all rose, and he was amazed at a sight of which he had never dreamed, a communion of monks.

They advanced in single file, silent and with downcast eyes, and when the first arrived before the altar, he turned round to embrace the comrade who followed; he in turn took in his arms the religious who followed him, and so on to the last. All, before receiving the Eucharist, exchanged the kiss of peace, then they knelt, communicated, and came back in single file, turning into the rotunda behind the altar.

And the return was unexpected; with the white fathers at the head of the line, they made their way very slowly with closed eyes and joined hands. The faces seemed to be somewhat altered; they were differently lit from within; it seemed that the soul, driven by the power of the Sacrament against the sides of the body, filtered through the pores and lit up the skin with a special light of joy, with that kind of brightness which pours from white souls, and makes way like a rose-coloured vapour along the cheeks, and shines, as if concentrated, on the brow.

Watching the mechanical and hesitating gait of these monks, it seemed as if their bodies were no more than automata moving from habit, and that the souls, being elsewhere, gave no heed to them.

Durtal recognized the old lay brother, bent so much that his face disappeared in his beard which pressed against his chest, and his two great knotty hands trembled as he clasped them; he also noticed the tall young brother, his features seeming drawn on a dissolved surface, gliding with short steps, his eyes closed.

By a fatal chance he thought upon himself. He was the only one who did not communicate, for he saw M. Bruno coming last from behind the altar and returning to his place with folded arms. This exclusion brought home to him clearly how different he was, and how far apart, from those around him! All were admitted, and he alone remained outside. His unworthiness was more apparent, and he grew sad at being put aside, looked on, as he deserved to be, as a stranger, separated like the goat of the Scriptures, penned, far from the sheep, on the left of Christ.

These reflections were of use to him, for they relieved him of the terror of confession which was again coming over him. This act seemed to him so natural and just, in his necessary humiliation and unavoidable suffering, that a desire came over him to accomplish it at once, so that he might appear in this chapel purified and washed, and with at least some resemblance to the others.

When the mass was over, he made his way towards his cell to get a tablet of chocolate.

At the top of the stairs M. Bruno, with a large apron round him, was getting ready to clean the steps.

Durtal looked on him with surprise. The oblate smiled and shook hands with him.

"This is an excellent task for the soul," he said, showing his broom; "it recalls modest sentiments which one is too inclined to forget after living in the world."

And he began sweeping vigorously, and collecting into a pan the dust which like pepper filled every crevice in the floor.

Durtal carried his tablet into the garden. "Let us consider," he said to himself as he nibbled it; "supposing I took another walk and tried an unknown part of the wood?" And he felt no wish to do so. "No, placed as I am, I would rather haunt the same spot and not leave the places to which I am accustomed; I am already so little under control, and so easily disturbed, that

I do not wish to risk anything by curiosity to see new places." And he went down to the cross pond. He went along the banks, and having reached the end, was astonished to find, a few steps farther, a stream spotted with green pellicules, hollowing its way between two hedges which fenced in the monastery. The fields stretched out beyond, and the roofs of a large farmhouse were visible in the trees, and all round the horizon on hills were forests which seemed to stop the way before the sky.

"I imagined the grounds were larger," he said to himself, retracing his steps; and having reached the end of the cross pond, he gazed on the huge wooden crucifix reared in the air which was reflected in that black mirror. It sank down, seen from behind, trembling in the small waves stirred up by the breeze, and seemed to fall whirling round in that stretch of ink. And as the body of the marble Christ was hidden by the wood, only the two white arms which hung below the tree could be seen, twisted in the blackness of the water.

Seated on the grass, Durtal gazed on the hazy image on the recumbent cross, and thinking of his soul, which, like the pond, was tanned and stained by a bed of dead leaves and a dunghill of sins, he pitied the Saviour whom he was about to invite to bathe Himself there, for it would no longer be the Martyr of Golgotha to whom at all events death came on a hill, His head high, by daylight, in the open air! but it would be by an increase of outrages, the abominable plunging of the crucified body, the head low, by night, into a depth of mud.

"Ah! it would be time to spare Him, in filtering and clarifying me," he cried to himself. And the swan, till then motionless in an arm of the pond, swept over the lamentable image in advancing, and whitened the moving mourning of the waters with its peaceful reflection.

And Durtal thought of the absolution which he would perhaps obtain, and he reopened his prayer-book and numbered his faults; and, slowly, as on the day before, he tapped, in his innermost being, a fountain of tears. . . .

He shook off his sadness, left the pond, and returning to the lime avenue, he interested himself in a closer inspection of the trees. They raised huge trunks, covered with reddish-brown stonecrop, silvered grey by mosses; and several that morning were wrapped as in a mantle trimmed with pearls, gossamer threads studded with drops of dew.

He sat down on a bench, but fearing a shower, for it looked threatening, he retired to his cell.

He felt no desire to read; he was eager for, while yet he dreaded, the arrival of nine o'clock, to have done with, to get rid of the weight upon his soul, and he prayed mechanically, without knowing what he mumbled, always thinking on this confession, full of alarm and harassed with fears.

He went down a little before the time, and when he entered the auditorium his heart failed him.

In spite of himself, his eyes were fixed upon the prie-Dieu, where he had suffered so cruelly.

To think that he had to put himself on that hurdle again, to stretch himself on that rack of torture! He tried to collect himself, to compose himself—and he drew himself up quickly; he heard the footsteps of the monk. The door opened, and, for the first time, Durtal dared to look the prior in the face; it seemed to be hardly the same man, nor the face, he had noticed from a distance; the profile was so haughty, and the full face so sweet; the eye dulled the proud energy of the features, an eye familiar and deep, when at the same time there was a quiet joy and a sad pity.

"Come," he said, "do not be disturbed, you are about to speak to our Saviour alone, who knows all your faults." And he knelt down and prayed for some time and came, as on the day before, to sit by the prie-Dieu; he bent towards Durtal and listened.

Somewhat reassured, the penitent began without too great anguish. He accused himself of faults common to all men, want of charity towards his neighbour, evil speaking, hate, rash judgment, abuse, lies, vanity, anger, etc.

The monk interrupted him for a moment.

"You said, just now, I think, that in your youth you contracted debts; have you paid them?"

And on an affirmative sign from Durtal, he said, "Good," and went on,

"Have you belonged to any secret society? have you fought a duel?—I am obliged to ask these questions for they are reserved cases."

"No?—Good"—and he was silent.

"Before God, I accuse myself of everything," resumed Durtal; "as I confessed to you, yesterday, since my first communion I have given up everything; prayers, mass, everything; I have denied God, I have blasphemed, I had entirely lost faith."

And Durtal stopped.

He was reaching the sins of the flesh. His voice fell.

"Here I do not know how to explain myself," he said, keeping back his tears.

"Let us see," the monk said gently; "you told me yesterday that you had committed all those acts which are comprised in the sin of lust."

"Yes, father"; and trembling, he added, "Must I go into the details?"

"No, it is useless. I will confine myself to asking you, for it alters the nature of the sin, whether in your case there have been any private sins, or any sins committed between persons of the same sex?"

"Not since I left school."

"Have you committed adultery?"

"Yes."

"Am I to undertstand that in your relations with women, you have committed every possible excess?'

Durtal made an affirmative sign.

"That is sufficient."

And the monk was silent.

Durtal choked with disgust; the avowal of these horrors was a terrible effort to him; yet crushed as he was by shame, he was beginning to breathe, when suddenly he plunged his head again in his hands.

The remembrance of the sacrilege in which Madame Chantelouve had made him share, came back to him.

Hesitatingly he confessed that he had from curiosity assisted at a black mass, and that afterwards, without wishing it, he had defiled a Host which that woman, saturated with Satanism, concealed about her.

The prior listened without moving.

"Did you continue your visits to that woman?"

"No; that had given me a horror of her."

The Trappist reflected and said,

"That is all?"

"I think I have confessed everything," replied Durtal.

The confessor was silent for some minutes, and then in a pensive voice, he murmured,

"I am struck, even more than yesterday, by the astonishing miracle which Heaven has worked in you.

"You were sick, so sick that what Martha said of the body of Lazarus might truly have been said of your soul, 'Iam foetet!' And Christ has, in some manner, raised you. Only do not deceive yourself, the conversion of a sinner is not his cure, but only his convalescence; and this convalescence sometimes lasts for several years and is often long.

"It is expedient that you should determine from this moment to fortify yourself against any falling back, and to do all in your power for recovery. The preventive treatment consists of prayer, the sacrament of penance, and holy communion.

"Prayer?—you know it, for without much prayer you could not have decided to come here after the troubled life you had led."

"Ah! but I prayed so badly!"

"It does not matter, as your wish was to pray well! Confession?—It was painful to you; it will be less so now that you no longer have to avow the accumulated sins of years. The communion troubles me more; for it is to be feared that when you have triumphed over the flesh the Demon should await you there, and endeavour to draw you away, for he knows well that, without this divine government, no healing is possible. You will therefore have to give this matter all your attention."

The monk reflected a minute, and then went on,

"The holy Eucharist . . . you will have more need of it than others, for you will be more unhappy than less cultured and simpler beings. You will be tortured by the imagination. It has made you sin much; and, by a just recompense, it will make you suffer much; it will be the badly closed door of your soul by which the Demon will enter and spread himself in you. Watch over this, and pray fervently that the Saviour may help you. Tell me, have you a rosary?"

"No, father."

"I feel," said the monk, "that the tone in which you said 'No' shows a certain hostility to the rosary."

"I admit that this mechanical manner of saying prayers wearies me a little; I do not know why, but it seems to me that at the end of some seconds I can no longer think of what I am saying; I should mock, and should certainly end by stammering out something stupid."

"You have known," quietly answered the prior, "some fathers of families. Their children stammer forth caresses, and tell them no matter what, and yet they are delighted to listen! Why should not our Lord, who is a good Father, love to hear His children when they drawl, or even when they talk nonsense?"

And after a pause he went on,

"I scent the devil's artifice in what you say, for the highest graces are attached to this crown of prayers. The most Blessed Virgin herself revealed to the saints this means of prayer; she declared she delighted in it; that should be enough to make us love it.

"Do it, then, for her who has powerfully assisted in your conversion, who has interceded with her Son to save you. Remember, also, that God wished that all graces should come to us through her. St. Bernard expressly declares 'Totum nos habere voluit per Mariam.' "

The monk paused anew, and added,

"However, the rosary enrages fools, and that is a sure sign. You will for a penance recite ten every day for a month."

He ceased, and then went on again, slowly,

"All of us, alas! retain that scar of original sin which is the inclination towards evil; each man encourages it more or less; as for you, since you grew up, the scar has been always open, but as you hate the wound God will close it.

"So I will say nothing of your past, as your repentance and your firm resolve to sin no more efface it. Tomorrow, you will receive the pledge of reconciliation, you will communicate; after so many years the Lord will set out on the way to your soul and will rest there; approach Him with great humility, and prepare yourself from this moment, by prayer, for this mysterious meeting of hearts which His goodness desires. Now say your act of contrition and I will give you holy absolution."

The monk raised his arms, and the sleeves of his white cowl rose above him like two wings. With uplifted eyes he uttered the imperious formula which breaks the bonds, and the three words, "Ego te absolvo," spoken more distinctly and slowly, fell upon Durtal, who trembled from head to foot. He almost sank to the ground, incapable of collecting himself or understanding himself, only feeling, in the clearest manner, that Christ Himself was present, near him in that place, and finding no word of thanks, he wept, ravished and bowed down under the great sign of the cross with which the monk enveloped him.

He seemed to be waking from a dream as the prior said to him,

"Rejoice, your life is dead; it is buried in a cloister, and in a cloister it will be born again; it is a good omen; have confidence in our Lord and go in peace."

Like Sergei Bulgakov and others in this section, the Danish writer Johannes Jørgensen was influenced by the great secular credos of his day, particularly socialism. Yet, as he wrote in his autobiography concerning his life as a student and emerging writer in Copenhagen in the 1880s, "such a state of spiritual ignorance had been reached that no one knew what love was." In 1896 Jørgensen converted to Catholicism, a radical and personally excruciating decision that caused him to fall out with many of his antireligious friends. His autobiography (*Mit livs legende*, 1916–28) portrays a rationalism often at odds with Catholic dogma, but against which the promise of escape from egoism and moral relativism ultimately won out.

Since Jørgensen spent much of the early part of his life searching for meaning through materialist philosophies, it is appropriate that he later wrote a life of Saint Francis of Assisi, who gave up all his considerable material goods to pursue the spiritual life. Still, Jørgensen never attained the quiescence of the saints he so admired and wrote about. His autobiography portrays the enduring effect of

JOHANNES JØRGENSEN

[1 8 6 6 – 1 9 5 6]

I began my youth . . . in looking back for a lost Paradise.

the Romantic poets, particularly Goethe: because of his love not only for Jesus but also for Pan, Jørgensen always felt the striving for knowledge and restlessness that characterized that poet's most famous creation, Faust. [EP]

FROM HIS AUTOBIOGRAPHY

. . . Then late one evening, one night when the snow was whirling round my low house and I alone was awake, I began to prepare my confession, to put my life in order, to settle up with the past and make up the books. The diary says:

"Jan. 15. A night of snow-fall—all over the room letters from the last fourteen years. What a long, extraordinary life! What a crowd of all kinds of people—relations, friends, benefactors, publishers, editors, lawyers, creditors, sisters, sweethearts, men on the Exchange, writers, students, comrades, artists, zoologists, journalists, professors, socialists, monks—and so much takes on a quite different meaning now! It is as if my egoism had prevented me from seeing—I have deceived those who were good to me and I have believed the deceivers—Photographs, letters written by some now dead—everywhere lying, defection, and playing with life—no relationship in which I have done right. Promising rashly, running into debt, never a thought of payment. A monomaniac egoist who shakes off all obligations—a bad, incapable person—useless, worthless.

"Only now do I see myself. At that time I always thought I was right. Now I see how I was in the wrong, how hideous, how mean. How petty and exacting I was. To think that I was *tolerated* at all!

"The storm is growling, the snow is drifting. Packet after packet of letters is taken out. I live again through forgotten events, through dangers long since passed, festivals of which the joy is gone—friends who now are enemies—embarrassments, business matters, love affairs, despairs—all of them far away, forgotten, dead, lost . . .

"The first halting letters to editors—in a writing which I hardly recognise as my own—and the editor's answer to Mr. J. J. Letters from schoolmasters and assistant masters, administrators of bequests and from 'The Social Democrat,' *Testimonium paupertatis*, testimonials, certificates—letters from the 'Small Loan Fund,' violet and pink feminine envelopes, dried flowers, bunches of violets and snowdrops, scraps of manuscripts of poems, with many sketches in the margin—old newspapers, old Press notices, old joys and feuds—layer upon layer of the past.

"The most varied handwritings, conventional, dashing, honest, affected, vague, firm. Old addresses, post-marks and dates. All my old life—arrangements about work; prescriptions and bills, engagement cards of friends, and continually my own name, which seems to me like the name of one dead—over and over again on all the hundreds of envelopes—the estate of one *deceased*.

"Again and again have I been in the wrong. My life has been childish—and shameful. The egoism of a boy.

"And nothing at all of it is anything to me any more. It is done with, my God—and I thank Thee!"

"VERY WELL, THEN," SAID FATHER BRINKMANN, "WE WILL FIX THE day for your first confession on February 15th and the day for your reception into the Holy Catholic Church on the 16th. Are you satisfied with that?" ...

I prepared, then, for this first confession during the days preceding February 15th. Following Father Brinkmann's advice, I wrote it down in order not to forget anything. That night of snow, when I had set my past in order, had been a good preparation—one forgets one's life so easily, especially those things in it on which one does not like to dwell. One by one I went through the old Ten Commandments and examined the years that had passed in the stern light from Sinai. Point by point I had to admit with the Psalmist: "If Thou, O Lord, wilt observe iniquities: Lord, who shall bear it?"

During that time I had a long talk—it lasted until three o'clock in the morning—with one of the old acquaintances of the days of "The Tower." He came out of interest, out of sympathy, out of curiosity—came also, perhaps, because like me he had come into contact with the new, Catholicising and Catholic France, had read Villiers and Verlaine, Hello and Huysmans. ... "But, after all, have you been such a great sinner?" he said with a smile, over the third or fourth whisky. "Have you been any worse than the rest of us? And have we been so bad, after all? We have not always been faithful to our wives, we have run into debt, we have caroused rather freely at times, but are we any less decent than other fellows?"

Perhaps not. Perhaps we were decent men—as men go, and as most decent men are. But how was it, oh decent man, that time in your wild youth, long before you became a bank director or a co-partner in the firm of wholesale linen goods? Deep down in the past, far down amongst the dead years, is not something stirring there—like a pale worm? Do you remember that little girl—she was only fifteen or sixteen, wasn't she—in the house where you had a room? She kept your room in order because the family was poor, and you played with her, made her believe that you were fond of her, got her into your room in the dusk when her parents were out and sat there crumpling her and breaking her modesty. Where is she now? What did she become, after you? . . . Or do you remember your first clerkship, you had just proudly become a member of the Commercial Society and had your dinner at the Society's rooms. Your salary was insufficient and you pilfered from the petty cash box which was in your care, and when the shortage was discovered, you turned suspicion away from yourself by lies, so that the blame fell on the office porter. Was he dismissed? Or what happened? Or do you recall that time when you must needs have a new suit to go out with Elna? It was no use going to a fashionable tailor, shabby as you were in your old winter coat. Then a fellow-clerk gave you the address of a little cheap tailor living on the top floor of a house in a third-rate street. Do you remember his flat— the room which was a workshop at one end, a bedroom at the other? Do you remember how over-heated it was, and how it smelt of the pressing-iron?— and his worn-looking wife and the grey faces of the little children playing on the floor? Do you remember that he wanted you to pay something on deposit —"it is far too great an expense for me to buy that fine, blue serge," he said, looking so anxiously at you. "I am only a small tailor," he added, with a pleading look, hoping you might be an honest fellow and not a swindler, like so many young fellows nowadays—And you got your fine blue serge suit; it came late on the eve of Whitsunday, and you had taken care not to be at home. The next day you were out in the woods with Elna and your fine new clothes were admired, and you had lunch in the Deer Park, but was the suit ever paid for?

Ah, all of us who became honest men later—is our past any different? Was not our youth like that? And later, much later, that evening after a men's dinner at a fashionable restaurant—oh well, dash it all, it was too bad of Petersen to be so lavish with the champagne—of course that kind of thing *ought not* to happen when one is a married man—but after all one is only human. . . .

Ah, all of us, who pass for decent men—who amongst us dares to cast the first stone?

But when at last everything had been ransacked, found, classified and written down, I went for a walk. It was early spring, the first eranthis were peeping up in the villa gardens, there was warm sun over withered grass, a racing wind was snapping the dead branches from the trees in the parks. I went out to Söndermarken, followed the path on the right alongside the Roskilde road, until I came to the bench opposite the gardener's house where we had lived two years before. There I sat down, for this bench was a particular bench in my life, a bench of benches—I had found it on my nineteenth birthday, when as a newly-hatched student I strolled about in the Copenhagen parks, with Goethe's poems in my pocket. A foggy grey, foggy mild November day I had sat here—the very day for me, with a spicy smell of fallen leaves from the thick carpet of wet, golden-brown foliage under the trees, with clear strings of pearly drops on all the bushes, with heavy mist dripping from the tall, black trees. Not a sound, save now and then the cry of a rook, or the crowing of a cock behind the hedge, the rumbling of cart wheels out in the broad, misty country. Otherwise silence and peace, the great, healing peace of November—soothing Nirvana. To this bench I had returned again and again, on bright summer mornings, in the dusk of grey autumn afternoons, and that hopeless morning in May, 1889, when I felt as one who is at home nowhere, belonging neither to the day nor the night. On this bench I was now sitting again, seven years after, and looking across at the yellow two-storied house in which we had had the flat on the first floor. It was occupied again, there were curtains at the windows and plants in pots on the window-sills. I saw the balcony where my son had played and on which I had so often stood and looked at the stars and heard the hooting of the owls. Behind the house was the wide country—the country which I had roamed with Gottschalk and with Viggo and Ingeborg Stuckenberg—the home-country of my restless, unhappy, roaming youth. There it lay—out there were still the lake and the inn and the arms of the windmill against the horizon, and one could still walk out to "The Three Flagons" and eat fried eggs with good, fresh, country bread and drink bitters. One night I had dreamed of this country and had written verses about it.

The land that in the night I saw in dreams
was flat and green and full of rushing streams;
I wandered on, the breeze was moist and keen,
the clouds of storms and harvest bore the mien,
and about my feet the grass did whip me as I walked.
I wandered on until my eye perceived
a narrow streak of silver-grey upon the sea
which lay along the border-line of earth and sky.
There did I halt and hear the screaming of the gulls
and poplars whispering from a grass-grown dyke.
Then did I see whence I this land did know
and that here my life for me was waiting,
prepared for me who wandered lost,
and prayed, in exile, to an image strange to me.

Yes, this was "my own life," that I looked out across once again—"my own life in good and evil—and nothing but this," as Stuckenberg was soon after to call out to me. But "my own life" was not enough for me. It had been weighed in the scales of existence and found wanting. Others, perhaps, might find it enough to live their own lives. I did not deny it. But my path went inexorably to the kneeling-bench before that which the poem had called "a strange image"—to Our Lady's carved, many-coloured and gilded altar in the church of the Sacred Heart. My path led to the confessional.

I rose from the bench and looked neither to the right nor the left until I stood in Stenosgade. It was about midday, the church was sunny and warm. I knelt down, I could not pray, I only waited. A door was opened in the chancel, a priest came, genuflected to the altar, strode with slow and digni-fied steps down through the church and disappeared into one of the two confessionals in the south transept. I understood that it was Father Joseph Schmidt—and that now I had to get up and take my place—that of the penitent sinner—

Then for the first time I approached the lattice of the confessional. "Not even we old Catholics draw near to Sinai without trembling," Father Brink-mann had said to me the day before, during a last talk. And in spite of all practical and theoretical preparation, in spite of all good will, it was a strange and difficult moment for a young disciple of Brandes of the year 1884, for a recent Bohemian of "Bernina," when the step was taken into the dim confes-sional—the step away from the bright world of freedom of thought and action, the step in beneath law and dogma, the step in behind the concealing curtain, in before the delegate of Rome, who sat there waiting motionless in the gloom, with the magic stole over his shoulders, with authority to remit sins or to retain them, to open the door to heaven or to the abyss.

Like many members of the Russian intelligentsia at the turn of the century, Sergei Bulgakov became involved in revolutionary activities, embracing Marxist doctrine and publishing widely respected scholarly works on the market economy and agricultural society. But, sickened by the bloodshed and corrupt politics of the revolutionary events of 1905, Bulgakov turned from the study of political economics to Russian Orthodox theology and found himself increasingly drawn toward faith in God. His return to the Russian Orthodox Church of his childhood and his declared intent to seek ordination led to difficulties with the Soviet authorities. Eventually he was forced to emigrate to Paris, where he became dean of the widely influential Orthodox Theological Academy, whose faculty included some of the major Eastern Orthodox theologians of this century: Nikolai Berdiaev and Nikolai Zernov.

Bulgakov is best known and gaining increasing popularity for his "sophiology" —a theology based on the concept of spiritual enlightenment as the feminine figure of wisdom, Sophia, who appears in the Old Testament Book of Proverbs and

SERGEI
BULGAKOV

[1 8 7 1 – 1 9 4 4]

I doomed myself voluntarily to go

through this purgatory.

in some of the statements of Christ. The veneration of Divine Sophia was also a signal feature of the Russian Symbolist movement in the arts at the turn of the century. The poet and philosopher Vladimir Soloviev and the poets Aleksandr Blok and Andrei Bely considered themselves "knights" of the Divine Sophia. The poetry of Soloviev and Blok especially contains numerous references to the "beautiful and unknown Lady."

Discerning a feminine element in God's character, Bulgakov anticipates many of the current trends in Christian theology. The sense of God as maternal and of a return to faith as finding one's home reflects Russian cultural predilections to invest *patria* and church with motherly qualities. In the passage that follows, Bulgakov's spiritual journey becomes a home-coming.   [AM]

FROM HIS AUTOBIOGRAPHY

I was born in a priest's family, and Levite blood of six generations flowed in my veins. I grew up near the parish church of St. Sergius, in the gracious atmosphere of its prayers and within the sound of its bells. The aesthetic, moral, and everyday recollections of my childhood are bound up with the life of that parish church. Within its walls my heart rejoiced in prayer and mourned the departed. Until I was an adolescent I was faithful to my birth and upbringing as a son of the Church. I attended the parochial school in my native town, Livny, for four years and was then sent to the Theological Seminary in Oryol for three years.

In early adolescence, during my first or second year at the Seminary, I went through a religious crisis—painful but not tragic—which ended in my losing religious faith for many, many years. From the age of fourteen to about thirty the prodigal son withdrew into a far country to the sorrow and dismay of many, principally of his parents. I had a great deal to lose, and I gave it up with seeming ease, without any struggle (though in my godlessness I did think of suicide). . . .

In losing religious faith I naturally and, as it were, automatically adopted the revolutionary mood then prevalent among the intelligentsia. Without belonging to any particular party, I was bitterly opposed to the monarchism which was dominant in our clerical circles. In short, at that period in my life I went through the same experience as my predecessors in the Seminaries

(Chernyshevsky, Dobrolyubov, and others). I fell victim to a gloomy revolutionary nihilism, though in my case it was always combined with a love of art and literature which saved me. The general atmosphere of the theological schools, based on tradition and compulsion, was impotent to combat this nihilism and grew more and more unendurable to a proud and independent boy who genuinely loved truth and freedom.

The Seminary authorities intended me for the Theological Academy, but I felt that my only hope of salvation was to escape from the Seminary at once, without looking back. Where might I escape? "To be useful," to serve mankind and progress by scientific thought—towards which I always had a leaning. It was not easy for me to carry out my plan. It demanded sacrifices, not only from me but from my family, and in the first place from my parents (whom, in my youthful egoism, I considered least of all). Nevertheless, in the summer of 1888 I left the Oryol Seminary. After attending the classical school at Yalets for two years, I entered Moscow University as a student in the Faculty of Law in the autumn of 1890.

In my choice of faculty I followed the herd of the intelligentsia against my personal inclination. I was attracted by philology, philosophy, and literature, but chose law, which did not appeal to me. I did this with the idea that I might help save my country from Tsarist tyranny. And to this end I had to take up the social sciences and bind myself to political economy like a galley slave chained to his bench. I doomed myself voluntarily to go through this purgatory that I might redeem my sin as a prodigal son.

I entered the University with the firm intention of devoting myself to a discipline alien to me, and I carried out my decision. After graduation I was called by Moscow University to be a lecturer in political economy. My appointment was made by Professor A. I. Chuprov, the kindest and nicest man imaginable, whose fate was similar to mine: he too had been a theological student and recalled his past as a lost-paradise, but he was not destined to reach the promised land beyond the "intellectualistic wilderness." I can well fancy how perturbed he would have been at seeing me in a cassock; but he did not live to see such a shocking thing.

My mind developed along the lines of social and socialistic thought. Consecutively, and almost automatically, I then passed from one form of thought to another until finally I appeared enslaved by Marxism, which suited me about as well as a saddle fits a cow. In the years 1898 to 1900 the University sent me to study abroad. Naturally, I went first to Germany—the land of Marxism and Social Democracy. But there, contrary to all my expectations, I soon met with disappointment, and my *Weltanschauung* began to disintegrate all along the line.

At last I returned to Russia to occupy the chair of political economy I had longed for. By that time I was in a state of complete spiritual resignation, through which the voice of religious faith sounded, at first timidly and uncertainly but then more and more victoriously. I began to profess this faith in my writings from 1901 and 1902 onwards, much to the surprise and indignation of my former comrades in thought. But basically, even as a Marxist in a state of spiritual barbarism, I always longed for religion and I was never indifferent to faith. Initially, I had a passionate emotional belief in an earthly paradise. Then, after a certain moment when I gave myself permission to do so, I took a sharp turn and went quickly and decidedly straight from the far country to my spiritual fatherland. Having regained faith in a "personal" God, instead of the impersonal idol of progress, I accepted Christ—whom I had loved and carried in my heart as a child. And finally, I returned to Orthodoxy.

I was irresistibly drawn to my native Church. However, for years the thought of returning to my Father's house and the longing to do so remained unrealized. Secret suffering was the price I had to pay for my return. I was returning, of course, not only in heart but in mind as well. From a sociologist I was turning into a theologian (I note with gratitude the spiritual influence of Dostoyevsky and Vladimir Solovyov upon me in those years). At the same time there arose within me a desire, which secretly indeed had never left me, to return to my Father's house completely and become a priest. In those years I sometimes spoke of myself to my friends as a "traitor to the altar." It was not enough that I should have changed my philosophy of life. My Levite blood asserted itself more and more: my soul longed for priesthood and the altar. Prince E. N. Trubetskoy said to me once that he felt as though I "had been born in a cassock." . . .

How did I come to lose my faith? I lost it without noticing it myself. It occurred as something self-evident and unavoidable when the poetry of my childhood was squeezed out of my life by the prose of seminary education. As soon as I experienced my first doubts, and my critical faculty was early awakened, I realized that I could not be satisfied with the apologetics of the text-books. Instead of helping me, they further undermined my faith. My seminary education constantly raised before me many religious problems, but I was unable to cope with them, and the instructions given to me by my teachers only confused my mind. This conflict was further aggravated by compulsory attendance at the long services. Orthodox piety only irritated me, for its mystical side had ceased to exist for me.

I was twenty-four years old. For a decade I had lived without faith and, after early stormy doubts, a religious emptiness reigned in my soul. One evening we were driving across the southern steppes of Russia, and the strong-scented spring grass was gilded by the rays of a glorious sunset. Far in the distance I saw the blue outlines of the Caucasus. This was my first sight of the mountains. I looked with ecstatic delight at their rising slopes. I drank in the light and the air of the steppes. I listened to the revelation of nature. My soul was accustomed to the dull pain of seeing nature as a lifeless desert and of treating its surface beauty as a deceptive mask. Yet, contrary to my intellectual convictions, I could not be reconciled to nature without God.

Suddenly, in that evening hour, my soul was joyfully stirred. I started to wonder what would happen if the cosmos were not a desert and its beauty not a mask or deception—if nature were not death, but life. If he existed, the merciful and loving Father, if nature was the vesture of his love and glory, and if the pious feelings of my childhood, when I used to live in his presence, when I loved him and trembled because I was weak, were true, then the tears and inspiration of my adolescence, the sweetness of my prayers, my innocence and all those emotions which I had rejected and trodden down would be vindicated, and my present outlook with its emptiness and deadness would appear nothing more than blindness and lies, and what a transformation it would bring to me!

In 1898 a new wave of intoxication with this world came upon me. I experienced "personal happiness." I met the West for the first time. My admiration of its culture, its comfort, and its social democracy was boundless; and then suddenly a wonderful encounter with Raphael's Sistine Madonna took place in Dresden. It was a foggy autumn morning. I went to the art gallery in order to do my duty as a tourist. My knowledge of European painting was negligible. I did not know what to expect. The eyes of the Heavenly Queen, the Mother who holds in her arms the Eternal Infant, pierced my soul. I cried joyful and yet bitter tears, and with them the ice melted from my soul, and some of my psychological knots were loosened. This was an aesthetic emotion, but it was also a new knowledge; it was a miracle. I was then still a Marxist, but I was obliged to call my contemplation of the Madonna by the name of "prayer." I went to the Zwinger gallery early in the mornings in order to be there before others arrived. I ran there every day to pray and weep in front of the Virgin, and few experiences in my life were more blessed than those unexpected tears.

One sunny autumn day in 1908 I made my way to a solitary hermitage lost in the forest, where I was surrounded by the familiar sights of northern nature. I was still in the clutches of doubt and hesitation. I had come there as a companion of a friend; secretly I hoped that I might meet God. But my determination deserted me, and while I was at Vespers I remained cold and unfeeling. When the prayers for those preparing for confession began, I almost ran out of the church. I walked in deep distress towards the guest house, seeing nothing around me, and suddenly found myself in front of the elder's cell. I had been led there. I intended to go in another direction but absent-mindedly made a wrong turn in the confusion of my distress.

A miracle had happened to me. I realized it then without any doubt. The

Father, seeing his prodigal son, ran to meet me. I heard from the elder that all human sin was like a drop of water in comparison with the ocean of divine love. I left him, pardoned and reconciled, trembling and in tears, feeling myself returned as on wings within the precincts of the Church. At the door of the chapel I met my surprised and delighted companion, who had seen me leave in a state of acute distress. He was the witness of this conversion in my life.

It was another evening and another sunset, but this time a northern and not a southern one. The bells were calling to prayer. I listened to them as if I heard them for the first time in my life, for they invited me also to join the fellowship of believers. I looked on the world with new eyes. The next morning at the Eucharist I knew that I was a participant in the Covenant, that our Lord hung on the cross and shed his blood for me and because of me; that the most blessed meal was being prepared by the priest for me, and that the gospel narrative about the feast in the house of Simon the leper and about the woman who loved much was addressed personally to me. It was on that day when I partook of the blessed body and blood of my Lord.

Perhaps the best known of any work to issue from the stillness of the monastery is the autobiography of the poet, journalist, and Trappist monk Thomas Merton. The years following the publication of his autobiography, *The Seven Storey Mountain* (1948), witnessed a tremendous upsurge in conversions to Catholicism and vocations to Trappist monasteries.

Before becoming a monk, Thomas Merton was a successful journalist, novelist, and poet. Educated in Europe and the United States, he was, like Sergei Bulgakov, attracted to a variety of political philosophies, and joined various branches of socialism and communism. Throughout his flirtations with social action, he became increasingly aware of the need for a spiritual foundation for his political beliefs. After a failed attempt to become a priest, he worked for a time with Dorothy Day's Catholic Workers social outreach programs in Harlem, New York.

Because the Trappist order requires a vow of silence, Merton initially perceived his muse as being in conflict with his vocation. In a famous statement, he claimed, "One of us (the poet or the

THOMAS
MERTON

[1 9 1 5 – 1 9 6 8]

Enfolded in silence and

holiness . . .

monk) must die." Originally amused by a monk who would compose poetry on his first day in his cell, his superiors encouraged Merton to continue writing and publishing. Inspired by an abiding interest in the contemplative traditions of East and West, Merton remade the poetic meditation in modern form. His death in 1968 was tragic and untimely.   [AM]

FROM *THE SEVEN-STOREY MOUNTAIN*

It was very hot on Church Street. The street was torn up, and the dust swirled in the sun like gold around the crawling busses and the trucks and taxis. There were crowds of people on the sidewalks.

I stood under the relatively cool, white walls of the new Post Office building. And then, suddenly, walking in the crowd I saw my brother who was supposed to be at Ithaca. He was coming out of the building, and walking with more of a purpose, more of a swing. He almost ran into me.

"Oh," he said, "hello. Are you going out to Douglaston? I'll give you a ride. I've got the car here, just around the corner."

"What are you doing here?" I said.

Under the arching door of the big building were placards about joining the Navy, the Army, the Marines. The only question in my mind was which one he had been trying to join.

"Did you read about this new Naval Reserve scheme they've got?" he said. I knew something about it. That was what he was trying to get into. It was practically settled.

"You go on a cruise," he said, "and then you get a commission."

"Is it as easy as that?"

"Well, I guess they're anxious to get men. Of course, you have to be a college man."

When I told him I was not going to enter the novitiate after all, he said: "Why don't you come in to the Naval Reserve."

"No," I said, "no, thanks."

Presently he said: "What's that package you've got under your arm? Buy some books?"

"Yes."

When he had unlocked the car, I ripped the paper off the package, and took out the cardboard box containing the set of four books, bound in black leather, marked in gold.

I handed him one of the volumes. It was sleek and smelled new. The pages were edged in gold. There were red and green markers.

"What are they?" said John Paul.

"Breviaries."

The four books represented a decision. They said that if I could not live in the monastery, I should try to live in the world as if I were a monk in a monastery. They said that I was going to get as close as possible to the life I was not allowed to lead. If I could not wear the religious habit, I would at least join a Third Order and would try my best to get a job teaching in some Catholic College where I could live under the same roof as the Blessed Sacrament.

There could be no more question of living just like everybody else in the world. There could be no more compromises with the life that tried, at every turn, to feed me poison. I had to turn my back on these things.

God had kept me out of the cloister: that was His affair. He had also given me a vocation to live the kind of a life that people led in cloisters. If I could not be a religious, a priest—that was God's affair. But nevertheless He still wanted me to lead something of the life of a priest or of a religious. . . .

If I had ever thought I had become immune from passion, and that I did not have to fight for freedom, there was no chance of that illusion any more. It seemed that every step I took carried me painfully forward under a burden of desires that almost crushed me with the monotony of their threat, the intimate, searching familiarity of their ever-present disgust.

I did not have any lofty theories about the vocation of a lay-contemplative. In fact, I no longer dignified what I was trying to do by the name of a vocation. All I knew was that I wanted grace, and that I needed prayer, and that I was helpless without God, and that I wanted to do everything that people did to keep close to Him.

It was no longer possible to consider myself, abstractly, as being in a certain "state of life" which had special technical relations to other "states of life." All that occupied me now was the immediate practical problem of getting up my hill with this terrific burden I had on my shoulders, step by step, begging God to drag me along and get me away from my enemies and from those who were trying to destroy me. . . .

Yes, and from the secret places of His essence, God began to fill my soul with grace in those days, grace that sprung from deep within me, I could not know how or where. But yet I would be able, after not so many months, to realize what was there, in the peace and the strength that were growing in me through my constant immersion in this tremendous, unending cycle of prayer, ever renewing its vitality, its inexhaustible, sweet energies, from hour to hour, from season to season in its returning round. And I, drawn into that atmosphere, into that deep, vast universal movement of vitalizing prayer, which is Christ praying in men to His Father, could not help but begin at last to live, and to know that I was alive. And my heart could not help but cry out within me: "I will sing to the Lord as long as I live: I will sing praise to my God while I have my being. Let my speech be acceptable to Him: but I will take delight in the Lord."

Truly, He was sending forth His Spirit, uttering His divine Word and binding me to Himself through His Spirit preceding from the Word spoken within me. As the months went on, I could not help but realize it. . . .

But I am getting ahead of my story. For in these days, in the late summer of 1940, it was not yet that way. The Breviary was hard to learn, and every step was labor and confusion, not to mention the mistakes and perplexities I got myself into. However, Father Irenaeus helped to straighten me out, and told me how the various feasts worked together, and how to say first Vespers for the proper feast, and all the other things one needs to find out. Apart from him, however, I didn't even speak of the Breviary to any other priest. I kept quiet about it, half fearing that someone would make fun of me, or think I was eccentric, or try to snatch my books away from me on some pretext. I would have been better off if I had been acting under the guidance of a director, but I had no understanding of such a thing in those days.

Meanwhile, I put on my best blue suit and hitch-hiked out to St. Bonaventure and spoke with Father Thomas Plassman, who was the president of the college, and the picture of benevolence. He listened kindly and soberly to my answers to his questions, filling a chair with his huge frame and looking at me through his glasses, out of a great kind face built on pontifical lines and all set for smiles paternal enough to embrace an archdiocese. Father Thomas would make a wonderful prelate, and, as a matter of fact, all the students and seminarians at St. Bonaventure held him in great awe for his learning and piety.

Back in Olean his reputation was even greater. Once I had someone whisper to me that Father Thomas was the third best educated man in America. I was not able to find out who were the other two ahead of him, or how it was possible to determine who was the best educated, or what that might precisely mean.

But in any case, he gave me a job at St. Bonaventure's, teaching English, for it fell out that Father Valentine Long, who wrote books and taught literature to the sophomores, had been transferred to Holy Name College, in Washington.

In the second week of September, with a trunkful of books and a typewriter and the old portable phonograph that I had bought when I was still at Oakham, I moved in to the little room that was assigned to me on the second floor of the big, red-brick building that was both a dormitory and a monastery. Out of my window I could look beyond the chapel front to the garden and fields and the woods. There was a little astronomical observatory out there behind the greenhouses, and in the distance you could tell where the river was by the line of trees at the end of the pasture. And then, beyond that, were the high, wooded hills, and my gaze travelled up Five Mile Valley beyond the farms to Martinny's Rocks. My eyes often wandered out there, and rested in that peaceful scene, and the landscape became associated with my prayers, for I often prayed looking out of the window. And even at night, the tiny, glowing light of a far farmhouse window in Five Mile Valley attracted my eye, the only visible thing in the black darkness, as I knelt on the floor and said my last prayer to Our Lady.

And as the months went on, I began to drink poems out of those hills.

Yet the room was not quiet, either. It was right on a corner next to the stairs, and when anybody on our floor was wanted on the telephone, someone would rush up the stairs and stick his head into the corridor right by my door and yell down the echoing hall. All day long I heard those voices bellowing, "Hey, Cassidy! Hey, Cassidy!" but I did not mind. It did not stop me from doing twice as much work in that room, in one year, as I had done in all the rest of my life put together.

It amazed me how swiftly my life fell into a plan of fruitful and pleasant organization, here under the roof with these Friars, in this house dedicated to God. The answer to this was, of course, the God Who lived under that same roof with me, hidden in His Sacrament, the heart of the house, diffusing His life through it from the chapel Tabernacle: and also the Office I recited every day was another answer. Finally, there was the fact of my seclusion.

By this time, I had managed to get myself free from all the habits and luxuries that people in the world think they need for their comfort and amusement. My mouth was at last clean of the yellow, parching salt of nicotine, and I had rinsed my eyes of the grey slops of movies, so that now my taste and my vision were clean. And I had thrown away the books that soiled my heart. And my ears, too, had been cleansed of all wild and fierce noises and had poured into them peace, peace—except for that yell, "Hey, Cassidy," which, after all, did not make much difference.

Best of all, my will was in order, my soul was in harmony with itself and with God, though not without battle, and not without cost. That was a price I had to pay, or lose my life altogether, so there was no alternative but wait in patience, and let myself be ground out between the upper and nether millstones of the two conflicting laws within me. Nor could I taste anything of the sense that this is really a martyrdom full of merit and pleasing to God: I was still too obsessed with the sheer, brute difficulty of it, and the crushing humiliation that faced me all the time. *Peccatum meum contra me est semper.*

Yet, in spite of all that, there was in me the profound, sure certitude of liberty, the moral certitude of grace, of union with God, which bred peace that could not be shattered or overshadowed by any necessity to stand armed and ready for conflict. And this peace was all-rewarding. It was worth everything. And every day it brought me back to Christ's altars, and to my daily Bread, that infinitely holy and mighty and secret wholesomeness that was cleansing and strengthening my sick being through and through, and feeding, with His infinite life, my poor shredded sinews of morality.

I was writing a book—it was not much of a book—and I had classes to prepare. It was the latter work that had the most in it of health and satisfaction and reward. I had three big classes of sophomores, ninety students in all, to bring through English Literature from Beowulf to the Romantic Revival in one year. And a lot of them didn't even know how to spell. But that did not worry me very much, and it could not alter my happiness with *Piers Plowman* and the *Nun's Priest's Tale* and *Sir Gawain and the Green Knight:* I was back again in that atmosphere that had enthralled me as a child, the serene and simple and humorous Middle Ages, not the lute and goblin and moth-ball Middle Ages of Tennyson, but the real Middle Ages, the twelfth and thirteenth and fourteenth centuries, full of fresh air and simplicity, as solid as wheat bread and grape wine and water-mills and ox-drawn wagons: the age of Cistercian monasteries and of the first Franciscans.

And so, in my innocence, I stood up and talked about all these things in front of those rooms full of football players with long, unpronounceable names: and because they saw that I myself liked my own subject matter, they tolerated it, and even did a certain amount of work for me without too much complaint.

The classes were a strange mixture. The best elements in them were the football players and the seminarians. The football players were mostly on scholarships, and they did not have much money, and they stayed in at night most of the time. As a group, they were the best-natured and the best-tempered and worked as hard as the seminarians. They were also the most vocal. They liked to talk about these books when I stirred them up to argue. They liked to open their mouths and deliver rough, earnest and sometimes sardonic observations about the behavior of these figures in literature.

Also, some of them were strong and pious Catholics with souls full of faith and simplicity and honesty and conviction, yet without the violence and intemperance that come from mere prejudice. At Columbia it had been pretty much the fashion to despise football players as stupid: and I don't maintain that they are, as a class, geniuses. But the ones at St. Bona's taught me much more about people than I taught them about books, and I learned to have a lot of respect and affection for these rough, earnest, good-natured and patient men who had to work so hard and take so many bruises and curses to entertain the Friars and the Alumni on the football field, and to advertise the school.

I wonder what has happened to them all: how many of them got shot up in Africa or the Philippines? What became of that black-haired, grinning Mastrigiacomo who confided to me all his ambitions about being a band-leader; or that lanky, cat-faced villain Chapman whom I saw one night, after a dance, walking around chewing on a whole ham? What have they done with that big, quiet Irishman Quinn, or Woody McCarthy with his bulbous nose and eyebrows full of perplexity and his sallies of gruff wit? . . .

ALREADY, IN FEBRUARY, OR BEFORE THAT, THE IDEA CAME TO ME that I might make a retreat in some monastery for Holy Week and Easter. Where would it be? The first place that came into my mind was the Trappist abbey Dan Walsh had told me about, in Kentucky. And as soon as I thought about it, I saw that this was the only choice. That was where I needed to go. Something had opened out, inside me, in the last months, something that required, demanded at least a week in that silence, in that austerity, praying together with the monks in their cold choir.

And my heart expanded with anticipation and happiness.

Meanwhile, suddenly, one day, towards the beginning of Lent, I began to write poems. I cannot assign any special cause for the ideas that began to crowd on me from every side. I had been reading the Spanish poet, Lorca, with whose poetic vein I felt in the greatest sympathy: but that was not enough, in itself, to account for all the things I now began to write. In the first weeks of Lent, the fasting I took on myself—which was not much, but at least it came up to the standard required by the Church for an ordinary Christian, and did not evade its obligations under some privilege to which I was not entitled—instead of cramping my mind, freed it, and seemed to let loose the string of my tongue.

Sometimes I would go several days at a time, writing a new poem every day. They were not all good, but some of them were better than I had written before. In the end, I did not altogether reject more than half a dozen of them. And, having sent many of the others to various magazines, I at last had the joy of seeing one or two of them accepted.

Towards the beginning of March, I wrote to the Trappists at Gethsemani asking if I could come down there for a retreat during Holy Week. I had barely received their reply, telling me they would be glad to have me there, when another letter came.

It was from the Draft Board, telling me that my number was up for the army.

I was surprised. I had forgotten about the draft, or rather I had made calculations that put all this off until at least after Easter. However, I had thought out my position with regard to the war, and knew what I had to do in conscience. I made out my answers to the questionnaires with peace in my heart, and not much anticipation that it would make any difference to my case.

It was about eight years since we had all stood under the banner in the gymnasium at Columbia, and the Reds had shouted and stamped on the platform, and we had all loudly taken a pledge that we weren't going to fight in any war whatever. Now America was moving into position to enter a war as the ally of countries that had been attacked by the Nazis: and the Nazis had, as their ally, Communist Russia.

Meanwhile in those eight years, I had developed a conscience. If I had objected to war before, it was more on the basis of emotion than anything else. And my unconditional objection had, therefore, been foolish in more ways than one. On the other hand, I was not making the mistake of switching from one emotional extreme to the other. This time, as far as I was able, I felt that I was called upon to make clear my own position as a moral duty. . . .

And therefore I made out my papers with an application to be considered as a non-combatant objector: that is, one who would willingly enter the army, and serve in the medical corps, or as a stretcher bearer, or a hospital orderly or any other thing like that, so long as I did not have to drop bombs on open cities, or shoot at other men. . . .

I put down all my reasons, and quoted St. Thomas for the edification of the Draft Board and got the whole business notarized and sealed and put it in an envelope and dropped it in the wide-open mouth of the mailbox in the Olean post office.

And when it was done, I walked out into the snowy street, and an ineffable sense of peace settled in my heart.

It was a late, cold afternoon. The frozen piles of snow lay along the swept sidewalks, in the gutters, in front of the small, one-story buildings on State Street. Presently Bob O'Brien, the plumber at the Olean house, who lived in Alleghany, and who used to fix the pipes when they went wrong up at the cottage, came by in his car. He stopped to give me a ride.

He was a big, jovial, family man, with white hair and several sons who served as altar boys at St. Bonaventure's Church in Alleghany, and as we passed out of town on the wide road, he was talking about peaceful and ordinary things.

The country opened out before us. The setting sun shone as bright as blood, along the tops of the hills, but the snow in the valleys and hollows was blue and even purple with shadows. On the left of the road, the antennae of the radio station stood up into the clean sky, and far ahead of us lay the red-brick buildings of the College, grouped in an imitation Italy in the midst of the alluvial valley. Beyond that, on the side of the hill were the redder buildings of St. Elizabeth's convent, past the high bridge over the railroad tracks.

My eyes opened and took all this in. And for the first time in my life I realized that I no longer cared whether I preserved my place in all this or lost it: whether I stayed here or went to the army. All that no longer mattered. It was in the hands of One Who loved me far better than I could ever love myself: and my heart was filled with peace.

It was a peace that did not depend on houses, or jobs, or places, or times, or external conditions. It was a peace that time and material created situations could never give. It was peace that the world could not give.

The weeks went by, and I wrote some more poems, and continued to fast and keep my Lent. All I prayed was that God should let me know His will —and, if it pleased Him, there was only one other thing I asked for myself besides: if I had to go to the army, I begged Him at least to let me make a retreat with the Trappist monks before I went.

However, the next thing I got from the Draft Board was a notice to present myself for medical examination before the doctors in Olean.

I had not been expecting things to develop that way, and at first I interpreted this to mean that my request for consideration as a non-combatant had simply been ignored. There were three days before the examination, and so I got permission to go down to New York. I thought I might see the Draft Board and talk to them: but that was not possible. In any case, it was not necessary.

So the week-end turned out to be a sort of a festival with my friends. I saw Lax, who was now working for the *New Yorker*, and had a desk of his own in a corner of their offices where he wrote letters to pacify the people who complained about the humor, or the lack of it, in the pages of the magazine. Then we went out to Long Beach and saw Seymour. And then Seymour and I and Lax all together got in a car and went to Port Washington and saw Gibney.

The next day was St. Patrick's Day, and the massed bands of all the boys and girls in Brooklyn who had never had an ear for music were gathering under the windows of the *New Yorker* offices and outside the Gotham Book Mart. And I, an Englishman, wearing a shamrock which I had bought from a Jew, went walking around the city, weaving in and out of the crowds, and thinking up a poem called April, although it was March. It was a fancy poem about javelins and leopards and lights through trees like arrows and a line that said: "The little voices of the rivers change." I thought it up in and out of the light and the shade of the Forties, between Fifth and Sixth avenues, and typed it on Lax's typewriter in the *New Yorker* office, and showed it to Mark Van Doren in a subway station.

And Mark said, of the shamrock I was wearing:

"That is the greenest shamrock I have ever seen."

It was a great St. Patrick's Day. That night I got on the Erie train, and since I was so soon, I thought, to go to the army, I paid money to sleep in the Pullman. Practically the only other Pullman passenger was a sedate Franciscan nun, who turned out to be going to St. Elizabeth's: and so we got off at Olean together and shared a taxi out to Alleghany.

On Monday I prepared to go and be examined for the army. I was the first one there. I climbed the ancient stairs to the top floor of the Olean City Hall. I tried the handle of the room marked for the medical board, and the door opened. I walked in and stood in the empty room. My heart was still full of the peace of Communion.

Presently the first of the doctors arrived.

"You got here early," he said, and began to take off his coat and hat.

"We might as well begin," he said, "the others will be along in a minute."

So I stripped, and he listened to my chest, and took some blood out of my arm and put it in a little bottle, in a water-heater, to keep it cosy and warm for the Wassermann test. And while this was going on, the others were coming in, two other doctors to do the examining, and lanky young farm boys to be examined.

"Now," said my doctor, "let's see your teeth."

I opened my mouth.

"Well," he said, "you've certainly had a lot of teeth out!"

And he began to count them.

The doctor who was running the Medical Board was just coming in. My man got up and went to talk to him. I heard him say:

"Shall we finish the whole examination? I don't see much point to it."

The head doctor came over and looked at my mouth.

"Oh, well," he said, "finish the examination anyway."

And he sat me down and personally took a crack at my reflexes and went through all the rest of it. When it was over, and I was ready to get back into my clothes, I asked:

"What about it, Doctor?"

"Oh, go home," he said, "you haven't got enough teeth."

Once again I walked out into the snow street.

So they didn't want me in the army after all, even as a stretcher bearer! The street was full of quiet, full of peace.

And I remembered that it was the Feast of St. Joseph.

THE RE WERE STILL ABOUT THREE WEEKS LEFT UNTIL EASTER. Thinking more and more about the Trappist monastery where I was going to spend Holy Week, I went to the library one day and took down the *Catholic Encyclopaedia* to read about the Trappists. I found out that the Trappists were Cistercians, and then, in looking up Cistercians, I also came across the Carthusians, and a great big picture of the hermitages of the Camaldolese.

What I saw on those pages pierced me to the heart like a knife.

What wonderful happiness there was, then, in the world! There were still men on this miserable, noisy, cruel earth, who tasted the marvelous joy of silence and solitude, who dwelt in forgotten mountain cells, in secluded monasteries, where the news and desires and appetites and conflicts of the world no longer reached them.

They were free from the burden of the flesh's tyranny, and their clear vision, clean of the world's smoke and of its bitter sting, were raised to heaven and penetrated into the deeps of heaven's infinite and healing light.

They were poor, they had nothing, and therefore they were free and possessed everything, and everything they touched struck off something of the fire of divinity. And they worked with their hands, silently ploughing and harrowing the earth, and sowing seed in obscurity, and reaping their small harvests to feed themselves and the other poor. They built their own houses and made, with their own hands, their own furniture and their own coarse clothing, and everything around them was simple and primitive and poor, because they were the least and the last of men, they had made themselves outcasts, seeking, outside the walls of the world, Christ poor and rejected of men.

Above all, they had found Christ, and they knew the power and the sweetness and the depth and the infinity of His love, living and working in them. In Him, hidden in Him, they had become the "Poor Brothers of God." And for His love, they had thrown away everything, and concealed themselves in the Secret of His Face. Yet because they had nothing, they were the richest men in the world, possessing everything: because in proportion as grace emptied their hearts of created desire, the Spirit of God entered in and filled the place that had been made for God. And the Poor Brothers of God, in their cells, they tasted within them the secret glory, the hidden manna, the infinite nourishment and strength of the Presence of God. They tasted the sweet exultancy of the fear of God, which is the first intimate touch of the reality of God, known and experienced on earth, the beginning of heaven. The fear of the Lord is the beginning of heaven. And all day long, God spoke to them: the clean voice of God, in His tremendous peacefulness, spending truth within them as simply and directly as water wells up in a spring. And grace was in them, suddenly, always in more and more abundance, they knew not from where, and the coming of this grace to them occupied them altogether, and filled them with love, and with freedom.

And grace, overflowing in all their acts and movements, made everything they did an act of love, glorifying God not by drama, not by gesture, not by outward show, but by the very simplicity and economy of utter perfection, so utter that it escapes notice entirely.

Outside in the world were holy men who were holy in the sense that they went about with portraits of all the possible situations in which they could show their love of God displayed about them: and they were always conscious of all these possibilities. But these other hidden men had come so close to God in their hiddenness that they no longer saw anyone but Him. They themselves were lost in the picture: there was no comparison between them receiving and God giving, because the distance by which such comparison could be measured had dwindled to nothing. They were in Him. They had dwindled down to nothing and had been transformed into Him by the pure and absolute humility of their hearts.

And the love of Christ overflowing in those clean hearts made them children and made them eternal. Old men with limbs like the roots of trees had the eyes of children and lived, under their grey woolen cowls, eternal. And all of them, the young and the old, were ageless, the little brothers of God, the little children for whom was made the Kingdom of Heaven.

Day after day the round of the canonical hours brought them together and the love that was in them became songs as austere as granite and as sweet as wine. And they stood and they bowed in their long, solemn psalmody. Their prayer flexed its strong sinews and relaxed again into silence, and suddenly flared up again in a hymn, the color of flame, and died into silence: and you could barely hear the weak, ancient voice saying the final prayer. The whisper of the *amens* ran around the stones like sighs, and the monks broke up their ranks and half emptied the choir, some remaining to pray.

And in the night they also rose, and filled the darkness with the strong, patient anguish of their supplication to God: and the strength of their prayer (the Spirit of Christ concealing His strength in the words their voices uttered) amazingly held back the arm of God from striking and breaking at last the foul world full of greed and avarice and murder and lust and all sin.

The thought of those monasteries, those remote choirs, those cells, those hermitages, those cloisters, those men in their cowls, the poor monks, the men who had become nothing, shattered my heart.

In an instant the desire of those solitudes was wide open within me like a wound.

I had to slam the book shut on the picture of Camaldoli and the bearded hermits standing in the stone street of cells, and I went out of the library, trying to stamp out the embers that had broken into flame, there, for an instant, within me.

No, it was useless: I did not have a vocation, and I was not for the cloister, for the priesthood. Had I not been told that definitely enough? Did I have to have that beaten into my head all over again before I could believe it?

Yet I stood in the sun outside the dining hall, waiting for the noon Angelus, and one of the Friars was talking to me. I could not contain the one thing that filled my heart:

"I am going to a Trappist monastery to make a retreat for Holy Week," I said. The things that jumped in the Friar's eyes gave him the sort of expression you would expect if I had said: "I am going to go and buy a submarine and live on the bottom of the sea." . . .

It was a safe, oblique way of admitting what was in my heart—the desire to go to that monastery and stay for good.

. . . WE GOT IN THE CAR TOGETHER, AND STARTED UP THE ROAD, AND in a minute we were in the midst of moonlit fields.

"Are the monks in bed?" I asked the driver. It was only a few minutes past eight.

"Oh, yes, they go to bed at seven o'clock."

"Is the monastery far?"

"Mile and a half."

I looked at the rolling country, and at the pale ribbon of road in front of us, stretching out as grey as lead in the light of the moon. Then suddenly I saw a steeple that shone like silver in the moonlight, growing into sight from behind a rounded knoll. The tires sang on the empty road, and, breathless, I looked at the monastery that was revealed before me as we came over the rise. At the end of an avenue of trees was a big rectangular block of buildings, all dark, with a church crowned by a tower and a steeple and a cross: and the steeple was as bright as platinum and the whole place was as quiet as midnight and lost in the all-absorbing silence and solitude of the fields. Behind the monastery was a dark curtain of woods, and over to the west was a wooded valley, and beyond that a rampart of wooded hills, a barrier and a defence against the world.

And over all the valley smiled the mild, gentle Easter moon, the full moon in her kindness, loving this silent place.

At the end of the avenue, in the shadows under the trees, I could make out the lowering arch of the gate, and the words: *"Pax Intrantibus."*

The driver of the car did not go to the bell rope by the heavy wooden door. Instead he went over and scratched on one of the windows and called, in a low voice:

"Brother! Brother!"

I could hear someone stirring inside.

Presently the key turned in the door. I passed inside. The door closed quietly behind me. I was out of the world.

The effect of that big, moonlit court, the heavy stone building with all those dark and silent windows, was overpowering. I could hardly answer the Brother's whispered questions.

I looked at his clear eyes, his greying, pointed beard.

When I told him I came from St. Bonaventure's, he said drily:

"I was a Franciscan once."

We crossed the court, climbed some steps, entered a high, dark hall. I hesitated on the brink of a polished, slippery floor, while the Brother groped for the light switch. Then, above another heavy door, I saw the words: "God alone."

"Have you come here to stay?" said the Brother.

The question terrified me. It sounded too much like the voice of my own conscience.

"Oh, no!" I said. "Oh, no!" And I heard my whisper echoing around the hall and vanishing up the indefinite, mysterious heights of a dark and empty stair-well above our heads. The place smelled frighteningly clean: old and clean, an ancient house, polished and swept and repainted and repainted over and over, year after year.

"What's the matter? Why can't you stay? Are you married or something?" said the Brother.

"No," I said lamely, "I have a job . . ."

We began to climb the wide stairs. Our steps echoed in the empty darkness. One flight and then another and a third and a fourth. There was an immense distance between floors; it was a building with great high ceilings. Finally we came to the top floor, and the Brother opened the door into a wide room, and put down my bag, and left me.

I heard his steps crossing the yard below, to the gate house.

And I felt the deep, deep silence of the night, and of peace, and of holiness enfold me like love, like safety.

The embrace of it, the silence! I had entered into a solitude that was an impregnable fortress. And the silence that enfolded me, spoke to me, and spoke louder and more eloquently than any voice, and in the middle of that quiet, clean-smelling room, with the moon pouring its peacefulness in through the open window, with the warm night air, I realized truly whose house that was, O glorious Mother of God!

How did I ever get back out of there, into the world, after tasting the sweetness and the kindness of the love with which you welcome those that come to stay in your house, even only for a few days, O Holy Queen of Heaven, and Mother of my Christ?

. . .

BELLS WERE FLYING OUT OF THE TOWER IN THE HIGH, ASTOUNDING
darkness as I groped half blind with sleep for my clothing, and hastened into
the hall and down the dark stairs. I did not know where to go, and there was
no one to show me, but I saw two men in secular clothes, at the bottom of
the stairs, going through a door. One of them was a priest with a great head
of white hair, the other was a young man with black hair, in a pair of dunga-
rees. I went after them, through the door. We were in a hallway, completely
black, except I could see their shadows moving towards a big window at the
end. They knew where they were going, and they had found a door which
opened and let some light into the hall.

I came after them to the door. It led into the cloister. The cloister was
cold, and dimly lit, and the smell of damp wool astounded me by its unearth-
liness. And I saw the monks. There was one, right there, by the door; he had
knelt, or rather thrown himself down before a *pietà* in the cloister corner, and
had buried his head in the huge sleeves of his cowl there at the feet of the
dead Christ, the Christ Who lay in the arms of Mary, letting fall one arm and
a pierced hand in the limpness of death. It was a picture so fierce that it
scared me: the abjection, the dereliction of this seemingly shattered monk
at the feet of the broken Christ. I stepped into the cloister as if into an abyss.

The silence with people moving in it was ten times more gripping than it
had been in my own empty room.

And now I was in the church. The two other seculars were kneeling there
beside an altar at which the candles were burning. A priest was already at
the altar, spreading out the corporal and opening the book. I could not figure
out why the secular priest with the great shock of white hair was kneeling
down to serve Mass. Maybe he wasn't a priest after all. But I did not have
time to speculate about that: my heart was too full of other things in that
great dark church, where, in little chapels, all around the ambulatory behind
the high altar, chapels that were caves of dim candlelight, Mass was simula-
neously beginning at many altars.

How did I live through that next hour? It is a mystery to me. The silence,
the solemnity, the dignity of these Masses and of the church, and the overpowering atmosphere of prayers so fervent that they were almost tangible
choked me with love and reverence that robbed me of the power to breathe.
I could only get the air in gasps.

O my God, with what might You sometimes choose to teach a man's soul
Your immense lessons! Here, even through only ordinary channels, came to
me graces that overwhelmed me like a tidal wave, truths that drowned me
with the force of their impact: and all through the plain, normal means of
the liturgy—but the liturgy used properly, and with reverence, by souls
inured to sacrifice.

What a thing Mass becomes, in hands hardened by gruelling and sacrificial labor, in poverty and abjection and humiliation! "See, see," said those lights, those shadows in all the chapels. "See Who God is! Realize what this Mass is! See Christ here, on the Cross! See His wounds, see His torn hands, see how the King of Glory is crowned with thorns! Do you know what Love is? Here is Love, Here on this Cross, here is Love, suffering these nails, these thorns, that scourge loaded with lead, smashed to pieces, bleeding to death because of your sins and bleeding to death because of people that will never know Him, and never think of Him and will never remember His Sacrifice. Learn from Him how to love God and how to love men! Learn of this Cross, this Love, how to give your life away to Him."

Almost simultaneously all around the church, at all the various altars, the bells began to ring. These monks, they rang no bells at the *Sanctus* or the *Hanc igitur*, only at the Consecration: and now, suddenly, solemnly, all around the church, Christ was on the Cross, lifted up, drawing all things to Himself, that tremendous Sacrifice tearing hearts from bodies, and drawing them out to Him.

"See, see Who God is, see the glory of God, going up to Him out of this incomprehensible and infinite Sacrifice in which all history begins and ends, all individual lives begin and end, in which every story is told, and finished, and settled for joy or for sorrow: the one point of reference for all the truths that are outside of God, their center, their focus: Love."

Faint gold fire flashed from the shadowy flanks of the upraised chalice at our altar.

"Do you know what Love is? You have never known the meaning of Love, never, you who have always drawn all things to the center of your own nothingness. Here is Love in this chalice full of Blood, Sacrifice, mactation. Do you not know that to love means to be killed for glory of the Beloved? And where is your love? Where is now your Cross, if you say you want to follow Me, if you pretend you love Me?"

All around the church the bells rang as gentle and fresh as dew.

"But these men are dying for Me. These monks are killing themselves for Me: and for you, for the world, for the people who do not know Me, for the millions that will never know them on this earth . . ."

After Communion I thought my heart was going to explode. . . .

BACK IN THE WORLD, I FELT LIKE A MAN THAT HAD COME DOWN FROM the rare atmosphere of a very high mountain. When I got to Louisville, I had already been up for four hours or so, and my day was getting on towards its noon, so to speak, but I found that everybody else was just getting up and having breakfast and going to work. And how strange it was to see people walking around as if they had something important to do, running after busses, reading the newspapers, lighting cigarettes.

How futile all their haste and anxiety seemed.

My heart sank within me. I thought: "What am I getting into? Is this the sort of a thing I myself have been living in all these years?"

At a street corner, I happened to look up and caught sight of an electric sign, on top of a two-storey building. It read: "Clown Cigarettes."

I turned and fled from the alien and lunatic street, and found my way into the nearby cathedral, and knelt, and prayed, and did the Stations of the Cross.

Afraid of the spiritual pressure in that monastery? Was that what I had said the other day? How I longed to be back there now: everything here, in the world outside, was insipid and slightly insane.

IT WAS A THURSDAY NIGHT. THE ALUMNI HALL WAS BEGINNING TO fill. They were going to have a movie. But I hardly noticed it: it did not occur to me that perhaps Father Philotheus might go to the movie with the rest. In the silence of the grove my feet were loud on the gravel. I walked and prayed. It was very, very dark by the shrine of the Little Flower. "For Heaven's sake, help me!" I said.

I started back towards the buildings. "All right. Now I am really going to go in there and ask him. Here's the situation, Father. What do you think? Should I go and be a Trappist?"

There was still a light in Father Philotheus' room. I walked bravely into the hall, but when I got within about six feet of his door it was almost as if someone had stopped me and held me where I was with physical hands. Something jammed in my will. I couldn't walk a step further, even though I wanted to. I made a kind of push at the obstacle, which was perhaps a devil, and then turned around and ran out of the place once more.

And again I headed for the grove. The Alumni Hall was nearly full. My feet were loud on the gravel. I was in the silence of the grove, among wet trees.

I don't think there was ever a moment in my life when my soul felt so urgent and so special an anguish. I had been praying all the time, so I cannot say that I began to pray when I arrived there where the shrine was: but things became more definite.

"Please help me. What am I going to do? I can't go on like this. You can

see that! Look at the state I am in. What ought I to do? Show me the way."
As if I needed more information or some kind of a sign!

But I said this time to the Little Flower: "You show me what to do." And
I added, "If I get into the monastery, I will be your monk. Now show me
what to do."

It was getting to be precariously near the wrong way to pray—making
indefinite promises that I did not quite understand and asking for some sort
of a sign.

Suddenly, as soon as I had made that prayer, I became aware of the wood,
the trees, the dark hills, the wet night wind, and then, clearer than any of
these obvious realities, in my imagination, I started to hear the great bell of
Gethsemani ringing in the night—the bell in the big grey tower, ringing and
ringing, as if it were just behind the first hill. The impression made me
breathless, and I had to think twice to realize that it was only in my imagination that I was hearing the bell of the Trappist Abbey ringing in the dark.
Yet, as I afterwards calculated, it was just about that time that the bell is
rung every night for the *Salve Regina,* towards the end of Compline.

The bell seemed to be telling me where I belonged—as if it were calling
me home.

This fancy put such determination into me that I immediately started
back for the monastery—going the long way 'round, past the shrine of Our
Lady of Lourdes and the far end of the football field. And with every step I
took my mind became more and more firmly made up that now I would
have done with all these doubts and hesitations and questions and all the
rest, and get this thing settled, and go to the Trappists where I belonged.

When I came into the courtyard, I saw that the light in Father Philotheus'
room was out. In fact, practically all the lights were out. Everybody had gone
to the movies. My heart sank.

Yet there was one hope. I went right on through the door and into the
corridor, and turned to the Friars' common room. I had never even gone near
that door before. I had never dared. But now I went up and knocked on the
glass panel and opened the door and looked inside.

There was nobody there except one Friar alone, Father Philotheus.

I asked if I could speak with him and we went to his room.

That was the end of all my anxiety, all my hesitation.

As soon as I proposed all my hesitations and questions to him, Father
Philotheus said that he could see no reason why I shouldn't want to enter a
monastery and become a priest.

It may seem irrational, but at that moment, it was as if scales fell off my
own eyes, and looking back on all my worries and questions, I could see
clearly how empty and futile they had been. Yes, it was obvious that I was
called to the monastic life: and all my doubts about it had been mostly

shadows. Where had they gained such a deceptive appearance of substance and reality? Accident and circumstances had all contributed to exaggerate and distort things in my mind. But now everything was straight again. And already I was full of peace and assurance—the consciousness that everything was right, and that a straight road had opened out, clear and smooth, ahead of me.

Father Philotheus had only one question:

"Are your sure you want to be a *Trappist?*" he asked me.

"Father," I answered, "I want to give God everything."

I could see by the expression on his face that he was satisfied.

I went upstairs like somebody who had been called back from the dead. Never had I experienced the calm, untroubled peace and certainty that now filled my heart. . . .

I PACKED UP MOST OF MY CLOTHES, AND PUT THEM IN A BIG BOX FOR Friendship House and the Negroes of Harlem. I left most of my books on my shelf for Father Irenaeus and his library, and gave some to a friend in the Seminary, who had been reading Duns Scotus with me, under Father Philotheus. The rest I put in a box to take with me to Gethsemani. Apart from that, all my possessions fitted into one suitcase, and that was too much: except that the Trappists might not receive me in their monastery.

I took the manuscripts of three finished novels and one half-finished novel and ripped them up and threw them in the incinerator. I gave away some notes to people who might be able to use them, and I packed up all the poems I had written, and the carbon copy of the *Journal of My Escape from the Nazis*, and another *Journal* I had kept, and some material for an anthology of religious verse, and sent it all to Mark Van Doren. Everything else I had written I put in a binder and sent to Lax and Rice who were living on 114th Street, New York. I closed my checking account at the Olean bank, and collected a check, with a bonus, for my services in the English Department from the bursar who couldn't figure out why a man would want to collect his wages in the middle of the month. I wrote three letters—to Lax, the Baroness and my relatives—and some postcards, and by the afternoon of the following day, Tuesday, with an amazing and joyous sense of lightness, I was ready to go.

My train was in the evening. It was already dark when the taxi called for me at the College.

"Where you going, Prof?" said somebody, as I passed out of the building with my suitcase.

The cab door slammed on my big general good-bye, and we drove away. I did not turn to see the collection of heads that watched the parting cab from the shelter of the arched door.

I RANG THE BELL AT THE GATE. IT LET FALL A DULL, UNRESONANT note inside the empty court. My man got in his car and went away. Nobody came. I could hear somebody moving around inside the Gatehouse. I did not ring again. Presently, the window opened, and Brother Matthew looked out between the bars, with his clear eyes and greying beard.

"Hullo, Brother," I said.

He recognized me, glanced at the suitcase and said: "This time have you come to stay?"

"Yes, Brother, if you'll pray for me," I said.

Brother nodded, and raised his hand to close the window.

"That's what I've been doing," he said, "praying for you."

Madeleine L'Engle is best known for her Newbery Medal–winning children's book *A Wrinkle in Time*, which she describes as a "hymn of praise" to God. The author of numerous children's books, novels, and three autobiographical works, her themes are ecological and Christological; she probes the ethical complexities of modern science through fantasy and speculation, at the same time creating eccentric but recognizable characters who live at the outer edge of the pursuit of knowledge and wisdom.

A consistent winner of prizes and honors, she had to overcome a long and difficult period of literary rejection while her children were young. The first part of her autobiography, *A Circle of Quiet*, describes her youth in postwar Europe, her stint in the New York theater, her marriage to the actor Hugh Franklin, and their decision to raise their children in the country. During that time, the Franklins became involved with their local church, the beginning of L'Engle's odyssey to faith. Impressed by the idea of Christian community, the Franklins became foster parents to orphaned children

MADELEINE
L'ENGLE

[1 9 1 8 –   ]

We desperately need the foolishness

of God.

and troubled teenagers. The creation of a home circle of family and friends became as important to L'Engle as her writing. When a publisher finally took a chance on *A Wrinkle in Time*, she was stunned by the immediate acclaim that followed its appearance.

Relocating to New York City brought L'Engle into contact with deeply committed Christians at the Cathedral of St. John the Divine. In the selection presented here, L'Engle describes her final steps toward acceptance of the Christian doctrine, which for her, in its emphasis on love, encompasses the greatest of forces that endure outside of time.   [AM]

FROM *A CIRCLE OF QUIET*

When I do something wrong I tend to alibi, to make excuses, blame someone else. Until I can accept whatever it is that I have done, I am only widening the gap between my real and my ontological self, and I am thus excluding myself so that I begin to think that I am unforgivable.

We need to be forgiven:

To be forgiven in this time when fish are dying in our rivers; in this time of poison gas dumped on the ocean floor and in the less and less breathable air of our cities, of children starving; being burned to death in wars which stumble on; being attacked by rats in their cribs . . .

We need to be forgiven in this grey atmosphere which clogs the lungs so that we cannot breathe, and breathless, spiritless, can no longer discern what is right and what is wrong, what is our right hand and what is our left, what is justice and what tyranny, what is life and what is death.

I heard a man of brilliance cry out that God has withdrawn from nations when they have turned from Him, and surely we are stiff-necked people; why should He not withdraw?

But then I remember Jonah accusing God of overlenience, of foolishness, mercy, and compassion.

We desperately need the foolishness of God.

DURING MY LAST YEAR IN BOARDING SCHOOL I HAD ATTAINED THE elevated position of Head of School; I was editor of the yearbook and literary magazine, played leading roles in the school plays. I had finally made it. I also had all the answers, theologically speaking. I went, with all the other Episcopalians in the school, to the Episcopal church on Sunday; it bored me totally, and it was then that I picked up the habit of writing poetry during sermons. When it came to the General Confession in Morning Prayer I was, with proper humility, willing to concede that I occasionally left undone a few things which I ought to have done (I was, after all, very busy), and I occasionally did a few things which I ought not to have done (I was, after all, not "pi"); but I was not willing to say that I was a miserable offender and that there was no health in me.

It's a stage we all go through; it takes a certain amount of living to strike the strange balance between the two errors either of regarding ourselves as unforgivable or as not needing forgiveness.

During the Crosswicks years when the children were little, a new hymnal was put out for the Congregational church. In the back is a section of prayers, and it includes the General Confession from the Book of Common Prayer. It is an interesting commentary on human nature in this confused century that precisely those words which I could not, would not say as an adolescent were deleted from the Congregational prayers.

By that time, in the midst of my fumbling agnosticism, it had become very clear to me that I *was* a miserable offender, and that there was very little health in me. I wasn't falling into that peculiar trap of *hubris* which tempts one into thinking that one is sinfuler than thou. If I never got through a day when I didn't do at least one thing I regretted, this was assuredly true of everybody else I knew. Perhaps my friends were not tempted, as I was, to do a Gauguin, but they had their own major temptations. Perhaps their sins of omission were less in the housewifely area than mine, but surely they had their own equivalent. I was rather upset by the mutilation of the Confession.

"It's all right to think you can be virtuous if you try just a little harder when you're an adolescent," I told Quinn, "but I don't like having the church behave like an adolescent."

When we moved back to New York a series of those noncoincidences started me back into the church in which I was born, the church of John Donne, Lancelot Andrewes, Shakespeare. A friend of Alan's, doing his Ph.D. in seventeenth-century English literature, became an Anglican, saying that one can hardly spend so much time with all these people without sharing their beliefs. When, shortly after our return, the Episcopal church put out a trial liturgy, I was unhappy with it for two major reasons: it was not worded in the best language of which we are capable; and it made the confession before receiving communion optional.

We haven't done a very good job of righting the wrongs of our parents or our peers, my generation. We can't say to our children, here is a green and peaceful world we have prepared for you and your children: enjoy it. We can offer them only war and pollution and senility. And this is the time we decide, in our churches, that we're so virtuous we don't need to be forgiven: symbolically, ironically forgiven.

If the Lord's table is the prototype of the family table, then, if I think in terms of the family table, I know that I cannot sit down to bread and wine until I've said I'm sorry, until reparations have been made, relations restored. When one of our children had done something particularly unworthy, if it had come out into the open before dinner, if there had been an "I'm sorry," and there had been acceptance, and love, then would follow the happiest dinner possible, full of laughter and fun. If there was something still hidden; if one child, or as sometimes happens, one parent, was out of joint with the family and the world, that would destroy the atmosphere of the whole meal.

What is true of the family table is, in another sense, true of the conjugal bed. Twin beds make no sense to me. I can understand an occasional need for a separate room, but not separate beds. If a man and wife get into bed together it is very difficult to stay mad. Both Hugh and I have tried, and it hasn't worked. The touch of a hand is enough to dissolve me into tenderness; the touch of a cold foot enough to dissolve me into laughter. One way or another, reparation is made, relations restored, love returned.

Only a human being can say *I'm sorry. Forgive me.* This is part of our particularity. It is part of what makes us capable of tears, capable of laughter. . . .

ONE OF THE THINGS I AM MOST GRATEFUL FOR IS MY VERY LACK OF ability as a pastry cook. A decade ago when we first moved back to New York from Crosswicks, we put our children in a nearby school, St. Hilda's and St. Hugh's. . . .

One day the children came home with the usual mimeographed petition for a cake for the bazaar. They were new at the school and they wanted their mother to do the right thing. "Please, Mother." So I baked a cake.

I'm as bad at cakes as I am at cherry pies. The last cherry pie I made was shortly after we were married and Hugh had some people from the Theatre Guild in for dinner, and I was determined to impress them with my wifely virtues. When it was time for dessert I didn't think the pie crust was brown enough, so I put it under the broiler. We had to get the fire extinguisher.

So I made a cake for my children's sake. It tasted delicious. But it didn't look the way it tasted. It was lopsided: a mess. I wrote the headmistress a note which ran more or less like this: "I tried. I baked a cake. Because my family loves me, they will eat it. But it is obvious that this is not the way in which I can be of use to the school. Is there anything else I could do, more in line with my talents? Is there a play we could help with, or anything like that?"

Within a few days Hugh and I found that we were directing the Christmas pageant, with the entire Cathedral of St. John the Divine as our stage: Mr. and Mrs. Max Reinhardt. It's quite something to see the three kings march in their glorious costumes the length of two city blocks.

If I had been able to bake that cake for the school cake sale I might still be in darkness. Father Anthony (I speak of him so casually: he is Metropolitan of Surozh and Exarch of the Russian Patriarchal in Western Europe) said last spring that it is good to have turned to God as he did, as I did, after a time of darkness, because then one truly knows what it is like to be dead, and now to be alive.

Hugh and I first ran into Canon Tallis when we were directing the pageant at the Cathedral, after my cake-baking fiasco. Ran into is right. We clashed. He did not like vast quantities of school children in the Cathedral during Advent, that austere time of eschatology, reenacting the Christmas story out of chronology. He bristled when he saw us. We bristled when we saw him. We could conceive of no reason why the pageant wasn't the most important thing in the world, why he didn't put at our disposal all the facilities of the Cathedral.

Later, when I knew him better, I explained to him, passionately, that the chronology of the pageant wasn't really what was important; Christmas is an arbitrary date anyhow; the important thing was that the children should have some idea of Christmas beyond street-corner Santa Clauses and loudspeakers braying out Christmas carols. "Don't you understand that many of them won't have any Christmas otherwise? They won't even go to church. If it's not to be a blasphemy they'll have to have it here, now, before the school vacation begins, out of chronology—but in real time."

Thus Madeleine the agnostic.

But we did, after that, have all the cooperation possible from the Cathedral staff.

Later on I went to Canon Tallis, almost by accident, when I was in trouble. I'd made an appointment with another canon at the Cathedral, and his secretary forgot to put the appointment in his book. He was full of apologies, but had to be away, so couldn't see me later, and suggested Tallis. Canon Tallis was the last person I wanted to see. Something told me that it would either work magnificently or be totally horrible.

It worked magnificently.

It wasn't that my problem was solved but that I had help in bearing it. I also told him all my intellectual doubts, my total incredulity about the incarnation; the idea that God could pitch his tent among men was absurd. Of course! It still is.

I had talked with several Congregational minister friends about my intellectual doubts. I was eager to be converted—I didn't like atheism or agnosticism; I was by then well aware that I am not self-sufficient, that I needed the dimension of transcendence. They were eager to convert me. But they explained everything. For every question I asked, they had an answer. They tried to reach me through my mind.

First of all, my mind is not that good. I'm not stupid; I did graduate from Smith with honors. But I am, basically, not an intellectual. Nevertheless, I knew that I could not throw away my mind, and it was not the discoveries of science that bothered me. On the contrary. The book I read during this period which brought me closest to God was one that never mentioned God, *The Limitations of Science*, by J. W. N. Sullivan.

My minister friends gave me all kinds of theological books to read, mostly by German theologians. The more I read, the further I was shoved away from any kind of acceptance. I would read logical explanations of the totally mysterious scandal of particularity and think: if I have to believe all this bunk, then Christianity is not for me. One line in the Book of Common Prayer made sense to me: *the mystery of the word made flesh.* If only my friends would admit that it *was* a mystery, and stop giving me explanations! I wrote in my journal: "I talk to people—oh, people I respect, people I like—and yet I never feel any sense of terrific excitement in their own lives about Jesus, in the way that the early Christians must have been excited so that they were transfigured by Jesus. In no one, no one, no matter how loudly they talk about salvation being possible only through Jesus, do I find this great thing *showing* in them, glowing in them, lighting their lives, as it must if it is to make any sense today at all." I was, I am sure, less than fair; nevertheless that was what reasonable explanations did to me.

Canon Tallis did not explain anything. He listened to my doubts in silence. I think he thought they were really very unimportant. As far as my specific, daily problems were concerned, I found that I could take them more lightly, could laugh more easily.

Then spring came. Hugh was away with the tour of *Luther.* He'd had a fine time playing Cardinal Cajetan on Broadway, and we felt that he should go on tour. But all kinds of things happened that spring. Bion, eleven, started running a high fever, for which no explanation could be found. At the hospital the doctor assured me that there was a physical cause, and they would go on testing until they found it. For forty-eight hours I lived with the knowledge that the doctor thought that Bion had cancer of the liver. He had been talking to me in abstruse medical terms, but one of my closest friends is a doctor, and I more or less went through medical school with her, and suddenly the doctor looked at me and said, "Do you know what I am talking about?"

"Yes. I'm afraid I do."

"We're re-testing, and I'll call you as soon as the results are in."

Hugh and I were trying not to phone each other too often; we called about every three days. He would be phoning the evening that we would know the results. By shortly after six, when Hugh usually called, I had not heard anything. Then the phone rang, and I dreaded telling Hugh what we feared; there was never any question of keeping it from him; he'd hear it in my voice. But it was not Hugh, it was the doctor, and it was not cancer.

Then Hugh's father died, and he had to fly from Chicago to Tulsa for the funeral. He called me from Chicago before leaving; I already knew, because I had talked to his sister that morning. While Hugh and I were talking, I could hear his voice break, and he said in astonishment, "Isn't it extraordinary, this is the first time I've felt anything about Dad, talking to you." But of course we both knew that it wasn't extraordinary at all.

Then happy news. Josephine was to be salutatorian of her class, graduating at sixteen. We were joyful and proud. But Hugh couldn't come for graduation, because he had taken time off from the play for his father's funeral. And Bion was still in the hospital.

Then something happened, something so wounding that it cannot possibly be written down. Think of two of the people you love most in the world; think of a situation in which both are agonizingly hurt and you are powerless to do anything to help. It is far easier to bear pain for ourselves than for those we love, especially when part of it is that we cannot share the pain but must stand by, unable to alleviate it.

Canon Tallis hardly knew us at all, then. But he stepped in. What he did is involved with all that I cannot write. The point right now is that this was the moment of light for me, because it was an act of love, Love made visible.

And that did it. Possibly nothing he could have done for me, myself, would have illuminated the world for me as did this act of love towards those I love. Because of this love, this particular (never general) Christian love, my intellectual reservations no longer made the least difference. I had seen love in action, and that was all the proof I needed.

THERE IS NO MORE BEAUTIFUL WITNESS TO THE MYSTERY OF THE word made flesh than a baby's naked body. I remember with sensory clarity sitting with one of my babies on my lap and running my hand over the incredibly pure smoothness of the bare back and thinking that any mother, holding her child thus, must have at least an echo of what it is like to be Mary; that in touching the particular created matter, flesh, of our child, we are touching the Incarnation. Alan, holding his daughter on his lap, running his hand over her bare back with the same tactile appreciation with which I had touched my children, made a similar remark.

Once, when I was in the hospital, the smooth and beautiful white back of the woman in the bed next to mine, a young woman dying of cancer, was a stabbing and bitter reminder of the ultimate end of all matter.

But not just our human bodies: all matter: the stars in their courses: everything: the end of time.

Meanwhile we are in time, and the flesh is to be honored. At all ages. For me, this summer, this has been made clear in a threefold way: I have fed, bathed, played pat-a-cake with my grandbabies. In the night when I wake up, as I usually do, I always reach out with a foot, a hand, to touch my husband's body; I go back to sleep with my hand on his warm flesh. And my mother is almost ninety and preparing to move into a different country. I do not understand the mysteries of the flesh, but I know that we must not be afraid to reach out to each other, to hold hands, to touch.

In our bedroom there is a large old rocking chair which was in the attic of Crosswicks when we bought it. It seems to have been made especially for mothers and babies. I have sat in it and nursed my babe in the middle of the night. I have sung innumerable lullabies from it. When Hugh was in *Medea*, which was sent overseas in 1951 by the State Department, I sat in the rocking chair, carrying his child within me and holding out first-born in my arms, singing all the old lullabies, but especially *Sweet and Low* because of "over the Western sea," and "Bring him again to me."

This summer I sit in the rocking chair and rock and sing with one or other of my granddaughters. I sing the same songs I sang all those years ago. It feels utterly right. Natural. The same.

But it isn't the same. I may be holding a baby just as I used to hold a baby, but chronology has done many things in the intervening years, to the world, to our country, to my children, to me. I may feel, rocking a small, loving body, no older than I felt rocking that body's mother. But I am older bodily; my energy span is not as long as it used to be; at night my limbs ache with fatigue; my eyes are even older than the rest of me. It is going to seem very early—it is going to *be* very early—when the babies wake up: Alan, Josephine, Cynthia, and I take turns getting up and going downstairs with them, giving them breakfast, making the coffee. Is it my turn again so quickly?

Chronology: the word about the measurable passage of time, although its duration varies: how long is a toothache? how long is standing in line at the supermarket? how long is a tramp through the fields with the dogs? or dinner with friends, or a sunset, or the birth of a baby?

Chronology, the time which changes things, makes them grow older, wears them out, and manages to dispose of them, chronologically, forever.

Thank God there is kairos, too: again the Greeks were wiser than we are. They had two words for time: *chronos* and *kairos*.

Kairos is not measurable. Kairos is ontological. In kairos we *are*, we are fully in isness, not negatively, as Sartre saw the isness of the oak tree, but fully, wholly, positively. Kairos can sometimes enter, penetrate, break through chronos: the child at play, the painter at his easel, Serkin playing the *Appassionata*, are in kairos. The saint at prayer, friends around the dinner table, the mother reaching out her arms for her newborn baby, are in kairos. The bush, the burning bush, is in kairos, not any burning bush, but the very particular burning bush before which Moses removed his shoes; the bush I pass on my way to the brook. In kairos that part of us which is not consumed in the burning is wholly awake. We too often let it fall asleep, not as the baby in my arms droops into sleepiness, but dully, bluntingly.

I sit in the rocking chair with a baby in my arms, and I am in both kairos and chronos. In chronos I may be nothing more than some cybernetic salad on the bottom left-hand corner of a check; or my social-security number; or my passport number. In kairos I am known by name: Madeleine.

The baby doesn't know about chronos yet.

CHARLES W. COLSON

[1 9 3 1 –]

Something inside me was urging me

to surrender.

In one of the most documented and public conversions to Christianity in the twentieth century, Chuck Colson, facing criminal charges associated with the Watergate crimes of the Nixon administration, announced to the media that he had "accepted Jesus Christ." Renowned as a hatchet man who would, by his own account, walk over his own grandmother to accomplish his goals, Colson abruptly changed course to join with former political enemies in prayer breakfasts at the White House.

During his term in prison, he found himself periodically tempted to return to his former ruthless procedures in obtaining goods or legal services for his fellow inmates. His increasing discomfort with old habits, and the vitality of his new faith when shared with fellow Christians on the inside and outside, signaled for him a genuine spiritual transformation. Once released, believing his experiences were ordained to prepare him for missionary work, Colson established Prison Fellowship and its subsidiary program, Angel Tree, as ministries to prisoners and their families.

In the selections presented here from his now-classic autobiography, *Born*

Again, Colson describes the moment of his spiritual rebirth, stimulated by the counseling of his friend Tom Phillips, then president of the Raytheon Corporation. Colson's public announcement that he had become a Christian, issued at a time of intense media attention to White House events, caused considerable exposure for Colson amid the turmoil of the Watergate convictions.

[AM]

FROM  *BORN AGAIN*

Sitting there on the dimly lit porch, my self-centered past was washing over me in waves. It was painful. Agony. Desperately I tried to defend myself. What about my sacrifices for government service, the giving up of a big income, putting my stocks into a blind trust? The truth, I saw in an instant, was that I'd wanted the position in the White House more than I'd wanted money. There was no sacrifice. And the more I had talked about my own sacrifices, the more I was really trying to build myself up in the eyes of others. I would eagerly have given up everything I'd ever earned to prove myself at the mountaintop of government. It was pride—Lewis's "great sin" —that had propelled me through life.

Tom finished the chapter on pride and shut the book. I mumbled something noncommittal to the effect that "I'll look forward to reading that." But Lewis's torpedo had hit me amidships. I think Phillips knew it as he stared into my eyes. That one chapter ripped through the protective armor in which I had unknowingly encased myself for forty-two years. Of course, I had not known God. *How could I?* I had been concerned with myself. *I* had done this and that, *I* had achieved, *I* had succeeded and *I* had given God none of the credit, never once thanking Him for any of His gifts to me. I had never thought of anything being "immeasurably superior" to myself, or if I had in fleeting moments thought about the infinite power of God, I had not related Him to my life. In those brief moments while Tom read, I saw myself as I never had before. And the picture was ugly.

"How about it, Chuck?" Tom's question jarred me out of my trance. I knew precisely what he meant. Was I ready to make the leap of faith as he had in New York, to "accept" Christ?

"Tom, you've shaken me up. I'll admit that. That chapter describes me. But I can't tell you I'm ready to make the kind of commitment you did. I've got to be certain. I've got to learn a lot more, be sure all my reservations are satisfied. I've got a lot of intellectual hang-ups to get past."

For a moment Tom looked disappointed, then he smiled. "I understand, I understand."

"You see," I continued, "I saw men turn to God in the Marine Corps; I did once myself. Then afterwards it's all forgotten and everything is back to normal. Foxhole religion is just a way of using God. How can I make a commitment now? My whole world is crashing down around me. How can I be sure I'm not just running for shelter and that when the crisis is over I'll forget it? I've got to answer all the intellectual arguments first and if I can do that, I'll be sure."

"I understand," Tom repeated quietly.

I was relieved he did, yet deep inside of me something wanted to tell Tom to press on. He was making so much sense, the first time anyone ever had in talking about God.

But Tom did not press on. He handed me his copy of *Mere Christianity*. "Once you've read this, you might want to read the Book of John in the Bible." I scribbled notes of the key passages he quoted. "Also there's a man in Washington you should meet," he continued, "name of Doug Coe. He gets people together for Christian fellowship—prayer breakfasts and things like that. I'll ask him to contact you."

Tom then reached for his Bible and read a few of his favorite psalms. The comforting words were like a cold soothing ointment. For the first time in my life, familiar verses I'd heard chanted lifelessly in church came alive. "Trust in the Lord," I remember Tom reading, and I wanted to, right that moment I wanted to—if only I knew how, if only I could be sure.

"Would you like to pray together, Chuck?" Tom asked, closing his Bible and putting it on the table beside him.

Startled, I emerged from my deep thoughts. "Sure—I guess I would—Fine." I'd never prayed with anyone before except when someone said grace before a meal. Tom bowed his head, folded his hands, and leaned forward on the edge of his seat. "Lord," he began, "we pray for Chuck and his family, that You might open his heart and show him the light and the way. . . ."

As Tom prayed, something began to flow into me—a kind of energy. Then came a wave of emotion which nearly brought tears. I fought them back. It sounded as if Tom were speaking directly and personally to God, almost as if He were sitting beside us. The only prayers I'd ever heard were formal and stereotyped, sprinkled with *Thees* and *Thous*.

When he finished, there was a long silence. I knew he expected me to pray but I didn't know what to say and was too self-conscious to try. We walked to the kitchen together where Gert was still at the big table, reading. I thanked her and Tom for their hospitality.

"Come back, won't you?" she said. Her smile convinced me she meant it.

"Take care of yourself, Chuck, and let me know what you think of that book, will you?" With that, Tom put his hand on my shoulder and grinned. "I'll see you soon."

I didn't say much; I was afraid my voice would crack, but I had the strong feeling that I *would* see him soon. And I couldn't wait to read his little book.

Outside in the darkness, the iron grip I'd kept on my emotions began to relax. Tears welled up in my eyes as I groped in the darkness for the right key to start my car. Angrily I brushed them away and started the engine. "What kind of weakness is this?" I said to nobody.

The tears spilled over and suddenly I knew I had to go back into the house and pray with Tom. I turned off the motor, got out of the car. As I did, the kitchen light went out, then the light in the dining room. Through the hall window I saw Tom stand aside as Gert started up the stairs ahead of him. Now the hall was in darkness. It was too late. I stood for a moment staring at the darkened house, only one light burning now in an upstairs bedroom. Why hadn't I prayed when he gave me the chance? I wanted to so badly. Now I was alone, really alone.

As I drove out of Tom's driveway, the tears were flowing uncontrollably. There were no streetlights, no moonlight. The car headlights were flooding illumination before my eyes, but I was crying so hard it was like trying to swim underwater. I pulled to the side of the road not more than a hundred yards from the entrance to Tom's driveway, the tires sinking into soft mounds of pine needles.

I remember hoping that Tom and Gert wouldn't hear my sobbing, the only sound other than the chirping of crickets that penetrated the still of the night. With my face cupped in my hands, head leaning forward against the wheel, I forgot about machismo, about pretenses, about fears of being weak. And as I did, I began to experience a wonderful feeling of being released. Then came the strange sensation that water was not only running down my cheeks, but surging through my whole body as well, cleansing and cooling as it went. They weren't tears of sadness and remorse, nor of joy— but somehow, tears of relief.

And then I prayed my first real prayer. "God, I don't know how to find You, but I'm going to try! I'm not much the way I am now, but somehow I want to give myself to You." I didn't know how to say more, so I repeated over and over the words: *Take me.*

I had not "accepted" Christ—I still didn't know who He was. My mind told me it was important to find that out first, to be sure that I knew what I was doing, that I meant it and would stay with it. Only, that night, something inside me was urging me to surrender—to what or to whom I did not know.

I stayed there in the car, wet-eyed, praying, thinking, for perhaps half an hour, perhaps longer, alone in the quiet of the dark night. Yet for the first time in my life I was not alone at all. . . .

BACK AT THE INN DOUBTS ABOUT MY MOTIVES CONTINUED TO NAG
at me. Was I seeking a safe port in the storm, a temporary hiding place? Was
that what happened in Tom Phillips's driveway? Despite the arrow to the
heart and my awakening on the Maine coast to the incredible realization
about Jesus Christ, was I somehow looking to religion as a last-gasp effort to
save myself as everything else in my world was crashing down about me?

Did I hope that God would keep my world intact? Legitimate doubts, I
suppose. Certainly many people would accuse me of copping out in time
of trouble. But could I make a decision based on how the world might
judge it?

No, I knew the time had come for me: I could not sidestep the central
question Lewis (or God) had placed squarely before me. Was I to accept
without reservations Jesus Christ as Lord of my life? It was like a gate before
me. There was no way to walk around it. I would step through, or I would
remain outside. A "maybe" or "I need more time" was kidding myself.

And as something pressed that question home, less and less was I troubled
by the curious phrase "accept Jesus Christ." It had sounded at first both
pious and mystical, language of the zealot, maybe black-magic stuff. But "to
accept" means no more than "to believe." Did I believe what Jesus said? If
I did, if I took it on faith or reason or both, then I accepted. Not mystical or
weird at all, and with no in-between ground left. Either I would believe or I
would not—and believe it all or none of it.

The search that began that week on the coast of Maine, as I pondered it,
was not quite as important as I had thought. It simply returned me to where
I had been when I asked God to "take me" in that moment of surrender on
the little country road in front of the Phillipses' home. What I studied so
intently all week opened a little wider the new world into which I had
already taken my first halting, shaky steps. One week of study on the Maine
coast would hardly qualify, even in the jet age, as much of an odyssey, but I
felt as if I'd been on a journey of thousands of miles.

And so early that Friday morning, while I sat alone staring at the sea I
love, words I had not been certain I could understand or say fell naturally
from my lips: "Lord Jesus, I believe You. I accept You. Please come into my
life. I commit it to You."

With these few words that morning, while the briny sea churned, came a
sureness of mind that matched the depth of feeling in my heart. There came
something more: strength and serenity, a wonderful new assurance about
life, a fresh perception of myself and the world around me. In the process, I
felt old fears, tensions, and animosities draining away. I was coming alive to
things I'd never seen before; as if God was filling the barren void I'd known
for so many months, filling it to its brim with a whole new kind of awareness.

I wrote Tom Phillips, telling him of the step I had taken, of my gratitude for his loving concern, and asked his prayers for the long and difficult journey I sensed lay ahead.

I could not possibly in my wildest dreams have imagined what it would involve. How fortunate it is that God does not allow us to see into the future. . . .

EACH MORNING SHORTLY AFTER EIGHT, THE MEN OF POWER IN THE executive branch of government assemble around a long antique mahogany table in the historic Roosevelt Room just across a narrow corridor from the President's Oval Office. For over three years I was always present, listening to Kissinger's briefing on whatever troubled area of the globe demanded our attention, joining in the discussion of pressing domestic issues with John Ehrlichman or George Shultz, jotting down notes about the President's schedule as Bob Haldeman reviewed it.

Small wonder, I suppose, that all through those frantic years I had not known that at the very same time, one morning every two weeks, another group was also meeting around a table in the basement of the White House west wing. Those present would include a departmental Under Secretary or two, sometimes a Cabinet member and a handful of White House staffers sharing their faith with one another, reading from the Scriptures and praying together. Even if I had known there was a White House prayer group, I would have considered myself too busy to attend.

Although President Nixon had refused to invite his arch foe Harold Hughes inside the executive mansion, the small group meeting biweekly in the basement was eager for the senator's fellowship. Harold accepted their invitation to attend a breakfast meeting scheduled for December 6. Since he had been inside the White House only once during Nixon's term, and since these were bitter days, with Washington divided into hostile camps, Harold and Doug suggested I go along. Perhaps I could help in case some overly zealous Nixon partisan took offense at Hughes's mere presence there.

I arrived a minute before eight, walking briskly through the Southwest Gate, past the familiar faces of the guards who waved cheerily. It was such a beautiful sunny day, and I felt so jubilant over the prospect of Hughes praying in the White House, that I even smiled at the sleepy-eyed reporters who were always about, making notes on everyone coming and going.

I walked through the basement door entrance to the west wing, down the low-ceilinged corridor lined with huge color photographs of Nixon and his travels, past a door marked simply SITUATION ROOM, the nerve center of the National Security Council, whose offices stretch through a subterranean labyrinth beneath the South Lawn. The breakfast was being held in the paneled Conference Dining Room, reserved for senior White House staffers and Cabinet members. This morning three tables had been pushed together and places set for fourteen. Already seated, with his back to the wall—I thought he chose it that way—was Harold Hughes looking stiff and uncomfortable, surrounded by half a dozen staunch Nixonites.

The senator looked up at my entrance, brightened noticeably, and shouted, "Hi, brother!" I greeted my friends and took a seat at a far corner of the long table. One by one, others arrived, filling all of the chairs except the one immediately to my right. Under Secretary of Labor Dick Shubert was there, as was Ken Belieu, who had been coaxed out of retirement to help the new Vice-President Gerald Ford organize his office. There were other old friends; most I had not known to be interested in this sort of thing. The red-jacketed Filipino stewards began shuttling silver pots of hot coffee and trays of buns from the kitchen. We had started to eat when the door swung open and the chairman of the Federal Reserve Board, Arthur Burns, entered.

"What is Arthur Burns doing here?" I asked in astonishment to the man on my left, Father John McLaughlin, the Jesuit priest and staff speech writer for the President. Aware of the "dirty trick" episode several years before when I falsely accused Burns of seeking a pay raise, Father John chuckled. "Arthur is a regular participant in these breakfasts," he told me.

"But he's Jewish," I protested. Not that this really made any difference; it was simply the first thing I could think to say to explain my obvious distress. As I am sure McLaughlin realized, I dreaded the confrontation.

"He is not only Jewish," McLaughlin went on, "he is the chairman of this breakfast meeting."

Burns looked just as uncomfortable at the sight of me, and even more so at the realization, as his eyes quickly scanned the table, that the only empty chair was next to me. He hesitated for a moment, then leaned across the table to introduce himself to Hughes, greeted the others, and with the barest nod in my direction sat down.

Hughes proved to be more of an attraction than the organizers of the breakfast had expected. Soon the room which seats fifty was almost full, sending the stewards scurrying to the kitchen for additional plates of scrambled eggs. But the turnout, though large, was scarcely welcoming; the atmosphere was charged with skepticism.

At 8:20 Burns, who had picked nervously at his breakfast, welcomed the overflow crowd and explained how happy the White House prayer group was to have Senator Hughes present to discuss his reasons for leaving the Senate to enter a full-time lay ministry. Then with none of the flowery superlatives normally passed among politicians at Washington gatherings, Burns turned the meeting over to Hughes.

After a few opening moments of uncharacteristic nervousness, Harold was in charge, his eloquent commanding self. For twenty minutes there was not another sound in that room other than his deep, powerful voice. He spoke with devastating honesty about his past, the power of Christ in his changed life, the conflicts he had faced as a Christian in government, and then for the final few minutes, how he had come to know his brother in Christ, Chuck Colson.

If it had not been such a moving moment, I would have laughed aloud at the astonished expressions around the room. Out of the corner of my eye I saw Arthur Burns sitting absolutely motionless, eyes fixed on Hughes, a soft shock of gray hair hanging over his brow, his mouth open. The pipe he had been smoking furiously at the outset now lay cold in his right hand.

"I've learned how wrong it is to hate," Hughes went on. "For years there were men towards whom I felt consuming bitterness. I wasn't hurting them, only myself. By hating I was shutting Christ's love out of my life. One of the men I hated most was Chuck Colson, but now that we share a commitment together in Christ, I love him as my brother. I would trust him with my life, my family, with everything I have."

When he finished there was a long silence—no one could take his eyes off the senator. Seconds ticked by, a minute perhaps, almost as if the whole room was in silent prayer.

Arthur Burns, who was to close the meeting, seemed unable to find the words. Finally, he very deliberately laid his pipe on the table, stared at it for a moment, folded his hands in front of him, and slowly lifted his eyes. In a voice so low I doubted if those across the room could hear, he began. "Senator—I just want to say—that is one of the most beautiful and moving things I have ever heard from any man."

He cleared his throat and it was plain that he was choking back tears. "I don't want to say anything else," he said. "Just this—on behalf of this group, would you please come back again?" With that he arose, took my right hand in his left and said, "Now I would like to ask Mr. Colson to lead us in prayer."

Everyone in the room joined hands. I was so surprised that it was a moment before I found my voice. There was no time to compose a prayer in my mind; I would have to depend on the Holy Spirit. The words which came out were a plea for all of us in the room, regardless of our position in government, to come before Him in humility and submission, in the knowledge that we were nothing, that He was everything, and that without His hand on our shoulders we could not possibly attend the affairs of our nation. As I ended the prayer, asking it all in the name of our Lord Jesus Christ, I felt Burns's grip tighten. . . . Then he stammered, "I've never, never felt—I've never known—well, this has been quite a morning." With that he squeezed my arm, turned, and walked into the bright sunlight outside.

I walked back to my office praising God. . . .

The following is taken directly from the transcript of the [press briefing] (White House News Conference Transcript #1869, December 6, 1973) beginning with Dan Rather of CBS News:

RATHER: Jerry, what is the President doing continuing to see Charles Colson?

WARREN: I don't think he is.

RATHER: What was Mr. Colson doing at the White House today?

WARREN: (pause) Well . . . (pause) he was attending a meeting in the dining room downstairs which is held every other Thursday. A group of White House staff members get together for a prayer breakfast and Mr. Colson was attending that. . . .

UNIDENTIFIED VOICE: Prayer!

ANOTHER UNIDENTIFIED VOICE: Is he going to be the next preacher?

Several minutes of the proceedings here became unintelligible because of the laughter which apparently rocked the room. Jerry told me later there hadn't been such merriment in the Press Room since before Watergate began eighteen months earlier.

RATHER: I would like an answer.

WARREN: That is the answer.

RATHER: That he was attending a prayer breakfast?

The transcript shows that Warren launched into a lengthy explanation about Senator Hughes's appearance at the breakfast that morning, those who attended, the frequency of the breakfasts, and the fact that former staff members such as myself did attend. The laughter evidently was gone.

RATHER: Jerry, isn't this a little unusual, to have a full-time paid lobbyist for very large associations and individuals in and out of the White House to attend things such as a prayer breakfast?

WARREN: Dan, I don't think so at all. I think that is stretching it a great deal. When a group of individuals who have worked together, sit down together to practice what they believe in, and that is a prayer breakfast, I see just no connection at all. I think you are stretching it.

RATHER: If I may follow on this, let the record show I am not antiprayer or prayer breakfasts or anything, but I do think there is a fairly important question involved here. While Charles Colson was, at one time, a member of the White House staff, he is now operating for people such as the Teamsters Union. Now we all know the way Washington works. These people ingratiate themselves with people in positions of power, and at such things as, yes, a prayer breakfast, they do their business. Isn't someone around here worried at least about the symbolism of this?

WARREN: No more than we are worried about the symbolism of Senator Hughes being the main speaker.

QUESTIONS FROM UNIDENTIFIED VOICE: Is he representing some outside business interest?

QUESTION: What is the parallel?

WARREN: The parallel is that these are human beings who are expressing their belief together, and I see no problem with that whatsoever.

QUESTION: Senator Hughes is going to go into the clergy. Are you comparing that with the Teamsters Union? (laughter).

WARREN: I think this has gone far enough.

With that Warren turned and walked away from the podium, leaving a roomful of bemused reporters and only one news story of the day—Colson at a prayer breakfast.

Shortly before noon every button on my telephone lighted up at once. Nothing unusual. It happened often enough through the long night of Watergate. Whenever a new accusation was hurled my way, reporters reached for their phones to call for my comment, a standard practice. "The *Chicago Tribune*, the *Post*, the *New York Times*, AP," Holly reported. "All of them calling at once."

My heart raced. There had not been much about me in the press lately. Could it be the long-expected indictment? I took the *Chicago Tribune* call first, because I liked Aldo Beckman, its Washington Bureau chief who was on the line.

"There's a story moving on the wires, Chuck, about your attending a prayer meeting at the White House this morning, about you and Senator Harold Hughes of Iowa becoming close friends." The skepticism in his voice increased: "And then something else here about your having found religion."

In a flush of anger I protested, "Come on, Aldo, you guys have printed everything there is to print about me. But my religion is my own business and I'm not about to talk about it in the public press. Enough is enough."

"Warren has announced that you were at a prayer breakfast this morning at the White House. It's already public."

"Warren announced it?" I was stunned. "Well, then let Warren tell you all about it." With that I hung up.

By now the calls were coming in a torrent. "What shall I tell them?" Holly asked.

"Tell them to . . ." And then I thought better of it. "Just take down the names. Maybe I'll call back."

I placed a call to Jerry Warren who explained what had happened. "I guess someone saw you come in today, Chuck. These vultures are grabbing for every little straw. They had a field day with the prayer-breakfast bit. You should have seen their faces," he chuckled.

"But I've been in the White House over and over these past months, Jerry, and they've watched me come and go all the time. Why should they ask about it today?"

I called Doug Coe, who told me that reporters were calling Hughes and Fellowship House, too, and were piecing the story together. "Just be careful, Chuck. Don't lose your temper," Doug advised.

The question I had asked Jerry Warren began to plague me: "Why today?" Dan Rather might have asked that question almost any day of the week over the prior nine months. There were times just before a major Presidential announcement, or after the "Saturday Night Massacre," or when the Ervin Committee was in full swing when my visits should have drawn suspicious attention. They never had. Why now?

Was it possible that it wasn't chance at all? I was learning that the Lord works in mysterious ways—although it was hard for me to see how His purposes could be served by cynical articles about my conversion. Yet the thought persisted. Why had not Warren brushed Rather's question aside, said simply that I had not been to see Nixon? Or that he didn't know? Why bring in the prayer breakfast? That wasn't Warren's usual style.

And yet how could this be God's doing? Attention from the press was the last thing we wanted now; the lower my profile the better, my lawyers believed. And the cynics would have a circus; there would be a lot of snickering, especially from old friends. Finally, if the story ever came out with my verification, I'd be locked completely into a new life, no falling back into my old ways.

And suddenly I found myself remembering how Tom Phillips had proclaimed his faith to me. He risked embarrassment in doing so, but his courage helped change my life. The teaching of Scripture was as clear as the sparkle of sun now streaming in my office windows. "Never be ashamed of bearing witness to our Lord," Paul wrote to Timothy (*see* 2 Timothy 1:8 PHILLIPS). We had discussed this recently at a Monday meeting. Not to verify the story would be almost to deny the reality of what had happened to me. There was no other way, I concluded, no way to modify it, condition it, or call it something else, no socially acceptable middle ground.

The decision was made. If Rather's question was the result of a one-in-a-thousand coincidence, so be it. But if it was God's doing, I must do my part. So I called the reporters back and did my best to explain my commitment. Even as I listened to the words coming out of my mouth against the clattering of typewriter keys on the other end of the phone it sounded unreal: "Accepting Christ . . . Jesus Christ in my life." What this was going to look like in the stark black of printer's ink! The occasional titters, the "Would you repeat that—more slowly—this time," confirmed my worst fears.

"TOUGH GUY" COLSON HAS TURNED RELIGIOUS proclaimed the *Los Angeles*

Times; COLSON HAS "FOUND RELIGION" in the *New York Times. Time* magazine summed up the press reports the following week (December 17, 1973) under the heading "Conversion":

> *Of all the Watergate cast, few had a reputation for being tougher, wilier, nastier or more tenaciously loyal to Richard Nixon than onetime Presidential Adviser Charles W. Colson. The former Marine captain is alleged by Jeb Stuart Magruder to have urged the original Watergate bugging and has been implicated in a host of other dirty tricks, including the forgery of a State Department cable. At the peak of his influence, he proudly boasted that his commitment to the re-election of the President was such that "I would walk over my grandmother if necessary."*
>
> *At a White House staff prayer breakfast last week, Colson, 42, revealed a new aspect. He said that he has "come to know Christ. . . ." Suspecting that his newfound faith may go down hard with some, Tough Guy Colson had a forthright response for scoffers. Said he: "If anyone wants to be cynical about it, I'll pray for him."*

ELDRIDGE
CLEAVER

[1 9 3 5 –]

I saw a path of light leading

through a prison cell . . .

As leader of the Black Panthers and an avowed Marxist, Cleaver wrote his first autobiographical work, *Soul on Ice,* from a prison cell. In that work he recounts the story of a childhood and youth given over to crime, followed by a series of imprisonments that he turned to good use by spending the time to educate himself. Soon after his release, Cleaver, now a Black Muslim and Minister of Information for the revolutionary Black Panthers, again came into conflict with the police, who revoked his parole. Desperately seeking to avoid another term in prison, he fled to France by way of Cuba, Algeria, and North Korea. While in exile, he suffered from a crippling, deep depression and terrifying suicidal moods. He was able to break through this period of psychic darkness only as the result of a vision in which Christ appeared, replacing all his former heroes and offering him a new spiritual life.

Like Thomas Merton or Sergei Bulgakov, Cleaver found his empathy for the oppressed and impoverished amplified and secured by his new Christian faith. He also found the strength to return to the United States and complete his term in prison. In this excerpt from his second autobiographical work, *Soul on Fire*, Cleaver describes the moment of his spiritual crisis and his subsequent elation and sense of interior liberation, even at the prospect of future imprisonment.   [AM]

FROM *SOUL ON FIRE*

I began to experience a severe depression. Perhaps I have been crazy all my life, but I never went around depressed or brooding or tormented or anything like that. In this situation in France, I began to be terribly depressed. I began to feel completely, totally useless, burdened. I began to put a lot of pressure on my wife with the idea of driving her away and forcing her to go back to the United States and take the children. I was the obstacle. Kathleen had never been arrested in her life. My children had never been arrested. They were free. I was the fugitive and it was my fault we were locked out; and I began to feel guilty to the extent that I could hardly face them. To be around them I felt miserable, guilty, seeing the emptiness that had become our life.

In addition to our house in Paris, we had an apartment on the Mediterranean coast near Cannes and Nice. Here I had all of my books and filing cabinets, typewriter, manuscripts; and I could go there to be alone to write. I would go there and just sit and stare out in space with a blank mind—just miserable—becoming more and more miserable as if there were no end to misery—just becoming worse and worse and worse. I would return to Paris, and that didn't help. I'd go back down to the coast, and that didn't help. I was running back and forth—getting worse and worse.

Finally, one night in Paris I became aware of the hopelessness of our situation. We were sitting down to dinner and we had two candles on the table. All the lights in the house were out, and I was suddenly struck that this was a perfect metaphor for our life: our life was empty—there was no light in our life. We were going through an empty ritual, eating in the same spirit in which you might drive to a gas station and fill up the tank. It was meaningless, pointless, getting nowhere.

I returned to the Mediterranean Coast and began thinking of putting an end to it all by committing suicide. I really began to think about that. I was sitting up on my balcony, one night, on the thirteenth floor—just sitting there. It was a beautiful Mediterranean night—sky, stars, moon hanging there in a sable void. I was brooding, downcast, at the end of my rope. I looked up at the moon and saw certain shadows . . . and the shadows became a man in the moon, and I saw a profile of myself (a profile that we had used on posters for the Black Panther Party—something I had seen a thousand times). I was already upset and this scared me. When I saw that image, I started trembling. It was a shaking that came from deep inside, and it had a threat about it that this mood was getting worse, that I could possibly disintegrate on the scene and fall apart. As I stared at this image, it changed, and I saw my former heroes paraded before my eyes. Here were Fidel Castro, Mao Tse-tung, Karl Marx, Frederick Engels, passing in review—each one appearing for a moment of time, and then dropping out of sight, like fallen heroes. Finally, at the end of the procession, in dazzling, shimmering light, the image of Jesus Christ appeared. That was the last straw.

I just crumbled and started crying. I fell to my knees, grabbing hold of the banister; and in the midst of this shaking and crying the Lord's Prayer and the 23rd Psalm came into my mind. I hadn't thought about these prayers for years. I started repeating them, and after a time I gained some control over the trembling and crying. Then I jumped up and ran to my bookshelf and got the Bible. It was the family Bible my mother had given to me because I am the oldest boy—the oldest son. And this Bible . . . when Kathleen left the United States, she brought with her a very small bag, and instead of grabbing the Communist Manifesto or *Das Kapital*, she packed that Bible. That is the Bible that I grabbed from the shelf that night and in which I turned to the 23rd Psalm. I discovered that my memory really had not served me that well. I got lost somewhere between the Valley of the Shadow of Death and the overflowing cup. But it was the Bible in which I searched and found that psalm. I read through it. At that time I didn't even know where to find the Lord's Prayer. I looked for it desperately. Pretty soon the type started swimming before my eyes, and I lay down on the bed and went to sleep.

That night I slept the most peaceful sleep I have ever known in my life. I woke up the next morning with a start, as though someone had touched me, and I could see in my mind the way, all the way back home, just as clear as I've ever seen anything. I saw a path of light that ran through a prison cell. . . . This prison cell was a dark spot on this path of light, and the meaning, which was absolutely clear to me, was that I didn't have to wait on any politician to help me get back home. I had it within my power to get back home by taking that first step, by surrendering; and it was a certainty that everything was going to be all right. I just knew that—that was the solution, and I would be all right if I would take that step.

Kathleen Norris charts her spiritual journey in the extreme landscapes and weather conditions of her home state, South Dakota. Educated at Bennington College, Norris established herself as a poet, winning grants and fellowships from the State of New York. Although entrenched in the intellectual and artistic world of New York City and the East Coast, Norris and her husband decided to relocate to her hometown of Lemmon, South Dakota, upon inheriting her family homestead.

In attempting to define the quality of life in the Dakotas, Norris found herself engaged in a more unsettling search, one that forced her to reengage with her family's past and her own deepest fears. In *Dakota: A Spiritual Geography,* she finds in the desolation of the prairie wilderness the same spiritual challenges faced by communities of desert contemplatives, hermitages, and modern-day cloisters. In the spiritual tradition of ascetic recluses, the vast solitude of the empty prairie becomes synonomous with the spare chill of a cloistered cell. Norris reconnects with the pragmatic spiritual life of her homesteading ancestors and begins to

KATHLEEN NORRIS

[1 9 4 7 –   ]

When we journey here, we discover it is no less old than new.

explore the religious practices of Native Americans and itinerant missionaries.

In the inner reaches of herself and in the traces of her family heritage,
Norris discovers both the limits of her own mental space and the spiritual
capacity to transcend them.   [AM]

FROM *DAKOTA: A SPIRITUAL GEOGRAPHY*

My spiritual geography is a study in contrasts. The three places with which I
have the deepest affinity are Hawaii, where I spent my adolescent years; New
York City, where I worked after college; and western South Dakota. Like many
Americans of their generation, my parents left their small-town roots in the
1930s and moved often. Except for the family home in Honolulu—its yard
rich with fruits and flowers (pomegranate, tangerine, lime, mango, plumeria,
hibiscus, lehua, ginger, and bird-of-paradise)—and my maternal grandparents'
house in a remote village in western Dakota—its modest and hard-won garden
offering columbine, daisies and mint—all my childhood places are gone.

When my husband and I moved nearly twenty years ago from New York
to that house in South Dakota, only one wise friend in Manhattan understood
the inner logic of the journey. Others, appalled, looked up Lemmon, South
Dakota (named for G. E. "Dad" Lemmon, a cattleman and wheeler-dealer
of the early 1900s, and home of the Petrified Wood Park—the world's largest
—a gloriously eccentric example of American folk art) in their atlases and
shook their heads. How could I leave the artists' and writers' community in
which I worked, the diverse and stimulating environment of a great city, for
such barrenness? Had I lost my mind? But I was young, still in my twenties,
an apprentice poet certain of the rightness of returning to the place where I
suspected I would find my stories. As it turns out, the Plains have been
essential not only for my growth as a writer, they have formed me spiritually.
I would even say they have made me a human being.

St. Hilary, a fourth-century bishop (and patron saint against snake bites)
once wrote, "Everything that seems empty is full of the angels of God." The
magnificent sky above the Plains sometimes seems to sing this truth; angels
seem possible in the wind-filled expanse. A few years ago a small boy named
Andy who had recently moved to the Plains from Pennsylvania told me he
knew an angel named Andy Le Beau. He spelled out the name for me and
I asked him if the angel had visited him here. "Don't you know?" he said
in the incredulous tone children adopt when adults seem stupefyingly igno-

rant. "Don't you know?" he said, his voice rising. "*This* is where angels drown."

Andy no more knew that he was on a prehistoric sea bed than he knew what *le beau* means in French, but some ancient wisdom in him had sensed great danger here; a terrifying but beautiful landscape in which we are at the mercy of the unexpected, and even angels proceed at their own risk. . . .

THE GRIM SURROUNDINGS USED TO OVERWHELM ME, AND IT WAS only when I began to apply what I had learned from the fourth-century desert monks I was reading that I found I could flourish there. I began to see those forlorn motel rooms as monks' cells, full of the gifts of silence and solitude. While this caused no end of amusement among the staff at the North Dakota Arts Council, it worked. Instead of escaping into television every night, I found that I could knit, work on my writing, and do serious reading; in short, be in the desert and let it bloom.

I had stumbled onto a basic truth of asceticism: that it is not necessarily a denigration of the body, though it has often been misapplied for that purpose. Rather, it is a way of surrendering to reduced circumstances in a manner that enhances the whole person. It is a radical way of knowing exactly who, what, and where you are, in defiance of those powerful forces in society—alcohol, drugs, television, shopping malls, motels—that aim to make us forget. A monk I know who directs retreats for other monasteries, and therefore must travel more than most Benedictines, has come to see air travel as a modern form of his ascetic practice. He finds the amenities offered, the instructions to relax and enjoy the flight laughable when he stops to realize where he is.

The insight of one fourth-century monk, Evagrius, that in the desert, most of one's troubles come from distracting "thoughts of one's former life" that don't allow us to live in the present, reflects what I regard as the basic principle of desert survival: not only to know where you are but to learn to love what you find there. I live in an American desert, without much company, without television, because I am trying to know where on earth I am. Dakota discipline, like monastic discipline, requires me to know. In a blizzard, or one of our sudden cold snaps that can take the temperature from thirty degrees above to thirty-five below in a matter of hours, not knowing can kill you.

Whether the desert is a monastery, a one-room schoolhouse forty miles from the nearest small town, where the children are telling you that "poetry's dumb," or a cinderblock motel room whose windows rattle in the fierce winter winds, a healthy ascetic discipline asks you to rejoice in these gifts of deprivation, to learn from them, and to care less for amenities than for that which refreshes from a deeper source. Desert wisdom allows you to be at home, wherever you are.

A brother came to Scetis to visit Abba Moses and asked him for a word. The old man said to him, "Go, sit in your cell, and your cell will teach you everything."

Weather Report: February 10

I walk downtown, wearing a good many of the clothes I own, keeping my head down and breathing through several thicknesses of a wool scarf. A day so cold it hurts to breathe; dry enough to freeze spit. Kids crack it on the sidewalk.

Walking with care, snow barely covering the patches of ice, I begin to recall a canticle or a pslam—I can't remember which—and my body keeps time:

> *Cold and chill, bless the Lord*
> *Dew and rain, bless the Lord*
> *Frost and chill, bless the Lord*
> *Ice and snow, bless the Lord*
> *Nights and days, bless the Lord*
> *Light and darkness, bless the Lord.*

Another line comes to mind: "at the breath of God's mouth the waters flow." Spring seems far off, impossible, but it is coming. Already there is dusk instead of darkness at five in the afternoon; already hope is stirring at the edges of the day. . . .

FEAR IS NOT A BAD PLACE TO START A SPIRITUAL JOURNEY. IF YOU know what makes you afraid, you can see more clearly that the way out is through the fear. For me, this has meant acknowledging that the strong emotions dredged up by the few Christian worship services—usually weddings or funerals—I attended during the twenty-year period when I would have described my religion as "nothing," were trying to tell me something. It has meant coming to terms with my fundamentalist Methodist ancestors, no longer ignoring them but respecting their power.

Conversion means starting with who we are, not who we wish we were. It means knowing where we come from. It means taking to heart the words of Native American writer Andy Smith, who writes in *Ms.,* "a true medicine woman would . . . advise a white woman to look into her own culture and find what is liberating in it." And this is what I hope I have done, beginning with my move back to Dakota. My path of conversion may have a few elements of Indianness, because of the spirits of the land where I live, and because I understand that my faith comes from my grandmothers. It was in moving back to the Plains that I found my old ones, my flesh and blood ancestors as well as the desert monks and mystics of the Christian church. Dakota is where it all comes together, and surely that is one definition of the sacred.

It came as an unwelcome surprise that my old ones led me back to church. It continues to surprise me that the church is for me both a new and an old frontier. And it astonishes me as much as it delights me that moving to the Dakota grasslands led me to a religious frontier where the new growth is fed by something very old, the 1,500-year tradition of Benedictine monasticism. It grounds me; I use it as compost to "work the earth of my heart," to borrow a phrase from a fourth-century monk. I can long for change, for a "new earth," as Gregory of Nyssa defines it, "a good heart, a heart like the earth, which drinks up the rain that falls on it and yields a rich harvest."

Conversion doesn't offer a form of knowledge that can be bought and sold, quantified, or neatly packaged. It is best learned slowly and in community, the way a Native American child learns his or her traditional religion, the way an adult learns to be a Benedictine, not by book learning or weekend workshops but by being present at the ceremonies. Truly present, with a quiet heart that allows you to become a good listener, an observer of those —plants, animals, cloud formations, people, and words—who know and define the territory.

One of the earliest Christian monks, the fourth-century Anthony of the Desert, told a visiting philosopher who had apparently commented on his lack of reading material, "My book, O philosopher, is the nature of created things, and any time I wish to read the words of God, the book is before me." I know plenty of Dakotans, white and Native American alike, who feel the same way. In his *Life of Anthony,* Athanasius describes the mountain in the desert where the saint finally settled as a hermit, saying that "Anthony, as though inspired by God, fell in love with the place." Ecologist Susan Bratton has pointed out that the Greek verb used for "fell in love" in this sentence is a form of *agapao,* which implies a love that is divinely ordained.

The hermit stories of desert and Celtic monasticism are full of monks in love with a place, and the Christian mystical and monastic tradition often acts as a countercultural stream in a religion which has over-emphasized the spiritual. Bernard of Clairvaux, a monk in the tradition of Anthony, wrote in

1130 to a man who wanted to found a monastery, "Believe us who have experience, you will find much more laboring amongst woods than ever you will amongst books. Woods and stones will teach you more than any master."

Bernard's words remind me that it is the land of western Dakota that has taught me that communal worship is something I need; that it is an experience, not a philosophy or even theology. Whatever the pitch of my religious doubts, it is available to me for the asking. It seems a wonder to me that in our dull little town we can gather together to sing some great hymns, reflect on our lives, hear some astonishing scriptures (and maybe a boring sermon; you take your chances), offer some prayers and receive a blessing.

At its Latin root, the word religion is linked to the words ligature and ligament, words having both negative and positive connotations, offering both bondage and freedom of movement. For me, religion is the ligament that connects me to my grandmothers, who, representing so clearly the negative and positive aspects of the Christian tradition, made it impossible for me either to reject or accept the religion wholesale. They made it unlikely that I would settle for either the easy answers of fundamentalism or the overintellectualized banalities of a conventionally liberal faith. Instead, the more deeply I've reclaimed what was good in their faith, the more they have set me free to find my own way.

Step by step, as I made my way back to church, I began to find that many of the things modern people assume are irrelevant—the liturgical year, the liturgy of the hours, the Incarnation as an everyday reality—are in fact essential to my identity and my survival. I'm not denying the past, or trying to bring it back, but am seeking in my inheritance what theologian Letty Russell terms "a usable past." Perhaps I am also redefining frontier not as a place you exploit and abandon but as a place where you build on the past for the future. When we journey here, we discover it is no less old than new. T. S. Eliot wrote, "The end of all our exploring / Will be to arrive where we started / And know the place for the first time." Against all the odds, I rediscovered the religion I was born to, and found in it a home.

PART TWO

PILGRIMS
& MISSIONARIES

ONE OF THE MORE FAMILIAR TYPES OF SPIRITUAL AUTOBIOGRAPHY is a life story described in terms of a pilgrimage. In both fiction and autobiography, picturing spiritual struggles as a journey through perilous geography is a common practice. Saint John of the Cross created an elaborate drawing of the paths leading up Mount Carmel to illustrate spiritual discipline; Dante traveled up and down the mountains of Hell and Purgatory, while John Bunyan's Christian must slog his way through sloughs, swamps, and mountain paths in *Pilgrim's Progress*. The origins of this idea are located in the Biblical account of the forty years the Israelites were forced to spend wandering in the desert. Many authors in this volume characterize their psychic experiences in terms of dangerous travels: Leo Tolstoy's rowing toward God, Saint John of the Cross's ascent of Mount Carmel, Petrarch's mountain climb, Kathleen Norris's exploration of the prairie vastness.

In this section of *Pilgrim Souls*, we include many authors who were, in fact, pilgrims—for example, the men and women who founded Plymouth Plantation as an asylum for religious freedom, and who often compared themselves and their experiences to those of the wandering Israelites. Because a written testimony of personal conversion was required of all members of the Puritan colony, some of the most profound reflections on the life of the soul were penned by Puritans like Anne Bradstreet, Jonathan Edwards, and John Bunyan. More modern treatments of spiritual pilgrimages, like that of Christina Rossetti, reflect the impulse to reject the world in favor of spiritual retreat.

What these different writers have in common is a lifelong commitment to spiritual training, sacrificing all concerns and pleasures that might interfere with their overwhelming desire to be close to God. As in John Donne's account of experiencing three births—physical birth, spiritual rebirth in Christ, and return to life after illness—pilgrims and missionaries, tested by hardships and deprivation, describe a continual sense of spiritual renewal.

The pilgrims and missionaries whose lives are told here respond to calls to abandon all comfort and fame in order to pursue their spiritual vocations. In some cases, like David Livingstone or Albert Schweitzer, the call is perceived as a summons to service. In other cases, like Saint Ignatius of Loyola or the anonymous Russian pilgrim, the soul embarks on a passage to greater illumination through the practice of spiritual exercises. In all cases, an indifference to the affairs of the world in favor of an intimate relationship with God is the essential fact of each author's existence: the arduous, even crippling experiences of poverty, pain, and martyrdom described by such authors as Rabbi Leon Modena or Arch-priest Avvakum vanish in the joy of the spiritual life that sustains them.
[AM]

Although the events of Moses' life are written in the third person, if the authorship of the Pentateuch (the five books of Moses) is ascribed to Moses, then he is the author of his own biography. According to Exodus, Moses, raised in the Egyptian palace by the pharaoh's daughter, became the leader and liberator of the Hebrew slaves, the giver of the Law for the new nation of Israel, and the guide of the Israelites during their forty-year exile in the wilderness. Scholars disagree about the time frame of the Exodus, but the most popular version sets the events at the time of Ramses II (reigned 1304–1237 B.C.). The selections presented here from Exodus and Deuteronomy focus on Moses' relationship with God and his experiences on Mount Sinai.

While the prophets and patriarchs of Israel were permitted only to hear the word of God, Moses spoke with God face to face; his own face was so irradiated by these encounters he was forced to wear a veil while walking among the tents of the Israelites. A mistranslation of this phenomenon prompted Michelangelo's famous depiction of a horned Moses in the

MOSES

[CA. 14TH–13TH

CENTURY B.C.]

I will publish the name of the Lord.

Church of San Pietro in Vincoli. Moses experienced a double passion—for his God, with whom he engaged in constant dialogue, and for his people. Because of the constant grumbling of the Israelites and their apostasy with the Golden Calf, Moses offered himself as their intercessor and willingly shared their punishment of the forty-year exile in the wilderness.

A man given to tempestuous rages, Moses was forced to flee Egypt because he had murdered an Egyptian; later he claimed God's power as his own when miraculously bringing water from a rock; he was prohibited from entering the promised land because of this last infringement. Initially unwilling to lead his people out of Egypt, claiming a stammering tongue, Moses grew sufficiently bold to demand to see the glory of God on Mount Sinai and thus became the only prophet to have seen the glory of God and live.

[AM]

FROM EXODUS

CHAPTER 2

1 And there went a man of the house of Levi, and took *to wife* a daughter of Levi.

2 And the woman conceived, and bare a son: and when she saw him that he *was* a goodly *child*, she hid him three months.

3 And when she could not longer hide him, she took for him an ark of bulrushes, and daubed it with slime and with pitch, and put the child therein; and she laid *it* in the flags by the river's brink.

4 And his sister stood afar off, to wit what would be done to him.

5 And the daughter of Pharaoh came down to wash *herself* at the river; and her maidens walked along by the river's side; and when she saw the ark among the flags, she sent her maid to fetch it.

6 And when she had opened *it* she saw the child: and, behold, the babe wept. And she had compassion on him, and said, This *is one* of the Hebrews' children.

7 Then said his sister to Pharaoh's daughter, Shall I go and call to thee a nurse of the Hebrew women, that she may nurse the child for thee?

8 And Pharaoh's daughter said to her, Go. And the maid went and called the child's mother.

9 And Pharaoh's daughter said unto her, Take this child away, and nurse it for me, and I will give *thee* thy wages. And the woman took the child, and nursed it.

10 And the child grew, and she brought him unto Pharaoh's daughter, and he became her son. And she called his name Moses: and she said, Because I drew him out of the water.

11 And it came to pass in those days, when Moses was grown, that he went out unto his brethren, and looked on their burdens: and he spied an Egyptian smiting an Hebrew, one of his brethren.

12 And he looked this way and that way, and when he saw that *there was* no man, he slew the Egyptian, and hid him in the sand.

13 And when he went out the second day, behold, two men of the Hebrews strove together: and he said to him that did the wrong, Wherefore smitest thou thy fellow?

14 And he said, Who made thee a prince and a judge over us? intendest thou to kill me, as thou killedst the Egyptian? And Moses feared, and said, Surely this thing is known.

15 Now when Pharaoh heard this thing, he sought to slay Moses. But Moses fled from the face of Pharaoh, and dwelt in the land of Midian: and he sat down by a well.

16 Now the priest of Midian had seven daughters: and they came and drew *water*, and filled the troughs to water their father's flock.

17 And the shepherds came and drove them away: but Moses stood up and helped them, and watered their flock.

18 And when they came to Reuel their father, he said, How *is it that* ye are come so soon to day?

19 And they said, An Egyptian delivered us out of the hand of the shepherds, and also drew *water* enough for us, and watered the flock.

20 And he said unto his daughters, And where *is* he? why *is* it *that* ye have left the man? call him, that he may eat bread.

21 And Moses was content to dwell with the man: and he gave Moses Zipporah his daughter.

22 And she bare *him* a son, and he called his name Gershom: for he said, I have been a stranger in a strange land.

23 And it came to pass in process of time, that the king of Egypt died: and the children of Israel sighed by reason of the bondage, and they cried, and their cry came up unto God by reason of the bondage.

24 And God heard their groaning, and God remembered his covenant with Abraham, with Isaac and with Jacob.

25 And God looked upon the children of Israel, and God had respect unto *them*.

CHAPTER 3

1 Now Moses kept the flock of Jethro his father in law, the priest of Midian: and he led the flock to the backside of the desert, and came to the mountain of God, *even* to Horeb.

2 And the angel of the LORD appeared unto him in a flame of fire out of the midst of a bush: and he looked, and, behold, the bush burned with fire, and the bush *was* not consumed.

3 And Moses said, I will now turn aside, and see this great sight, why the bush is not burnt.

4 And when the LORD saw that he turned aside to see. God called unto him out of the midst of the bush, and said. Moses, Moses. And he said. Here *am* I.

5 And he said, Draw not nigh hither: put off they shoes from off thy feet, for the place whereon thou standest *is* holy ground.

6 Moreover he said, I *am* the God of thy father, the God of Abraham, the God of Isaac, and the God of Jacob. And Moses hid his face: for he was afraid to look upon God.

7 And the LORD said, I have surely seen the affliction of my people which *are* in Egypt, and have heard their cry by reason of their taskmasters: for I know their sorrows;

8 And I am come down to deliver them out of the hand of the Egyptians, and to bring them up out of that land unto a good land and a large, unto a land flowing with milk and honey; unto the place of the Canaanites, and the Hittites, and the Amorites, and the Perizzites, and the Hivites, and the Jebusites.

9 Now therefore, behold, the cry of the children of Israel is come unto me: and I have also seen the oppression wherewith the Egyptians oppress them.

10 Come now therefore, and I will send thee unto Pharaoh, that thou mayest bring forth my people the children of Israel out of Egypt.

11 And Moses said unto God, Who *am* I, that I should go unto Pharaoh, and that I should bring forth the children of Israel out of Egypt?

12 And he said, Certainly I will be with thee; and this *shall be* a token unto thee, that I have sent thee: When thou hast brought forth the people out of Egypt, ye shall serve God upon this mountain.

13 And Moses said unto God. Behold, *when* I come unto the children of Israel, and shall say unto them, The God of your fathers hath sent me unto you: and they shall say to me, What *is* his name? what shall I say unto them?

14 And God said unto Moses, I AM THAT I AM: and he said, Thus shalt thou say unto the children of Israel, I AM hath sent me unto you.

15 And God said moreover unto Moses. Thus shalt thou say unto the children of Israel. The LORD God of your fathers, the God of Abraham, the God of Isaac, and the God of Jacob, hath sent me unto you: this is my name for ever, and this *is* my memorial unto all generations.

16 Go, and gather the elders of Israel together, and say unto them, The LORD God of your fathers, the God of Abraham, of Isaac, and of Jacob, appeared unto me, saying. I have surely visited you, and *seen* that which is done to you in Egypt:

17 And I have said. I will bring you up out of the affliction of Egypt unto the land of the Canaanites, and the Hittites, and the Amorites, and the Perizzites, and the Hivites, and the Jebusites, unto a land flowing with milk and honey.

18 And they shall hearken to thy voice: and thou shalt come, thou and the elders of Israel, unto the king of Egypt, and ye shall say unto him, The LORD God of the Hebrews hath met with us: and now let us go, we beseech thee, three days' journey into the wilderness, that we may sacrifice to the LORD our God.

19 And I am sure that the king of Egypt will not let you go, no, not by a mighty hand.

20 And I will stretch out my hand and smite Egypt with all my wonders which I will do in the midst thereof: and after that he will let you go.

21 And I will give this people favour in the sight of the Egyptians: and it shall come to pass, that, when ye go, ye shall not go empty:

22 But every woman shall borrow of her neighbour, and of her that sojourneth in her house, jewels of silver, and jewels of gold, and raiment: and ye shall put *them* upon your sons, and upon your daughters; and ye shall spoil the Egyptians.

CHAPTER 4

1 And Moses answered and said, But, behold, they will not believe me, nor hearken unto my voice: for they will say, The LORD hath not appeared unto thee.

2 And the LORD said unto him, What *is* that in thine hand? And he said. A rod.

3 And he said. Cast it on the ground. And he cast it on the ground, and it became a serpent; and Moses fled from before it.

4 And the LORD said unto Moses, Put forth thine hand, and take it by the tail. And he put forth his hand, and caught it, and it became a rod in his hand:

5 That they may believe that the LORD God of their fathers, the God of Abraham, the God of Isaac, and the God of Jacob, hath appeared unto thee.

6 And the LORD said furthermore unto him, Put now thine hand into thy bosom. And he put his hand into his bosom: and when he took it out, behold, his hand *was* leprous as snow.

7 And he said, Put thine hand into they bosom again. And he put his hand into his bosom again; and plucked it out of his bosom, and, behold, it was turned again as his *other* flesh.

8 And it shall come to pass, if they will not believe thee, neither hearken to the voice of the first sign, that they will believe the voice of the latter sign.

9 And it shall come to pass, if they will not believe also these two signs, neither hearken unto thy voice, that thou shalt take of the water of the river, and pour *it* upon the dry *land*: and the water which thou takest out of the river shall become blood upon the dry *land*.

10 And Moses said unto the LORD, O my Lord, I *am* not eloquent, neither heretofore, nor since thou hast spoken unto thy servant: but I *am* slow of speech, and of a slow tongue.

11 And the LORD said unto him, Who hath made man's mouth? or who maketh the dumb, or deaf, or the seeing, or the blind? have not I the LORD?

12 Now therefore go, and I will be with thy mouth, and teach thee what thou shalt say.

13 And he said, O my Lord, send, I pray thee, by the hand *of him whom* thou wilt send.

14 And the anger of the LORD was kindled against Moses, and he said, *Is* not Aaron the Levite thy brother? I know that he can speak well. And also, behold, he cometh forth to meet thee: and when he seeth thee, he will be glad in his heart.

15 And thou shalt speak unto him, and put words in his mouth: and I will be with thy mouth, and with his mouth, and will teach you what ye shall do.

16 And he shall be thy spokesman unto the people: and he shall be, *even* he shall be to thee instead of a mouth, and thou shalt be to him instead of God.

17 And thou shalt take this rod in thine hand, wherewith thou shalt do signs.

[Exodus 4:18–19:2 recounts the exodus of the Israelites from Egypt under Moses' leadership.]

CHAPTER 19

3 And Moses went up unto God, and the LORD called unto him out of the mountain, saying, Thus shalt thou say to the house of Jacob, and tell the children of Israel;

4 Ye have seen what I did unto the Egyptians, and *how* I bare you on eagles' wings, and brought you unto myself.

5 Now therefore, if ye will obey my voice indeed, and keep my covenant, then ye shall be a peculiar treasure unto me above all people: for all the earth *is* mine:

6 And ye shall be unto me a kingdom of priests, and an holy nation. These *are* the words which thou shalt speak unto the children of Israel.

7 And Moses came and called for the elders of the people, and laid before their faces all these words which the LORD commanded him.

8 And all the people answered together, and said, All that the LORD hath spoken we will do. And Moses returned the words of the people unto the LORD.

9 And the LORD said unto Moses, Lo, I come unto thee in a thick cloud, that the people may hear when I speak with thee, and believe thee for ever. And Moses told the words of the people unto the LORD.

10 And the LORD said unto Moses, Go unto the people, and sanctify them to day and to morrow, and let them wash their clothes,

11 And be ready against the third day: for the third day the LORD will come down in the sight of all the people upon mount Sinai.

12 And thou shalt set bounds unto the people round about, saying, Take heed

to yourselves, *that ye* go *not* up into the mount, or touch the border of it: whosoever toucheth the mount shall be surely put to death:

13 There shall not an hand touch it, but he shall surely be stoned, or shot through; whether it *be* beast or man, it shall not live: when the trumpet soundeth long, they shall come up to the mount.

14 And Moses went down from the mount unto the people, and sanctified the people; and they washed their clothes.

15 And he said unto the people, Be ready against the third day: come not at *your* wives.

16 And it came to pass on the third day in the morning, that there were thunders and lightnings, and a thick cloud upon the mount, and the voice of the trumpet exceeding loud; so that all the people that *was* in the camp trembled.

17 And Moses brought forth the people out of the camp to meet with God; and they stood at the nether part of the mount.

18 And mount Sinai was altogether on a smoke, because the LORD descended upon it in fire: and the smoke thereof ascended as the smoke of a furnace, and the whole mount quaked greatly.

19 And when the voice of the trumpet sounded long, and waxed louder and louder, Moses spake, and God answered him by a voice.

20 And the LORD came down upon mount Sinai, on the top of the mount: and the LORD called Moses *up* to the top of the mount; and Moses went up.

21 And the LORD said unto Moses, Go down, charge the people, lest they break through unto the LORD to gaze, and many of them perish.

22 And let the priests also, which come near to the LORD, sanctify themselves, lest the LORD break forth upon them.

23 And Moses said unto the LORD. The people cannot come up to mount Sinai: for thou chargedst us, saying, Set bounds about the mount, and sanctify it.

24 And the LORD said unto him, Away, get thee down, and thou shalt come up, thou, and Aaron with thee: but let not the priests and the people break through to come up unto the LORD, lest he break forth upon them.

25 So Moses went down unto the people, and spake unto them.

[Exodus 20:1–24:8 has been omitted.]

CHAPTER 24

9 Then went up Moses, and Aaron, Nadab, and Abihu, and seventy of the elders of Israel:

10 And they saw the God of Israel: and *there was* under his feet as it were a paved work of a sapphire stone, and as it were the body of heaven in *his* clearness.

11 And upon the nobles of the children of Israel he laid not his hand: also they saw God, and did eat and drink.

12 And the LORD said unto Moses, Come up to me into the mount, and be there: and I will give thee tables of stone, and a law, and commandments which I have written; that thou mayest teach them.

13 And Moses rose up, and his minister Joshua: and Moses went up into the mount of God.

14 And he said unto the elders, Tarry ye here for us, until we come again unto you: and behold, Aaron and Hur *are* with you: if any man have any matters to do, let him come unto them.

15 And Moses went up into the mount, and a cloud covered the mount.

16 And the glory of the LORD abode upon mount Sinai, and the cloud covered it six days: and the seventh day he called unto Moses out of the midst of the cloud.

17 And the sight of the glory of the LORD *was* like devouring fire on the top of the mount in the eyes of the children of Israel.

18 And Moses went into the midst of the cloud, and gat him up into the mount: and Moses was in the mount forty days and forty nights.

[Exodus 25:1–33:11 has been omitted.]

CHAPTER 33

12 And Moses said unto the LORD See, thou sayest unto me, Bring up this people: and thou hast not let me know whom thou wilt send with me. Yet thou hast said, I know thee by name, and thou hast also found grace in my sight:

13 Now therefore, I pray thee, if I have found grace in thy sight, shew me now thy way, that I may know thee, that I may find grace in thy sight: and consider that this nation is thy people.

14 And he said, My presence shall go *with thee*, and I will give thee rest.

15 And he said unto him, If thy presence go not *with me*, carry us not up hence.

16 For wherein shall it be known here that I and thy people have found grace in thy sight? *is it* not in that thou goest with us? so shall we be separated, I and thy people, from all the people that *are* upon the face of the earth.

17 And the LORD said unto Moses, I will do this thing also that thou hast spoken: for thou hast found grace in my sight, and I know thee by name.

18 And he said, I beseech thee, shew me thy glory.

19 And he said, I will make all my goodness pass before thee, and I will proclaim the name of the LORD before thee; and will be gracious to whom I will be gracious, and will shew mercy on whom I will shew mercy.

20 And he said, Thou canst not see my face: for there shall no man see me, and live.

21 And the LORD said, Behold, *there is* a place by me, and thou shalt stand upon a rock:

22 And it shall come to pass, while my glory passeth by, that I will put thee in a clift of the rock, and will cover thee with my hand while I pass by:

23 And I will take away mine hand, and thou shalt see my back parts: but my face shall not be seen.

CHAPTER 34

1 And the LORD said unto Moses, Hew thee two tables of stone like unto the first: and I will write upon *these* tables the words that were in the first tables, which thou brakest.

2 And be ready in the morning, and come up in the morning unto mount Sinai, and present thyself there to me in the top of the mount.

3 And no man shall come up with thee, neither let any man be seen throughout all the mount: neither let the flocks nor herds feed before that mount.

4 And he hewed two tables of stone like unto the first; and Moses rose up early in the morning, and went up unto mount Sinai, as the LORD had commanded him, and took in his hand the two tables of stone.

5 And the LORD descended in the cloud, and stood with him there, and proclaimed the name of the LORD.

6 And the LORD passed by before him, and proclaimed. The LORD, The LORD God, merciful and gracious, longsuffering, and abundant in goodness and truth.

7 Keeping mercy for thousands, forgiving iniquity and transgression and sin, and that will by no means clear *the guilty;* visiting the iniquity of the fathers upon the children, and upon the children's children, unto the third and to the fourth *generation.*

8 And Moses made haste, and bowed his head toward the earth, and worshipped.

FROM DEUTERONOMY

CHAPTER 31

30 And Moses spake in the ears of all the congregation of Israel the words of this song, until they were ended.

CHAPTER 32

1 Give ear, O ye heavens, and I will speak; and hear, O earth, the words of my mouth.

2 My doctrine shall drop as the rain, my speech shall distil as the dew, as the small rain upon the tender herb, and as the showers upon the grass:

3 Because I will publish the name of the LORD: ascribe ye greatness unto our God.

4 He *is* the Rock, his work *is* perfect: for all his ways *are* judgment: a God of truth and without iniquity, just and right *is* he.

Saul of Tarsus, a pupil of the renowned Rabbi Gamaliel, was engaged in active persecution of the early Christians when, in about 33 A.D., he experienced a dramatic conversion on the road to Damascus. Blinded by a vision of Jesus of Nazareth, he experienced a miraculous healing at the hands of a Christian in Damascus. Upon regaining his sight, he designated himself the thirteenth apostle of Christ and took the name Paul. He spent the remainder of his life in extensive missionary journeys throughout the Middle East and Asia Minor, until he was arrested and reputedly executed by Nero. Most of his writings were circular letters meant to be passed among the various churches. He wrote from captivity, rating his own trials as great honors in the Christian life and exhorting the young churches to lives of holiness.

Accounts of Paul's travels and testimonies are also given in the Book of Acts, usually attributed to Luke. The conversion narrative of Saint Paul actually exists in several forms in the New Testament. Paul felt compelled to deliver his testimony frequently to defend

SAINT PAUL
(SAUL OF TARSUS)

[1 0 – 6 7 A . D .]

I count all things but loss.

his claim for the title of Apostle, one who has seen and walked with the Lord.

These early stories are the foundations for the genre of spiritual autobiography. The basic outline of events, from blindness to enlightenment, is mediated by an encounter with a blinding spiritual truth and the mandate for spiritual redirection. Paul, looking back on his life as Saul, counts his gains as losses and embraces his losses as gains. Laying his accomplishments at the feet of Christ, he compares spiritual ignorance to the deceptions of a dark looking glass and the vicissitudes of childish impulses. The accomplishment of spiritual rebirth illuminates the past and renders the preoccupations of everyday life transparent in the light of spiritual joys.

This narrative pattern, adapted by Saint Augustine, becomes part of the standard form for literary accounts of the spiritual life. The transforming experience of divine revelation and a call to pilgrimage and missionary service, as expressed for the first time by Saint Paul, is echoed in the writings of the pilgrims and missionaries included in this section.   [AM]

FROM HIS LETTERS

Acts 22:1–21
[skips 22:2]

1 Men, brethren, and fathers, hear ye my defence *which I make* now unto you. . . .

3 I am verily a man *which am* a Jew, born in Tarsus, *a city* in Cilicia, yet brought up in this city at the feet of Gamaliel, *and* taught according to the perfect manner of the law of the fathers, and was zealous toward God, as ye all are this day.

4 And I persecuted this way unto the death, binding and delivering into prisons both men and women.

5 As also the high priest doth bear me witness, and all the estate of the elders: from whom also I received letters unto the brethren, and went to Damascus, to bring them which were there bound unto Jerusalem, for to be punished.

6 And it came to pass, that, as I made my journey, and was come nigh unto Damascus about noon, suddenly there shone from heaven a great light round about me.

7 And I fell unto the ground, and heard a voice saying unto me, Saul, Saul, why persecutest thou me?

8 And I answered, Who art thou, Lord? And he said unto me, I am Jesus of Nazareth, whom thou persecutest.

9 And they that were with me saw indeed the light, and were afraid; but they heard not the voice of him that spake to me.

10 And I said, What shall I do, Lord? And the Lord said unto me, Arise, and go into Damascus; and there it shall be told thee of all things which are appointed for thee to do.

11 And when I could not see for the glory of that light, being led by the hand of them that were with me, I came into Damascus.

12 And one Ananias, a devout man according to the law, having a good report of all the Jews which dwelt *there*,

13 Came unto me, and stood, and said unto me, Brother Saul, receive thy sight. And the same hour I looked up upon him.

14 And he said, The God of our fathers hath chosen thee, that thou shouldest know his will, and see that Just One, and shouldest hear the voice of his mouth.

15 For thou shalt be his witness unto all men of what thou hast seen and heard.

16 And now why tarriest thou? arise, and be baptized, and wash away thy sins, calling on the name of the Lord.

17 And it came to pass, that, when I was come again to Jerusalem, even while I prayed in the temple, I was in a trance;

18 And saw him saying unto me, Make haste, and get thee quickly out of Jerusalem: for they will not receive thy testimony concerning me.

19 And I said, Lord, they know that I imprisoned and beat in every synagogue them that believed on thee:

20 And when the blood of thy martyr Stephen was shed, I also was standing by, and consenting unto his death, and kept the raiment of them that slew him.

21 And he said unto me, Depart: for I will send thee far hence unto the Gentiles.

I Corinthians 13:1–13

1 Though I speak with the tongues of men and of angels, and have not charity, I am become *as* sounding brass, or a tinkling cymbal.

2 And though I have *the gift of* prophecy, and understand all mysteries, and

all knowledge; and though I have all faith, so that I could remove mountains, and have not charity, I am nothing.

3 And though I bestow all my goods to feed *the poor*, and though I give my body to be burned, and have not charity, it profiteth me nothing.

4 Charity suffereth long, *and* is kind; charity envieth not; charity vaunteth not itself, is not puffed up,

5 Doth not behave itself unseemly, seeketh not her own, is not easily provoked, thinketh no evil;

6 Rejoiceth not in iniquity, but rejoiceth in the truth;

7 Beareth all things, believeth all things, hopeth all things, endureth all things.

8 Charity never faileth: but whether *there be* prophecies, they shall fail; whether *there be* tongues, they shall cease; whether *there be* knowledge, it shall vanish away.

9 For we know in part, and we prophesy in part.

10 But when that which is perfect is come, then that which is in part shall be done away.

11 When I was a child, I spake as a child, I understood as a child, I thought as a child: but when I became a man, I put away childish things.

12 For now we see through a glass, darkly; but then face to face: now I know in part; but then shall I know even as also I am known.

13 And now abideth faith, hope, charity, these three; but the greatest of these *is* charity.

II Corinthians 12:1–10

1 It is not expedient for me doubtless to glory. I will come to visions and revelations of the Lord.

2 I knew a man in Christ above fourteen years ago, (whether in the body, I cannot tell; or whether out of the body, I cannot tell: God knoweth;) such an one caught up to the third heaven.

3 And I knew such a man, (whether in the body, or out of the body, I cannot tell: God knoweth;)

4 How that he was caught up into paradise, and heard unspeakable words, which it is not lawful for a man to utter.

5 Of such an one will I glory: yet of myself I will not glory, but in mine infirmities.

6 For though I would desire to glory, I shall not be a fool; for I will say the truth: but *now* I forbear, lest any man should think of me above that which he seeth me *to be*, or *that* he heareth of me.

7 And lest I should be exalted above measure through the abundance of the revelations, there was given to me a thorn in the flesh, the messenger of Satan to buffet me, lest I should be exalted above measure.

8 For this thing I besought the Lord thrice, that it might depart from me.

9 And he said unto me, My grace is sufficient for thee: for my strength is made perfect in weakness. Most gladly therefore will I rather glory in my infirmities, that the power of Christ may rest upon me.

10 Therefore I take pleasure in infirmities, in reproaches, in necessities, in persecutions, in distresses for Christ's sake: for when I am weak, then am I strong.

Philippians 1:19–26

19 For I know that this shall turn to my salvation through your prayer, and the supply of the Spirit of Jesus Christ,

20 According to my earnest expectation and *my* hope, that in nothing I shall be ashamed, but *that* with all boldness, as always, *so* now also Christ shall be magnified in my body, whether *it be* by life, or by death.

21 For to me to live *is* Christ, and to die *is* gain.

22 But if I live in the flesh, this *is* the fruit of my labour: yet what I shall choose I wot not.

23 For I am in a strait betwixt two, having a desire to depart, and to be with Christ; which is far better:

24 Nevertheless to abide in the flesh *is* more needful for you.

25 And having this confidence, I know that I shall abide and continue with you all for your furtherance and joy of faith;

26 That your rejoicing may be more abundant in Jesus Christ for me by my coming to you again.

II Timothy 2:9–10

9 Wherein I suffer trouble, as an evildoer, *even* unto bonds; but the word of God is not bound.

10 Therefore I endure all things for the elect's sakes; that they may also obtain the salvation which is in Christ Jesus with eternal glory.

MARTIN LUTHER

[1 4 8 3 – 1 5 4 6]

I was altogether born again and entered paradise itself.

A devout German monk in the strict Augustinian order, Martin Luther singlehandedly initiated the chain of events leading to the Reformation by nailing to the door of Wittenberg Cathedral his Ninety-five Theses protesting abuses in the Church. In his extensive commentaries on the Old and New Testaments, Luther elaborated a position on the doctrines of grace and salvation that became the cornerstone of Protestant theology.

Initally hoping to achieve reform within the church, Luther found himself facing trial and excommunication for heresy, but did not back down, as his famous "Here I stand" defense asserts. In his interpretation of salvific grace, Luther was influenced by Saint Augustine's definitions, but ascribed his insights primarily to his reading of Scripture.

Emphasizing the writings of Paul and especially his Epistle to the Galatians, Luther issued the famous rallying cry of the Reformation, *"sola gratia, sola fide, sola scriptura."* According to these three principles, humanity is saved by the grace of God alone rather than by religious observances or moral living ("sola gratia"); faith alone is sufficient for salvation ("sola fide"); and Holy Scripture is the sole reliable guide in spiritual matters ("sola scriptura").

In a sermon of 1545 and in prefaces to Latin works written in the same year, Luther describes the unfolding of his thoughts, beginning with an account of his pilgrimage to Rome when he became deeply disillusioned over corrupt church practices. As a monk, he had been noted for scrupulosity, spending up to five hours a day in confession and still experiencing an anxious dread that his salvation was not secure. His meticulous enactment of prescribed ritual during his Roman pilgrimage began to strike him as no longer efficacious. Captivated by Paul's description of his helplessness to root out evil in his own soul, and by Saint Augustine's theological treatment of the same problem, Luther began to insist on the necessity for reliance on the power of Christ to attain victory in the spiritual warfare of the psyche, rather than on one's own efforts for personal sanctification. The concluding selection presented here is drawn from a discussion of this point in his commentaries. [AM]

FROM HIS WRITINGS

I was a devout monk and wanted to force God to justify me because of my works and the severity of my life. I was a good monk, and kept the rule of my order so strictly that I may say that if ever a monk got to heaven by his monkery, I would have gotten there as well. All my brothers in the monastery who knew me will bear me out. If I had kept on any longer, I would have killed myself with vigils, prayers, readings, and other works.

I WAS VERY PIOUS IN THE MONASTERY, YET I WAS SAD BECAUSE I thought God was not gracious to me....

When I made my pilgrimage to Rome, I was such a fanatical saint that I dashed through all the churches and crypts, believing all the stinking forgeries of those places. I ran through about a dozen Masses in Rome and was almost prostrated by the thought that my mother and father were still alive, because I should gladly have redeemed them from purgatory with my Masses and other excellent works and prayers. . . . But it was too crowded, and I could not get in; so I ate a smoked herring instead. . . .

I was not in Rome very long, but I celebrated many Masses there and also saw many Masses; it horrifies me to think of it. I overheard the officials at mealtime laughing and boasting about how some Masses were done, saying over bread and wine, "Bread you are, and bread you will remain," and then holding up the bread and wine [at the elevation]. Now I was a young and truly pious monk, and I was shocked by such words. Indeed I was disgusted that they could celebrate the Mass so flippantly, as if they were performing some kind of trick. Before I had even gotten to the Gospel [to its reading in the Mass], the priest beside me had already concluded a Mass and shouted at me: 'Passa, Passa—enough now, finish it off.' We were simply laughed at because we were such pious monks. A Christian was taken to be nothing but a fool. . . .

I know priests who said six or seven Masses while I said only one. They took money for them and I didn't. . . .

Whoever came to Rome with money received the forgiveness of sins. Like a fool, I carried onions to Rome and brought back garlic. . . .

I wouldn't take one thousand florins for not having seen Rome because I wouldn't have been able to believe such things if I had been told by somebody without having seen them for myself.

IN ORDER TO RELEASE MY GRANDFATHER FROM PURGATORY, I climbed the stairs of Pilate [*Santa Scala*], praying a *Paternoster* on each step, for it was the prevailing belief that whoever prayed in this way could free a soul [from purgatory]. But when I arrived at the top, I thought, "Who knows whether it is true? Such a prayer is worth nothing."

MEANWHILE, I HAD ALREADY DURING THAT YEAR RETURNED TO IN- terpret the Psalter anew. I had confidence in the fact that I was more skillful, after I had lectured in the university on St. Paul's epistles to the Romans, to the Galatians, and the one to the Hebrews. I had indeed been captivated with an extraordinary ardor for understanding Paul in the Epistle to the Romans. But up till then it was not the cold blood about the heart, but a single word in Chapter 1 [:17], "In it the righteousness of God is revealed," that had stood in my way. For I hated that word "righteousness of God," which, according to the use and custom of all the teachers, I had been taught to understand philosophically regarding the formal or active rightousness, as they called it, with which God is righteous and punishes the unrighteous sinner.

Though I lived as a monk without reproach, I felt that I was a sinner before God with an extremely disturbed conscience. I could not believe that he was placated by my satisfaction. I did not love, yes, I hated the righteous God who punishes sinners, and secretly, if not blasphemously, certainly murmuring greatly, I was angry with God, and said, "As if, indeed, it is not enough, that miserable sinners, eternally lost through original sin, are crushed by every kind of calamity by the law of the decalogue, without having God add pain to pain by the gospel and also the gospel threatening us with his righteousness and wrath!" Thus I raged with a fierce and troubled conscience. Nevertheless, I beat importunately upon Paul at that place, most ardently desiring to know what St. Paul wanted.

At last, by the mercy of God, meditating day and night, I gave heed to the content of the words, namely, "In it the righteousness of God is revealed, as it is written, 'He who through faith is righteous shall live.'" There I began to understand that the righteousness of God is that which the righteous lives by a gift of God, namely by faith. And this is the meaning: the righteousness of God is revealed by the gospel, namely, the passive righteousness with which merciful God justifies us by faith, as it is written, "He who through faith is righteous shall live." Here I felt that I was altogether born again and had entered paradise itself through open gates. There a totally other face of the entire Scripture showed itself to me. Thereupon I ran through the Scriptures from memory. I also found in other terms an analogy, as, the work of God, that is, what God does in us, the power of God, with which he makes us strong, the wisdom of God, with which he makes us wise, the strength of God, the salvation of God, the glory of God.

And I extolled my sweetest word with a love as great as the hatred with which I had before hated the word "righteousness of God." Thus that place in Paul was for me truly the gate to paradise. Later I read Augustine's *The Spirit and the Letter*, where contrary to hope I found that he, too, interpreted God's righteousness in a similar way, as the righteousness with which God clothes us when he justifies us. Although this was heretofore said imperfectly and he did not explain all things concerning imputation clearly, it nevertheless was pleasing that God's righteousness with which we are justified was taught.

SAINT
IGNATIUS
OF LOYOLA

[1491-1556]

Thoughts of the past were soon

forgotten in the presence of these

holy desires.

Ignatius of Loyola was born the youngest son of a noble and wealthy Spanish family. His autobiography, a third-person narrative called in some versions "The Pilgrim's Story" because Ignatius often refers to himself as "the Pilgrim," was dictated in Spanish about 1555. This was more than a decade after he founded the Jesuits, or Society of Jesus, which became one of the most influential agents of the Catholic Counter-Reformation of the sixteenth century.

The first chapter tells of the year of his spiritual conversion, in 1521. In that year, while participating in the defense of the kingdom of Navarre against troops of the French king, he was wounded. His long convalescence from his nearly fatal injury was filled with meditation and reflection on two different states of soul: one was full of fantasies of the rigors of chivalric life and the service of high-born ladies, while the other offered the prospect of a life of spiritual stringency in imitation of Christian saints. Although spiritual warfare is not an uncommon image in the descriptions of the inner life written by other pilgrims in this section —see, for example, the accounts of John

Bunyan or Archpriest Avvakum—Saint Ignatius is unique in portraying the refinement of the soul as an exercise even more rigorous than the training of an athlete or soldier. [EP]

FROM *SAINT IGNATIUS'S OWN STORY*

1 Up to his twenty-sixth year he was a man given over to the vanities of the world, and took a special delight in the exercise of arms, with a great and vain desire of winning glory. He was in a fortress which the French were attacking, and although the others were of the opinion that they should surrender on terms of having their lives spared, as they clearly saw there was no possibility of a defense, he gave so many reasons to the governor that he persuaded him to carry on the defense against the judgment of the officers, who found some strength in his spirit and courage. On the day on which they expected the attack to take place, he made his confession to one of his companions in arms. After the assault had been going on for some time, a cannon ball struck him in the leg, crushing its bones, and because it passed between his legs it also seriously wounded the other.

2 With his fall, the others in the fortress surrendered to the French, who took possession, and treated the wounded man with great kindliness and courtesy. After twelve or fifteen days in Pamplona they bore him in a litter to his own country. Here he found himself in a very serious condition. The doctors and surgeons whom he had called from all parts were of the opinion that the leg should be operated on again and the bones reset, either because they had been poorly set in the first place, or because the jogging of the journey had displaced them so that they would not heal. Again he went through this butchery, in which as in all the others that he had suffered he uttered no word, nor gave any sign of pain other than clenching his fists.

3 His condition grew worse. Besides being unable to eat he showed other symptoms which are usually a sign of approaching death. The feast of St. John drew near, and as the doctors had very little hope of his recovery, they advised him to make his confession. He received the last sacraments on the eve of the feast of Sts. Peter and Paul, and the doctors told him that if he showed no improvement by midnight, he could consider himself as good as dead. The patient had some devotion to St. Peter, and so our Lord wished that his improvement should begin that very midnight. So rapid was his recovery that within a few days he was thought to be out of danger of death.

4 When the bones knit, one below the knee remained astride another, which caused a shortening of the leg. The bones so raised caused a protuber-

ance that was not pleasant to the sight. The sick man was not able to put up with this, because he had made up his mind to seek his fortune in the world. He thought the protuberance was going to be unsightly and asked the surgeons whether it could be cut away. They told him that it could be cut away, but that the pain would be greater than all he had already suffered, because it was now healed and it would take some time to cut it off. He determined, nevertheless, to undergo this martyrdom to gratify his own inclinations. His elder brother was quite alarmed and declared that he would not have the courage to undergo such pain. But the wounded man put up with it with his usual patience.

5 After the superfluous flesh and the bone were cut away, means were employed for preventing the one leg from remaining shorter than the other. Many ointments were applied and devices employed for keeping the leg continually stretched which caused him many days of martyrdom. But it was our Lord Who restored his health. In everything else he was quite well, but he was not able to stand upon that leg, and so had to remain in bed. He had been much given to reading worldly books of fiction and knight errantry, and feeling well enough to read he asked for some of these books to help while away the time. In that house, however, they could find none of those he was accustomed to read, and so they gave him a Life of Christ and a book of the Lives of the Saints in Spanish.

6 By the frequent reading of these books he conceived some affection for what he found there narrated. Pausing in his reading, he gave himself up to thinking over what he had read. At other times he dwelt on the things of the world which formerly had occupied his thoughts. Of the many vain things that presented themselves to him, one took such possession of his heart that without realizing it he could spend two, three, or even four hours on end thinking of it, fancying what he would have to do in the service of a certain lady, of the means he would take to reach the country where she was living, of the verses, the promises he would make her, the deeds of gallantry he would do in her service. He was so enamored with all this that he did not see how impossible it would all be, because the lady was of no ordinary rank; neither countess, nor duchess, but of a nobility much higher than any of these.

7 Nevertheless, our Lord came to his assistance, for He saw to it that these thoughts were succeeded by others which sprang from the things he was reading. In reading the Life of our Lord and the Lives of the Saints, he paused to think and reason with himself. "Suppose that I should do what St. Francis did, what St. Dominic did?" He thus let his thoughts run over many things that seemed good to him, always putting before himself things that were difficult and important which seemed to him easy to accomplish when he proposed them. But all his thought was to tell himself, "St. Dominic did

this, therefore, I must do it. St. Francis did this; therefore, I must do it." These thoughts also lasted a good while. And then other things taking their place, the worldly thoughts above mentioned came upon him and remained a long time with him. This succession of diverse thoughts was of long duration, and they were either of worldly achievements which he desired to accomplish, or those of God which took hold of his imagination to such an extent, that worn out with the struggle, he turned them all aside and gave his attention to other things.

8 There was, however, this difference. When he was thinking of the things of the world he was filled with delight, but when afterwards he dismissed them from weariness, he was dry and dissatisfied. And when he thought of going barefoot to Jerusalem and of eating nothing but herbs and performing the other rigors he saw that the saints had performed, he was consoled, not only when he entertained these thoughts, but even after dismissing them he remained cheerful and satisfied. But he paid no attention to this, nor did he stop to weigh the difference until one day his eyes were opened a little and he began to wonder at the difference and to reflect on it, learning from experience that one kind of thoughts left him sad and the other cheerful. Thus, step by step, he came to recognize the difference between the two spirits that moved him, the one being from the evil spirit, the other from God.

9 He acquired no little light from his reading and began to think more seriously of his past life and the great need he had of doing penance for it. It was during this reading that these desires of imitating the saints came to him, but with no further thought of circumstances than of promising to do with God's grace what they had done. What he desired most of all to do, as soon as he was restored to health, was to go to Jerusalem, as above stated, undertaking all the disciplines and abstinences which a generous soul on fire with the love of God is wont to desire.

10 The thoughts of the past were soon forgotten in the presence of these holy desires, which were confirmed by the following vision. One night, as he lay awake, he saw clearly the likeness of our Lady with the holy Child Jesus, at the sight of which he received most abundant consolation for a considerable interval of time. He felt so great a disgust with his past life, especially with its offenses of the flesh, that he thought all such images which had formerly occupied his mind were wiped out. And from that hour until August of 1553, when this is being written, he never again consented to the least suggestion of the flesh. This effect would seem to indicate that the vision was from God, although he never ventured to affirm it positively, or claim that it was anything more than he had said it was. But his brother and other members of the family easily recognized the change that had taken place in the interior of his soul from what they saw in his outward manner.

11 Without a care in the world he went on with his reading and his good resolutions. All the time he spent with the members of the household he devoted to the things of God, and in this way brought profit to their souls. He took great delight in the books he was reading, and the thought came to him to select some short but important passages from the Life of Christ and the Lives of the Saints. And so he began to write very carefully in a book, as he had already begun to move a little about the house. The words of Christ he wrote in red ink and those of our Lady in blue, on polished and lined paper in a good hand, for he was an excellent penman. Part of his time he spent in writing, part in prayer. It was his greatest consolation to gaze upon the heavens and the stars, which he often did, and for long stretches at a time, because when doing so he felt within himself a powerful urge to be serving our Lord. He gave much time to thinking about his resolve, desiring to be entirely well so that he could begin his journey.

12 As he was going over in his mind what he should do on his return from Jerusalem, so as to live in perpetual penance, the thought occurred to him of joining the Carthusians of Seville. He could there conceal his identity so as to be held in less esteem, and live there on a strictly vegetable diet. But as the thought returned of a life of penance which he wanted to lead by going about the world, the desire of the Carthusian life grew cool, since he felt that there he would not be able to indulge the hatred he had conceived against himself. And yet, he instructed a servant of the house who was going to Burgos to bring back information about the Carthusian Rule, and the information brought to him seemed good. But for the reason given above, and because his attention was entirely occupied with the journey he was thinking of making at once, he gave up thinking about the Carthusians as it was a matter that could await his return. Indeed, feeling that he was pretty well restored, he thought it was time to be up and going and told his brother so. "You know, my lord, the Duke of Nájera is aware that I have recovered. It will be good for me to go to Navarette." The Duke was there at the time. His brother led him from one room to another, and with a great show of affection, begged him not to make a fool of himself. He wanted him to see what hopes the people placed in him and what influence he might have, along with other like suggestions, all with the intention of turning him from the good desire he had conceived. But, without departing from the truth, for he was very scrupulous about that, he reassured him in a way that allowed him to slip away from his brother.

Leon Modena da Venezia was a complex personality. His autobiography focuses on his travails—his obsession with gambling, the terrible fates of his sons, the restrictions against Jews in Italy at the time of the Counter-Reformation. Unlike most other autobiographies in this collection, it is not a summation of a life viewed in retrospect. Instead, begun in 1618 and completed in 1648, it was meant instead to stand as a memorial to Modena's reverence for the God of his ancestors and to his love for his children.

We would scarcely know from it that he was a man of immense intellectual accomplishments. He corresponded or was in personal contact with scholars from London to Prague and beyond, and Christians sought his instruction in Hebrew and biblical studies. The poetry he wrote shows his knowledge of Latin literature and rhetoric as well as traditional Jewish learning. His sermons were famous well beyond the Venetian ghetto. Often called upon to resolve disputes in local affairs, he also used his eloquence in an important communal matter: his presentation before the papal legate on the subject of Jewish moneylending

RABBI LEON MODENA

[1 5 7 1 – 1 6 4 8]

The hand of God weighed heavily on the Jews throughout Italy.

helped to reestablish that privilege for the Jews of Ferrara. The autobiography, while scanting these achievements, shows Modena as he saw himself: a weak man but one of profound faith, who was certain of God's guiding hand in all matters.   [EP]

FROM *THE LIFE OF JUDAH*

With God's help may we do this successfully, amen.

This is the life story of Judah Aryeh [*Aryeh* is Hebrew for *lion*, Italian *leone*], son of the noble and trustworthy Isaac of blessed memory, son of the gaon and physician, Rabbi Mordecai of blessed memory, son of the venerable Isaac of blessed memory, son of the wealthy Moses of blessed memory, Modena:

"Few and evil have been the days of the years of my life"
in this world.

Inasmuch as the King's [God's] word has power to remove man from this world on the day of his death—after which all is forgotten—for more than twenty-four years I have desired in the depths of my soul to set down in writing all the incidents that happened to me from my beginnings until the end of my life, so that I shall not die, but live. I thought that it would be of value to my sons, the fruit of my loins, and to their descendants, and to my students, who are called sons, just as it is a great pleasure to me to be able to know the lives of my ancestors, forebears, teachers, and all other important and beloved people.

In particular, I longed to bequeath it as a gift to my firstborn son, the apple of my eye, the root of my heart, whose bright countenance was similar to mine, a man of wisdom, Mordecai of blessed memory, who was known as Angelo. All my thoughts were of him. I was proud of him, and he was the source of all my joy. But for those twenty-four years up to the present I did not succeed in writing this down as a memoir in a book. Now that God has taken away my joy,—it being two months since God took him away, leaving me desolate and faint all day long—my soul has refused to be comforted, for I will go to my grave mourning for my son, waiting for death as for a solemnly appointed time.

And so, at the age of forty-seven, an old man, full of disquietude, I resolved, in the month of Tevet 5378 [December 29, 1617–January 26, 1618] to begin and to finish, God willing, giving an account of all the essential as well as of the incidental happenings in my life. Should my children or children's children or students or others who know me look at it, they will see the woes that befell me. From the moment I entered the world, I had neither tranquility nor quiet nor rest, and then disquietude came upon me, namely, disquietude over my son Mordecai of blessed memory. I await death, which does not come.

Subsequently, from year to year, at six-month intervals, I shall add to this account what new happens to me. After that will come my will concerning my body, soul, and literary remains—and God will do what is proper in his eyes.

I RECEIVED THE TRADITION FROM MY FATHER, MY TEACHER OF blessed memory, that our ancestors came from France. In his house there was a family tree going back more than five hundred years, which had been found among the writings of my grandfather, the gaon of blessed memory. From my uncle, Rabbi Solomon Modena of blessed memory, it had passed to his daughter's son, my kinsman Rabbi Aaron, the son of Moses of Modena, may God his Rock protect him and grant him long life, who lives at present in Modena. He told me that it had left his possession, and although I have searched for it thoroughly I have so far been unable to obtain it.

Nonetheless, I know that it is so, from tradition passed on by my elders, that this family has always combined Torah with stature, riches with honor, and great wealth with charitableness. He [Rabbi Aaron] told me that after our forebears left France, they dwelled for a long time in Viterbo, and then came to Modena, where they acquired property and became fruitful and multiplied. Because they were the first to establish a pawnshop there and become wealthy, they took their name from that city. To this day, control over the cemetery there is in the hands of my aforementioned kinsman Moses, because our first forebears in the city purchased it for their own use. The first house they acquired in Modena is still in the possession of Moses, and I have seen it. In some places therein is found our crest in marble, the figure of a leopard standing on its two hind legs with a palm branch in its paw. Moses told me that it [the crest] has been in our family for more than five hundred years. He also has in his possession in writing the privileges of all those who ruled Modena—popes, emperors, dukes, and the like—who confirmed it.

Apparently, in the days of Isaac, the grandfather of my revered father of blessed memory, they moved to Bologna, though they continued to keep their house and pawnshop in Modena. And there, too, they became great and prospered, yet retained the name Modena. As for me, because I was born and grew up in Venice, and have lived in its environs, and have been in Modena only during the past ten years and but two or three times, I sign my name in Italian, "Leon Modena da Venezia," and not "da Modena." For that city has become our byname instead of our toponym, and as such you will find it in my printed Italian writings. . . .

Because of the oppressive expulsion decreed by Pope Pius V in 532_, my revered father journeyed from Bologna, leaving behind his possessions—a house, a mansion, and notes of credit worth thousands of gold pieces. He took what he had in hand and came to live in Ferrara.

My revered father's wife Peninah died in the year [5]329 [1568/1569], and in the same year, on the holiday of Shavuot [May 22–23, 1569], he married Rachel, the daughter of Johanan Halevi of blessed memory, from Apulia, but from a family of Ashkenazim. She was at that time the widow of Mordecai, known as Gumpeln Parenzo, the brother of Meir Parenzo, who is mentioned by name in several printed books. She had one son by that Mordecai, named Abraham, who was nine years old at the time. Previously my father had asked the sage Rabbi Abraham Rovigo, who was well versed in several kinds of wisdom, whether he would succeed if he married that woman. He replied that with her my father would not be successful in material matters, and that if he married her, he should change her name. So he changed her name to Diana.

Diana became pregnant in 5331 [late 1570], at which time a huge and severe earthquake struck Ferrara, the likes of which had not been known in all the lands, all of which is related in the book *Me'or 'einayim* by the aforementioned sage de Rossi. My revered father and the members of his household fled for their lives to Venice.

While they were still there, on Monday the 28th day of Nisan—corresponding to the 23d day of April [5]331 [1571]—between the eighteenth and nineteenth hours [noon to 1:00 P.M.], I, the bitter and impetuous, was born. I would almost, like Job and Jeremiah, curse that day. For why did I go out [of the womb] to witness toil, anger, strife, and trouble—only evil continually? . . .

On the night of the 13th of Tevet 5377 [December 21, 1616] I had a dream in which I saw a man standing before me, and many people were saying to me, "Do you see that man? He is a prophet, and the spirit of God is in him." So I approached him and said, "Master, as they tell me you are a prophet, please tell me when I shall die and how much longer I shall live." The man immediately answered, "Four years and seven months," whereupon I awoke. In the morning I composed a poem as a reminder, in the style of a poem that A[zariah] de Rossi of blessed memory had composed, having had it revealed to him in a dream that later was fulfilled, and which is written [i.e., copied] from his hand in [a copy of] his book that is in my possession: "While resting on my bed, on the night of the 13th of Tevet 5377, I dreamed of a prophet, who foretold my end. Another four years and seven months, in Tammuz or Av [5]381, I'll go to my resting place."

I will not refrain from telling you here that from my youth I had had a passionate desire to learn from the astrologers, on the basis of my birth date, what would happen to me during the days of my life and how many they would be. I had seen the horoscope that a certain man named Alessandro Bivago had compiled for my revered father of blessed memory in Bologna when he was seventeen. He told him everything that would happen to him year by year, and not one word failed to come true. He said that he would live seventy-two and one-half years, and it turned out to be seventy-two and two months. From that time on, I yearned for something like it. A horoscope was compiled for me by four astrologers, two Jews and two Christians, and to this day, on account of my sins, what they wrote has proved accurate. The time of my death is predicted for the age of fifty-two, approximately, and I am fifty now. Palmistry also indicates that it will occur about the age of fifty.

I now regret having undertaken that endeavor, for man's only proper way is to be pure before God, and he should not make such inquiries. So here I am today, pained on account of the past and anxious about the future. But God will do as he pleases. My only prayer to him is that he should not take me away before I repent of my sins. Ever since I was born I have had no joy, that I should worry about lacking it; neither have I seen any good in this world, that I should have difficulty leaving it. These, my final days, are burdensome. May the Creator be praised for everything forever. If the time or any other that has been decreed for me according to the aforementioned persons should pass, I will write of that fact further on. But if their words prove to be true, one of the readers should write it here below.

My bowels, my bowels. I writhe in pain. The chambers of my heart moan within me as I come to tell with twofold brokenheartedness about the death of my son Mordecai of blessed memory. After the holiday of Sukkot 5376 [ended October 16, 1615], when he first began to bleed from his mouth, it recurred, at first once a month, after that once a week, and then from Passover [5]377 [began April 30, 1617] on, every day. I tried frantically to cure him, but could not find a remedy. I saw no sign of benefit in any of the many medicines that I gave him. Finally, in the month of Elul [September 1617], his illness grew worse. I had eleven doctors, Jewish and Christian, consulting about his malady, some during personal visits and others through correspondence. He wished very much for the remedies of the aforementioned priest Grillo, having seen an example of his treatment of others. But, as it differed from the ways of all the other doctors, I was afraid to treat him accordingly. Only close to his death, to satisfy his wishes, did I allow him to take them.

About that time I dreamed that he said to me, "I have taken a house for myself outside the ghetto." I responded, "Show me where, so that I may come and find you." He answered, "I do not want to tell you, for I do not want you to come to find me." Meanwhile, bedridden, he continued to wane.

On the Sabbath of Repentance [5]378 [October 7, 1617] he got up from his bed to come hear two of my sermons. That evening he returned to his bed and began to run a fever, the likes of which he had never previously known. Finally, on the night of the arrival of Tuesday the 9th of Heshvan 5378 [November 7, 1617], his appointed time drew near, and he confessed his sins and recited many psalms and confessional prayers. He lay dying for about three hours, and then, about the ninth hour [3:00 A.M.], his soul returned to the Lord who had given it to him.

Truthfully, were it not for the maxim of the talmudic sages of blessed memory, "Just as the Holy One, blessed be he, gives the righteous the strength to accept their reward, so he gives strength to the wicked to accept their punishment," I could not possibly live with the pain and sorrow that have seized me from then until now. Not a day passes that [his death] is not fresh to me, as if his corpse were lying before me. The saying, "It is decreed that the dead should be forgotten by the heart," does not apply to me, for it is today three years since his death, and wherever I turn he is there before me.

He was an average-looking man, slender and not fat, with a hairy body. His face was not pale, but he had a small, rounded beard. He pleased all who saw him, and was wise in all worldly matters, as well as in the advice he gave when anyone asked him about matters divine. He preached well in public, delivering sermons in Florence, Mantua, Ferrara, and Venice. He was neither a happy nor a sad person, and got along well with people. None surpassed him in respect for parents. We were like two brothers, for he was twenty-six years and two months old [at his death], and I was forty-six and a half. Alas for me, I lost him, and I do not even know how to count his praises.

Later on it was reported to me in Ferrara, as he had related it, that one year before his death he told a certain woman how he had asked in a dream to be shown the woman decreed to become his wife and was shown a coffin covered in black.

I thought that my son Zebulun, may God his Rock protect him and grant him long life, would bring me consolation, but to this day his ways have not been straight, and he adds trouble and sorrow to my pain. May God guide him in the path of his commandments, so that he may console me before I die.

Following the death of the apple of my eye and root of my heart, I returned out of great anxiety to the enemy that always drove me out of the world—namely, playing games of chance—from which I had abstained for two years in order to please my aforementioned son. Until Passover 5380 [began April 19, 1620], I compounded the evil day after day....

At the end of Tevet 5382 [ended January 11, 1622], a celebration was held in the Great Synagogue at the conclusion of the study of the talmudic tractate Ketubbot. Eighteen sermons were delivered, and on the last night, which was the second day of Shevat [January 13, 1622], I gave the sermon before a huge standing crowd, packed in as never before, with many Christians and noblemen among the listeners. Poems and melodies were composed [for the occasion], and Zebulun sang a song that I had written. The listeners could not stop praising his sweet voice. I was extremely happy because my term of duty in the school had ended, and I had emerged into the freedom for which my soul had longed all that time. Even though I was empty-handed and had many debts, I praised the living God. I decided after Passover to lead myself along the proper path with his help, may he be praised.

Passover 5382 [March 26–April 3, 1622] was transformed for me from a time of happiness to one of sorrow, and from a holiday to a time of mourning, gloom, trouble, and darkness. Alas, O Righteous One of the universe! Alas, O Judge of the universe! How my sins have multiplied and my transgressions have increased! It is now a full fifty-one years since my birth, with things getting worse and worse. There is never a day whose curse is not greater than the one before. I have had neither rest nor peace, with anxiety following anxiety and calamity following calamity, in money matters, in heart, and in body. I hardly have strength to hold the pen in my hand and to write down what happened to me as a result of God's disfavor. How can the paper fail to become wet from the tears that fall upon it? O, my heart, which moans like a piped instrument, break so that my life can end! Death seems to me so good. No other rest would be good for me, because for hundreds of years until now, there has been no evil like the one that God visited upon me on account of my many wicked deeds.

Four years beforehand my oppressed, bitter, and impetuous son Zebulun, may God avenge his blood, had been forced to serve at a trial as a witness against certain accursed scoundrels and treacherous murderers. Since the days of the violent men who lived at the time of the destruction of the Temple there had not been the likes of them, the accursed brothers—may their names be blotted out from this world and their bones be ground to dust in hell in the world to come—Shabbetai and Moses Benincasa, known as da Hindelina. May their names be blotted out, those brothers! May their portion be cursed in the earth. May their sons speedily become orphans and travel about in search of bread like the descendants of Canaan.

Because of this, they bore a permanent grudge against him. They did not show it in their faces or words, but rather always spoke peaceably with him and me, while harboring treachery in their hearts. Finally, in the month of Av [5]381 [July–August 1621], while my son, may God avenge his blood, was speaking with the violent Shabbetai, may his name be blotted out, the latter began to quarrel with him. He struck him on the cheek and pursued him with a slaughterhouse knife to Cannaregio. There, my son, may God avenge his blood, spotted a sword on a villager's shoulder, grabbed it, and became the pursuer himself. He struck him [Shabbetai] lightly on one arm, but the latter threw himself into the water and thus escaped from my son.

When I heard about this, and before the conflict went farther, I entreated the nobleman, my lord Signore Alvise Giustinian, and he made peace between them. Thus the brothers, may their names be blotted out, once again passed themselves off as friends, while the fire of hatred burned ever more fiercely in their hearts.

On the night of the burning of leaven [the night before the first evening of Passover], the night of the arrival of Friday, March 25, [5]382 [1622], the two brothers, may their names be blotted out, formed a conspiracy with the bastard Isaac of the Spagnoletta family and the bastard Abram Ciompo della Bel, who were called "mules" because they were bastards, and with four Sephardim—David Mocatto, may his name be blotted out; Moses Emmanuel, may his name be blotted out; and the brothers Isaac and Jacob Montalti, the sons of the midwife—eight men hated by God. They feared Zebulun because they knew of his courage, namely, that he had the heart of a lion and would not retreat in the face of battle.

The bastard Isaac stalked him on the way to the house of the Levantine. Just as I arrived, for I had been informed about it and had gone looking for him to bring him home, they came out of hiding, pretending that they wanted to beat up someone else. The bastard called to him and said, "Come down, your friends are in a fight; come to their aid!" On the run, the impetuous one came down, passing me by without my recognizing him. As soon as he emerged they surrounded him and struck him on the head, bruising him without drawing blood. Then they stabbed him in the throat with a sword or a spear, so that he fled, shouting, "Father, Father, I am dying!"

Blood spurted out like a spring, and as he could not make it home, he went to the house of my brother-in-law Johanan, may God his Rock protect him and grant him long life. There he threw himself into bed, rolling in blood. Before the doctor could arrive, he had lost his lifeblood. By the time [the physician] bandaged his wounds there was no longer enough of it left to keep him alive, and his entire right side lost all feeling. Immediately after reciting the confessional prayer and the prayers for mercy, he lost consciousness from the blow to his head and never again uttered an intelligible word. He lay near death for four nights and three days until Monday, the first of the intermediate days of the holiday [of Passover, Monday, March 28, 1622], when his soul departed and he passed on to eternal life.

He was buried that day next to his brother, my son Mordecai of blessed memory. Upon his coffin while it was being carried was placed his blood-soiled clothing. This sight, and the sound of my cries and those of my woebegone wife, caused every heart and eye to shed tears. Even Christians and Turks grieved. At the cemetery there was an eighteen-year-old Christian citizen from the Dolfin family who had known him, and he grieved so much that immediately after returning home he took to his bed and died within four days. There was no one who had ever spoken with him [my son]—including many Christian commoners who were acquaintances of his—who did not weep over his death. Such a cruel death!

He was thirteen days short of twenty-one years, good-looking and handsome. There was nobody like him in this community. He sang with a voice as sweet as that of God's angel. He was wise, understanding, and cheerful, and a writer of both prose and poetry. He was brave in battle, and none had a heart as courageous as his. Alas, I had always told him, "Your big heart will kill you!" His courage and weapons he only used in zeal for his God and to hallow his name, for he could not endure the debasement of any Jew. And he never touched one of his own people.

Four months before his death, the citizen Signore Lorenzo Sanudo had told his horoscope, saying that he would be killed between the ages of twenty-one and twenty-two. Alas, my eyes witnessed such a cruel death visited upon him! His bloody state will never disappear from before my eyes for the rest of my life. My tears have been my bread, day and night. My soul refuses to be comforted, for there can be no consolation. I simply pray to God: "Please unleash your hand and cut me off. Take my soul from me. Then I shall cease to have anxiety from sinning before you, and shall have rest and quiet." . . .

[5]391 [1630/1631]. From that time on the pestilence began to spread all over. The hand of God weighed heavily on the Jews throughout Italy, bringing war, famine, and plague. The sorrows that befell the holy community of Mantua had not been felt since the time of the destruction of the Temple, and the holy community of Modena was almost destroyed by the pestilence. Then it reached Venice, and after it began in the Ghetto Vecchio with Moses Tzarfati of blessed memory, during the Days of Repentance [September 7–16, 1630]; and during Sukkot [September 21–29, 1630] with Jacob Cohen, known as Scocco, it spread further, until by today, the beginning of the month of Second Adar 5391 [March 5, 1631], about 170 people have died. There has been great panic in the various congregations, and many, especially the Sephardim, have left the city for the Levant or for Verona.

Seven hundred and fifty bales worth much money were sent to Lazzaretto, and almost all of them were destroyed or lost. For approximately a year Jews have been forbidden to buy and sell or engage in business negotiations; hence there has been no earning. The government also took more than 120,000 ducats from the Jews. An unprecedented rise in prices has been the worst blow of all, causing many Jews in these communities to become impoverished, the rich becoming middling and the middling poor, and no one taking pity any longer on the poor, for there is no money.

AND I, IN MY POVERTY, NOT ONLY HAVE I HAD MY WIDOWED DAUGH-ter Diana and her son, may God his Rock protect him and grant him long life, in my house for the past two years, but my daughter Sterella, may she be blessed above all women of the house, whose husband has not been able to return home for a full year, has also become my financial responsibility. Indeed, all of them are my responsibility in these strange times. But despite all this, God in his mercy and truth has not ceased to deal wondrously with me, and this year I have spent more than five hundred ducats between household necessities and repayment of debts without having to resort to donations from anybody. I earned these [ducats] by using my pen, my tongue, and my wits, and God in his great kindness had mercy.

Indeed, he has continuously protected me, for his hand has struck all the surrounding dwellings, and even the [apartments on the] staircase where I live. Above and below me and on all sides, left and right, people have taken ill and died from the plague. But to this day God has not allowed the agent of destruction to enter my apartment to cause affliction. May he not abandon or desert me or the members of my household. Amen.

Anne Bradstreet (née Dudley) is best known for her poetry, in particular for her "contemplations." A Puritan of great passion and commitment, she suffered personal hardship to travel to the Bay Colony in Massachusetts, of which her father, and later her husband, were both governors. During her difficult life as a pilgrim, she endured several periods of debilitating illness, which became for her times of great spiritual blessing and growth. Despite the popular perception of Puritan life as grim, Anne Bradstreet's poetry is characterized by joy, especially in the delights of the natural world and its simple pleasures. In the following letter to her children, Bradstreet recounts her own spiritual struggles in the hope of strengthening her children's formation as Christians. Frequent illnesses disturbed her habitual tranquillity; these challenges deepened her commitment to faith in a transcendent being. As in the work of Emily Dickinson or Christina Rossetti, Bradstreet's verse conveys a continual awareness of death and the transcience of matter, lending her themes a metaphysical dimension approaching that of John Donne.   [AM]

ANNE BRADSTREET

[CA. 1612 – 1672]

Heaven without the love of God . . .

would have been a Hell to me.

A LETTER TO MY CHILDREN

This book by Any yet vnread,
I leaue for yov when I am dead,
That, being gone, here yov may find
What was your liueing mother's mind.
Make vſe of what I leaue in Loue
And God ſhall bleſſe yov from above.

A. B.

My dear Children,—

I, knowing by experience that the exhortations of parents take moſt effeĉt when the speakers leaue to ſpeak, and thoſe eſpecially ſink deepeſt which are ſpoke lateſt—and being ignorant whether on my death bed I ſhall haue opportvnity to ſpeak to any of yov, much leſſe to All—thought it the beſt, whilſt I was able to compoſe ſome ſhort matters, (for what elſe to call them I know not) and bequeath to yov, that when I am no more with yov, yet I may bee dayly in your remembrance, (Although that is the leaſt in my aim in what I now doe) but that yov may gain ſome ſpiritual Advantage by my experience. I haue not ſtudyed in this yov read to ſhow my ſkill, but to declare the Truth—not to ſett forth myſelf, but the Glory of God. If I had minded the former, it had been perhaps better pleaſing to yov,—but ſeing the laſt is the beſt, let it bee beſt pleaſing to yov.

The method I will obſerve ſhall bee this—I will begin with God's dealing with me from my childhood to this Day. In my yovng years, about 6 or 7 as I take it, I began to make conſcience of my wayes, and what I knew was ſinfull, as lying, diſobedience to Parents, &c. I avoided it. If at any time I was overtaken with the like evills, it was a great Trouble. I could not be at reſt 'till by prayer I had confeſt it vnto God. I was alſo troubled at the negleĉt of Private Dutyes, tho: too often tardy that way. I alſo fovnd much comfort in reading the Scriptures, eſpecially thoſe places I thought moſt concerned my Condition, and as I grew to haue more vnderſtanding, ſo the more ſolace I took in them.

In a long fitt of ſicknes which I had on my bed I often commvned with my heart, and made my ſupplication to the moſt High who ſett me free from that affliĉtion.

But as I grew vp to bee about 14 or 15 I fovnd my heart more carnall, and ſitting looſe from God, vanity and the follyes of youth take hold of me.

About 16, the Lord layd his hand ſore vpon me and ſmott mee with the fmall pox. When I was in my afflietion, I befovght the Lord, and confeffed my Pride and Vanity and he was entreated of me, and again reftored me. But I rendered not to him according to the benefitt received.

After a fhort time I changed my condition and was marryed, and came into this Covntry, where I fovnd a new world and new manners, at which my heart rofe. But after I was convinced it was the way of God, I fubmitted to it and joined to the church at Bofton.

After fome time I fell into a lingering ficknes like a confvmption, together with a lameneffe, which correetion I faw the Lord fent to humble and try me and doe mee Good: and it was not altogether ineffeetuall.

It pleafed God to keep me a long time without a child, which was a great greif to me, and coft mee many prayers and tears before I obtaind one, and after him gave mee many more, of whom I now take the care, that as I have brovght yov into the world, and with great paines, weaknes, cares, and feares brovght yov to this, I now travail in birth again of yov till Chrift bee formed in yov.

Among all my experiences of God's gratious Dealings with me I haue conftantly obferved this, that he hath never fuffered me long to fitt loofe from him, but by one afflietion or other hath made me look home, and fearch what was amiffe—fo vfually thvs it hath been with me that I haue expected correetion for it, which moft commonly hath been vpon my own perfon, in fickneffe, weaknes, paines, fometimes on my foul, in Doubts and feares of God's difpleafure, and my fincerity towards him, fometimes he hath fmott a child with ficknes, fometimes chafftened by loffes in eftate,—and thefe Times (thro: his great mercy) haue been the times of my greateft Getting and Advantage, yea I haue fovnd them the Times when the Lord hath manifefted the moft Love to me. Then haue I gone to fearching, and haue faid with David, Lord fearch me and try me, fee what wayes of wickednes are in me, and lead me in the way everlafting: and feldome or never but I haue fovnd either fome fin I lay vnder which God would haue reformed, or fome duty negleeted which he would haue performed. And by his help I haue layd Vowes and Bonds vpon my Soul to perform his righteous commands.

If at any time yov are chaftened by God, take it as thankfully and Joyfully as in greateft mercyes, for if yee bee his yee fhall reap the greateft benefitt by it. It hath been no fmall fupport to me in times of Darknes when the Almighty hath hid his face from me, that yet I haue had abundance of fweetnes and refrefhment after afflietion, and more circumfpeetion in my walking after I haue been afflieted. I haue been with God like an vntoward child, that no longer then the rod has been on my back (or at leaft in fight) but I haue been apt to forgett him and myfelf too. Before I was afflieted I went aftray, but now I keep thy ftatutes.

I haue had great experience of God's hearing my Prayers, and returning comfortable Anfwers to me, either in granting the Thing I prayed for, or elfe in fatiffying my mind without it; and I haue been confident it hath been from him, becavfe I have fovnd my heart through his goodnes enlarged in Thankfullnes to him.

I haue often been perplexed that I haue not found that conftant Joy in my Pilgrimage and refrefhing which I fuppofed moft of the fervants of God haue; althovgh he hath not left me altogether without the wittnes of his holy fpirit, who hath oft given mee his word and fett to his Seal that it fhall bee well with me. . . .

And, when I haue been in ficknes and haue thovght if the Lord would but lift vp the light of his Covntenance vpon me, altho: he grovnd me to powder, it would bee but light to me; yea, oft haue I thovght were it hell itfelf, and could there find the Love of God toward me, it would bee a Heaven. And, could I haue been in Heaven without the Love of God, it would haue been a Hell to me; for, in Truth, it is the abfence and prefence of God that makes Heaven or Hell.

Many times hath Satan troubled me concerning the verity of the fcriptures, many times by Atheifme how I could know whether there was a God; I never faw any miracles to confirm me, and thofe which I read of how did I know but they were feigned. That there is a God my Reafon would foon tell me by the wondrous workes that I fee, the vaft frame of the Heaven and the Earth, the order of all things, night and day, Summer and Winter, Spring and Autvmne, the dayly providing for this great hovfhold vpon the Earth, the preferving and directing of All to its proper end. The confideration of thefe things would with amazement certainly refolve me that there is an Eternall Being.

But how fhould I know he is fuch a God as I worfhip in Trinity, and fuch a Saviour as I rely upon? tho: this hath thovfands of Times been fvggefted to mee, yet God hath helped me over. I haue argved thvs with myfelf. That there is a God I fee. If ever this God hath revealed himfelf, it mvft bee in his word, and this mvft bee it or none. Haue I not fovnd that operation by it that no humane Invention can work vpon the Soul? hath not Judgments befallen Diverfe who haue fcorned and contemd it? hath it not been pre-ferved thro: All Ages maugre all the heathen Tyrants and all of the enemyes who haue oppofed it? Is there any ftory but that which fhowes the beginnings of Times, and how the world came to bee as wee fee? Doe wee not know the prophecyes in it fullfilled which could not haue been fo long foretold by any but God himfelf? . . .

The confideration of thefe things and many the like would foon turn me to my own Religion again.

But fome new Troubles I haue had fince the world has been filled with

Blaſphemy, and Sectaries, and ſome who haue been accounted ſincere Chriſtians haue been carryed away with them, that ſomtimes I haue ſaid, Is there ffaith vpon the earth? and I haue not known what to think. But then I haue remembred the words of Chriſt that ſo it muſt bee, and that, if it were poſſible, the very elect ſhould bee deceived. Behold, ſaith our Saviour, I have told yov before. That hath ſtayed my heart, and I can now ſay, Return, O my Soul, to thy Reſt, vpon this Rock Chriſt Jeſus will I build my faith; and, if I periſh, I periſh. But I know all the Powers of Hell ſhall neuer prevail againſt it. I know whom I haue trvſted, and whom I haue beleived, and that he is able to keep that I haue committed to his charge.

Now to the King, Immortall, Eternall, and inviſible, the only wife God, bee Honoure and Glory for ever and ever! Amen.

This was written in mvch ſickneſſe and weaknes, and is very weakly and imperfectly done; but, if yov can pick any Benefitt out of it, it is the marke which I aimed at.

ARCHPRIEST AVVAKUM (AVVAKUM PETROVICH)

[1 6 2 0 – 1 6 8 2]

Almighty miserable it was,

but sweet for my soul.

The Archpriest Avvakum was a leader of the Old Believer Schism that divided the Russian Church in the mid-seventeenth century. Because of various minor reforms being introduced by Patriarch Nikon into the Russian Orthodox liturgy to bring it into consistency with Western practices—for example, signing the cross with three fingers instead of two—a large number of "raskolniki" ("Schismatics") or "Old Believers" broke away from the official church. Without officially ordained priests, their clergy were denounced as heretical and widespread persecution followed. Imprisonment, exile, and the torching of schismatic churches, even with the congregation inside, became the norm. Avvakum himself endured beatings and tortures; he spent years in a subterranean prison cell consisting of no more than a rude hole in the ground. Some groups of Old Believers emigrated to the Americas and the Far East. Still adhering to their traditions today, the Old Believers resemble the American Amish and Mennonite communities in their insularity and cultural conservatism.

Avvakum's *Life of Archpriest Avvakum*

by Himself is a dramatically innovative work. Since Avvakum's motivation was to sanctify himself and justify his leadership of the Old Believers, he adopted, while changing forever, the traditional form of hagiographical literature. Stylistically and linguistically, Avvakum's *Life* breaks with traditional hagiography, as it is composed in the vernacular Old Russian rather than in Old Church Slavonic; uses vivid folkloric and colloquial expressions; and is written by the "saint" himself. The crude realism and almost barbaric simplicity of the narrative is a stark contrast to the sentimental and stylized saints' lives of traditional Church literature. While emphasizing his heroic capacity for martyrdom, Avvakum stresses his unreliability as a narrator; like Saint Augustine, he confesses his pride and feelings of self-righteousness and vanity as necessarily bound up with the very process of writing about himself. [AM]

FROM *THE LIFE OF ARCHPRIEST AVVAKUM BY HIMSELF*

The Archpriest
Avvakum hath been charged
to write his *Life* by the monk Epifanij
(as this monk is his confessor), so that the
works of God shall not pass into oblivion;
and to this end hath he been charged by
his confessor, to the glory of
Christ our God.
Amen.

All-holy Trinity, O God and Creator of all the world! Speed and direct my heart to begin with wisdom and to end with the good works about which I, an unworthy man, now desire to speak. Understanding my ignorance and bowing down I pray to thee; and as I beseech thee for aid, govern my mind and strengthen my heart to prepare for the fashioning of good works, so that illumined by good works I may have a place at thy right hand with all thine Elect on Judgment Day. And now, O Master, bless me so that sighing from my heart I might proclaim Dionysios the Areopagite on the divine names which are the eternally connatural and true names for God, those which are proximate and those which are consequent, that is to say, laudatory. These are the connatural: He is that is, Light, Truth, Life. Only four are of the essential, but of the consequent there are many. These are: Lord, the Almighty, the Unfathomable, the Unapproachable, the Thrice-radiant, the Trisubstantial, the King of Glory, the Omnipresent, Fire, Spirit, and God; understand others after this manner.

I WAS BORN IN THE NIŽNIJ NOVGOROD AREA, BEYOND THE KUDMA River, in the village of Grigorovo. My father was the priest Pëtr, my mother Marija, as a nun Marfa. My father was given to hard drink, but my mother fasted and prayed zealously and was ever teaching me the fear of God. Once I saw a dead cow at a neighbor's, and that night I arose and wept much over my soul before the icon, being mindful of death and how I too must die. And from that time I grew accustomed to praying every night. Then my mother was widowed and I, still young, orphaned, and we were driven out, away from our kin. My mother deigned to have me married. And I prayed to the most holy Mother of God that she might give me for a wife a helpmate to salvation. And in the same village there was a girl, also an orphan, who was accustomed to going to church unceasingly; her name was Anastasija. Her father was a blacksmith by the name of Marko, very rich, but when he died everything dwindled away. And she lived in poverty and prayed to God that she might be joined with me in marital union; and so it was, by the will of God. Afterwards my mother went to God amidst great feats of piety. And being banished I moved to another place. I was ordained a deacon at the age of twenty-one, and after two years I was made a priest. I lived as a priest for eight years and was then raised to archpriest by Orthodox bishops. Since then twenty years have passed, and in all it is thirty years that I have been in holy orders.

And when I was a priest I had many spiritual children; up to now it would be about five or six hundred. Never slumbering I, a sinner, was diligent in churches and in homes, at crossroads, in towns and villages, even in the capital and in the lands of Siberia, preaching and teaching the Word of God, this for about twenty-five years.

When I was still a priest, there came to me to confess a young woman burdened with many sins, guilty of fornication and self-abuse of every sort; and weeping she began to acquaint me with it all in detail, standing before the Gospel there in the church. But I, thrice-accursed healer, I was afflicted myself, burning inwardly with a lecherous fire, and it was bitter for me in that hour. I lit three candles and stuck them to the lectern, and raised my right hand into the flame and held it there until the evil conflagration within me was extinguished After dismissing the young woman, laying away my vestments and praying awhile, I went to my home deeply grieved. The hour was as midnight, and having come into my house I wept before the icon of the Lord so that my eyes swelled; and I prayed earnestly that God might separate me from my spiritual children, for the burden was heavy and hard to bear. And I fell to the ground on my face; I wept bitterly, and lying there sank into forgetfulness. Nothing could I ken, as I was weeping, but the eyes of my heart beheld the Volga. I saw two golden boats sailing gracefully, and their oars were of gold, and the masts of gold, and everything was of gold; each had one helmsman for the crew. And I asked, "Whose boats are these?" And they answered, "Luka's and Lavrentij's." They had been my spiritual children; they set me and my house on the path to salvation, and their passing was pleasing to God. And lo, I then saw a third boat, not adorned with gold but motley colored—red, and white, and blue, and black, and ashen; the mind of man could not take in all its beauty and excellence. A radiant youth sitting aft was steering. He raced toward me out of the Volga as if he wanted to swallow me whole. And I shouted. "Whose boat is this?" And he sitting in it answered, "Your boat. Sail in it with your wife and children if you're going to pester the Lord." And I was seized by trembling, and sitting down I pondered: "What is this vision? And what sort of voyage will it be?"

And lo, after a little while, as it is written, "The sorrows of death compassed me, and the afflictions of hell gat hold upon me; I found trouble and sorrow." An official carried off a widow's daughter, and I besought him that he should return the orphan to her mother. But scorning our entreaty he raised up a storm against me; coming in a multitude they trampled me to death near the church. And I lay dead for more than half an hour, and returned to life with a sign from God. And being terrified he yielded up the young woman to me. Afterwards he was instructed by the devil; he came into the church and beat me and dragged me by the legs along the ground, still in my vestments. But I was saying a prayer the while.

Later, another official at another time raged savagely against me. He rushed into my house, and having beaten me he gnawed the fingers of my hand with his teeth like a dog. And when his throat filled with blood, he loosed my hand from his teeth, and leaving me he went home. But I, thanking God and having wrapped my hand with a kerchief, I went to Vespers. And when I was on the way he leaped out at me again with two pistols, and being close to me he fired one. By God's will the powder flared in the pan, but the pistol didn't shoot. He threw it on the ground and again he fired the other in the same way, but God's will brought this to pass in the same way —that pistol didn't shoot either. And walking along I prayed earnestly to

God, and with one hand I signed him with the Cross and bowed down before him. He was barking away at me, but I said unto him, "Let grace be upon thy lips, Ivan Rodionovič!" Afterwards he took away my home and kicked me out, robbing me of everything, and he gave me no bread for the road. . . .

A little later others again drove me from that place for the second time. And I dragged myself to Moscow, and by God's will the Sovereign ordered that I be appointed archpriest in Jur'evec-on-the-Volga. I lived here only a little, just eight weeks. The devil instructed the priests and peasants and their females; they came to the patriarchal chancellery where I was busy with church business, and in a crowd they dragged me out of the chancellery (there were maybe fifteen hundred of them). And in the middle of the street they beat me with clubs and stomped me, and the females had at me with stove hooks. Because of my sins, they almost beat me to death and they cast me down near the corner of a house. The Commandant rushed up with his artillerymen, and seizing me they raced away on their horses to my poor home. And the Commandant stationed his men about the yard. But people came up to the yard, and the town was in tumult. Most of all, as I had cut short their fornicating, the priests and their females were howling, "Kill the crook, the son of a whore, and we'll pitch his carcass in the ditch for the dogs!"

After resting, two days later at night I abandoned wife and children and with two others headed along the Volga toward Moscow. I escaped to Kostroma—and sure enough, there they'd driven out the Archpriest Daniil too. Ah, what misery! the devil badgers a man to death! I trudged to Moscow and presented myself to Stefan, the Tsar's confessor, and he was troubled with me. "Why did you abandon your cathedral church?" he says. Again more misery for me! The Tsar came to his confessor that night to be blessed and saw me there—again more heartache. "And why," he says. "did you abandon your town?" And my wife and children and the help, some twenty people, had stayed in Jur'evec, no telling if they were living or dead. Still more misery. . . .

Later on Boris Neledinskij and his musketeers seized me during a vigil; about sixty people were taken with me. They were led off to a dungeon but me they put in the Patriarch's Court for the night, in chains. When the sun had risen on the Sabbath, they put me in a cart and stretched out my arms and drove me from the Patriarch's Court to the Andronikov Monastery, and there they tossed me in chains into a dark cell dug into the earth. I was locked up three days, and neither ate nor drank. Locked there in darkness I bowed down in my chains, maybe to the east, maybe to the west. No one came to me, only the mice and the cockroaches; the crickets chirped and there were fleas to spare. It came to pass that on the third day I was voracious, that is, I wanted to eat, and after Vespers there stood before me, whether an angel or whether a man I didn't know and to this day I still don't know, but only that he said a prayer in the darkness, and taking me by the shoulder led me with my chain to the bench and sat me down, and put a spoon in my hands and a tiny loaf, and gave me a dab of cabbage soup to sip—my, it was tasty, uncommonly good! And he said unto me, "Enough, that will suffice thee for thy strengthening." And he was gone. The doors didn't open, but he was gone! It's amazing if it was a man, but what about an angel? Then there's nothing to be amazed about, there are no barriers to him anywhere.

In the morning the Archimandrite came with the brethren and led me out; they scolded me: "Why don't you submit to the Patriarch?" But I blasted and barked at him from Holy Writ. They took off the big chain and put on a small one, turned me over to a monk for a guard, and ordered me hauled into the church. By the church they dragged at my hair and drummed on my sides; they jerked at my chain and spit in my eyes. God will forgive them in this age and that to come. It wasn't their doing but cunning Satan's. I was locked up there four weeks. . . .

After this they again led me on foot out of the monastery to the Patriarch's Court, as before stretching out my arms, and having contended much with me they led me away again the same way. Later, on St. Nikita's Day, there was a procession with crosses, but me they again carried in a cart, meeting the crosses on their way. And they carried me to the Cathredal Church to shear me, and kept me at the threshold for a long time during the Mass. The Sovereign came down from his place, and approaching the Patriarch he prevailed upon him. They didn't shear me, but led me off to the Siberia Office and handed me over to the secretary Tret'jak Bašmak, now the Elder Savatej who also suffers in Christ, locked up in a dungeon pit at Novospasskij. Save him, O Lord! And at that time he was good to me.

Later they exiled me to Siberia with my wife and children. And of our many privations on the road there is too much to tell, but maybe a small portion of them should be mentioned. The Archpriestess had a baby, and we carried her sick in a cart to Tobol'sk. For three thousand versts and about thirteen weeks we dragged along in carts, and by water and sledges one-half the way.

The Archbishop in Tobol'sk appointed me to a post. Here in this church great troubles overtook me. In a year and a half the Word of the Tsar was spoken against me five times, and one person in particular, the Secretary of the Archbishop's court Ivan Struna, he shook my soul. The Archbishop left for Moscow, and with him gone, because of the devil's instruction, he attacked me. . . .

Then a decree arrived. It was ordered that I be taken from Tobol'sk to the Lena river because I was blasting from Holy Writ and blistering the Nikonian heresy. During those times a short letter came to me from Moscow.

Two of my brothers lived up in the Tsarina's apartments, and both died during the plague along with their wives and children. And many of my friends and kinsmen died off. God poured forth the vials of his wrath upon the kingdom! And still those poor souls didn't come to their senses, and kept right on stirring up the Church. Then Neronov spoke, and he told the Tsar the three pestilences that come of schism in the Church: plague, the sword, and division. So it has come to pass now in our time. But the Lord is merciful. Having punished he has mercy on us in our repentance; having scattered the diseases of our bodies and souls he gives us peace I hope and trust in Christ. I await his compassion, and I tarry in hope for the resurrection of the dead.

So then I climbed into my boat again, the one that had been shown to me, of which I have spoken previously, and I journeyed to the Lena. But when I came to Yeniseisk another decree arrived; it ordered us to carry on into Daurija—this would be more than twenty thousand versts from Moscow. And they handed me over into the troop of Afanasij Paškov: the people there with him numbered six hundred. As a reward for my sins he was a harsh man; he burned and tortured and flogged people all the time. I had often tried to bring him to reason, and here I had fallen into his hands myself. And from Moscow he had orders from Nikon to afflict me.

After we had traveled out of Yeniseisk, when we were on the great Tunguska River, my prame was completely swamped by a storm; it filled full of water in the middle of the river, the sail was ripped to shreds, only the decks were above water, everything else had gone under. My wife, bareheaded, just barely dragged the children out of the water onto the decks. But looking to Heaven I shouted. "Lord, save us! Lord, help us!" And by God's will we were washed ashore. Much could be said about this! On another prame two men were swept away and drowned in the water. After putting ourselves to rights on the bank, we traveled on again.

When we came to the Šamanskij Rapids we met some people sailing the other way. With them were two widows, one about sixty and the other older; they were sailing to a convent to take the veil. But Paškov started to turn them around and wanted to give them in marriage. And I said to him, "According to the Canons it is not fitting to give such women in marriage." What would it cost him to listen to me and let the widows go? But no, being enraged he decided to afflict me. On another rapids, the Long Rapids, he started to kick me out of the prame. "Because of you," he says, "the prame don't go right! You're a heretic! Go walk through the mountains, you're not going with Cossacks!" Ah, misery came my way! The mountains were high, the forests dense, the cliffs of stone, standing like a wall—you'd crick your neck looking up! In those mountains are found great snakes; geese and ducklings with red plumage, black ravens, and grey jackdaws also live there. In those mountains are eagles and falcons and gerfalcons and mountain pheasants and pelicans and swans and other wild fowl, an endless abundance, birds of many kinds. In those mountains wander many wild beasts, goats and deer, Siberian stags and elk, wild boars, wolves, wild sheep—you'll lay your eyes on them but never your hands! Paškov drove me out into those mountains to live with the beasts and the snakes and the birds.

So I wrote him a short little epistle; the beginning went like this: "Man! Fear God, who sitteth above the Cherubim and gazeth into the abyss; before him the heavenly Powers do tremble and all creation together with mankind. Thou alone dost scorn and exhibit unseemliness"—and so on. A good bit was written there, and I sent it to him. And lo, about fifty men ran up, seized my prame, and rushed off to him (I was camped about three versts away from him). I cooked the Cossacks some porridge, and I fed them. The poor souls, they both ate and trembled, and others watching wept for me and pitied me. A prame was brought up, the executioners seized me and brought me before him. He stood there with a sword, all atremble, and started to speak to me. "Are you a frocked or unfrocked priest?" And I answered, "Verily, I am Avvakum the Archpriest. Speak! What is your business with me?" And he bellowed like a savage beast and hit me on one cheek, then on the other, again on top of my head, and knocked me down. Grabbing his commander's axe, he hit me three times on the back as I lay there, and stripping me, he laid seventy-two blows across that same back with a knout. But I was saying, "O Lord, Jesus Christ, Son of God, help me!" And I kept on saying the same thing, the same thing without let-up. So it was bitter for him that I was not saying, "Have mercy!" At every blow I said a prayer, but in the middle of the beating I cried out to him, "That's enough of this beating!" So he ordered it stopped. And I managed to say, "Why are you beating me? Do you know?" And he again ordered them to beat me, now on the ribs, and then they let me go. I began to tremble and fell down. And he ordered me dragged off to the ammunition prame; they chained my hands and feet and tossed me against the mast bracing.

It was autumn, rain was falling on me, and all night long I lay in the downpour. When they were beating, it didn't hurt then, what with the prayers, but lying there a thought strayed into my head: "O Son of God, why did you let him beat me so hard that way? You know I stood up for your widows! Who will set a judge between me and thee? You never shamed me this way when I thieved in the night! And this time I don't know how I've sinned!" There's a good man for you!—another shit-faced Pharisee wanting to drag the Lord to court! If Job spoke in this way, he was righteous and pure, and moreover had not fathomed Holy Writ; he was outside the Law, in a barbarous land, and knew God from his creation. But I, firstly, am sinful; secondly, I find repose in the Law and am supported in all things by Holy Writ, as "we must through tribulation enter into the Kingdom of God"—but I fell into such madness! Alas for me! Why wasn't that prame swamped by the water with me in it? And in those moments my bones started to ache, and my veins went stiff, and my heart gave out, yes and I started to die. Water splashed in my mouth, so I sighed and repented before God. The Lord our Light is merciful; he doth not recall against us our former transgressions, rewarding repentance. And again nothing was hurting.

In the morning they tossed me into a small boat and carried me onwards. When we reached the Padun Rapids, the biggest of them all—the river around that place is near a verst in width—they brought me right up to the rapids. Three cascades run across the whole river, fearfully steep; find the gates or your boat will be kindling! Down came the rain and snow, and only a poor little kaftan had been tossed across my shoulders. The water poured down my belly and back, terrible was my need. They dragged me out of the boat, then dragged me in chains across the rocks and around the rapids. Almighty miserable it was, but sweet for my soul! I wasn't grumbling at God a second time. The words spoken by the Prophet and Apostle came to mind: "My son, despise not thou the chastening of the Lord, nor faint when thou art rebuked of him. For whom God loveth he chasteneth, and scourgeth every son whom he receiveth. If ye endure chastening, God dealeth with you as with sons. But if ye partake of him without chastisement, then are ye bastards, and not sons." And with these words I comforted myself.

Afterwards they brought me to the Bratskij fortress and tossed me into the dungeon, and gave me a little pile of straw. And I was locked up till St. Philip's Fast in a freezing tower. Winter thrives there at that time, but God warmed me even without clothes! Like a little dog I lay on my lump of straw. Sometimes they fed me, sometimes not. The mice were plentiful, and I swatted them with my *skuf'ja*—the silly fools wouldn't even give me a stick. I lay on my belly all the time; my back was rotting. Plentiful too were the fleas and lice. I wanted to shout at Paškov, "Forgive me!" But the power of God did forefend it; it was ordained that I endure. He moved me to a warm hut, and there I lived the winter through in fetters along with hostages and dogs. But my wife and children were sent about twenty versts away from me. Her peasant woman Ksen'ja tormented her that whole winter long, all the time yapping and scolding. After Christmas my son Ivan, still a little boy, trudged over to stay with me awhile, and Paškov ordered him tossed into the freezing dungeon where I had been locked up. He spent the night, the little love, and almost froze to death. In the morning he ordered him thrown out, back to his mother. I didn't even get to see him. He dragged himself back to his mother—and frostbit his hands and feet.

In the spring we traveled on again. Not much space was given to supplies. One store was looted from top to bottom, books and extra clothes were taken away. But some other things still remained. On Lake Baikal I was swamped again. Along the river Xilok he made me haul on the tow-rope. The going was bitter hard on that river—there wasn't time for eating, much less for sleeping. All summer long we suffered. People keeled over and died from hauling in water, and my legs and belly turned blue. For two summers we tramped around in water, and in the winters we dragged ourselves over portages.

On that same Xilok River I was swamped for the third time. The little barge was torn away from the bank by the water; the other people's stayed there but mine was snatched up and away we went! My wife and children were left on the bank, and only the helmsman and I were swept away. The water was fast and it whirled the barge gunners high and bottom-side up, but I kept crawling up on it, and myself shouted, "Queen of Heaven, help us! Our Hope, don't drown us!" Sometimes my legs went under, sometimes I crawled up on top. We were carried more than a verst, then some people snared us. Everything was smashed to bits! But what could be done if Christ and the most immaculate Mother of God deigned it so? I was laughing after coming out of the water, but the people there were oh'ing and ah'ing as they hung my clothes around on bushes, satin and taffeta coats and some other trifles. We still had a good bit left in chests and sacks. After this everything rotted through, and we were left naked. But Paškov wanted to flog me again: "You're making a laughing-stock of yourself," he said. So once again I pestered our Light, the Mother of God: "Queen of Heaven, calm that fool!" So she, our great Hope, she calmed him down: he started to take pity on me.

Then we moved to Lake Irgen. A portage is there and during the winter we started hauling. He took away my workers but wouldn't order others hired in their places. And the children were little—many to eat but no one to work. All alone this poor, miseried old Archpriest made a dogsled, and the winter long he dragged himself over the portage....

And in these privations two of my little sons died, and with the others we somehow suffered on, roaming naked and barefoot through the mountains and over sharp rocks, keeping body and soul together with grasses and roots. And I myself, sinner that I am, I both willingly and unwillingly partook of the flesh of mares and the carrion of beasts and birds. Alas for my sinful soul! "Who will give my head water and a fountain of tears that I might weep for my poor soul," which I wickedly sullied with worldly pleasures? But we were helped in the name of Christ by the Boyarina, the Commander's daughter-in-law Evdokija Kirillovna, yes and by Afanasij's wife Fekla Simeonovna too. They gave us relief against starvation secretly, without his knowing. Sometimes they sent a little piece of meat, sometimes a small round loaf, sometimes a bit of flour and oats, as much as could be scraped together, a quarter pood and maybe a pound or two more, sometimes she saved up a good half pood and sent it over, and sometimes she raked feed out of the chicken trough. My daughter Agrafena, the poor little love, on the sly she would wander over under the Boyarina's window. And we didn't know whether to laugh or cry! Sometimes they'd drive the little child away from the window without the Boyarina's knowing, but sometimes she'd drag back a good bit. She was a little girl then, but now she's twenty-seven and still unmarried. My poor, dear daughter, now she lives in tears at Mezen with her younger sisters, keeping body and soul together somehow. And her mother and brothers sit locked up, buried in the earth. But what's to be done? Let those broken hearts suffer for the sake of Christ. So be it, with God's help. For it is ordained that we must suffer, we must suffer for the sake of the Christian faith. You loved, Archpriest, of the famed to be friend; love then to endure, poor wretch, to the end! It is written: "Blessed is not he that begins, but he that has finished." But enough of this. Let's get back to my story. . . . For five weeks we traveled by dogsled over naked ice. He gave me two miserable old nags for the little ones and for our pitiful belongings, but the Archpriestess and myself trudged along on foot; stumbling and hurting ourselves on the ice. The land was barbarous, the natives hostile. We dared not leave the horses at length; keeping up with them was outside our strength—starving and weary people we were. The poor Archpriestess tottered and trudged along, and then she'd fall in a heap—fearfully slippery it was! Once she was trudging along, and she caved in, and another just as weary trudged up into her and right there caved in himself. They were both ashouting, but they couldn't get up. The peasant was shouting, "Little mother, my Lady, forgive me!" But the Archpriestess was shouting, "Why'd you crush me, father?" I came up, and the poor dear started in on me, saying, "Will these sufferings go on a long time, Archpriest?" And I said, "Markovna, right up to our very death." And so she sighed and answered, "Good enough, Petrovič, then let's be getting on."

A preacher in the English Nonconformist Church, John Bunyan is best known for his allegorical work, *Pilgrim's Progress*, which describes the travels of Christian through various dangers to a secure position in the Kingdom of Heaven. In the work excerpted here, *Grace Abounding to the Chief of Sinners*, Bunyan gives us his own autobiography, composed in prison, to which he was sentenced for preaching without a license. In this uniquely probing and introspective work, Bunyan describes a psychic life of violent mood swings: from a momentary sense of security with God, Bunyan plunges into the anxious conviction that he is irredeemably destined for hellfire. At the end of his lengthy travail with his own doubts and fears, Bunyan grasps at the doctrine of the grace of God, which makes forgiveness and redemption available at all times to all souls without requirement of any action except the profession of faith.   [AM]

JOHN BUNYAN

[1 6 2 8 – 1 6 8 8]

I have encouragement

to come to God.

FROM *GRACE ABOUNDING*

1. In this my relation of the merciful working of God upon my soul, it will not be amiss, if, in the first place, I do, in a few words, give you a hint of my pedigree, and manner of bringing up; that thereby the goodness and bounty of God towards me, may be the more advanced and magnified before the sons of men.

2. For my descent then, it was, as is well known by many, of a low and inconsiderable generation; my father's house being of that rank that is mean-est and most despised of all the families in the land. Wherefore I have not here, as others, to boast of noble blood, or of a high-born state, according to the flesh; though, all things considered, I magnify the heavenly Majesty, for that by this door He brought me into this world, to partake of the grace and life that is in Christ by the gospel.

3. But yet, notwithstanding the meanness and inconsiderableness of my parents, it pleased God to put it into their hearts to put me to school, to learn both to read and write; the which I also attained, according to the rate of other poor men's children; though, to my shame I confess, I did soon lose that little I learned, and that even almost utterly, and that long before the Lord did work His gracious work of conversion upon my soul.

4. As for my own natural life, for the time that I was without God in the world, it was indeed according to the course of this world, and "the spirit that now worketh in the children of disobedience" (Eph. 2.2, 3). It was my delight to be "taken captive by the devil at his will" (II Tim. 2.26). Being filled with all unrighteousness, the which did also so strongly work and put forth itself, both in my heart and life, and that from a child, that I had but few equals, especially considering my years, which were tender, being few, both for cursing, swearing, lying, and blaspheming the holy name of God.

5. Yea, so settled and rooted was I in these things, that they became as a second nature to me; the which, as I also have with soberness considered since, did so offend the Lord, that even in my childhood He did scare and affright me with fearful dreams, and did terrify me with dreadful visions; for often, after I had spent this and the other day in sin, I have in my bed been greatly afflicted, while asleep, with the apprehensions of devils and wicked spirits, who still, as I then thought, laboured to draw me away with them, of which I could never be rid.

6. Also I should, at these years, be greatly afflicted and troubled with the thoughts of the day of judgment, and that both night and day, and should tremble at the thoughts of the fearful torments of hell fire; still fearing that

it would be my lot to be found at last amongst those devils and hellish fiends, who are there bound down with the chains and bonds of eternal darkness, "unto the judgment of the great day."

7. These things, I say, when I was but a child but nine or ten years old, did so distress my soul, that when in the midst of my many sports and childish vanities, amidst my vain companions, I was often much cast down and afflicted in my mind therewith, yet could I not let go my sins. Yea, I was also then so overcome with despair of life and heaven, that I should often wish either that there had been no hell, or that I had been a devil—supposing they were only tormentors; that if it must needs be that I went thither, I might be rather a tormentor, than be tormented myself.

8. A while after, these terrible dreams did leave me, which also I soon forgot; for my pleasures did quickly cut off the remembrance of them, as if they had never been: wherefore, with more greediness, according to the strength of nature, I did still let loose the reins to my lusts, and delighted in all transgression against the law of God: so that, until I came to the state of marriage, I was the very ringleader of all the youth that kept me company, into all manner of vice and ungodliness.

9. Yea, such prevalency had the lusts and fruits of the flesh in this poor soul of mine, that had not a miracle of precious grace prevented, I had not only perished by the stroke of eternal justice, but had also laid myself open, even to the stroke of those laws, which bring some to disgrace and open shame before the face of the world.

10. In these days, the thoughts of religion were very grievous to me; I could neither endure it myself, nor that any other should; so that, when I have seen some read in those books that concerned Christian piety, it would be as it were a prison to me. Then I said unto God, "Depart from me, for I desire not the knowledge of thy ways" (Job 21.14). I was now void of all good consideration, heaven and hell were both out of sight and mind; and as for saving and damning, they were least in my thoughts. O Lord, thou knowest my life, and my ways were not hid from Thee.

11. Yet this I well remember, that though I could myself sin with the greatest delight and ease, and also take pleasure in the vileness of my companions; yet, even then, if I have at any time seen wicked things, by those who professed goodness, it would make my spirit tremble. As once, above all the rest, when I was in my height of vanity, yet hearing one to swear that was reckoned for a religious man, it had so great a stroke upon my spirit, that it made my heart to ache. . . .

13. This also have I taken notice of with thanksgiving; when I was a soldier, I, with others, were drawn out to go to such a place to besiege it; but when I was just ready to go, one of the company desired to go in my room; to which, when I had consented, he took my place; and coming to the siege,

as he stood sentinel, he was shot into the head with a musket bullet, and died.

14. Here, as I said, were judgments and mercy, but neither of them did awaken my soul to righteousness; wherefore I sinned still, and grew more and more rebellious against God, and careless of mine own salvation.

15. Presently after this, I changed my condition into a married state, and my mercy was to light upon a wife whose father was counted godly. This woman and I, though we came together as poor as poor might be, not having so much household stuff as a dish or spoon betwixt us both, yet this she had for her part, *The Plain Man's Pathway to Heaven*, and *The Practice of Piety*, which her father had left her when he died. In these two books I should sometimes read with her, wherein I also found some things that were somewhat pleasing to me; but all this while I met with no conviction. She also would be often telling of me, what a godly man her father was, and how he would reprove and correct vice, both in his house, and amongst his neighbours; what a strict and holy life he lived in his day, both in word and deed.

16. Wherefore these books with this relation, though they did not reach my heart, to awaken it about my sad and sinful state, yet they did beget within me some desires to religion: so that, because I knew no better, I fell in very eagerly with the religion of the times; to wit, to go to church twice a day, and that too with the foremost; and there should very devoutly, both say and sing as others did, yet retaining my wicked life; but withal, I was so overrun with a spirit of superstition, that I adored, and that with great devotion, even all things, both the high place, priest, clerk, vestment, service, and what else belonging to the church; counting all things holy that were therein contained, and especially the priest and clerk most happy, and without doubt, greatly blessed, because they were the servants, as I then thought, of God, and were principal in the holy temple, to do His work therein.

17. This conceit grew so strong in little time upon my spirit, that had I but seen a priest, though never so sordid and debauched in his life, I should find my spirit fall under him, reverence him, and knit unto him: yea, I thought for the love I did bear unto them, supposing they were the ministers of God, I could have lain down at their feet, and have been trampled upon by them; their name, their garb, and work, did so intoxicate and bewitch me. . . .

19. But all this while, I was not sensible of the danger and evil of sin; I was kept from considering that sin would damn me, what religion soever I followed, unless I was found in Christ. Nay, I never thought of Him, nor whether there was one, or no. Thus man, while blind, doth wander, but wearieth himself with vanity, for he knoweth not the way to the city of God (Eccl. 10.15).

20. But one day, amongst all the sermons our parson made, his subject

was, to treat of the Sabbath-day, and of the evil of breaking that, either with labour, sports or otherwise. Now I was, notwithstanding my religion, one that took much delight in all manner of vice, and especially that was the day that I did solace myself therewith, wherefore I fell in my conscience under his sermon, thinking and believing that he made that sermon on purpose to show me my evil doing; and at that time I felt what guilt was, though never before, that I can remember; but then I was, for the present, greatly loaden therewith, and so went home when the sermon was ended, with a great burden upon my spirit.

21. This, for that instant, did benumb the sinews of my best delights, and did imbitter my former pleasures to me; but behold, it lasted not, for before I had well dined, the trouble began to go off my mind, and my heart returned to his old course: but oh! how glad was I, that this trouble was gone from me, and that the fire was put out, that I might sin again without control! Wherefore, when I had satisfied nature with my food, I shook the sermon out of my mind, and to my old custom of sports and gaming I returned with great delight.

22. But the same day, as I was in the midst of a game at cat, and having struck it one blow from the hole, just as I was about to strike it the second time, a voice did suddenly dart from heaven into my soul, which said, Wilt thou leave thy sins and go to heaven, or have thy sins and go to hell? At this I was put to an exceeding maze; wherefore, leaving my cat upon the ground, I looked up to heaven, and was as if I had, with the eyes of my understanding, seen the Lord Jesus looking down upon me, as being very hotly displeased with me, and as if He did severely threaten me with some grievous punishment for these and other my ungodly practices.

23. I had no sooner thus conceived in my mind, but suddenly this conclusion was fastened on my spirit, for the former hint did set my sins again before my face, that I had been a great and grievous sinner, and that it was now too late for me to look after heaven; for Christ would not forgive me, nor pardon my transgressions. Then I fell to musing upon this also; and while I was thinking on it and fearing lest it should be so, I felt my heart sink in despair, concluding it was too late; and therefore I resolved in my mind I would go on in sin; for, thought I, if the case be thus, my state is surely miserable; miserable if I leave my sins, and but miserable if I follow then; I can but be damned, and if I must be so, I had as good be damned for many sins, as to be damned for few.

24. Thus I stood in the midst of my play, before all that then were present; but yet I told them nothing: but I say, I having made this conclusion, I returned desperately to my sport again; and I well remember, that presently this kind of despair did so possess my soul, that I was persuaded I could never attain to other comfort than what I should get in sin; for heaven was

gone already, so that on that I must not think; wherefore I found within me a great desire to take my fill of sin, still studying what sin was set to be committed, that I might taste the sweetness of it; and I made as much haste as I could to fill my belly with its delicates, lest I should die before I had my desire; for that I feared greatly. In these things, I protest before God, I lie not, neither do I feign this sort of speech; these were really, strongly, and with all my heart, my desires; the good Lord, whose mercy is unsearchable, forgive me my transgressions. . . .

26. Now therefore I went on in sin with great greediness of mind, still grudging that I could not be so satisfied with it as I would. . . .

29. But quickly after this, I fell in company with one poor man that made profession of religion; who, as I then thought, did talk pleasantly of the Scriptures, and of the matters of religion; wherefore, falling into some love and liking to what he said, I betook me to my Bible, and began to take great pleasure in reading, but especially with the historical part thereof; for, as for Paul's epistles, and Scriptures of that nature, I could not away with them, being as yet but ignorant, either of the corruptions of my nature, or of the want and worth of Jesus Christ to save me.

30. Wherefore I fell to some outward reformation, both in my words and life, and did set the commandments before me for my way to heaven; which commandments I also did strive to keep, and, as I thought, did keep them pretty well sometimes, and then I should have comfort: yet now and then should break one, and so afflict my conscience: but then I should repent, and say I was sorry for it, and promise God to do better next time, and there get help again, for then I thought I pleased God as well as any man in England. . . .

36. But, poor wretch as I was, I was all this while ignorant of Jesus Christ, and going about to establish my own righteousness; and had perished therein, had not God, in mercy, showed me more of my state of nature.

37. But upon a day, the good providence of God did cast me to Bedford, to work on my calling; and in one of the streets of that town, I came where there were three or four poor women sitting at a door in the sun, and talking about the things of God; and being now willing to hear them discourse, I drew near to hear what they said, for I was now a brisk talker also myself in the matters of religion, but now I may say, I heard, but I understood not; for they were far above, out of my reach, for their talk was about a new birth, the work of God on their hearts, also how they were convinced of their miserable state by nature; they talked how God had visited their souls with His love in the Lord Jesus, and with what words and promises they had been refreshed, comforted, and supported against the temptations of the devil. Moreover, they reasoned of the suggestions and temptations of Satan in particular; and told to each other by which they had been afflicted, and how

they were borne up under his assaults. They also discoursed of their own wretchedness of heart, of their unbelief; and did contemn, slight, and abhor their own righteousness, as filthy and insufficient to do them any good.

38. And methought they spake as if joy did make them speak; they spake with such pleasantness of Scripture language, and with such appearance of grace in all they said, that they were to me as if they had found a new world, as if they were people that dwelt alone, and were not to be reckoned among their neighbours (Num. 23.9).

39. At this I felt my own heart began to shake, as mistrusting my condition to be naught; for I saw that in all my thoughts about religion and salvation, the new birth did never enter into my mind, neither knew I the comfort of the Word and promise, nor the deceitfulness and treachery of my own wicked heart. As for secret thoughts, I took no notice of them; neither did I understand what Satan's temptations were, nor how they were to be withstood and resisted, etc.

40. Thus, therefore, when I had heard and considered what they said, I left them, and went about my employment again, but their talk and discourse went with me; also my heart would tarry with them, for I was greatly affected with their words, both because by them I was convinced that I wanted the true tokens of a truly godly man, and also because by them I was convinced of the happy and blessed condition of him that was such a one.

41. Therefore I should often make it my business to be going again and again into the company of these poor people, for I could not stay away; and the more I went amongst them, the more I did question my condition; and as I still do remember, presently I found two things within me, at which I did sometimes marvel, especially considering what a blind, ignorant, sordid, and ungodly wretch but just before I was; the one was a great softness and tenderness of heart, which caused me to fall under the conviction of what by Scripture they asserted; and the other was a great bending in my mind to a continual meditating on it. and on all other good things which at any time I heard or read of.

42. By these things my mind was now so turned, that it lay like a horse leech at the vein, still crying out, Give, give (Prov. 30.15); yea, it was so fixed on eternity, and on the things about the kingdom of heaven, that is, so far as knew, though as yet, God knows, I knew but little; that neither pleasures nor profits, nor persuasions, nor threats, could loosen it, or make it let go his hold; and though I may speak it with shame, yet it is in very deed a certain truth, it would then have been as difficult for me to have taken my mind from heaven to earth, as I have found it often since to get it again from earth to heaven. . . .

46. And now, methought, I began to look into the Bible with new eyes, and read as I never did before; and especially the epistles of the apostle Paul

were sweet and pleasant to me; and, indeed, I was then never out of the Bible, either by reading or meditation; still crying out to God, that I might know the truth, and way to heaven and glory. . . .

I found, by reading the Word, that those that must be glorified with Christ in another world must be called by Him here; called to the partaking of a share in His Word and righteousness, and to the comforts and first fruits of His Spirit, and to a peculiar interest in all those heavenly things which do indeed fore fit the soul for that rest and house of glory which is in heaven above.

72. Here, again, I was at a very great stand, not knowing what to do, fearing I was not called; for, thought I, if I be not called, what then can do me good? None but those who are effectually called, inherit the kingdom of heaven. But oh! how I now loved those words that spake of a Christian's calling! as when the Lord said to one, "Follow me," and to another, "Come after me." And oh! Thought I, that He would say so to me too, how gladly would I run after him!

73. I cannot now express with what longings and breakings in my soul I cried to Christ to call me. Thus I continued for a time, all on a flame to be converted to Jesus Christ; and did also see at that day, such glory in a converted state, that I could not be contented without a share therein. Gold! could it have been gotten for gold, what could I have given for it! had I a whole world it had all gone ten thousand times over for this, that my soul might have been in a converted state. . . .

187. Thus was I always sinking, whatever I did think or do. So one day I walked to a neighbouring town, and sat down upon a settle in the street, and fell into a very deep pause about the most fearful state my sin had brought me to; and, after long musing, I lifted up my head, but methought I saw as if the sun that shineth in the heavens did grudge to give light, and as if the very stones in the street, and tiles upon the houses, did bend themselves against me; methought that they all combined together to banish me out of the world; I was abhorred of them, and unfit to dwell among them, or be partaker of their benefits, because I had sinned against the Saviour. O how happy, now, was every creature over what I was; for they stood fast and kept their station, but I was gone and lost.

188. Then breaking out in the bitterness of my soul, I said to myself, with a grievous sigh, How can God comfort such a wretch as I? I had no sooner said it but this returned upon me, as an echo doth answer a voice, This sin is not unto death. At which I was as if I had been raised out of a grave, and cried out again, Lord, how couldest Thou find out such a word as this? for I was filled with admiration at the fitness, and, also, at the unexpectedness of the sentence, the fitness of the word, the rightness of the timing of it, the power, and sweetness, and light, and glory that came with it, was marvellous

to me to find. I was now, for the time, out of doubt as to that about which I so much was in doubt before; my fears before were, that my sin was not pardonable, and so that I had no right to pray, to repent, etc., or that if I did, it would be of no advantage or profit to me. But now, thought I, if this sin is not unto death, then it is pardonable; therefore, from this I have encouragement to come to God, by Christ, for mercy, to consider the promise of forgiveness as that which stands with open arms to receive me, as well as others. This, therefore, was a great easement to my mind; to wit, that my sin was pardonable, that it was not the sin unto death (I John 5.16, 17). None but those that know what my trouble, by their own experience, was, can tell what relief came to my soul by this consideration; it was a release to me from my former bonds, and a shelter from my former storm. I seemed now to stand upon the same ground with other sinners, and to have as good right to the word and prayer as any of them.

JONATHAN
EDWARDS

[1 7 0 3 – 1 7 5 8]

I felt . . . an ardency of the soul to

be . . . emptied and annihilated; to

lie in the dust.

Because of his great erudition and literary genius, Jonathan Edwards, the leading Puritan theologian, scholar, and preacher of his time, has been called the American Milton or Saint Augustine. Certainly his scholarship—he was the most published American man of letters before 1800—and his role as the pastor of the "Great Awakening" revivalist movement, which spread from Northampton, Massachusetts, have made him the most notable Puritan in American history. His reputation as a "hellfire and damnation" preacher, based on the text of his most-read work, the sermon "Sinners in the Hands of an Angry God," does not convey what is actually known of his dry, reserved, and intellectual manner in the pulpit.

Edwards's firsthand observations of the religious revival in his own parish are entered in *A Faithful Narrative of the Surprising Work of God.* By all accounts happily married, Edwards frequently expressed envy at his wife's spiritual life, which spurred him to scholarly investigations of the shape of religious experience. He was one of the few scholars of his day uniquely fitted to the task as a result of his close observation of the revivals of Northampton and because of his unusual erudition in the fields of contemporary philosophy and psychology. He approached the analysis of spiritual conversion according to the epistemological doctrines of John Locke in his work *Religious Affections*. He also directed this type of analysis toward himself, writing a spiritual autobiography that simultaneously exemplifies and transcends the typical Puritan conversion testimonial. His love of the natural world and his early naturalist studies contribute to his experience of God as the superior creator of a sublime world and the lover of a crushed humanity.   [AM]

PERSONAL NARRATIVE

I had a variety of concerns and exercises about my soul from my childhood; but had two more remarkable seasons of awakening, before I met with that change, by which I was brought to those new dispositions, and that new sense of things, that I have since had. The first time was when I was a boy, some years before I went to college, at a time of remarkable awakening in my father's congregation. I was then very much affected for many months, and concerned about the things of religion, and my soul's salvation; and was abundant in duties. I used to pray five times a day in secret, and to spend much time in religious talk with other boys; and used to meet with them to pray together. I experienced I know not what kind of delight in religion. My mind was much engaged in it, and had much self-righteous pleasure; and it was my delight to abound in religious duties. I, with some of my schoolmates joined together, and built a booth in a swamp, in a very secret and retired place, for a place of prayer. And besides, I had particular secret places of my own in the woods, where I used to retire by myself; and used to be from time to time much affected. My affections seemed to be lively and easily moved, and I seemed to be in my element, when engaged in religious duties. And I am ready to think, many are deceived with such affections, and such a kind of delight, as I then had in religion, and mistake it for grace.

But in process of time, my convictions and affections wore off; and I entirely lost all those affections and delights, and left off secret prayer, at least as to any constant performance of it; and resumed like a dog to his vomit, and went on in ways of sin.

Indeed, I was at some times very uneasy, especially towards the latter part of the time of my being at college. Till it pleased God, in my last year at

college, at a time when I was in the midst of many uneasy thoughts about
the state of my soul, to seize me with a pleurisy; in which he brought me
nigh to the grave, and shook me over the pit of hell.

But yet, it was not long after my recovery, before I fell again into my old
ways of sin. But God would not suffer me to go on with any quietness; but I
had great and violent inward struggles: till after many conflicts with wicked
inclinations, and repeated resolutions, and bonds that I laid myself under by
a kind of vows to God, I was brought wholly to break off all former wicked
ways, and all ways of known outward sin; and to apply myself to seek my
salvation, and practice the duties of religion: but without that kind of affection and delight, that I had formerly experienced. My concern now
wrought more by inward struggles and conflicts, and self-reflections, I made
seeking my salvation the main business of my life. But yet it seems to me, I
sought after a miserable manner: which has made me sometimes since to
question, whether ever it issued in that which was saving, being ready to
doubt, whether such miserable seeking was ever succeeded. But yet I was
brought to seek salvation, in a manner that I never was before. I felt a spirit
to part with all things in the world, for an interest in Christ. My concern
continued and prevailed, with many exercising things and inward struggles;
but yet it never seemed to be proper to express my concern that I had, by
the name of terror.

From my childhood up, my mind had been wont to be full of objections
against the doctrine of God's sovereignty, in choosing whom he would to
eternal life, and rejecting whom he pleased; leaving them eternally to perish,
and be everlastingly tormented in hell. It used to appear like a horrible
doctrine to me. But I remember the time very well, when I seemed to be
convinced, and fully satisfied, as to this sovereignty of God, and his justice
in thus eternally disposing of men, according to his sovereign pleasure. But
never could give an account, how, or by what means, I was thus convinced;
not in the least imagining, in the time of it, nor a long time after, that there
was any extraordinary influence of God's Spirit in it but only that now I saw
further, and my reason apprehended the justice and reasonableness of it.
However, my mind rested in it; and it put an end to all those cavils and
objections, that I had till then abode with me, all the preceding part of my
life. And there has been a wonderful alteration in my mind, with respect to
the doctrine of God's sovereignty, from that day to this; so that I scarce ever
have found so much as the rising of an objection against God's sovereignty,
in the most absolute sense, in showing mercy on whom he will show mercy,
and hardening and eternally damning whom he will. God's absolute sovereignty, and justice, with respect to salvation and damnation, is what my mind
seems to rest assured of, as much as of anything that I see with my eyes; at
least it is so at times. But I have oftentimes since that first conviction, had
quite another kind of sense of God's sovereignty, than I had then. I have

often since, not only had a conviction, but a *delightful* conviction. The doctrine of God's sovereignty has very often appeared, an exceeding pleasant, bright and sweet doctrine to me: and absolute sovereignty is what I love to ascribe to God. But my first conviction was not with this.

The first that I remember that ever I found anything of that sort of inward, sweet delight in God and divine things, that I have lived much in since, was on reading those words, I Tim. 1:17. "Now unto the King eternal, immortal, invisible, the only wise God, be honor and glory forever and ever, Amen." As I read the words, there came into my soul, and was as it were diffused through it, a sense of the glory of the Divine Being; a new sense, quite different from anything I ever experienced before. Never any words of Scripture seemed to me as these words did. I thought with myself, how excellent a Being that was; and how happy I should be, if I might enjoy that God, and be wrapped up to God in heaven, and be as it were swallowed up in him. I kept saying, and as it were singing over these words of Scripture to myself; and went to prayer, to pray to God that I might enjoy him; and prayed in a manner quite different from what I used to do; with a new sort of affection. But it never came into my thought, that there was anything spiritual, or of a saving nature in this.

From about that time, I began to have a new kind of apprehensions and ideas of Christ, and the work of redemption, and the glorious way of salvation by him. I had an inward, sweet sense of these things, that at times came into my heart; and my soul was led away in pleasant views and contemplations of them. And my mind was greatly engaged, to spend my time in reading and meditating on Christ; and the beauty and excellency of his person, and the lovely way of salvation, by free grace in him. I found no books so delightful to me, as those that treated of these subjects. Those words, Cant. 2:1, used to be abundantly with me: "I am the rose of Sharon, the lily of the valleys." The words seemed to me, sweetly to represent, the loveliness and beauty of Jesus Christ. And the whole Book of Canticles used to be pleasant to me; and I used to be much in reading it, about that time. And found, from time to time, an inward sweetness, that used, as it were, to carry me away in my contemplations; in what I know not how to express otherwise, than by a calm, sweet abstraction of soul from all the concerns of this world; and a kind of vision, or fixed ideas and imaginations, of being alone in the mountains, or some solitary wilderness, far from all mankind, sweetly conversing with Christ, and wrapped and swallowed up in God. The sense I had of divine things, would often of a sudden as it were, kindle up a sweet burning in my heart; an ardor of my soul, that I know not how to express.

Not long after I first began to experience these things, I gave an account to my father, of some things that had passed in my mind. I was pretty much affected by the discourse we had together. And when the discourse was ended, I walked abroad alone, in a solitary place in my father's pasture, for contemplation. And as I was walking there, and looked up on the sky and clouds; there came into my mind, a sweet sense of the glorious majesty and grace of God, that I know not how to express. I seemed to see them both in a sweet conjunction: majesty and meekness joined together: it was a sweet and gentle, and holy majesty, and also a majestic meekness; an awful sweetness; a high, and great, and holy gentleness.

After this my sense of divine things gradually increased, and became more and more lively, and had more of that inward sweetness. The appearance of everything was altered: there seemed to be, as it were, a calm, sweet cast, or appearance of divine glory, in almost everything. God's excellency, his wisdom, his purity and love, seemed to appear in everything; in the sun, moon and stars; in the clouds, and blue sky, in the grass, flowers, trees; in the water, and all nature; which used greatly to fill my mind. I often used to sit and view the moon, for a long time; and so in the daytime, spent much time in viewing the clouds and sky, to behold the sweet glory of God in these things: in the meantime, singing forth with a low voice, my contemplations of the Creator and Redeemer. And scarce anything, among all the works of nature, was so sweet to me as thunder and lightning. Formerly, nothing had been so terrible to me. I used to be a person uncommonly terrified with thunder and it used to strike me with terror, when I saw a thunderstorm rising. But now, on the contrary, it rejoiced me. I felt God at the first appearance of a thunderstorm. And used to take the opportunity at such times, to fix myself to view the clouds, and see the lightnings play, and hear the majestic and awful voice of God's thunder: which oftentimes was exceeding entertaining, leading me to sweet contemplations of my great and glorious God. And while I viewed, used to spend my time, as it always seemed natural to me, to sing or chant forth my meditations; to speak my thoughts in soliloquies, and speak with a singing voice.

I felt then a great satisfaction as to my good estate. But that did not content me. I had vehement longings of soul after God and Christ, and after more holiness; wherewith my heart seemed to be full, and ready to break. . . .

My sense of divine things seemed gradually to increase, till I went to preach at New York; which was about a year and a half after they began. While I was there, I felt them, very sensibly, in a much higher degree, than I had done before. My longings after God and holiness, were much increased. Pure and humble, holy and heavenly Christianity, appeared exceeding amiable to me. I felt in me a burning desire to be in everything a complete Christian; and conformed to the blessed image of Christ: and that I might live in all things, according to the pure, sweet and blessed rules of the gospel. I had an eager thirsting after progress in these things. My longings after it, put me upon pursuing and pressing after them. It was my continual strife day and night, and constant inquiry, how I should be more holy, and live more holily, and more becoming a child of God, and disciple of Christ. I sought an increase of grace and holiness, and that I might live an holy life, with vastly more earnestness, than ever I sought grace, before I had it. . . .

The soul of a true Christian, as I then wrote my meditations, appeared like . . . a little white flower, as we see in the spring of the year; low and humble on the ground, opening its bosom, to receive the pleasant beams of the sun's glory; rejoicing as it were, in a calm rapture; diffusing around a sweet fragrancy, standing peacefully and lovingly, in the midst of other flowers round about; all in like manner opening their bosoms, to drink in the light of the sun.

There was no part of creature-holiness, that I then, and at other times, had so great a sense of the loveliness of, as humility, brokenness of heart and poverty of spirit: and there was nothing that I had such a spirit to long for. My heart as it were panted after this, to lie low before God, and in the dust; that I might be nothing, and that God might be all; that I might become as a little child.

While I was there at New York, I sometimes was much affected with reflections on my past life, considering how late it was, before I began to be truly religious; and how wickedly I had lived till then: and once so as to weep abundantly, and for a considerable time together.

On January 12, 1722–23, I made a solemn dedication of myself to God, and wrote it down; giving up myself, and all that I had to God; to be for the future in no respect my own; to act as one that had no right to himself, in any respect. And solemnly vowed to take God for my whole portion and felicity; looking on nothing else as any part of my happiness, nor acting as if it were: and his law for the constant rule of my obedience: engaging to fight with all my might, against the world, the flesh and the devil, to the end of my life. But have reason to be infinitely humbled, when I consider, how much I have failed of answering my obligation.

I had then abundance of sweet religious conversation in the family where I lived, with Mr. John Smith, and his pious mother. My heart was knit in affection to those, in whom were appearances of true piety; and I could bear the thoughts of no other companions, but such as were holy, and the disciples of the blessed Jesus.

I had great longings for the advancement of Christ's kingdom in the world. My secret prayer used to be in great part taken up in praying for it. . . . It was my comfort to think of that state, where there is fullness of joy; where reigns heavenly, sweet, calm and delightful love, without alloy; where there are continually the dearest expressions of this love; where is the enjoyment of the persons loved, without ever parting; where these persons that appear so lovely in this world, will really be inexpressibly more lovely, and full of love to us. And how sweetly will the mutual lovers join together to sing the praises of God and the Lamb! How full will it fill us with joy, to think, that this enjoyment, these sweet exercises will never cease or come to an end; but will last to all eternity!

Continued much in the same frame in the general, that I had been in at New York, till I went to New Haven, to live there as tutor of the College; having one special season of uncommon sweetness: particularly once at Bolton, in a journey from Boston, walking out alone in the fields. After I went to New Haven, I sunk in religion; my mind being diverted from my eager and violent pursuits after holiness, by some affairs that greatly perplexed and distracted my mind.

In September 1725, was taken ill at New Haven; and endeavoring to go home to Windsor, was so ill at the North Village, that I could go no further: where I lay sick for about a quarter of a year. And in this sickness, God was pleased to visit me again with the sweet influences of his Spirit. My mind was greatly engaged there on divine, pleasant contemplations, and longings of soul. I observed that those who watched with me, would often be looking out for the morning, and seemed to wish for it. Which brought to my mind those words of the Psalmist, which my soul with sweetness made its own language. "My soul waiteth for the Lord more than they that watch for the morning I say, more than they that watch for the morning" [Ps. 130:6]. And when the light of the morning came, and the beams of the sun came in at the windows, it refreshed my soul from one morning to another. It seemed to me to be some image of the sweet light of God's glory.

I remember, about that time, I used greatly to long for the conversion of some that I was concerned with. It seemed to me, I could gladly honor them, and with delight be a servant to them, and lie at their feet, if they were but truly holy.

But some time after this, I was again greatly diverted in my mind, with some temporal concerns, that exceedingly took up my thoughts, greatly to the wounding of my soul: and went on through various exercises, that it would be tedious to relate, that gave me much more experience of my own heart, than ever I had before.

Since I came to [Northampton], I have often had sweet complacency in God in views of his glorious perfections, and the excellency of Jesus Christ. God has appeared to me, a glorious and lovely Being, chiefly on the account of his holiness. The holiness of God has always appeared to me the most lovely of all his attributes. The doctrines of God's absolute sovereignty, and free grace, in showing mercy to whom he would show mercy, and man's absolute dependence on the operations of God's Holy Spirit, have very often appeared to me as sweet and glorious doctrines. These doctrines have been much my delight. God's sovereignty has ever appeared to me, as great part of his glory. It has often been sweet to me to go to God, and adore him as a sovereign God, and ask sovereign mercy of him.

I have loved the doctrines of the gospel: they have been to my soul like green pastures. The gospel has seemed to me to be the richest treasure; the treasure that I have most desired, and longed that it might dwell richly in me. The way of salvation by Christ, has appeared in a general way, glorious and excellent, and most pleasant and beautiful. It has often seemed to me, that it would in a great measure spoil heaven, to receive it in any other way. That text has often been affecting and delightful to me, Is. 32:2, "A man shall be an hiding place from the wind, and a covert from the tempest; as rivers of water in a dry place, as the shadow of a great rock in a weary land."

It has often appeared sweet to me, to be united to Christ, to have him for my head, and to be a member of his body, and also to have Christ for my teacher and prophet. I very often think with sweetness and longings and partings of soul, of being a little child, taking hold of Christ, to be led by him through the wilderness of this world. That text, Matt. 18, at the beginning, has often been sweet to me: "Except ye be converted, and become as little children, ye shall not enter into the kingdom of heaven." I love to think of coming to Christ, to receive salvation of him, poor in spirit, and quite empty of self; humbly exalting him alone; cut entirely off from my own root, and to grow into, and out of Christ: to have God in Christ to be all in all; and to live by faith on the Son of God, a life of humble, unfeigned confidence in him. That Scripture has often been sweet to me, Ps. 115:1, "Not unto us, O Lord, not unto us, but unto thy name give glory, for thy mercy, and for thy truth's sake." And those words of Christ, Luke 10:21, "In that hour Jesus rejoiced in spirit, and said, I thank thee, O Father, Lord of heaven and earth, that thou hast hid these things from the wise and prudent, and hast revealed them unto babes: even so, Father; for so it seemed good in thy sight." That sovereignty of God that Christ rejoiced in, seemed to me to be worthy to be rejoiced in; and that rejoicing of Christ, seemed to me to show the excellency of Christ, and the Spirit that he was of.

Sometimes only mentioning a single word, causes my heart to burn within me: or only seeing the name of Christ, or the name of some attribute of God. And God has appeared glorious to me, on account of the Trinity. It has made me have exalting thoughts of God, that he subsists in three persons; Father, Son, and Holy Ghost.

The sweetest joys of delights I have experienced, have not been those that have arisen from a hope of my own good estate; but in a direct view of the glorious things of the gospel. When I enjoy this sweetness, it seems to carry me above the thoughts of my own safe estate. It seems at such times a loss that I cannot bear, to take off my eye from the glorious, pleasant object I behold without me, to turn my eye in upon myself, and my own good estate.

My heart has been much on the advancement of Christ's kingdom in the world. The histories of the past advancement of Christ's kingdom, have been sweet to me. When I have read histories of past ages, the pleasantest thing in all my reading has been, to read of the kingdom of Christ being promoted. And when I have expected in my reading, to come to any such thing, I have plotted upon it all the way as I read. And my mind has been much entertained and delighted, with the Scripture promises and prophecies, of the future glorious advancement of Christ's kingdom on earth.

I have sometimes had a sense of the excellent fullness of Christ, and his meetness and suitableness as a Savior; whereby he has appeared to me, far above all, the chief of ten thousands. And his blood and atonement has appeared sweet, and his righteousness sweet, which is always accompanied with an ardency of spirit, and inward strugglings and breathings and groanings, that cannot be uttered, to be emptied of myself, and swallowed up in Christ.

Once, as I rid out into the woods for my health, anno 1737; and having lit from my horse in a retired place, as my manner commonly has been, to walk for divine contemplation and prayer; I had a view, that for me was extraordinary, of the glory of the Son of God; as mediator between God and man; and his wonderful, great, full, pure and sweet grace and love, and meek and gentle condescension. This grace, that appeared to me so calm and sweet, appeared great above the heavens. The person of Christ appeared ineffably excellent, with an excellency great enough to swallow up all thought and conception. Which continued, as near as I can judge, about an hour; which kept me, the bigger part of the time, in a flood of tears, and weeping aloud. I felt withal, an ardency of soul to be, what I know not otherwise how to express, than to be emptied and annihilated; to lie in the dust, and to be full of Christ alone; to love him with a holy and pure love; to trust in him; to live upon him; to serve and follow him, and to be totally wrapped up in the fullness of Christ, and to be perfectly sanctified and made pure, with a divine and heavenly purity. I have several other times, had views very much of the same nature, and that have had the same effects.

I have many times had a sense of the glory of the third person in the Trinity, in his office of sanctifier; in his holy operations communicating divine light and life to the soul. God in the communications of his Holy Spirit, has appeared as an infinite fountain of divine glory and sweetness; being full and sufficient to fill and satisfy the soul: pouring forth itself in sweet communications, like the sun in its glory, sweetly and pleasantly diffusing light and Life.

I have sometimes had an affecting sense of the excellency of the Word of God, as a Word of life; as the light of life; a sweet, excellent, life-giving Word: accompanied with a thirsting after that Word, that it might dwell richly in my heart.

I have often since I lived in this town, had very affecting views of my own sinfulness and vileness; very frequently so as to hold me in a kind of loud weeping, sometimes for a considerable time together: so that I have often been forced to shut myself up. I have had a vastly greater sense of my own wickedness, and the badness of my heart, since my conversion, than ever I had before. It has often appeared to me, that if God should mark iniquity against me, I should appear the very worst of all mankind; of all that have been since the beginning of the world to this time: and that I should have by far the lowest place in hell. When others that have come to talk with me about their soul concerns, have expressed the sense they have had of their own wickedness, by saying that it seemed to them, that they were as bad as the devil himself; I thought their expressions seemed exceeding faint and feeble, to represent my wickedness. I thought I should wonder, that they should content themselves with such expressions as these, if I had any reason to imagine, that their sin bore any proportion to mine. It seemed to me, I should wonder at myself, if I should express *my* wickedness in such feeble terms as they did.

My wickedness, as I am in myself, has long appeared to me perfectly ineffable, and infinitely swallowing up all thought and imagination; like an infinite deluge, or infinite mountains over my head. I know not how to express better, what my sins appear to me to be, than by heaping infinite upon infinite, and multiplying infinite by infinite. I go about very often, for this many years, with these expressions in my mind, and in my mouth, "Infinite upon Infinite. Infinite upon Infinite!" When I look into my heart, and take a view of my wickedness, it looks like an abyss infinitely deeper than hell. And it appears to me, that were it not for free grace, exalted and raised up to the infinite height of all the fullness and glory of the great Jehovah, and the arm of his power and grace stretched forth, in all the majesty of his power, and in all the glory of his sovereignty; I should appear sunk down in my sins infinitely below hell itself, far beyond sight of everything, but the piercing eye of God's grace, that can pierce even down to such a depth, and to the bottom of such an abyss.

And yet, I ben't in the least inclined to think, that I have a greater conviction of sin than ordinary. It seems to me, my conviction of sin is exceeding small, and faint. It appears to me enough to amaze me, that I have no more sense of my sin. I know certainly, that I have very little sense of my sinfulness. That my sins appear to me so great, don't seem to me to be, because I have so much more conviction of sin than other Christians, but because I am so much worse, and have so much more wickedness to be convinced of. When I have had these turns of weeping and crying for my sins, I thought I knew in the time of it, that my repentance was nothing to my sin.

I have greatly longed of late, for a broken heart, and to lie low before

God. And when I ask for humility of God, I can't bear the thoughts of being no more humble, than other Christians. It seems to me, that though their degrees of humility may be suitable for them; yet it would be a vile self-exaltation in me, not to be the lowest in humility of all mankind. Others speak of their longing to be humbled to the dust. Though that may be a proper expression for them, I always think for myself; that I ought to be humbled down below hell. 'Tis an expression that it has long been natural for me to use in prayer to God. I ought to lie infinitely low before God.

It is affecting to me to think, how ignorant I was, when I was a young Christian, of the bottomless, infinite depths of wickedness, pride, hypocrisy and deceit left in my heart.

I have vastly a greater sense, of my universal, exceeding dependence on God's grace and strength, and mere good pleasure, of late, than I used formerly to have; and have experienced more of an abhorrence of my own righteousness. The thought of any comfort or joy, arising in me, on any consideration, or reflection on my own amiableness, or any of my perfor-mances or experiences, or any goodness of heart or life, is nauseous and detestable to me. And yet I am greatly afflicted with a proud and self-righteous spirit; much more sensibly, than I used to be formerly. I see that serpent rising and putting forth its head, continually, everywhere, all around me.

Though it seems to me, that in some respects I was a far better Christian, for two or three years after my first conversion, than I am now, and lived in a more constant delight and pleasure: yet of late years, I have had a more full and constant sense of the absolute sovereignty of God, and a delight in that sovereignty, and have had more of a sense of the glory of Christ, as a media-tor, as revealed in the gospel. On one Saturday night in particular, I had a particular discovery of the excellency of the gospel of Christ, above all other doctrines; so that I could not but say to myself; "This is my chosen light, my chosen doctrine": and of Christ, "This is my chosen prophet." It appeared to me to be sweet beyond all expression, to follow Christ, and to be taught and enlightened and instructed by him; to learn of him, and live to him.

Another Saturday night, January 1738–39, I had such a sense, how sweet and blessed a thing it was, to walk in the way of duty, to do that which was right and meet to be done, and agreeable to the holy mind of God; that it caused me to break forth into a kind of a loud weeping, which held me some time; so that I was forced to shut myself up, and fasten the doors. I could not but as it were cry out, "How happy are they which do that which is right in the sight of God! They are blessed indeed, they are the happy ones!" I had at the same time, a very affecting sense, how meet and suitable it was that God should govern the world, and order all things according to his own pleasure; and I rejoiced in it, that God reigned, and that his will was done.

Founder of the Methodist movement in the Church of England, John Wesley was influenced by the Moravian Brotherhood, a sect emphasizing reliance on faith, and by Martin Luther's theology. Convinced that his calling was to teach his understanding of salvation by faith, Wesley adopted the life of an itinerant missionary, only returning home in his late eighties. Educated at Oxford and ordained a priest, Wesley and his brother Charles—later the author of more than seven thousand hymns—founded a Bible study group at Oxford called the Holy Club. The members of this club were often derisively referred to as "methodists," a designation that came to define an entire denomination. In the passage presented here, John Wesley recounts his early struggles to approach God.   [AM]

JOHN WESLEY

[1 7 0 3 – 1 7 9 1]

My soul waiting on Him

continually . . .

FROM *THE JOURNAL OF JOHN WESLEY*

What occurred on *Wednesday* the 24th, I think best to relate at large, after premissing what may make it the better understood. Let him that cannot receive it ask of the Father of lights that He would give more light to him and me.

1. I believe, till I was about ten years old I had not sinned away that "washing of the Holy Ghost" which was given me in baptism, having been strictly educated and carefully taught that I could only be saved "by universal obedience, by keeping all the commandments of God"; in the meaning of which I was diligently instructed. And those instructions, so far as they respected outward duties and sins, I gladly received and often thought of. But all that was said to me of inward obedience or holiness I neither understood nor remembered. So that I was indeed as ignorant of the true meaning of the law as I was of the gospel of Christ.

2. The next six or seven years were spent at school; where, outward restraints being removed, I was much more negligent than before, even of outward duties, and almost continually guilty of outward sins, which I knew to be such, though they were not scandalous in the eye of the world. However, I still read the Scriptures, and said my prayers morning and evening. And what I now hoped to be saved by, was (1) not being so bad as other people; (2) having still a kindness for religion; and (3) reading the Bible, going to church, and saying my prayers.

3. Being removed to the University for five years, I still said my prayers both in public and in private, and read, with the Scriptures, several other books of religion, especially comments on the New Testament. Yet I had not all this while so much as a notion of inward holiness; nay, went on habitually, and for the most part very contentedly, in some or other known sin: indeed, with some intermission and short struggles, especially before and after the Holy Communion, which I was obliged to receive thrice a year. I cannot well tell what I hoped to be saved by now, when I was continually sinning against that little light I had; unless by those transient fits of what many divines taught me to call repentance.

4. When I was about twenty-two, my father pressed me to enter into holy orders. At the same time, the providence of God directing me to Kempis's *Christian Pattern*, I began to see, that true religion was seated in the heart, and that God's law extended to all our thoughts as well as words and actions. I was, however, very angry at Kempis for being too strict; though I read him only in Dean Stanhope's translation. Yet I had frequently much sensible comfort in reading him, such as I was an utter stranger to before; and meeting

likewise with a religious friend, which I never had till now, I began to alter the whole form of my conversation, and to set in earnest upon a new life. I set apart an hour or two a day for religious retirement. I communicated every week. I watched against all sin, whether in word or deed. I began to aim at, and pray for, inward holiness. So that now, "doing so much, and living so good a life," I doubted not but I was a good Christian.

5. Removing soon after to another College, I executed a resolution which I was before convinced was of the utmost importance,—shaking off at once all my trifling acquaintance—I began to see more and more the value of time. I applied myself closer to study. I watched more carefully against actual sins; I advised others to be religious, according to that scheme of religion by which I modelled my own life. But meeting now with Mr. Law's *Christian Perfection* and *Serious Call*, although I was much offended at many parts of both, yet they convinced me more than ever of the exceeding height and breadth and depth of the law of God. The light flowed in so mightily upon my soul, that everything appeared in a new view. I cried to God for help, and resolved not to prolong the time of obeying Him as I had never done before. And by my continued endeavour to keep His whole law, inward and outward, to the utmost of my power, I was persuaded that I should be accepted of Him, and that I was even then in a state of salvation.

6. In 1730 I began visiting the prisons; assisting the poor and sick in town; and doing what other good I could, by my presence or my little fortune, to the bodies and souls of all men. To this end I abridged myself of all superfluities, and many that are called necessaries of life. I soon became a by-word for so doing, and I rejoiced that my name was cast out as evil. The next spring I began observing the Wednesday and Friday Fasts commonly observed in the ancient Church: tasting no food till three in the afternoon. And now I knew not how to go any further. I diligently strove against all sin. I omitted no sort of self-denial which I thought lawful; I carefully used, both in public and in private, all the means of grace at all opportunities. I omitted no occasion of doing good; I for that reason suffered evil. And all this I knew to be nothing, unless as it was directed toward inward holiness. Accordingly this, the image of God, was what I aimed at in all, by doing His will, not my own. Yet when, after continuing some years in this course, I apprehended myself to be near death, I could not find that all this gave me any comfort or any assurance of acceptance with God. At this I was then not a little surprised; not imagining I had been all this time building on the sand, nor considering that "other foundation can no man lay than that which is laid" by God, "even Christ Jesus."

7. Soon after, a contemplative man "convinced me still more than I was convinced before, that outward works are nothing, being alone; and in several conversations instructed me how to pursue inward holiness, or a union of the

soul with God. But even of his instructions (though I then received them as the words of God) I cannot but now observe (1) that he spoke so incautiously against trusting in outward works, that he discouraged me from doing them at all; (2) that he recommended (as it were, to supply what was wanting in them) *mental prayer,* and the like exercises, as the most effectual means of purifying the soul and uniting it with God. Now these were, in truth, as much my own works as visiting the sick or clothing the naked; and the union with God thus pursued was as really my own righteousness as any I had before pursued under another name.

8. In this refined way of trusting to my own works and my own righteousness (so zealously inculcated by the Mystic writers), I dragged on heavily, finding no comfort or help therein till the time of my leaving England. On shipboard, however, I was again active in outward works; where it pleased God of His free mercy to give me twenty-six of the Moravian brethren for companions, who endeavoured to show me "a more excellent way." But I understood it not at first. I was too learned and too wise. So that it seemed foolishness unto me. And I continued preaching, and following after, and trusting in, that righteousness whereby no flesh can be justified.

9. All the time I was at Savannah I was thus beating the air. Being ignorant of the righteousness of Christ, which, by a living faith in Him, bringeth salvation "to every one that believeth," I sought to establish my own righteousness; and so labored in the fire all my days. I was now properly "under the law"; I knew that "the law" of God was "spiritual; I consented to it that it was good." Yea, "I delighted in it, after the inner man." Yet was I "carnal, sold under sin." Every day was I constrained to cry out, "What I do, I allow not: for what I would, I do not; but what I hate, that I do." To will is indeed "present with me: but how to perform that which is good, I find not. For the good which I would, I do not; but the evil which I would not, that I do. I find a law, that when I would do good, evil is present with me": even "the law in my members, warring against the law of my mind," and still "bringing me into captivity to the law of sin."

10. In this vile, abject state of bondage to sin, I was indeed fighting continually, but not conquering. Before, I had willingly served sin: now it was unwillingly; but still I served it. I fell, and rose, and fell again. Sometimes I was overcome, and in heaviness: sometimes I overcame, and was in joy. For as in the former state I had some foretastes of the terrors of the law; so had I in this, of the comforts of the gospel. During this whole struggle between nature and grace, which had now continued above ten years, I had many remarkable returns to prayer, especially when I was in trouble; I had many sensible comforts, which are indeed no other than short anticipations of the life of faith. But I was still "under the law," not "under grace" (the state most who are called Christians are content to live and die in); for I was only striving with, not freed from, sin. Neither had I the witness of the Spirit

with my spirit, and indeed could not; for I "sought it not by faith, but as it were by the works of the law."

11. In my return to England, January 1738, being in imminent danger of death, and very uneasy on that account, I was strongly convinced that the cause of that uneasiness was unbelief; and that the gaining a true, living faith was the "one thing needful" for me. But still I fixed not this faith on its right object: I meant only faith in God, not faith in or through Christ. Again, I knew not that I was wholly void of this faith; but only thought I had not enough of it. So that when Peter Böhler, whom God prepared for me as soon as I came to London, affirmed of true faith in Christ (which is but one) that it had those two fruits inseparably attending it, "dominion over sin and constant peace from a sense of forgiveness," I was quite amazed, and looked upon it as a new gospel. If this was so, it was clear I had not faith. But I was not willing to be convinced of this. Therefore I disputed with all my might, and laboured to prove that faith might be where these were not: for all the scriptures relating to this I had been long since taught to construe away; and to call all Presbyterians who spoke otherwise. Besides, I well saw no one could, in the nature of things, have such a sense of forgiveness, and not *feel* it. But I felt it not. If, then, there was no faith without this, all my pretensions to faith dropped at once.

12. When I met Peter Böhler again, he consented to put the dispute upon the issue which I desired, namely, Scripture and experience. I first consulted the Scripture. But when I set aside the glosses of men, and simply considered the words of God, comparing them together, endeavouring to illustrate the obscure by the plainer passages, I found they all made against me, and was forced to retreat to my last hold, "that experience would never agree with the *literal interpretation* of those scriptures. Nor could I therefore allow it to be true, till I found some living witnesses of it." He replied, he could show me such at any time; if I desired it, the next day. And accordingly the next day he came again with three others, all of whom testified, of their own personal experience, that a true living faith in Christ is inseparable from a sense of pardon for all past and freedom from all present sins. They added with one mouth that this faith was the gift, the free gift of God; and that He would surely bestow it upon every soul who earnestly and perseveringly sought it. I was now thoroughly convinced; and, by the grace of God, I resolved to seek it unto the end, (1) By absolutely renouncing all dependence, in whole or in part, upon *my own* works or righteousness; on which I had really grounded my hope of salvation, though I knew it not, from my youth up; (2) by adding to the constant use of all the other means of grace, continual prayer for this very thing, justifying, saving faith, a full reliance on the blood of Christ shed for *me;* a trust in Him, as *my* Christ, as *my* sole justification, sanctification, and redemption.

13. I continued thus to seek it (though with strange indifference, dullness,

and coldness, and unusually frequent relapses into sin) till *Wednesday*, May 24. I think it was about five this morning, that I opened my Testament on those words, Τὰ μέγιστα ἡμῖν καὶ τίμια ἐπαγγέλματα δεδώρηται, ἵνα γένησθε θείας κοινωνοὶ φύσεως. "There are given unto us exceeding great and precious promises, even that ye should be partakers of the divine nature" (2 Pet. i. 4). Just as I went out, I opened it again on those words, "Thou art not far from the kingdom of God." In the afternoon I was asked to go to St. Paul's. The anthem was, "Out of the deep have I called unto Thee, O Lord: Lord, hear my voice. O let Thine ears consider well the voice of my complaint. If Thou, Lord, wilt be extreme to mark what is done amiss, O Lord, who may abide it? For there is mercy with Thee; therefore shalt Thou be feared. O Israel, trust in the Lord: for with the Lord there is mercy, and with Him is plenteous redemption. And He shall redeem Israel from all his sins."

14. In the evening I went very unwillingly to a society in Aldersgate Street, where one was reading Luther's preface to the *Epistle to the Romans*. About a quarter before nine, while he was describing the change which God works in the heart through faith in Christ, I felt my heart strangely warmed. I felt I did trust in Christ, Christ alone for salvation; and an assurance was given me that He had taken away *my* sins, even *mine*, and saved *me* from the law of sin and death.

15. I began to pray with all my might for those who had in a more especial manner despitefully used me and persecuted me. I then testified openly to all there what I now first felt in my heart. But it was not long before the enemy suggested, "This cannot be faith; for where is thy joy?" Then was I taught that peace and victory over sin are essential to faith in the Captain of our salvation; but that, as to the transports of joy that usually attend the beginning of it, especially in those who have mourned deeply, God sometimes giveth, sometimes withholdeth them, according to the counsels of His own will.

16. After my return home, I was much buffeted with temptations; but cried out, and they fled away. They returned again and again. I as often lifted up my eyes, and He "sent me help from His holy place." And herein I found the difference between this and my former state chiefly consisted. I was striving, yea, fighting with all my might under the law, as well as under grace. But then I was sometimes, if not often, conquered; now, I was always conqueror.

17. *Thur. 25.*—The moment I awaked, "Jesus, Master," was in my heart and in my mouth; and I found all my strength lay in keeping my eye fixed upon Him, and my soul waiting on Him continually. Being again at St. Paul's in the afternoon, "My song shall be always of the loving-kindness of the Lord: with my mouth will I ever be showing forth Thy truth from one generation to another." Yet the enemy injected a fear, "If thou dost believe,

why is there not a more sensible change?" I answered (yet not I), "That I know not. But this I know, I have 'now peace with God.' And I sin not to-day, and Jesus my Master has forbid me to take thought for the morrow."

18. "But is not any sort of fear," continued the tempter, "a proof that thou dost not believe?" I desired my Master to answer for me, and opened His Book upon those words of St. Paul, "Without were fightings, within were fears." Then, inferred I, well may fears be within me; but I must go on, and tread them under my feet.

DAVID
LIVINGSTONE

[1 8 1 3 – 1 8 7 3]

His mercy has influenced my

conduct ever since.

One of the most re-
nowned of missionary
explorers, David Liv-
ingstone was sent to
Africa by the London Missionary Society.
His indomitable spirit enabled him to
push farther into the interior of Africa
than previous efforts. He discovered Vic-
toria Falls and furthered the search for
the origin of the Nile. An advocate for
the abolition of slavery, he championed
the cause of African self-rule and auton-
omy. The brief passage that follows describes his state of mind at the time of
making the commitment to missionary
life. It is excerpted from his autobiographical work, *Missionary Travels and Researches in South Africa.* [AM]

FROM *MISSIONARY TRAVELS AND RESEARCHES*
IN SOUTH AFRICA

Great pains had been taken by my parents to instill the doctrines of Christianity into my mind, and I had no difficulty in understanding the theory of our free salvation by the atonement of our Savior, but it was only about this time that I really began to feel the necessity and value of a personal application of the provisions of that atonement to my own case. The change was like what may be supposed would take place were it possible to cure a case of "color blindness." The perfect freeness with which the pardon of all our guilt is offered in God's book drew forth feelings of affectionate love to Him who bought us with his blood, and a sense of deep obligation to Him for his mercy has influenced, in some small measure, my conduct ever since. But I shall not again refer to the inner spiritual life which I believe then began, nor do I intend to specify with any prominence the evangelistic labors to which the love of Christ has since impelled me. This book will speak, not so much of what has been done, as of what still remains to be performed, before the Gospel can be said to be preached to all nations.

In the glow of love which Christianity inspires, I soon resolved to devote my life to the alleviation of human misery. Turning this idea over in my mind, I felt that to be a pioneer of Christianity in China might lead to the material benefit of some portions of that immense empire; and therefore set myself to obtain a medical education, in order to be qualified for that enterprise.

ANONYMOUS RUSSIAN PILGRIM

[CA. 1835]

My whole desire was fixed upon one

thing only.

The manuscript entitled "Candid Narratives of a Pilgrim to His Spiritual Father" was written by an unknown Russian serf at about the time of the Crimean War. In 1884, the manuscript was taken from the monastery at Mount Athos where it had been preserved; it was then copied and disseminated by the Abbot of Saint Michael's monastery at Kazan. In the two parts of the manuscript presented here, the pilgrim relates the story of his own life as a peasant, the hardships that induced him to take up pilgrimage as a way of life, and his spiritual apprenticeship to an elder in a monastery where he was initiated into the practice of continual inner prayer.

Wandering pilgrims were common in Russia; like the pilgrim in this account, they made their way from shrine to shrine, often in small groups, and were hosted along the way, often by noble families. Pilgrims and novices in the Russian monastic system usually attached themselves to a *starets*, or elder, who served as a spiritual director. The practice of unceasing internal prayer is a unique feature of Eastern Orthodox devotion, introduced in the tenth century by Saint Symeon the New Theologian. Similar to a chanted mantra, the unceasing prayer becomes the automatic center of each moment in the practitioner's life. This devotional practice became widespread in Russian monasteries in a movement called *hesychasm*. The writings of various hesychast theologians were collected in a volume entitled *The Philokalia*, a copy of which constituted this Russian pilgrim's only possession.   [AM]

FROM *THE WAY OF A PILGRIM*

By the grace of God I am a Christian man, by my actions a great sinner, and by calling a homeless wanderer of the humblest birth who roams from place to place. My worldly goods are a knapsack with some dried bread in it on my back, and in my breast-pocket a Bible. And that is all. . . .

I WAS BORN IN A VILLAGE IN THE GOVERNMENT OF OREL. AFTER THE death of our parents, there were just the two of us left, my brother and I, he was ten years old and I was two. We were adopted by our grandfather, a worthy old man and comfortably off. He kept an inn which stood on the main road, and thanks to his sheer goodness of heart, a lot of travellers put up there. My brother, who was a madcap child, spent most of his time running about in the village, but for my part I liked better to stay near my grandfather. On Sundays and festivals we used to go to church together, and at home my grandfather often used to read the Bible, this very Bible here, which now belongs to me. When my brother grew up he took to drink. Once when I was seven years old and we were both of us lying down on the stove, he pushed me so hard that I fell off and hurt my left arm, so that I have never been able to use it since, it is all withered up. My grandfather saw that I should never be fit to work on the land and taught me to read. As we had no spelling-book, he did so from this Bible. He pointed out the A's, and made me form words and learn to know the letters when I saw them. I scarcely know how myself, but, somehow, by saying things after him over and over again, I learned to read in the course of time. And later on, when my grandfather's sight grew weak he often made me read the Bible aloud to him, and he corrected me as he listened. There was a certain clerk who often came to our inn. He wrote a good hand and I liked watching him write. I copied his writing, and he began to teach me. He gave me paper and ink, he made me quill pens, and so I learned to write also. Grandfather was very pleased, and charged me thus, "God has granted you the gift of learning; it will make a man of you. Give thanks to God, and pray very often."

We used to attend all the services at church and we often had prayers at home. It was always my part to read the fifty-first psalm, and while I did so grandfather and grandmother made their prostrations or knelt. When I was seventeen I lost my grandmother. Then grandfather said to me, "This house of ours no longer has a mistress, and that is not well. Your brother is a worthless fellow. I am going to look for a wife for you, you must get married." I was against the idea, saying that I was a cripple, but my grandfather would not give way. He found a worthy and sensible young girl about twenty years of age and I married her. A year later my grandfather fell very ill. Knowing that his death was near, he called for me, and bade me farewell, saying, "I leave you my house and all I have. Obey your conscience, deceive no one, and above all pray to God; everything comes from Him. Trust in Him only. Go to church regularly, read your Bible, and remember me and your grand-mother in your prayers. Here is my money, that also I give you; there is a thousand roubles. Take care of it. Do not waste it, but do not be miserly either; give some of it to the poor and to God's church." After this he died, and I buried him.

My brother grew envious because the property had been left wholly to me. His anger against me grew, and the Enemy prompted him in this to such an extent that he even laid plans to kill me. In the end this is what he did one night while we were asleep and no guests were in the house. He broke into the room where the money was kept, stole the money from a chest and then set fire to the room. The fire had got a hold upon the whole building before we knew of it, and we only just escaped by jumping out of a window in our night clothes. The Bible was lying under our pillow, so we snatched it up and took it with us. As we watched our house burning we said to one another, "Thank God, the Bible is saved, that at least is some consolation in our grief." So everything we had was burnt, and my brother went off without a trace. Later on we heard that when he was in his cups he boasted of the fact that he had taken the money and burnt the house.

We were left naked and ruined, absolutely beggars. We borrowed some money as best we could, built a little hut, and took up the life of landless peasants. My wife was clever with her hands. She knitted, spun and sewed. People gave her jobs, and day and night she worked and kept me. Owing to the uselessness of my arm I could not even make bark shoes. She would do her knitting and spinning, and I would sit beside her and read the Bible. She would listen, and sometimes begin to cry. When I asked, "What are you crying about? At least we are alive, thank God!" she would answer, "It touches me so, that beautiful writing in the Bible."

Remembering what my grandfather had bidden us, we often fasted, every morning we said the Acathist of Our Lady, and at night we each made a thousand prostrations to avoid falling into temptation. Thus we lived quietly enough for two years. But this is what is so surprising—although we had no understanding of interior prayer offered in the heart and indeed had never heard of it, but prayed with the tongue only, and made our prostrations without thought like buffoons turning somersaults, yet in spite of all this the wish for prayer was there, and the long prayers we said without understanding did not seem tiring, indeed we liked them. Clearly it is true, as a certain teacher once told me, that a secret prayer lies hidden within the human heart. The man himself does not know it, yet working mysteriously within his soul, it urges him to prayer according to each man's knowledge and power.

After two years of this sort of life that we were leading, my wife was taken suddenly ill with a high fever. She was given her Communion and on the ninth day of her illness she died. I was now left entirely alone in the world. There was no sort of work that I could do; still I had to live, and it went against my conscience to beg. Beside that, I felt such grief at the loss of my wife that I did not know what to do with myself. When I happened to go into our little hut and caught sight of her clothes or perhaps a scarf, I burst into tears and even fell down senseless. So feeling I could no longer bear my grief living at home, I sold the hut for twenty roubles, and such clothes as there were of my own and my wife's I gave away to the poor. Because of my crippled arm I was given a passport which set me free once for all from public duties, and taking my beloved Bible I set straight off, without caring or thinking where I was going.

But after a while I began to think where I would go, and said to myself, "First of all I will go to Kiev. I will venerate the shrines of those who were pleasing to God, and ask for their help in my trouble." As soon as I had made up my mind to this, I began to feel better, and, a good deal comforted, I made my way to Kiev. Since that time, for the last thirteen years that is, I have gone on wandering from place to place, I have made the round of many churches and monasteries, but nowadays I am taking more and more to wandering over the steppes and fields. I do not know whether God will vouchsafe to let me go to Jerusalem. If it be His will, when the time comes my sinful bones may be laid to rest there.

ON THE 24TH SUNDAY AFTER PENTECOST I WENT TO CHURCH TO say my prayers there during the Liturgy. The first Epistle of St. Paul to the Thessalonians was being read, and among other words I heard these—*"Pray*

without ceasing." It was this text, more than any other, which forced itself upon my mind, and I began to think how it was possible to pray without ceasing, since a man has to concern himself with other things also in order to make a living. I looked at my Bible, and with my own eyes read the words which I had heard, *i.e.,* that we ought always, at all times and in all places, to pray with uplifted hands. I thought and thought, but knew not what to make of it. "What ought I to do?" I thought. "Where shall I find someone to explain it to me? I will go to the churches where famous preachers are to be heard; perhaps there I shall hear something which will throw light on it for me." I did so. I heard a number of very fine sermons on prayer; what prayer is, how much we need it, and what its fruits are; but no one said how one could succeed in prayer. I heard a sermon on spiritual prayer, and unceasing prayer, but how it was to be done was not pointed out.

Thus listening to sermons failed to give me what I wanted, and having had my fill of them without gaining understanding, I gave up going to hear public sermons. I settled on another plan—by God's help to look for some experienced and skilled person who would give me in conversation that teaching about unceasing prayer which drew me so urgently.

For a long time I wandered through many places. I read my Bible always, and everywhere I asked whether there was not in the neighbourhood a spiritual teacher, a devout and experienced guide, to be found. One day I was told that in a certain village a gentleman had long been living and seeking the salvation of his soul. He had a chapel in his house. He never left his estate, and he spent his time in prayer and reading devotional books. Hearing this, I ran rather than walked to the village named. I got there and found him.

"What do you want of me?" he asked.

"I have heard that you are a devout and clever person," said I. "In God's name please explain to me the meaning of the Apostle's words, *'Pray without ceasing.'* How is it possible to pray without ceasing? I want to know so much, but I cannot understand it all."

He was silent for a while and looked at me closely. Then he said: "Ceaseless interior prayer is a continual yearning of the human spirit towards God. To succeed in this consoling exercise we must pray more often to God to teach us to pray without ceasing. Pray more, and pray more fervently. It is prayer itself which will reveal to you how it can be achieved unceasingly; but it will take some time."

So saying, he had food brought to me, gave me money for my journey, and let me go.

He did not explain the matter.

Again I set off. I thought and thought, I read and read, I dwelt over and over again upon what this man had said to me, but I could not get to the bottom of it. Yet so greatly did I wish to understand that I could not sleep at night.

I walked at least a hundred and twenty-five miles, and then I came to a large town, a provincial capital, where I saw a monastery. At the inn where I stopped I heard it said that the Abbot was a man of great kindness, devout and hospitable. I went to see him. He met me in a very friendly manner, asked me to sit down, and offered me refreshment.

"I do not need refreshment, holy Father," I said, "but I beg you to give me some spiritual teaching. How can I save my soul?"

"What? Save your soul? Well, live according to the commandments, say your prayers, and you will be saved."

"But I hear it said that we should pray without ceasing, and I don't know how to pray without ceasing. I cannot even understand what unceasing prayer means. I beg you, Father, explain this to me."

"I don't know how to explain further, dear brother. But, stop a moment, I have a little book, and it is explained there." And he handed me St. Dmitri's book on *The Spiritual Education of the Inner Man*, saying, "Look, read this page."

I began to read as follows: "The words of the Apostle '*Pray without ceasing*' should be understood as referring to the creative prayer of the understanding. The understanding can always be reaching out towards God, and pray to Him unceasingly."

"But," I asked, "what is the method by which the understanding can always be turned towards God, never be disturbed, and pray without ceasing?"

"It is very difficult, even for one to whom God Himself gives such a gift," replied the Abbot.

He did not give me the explanation.

I spent the night at his house, and in the morning, thanking him for his kindly hospitality, I went on my way; where to, I did not know myself. My failure to understand made me sad, and by way of comforting myself I read my Bible. In this way I followed the main road for five days.

At last towards evening I was overtaken by an old man who looked like a cleric of some sort. In answer to my question he told me that he was a monk belonging to a monastery some six miles off the main road. He asked me to go there with him. "We take in pilgrims," said he, "and give them rest and food with devout persons in the guest house." I did not feel like going. So in reply I said that my peace of mind in no way depended upon my finding a resting-place, but upon finding spiritual teaching. Neither was I running after food, for I had plenty of dried bread in my knapsack.

"What sort of spiritual teaching are you wanting to get?" he asked me. "What is it puzzling you? Come now! Do come to our house, dear brother.

We have *startsi* [plural form of *starets*, elder] of ripe experience well able to give guidance to your soul and to set it upon the true path, in the light of the word of God and the writings of the holy Fathers."

"Well, it's like this, Father," said I. "About a year ago, while I was at the Liturgy, I heard a passage from the Epistles which bade men pray without ceasing. Failing to understand, I began to read my Bible, and there also in many places I found the divine command that we ought to pray at all times, in all places; not only while about our business, not only while awake, but even during sleep. *'I sleep, but my heart waketh.'* This surprised me very much, and I was at a loss to understand how it could be carried out and in what way it was to be done. A burning desire and thirst for knowledge awoke in me. Day and night the matter was never out of my mind. So I began to go to churches and to listen to sermons. But however many I heard, from not one of them did I get any teaching about how to pray without ceasing. They always talked about getting ready for prayer, or about its fruits and the like, without teaching one *how* to pray without ceasing, or what such prayer means. I have often read the Bible and there made sure of what I have heard. But meanwhile I have not reached the understanding that I long for, and so to this hour I am still uneasy and in doubt."

Then the old man crossed himself and spoke. "Thank God, my dear brother, for having revealed to you this unappeasable desire for unceasing interior prayer. Recognise in it the call of God, and calm yourself. Rest assured that what has hitherto been accomplished in you is the testing of the harmony of your own will with the voice of God. It has been granted to you to understand that the heavenly light of unceasing interior prayer is attained neither by the wisdom of this world, nor by the mere outward desire for knowledge, but that on the contrary it is found in poverty of spirit and in active experience in simplicity of heart. That is why it is not surprising that you have been unable to hear anything about the essential work of prayer, and to acquire the knowledge by which ceaseless activity in it is attained. Doubtless a great deal has been preached about prayer, and there is much about it in the teaching of various writers. But since for the most part all their reasonings are based upon speculation and the working of natural wisdom, and not upon active experience, they sermonise about the qualities of prayer, rather than about the nature of the thing itself. One argues beautifully about the necessity of prayer, another about its power and the blessing which attend it, a third again about the things which lead to perfection in prayer, *i.e.*, about the absolute necessity of zeal, an attentive mind, warmth of heart, purity of thought, reconciliation with one's enemies, humility, contrition, and so on. But what is prayer? And how does one learn to pray? Upon these questions, primary and essential as they are, one very rarely gets any precise enlightenment from present-day preachers. For these questions are more difficult to understand than all their arguments that I have just spoken of, and require mystical knowledge, not simply the learning of the schools. And the most deplorable thing of all is that the vain wisdom of the world compels them to apply the human standard to the divine. Many people reason quite the wrong way round about prayer, thinking that good actions and all sorts of preliminary measures render us capable of prayer. But quite the reverse is the case, it is prayer which bears fruit in good works and all the virtues. Those who reason so, take, incorrectly, the fruits and the results of prayer for the means of attaining it, and this is to depreciate the power of prayer. And it is quite contrary to Holy Scripture, for the Apostle Paul says, '*I exhort therefore that first of all supplications be made*' (I Tim., ii, 1). The first thing laid down in the Apostle's words about prayer is that the work of prayer comes before everything else: '*I exhort therefore that first of all . . .*' The Christian is bound to perform many good works, but before all else what he ought to do is to pray, for without prayer no other good work whatever can be accomplished. Without prayer he cannot find the way to the Lord, he cannot understand the truth, he cannot crucify the flesh with its passions and lusts, his heart cannot be enlightened with the light of Christ, he cannot be savingly united to God. None of those things can be effected unless they are preceded by constant prayer. I say 'constant,' for the perfection of prayer does not lie within our power; as the Apostle Paul says, '*For we know not what we should pray for as we ought*' (Rom. viii, 26). Consequently it is just to pray often, to pray always, which falls within our power as the means of attaining purity of prayer, which is the mother of all spiritual blessings." . . .

During this talk, we had almost reached the monastery. And so as not to lose touch with this wise old man, and to get what I wanted more quickly, I hastened to say, "Be so kind, Reverend Father, as to show me what prayer without ceasing means and how it is learnt. I see you know all about these things."

He took my request kindly and asked me into his cell. "Come in," said he; "I will give you a volume of the holy Fathers from which with God's help you can learn about prayer clearly and in detail."

We went into his cell and he began to speak as follows. "The continuous interior Prayer of Jesus is a constant uninterrupted calling upon the divine Name of Jesus with the lips, in the spirit, in the heart; while forming a mental picture of His constant presence, and imploring His grace, during every occupation, at all times, in all places, even during sleep. The appeal is couched in these terms, 'Lord Jesus Christ, have mercy on me.' One who accustoms himself to this appeal experiences as a result so deep a consolation and so great a need to offer the prayer always, that he can no longer live without it, and it will continue to voice itself within him of its own accord. Now do you understand what prayer without ceasing is?"

"Yes indeed, Father, and in God's name teach me how to gain the habit of it," I cried, filled with joy.

"Read this book," he said. "It is called *The Philokalia*, and it contains the full and detailed science of constant interior prayer, set forth by twenty-five holy Fathers. The book is marked by a lofty wisdom and is so profitable to use that it is considered the foremost and best manual of the contemplative spiritual life. As the revered Nicephorus said, 'It leads one to salvation without labour and sweat.' "

"Is it then more sublime and holy than the Bible?" I asked.

"No, it is not that. . . . Holy Scripture is a dazzling sun, and this book, *The Philokalia*, is the piece of glass which we use to enable us to contemplate the sun in its imperial splendour. Listen now, I am going to read you the sort of instruction it gives on unceasing interior prayer."

He opened the book, found the instruction by St. Simeon the New Theologian, and read: "Sit down alone and in silence. Lower your head, shut your eyes, breathe out gently and imagine yourself looking into your own heart. Carry your mind, *i.e.*, your thoughts, from your head to your heart. As you breathe out, say 'Lord Jesus Christ, have mercy on me.' Say it moving your lips gently, or simply say it in your mind. Try to put all other thoughts aside. Be calm, be patient, and repeat the process very frequently.". . .

The *starets* sent me away with his blessing and told me that while learning the Prayer I must always come back to him and tell him everything, making a very frank confession and report; for the inward process could not go on properly and successfully without the guidance of a teacher.

In church I felt a glowing eagerness to take all the pains I could to learn unceasing interior prayer, and I prayed to God to come to my help. Then I began to wonder how I should manage to see my *starets* again for counsel or confession, since leave was not given to remain for more than three days in the monastery guesthouse, and there were no houses near.

However, I learned that there was a village between two and three miles from the monastery. I went there to look for a place to live, and to my great happiness God showed me the thing I needed. A peasant hired me for the whole summer to look after his kitchen garden, and what is more gave me the use of a little thatched hut in it where I could live alone. God be praised! I had found a quiet place. And in this manner I took up my abode and began to learn interior prayer in the way I had been shown, and to go to see my *starets* from time to time.

For a week, alone in my garden, I steadily set myself to learn to pray without ceasing exactly as the *starets* had explained. At first things seemed to go very well. But then it tired me very much. I felt lazy and bored and overwhelmingly sleepy, and a cloud of all sorts of other thoughts closed round me. I went in distress to my *starets* and told him the state I was in.

He greeted me in a friendly way and said, "My dear brother, it is the attack of the world of darkness upon you. To that world, nothing is worse than heartfelt prayer on our part. And it is trying by every means to hinder you and to turn you aside from learning the Prayer. But all the same the enemy only does what God sees fit to allow, and no more than is necessary for us. It would appear that you need a further testing of your humility, and that it is too soon, therefore, for your unmeasured zeal to approach the loftiest entrance to the heart. You might fall into spiritual covetousness. I will read you a little instruction from *The Philokalia* upon such cases."

He turned to the teaching of Nicephorus and read, " 'If after a few attempts you do not succeed in reaching the realm of your heart in the way you have been taught, do what I am about to say, and by God's help you will find what you seek. The faculty of pronouncing words lies in the throat. Reject all other thoughts (you can do this if you will) and allow that faculty to repeat only the following words constantly, "Lord Jesus Christ, have mercy on me." Compel yourself to do it always. If you succeed for a time, then without a doubt your heart also will open to prayer. We know it from experience.'

"There you have the teaching of the holy Fathers on such cases," said my *starets*, "and therefore you ought from to-day onwards to carry out my directions with confidence, and repeat the Prayer of Jesus as often as possible. Here is a rosary. Take it, and to start with say the Prayer three thousand times a day. Whether you are standing or sitting, walking or lying down, continually repeat, 'Lord Jesus Christ, have mercy on me.' Say it quietly and without hurry, but without fail exactly three thousand times a day without deliberately increasing or diminishing the number. God will help you and by this means you will reach also the unceasing activity of the heart."

I gladly accepted this guidance and went home and began to carry out faithfully and exactly what my *starets* had bidden. For two days I found it rather difficult, but after that it became so easy and likeable, that as soon as I stopped, I felt a sort of need to go on saying the Prayer of Jesus, and I did it freely and willingly, not forcing myself to it as before.

I reported to my *starets*, and he bade me say the Prayer six thousand times a day, saying, "Be calm, just try as faithfully as possible to carry out the set number of prayers. God will vouchsafe you His grace."

In my lonely hut I said the Prayer of Jesus six thousand times a day for a whole week. I felt no anxiety. Taking no notice of any other thoughts however much they assailed me, I had but one object, *i.e.*, to carry out my *starets'* bidding exactly. And what happened? I grew so used to my Prayer that when I stopped for a single moment, I felt, so to speak, as though something were missing, as though I had lost something. The very moment I started the Prayer again, it went on easily and joyously. If I met anyone I had no wish to talk to him. All I wanted was to be alone and to say my Prayer, so used to it had I become in a week.

My *starets* had not seen me for ten days. On the eleventh day he came to see me himself, and I told him how things were going. He listened and said, "Now you have got used to the Prayer. See that you preserve the habit and strengthen it. Waste no time, therefore, but make up your mind by God's help from to-day to say the Prayer of Jesus twelve thousand times a day. Remain in your solitude, get up early, go to bed late, and come and ask advice of me every fortnight."

I did as he bade me. The first day I scarcely succeeded in finishing my task of saying twelve thousand prayers by late evening. The second day I did it easily and contentedly. To begin with, this ceaseless saying of the Prayer brought a certain amount of weariness, my tongue felt numbed, I had a stiff sort of feeling in my jaws, I had a feeling at first pleasant but afterwards slightly painful in the roof of my mouth. The thumb of my left hand, with which I counted my beads, hurt a little. I felt a slight inflammation in the whole of that wrist, and even up to the elbow, which was not unpleasant. Moreover, all this aroused me, as it were, and urged me on to frequent saying of the Prayer. For five days I did my set number of twelve thousand prayers, and as I formed the habit I found at the same time pleasure and satisfaction in it.

Early one morning the Prayer woke me up as it were. I started to say my usual morning prayers, but my tongue refused to say them easily or exactly. My whole desire was fixed upon one thing only—to say the Prayer of Jesus, and as soon as I went on with it I was filled with joy and relief. It was as though my lips and my tongue pronounced the words entirely of themselves without any urging from me. I spent the whole day in a state of the greatest contentment, I felt as though I was cut off from everything else. I lived as though in another world, and I easily finished my twelve thousand prayers by the early evening. I felt very much like still going on with them, but I did not dare to go beyond the number my *starets* had set me. Every day following I went on in the same way with my calling on the Name of Jesus Christ, and that with great readiness and liking. Then I went to see my *starets* and told him everything frankly and in detail.

He heard me out and then said, "Be thankful to God that this desire for the Prayer and this facility in it have been manifested in you. It is a natural consequence which follows constant effort and spiritual achievement. So a machine to the principal wheel of which one gives a drive, works for a long while afterwards by itself; but if it is to go on working still longer, one must oil it and give it another drive. Now you see with what admirable gifts God in His love for mankind has endowed even the bodily nature of man. You see what feelings can be produced even outside a state of grace in a soul which is sinful and with passions unsubdued, as you yourself have experienced. But how wonderful, how delightful and how consoling a thing it is when God is pleased to grant the gift of self-acting spiritual prayer, and to cleanse the soul from all sensuality! It is a condition which is impossible to describe, and the discovery of this mystery of prayer is a foretaste on earth of the bliss of Heaven. Such happiness is reserved for those who seek after God in the simplicity of a loving heart. Now I give you my permission to say your Prayer as often as you wish and as often as you can. Try to devote every moment you are awake to the Prayer, call on the Name of Jesus Christ without counting the number of times, and submit yourself humbly to the will of God, looking to Him for help. I am sure He will not forsake you, and that He will lead you into the right path."

Under this guidance I spent the whole summer in ceaseless oral prayer to Jesus Christ, and I felt absolute peace in my soul. During sleep I often dreamed that I was saying the Prayer. And during the day if I happened to meet anyone, all men without exception were as dear to me as if they had been my nearest relations. But I did not concern myself with them much. All my ideas were quite calmed of their own accord. I thought of nothing whatever but my Prayer, my mind tended to listen to it, and my heart began of itself to feel at times a certain warmth and pleasure. If I happened to go to church the lengthy service of the monastery seemed short to me, and no longer wearied me as it had in time past. My lonely hut seemed like a splendid palace, and I knew not how to thank God for having sent to me, a lost sinner, so wholesome a guide and master.

But I was not long to enjoy the teaching of my dear *starets*, who was so full of divine wisdom. He died at the end of the summer. Weeping freely I bade him farewell, and thanked him for the fatherly teaching he had given my wretched self, and as a blessing and a keepsake I begged for the rosary with which he said his prayers.

And so I was left alone. Summer came to an end and the kitchen garden was cleared. I had no longer anywhere to live. My peasant sent me away, giving me by way of wages two roubles, and filling up my bag with dried bread for my journey. Again I started off on my wanderings. But now I did not walk along as before, filled with care. The calling upon the Name of Jesus Christ gladdened my way. Everybody was kind to me, it was as though everyone loved me.

Then it occurred to me to wonder what I was to do with the money I had earned by my care of the kitchen garden. What good was it to me? Yet stay! I no longer had a *starets*, there was no one to go on teaching me. Why not buy *The Philokalia* and continue to learn from it more about interior prayer?

I crossed myself and set off with my Prayer. I came to a large town, where I asked for the book in all the shops. In the end I found it, but they asked me three roubles for it, and I had only two. I bargained for a long time, but the shopkeeper would not budge an inch. Finally, he said, "Go to this church near by, and speak to the churchwarden. He has a book like that, but it's a very old copy. Perhaps he will let you have it for two roubles." I went, and sure enough I found and bought for my two roubles a worn and old copy of *The Philokalia*. I was delighted with it. I mended my book as much as I could, I made a cover for it with a piece of cloth, and put it into my breast pocket with my Bible.

And that is how I go about now, and ceaselessly repeat the Prayer of Jesus, which is more precious and sweet to me than anything in the world. At times I do as much as forty-three or -four miles a day, and do not feel that I am walking at all. I am aware only of the fact that I am saying my Prayer. When the bitter cold pierces me, I begin to say my Prayer more earnestly and I quickly get warm all over. When hunger begins to overcome me, I call more often on the Name of Jesus, and I forget my wish for food. When I fall ill and get rheumatism in my back and legs, I fix my thoughts on the Prayer and do not notice the pain. If anyone harms me I have only to think, "How sweet is the Prayer of Jesus!" and the injury and the anger alike pass away and I forget it all. I have become a sort of half-conscious person. I have no cares and no interests. The fussy business of the world I would not give a glance to. The one thing I wish for is to be alone, and all by myself to pray, to pray without ceasing; and doing this, I am filled with joy. God knows what is happening to me! Of course, all this is sensuous, or as my departed *starets* said, an artificial state which follows naturally upon routine. But because of my unworthiness and stupidity I dare not venture yet to go on further, and learn and make my own, spiritual prayer within the depths of my heart. I await God's time. And in the meanwhile I rest my hope on the prayers of my departed *starets*. Thus, although I have not yet reached that ceaseless spiritual prayer which is self-acting in the heart, yet I thank God I do now understand the meaning of those words I heard in the Epistle—*"Pray without ceasing."*

The sister of Dante Gabriel Rossetti and the subject of numerous Pre-Raphaelite paintings, Christina Rossetti was a poet in her own right who was widely read during and after her lifetime. She shared the interests of the Pre-Raphaelite Brotherhood: medievalism, intricacy in poetic or artistic line, symbolism, religious and spiritual imagery and themes. As a woman, she was excluded from actual membership in the circle. The autobiographical novella *Maude*, written during a period in her late adolescence when she suffered several debilitating illnesses, was not published until three years after her death in 1894.

Rossetti's increasing sense of alienation from the types of social activities expected of her—garden parties, soirées, teas—and her persistence in adopting a semi-cloistered life at home in order to pursue her art caused her some difficulties with friends and family who admired her talent but could not regard her writing as a serious occupation. The first half of Maude relates the narrator's increasing frustration and her desire for a contemplative community life, such as the Pre-Raphaelite Brotherhood, that would take

CHRISTINA ROSSETTI

[1 8 3 0 – 1 8 9 4]

Shut out all the troublesome noise of life; I would be dumb . . .

her out of the world and sustain her as an artist. Only the sisterhoods of the High Anglican Church offered such an option at that time, and therefore taking the veil figures prominently as a theme in the poems that accompany the novel. Maude/Rossetti's own temperament and search for spiritual enlightenment through poetic rather than religious practice precluded that choice. The narrator's resistance to religious observance and the cloistered life of a nun constitutes the dramatic tension of the second half of the novella.

[AM]

FROM *MAUDE*

It was Christmas Eve. All day long Maude and her cousins were hard at work putting up holly and mistletoe in wreaths, festoons, or bunches, wherever the arrangement of the rooms admitted of such embellishment. The picture-frames were hidden behind foliage and bright berries; the bird-cages were stuck as full of green as though it had been Summer. A fine sprig of holly was set apart as a centre-bit for the pudding of next day: scratched hands and injured gowns were disregarded: hour after hour the noisy bustle raged until Mrs Foster, hunted from place to place by her young relatives, heard, with inward satisfaction, that the decorations were completed.

After tea Mary set the backgammon board in array and challenged her Aunt to their customary evening game: Maude, complaining of a headache, and promising either to wrap herself in a warm shawl or to go to bed, went to her room and Agnes, listening to the rattle of the dice, at last came to the conclusion that her presence was not needed down stairs, and resolved to visit the upper regions. Thinking that her cousin was lying down tired and might have fallen asleep, she forbore knocking; but opened the door softly and peeped in.

Maude was seated at a table, surrounded by the old chaos of stationery; before her lay the locking manuscript-book, into which she had just copied something. That day she had appeared more than usually animated: and now supporting her forehead upon her hand, her eyes cast down till the long lashes nearly rested upon her cheeks, she looked pale, languid, almost in pain. She did not move, but let her visitor come close to her without speaking: Agnes thought she was crying.

"Dear Maude, you have overtired yourself. Indeed, for all our sakes, you should be more careful:" here Agnes passed her arm affectionately round her friend's neck: "I hoped to find you fast asleep, and instead of this you have been writing in the cold. Still, I did not come to lecture; and am even ready to show my forgiving disposition by reading your new poem: may I?"

Maude glanced quickly up at her cousin's kind face, then answered: "Yes, if you like;" and Agnes read as follows:

> *Vanity of vanities, the Preacher saith,*
> *All things are vanity. The eye and ear*
> *Cannot be filled with what they see and hear:*
>   *Like early dew, or like the sudden breath*
>   *Of wind, or like the grass that withereth*
> *Is man, tossed to and fro by hope and fear:*
> *So little joy hath he, so little cheer,*
>   *Till all things end in the long dust of death.*
> *Today is still the same as yesterday,*
>   *Tomorrow also even as one of them;*
>   *And there is nothing new under the sun.*
>   *Until the ancient race of time be run,*
>   *The old thorns shall grow out of the old stem,*
> *And morning shall be cold and twilight grey.—*

This sonnet was followed by another, written like a postscript:

> *I listen to the holy antheming*
> *That riseth in thy walls continually,*
> *What while the organ pealeth solemnly*
>   *And white-robed men and boys stand up to sing.*
> *I ask my heart with a sad questioning:*
> *"What lov'st thou here?" and my heart answers me:*
> *"Within the shadows of this sanctuary*
>   *To watch and pray is a most blessed thing."*
> *To watch and pray, false heart? it is not so:*
>   *Vanity enters with thee, and thy love*
> *Soars not to Heaven, but grovelleth below.*
>   *Vanity keepeth guard, lest good should reach*
>   *Thy hardness; not the echoes from above*
> *Can rule thy stubborn feelings or can teach.—*

"Was this composed after going to S. Andrew's?"

"No; I wrote it just now, but I was thinking of S. Andrew's. It is horrible to feel such a hypocrite as I do."

"Oh! Maude, I only wish I were as sensible of my faults as you are of yours. But a hypocrite you are not: don't you see that every line of these sonnets attests your sincerity?"

"You will stay to Communion tomorrow?" asked Maude after a short silence, and without replying to her cousin's speech; even these few words seemed to cost her an effort.

"Of course I shall; why, it is Christmas Day:—at least I trust to do so. Mary and I have been thinking how nice it will be for us all to receive together: so I want you to promise that you will pray for us at the Altar, as I shall for you. Will you?"

"I shall not receive tomorrow," answered Maude; then hurrying on as if to prevent the other from remonstrating: "No: at least I will not profane Holy Things; I will not add this to all the rest. I have gone over and over again, thinking I should come right in time, and I do not come right: I will go no more."

Agnes turned quite pale: "Stop," she said interrupting her cousin: "Stop; you cannot mean,—you do not know what you are saying. You will go no more? Only think, if the struggle is so hard now, what it will be when you reject all help."

"I do not struggle."

"You are ill tonight," rejoined Agnes very gently: "you are tired and over-excited. Take my advice, dear; say your prayers and get to bed. But do not be very long; if there is anything you miss and will tell me of, I will say it in your stead. Don't think me unfeeling: I was once on the very point of acting as you propose. I was perfectly wretched: harassed and discouraged on all sides. But then it struck me—you won't be angry?—that it was so ungrateful to follow my own fancies, instead of at least endeavouring to do God's Will: and so foolish too; for if our safety is not in obedience, where is it?"

Maude shook her head: "Your case is different. Whatever your faults may be, (not that I perceive any,) you are trying to correct them; your own conscience tells you that. But I am not trying. No one will say that I cannot avoid putting myself forward and displaying my verses. Agnes, you must admit so much."

Deep-rooted indeed was that vanity which made Maude take pleasure, on such an occasion, in proving the force of arguments directed against herself. Still Agnes would not yield; but resolutely did battle for the truth.

"If hitherto it has been so, let it be so no more. It is not too late: besides, think for one moment what will be the end of this. We must all die: what if you keep to your resolution, and do as you have said, and receive the Blessed Sacrament no more?"—Her eyes filled with tears.

Maude's answer came in a subdued tone: "I do not mean never to Communicate again. You remember Mr Paulson told us last Sunday that sickness and suffering are sent for our correction. I suffer very much. Perhaps a time will come when these will have done their work on me also; when I shall be purified indeed and weaned from the world. Who knows? the lost have been found, the dead quickened." She paused as if in thought; then continued: "You partake of the Blessed Sacrament in peace, Agnes, for you are good; and Mary, for she is harmless: but your conduct cannot serve to direct mine because I am neither the one nor the other. Some day I may be fit again to approach the Holy Altar, but till then I will at least refrain from dishonouring it."

Agnes felt almost indignant: "Maude, how can you talk so? this is not reverence. You cannot mean that for the present you will indulge vanity and display; that you will court admiration and applause; that you will take your fill of pleasure until sickness, or it may be death, strips you of temptation and sin together. Forgive me; I am sure you never meant this: yet what else does a deliberate resolution to put off doing right come to?—and if you are determined at once to do your best, why deprive yourself of the appointed means of grace? Dear Maude, think better of it;" and Agnes knelt beside her cousin, and laid her head against her bosom.

But still Maude, with a sort of desperate wilfulness, kept saying: "It is of no use; I cannot go tomorrow; it is of no use." She hid her face, leaning upon the table and weeping bitterly; while Agnes, almost discouraged, quitted the room.

Maude, once more alone, sat for some time just as her cousin left her. Gradually the thick, low sobs became more rare; she was beginning to feel sleepy. At last she roused herself with an effort and commenced undressing; then it struck her that her prayers had still to be said. The idea of beginning them frightened her, yet she could not settle to sleep without saying something. Strange prayers they must have been, offered with a divided heart and a reproachful conscience. Still they were said at length; and Maude lay down harassed, wretched, remorseful, everything but penitent. She was nearly asleep, nearly unconscious of her troubles, when the first stroke of midnight sounded. Immediately a party of Christmas waits and carollers burst forth with their glad music. The first part was sung in full chorus:

> *"Thank God, thank God, we do believe;*
> *Thank God that this is Christmas Eve.*
> *Even as we kneel upon this day,*
> *Even so the ancient legends say,*
> *Nearly two thousand years ago*
> *The stalled ox knelt, and even so*
> *The ass knelt full of praise, which they*
> *Could not express, while we can pray.*
> *Thank God, thank God, for Christ was born*

Ages ago, as on this morn.
In the snow-season undefiled
God came to earth a Little Child:
He put His ancient Glory by
To love for us and then to die."—

—Then half the voices sang the following stanza:

"How shall we thank God? how shall we
Thank Him and praise Him worthily?
What will He have Who loved us thus?
What presents will He take from us?—
Will He take gold? or precious heap
Of gems? or shall we rather steep
The air with incense? or bring myrrh?—
What man will be our messenger
To go to Him and ask His Will?
Which having learned, we will fulfil
Though He choose all we most prefer:
What man will be our messenger?"—

—This was answered by the other half:

"Thank God, thank God, the Man is found,
Sure-footed, knowing well the ground.
He knows the road, for this the way
He travelled once, as on this day.
He is our Messenger; beside,
He is our Door and Path and Guide;
He also is our Offering;
He is the Gift That we must bring."—

—Finally all the singers joined in the conclusion:

"Let us kneel down with one accord
And render thanks unto the Lord:
For unto us a Child is born
Upon this happy Christmas morn;
For unto us a Son is given,
Firstborn of God, and Heir of Heaven."—

As the echoes died away Maude fell asleep.

MAUDE FOSTER TO AGNES CLIFTON.

2nd July 18—

My dear Agnes,

You have heard of my mishap? it keeps me not bedridden, but sofa-ridden. My side is dreadfully hurt; I looked at it this morning for the first time, but hope never again to see so shocking a sight. The pain now and then is extreme, though not always so; sometimes, in fact, I am unconscious of any injury.

Will you convey my best love and wishes to Mary, and tell her how much I regret being away from her at such a time; especially as Mamma will not hear of leaving me. A day or two ago I tried to compose an Epithalamium for our fair fiancée; which effort resulted in my present enclosure: not much to the purpose, we must admit. You may read it when no better employment offers. The first Nun no one can suspect of being myself, partly because my hair is far from yellow and I do not wear curls; partly because I never did anything half so good as profess. The second might be Mary, had she mistaken her vocation. The third is Magdalen, of course. But whatever you miss, pray read the mottoes. Put together they form a most exquisite little song which the Nuns sing in Italy. One can fancy Sister Magdalen repeating it with her whole heart.

The Surgeon comes twice a day to dress my wounds; still, all the burden of nursing falls on poor Mamma. How I wish you were here to help us both: we should find plenty to say.

But perhaps ere many months are passed I shall be up and about, when we may go together on a visit to Mary; a most delightful possibility. By the way, how I should love a baby of hers, and what a pretty little creature it ought to be. Do you think Mr Herbert handsome? hitherto I have only heard a partial opinion.

Ugh, my side! it gives an awful twinge now and then. You need not read my letter; but I must write it, for I am unable to do anything else. Did the pillow reach safely? It gave me so much pleasure to work it for Mary, who, I hope, likes it. At all events, if not to her taste, she may console herself with the reflection that it is unique; for the pattern was my own designing.

Here comes dinner; goodbye. When will anything so welcome as your kind face gladden the eyes of

Your affectionate
Maude Foster?———

Three Nuns.
1.

> *"Sospira questo core*
> *E non so dir perchè."*
> *[This heart sighs*
> *I know not wherefore.]*

Shadow, shadow on the wall
  Spread thy shelter over me;
Wrap me with a heavy pall,
  With the dark that none may see.
Fold thyself around me; come:
Shut out all the troublesome
Noise of life; I would be dumb.

Shadow thou hast reached my feet,
  Rise and cover up my head;
Be my stainless winding sheet,
  Buried before I am dead.
Lay thy cool upon my breast:
Once I thought that joy was best,
Now I only care for rest.

By the grating of my cell
  Sings a solitary bird;
Sweeter than the vesper bell,
  Sweetest song was ever heard.
Sing upon thy living tree:
Happy echoes answer thee,
Happy songster, sing to me.

When my yellow hair was curled
  Though men saw and called me fair,
I was weary in the world
  Full of vanity and care.
Gold was left behind, curls shorn
When I came here; that same morn
Made a bride no gems adorn.

Here wrapped in my spotless veil,
  Curtained from intruding eyes,
I whom prayers and fasts turn pale
  Wait the flush of Paradise.
But the vigil is so long

My heart sickens:—sing thy song,
Blithe bird that canst do no wrong.

Sing on, making me forget
  Present sorrow and past sin.
Sing a little longer yet:
  Soon the matins will begin;
And I must turn back again
To that aching worse than pain
I must bear and not complain.

Sing, that in thy song I may
  Dream myself once more a child
In the green woods far away
  Plucking clematis and wild
Hyacinths, till pleasure grew
Tired, yet so was pleasure too,
Resting with no work to do.

In the thickest of the wood,
  I remember, long ago
How a stately oak tree stood,
  With a sluggish pool below
Almost shadowed out of sight.
On the waters dark as night,
Water-lilies lay like light.

There, while yet a child, I thought
  I could live as in a dream,
Secret, neither found nor sought:
  Till the lilies on the stream,
Pure as virgin purity,
Would seem scarce too pure for me:—
Ah, but that can never be.

2.

"Sospirerà d'amore,
    Ma non lo dice a me."
[It may be sighing for love
    but will not tell me so.]

I loved him, yes, where was the sin?
  I loved him with my heart and soul.
  But I pressed forward to no goal,

There was no prize I strove to win.
Show me my sin that I may see:—
Throw the first stone, thou Pharisee.

I loved him, but I never sought
*   That he should know that I was fair.*
*   I prayed for him; was my sin prayer?*
I sacrificed, he never bought.
He nothing gave, he nothing took;
We never bartered look for look.

My voice rose in the sacred choir,
*   The choir of Nuns; do you condemn*
*   Even if, when kneeling among them,*
Faith, zeal and love kindled a fire
And I prayed for his happiness
Who knew not? was my error this?

I only prayed that in the end
*   His trust and hope may not be vain.*
*   I prayed not we may meet again:*
I would not let our names ascend,
No, not to Heaven, in the same breath;
Nor will I join the two in death.

Oh sweet is death; for I am weak
*   And weary, and it giveth rest.*
*   The Crucifix lies on my breast,*
And all night long it seems to speak
Of rest; I hear it through my sleep,
And the great comfort makes me weep.

Oh sweet is death that bindeth up
*   The broken and the bleeding heart.*
*   The draught chilled, but a cordial part*
Lurked at the bottom of the cup;
And for my patience will my Lord
Give an exceeding great reward.

Yea, the reward is almost won,
*   A crown of glory and a palm.*
*   Soon I shall sing the unknown psalm;*
Soon gaze on light, not on the sun;
And soon, with surer faith, shall pray
For him, and cease not night nor day.

My life is breaking like a cloud;
    God judgeth not as man doth judge—
    Nay, bear with me; you need not grudge
This peace; the vows that I have vowed
Have all been kept: Eternal Strength
Holds me, though mine own fails at length.

Bury me in the Convent ground
    Among the flowers that are so sweet;
    And lay a green turf at my feet,
Where thick trees cast a gloom around.
At my head let a Cross be, white
Through the long blackness of the night.

Now kneel and pray beside my bed
    That I may sleep being free from pain:
    And pray that I may wake again
After His Likeness, Who hath said
(Faithful is He Who promiseth,)
We shall be satisfied Therewith.

3.

    "Rispondimi, cor mio,
      Perchè sospiri tu?
    Risponde: Voglio Iddio,
      Sospiro per Gesù."
    [Answer me, my heart
      What do you sigh for?
    It replies: I desire God,
      I sigh for Jesus.]

My heart is as a freeborn bird
    Caged in my cruel breast,
That flutters, flutters evermore,
    Nor sings, nor is at rest.
But beats against the prison bars,
    As knowing its own nest
Far off beyond the clouded West.

My soul is as a hidden fount
    Shut in by clammy clay,
That struggles with an upward moan;
    Striving to force its way

Up through the turf, over the grass,
*   Up, up into the day,*
Where twilight no more turneth grey.

Oh for the grapes of the True Vine
*   Growing in Paradise.*
Whose tendrils join the Tree of Life
*   To that which maketh wise.*
Growing beside the Living Well
*   Whose sweetest waters rise*
Where tears are wiped from tearful eyes.

Oh for the waters of that Well
*   Round which the Angels stand.*
Oh for the Shadow of the Rock
*   On my heart's weary land.*
Oh for the Voice to guide me when
*   I turn to either hand,*
Guiding me till I reach Heaven's strand.

Thou World from which I am come out,
*   Keep all thy gems and gold;*
Keep thy delights and precious things,
*   Thou that art waxing old.*
My heart shall beat with a new life,
*   When thine is dead and cold:*
When thou dost fear I shall be bold.

When Earth shall pass away with all
*   Her pride and pomp of sin,*
The City builded without hands
*   Shall safely shut me in.*
All the rest is but vanity
*   Which others strive to win:*
Where their hopes end my joys begin.

I will not look upon a rose
*   Though it is fair to see:*
The flowers planted in Paradise
*   Are budding now for me.*
Red roses like love visible
*   Are blowing on their tree,*
Or white like virgin purity.

I will not look unto the sun
*   Which setteth night by night:*

In the untrodden courts of Heaven
  My crown shall be more bright.
Lo, in the New Jerusalem
  Founded and built aright
My very feet shall tread on light.

With foolish riches of this World
  I have bought treasure, where
Nought perisheth: for this white veil
  I gave my golden hair;
I gave the beauty of my face
  For vigils, fasts and prayer;
I gave all for this Cross I bear.

My heart trembled when first I took
  The vows which must be kept;
At first it was a weariness
  To watch when once I slept.
The path was rough and sharp with thorns;
  My feet bled as I stepped;
The Cross was heavy and I wept.

While still the names rang in mine ears
  Of daughter, sister, wife;
The outside world still looked so fair
  To my weak eyes, and rife
With beauty; my heart almost failed;
  Then in the desperate strife
I prayed, as one who prays for life.

Until I grew to love what once
  Had been so burdensome.
So now when I am faint, because
  Hoped deferred seems to numb
My heart, I yet can plead; and say
  Although my lips are dumb:
"The Spirit and the Bride say, Come."—

ALBERT SCHWEITZER

[1875–1965]

In addition to the outward, I now had inner happiness.

A polymath of great vitality and faith, Albert Schweitzer earned doctorates in music, theology, and medicine. Because he adopted a theological interpretation of Christ that deviated from that of his university, he was often considered a maverick within the church and seminary. He was educated at Strasbourg, received his doctorate in music in 1899 and his doctorate in theology the following year. Simultaneously, Schweitzer distinguished himself as a leading organist and musicologist, publishing *J. S. Bach: le musicien-poète* in 1905.

Despite his great academic and musical successes, Schweitzer chose to answer what he felt was Christ's summons to him to serve humanity; he planned to become a medical missionary. Although noted for his eloquence in the pulpit, Schweitzer felt called to a form of silent evangelization, by caring for the physical needs of communities without established medical care. Following eight years of medical study, he founded a successful hospital in Africa. While held a prisoner of war by the French during World War I, he assisted other prisoners medically and spiritually, while writing his *Philosophy of Culture*, in which he expressed his belief in the necessity of "reverence for all living things." His theological writings include *The Mysticism of Paul the Apostle* (1930), *The Kingdom of God and Primitive Christianity* (1950), and his famous *Quest for the Historical Jesus*.

His memoirs reflect his endless concern for the sufferings of humanity and his eagerness to serve. After the war, he returned to Africa to expand his hospital with the addition of a leper colony. His great service in Africa earned him the Goethe Prize in 1928 and the Nobel Peace Prize in 1952.   [AM]

FROM *OUT OF MY LIFE AND THOUGHT: AN AUTOBIOGRAPHY*

On October 13th, 1905, a Friday, I dropped into a letter-box in the Avenue de la Grande Armée in Paris letters to my parents and to some of my most intimate acquaintances, telling them that at the beginning of the winter term I should enter myself as a medical student, in order to go later on to Equatorial Africa as a doctor. In one of them I sent in the resignation of my post as Principal of the Theological College of S. Thomas's, because of the claim on my time that my intended course of study would make.

The plan which I meant now to put into execution had been in my mind for a long time, having been conceived so long ago as my student days. It struck me as incomprehensible that I should be allowed to lead such a happy life, while I saw so many people around me wrestling with care and suffering. Even at school I had felt stirred whenever I got a glimpse of the miserable home surroundings of some of my schoolfellows and compared them with the absolutely ideal conditions in which we children of the parsonage at Günsbach lived. While at the University and enjoying the happiness of being able to study and even to produce some results in science and art, I could not help thinking continually of others who were denied that happiness by their material circumstances or their health. Then one brilliant summer morning at Günsbach, during the Whitsuntide holidays—it was in 1896— there came to me, as I awoke, the thought that I must not accept this happiness as a matter of course, but must give something in return for it. Proceeding to think the matter out at once with calm deliberation, while the birds were singing outside, I settled with myself before I got up, that I would consider myself justified in living till I was thirty for science and art, in order to devote myself from that time forward to the direct service of humanity.

Many a time already had I tried to settle what meaning lay hidden for me in the saying of Jesus! "Whosoever would save his life shall lose it, and whosoever shall lose his life for My sake and the Gospels shall save it." Now the answer was found. In addition to the outward, I now had inward happiness.

What would be the character of the activities thus planned for the future was not yet clear to me. I left it to circumstances to guide me. One thing only was certain, that it must be directly human service, however inconspicuous the sphere of it.

MY THIRTIETH BIRTHDAY A FEW MONTHS LATER I SPENT LIKE THE man in the parable who "desiring to build a tower, first counts the cost whether he have wherewith to complete it." The result was that I resolved to realize my plan of direct human service in Equatorial Africa.

MY RELATIVES AND MY FRIENDS ALL JOINED IN EXPOSTULATING with me on the folly of my enterprise. I was a man, they said, who was burying the talent entrusted to him and wanted to trade with false currency. Work among savages I ought to leave to those who would not thereby be compelled to leave gifts and acquirements in science and art unused. Widor, who loved me as if I were his son, scolded me as being like a general who wanted to go into the firing-line—there was no talk about trenches at that time—with a rifle. A lady who was filled with the modern spirit proved to me that I could do much more by lecturing on behalf of medical help for natives than I could by the action I contemplated. That saying from Goethe's *Faust* ("In the beginning was the Deed"), was now out of date, she said. To-day propaganda was the mother of happenings.

In the many verbal duels which I had to fight, as a weary opponent, with people who passed for Christians, it moved me strangely to see them so far from perceiving that the effort to serve the love preached by Jesus may sweep a man into a new course of life, although they read in the New Testament that it can do so, and found it there quite in order. I had assumed as a matter of course that familiarity with the sayings of Jesus would produce a much better appreciation of what to popular logic is non-rational, than my own case allowed me to assert. Several times, indeed, it was my experience that my appeal to the act of obedience which Jesus' command of love may under special circumstances call for, brought upon me an accusation of conceit, although I had, in fact, been obliged to do violence to my feelings to employ this argument at all. In general, how much I suffered through so many people assuming a right to tear open all the doors and shutters of my inner self!

As a rule, too, it was of no use allowing them, in spite of my repugnance, to have a glimpse of the thoughts which had given birth to my resolution. They thought there must be something behind it all, and guessed at disappointment at the slow growth of my reputation. For this there was no ground at all, seeing that I had received, even as a young man, such recognition as others usually get only after a whole life of toil and struggle. Unfortunate love experiences were also alleged as the reason for my decision.

I felt as a real kindness the action of persons who made no attempt to dig their fists into my heart, but regarded me as a precocious young man, not quite right in his head, and treated me correspondingly with affectionate mockery.

I felt it to be, in itself, quite natural that relations and friends should put before me anything that told against the reasonableness of my plan. As one who demands that idealists shall be sober in their views, I was conscious that every start upon an untrodden path is a venture which only in unusual circumstances looks sensible and likely to be successful. In my own case I held the venture to be justified, because I had considered it for a long time and from every point of view, and credited myself with the possession of health, sound nerves, energy, practical common sense, toughness, prudence, very few wants, and everything else that might be found necessary by anyone wandering along the path of the idea. I believed myself, further, to wear the protective armour of a temperament quite capable of enduring an eventual failure of my plan. . . .

What seemed to my friends the most irrational thing in my plan was that I wanted to go to Africa, not as a missionary, but as a doctor, and thus when already thirty years of age burdened myself as a beginning with a long period of laborious study. And that this study would mean for me a tremendous effort, I had no manner of doubt. I did, in truth, look forward to the next few years with dread. But the reasons which determined me to follow the way of service I had chosen, as a doctor, weighed so heavily that other considerations were as dust in the balance.

I wanted to be a doctor that I might be able to work without having to talk. For years I had been giving myself out in words, and it was with joy that I had followed the calling of theological teacher and of preacher. But this new form of activity I could not represent to myself as being talking about the religion of love, but only as an actual putting it into practice. Medical knowledge made it possible for me to carry out my intention in the best and most complete way, wherever the path of service might lead me.

DAG
HAMMARSKJÖLD

[1 9 0 5 – 1 9 6 1]

Not I, but God in me.

Known as the secretary general of the United Nations, an office to which he was twice elected, Dag Hammarskjöld was also an international banker and a Swedish governmental minister of some distinction, as well as an erstwhile professor of political economy. Hailed as a great worker for world peace and an indefatigable leader of the United Nations, Hammarskjöld drew on his Christian faith to sustain his activity on behalf of humanity. He described his spiritual struggles and his battle with depression in a private journal that was published posthumously under the title *Markings*. For the most part a collection of thoughts, aphorisms, and selections from the Bible and other inspirational literature, *Markings* gives some suggestion of Hammarskjöld's thoughts, and relates somewhat elliptically his sense of release from anxiety in turning to divine providence. The passages describing that transition are presented here. [AM]

FROM *MARKINGS*

Maturity: among other things—not to hide one's strength out of fear and, consequently, live below one's best.

Goodness is something so simple: always to live for others, never to seek one's own advantage.

When in decisive moments—as now—God acts, it is with a stern purposefulness, a Sophoclean irony. When the hour strikes, He takes what is His. What have *you* to say?—Your prayer has been answered, as you know. God has a use for you, even though what He asks doesn't happen to suit you at the moment. God, who "abases him whom He raises up."

> *Will it come, or will it not,*
> *The day when the joy becomes great,*
> *The day when the grief becomes small?*
> *(Gunnar Ekelöf)*

It *did* come—the day when the grief became small. For what had befallen me and seemed so hard to bear became significant in the light of the demands which God was now making. But how difficult it is to feel that this was also, and for that very reason, the day when the joy became great.

Not I, but God in me.

Maturity: among other things, a new lack of self-consciousness—the kind you can only attain when you have become entirely indifferent to yourself through an absolute assent to your fate.

He who has placed himself in God's hands stands free vis-à-vis men: he is entirely at his ease with them, because he has granted them the right to judge.

"Their lives grounded in and sustained by God, they are incapable of any kind of pride; because they give back to God all the benefits He has bestowed on them, they do not glorify each other, but do all things to the Glory of God alone." *(Thomas Aquinas)*

I am the vessel. The draught is God's. And God is the thirsty one.

In the last analysis, what does the word "sacrifice" mean? Or even the word "gift"? He who has nothing can give nothing. The gift is God's—to God.

He who has surrendered himself to it knows that the Way ends on the Cross—even when it is leading him through the jubilation of Gennesaret or the triumphal entry into Jerusalem.

TO BE FREE, TO BE ABLE TO STAND UP AND LEAVE *EVERYTHING* behind—without looking back. To say *Yes*—

Except in faith, nobody is humble. The mask of weakness or of Phariseeism is not the naked face of humility.

And, except in faith, nobody is proud. The vanity displayed in all its varieties by the spiritually immature is not pride.

To be, in faith, both humble and proud: that is, to *live*, to know that in God I am nothing, but that God is in me.

To say Yes to life is at one and the same time to say Yes to oneself.

Yes—even to that element in one which is most unwilling to let itself be transformed from a temptation into a strength. . . .

THE "UNHEARD-OF"—TO BE IN THE HANDS OF GOD.

Once again a reminder that this is all that remains for you to live for—and once more the feeling of disappointment which shows how slow you are to learn. . . .

So long as you abide in the Unheard-of, you are beyond and above—to hold fast to this must be the First Commandment in your spiritual discipline. . . .

To have faith—not to hesitate!

"If I take the wings of the morning and remain in the uttermost parts of the sea;

even there also shall thy hand lead me." (*Psalm* 139:8)

PART THREE

MYSTICS
& VISIONARIES

THE AUTOBIOGRAPHICAL TRADITION OF MYSTIC, VISIONARY, AND seer is well established; usually these authors have been urged by their spiritual directors to give an account of their experiences. Their stories are similar in describing how they alternately have been overjoyed by the beauty of revelation and have endured an exquisitely painful sense of the withdrawal of God's presence.

Mystical spiritual autobiographies verge on the fantastic or supernatural; we might expect a heightened tone or inflated rhetoric in keeping with the subject matter. Instead, a simple exercise for finding God is delivered by Brother Lawrence, the "kitchen saint," with the same brevity and clarity as directions for baking bread; Teresa of Avila describes with precision and intelligence the daily events of convent life in the same breath as she relates mind-piercing encounters with Christ, the transformation of wooden crosses into jewel-studded crucifixes, the appearance of angels who plunge fiery darts into a waiting breast.

The range of mystical and visionary expression is immense. In earlier centuries, revelations focused on more traditional religious subjects, like the crucifixion of Christ. Julian of Norwich and Saint Margaret Mary Alacoque share in devotions and revelations of this kind. In the modern period, mystical experience is shaped and cleanly focused as a purely supernatural event; the role of the mystic is to perceive the salience of the supernatural in the quotidian.

The mystic's all-encompassing desire for purity and holiness, for uninterrupted union with God, is often figured as the romantic passion of lovers. A long literary tradition, beginning with Solomon's *Song of Songs*, treats romantic love as an allegory of God's relationship with humanity, Israel as the faithless bride of the Almighty, the church as the stainless bride of Christ. The tradition culminates in the troubadour's concept of courtly love, represented here in Dante's *La vita nuova*, where the beloved woman becomes a spiritual guide, in her death and assumption leading the poet to God and heaven. The poetry of Saint John of the Cross, like the canticles of Saint Francis of Assisi, who called himself a troubadour for God, expresses a passion for the Beloved who unites with the world—brother sun, sister moon—in a holy covenant of marriage. In this poetic tradition, the soul cries out to its beloved in anguish at every separation, in ecstasy at every intimation of response. The transfiguring power of love for God, the desire to suffer for the good of one's soul, and the intense absorption in the inner life, as seen in the piety of Madame Guyon, for example, leave the mystic vulnerably open to despair in the anxious perception of the withdrawal of grace.

The dark night of the soul, the trials of spiritual aridity express a very modern anguish at God's apparent silence. The urgent need of the visionary to see beyond the emptiness of earthly shadows and hollow echoes informs even the naive and childlike ideas of Saint Thérèse de Lisieux, who depicts the silence of God in the form of Christ sleeping in a rocking boat on the Sea of Galilee. The practice of abstinence, self-laceration, self-imposed humiliation, or torture and martyrdom reveal the eagerness of the visionary to affiliate with the sufferings of Christ, which, as revealed by Julian of Norwich, become the source of all conso-lation. [AM]

Rābi'a al-'Adawīya, a freed slave girl from Basra, in what is present-day Iraq, has been referred to in the West as the Muslim Saint Teresa. She is associated with the large ascetic and mystical movement within Islam called Sufism. Sufis seek joy in an overwhelming and—in the best sense of the word —irrational love of God. Early anecdotes about Rābi'a tell us that she closed all the windows in spring in order not to be distracted by the beauties of nature from contemplation of the maker of such beauties. Despite such asceticism, her reported sayings are distinguished by the familiarity with which she addresses the deity along with utter confidence in His existence and His perfect love. Though Rābi'a characterizes herself as a "weak creature," accounts of her show her outwitting the learned, particularly the religious and secular leaders of her time.

In describing the blissful ecstasy felt by the soul in its direct and mystical apprehension of God, Rābi'a used a vocabulary of sensuous symbols. From her prayers, selections from which follow, is said to derive the element of selfless love of Sufism: even the thought of Paradise

RĀBI'A
AL-'ADAWĪYA

[D. 801]

Make my heart present.

is a distraction for the true Sufi mystic, a veil that hides the primordial divine beauty. Rābi'a's life embodied the central tenet of Sufism: to worship God out of love rather than from fear or hope.   [EP]

FROM HER PRAYERS

"O God, whatsoever Thou hast apportioned to me of worldly things, do Thou give that to Thy enemies; and whatsoever Thou has apportioned to me in the world to come, give that to Thy friends; for Thou sufficest me."

"O God, if I worship Thee for fear of Hell, burn me in Hell, and if I worship Thee in hope of Paradise, exclude me from Paradise; but if I worship Thee for Thy own sake, grudge me not Thy everlasting beauty."

"O God, my whole occupation and all my desire in this world, of all worldly things, is to remember Thee, and in the world to come, of all things of the world to come, is to meet Thee. This is on my side, as I have stated; now do Thou whatsoever Thou wilt."

"O Lord, if you send me to hell on the morrow of the resurrection, I will reveal a secret such that hell will flee from me, not to return for a thousand years."

"O Lord, if tomorrow you put me in hell, I will cry out, 'You have be-friended me. Is this how one treats friends?' " A voice called out, "Rābi'a, do not think ill of us. Be assured that we will bring you into the circle of our friends, so you may converse with us."

"O my God, my work and my desire, in all this world, is recollection of you and in the afterworld, meeting with you. This is what is mine—you do as you will."

And nightly she would say, "O Lord, make my heart present or accept my prayers without my heart."

When her death approached, important people were at her bedside. She said, "For the sake of God's prophets, arise and leave the room." They arose, went out, and closed the door. They heard a voice: "O soul now in peace, return to your Lord, well pleased and well pleasing."

The author of one of the greatest works of world literature, *The Divine Comedy*, Dante was a resident of Florence, where he took active part in politics. When his political enemies came to power in 1302, he was banished from Florence. He lived in various cities, spending his last years in Ravenna, where he remained until his death. According to Dante's poetry and his account of himself in *La vita nuova (The New Life)*, which is excerpted here, at the age of nine he fell in love with a young girl of noble birth, Beatrice (whom some scholars have identified as Beatrice Portinari). *La vita nuova* is an account of his poetry writing and his efforts to conceal his love for Beatrice from the world by establishing a "screen love," to whom he publicly paid court. With Beatrice's death, Dante becomes deeply depressed and then, directing his soul to remain in union with Beatrice as she enters the supernatural realms of purgatory and heaven, he finds his mind's eye drawn to the contemplation of spiritual realities. The result of this mystical experience is the composition of his masterpiece *La Divina Commedia: Inferno, Purgatorio, Paradiso.*

DANTE ALIGHIERI

[1 2 6 5 – 1 3 2 1]

Beyond the widest

of the circling spheres;

A sigh which leaves my heart

aspires to move.

In *La vita nuova*, Dante analyzes his poetry, his experiences in love, and his search to merge with Beatrice, who leads him to God. Dante's love for Beatrice situates his verse in the tradition of ecstatic poetry where the endless desire of unconsummated human love allegorizes the love between humanity and an unreachable God.   [AM]

FROM *LA VITA NUOVA*

In the book of my memory, after the first pages, which are almost blank, there is a section headed *Incipit vita nova* [Here begins my new life]. Beneath this heading I find the words which it is my intention to copy into this smaller book, or if not all, at least their meaning.

NINE TIMES THE HEAVEN OF THE LIGHT HAD REVOLVED IN ITS OWN movement since my birth and had almost returned to the same point when the woman whom my mind beholds in glory first appeared before my eyes. She was called Beatrice by many who did not know what it meant to call her this. She had lived in this world for the length of time in which the heaven of the fixed stars had circled one twelfth of a degree towards the East. Thus she had not long passed the beginning of her ninth year when she appeared to me and I was almost at the end of mine when I beheld her. She was dressed in a very noble colour, a decorous and delicate crimson, tied with a girdle and trimmed in a manner suited to her tender age. The moment I saw her I say in all truth that the vital spirit, which dwells in the inmost depths of the heart, began to tremble so violently that I felt the vibration alarmingly in all my pulses, even the weakest of them. As it trembled, it uttered these words: *Ecce deus fortior me, qui veniens dominabitur mihi* [Behold a god more powerful than I, who comes to rule over me]. At this point, the spirit of the senses which dwells on high in the place to which all our sense perceptions are carried, was filled with amazement and, speaking especially to the spirits of vision, made this pronouncement: *Apparuit iam beatitudo vestra* [The source of your joy has been revealed]. Whereupon the natural spirit, which dwells where our nourishment is digested, began to weep and, weeping, said: *Heu miser! Quia frequenter impeditus ero deinceps* [Alas, poor me! Henceforth I shall often be frustrated]. From then on indeed Love ruled over my soul,

which was thus wedded to him early in life, and he began to acquire such
assurance and mastery over me, owing to the power which my imagination
gave him, that I was obliged to fulfil all his wishes perfectly. He often
commanded me to go where perhaps I might see this angelic child and so,
while I was still a boy, I often went in search of her; and I saw that in all her
ways she was so praiseworthy and noble that indeed the words of the poet
Homer might have been said of her: "She did not seem the daughter of a
mortal man, but of a god." Though her image, which was always present in
my mind, incited Love to dominate me, its influence was so noble that it
never allowed Love to guide me without the faithful counsel of reason, in
everything in which such counsel was useful to hear. But, since to dwell on
the feelings and actions of such early years might appear to some to be
fictitious, I will move on and, omitting many things which might be copied
from the master-text from which the foregoing is derived, I come now to
words inscribed in my memory under more important headings.

WHEN EXACTLY NINE YEARS HAD PASSED SINCE THIS GRACIOUS
being appeared to me, as I have described, it happened that on the last day
of this intervening period this marvel appeared before me again, dressed in
purest white, walking between two other women of distinguished bearing,
both older than herself. As they walked down the street she turned her eyes
towards me where I stood in fear and trembling, and with her ineffable
courtesy, which is now rewarded in eternal life, she greeted me; and such
was the virtue of her greeting that I seemed to experience the height of
bliss. It was exactly the ninth hour of day when she gave me her sweet
greeting. As this was the first time she had ever spoken to me, I was filled
with such joy that, my senses reeling, I had to withdraw from the sight of
others. . . .

THEN IT HAPPENED THAT AS I WAS WALKING ALONG A PATH BESIDE
which flowed a stream of very clear water so strong an urge to write came
over me that I began to think how I should set about it. I thought it would
not be fitting to speak of my lady to anyone except other women, whom I
should address in the second person, and not to any woman but only to those
who are gracious, not merely feminine. Then my tongue spoke, almost as
though moved of its own accord, and said: "Ladies who know by insight

what love is." With great joy I stored these words away in my mind, intending to use them as an opening for my rhyme. Then when I had returned to the city, I pondered for several days and finally I began a *canzone* which opens with these words, and is composed in a manner which will appear evident when I come to divide it. The *canzone* begins: *Ladies who know . . .*

> *Ladies who know by insight what love is,*
>   *With you about my Lady I would treat,*
>   *Not that I think her praises I'll complete,*
>   *But seeking by my words to ease my mind.*
>   *When I consider all her qualities*
>   *I say that Love steals over me so sweet*
>   *That if my courage then did not retreat*
>   *By speaking I'd enamour all mankind.*
>   *Yet words not too exalted I would find,*
>   *Lest base timidity my mind possess;*
>   *But lightly touch upon her graciousness,*
>   *Leaving her worth by this to be divined,*
>   *With you, ladies and maidens who know love.*
>   *To others it may not be spoken of.*
>
> *To the all-knowing mind an angel prays:*
>   *"Lord, in the world a miracle proceeds,*
>   *In act and visible, from a soul's deeds,*
>   *Whose splendour reaches to this very height,"*
>   *One imperfection only Heaven has:*
>   *The lack of her; so now for her it pleads*
>   *And every saint with clamour intercedes.*
>   *Only compassion is our advocate.*
>   *God understands to whom their prayers relate*
>   *And answers them: "My loved ones, bear in peace*
>   *That she, your hope, remain until I please*
>   *Where one knows he must lose her, soon or late,*
>   *And who will say in Hell: 'Souls unconfessed!*
>   *I have beheld the hope of Heaven's blessed.' "*
>
> *My lady is desired in highest heaven.*
>   *Now of her excellence I'd have you hear.*
>   *All ladies who would noble be, draw near*
>   *And walk with her, for as she goes her way*
>   *A chill in evil hearts by Love is driven,*
>   *Causing all thoughts to freeze and perish there.*
>   *If any such endured to look on her*

He would be changed to good or die straightway.
If any man she find who worthy be
To look at her, her virtue then he knows,
For, greeting him, salvation she bestows,
In meekness melting every grudge away.
With further grace has God endowed her still:
Whoever speaks with her shall not fare ill.

Love says of her: "How can a mortal thing
Have purity and beauty such as hers?"
Then looks again and to himself he swears
A marvel she must be which God intends
Pearl-like, not to excess, her colouring,
As suited to a lady's face, appears.
She is the sum of nature's universe.
To her perfection all of beauty tends.
Forth from her eyes, where'er her gaze she bends,
Come spirits flaming with the power of love.
Whoever sees her then, those eyes they prove,
Passing within until the heart each finds.
You will see Love depicted in her face,
There where no man dare linger with his gaze.

My song, you will go parleying, I know,
With many ladies, when I give consent.
Since I have raised you without ornament
As Love's young daughter, hear now what I say.
Of those about you, beg assistance, so:
"Tell me which way to take, for I am sent
To her whose praise is my embellishment."
If you would journey there without delay
Among the base and vulgar do not stay.
Contrive to show your meaning, if you can,
Only to ladies or a courteous man.
They will conduct you by the quickest way.
You will find Love abiding with her beauty.
Commend me to my Lord, as is your duty.

... WHEN THIS *CANZONE* HAD CIRCULATED AMONG A NUMBER OF
people, a friend who heard it was moved to ask me to write saying what Love

is, having perhaps, because of the verses he had heard, greater confidence in me than I deserved. So, reflecting that after the development of my new theme it was appropriate to examine the subject of Love, and also to please my friend, I decided to write on this question. Then it was I wrote the sonnet which begins: *Love and the noble heart . . .*

> *Love and the noble heart are but one thing,*
>   *Even as the wise man tells us in his rhyme,*
>   *The one without the other venturing*
>   *As well as reason from a reasoning mind.*
>   *Nature, disposed to love, creates Love king,*
>   *Making the heart a dwelling-place for him*
>   *Wherein he lies quiescent, slumbering*
>   *Sometimes a little, now a longer time.*
> *Then beauty in a virtuous woman's face*
>   *Pleases the eyes, striking the heart so deep*
>   *A yearning for the pleasing thing may rise.*
>   *Sometimes so long it lingers in that place*
>   *Love's spirit is awakened from his sleep.*
>   *By a worthy man a woman's moved likewise.*

. . . I WAS STILL COMPOSING THIS *CANZONE* AND HAD COMPLETED the stanza which I give above when the Lord of justice called this most gracious lady to partake of glory under the banner of the blessed Queen, the Virgin Mary, whose name was always uttered in prayers of the utmost reverence by this blessed Beatrice. . . .

THERE ROSE UP ONE DAY WITHIN ME, ALMOST AT THE NINTH HOUR, a vivid impression in which I seemed to see Beatrice in glory, clothed in the crimson garments in which she first appeared before my eyes; and she seemed as young as when I first saw her. Then I began to think about her and as I recalled her through the sequence of time past my heart began to repent sorrowfully of the desire by which it had so basely allowed itself to be possessed for some days against the constancy of reason; and when this evil desire had been expelled all my thoughts returned once more to their most gracious Beatrice. And I say that from then onwards I began to think of her so much with the whole of my remorseful heart that frequently my sighs made this evident, expressing as they issued what my heart was saying, that is, the name of this most gracious soul and how she had departed from us. It often happened that a thought would be so laden with grief that I forgot what the thought had been and where I was. As a result of the rekindling of my sighs, my weeping which had abated was also refuelled to such an extent that my eyes were like two objects desirous only of shedding tears; and it often happened, because I wept for so long, that my eyes were ringed with dark red, which happens as a result of some illnesses which people suffer. Thus it seems that they were justly rewarded for their inconstancy, so much so that from then onwards I could not look at anyone who might return my gaze in such a way as to cause my eyes to weep again. Then, as I wanted this evil desire and vain temptation to be shown to be destroyed, so that the verses I had written previously should raise no doubts in anyone, I decided to write a sonnet to convey the substance of this narration. So I then wrote: *Alas! By the violence of many sighs.* I said "Alas" because I was ashamed that my eyes had indulged in such inconstancy.

I will not divide this sonnet because the foregoing account of it makes it quite clear.

> *Alas! By the violence of many sighs*
> *Born of the thoughts I harbour in my breast,*
> *I cannot meet the gaze of others, lest*
> *I bring new torment to my vanquished eyes:*
> *Two orbs of longing now, their solace is*
> *To flow with tears and only grief attest.*
> *So much they weep that Love makes manifest*
> *An encircling crown which suffering implies.*
> *These thoughts of mine and sighs which forth I send*
> *Within my heart to sharper anguish grow,*
> *Where Love in mortal pallor lies in pain;*
> *For in the deep recesses of their woe*
> *The sweet name of my Lady they have penned*
> *And many words to tell her death again.*

AFTER THIS TRIBULATION IT HAPPENED, AT THE TIME WHEN MANY people go on pilgrimages to see the blessed image which Jesus Christ has left us as an imprint of His most beautiful countenance, which my lady in glory now sees, that some pilgrims were passing along a road which runs almost through the centre of the city where that most gracious lady was born, lived and died. These pilgrims, it seemed to me, were very pensive as they went their way; and so, thinking about them, I said to myself: "These people seem to be journeying from far away, and I do not think they have ever even heard of my lady; they know nothing about her, indeed their thoughts are on quite other things than those that are around them here; perhaps they are thinking of their friends at home, of whom we know nothing." Then I said to myself: "I know that if they came from a nearby town they would look distressed as they passed through this sorrowing city." Then I said: "If I could detain them for a little while, I would surely make them weep before they left, for I would say things which would reduce to tears everyone who heard me." And so, when they had passed from my sight, I decided to write a sonnet in which I would set forth what I said to myself; and to make it more moving, I decided to write it as if I had spoken to them. So I wrote the sonnet which begins: *O Pilgrims....* I called them pilgrims in the general sense of the word; for "pilgrim" may be understood in two ways, one general and one particular, in as much as anyone journeying from his own country is a pilgrim. In the particular sense, pilgrim means someone who journeys to the sanctuary of St James and back. It should be understood that those who travel in the service of the Almighty are of three kinds. Those who travel overseas are called palmers, as they often bring back palms; those who go to St James's shrine in Galicia are called pilgrims, because the burial place of St James was further away from his country than that of any other apostle; and romeos are those who go to Rome, which is where those whom I call pilgrims were going.

I do not divide this sonnet since it is quite clear from the foregoing account.

> *O pilgrims, meditating as you go,*
> > *On matters, it may be, not near at hand,*
> > *Have you then journeyed from so far a land,*
> > *As from your aspect one may plainly know,*
> > *That in the sorrowing city's midst you show*
> > *No sign of grief, but onward tearless wend,*
> > *Like people how, it seems, can understand*
> > *No part of all its grievous weight of woe?*
> *If you will stay to hear the tale unfold*
> > *My sighing heart does truly promise this:*
> > *That you will go forth weeping when I've done.*
> > *This city's lost her source of blessedness,*
> > *And even words which may of her be told*
> > *Have power to move tears in everyone.*

. . .

. . . LATER TWO GRACIOUS LADIES SENT WORD TO ME, REQUESTING
me to send them certain of my verses. Reflecting on their noble lineage, I
decided to send them a new composition, written specially for them, together with those they had asked for, in order that I might fulfil their request
the more worthily. So I then wrote a sonnet describing my state and sent it
to them with the previous sonnet and with another which begins: *Come, gentle
hearts* . . .

The sonnet which I wrote specially for them begins: *Beyond the widest* . . .
It is divided into five parts. In the first I say where my thought goes, and I
call it a sigh, naming it thus after one of its effects; in the second I say why
it ascends where it does, that is, what causes it to ascend; in the third I say
what it sees, that is a lady in glory; and then I call it a pilgrim spirit, for
spiritually it ascends into the heavens, and there abides for a while, like a
pilgrim who is away from his own country; in the fourth I say that it sees her
so beatified, that is, possess of such attributes, that I cannot comprehend,
that is to say, my thought ascends so far into the quality of her being that my
intellect cannot follow it; for our intellect in the presence of those blessed
souls is as weak as our eyes before the sun; and this is confirmed by the
Philosopher in the second book of his *Metaphysics;* in the fifth part I say that
although I cannot comprehend the place to which my thought takes me,
that is, into the presence of her miraculous nature, I understand this at least,
that this thought of mine is entirely concerned with my lady, for frequently
I hear her name. At the end of this fifth part I say: "Beloved ladies," to
convey that it is to ladies to whom I write these lines. The second part
begins: *A new celestial;* the third: *As it nears* . . . ; the fourth: *Gazing at her* . . . ;
and the fifth: *That noble one* . . .

> *Beyond the widest of the circling spheres*
> *A sigh which leaves my heart aspires to move.*
> *A new celestial influence which Love*
> *Bestows on it by virtue of his tears*
> *Impels it ever upwards. As it nears*
> *Its goal of longing in the realms above*
> *The pilgrim spirit sees a vision of*
> *A soul in glory whom the host reveres.*
> *Gazing at her, it speaks of what it sees*
> *In subtle words I do not comprehend*
> *Within my heart forlorn which bids it tell.*
> *That noble one is named, I apprehend,*
> *For frequently it mentions Beatrice;*
> *This much, beloved ladies, I know well.*

. . .

AFTER THIS SONNET THERE APPEARED TO ME A MARVELLOUS VISION in which I saw things which made me decide to write no more of this blessed one until I could do so more worthily. And to this end I apply myself as much as I can, as she indeed knows. Thus, if it shall please Him by whom all things live that my life continue for a few years, I hope to compose concerning her what has never been written in rhyme of any woman. And then may it please Him who is the Lord of courtesy that my soul may go to see the glory of my lady, that is of the blessed Beatrice, who now in glory beholds the face of Him *qui est per omnia secula benedictus* [Who is blessed for ever].

Little is known of the life of Julian of Norwich beyond the information she provides in her account of the "showings of divine love" she received on her sickbed. She was anchoress of the Church of Saints Julian and Edward in Norwich, England, and apparently took her name from that of the patron saint. She is not known to have taken religious orders, neither does she appear to have been connected with the nearby Benedictine abbey. She is known for her autobiographical book *Revelations of Divine Love*, usually entitled *Showings*. Two versions of the manuscript exist: a shorter version written immediately after the events described, and a longer version written some fifteen years later, incorporating the results of her prayers, meditations, and interpretations of the revelations she received.

Like Brother Lawrence, who described peace with God in terms of a child at its mother's breast, Julian of Norwich also experienced divine love as a maternal manifestation. She believed the "showings" had been granted her for the benefit of her fellow Christians, and made it her mission to publish an account

JULIAN OF NORWICH

[1 3 4 2 – A F T E R 1 4 1 6]

The soul has become nothing

for love.

of her visions, originally entitled "Comfortable Words for Christ's Lovers."
Selections from the shorter version of *Showings* are presented here.   [A M]

FROM *SHOWINGS*

Here is a vision shown by the goodness of God to a devout woman, and her name is Julian, who is a recluse at Norwich and still alive, A.D. 1413, in which vision are very many words of comfort, greatly moving for all those who desire to be Christ's lovers.

I desired three graces by the gift of God. The first was to have recollection of Christ's Passion. The second was a bodily sickness, and the third was to have, of God's gift, three wounds. As to the first, it came into my mind with devotion; it seemed to me that I had great feeling for the Passion of Christ, but still I desired to have more by the grace of God. I thought that I wished that I had been at that time with Mary Magdalen and with the others who were Christ's lovers, so that I might have seen with my own eyes our Lord's Passion which he suffered for me, so that I might have suffered with him as others did who loved him, even though I believed firmly in all Christ's pains, as Holy Church shows and teaches, and as paintings of the Crucifixion represent, which are made by God's grace, according to Holy Church's teaching, to resemble Christ's Passion, so far as human understanding can attain. But despite all my true faith I desired a bodily sight, through which I might have more knowledge of our Lord and saviour's bodily pains, and of the compassion of our Lady and of all his true lovers who were living at that time and saw his pains, for I would have been one of them and have suffered with them. I never desired any other sight of God or revelation, until my soul would be separated from the body, for I trusted truly that I would be saved. My intention was, because of that revelation, to have had truer recollection of Christ's Passion. As to the second grace, there came into my mind with contrition—a free gift from God which I did not seek—a desire of my will to have by God's gift a bodily sickness, and I wished it to be so severe that it might seem mortal, so that I should in that sickness receive all the rites which Holy Church had to give me, whilst I myself should believe that I was dying, and everyone who saw me would think the same, for I wanted no comfort from any human, earthly life. In this sickness I wanted to have every kind of pain, bodily and spiritual, which I should have if I were dying, every fear and assault from devils, and every other kind of pain except the departure of the spirit, for I hoped that this would be profitable to me when I should die, because I desired soon to be with my God.

I desired these two, concerning the Passion and the sickness, with a condition, because it seemed to me that neither was an ordinary petition, and therefore I said: Lord, you know what I want. If it be your will that I have it, grant it to me, and if it be not your will, good Lord, do not be displeased, for I want nothing which you do not want. When I was young I desired to have that sickness when I was thirty years old. As to the third, I heard a man of Holy Church tell the story of St. Cecilia, and from his explanation I understood that she received three wounds in the neck from a sword, through which she suffered death. Moved by this, I conceived a great desire, and prayed our Lord God that he would grant me in the course of my life three wounds, that is, the wound of contrition, the wound of compassion and the wound of longing with my will for God. Just as I asked for the other two conditionally, so I asked for this third without any condition. The two desires which I mentioned first passed from my mind, and the third remained there continually.

AND WHEN I WAS THIRTY AND A HALF YEARS OLD, GOD SENT ME A bodily sickness in which I lay for three days and three nights; and on the fourth night I received all the rites of Holy Church, and did not expect to live until day. But after this I suffered on for two days and two nights, and on the third night I often thought that I was on the point of death; and those who were around me also thought this. But in this I was very sorrowful and reluctant to die, not that there was anything on earth that it pleased me to live for, or anything of which I was afraid, for I trusted in God. But it was because I wanted to go on living to love God better and longer, and living so, obtain grace to know and love God more as he is in the bliss of heaven. For it seemed to me that all the time that I had lived here was very little and short in comparison with the bliss which is everlasting. So I thought: Good Lord, is it no longer to your glory that I am alive? And my reason and my sufferings told me that I should die; and with all the will of my heart I assented wholly to be as was God's will.

So I lasted until day, and by then my body was dead from the middle downwards, it felt to me. Then I was moved to ask to be lifted up and supported, with cloths held to my head, so that my heart might be more free to be at God's will, and so that I could think of him whilst my life would last; and those who were with me sent for the parson, my curate, to be present at my end. He came with a little boy, and brought a cross; and by that time my eyes were fixed, and I could not speak. The parson set the cross before my face and said: Daughter, I have brought you the image of your saviour. Look at it and take comfort from it, in reverence of him who died for you and me. It seemed to me that I was well as I was, for my eyes were set upwards towards heaven, where I trusted that I was going; but nevertheless I agreed to fix my eyes on the face of the crucifix if I could, so as to hold out longer until my end came, for it seemed to me that I could hold out longer with my eyes set in front of me rather than upwards. After this my sight began to fail, and it was all dark around me in the room, dark as night, except that there was ordinary light trained upon the image of the cross, I never knew how. Everything around the cross was ugly to me, as if it were occupied by a great crowd of devils.

After that I felt as if the upper part of my body were beginning to die. My hands fell down on either side, and I was so weak that my head lolled to one side. The greatest pain that I felt was my shortness of breath and the ebbing of my life. Then truly I believed that I was at the point of death. And suddenly in that moment all my pain left me, and I was as sound, particularly in the upper part of my body, as ever I was before or have been since. I was astonished by this change, for it seemed to me that it was by God's secret doing and not natural; and even so, in this ease which I felt, I had no more confidence that I should live, nor was the ease complete, for I thought that I would rather have been delivered of this world, because that was what my heart longed for.

AND SUDDENLY IT CAME INTO MY MIND THAT I OUGHT TO WISH FOR the second wound, that our Lord, of his gift and of his grace, would fill my body full with recollection and feeling of his blessed Passion, as I had prayed before, for I wished that his pains might be my pains, with compassion which would lead to longing for God. So it seemed to me that I might with his grace have his wounds, as I had wished before; but in this I never wanted any bodily vision or any kind of revelation from God, but only the compassion which I thought a loving soul could have for our Lord Jesus, who for love was willing to become a mortal man. I desired to suffer with him, living in my mortal body, as God would give me grace. And at this, suddenly I saw the red blood trickling down from under the crown, all hot, flowing freely and copiously, a living stream, just as it seemed to me that it was at the time when the crown of thorns was thrust down upon his blessed head. Just so did he, both God and man, suffer for me. I perceived, truly and powerfully, that it was himself who showed this to me, without any intermediary; and then I said: Blessed be the Lord! This I said with a reverent intention and in a loud voice, and I was greatly astonished by this wonder and marvel, that he would so humbly be with a sinful creature living in this wretched flesh. I accepted it that at that time our Lord Jesus wanted, out of his courteous love, to show me comfort before my temptations began; for it seemed to me that I might well be tempted by devils, by God's permission and with his protection, before I died. With this sight of his blessed Passion and with his divinity, of which I speak as I understand, I saw that this was strength enough for me, yes, and for all living creatures who will be protected from all thc devils of hell and from all their spiritual enemies.

AND AT THE SAME TIME AS I SAW THIS CORPOREAL SIGHT, OUR LORD showed me a spiritual sight of his familiar love. I saw that he is to us everything which is good and comforting for our help. He is our clothing, for he is that love which wraps and enfolds us, embraces us and guides us, surrounds us for his love, which is so tender that he may never desert us. And so in this sight I saw truly that he is everything which is good, as I understand.

And in this he showed me something small, no bigger than a hazelnut, lying in the palm of my hand, and I perceived that it was as round as any ball. I looked at it and thought: What can this be? And I was given this general answer: It is everything which is made. I was amazed that it could last, for I thought that it was so little that it could suddenly fall into nothing. And I was answered in my understanding: It lasts and always will, because God loves it; and thus everything has being through the love of God....

EVERYTHING THAT I SAY ABOUT MYSELF I MEAN TO APPLY TO ALL MY fellow Christians, for I am taught that this is what our Lord intends in this spiritual revelation. And therefore I pray you all for God's sake, and I counsel you for your own profit, that you disregard the wretched worm, the sinful creature to whom it was shown, and that mightily, wisely, lovingly and meekly you contemplate God, who out of his courteous love and his endless goodness was willing to show this vision generally, to the comfort of us all. And you who hear and see this vision and this teaching, which is from Jesus Christ for the edification of your souls, it is God's will and my wish that you accept it with as much joy and delight as if Jesus had shown it to you as he did to me.... But God forbid that you should say or assume that I am a teacher, for that is not and never was my intention; for I am a woman ignorant, weak and frail. But I know very well that what I am saying I have received by the revelation of him who is the sovereign teacher. But it is truly love which moves me to tell it to you, for I want God to be known and my fellow Christians to prosper, as I hope to prosper myself, by hating sin more and loving God more. But because I am a woman, ought I therefore to believe that I should not tell you of the goodness of God, when I saw at that same time that it is his will that it be known? You will see this clearly in what follows, if it be well and truly accepted. Then will you soon forget me who am a wretch, and do this, so that I am no hindrance to you, and you will contemplate Jesus, who is every man's teacher. I speak of those who will be saved, for at this time God showed me no one else; but in everything I believe as Holy Church teaches, for I beheld the whole of this blessed revelation of our Lord as unified in God's sight, and I never understood anything from it which bewilders me or keeps me from the true doctrine of Holy Church.

ALL THIS BLESSED TEACHING OF OUR LORD WAS SHOWN TO ME IN three parts, that is by bodily vision and by words formed in my understanding and by spiritual vision. But I may not and cannot show the spiritual visions to you as plainly and fully as I should wish; but I trust in our Lord God Almighty that he will, out of his goodness and for love of you, make you accept it more spiritually and more sweetly than I can or may tell it to you, and so may it be, for we are all one in love. And in all this I was humbly moved in love towards my fellow Christians, that they might all see and know the same as I saw, for I wished it to be a comfort to them all, as it is to me; for this vision was shown for all men, and not for me alone. . . .

And after this I saw, in bodily vision, in the face of the crucifix which hung before me, a part of Christ's Passion: contempt, spitting to defoul his body, buffeting of his blessed face, and many woes and pains, more than I can tell; and his colour often changed, and all his blessed face was for a time caked with dry blood. This I saw bodily and sorrowfully and dimly; and I wanted more of the light of day, to have seen it more clearly. And I was answered in my reason that if God wished to show me more he would, but that I needed no light but him.

AND AFTER THIS I SAW GOD IN AN INSTANT OF TIME, THAT IS, IN MY understanding, and by this vision I saw that he is present in all things. I contemplated it carefully, knowing and perceiving through it that he does everything which is done. I marvelled at this vision with a gentle fear, and I thought: What is sin? For I saw truly that God does everything, however small it may be, and that nothing is done by chance, but it is of the endless providence of God's wisdom. Therefore I was compelled to admit that everything which is done is well done, and I was certain that God does no sin. Therefore it seemed to me that sin is nothing, for in all this sin was not shown to me. And I did not wish to go on feeling surprise at this, but I contemplated our Lord and waited for what he would show me. And on another occasion God did show me, nakedly in itself, what sin is, as I shall tell afterwards.

And after this as I watched I saw the body bleeding copiously, the blood hot, flowing freely, a living stream, just as I had before seen the head bleed. And I saw this in the furrows made by the scourging, and I saw this blood run so plentifully that it seemed to me that if it had in fact been happening there, the bed and everything around it would have been soaked in blood.

God has created bountiful waters on the earth for our use and our bodily comfort, out of the tender love he has for us. But it is more pleasing to him that we accept freely his blessed blood to wash us of our sins, for there is no drink that is made which it pleases him so well to give us; for it is so plentiful, and it is of our own nature.

AFTER THIS CHRIST SHOWED ME PART OF HIS PASSION, CLOSE TO his death. I saw his sweet face as it were dry and bloodless, with the pallor of dying, then more dead, pale and languishing, then the pallor turning blue and then more blue, as death took more hold upon his flesh. For all the pains which Christ suffered in his body appeared to me in his blessed face, in all that I could see of it, and especially in the lips. I saw there what had become of the four colours that I had seen before: his freshness, his ruddiness, his vitality and his beauty which I had seen. This was a grievous change to watch, this deep dying, and the nose shrivelled and dried up as I saw. The long torment seemed to me as if he had been dead for a week and had still gone on suffering pain, and it seemed to me as if the greatest and the last pain of his Passion was when his flesh dried up. And in this drying what Christ had said came to my mind: I thirst. For I saw in Christ a double thirst, one physical, the other spiritual. This saying was shown to me to signify the physical thirst, and what was revealed to me of the spiritual thirst I shall say afterwards; and concerning the physical thirst, I understood that the body was wholly dried up, for his blessed flesh and bones were left without blood or moisture. The blessed body was left to dry for a long time, with the wrenching of the nails and the sagging of the head and the weight of the body, with the blowing of the wind around him, which dried up his body and pained him with cold, more than my heart can think of, and with all his other pains I saw such pain that all that I can describe or say is inadequate, for it cannot be described. But each soul should do as St. Paul says, and feel in himself what is in Christ Jesus. This revelation of Christ's pains filled me full of pains, for I know well that he suffered only once, but it was now his will to show it to me and fill me with its recollection, as I had asked before. My mother, who was standing there with the others, held up her hand in front of my face to close my eyes, for she thought that I was already dead or had that moment died; and this greatly increased my sorrow, for despite all my pains, I did not want to be hindered from seeing, because of my love for him. And with regard to either, in all this time that Christ was present to me, I felt no pain except for Christ's pains; and then it came to me that I had little known what pain it was that I had asked for, for it seemed to me that my pains exceeded any mortal death. I thought: Is there any pain in hell like this? And in my reason I was answered that despair is greater, for that is a spiritual pain. But there is no greater physical pain than this; how could I suffer greater pain than to see him who is all my life, all my bliss and all my joy suffer? Here I felt truly that I loved Christ so much more than myself that I thought it would have been a great comfort to me if my body had died.

In this I saw part of the compassion of our Lady, St. Mary, for Christ and she were so united in love that the greatness of her love was the cause of the greatness of her pain. For her pain surpassed that of all others, as much as she loved him more than all others. And so all his disciples and all his true lovers suffered greater pains than they did at the death of their own bodies. For I am sure, by my own experience, that the least of them loved him more than they loved themselves. And here I saw a great unity between Christ and us; for when he was in pain we were in pain, and all creatures able to suffer pain suffered with him. And for those that did not know him, their pain was that all creation, sun and moon, ceased to serve men, and so they were all abandoned in sorrow at that time. So those who loved him suffered pain for their love, and those who did not love him suffered pain because the comfort of all creation failed them.

At this time I wanted to look to the side of the cross, but I did not dare, for I knew well that whilst I looked at the cross I was secure and safe. Therefore I would not agree to put my soul in danger, for apart from the cross there was no safety, but only the horror of devils.

Then there came a suggestion, seemingly friendly, to my reason. It was said to me: Look up to heaven to his Father. Then I saw clearly by the faith which I felt that there was nothing between the cross and heaven which could have grieved me, and that I must either look up or else answer. I answered, and said: No, I cannot, for you are my heaven. I said this because I did not want to look up, for I would rather have remained in that pain until Judgment Day than have come to heaven any other way than by him. For I knew well that he who had bought me so dearly would unbind me when it was his will.

THUS I CHOSE JESUS FOR MY HEAVEN, WHOM I SAW ONLY IN PAIN AT that time. No other heaven was pleasing to me than Jesus, who will be my bliss when I am there; and this has always been a comfort to me, that I chose Jesus as my heaven in all times of suffering and of sorrow. And that has taught me that I should always do so, and choose only him to be my heaven in well-being and in woe. And so I saw my Lord Jesus languishing for long, because of the union in him of man and God, for love gave strength to his humanity to suffer more than all men could. I mean not only more pain than any other one man could suffer, but also that he suffered more pain than would all men together, from the first beginning to the last day. No tongue may tell, no heart can fully think of the pains which our saviour suffered for us, if we have regard to the honour of him who is the highest, most majestic king, and to his shameful, grievous and painful death. For he who was highest and most honourable was most completely brought low, most utterly despised. But the love which made him suffer all this surpasses all his pains as far as heaven is above earth. For his pains were a deed, performed once through the motion of love; but his love was without beginning and is and ever will be without any end.

AND SUDDENLY, AS I LOOKED AT THE SAME CROSS, HE CHANGED TO an appearance of joy. The change in his appearance changed mine, and I was as glad and joyful as I could possibly be. And then cheerfully our Lord suggested to my mind: Where is there any instant of your pain or of your grief? And I was very joyful.

Then our Lord put a question to me: Are you well satisfied that I suffered for you? Yes, good Lord, I said; all my thanks to you, good Lord, blessed may you be! If you are satisfied, our Lord said, I am satisfied. It is a joy and a bliss and an endless delight to me that ever I suffered my Passion for you, for if I could suffer more, I would. In response to this, my understanding was lifted up into heaven, and there I saw three heavens; and at this sight I was greatly astonished, and I thought: I have seen three heavens, and all are of the blessed humanity of Christ. And none is greater, none is less, none is higher, none is lower, but all are equal in their joy.

For the first heaven, Christ showed me his Father, not in any corporeal likeness, but in his attributes and in his joy. For the Father's operation is this: He rewards his Son, Jesus Christ. This gift and this reward is so joyful to Jesus that his Father could have given him no reward which could have pleased him better. For the first heaven, which is the Father's bliss, appeared to me as a heaven, and it was full of bliss. For Jesus has great joy in all the deeds which he has done for our salvation, and therefore we are his, not only through our redemption but also by his Father's courteous gift. We are his bliss, we are his reward, we are his honour, we are his crown.

What I am describing now is so great a joy to Jesus that he counts as nothing his labour and his bitter sufferings and his cruel and shameful death. And in these words: If I could suffer more, I would suffer more, I saw truly that if he could die as often as once for every man who is to be saved, as he did once for all men, love would never let him rest till he had done it. And when he had done it, he would count it all as nothing for love, for everything seems only little to him in comparison with his love. And that he plainly said to me, gravely saying this: If I could suffer more. He did not say: If it were necessary to suffer more, but: If I could suffer more; for although it might not be necessary, if he could suffer more he would suffer more. This deed and this work for our salvation were as well done as he could devise it. It was done as honourably as Christ could do it, and in this I saw complete joy in Christ; but his joy would not have been complete if the deed could have been done any better than it was. And in these three sayings: It is a joy, a bliss and an endless delight to me, there were shown to me three heavens, and in this way. By "joy" I understood that the Father was pleased, by "bliss" that the Son was honoured, and by "endless delight" the Holy Spirit. The Father is pleased, the Son is honoured, the Holy Spirit takes delight. Jesus wants us to pay heed to this bliss for our salvation which is in the blessed Trinity, and to take equal delight, through his grace, whilst we are here. And this was shown to me when he said: Are you well satisfied? And by what Christ next said: If you are satisfied, I am satisfied, he made me understand that it was as if he had said: This is joy and delight enough for me, and I ask nothing else for my labour but that I may satisfy you. Generously and completely was this revealed to me.

So think wisely, how great this saying is: That ever I suffered my Passion for you; for in that saying was given exalted understanding of the love and the delight that he had in our salvation. . . .

. . .

THEN OUR LORD OPENED MY SPIRITUAL EYES, AND SHOWED ME MY soul in the midst of my heart. I saw my soul as wide as if it were a kingdom, and from the state which I saw in it, it seemed to me as if it were a fine city. In the midst of this city sits our Lord Jesus, true God and true man, a handsome person and tall, honourable, the greatest lord. And I saw him splendidly clad in honours. He sits erect there in the soul, in peace and rest, and he rules and he guards heaven and earth and everything that is. The humanity and the divinity sit at rest, and the divinity rules and guards, without instrument or effort. And my soul is blessedly occupied by the divinity, sovereign power, sovereign wisdom, sovereign goodness. . . .

And soon afterwards all was hidden, and I saw no more.

SAINT TERESA

OF AVILA

[1515–1582]

Nor is the soul content with less

than God.

By her own account, Teresa of Avila entered the convent with little zeal and for the succeeding twenty years experienced an agonizing spiritual struggle, culminating in the revelations and visions that have made her one of the most noted mystics in the Western European literary tradition. A reformer of the Carmelite order and correspondent with the leading religious and philosophical minds of her day, she was the author of several works on prayer and the contemplative life, notably *The Interior Castle*, as well as her own spiritual testimonies and autobiographies. In *The Book of Her Life*, excerpted here, she recounts several of her salvific visions, including the experience of being stabbed by an angel with a fiery dart, which has furnished the subject of numerous iconographic works, notably Giovanni Bernini's famous sculpture. In 1970, she was one of the first women saints to be named a Doctor of the Church. [AM]

FROM *THE BOOK OF HER LIFE*

Since my confessors commanded me and gave me plenty of leeway to write about the favors and the kind of prayer the Lord has granted me, I wish they would also have allowed me to tell very clearly and minutely about my great sins and wretched life. This would be a consolation. But they didn't want me to. In fact I was very much restricted in those matters. And so I ask, for the love of God, whoever reads this account to bear in mind that my life has been so wretched that I have not found a saint among those who were converted to God in whom I can find comfort. For I note that after the Lord called them, they did not turn back and offend Him. As for me, not only did I turn back and become worse, but it seems I made a study out of resisting the favors His Majesty was granting me. I was like someone who sees that she is obliged to serve more, yet understands that she can't pay the smallest part of her debt.

May God be blessed forever, He who waited for me so long! I beseech Him with all my heart to give me the grace to present with complete clarity and truthfulness this account of my life which my confessors ordered me to write. And I know, too, that even the Lord has for some time wanted me to do this, although I have not dared. May this account render Him glory and praise. And from now on may my confessors knowing me better through this narration help me in my weakness to give the Lord something of the service I owe Him, whom all things praise forever. Amen.

TO HAVE HAD VIRTUOUS AND GOD-FEARING PARENTS ALONG WITH the graces the Lord granted me should have been enough for me to have led a good life, if I had not been so wretched. My father was fond of reading good books, and thus he also had books in Spanish for his children to read. These good books together with the care my mother took to have us pray and be devoted to our Lady and to some of the saints began to awaken me when, I think, six or seven years old, to the practice of virtue. It was a help to me to see that my parents favored nothing but virtue. And they themselves possessed many.

My father was a man very charitable with the poor and compassionate toward the sick, and even toward servants. So great was his compassion that nobody was ever able to convince him to accept slaves. And his pity for them was such that once having in his home a slave owned by his brother, he treated her as though she were one of his children. He used to say that out of pity he couldn't bear seeing her held captive. He was very honest. No one ever saw him swear or engage in fault-finding. He was an upright man.

My mother also had many virtues. And she suffered much sickness during her life. She was extremely modest. Although very beautiful, she never gave occasion to anyone to think she paid any attention to her beauty. For at the time of her death at the age of thirty-three, her clothes were already those of a much older person. She was gentle and very intelligent. Great were the trials she suffered during her life. Her death was a truly Christian one.

We were in all three sisters and nine brothers. All resembled their parents in being virtuous, through the goodness of God, with the exception of myself —although I was the most loved of my father. And it seemed he was right— before I began to offend God. For I am ashamed when I recall the good inclinations the Lord gave me and how poorly I knew how to profit by them.

My brothers and sisters did not in any way hold me back from the service of God. I had one brother about my age. We used to get together to read the lives of the saints. (He was the one I liked most, although I had great love for them all and they for me.) When I considered the martyrdoms the saints suffered for God, it seemed to me that the price they paid for going to enjoy God was very cheap, and I greatly desired to die in the same way. I did not want this on account of the love I felt for God but to get to enjoy very quickly the wonderful things I read there were in heaven. And my brother and I discussed together the means we should take to achieve this. We agreed to go off to the land of the Moors and beg them, out of love of God, to cut off our heads there. It seemed to me the Lord had given us courage at so tender an age, but we couldn't discover any means. Having parents seemed to us the greatest obstacle. We were terrified in what we read about the suffering and the glory that was to last forever. We spent a lot of time talking about this and took delight in often repeating: forever and ever and ever. As I said this over and over, the Lord was pleased to impress upon me in childhood the way of truth.

When I saw it was impossible to go where I would be killed for God, we made plans to be hermits. And in a garden that we had in our house, we tried as we could to make hermitages piling up some little stones which afterward would quickly fall down again. And so in nothing could we find a remedy for our desire. It gives me devotion now to see how God gave me so early what I lost through my own fault.

I gave what alms I could, but that was little. I sought out solitude to pray my devotions, and they were many, especially the rosary, to which my mother was very devoted; and she made us devoted to it too. When I played with other girls I enjoyed it when we pretended we were nuns in a monastery, and it seemed to me that I desired to be one, although not as much as I desired the other things I mentioned.

I remember that when my mother died I was twelve years old or a little less. When I began to understand what I had lost, I went, afflicted, before an image of our Lady and besought her with many tears to be my mother. It seems to me that although I did this in simplicity it helped me. For I have found favor with this sovereign Virgin in everything I have asked of her, and in the end she has drawn me to herself. It wearies me now to see and think that I was not constant in the good desires I had in my childhood.

O my Lord, since it seems You have determined to save me, I beseech Your Majesty that it may be so. And since You have granted me as many favors as You have, don't You think it would be good (not for my gain but for Your honor) if the inn where You have so continually to dwell were not to get so dirty? It wearies me, Lord, even to say this, for I know that the whole fault was mine. It doesn't seem to me that there was anything more for You to do in order that from this age I would be all Yours. If I start to complain about my parents, I am not able to do so, for I saw nothing but good in them and solicitude for my own good.

As I grew older, when I began to know of the natural attractive qualities the Lord had bestowed on me (which others said were many), instead of thanking Him for them, I began to make use of them all to offend Him, as I shall now tell.

WHAT I AM GOING TO TELL ABOUT BEGAN, IT SEEMS TO ME, TO DO me much harm. I sometimes reflect on the great damage parents do by not striving that their children might always see virtuous deeds of every kind. For even though my mother, as I said, was virtuous, I did not, in reaching the age of reason, imitate her good qualities; in fact hardly at all. And the bad ones did me much harm. She loved books of chivalry. But this pastime didn't hurt her the way it did me, for she did not fail to do her duties; and we used to read them together in our free time. Perhaps she did this reading to escape thinking of the great trials she had to bear and to busy her children with something so that they would not turn to other things dangerous to them. Our reading such books was a matter that weighed so much upon my father that we had to be cautioned lest he see us. I began to get the habit of reading these books. And by that little fault, which I saw in my mother, I started to grow cold in my desires and to fail in everything else. I didn't think it was wrong to waste many hours of the day and night in such a useless practice, even though hidden from my father. I was so completely taken up with this reading that I didn't think I could be happy if I didn't have a new book.

I began to dress in finery and to desire to please and look pretty, taking great care of my hands and hair and about perfumes and all the empty things in which one can indulge, and which were many, for I was very vain. I had no bad intentions since I would not have wanted anyone to offend God on my account. For many years I took excessive pains about cleanliness and other things that did not seem in any way sinful. Now I see how wrong it must have been. . . .

The first eight days I felt very unhappy because of my being in [the] convent school, and more than that because of my suspicion that they knew about my vanity. For already I was wearied and did not fail to have great fear of God when I offended Him, trying to go to confession at once. Although at the beginning I was very unhappy, within eight days—and I think even less—I was much more content than when in my father's house. All were very pleased with me, for the Lord gave me the grace to be pleasing wherever I went, and so I was much loved. And although at that time I was strongly against my becoming a nun, it made me happy to see such good nuns, for there were many good ones in that house, very modest, religious and circumspect. Nonetheless, in spite of all, the devil didn't let up tempting me, through some outsiders who continued to send me messages. But since the opportunities were few, these persons stopped sending them. My soul began to return to the good habits of early childhood, and I saw the great favor God accords to anyone placed with good companions. It seems to me that His Majesty was considering and reconsidering in what way He could bring me back to Himself. May You be blessed, Lord, who put up with me so long! Amen.

One thing, it seems, that could have amounted to some excuse for me, should I not have had so many faults, was that the friendship with one of my cousins was in view of a possible marriage; and having inquired of my confessor and other persons about many things, I was told I was doing nothing against God.

There was a nun there in care of the dormitory for all of us who were lay persons. It was by means of her it seems that the Lord wished to begin to give me light, as I shall now tell.

BEGINNING, THEN, TO LIKE THE GOOD AND HOLY CONVERSATION OF this nun, I was glad to hear how well she spoke about God, for she was very discreet and saintly. There was no time it seems to me when I was not happy to hear about God. She began to tell me how she arrived at the decision to become a nun solely by reading what the Gospel says: *many are the called and few the chosen.* She told me about the reward the Lord grants those who give up all for Him. This good company began to help me get rid of the habits that the bad company had caused and to turn my mind to the desire for eternal things and for some freedom from the antagonism that I felt strongly within myself toward becoming a nun. And if I saw someone with the gift of tears when she prayed, or other virtues, I greatly envied her. For so hard was my heart that I could read the entire Passion without shedding a tear. This pained me.

After a year and a half in the convent school I was much better. I began to recite many vocal prayers and to seek that all commend me to God so that He might show me the state in which I was to serve Him. But still I had no desire to be a nun, and I asked God not to give me this vocation; although I also feared marriage.

By the end of this period of time in which I stayed there I was more favorable to the thought of being a nun, although not in that house, for there were things I was afterward to understand were most virtuous that seemed to me to be too extreme. And some of the youngest of the nuns contributed to my thinking this, for if all of them had been of one mind I would have greatly profited. Also, I had a good friend in another convent, and that was the reason why if I were to become a nun I would not have done so unless it were in the convent where she was. I looked more to pleasing my sensuality and vanity than to what was good for my soul. These good thoughts about being a nun sometimes came to me, and then would go away; and I could not be persuaded to be one. . . .

And although my will did not completely incline to being a nun, I saw that the religious life was the best and safest state, and so little by little I decided to force myself to accept it.

I was engaged in this battle within myself for three months, forcing myself with this reasoning: that the trials and hardships of being a nun could not be greater than those of purgatory and that I had really merited hell; that it would not be so great a thing while alive to live as though in purgatory; and that afterward I would go directly to heaven, for that was my desire.

And in this business of choosing a state, it seems to me I was moved more by servile fear than by love. The devil was suggesting that I would not be able to suffer the trials of religious life because I was too pampered. I resisted this with the thought of the trials Christ suffered and that it would be no great thing if I suffered some for Him; and that He would help me to bear them—I ought to have had this last thought, I don't remember if I did. I suffered very many temptations those days.

At that time I had together with a high fever, great fainting spells; for I always had poor health. My fondness for good books was my salvation. Reading the *Letters of St. Jerome* so encouraged me that I decided to tell my father about my decision to take the habit, for I was so persistent in points of honor that I don't think I would have turned back for anything once I told him. So great was his love for me that in no way was I able to obtain his permission or achieve anything through persons I asked to intercede for me. The most we could get from him was that after his death I could do whatever I wanted. I was afraid of myself and my frailty and of backing down; and since I could not wait so long, I tried to do it by another way, as I shall now tell. . . .

At this time they gave me *The Confessions of St. Augustine.* It seems the Lord ordained this, because I had not tried to procure a copy, nor had I ever seen one. I am very fond of St. Augustine, because the convent where I stayed as a lay person belonged to his order; and also because he had been a sinner, for I found great consolation in sinners whom, after having been sinners, the Lord brought back to Himself. It seemed to me I could find help in them and that since the Lord had pardoned them He could also pardon me. But there was one thing that left me inconsolable, as I have mentioned, and that was that the Lord called them only once, and they did not turn back and fall again; whereas in my case I had turned back so often that I was worn out from it. But by considering the love He bore me, I regained my courage, for I never lost confidence in His mercy; in myself, I lost it many times.

Oh, God help me, how it frightens me, my soul's blindness despite so much assistance from God! It made me fearful to see how little I could do by myself and how bound I became so that I was unable to resolve to give myself entirely to God.

As I began to read the *Confessions,* it seemed to me I saw myself in them. I began to commend myself very much to this glorious saint. When I came to the passage where he speaks about his conversion and read how he heard that voice in the garden, it only seemed to me, according to what I felt in my heart, that it was I the Lord called. I remained for a long time totally dissolved in tears and feeling within myself utter distress and weariness. Oh, how a soul suffers, God help me, by losing the freedom it should have in being itself; and what torments it undergoes! I marvel now at how I could have lived in such great affliction. May God be praised who gave me the life to rise up from a death so deadly.

It seemed to me my soul gained great strength from the Divine Majesty and that He must have heard my cries and taken pity on so many tears. The inclination to spend more time with Him began to grow. I started to shun the occasions of sin, because when they were avoided I then returned to loving His Majesty. In my opinion, I clearly understood that I loved Him; but I did not understand as I should have what true love of God consists in.

It doesn't seem to me I was yet finished preparing myself to desire to serve Him when His Majesty began to favor me again. Apparently, what others strive for with great labor, the Lord gains for me only through my desire to receive it, for He was now, in these later years, giving me delights and favors. I did not beseech Him to give me tenderness of devotion, never would I have dared to do that. I only begged Him to pardon my great sins and to give me the grace not to offend Him. Since I saw that my sins were so great, I would never have had the boldness to desire favors or delights. Clearly, it seems, He took pity on me and showed great mercy in admitting me before Him and bringing me into His presence, for I saw that if He Himself had not accomplished this, I would not have come.

Only once in my life, when in great dryness, do I recall having asked for spiritual delight. And when I became aware of what I was doing, I got so confused that the very annoyance at seeing myself with such lack of humility brought about what I had dared to ask for. I knew well that it was permissible to ask for this, but it seemed to me that such a request was licit for those who were prepared and determined to do every good and not to offend God. It seemed to me that the tears I shed were womanish and without strength since I did not obtain by them what I desired. But still, I believe they were valuable for me because, as I say, especially after these two instances of such great compunction and weariness of heart over my sins, I began to give myself more to prayer and to become less involved with things that did me harm, although I still did not avoid them completely; but—as I say—God was helping me turn aside from them. Since His Majesty was not waiting for anything other than some preparedness in me, the spiritual graces went on increasing in the manner I shall tell. It is not a customary thing for the Lord to give them save to those with greater purity of conscience.

I SOMETIMES EXPERIENCED, AS I SAID, ALTHOUGH VERY BRIEFLY, the beginning of what I will now speak about. It used to happen, when I represented Christ within me in order to place myself in His presence, or even while reading, that a feeling of the presence of God would come upon me unexpectedly so that I could in no way doubt He was within me or I totally immersed in Him. This did not occur after the manner of a vision. I believe they call the experience "mystical theology." The soul is suspended in such a way that it seems to be completely outside itself. The will loves; the memory, it seems to me, is almost lost. For, as I say, the intellect does not work, but it is as though amazed by all it understands because God desires that it understand, with regard to the things His Majesty represents to it, that it understands nothing.

. . .

WELL, TO RETURN TO THE ACCOUNT OF MY LIFE. I WAS ENDURING this difficult affliction, and, as I have said, many prayers were being offered up that the Lord might lead me by another safer path since this one, they told me, was so suspect. The truth of the matter is that even though I was beseeching God and however much I wanted to desire another path, it wasn't in my power to desire it, even though I always prayed for it, because I saw my soul so improved—except sometimes when I was very worn out from the things they told me and the fears they caused. I saw that I was a completely different person. I could not desire another path, but I placed myself in the hands of God that He would carry out His will completely in me; He knew what suited me. I saw that on this road I was being led to heaven, that previously I had been going to hell, and that I should want to follow this road and not believe that it had the devil as cause. Nor was I able to force myself, even though I did all I could, to believe and desire another road; it wasn't in my power to do so. I offered up what I did, if there was some good deed, for this intention. I invoked my favorite saints that they might free me from the devil. I made novenas. I recommended myself to St. Hilarion and to St. Michael the Archangel, of whom again I became a devotee for this purpose, and I begged many other saints that the Lord might show the truth —I mean that they might obtain this for me from His Majesty.

After two years of all these prayers of mine and those of others offered for the said intention (that the Lord would either lead me by another way or make known the truth, for the locutions I mentioned that the Lord granted me were experienced very repeatedly), the following happened to me. Being in prayer on the feastday of the glorious St. Peter, I saw or, to put it better, I felt Christ beside me; I saw nothing with my bodily eyes or with my soul, but it seemed to me that Christ was at my side—I saw that it was He, in my opinion, who was speaking to me. Since I was completely unaware that there could be a vision like this one, it greatly frightened me in the beginning; I did nothing but weep. However, by speaking one word alone to assure me, the Lord left me feeling as I usually did: quiet, favored, and without any fear. It seemed to me that Jesus Christ was always present at my side; but since this wasn't an imaginative vision, I didn't see any form. Yet I felt very clearly that He was always present at my right side and that He was the witness of everything I did. At no time in which I was a little recollected, or not greatly distracted, was I able to ignore that He was present at my side.

I immediately went very anxiously to my confessor to tell him. He asked me in what form I saw Him. I answered that I didn't see Him. He asked how I knew that it was Christ. I answered that I didn't know how, but that I couldn't help knowing that He was beside me, that I saw and felt Him

clearly, that my recollection of soul was greater, and that I was very continuously in the prayer of quiet, that the effects were much different from those
I usually experienced, and that it was very clear.

I could do nothing but draw comparisons in order to explain myself. And,
indeed, there is no comparison that fits this kind of vision very well. Since
this vision is among the most sublime (as I was afterward told by a very holy
and spiritual man, whose name is Friar Peter of Alcántara and of whom I
shall speak later, and by other men of great learning) and the kind in which
the devil can interfere the least of all, there are no means by which those of
us who know little here below can explain it. Learned men will explain it
better. For if I say that I see it with the eyes neither of the body nor of the
soul, because it is not an imaginative vision, how do I know and affirm that
He is more certainly at my side than if I saw Him? It is incorrect to think
that the vision is like that experience of those who are blind or in the dark
who don't see the other at their side. There is some likeness in this comparison but not a great deal, because in such a case these people experience
with their senses: either they hear the other person speak or stir, or they
touch them. In the vision there is nothing of this, nor do you see darkness;
but the vision is represented through knowledge given to the soul that is
clearer than sunlight. I don't mean that you see the sun or brightness, but
that a light, without your seeing light, illumines the intellect so that the soul
may enjoy such a great good. The vision bears with it wonderful blessings.

This vision is not like the presence of God that is often felt, especially by
those who experience the prayer of union or quiet, in which it seems that in
desiring to begin to practice prayer we find Him to speak to, and it seems
we know that He hears us through the effects and spiritual feelings of great
love and faith that we tenderly experience, and through other resolutions.
This presence is a great favor from God and should be highly esteemed by
the one He gives it to, for it is a very sublime prayer, but it is not a vision; in
this prayer of union or quiet one understands that God is present by the
effects that, as I say, He grants to the soul—that is the way His Majesty
wants to give the experience of Himself. In this vision it is seen clearly that
Jesus Christ, son of the Virgin, is present. In the prayer of union or quiet
some impressions of the Divinity are bestowed; in this vision, along with the
impressions, you see that also the most sacred humanity accompanies us and
desires to grant us favors.

Then the confessor asked me, "Who said it was Jesus Christ?" "He told
me many times," I answered. But before He told me He impressed upon
my intellect that it was He, and before doing this latter He told me He was
present—but I didn't see Him. If a person whom I had never seen but only
heard of should come to speak to me while I was blind or in the pitch dark
and tell me who he was, I would believe it; but I wouldn't be able to assert

as strongly that it was that person as I would if I saw him. In the case of this vision, I would; for, without being seen, it is impressed with such clear knowledge that I don't think it can be doubted. The Lord desires to be so engraved upon the intellect that this vision can no more be doubted than can what is seen; and even less, because when we see we sometimes suspect we may have fancied what we saw. In this vision, even though a suspicion may at first arise, there remains on the other hand such great certitude that the doubt has no force.

THE SPLENDOR IS NOT ONE THAT DAZZLES; IT HAS A SOFT WHITE-ness, is infused, gives the most intense delight to the sight, and doesn't tire it; neither does the brilliance, in which is seen the vision of so divine a beauty, tire it. It is a light so different from earthly light that the sun's brightness that we see appears very tarnished in comparison with that bright-ness and light represented to the sight, and so different that afterward you wouldn't want to open your eyes. It's like the difference between a sparkling, clear water that flows over crystal and on which the sun is reflecting and a very cloudy, muddy water flowing along the ground. This doesn't mean that the sun is represented or that the light resembles sunlight. It seems in fact like natural light, and the sunlight seems artificial. It is a light that has no night; nothing troubles it. In sum, it is of such a kind that a person couldn't imagine what it is like in all of life's days no matter how powerful the intellect. God gives it so suddenly that there wouldn't even be time to open your eyes, if it were necessary to open them. For when the Lord desires to give the vision, it makes no more difference if they are opened than if they are closed; even if we do not desire to see the vision, it is seen. No distraction is enough to resist it, nor is there power or diligence or care enough to do so. I have clearly experienced this, as I shall say.

FOR TWO AND A HALF YEARS GOD FREQUENTLY GRANTED ME THIS favor. It must be for over three years now that He has continually replaced this favor with another more sublime—as I shall perhaps afterward explain. And in being aware that He was speaking to me and that I was beholding that great beauty and the gentleness with which He spoke those words with His most beautiful and divine mouth—and at other times beholding His severity—and strongly desiring to know the color of His eyes, or how tall

He was, so that I could be able to describe these things, I never merited to see them. Nor was I able to obtain this knowledge; rather, by trying to do so, I would lose the vision entirely. Indeed I sometimes see Him looking at me with pity, but this kind of vision is so powerful that the soul cannot suffer it, and it remains in such a sublime rapture that in order to enjoy the beautiful vision more completely it loses it. Hence with respect to this vision there is nothing to desire or not to desire. It is clearly seen that the Lord desires nothing else than humility and confusion, and that we accept what is given and praise the one who gives it.

This is the case in all visions without exception; our effort can neither do nor undo anything when it comes to seeing more or seeing less. So that we may be made less capable of pride, the Lord desires us to be very clearly aware that this is not our work but His Majesty's work. Rather, it makes us humble and fearful when we observe that since the Lord takes away our power of seeing what we desire to see, He can take from us these favors and gifts—and we shall be left with nothing. We should always walk in fear as long as we live in this exile.

The Lord almost always showed Himself to me as risen, also when He appeared in the Host—except at times when He showed me His wounds in order to encourage me when I was suffering tribulation. Sometimes He appeared on the cross or in the garden, and a few times with the crown of thorns; sometimes He also appeared carrying the cross on account, as I say, of my needs and those of others. But His body was always glorified.

I suffered numerous affronts and trials in speaking about these visions, and very many persecutions. It seemed so certain to them that I had a devil that some persons wanted to exorcise me. This didn't matter much to me; but I grieved when I saw that my confessors were afraid to hear my confession or when I learned that others said something to them. Nonetheless, I was never able to regret having seen these heavenly visions, and I would not exchange even one for all the goods and delights of the world. I have always considered a vision a great favor from the Lord. It seems to me to be a most rich treasure, and the Lord Himself assured me of this many times. I saw that I was increasing very much in His love. I went to Him to complain about all these trials, and I always came away from prayer consoled and with new strength. I didn't dare contradict those who were judging my spirit, because I saw that everything would then become worse since my doing so would appear to them as a lack of humility. I talked with my confessor; he always consoled me greatly when he saw that I was troubled.

Since the visions were increasing, one from the group who previously helped me—for he sometimes heard my confession when the ordinary confessor wasn't able to do so—began to say that it was clearly the devil. He ordered that, since I didn't have the means to resist the visions, I should always bless myself when I saw one and make the gesture of scorn called the fig; he was certain the devil was the cause and that by my doing this the vision wouldn't return. He told me that I shouldn't be afraid, that God would protect me and take it away from me. Following this advice was very painful to me. Since I couldn't believe but that the vision was from God, it was a terrible thing for me to have to do what I was commanded; and neither could I desire, as I said, that the vision be taken away. But, finally, I did all they ordered me to do. I begged God persistently and with many tears that He would free me from deception. And I begged St. Peter and St. Paul; for since the first time the Lord appeared to me was on their feastday, He told me that they would protect me from being deceived. Thus I often saw them very clearly at my left, although not by an imaginative vision. These glorious saints were very much lords of mine.

Making the fig at this vision of the Lord caused me the greatest pain. When I saw Him present, I couldn't have believed it was the devil if they broke me in pieces; thus it was a kind of severe penance for me. So that I would not be forever blessing myself, I held a cross in my hand. I did this almost all the time; I didn't make the fig so continually, because it grieved me deeply to do so. I recalled the injuries the Jews caused Him and begged Him to pardon me since I was doing it in order to obey the one who stood in His place, and not to blame me, since they were the ministers that He had placed in His Church. He told me not to worry and that I did well in obeying, but that He would make the truth known. When they forbade me to practice prayer, it seemed to me He was annoyed. He told me to tell them that now what they were doing was tyranny. He gave me signs for knowing that the vision was not from the devil. I shall mention some afterward.

Once while I was holding the cross in my hand, for I had it on a rosary, He took it from me with His own hands; when He gave it back to me, it was made of four large stones incomparably more precious than diamonds— there is no appropriate comparison for supernatural things. A diamond seems to be something counterfeit and imperfect when compared with the precious stones that are seen there. The representation of the five wounds was of very delicate workmanship. He told me that from then on I would see the cross in that way; and so it happened, for I didn't see the wood from which it was made but these stones. No one, however, saw this except me.

When I began to try to obey the command to reject and resist these favors, there was a much greater increase in them. In seeking to distract myself, I never got free from prayer. It even seemed to me that I was in prayer while sleeping. There was an increase of love and of the loving complaints I was addressing to the Lord; the pain became unbearable, nor was it in my power to stop thinking of Him no matter how much I tried and even though I wanted to. Nonetheless, I obeyed when I could; but in this matter I was able to do little or nothing at all, and the Lord never took prayer from me. But even though He told me to do what they said, He assured me on the other hand and taught me what I should say to them—and so He does now. He gave me so many adequate reasons that these reasons made me feel completely secure.

After a short time His Majesty began as He had promised me to give further indication that it was He by increasing the love of God in me to such a degree that I didn't know where it came from (for it was very supernatural); nor did I procure it. I saw that I was dying with desire to see God, and I didn't know where to seek this life except in death. Some great impulses of this love came upon me in such a way that, even though they were not as unbearable as those I already mentioned before or of such value, I didn't know what to do with myself. For nothing satisfied me, nor could I put up with myself; it truly seemed as if my soul were being wrested from me. O superb contrivance of my Lord! What delicate skill You use with Your miserable slave! You hide Yourself from me and afflict me with Your love through a death so delightful that the soul would never want to escape from it. . . .

The Lord wanted me . . . to see . . . the following vision: I saw close to me toward my left side an angel in bodily form. I don't usually see angels in bodily form except on rare occasions; although many times angels appear to me, but without my seeing them, as in the intellectual vision I spoke about before. This time, though, the Lord desired that I see the vision in the following way: the angel was not large but small; he was very beautiful, and his face was so aflame that he seemed to be one of those very sublime angels that appear to be all afire. They must belong to those they call the cherubim, for they didn't tell me their names. But I see clearly that in heaven there is so much difference between some angels and others and between these latter and still others that I wouldn't know how to explain it. I saw in his hands a large golden dart and at the end of the iron tip there appeared to be a little fire. It seemed to me this angel plunged the dart several times into my heart and that it reached deep within me. When he drew it out, I thought he was carrying off with him the deepest part of me; and he left me all on fire with great love of God. The pain was so great that it made me moan, and the sweetness this greatest pain caused me was so superabundant that there is no desire capable of taking it away; nor is the soul content with less than God. The pain is not bodily but spiritual, although the body doesn't fail to share in some of it, and even a great deal. The loving exchange that takes place between the soul and God is so sweet that I beg Him in His goodness to give a taste of this love to anyone who thinks I am lying.

SAINT JOHN
OF THE CROSS

[1 5 4 2 – 1 5 9 1]

That I might take the prey
of this adventuring in God.

Saint John of the Cross was a Spanish Carmelite monk. *Ascent of Mount Carmel* and *The Dark Night of the Soul*, classic treatises in the literature of mysticism, were composed at the urging of John's mentor, Teresa of Avila. The books attempt to explicate one of John's poems, *"En Una Noche Oscura"* ("On a Dark Night"), which is excerpted here. For John, the soul consists of both sensual and spiritual parts that must be cleansed of imperfections before attaining union with God. To achieve this cleansing, the soul undergoes a journey through a "dark night" of spiritual annihilation, with faith as its guide, to the morning light of perfection—union with God. Written as guides for those already involved in the pursuit of the spiritual life, the treatises focus on extraordinary states of the soul. At the same time, the practical passages of John's expositions show keen insight into the passions of men and women.

As a person, John reveals himself best through his letters to Saint Teresa. With her, he was a reformer of Spanish monasticism and a founder of the contemplative order of Discalced (or barefoot) Carmelites. He sought always a strict rule that would shut out everything but the pursuit of pure spirit. He was known for his extreme frailty and for his complete and, to some, seemingly excessive devotion to God. [EP]

FROM ON  A DARK NIGHT

The Dark Night

Songs of the soul that rejoices in having reached the high state of perfection, which is union with God, by the path of spiritual negation.

1. One dark night,
fired with love's urgent longings
—ah, the sheer grace!—
I went out unseen,
my house being now all stilled.

2. In darkness, and secure,
by the secret ladder, disguised,
—ah, the sheer grace!—
in darkness and concealment,
my house being now all stilled.

3. On that glad night
in secret, for no one saw me,
nor did I look at anything
with no other light or guide
than the one that burned in my heart.

4. This guided me
more surely than the light of noon
to where he was awaiting me
—him I knew so well—
there in a place where no one appeared.

5. O guiding night!
O night more lovely than the dawn!
O night that has united
the Lover with his beloved,
transforming the beloved in her Lover.

6. *Upon my flowering breast,*
which I kept wholly for him alone,
there he lay sleeping,
and I caressing him
there in a breeze from the fanning cedars.

7. *When the breeze blew from the turret,*
as I parted his hair,
it wounded my neck
with its gentle hand,
suspending all my senses.

8. *I abandoned and forgot myself,*
laying my face on my Beloved;
all things ceased; I went out from myself,
leaving my cares
forgotten among the lilies.

The Living Flame of Love

Songs of the soul in the intimate communication of loving union with God.

1. *O living flame of love*
that tenderly wounds my soul
in its deepest center! Since
now you are not oppressive,
now consummate! if it be your will:
tear through the veil of this sweet encounter!

2. *O sweet cautery,*
O delightful wound!
O gentle hand! O delicate touch
that tastes of eternal life
and pays every debt!
In killing you changed death to life.

3. *O lamps of fire!*
in whose splendors
the deep caverns of feeling,
once obscure and blind,
now give forth, so rarely, so exquisitely,
both warmth and light to their Beloved.

4. *How gently and lovingly*
you wake in my heart,

where in secret you dwell alone;
and in your sweet breathing,
filled with good and glory,
how tenderly you swell my heart with love.

Stanzas concerning an ecstasy experienced in high contemplation.

I entered into unknowing,
and there I remained unknowing
transcending all knowledge.

1. I entered into unknowing,
yet when I saw myself there,
without knowing where I was,
I understood great things;
I will not say what I felt
for I remained in unknowing
transcending all knowledge.

2. That perfect knowledge
was of peace and holiness
held at no remove
in profound solitude:
it was something so secret
that I was left stammering,
transcending all knowledge.

3. I was so 'whelmed,
so absorbed and withdrawn,
that my senses were left
deprived of all their sensing,
and my spirit was given
an understanding while not understanding
transcending all knowledge.

4. He who truly arrives there
cuts free from himself:
all that he knew before
now seems worthless,
and his knowledge so soars
that he is left in unknowing
transcending all knowledge.

5. The higher he ascends
the less he understands,
because the cloud is dark
which lit up the night;
whoever knows this
remains always in unknowing
transcending all knowledge.

6. This knowledge in unknowing
is so overwhelming
that wise men disputing
can never overthrow it,
for their knowledge does not reach
to the understanding of not understanding,
transcending all knowledge.

7. And this supreme knowledge is so exalted
that no power of man or learning
can grasp it;
he who masters himself
will, with knowledge in unknowing,
always be transcending.

8. And if you should want to hear:
this highest knowledge lies
in the loftiest sense
of the essence of God;
this is a work of his mercy,
to leave one without understanding,
transcending all knowledge.

Stanzas of the soul that suffers with longing to see God.

I live, but not in myself,
and I have such hope
that I die because I do not die.

1. I no longer live within myself
and I cannot live without God,
for having neither him nor myself
what will life be?
It will be a thousand deaths,

longing for my true life
and dying because I do not die.

2. This life that I live
is no life at all,
and so I die continually
until I live with you;
hear me, my God:
I do not desire this life,
I am dying because I do not die.

3. When I am away from you
what life can I have
except to endure
the bitterest death known?
I pity myself,
for I go on and on living,
dying because I do not die.

4. A fish that leaves the water has this relief:
the dying it endures
ends at last in death.
What death can equal my pitiable life?
For the longer I live, the more drawn out is my dying.

5. When I try to find relief
seeing you in the Sacrament,
I find this greater sorrow:
I cannot enjoy you wholly.
All things are affliction
since I do not see you as I desire,
and I die because I do not die.

6. And if I rejoice, Lord,
in the hope of seeing you,
yet seeing I can lose you
doubles my sorrow.
Living in such fear
and hoping as I hope,
I die because I do not die.

7. Lift me from this death,
my God, and give me life:
do not hold me bound
with these bonds so strong;

see how I long to see you;
my wretchedness is so complete
that I die because I do not die.

8. I will cry out for death
and mourn my living
while I am held here
for my sins.
O my God, when will it be
that I can truly say:
now I live because I do not die?

Stanzas given a spiritual meaning.

I went out seeking love,
and with unfaltering hope
I flew so high, so high,
that I overtook the prey.

1. That I might take the prey
of this adventuring in God
I had to fly so high
that I was lost from sight;
and though in this adventure
I faltered in my flight,
yet love had already flown so high
that I took the prey.

2. When I ascended higher
my vision was dazzled,
and the most difficult conquest
came about in darkness;
but since I was seeking love
the leap I made was blind and dark,
and I rose so high, so high,
that I took the prey.

3. The higher I ascended
in this seeking so lofty
the lower and more subdued
and abased I became.
I said: No one can overtake it!
And sank, ah, so low,

that I was so high, so high,
that I took the prey.

4. In a wonderful way
my one flight surpassed a thousand,
for the hope of heaven
attains as much as it hopes for;
this seeking is my only hope,
and in hoping, I made no mistake,
because I flew so high, so high,
that I took the prey.

Stanzas applied spiritually to Christ and the soul.

1. A lone young shepherd lived in pain
withdrawn from pleasure and contentment,
his thoughts fixed on a shepherd-girl
his heart an open wound with love.

2. He weeps, but not from the wound of love,
there is no pain in such affliction,
even though the heart is pierced;
he weeps in knowing he's been forgotten.

3. That one thought: his shining one
has forgotten him, is such great pain
that he bows to brutal handling in a foreign land,
his heart an open wound with love.

4. The shepherd says: I pity the one
who draws herself back from my love,
and does not seek the joy of my presence,
though my heart is an open wound with love for her.

5. After a long time he climbed a tree,
and spread his shining arms,
and hung by them, and died,
his heart an open wound with love.

Song of the soul that rejoices in knowing God through faith.

For I know well the spring that flows and runs,
although it is night.

1. That eternal spring is hidden,
for I know well where it has its rise,
although it is night.

2. I do not know its origin, nor has it one,
but I know that every origin has come from it,
although it is night.

3. I know that nothing else is so beautiful,
and that the heavens and the earth drink there,
although it is night.

4. I know well that it is bottomless
and no one is able to cross it,
although it is night.

5. Its clarity is never darkened,
and I know that every light has come from it,
although it is night.

6. I know that its streams are so brimming
they water the lands of hell, the heavens, and earth,
although it is night.

7. I know well the stream that flows from this spring
is mighty in compass and power;
although it is night.

8. I know the stream proceeding from these two,
that neither of them in fact precedes it,
although it is night.

9. This eternal spring is hidden
in this living bread for our life's sake,
although it is night.

10. It is here calling out to creatures;
and they satisfy their thirst, although in darkness,
because it is night.

11. This living spring that I long for,
I see in this bread of life,
although it is night.

Perhaps the greatest of the English metaphysical poets, Donne is best known for his *Divine Poems,* "Holy Sonnets," and *Devotions upon Emergent Occasions.* The First Meditation and Prayer, reproduced here, follows the dedication of the latter work. Donne often observed that his family had suffered an undue share of persecution for its faith: he counted the martyr Sir Thomas More among his ancestors, and his own brother died in prison for providing asylum to a Catholic priest. Donne himself, as a recusant Catholic, was denied the privilege of receiving degrees from Oxford and Cambridge, although he matriculated at both institutions.

Donne entered the Anglican church without apparent conflict, although his spiritual life, as attested by his poetry, was marked by deep anxieties concerning his own salvation. Perhaps no other poet has captured so magisterially the evanescence of spiritual ecstasy and its reverse impulse, the dread of the fall from grace. The loss of his wife, whom he had married in the face of family opposition so great he was threatened with imprisonment, and the demise of his Parlia-

JOHN DONNE

[1 5 7 2 – 1 6 3 1]

I am my best part; I am my Soule.

mentary career, precipitated a deepening of his religious life. In the last decade of his life, he concentrated on his duties as dean of Saint Paul's Cathedral, London, and turned from poetry to composing sermons. Perhaps the most famous of his devotionals is his meditation on death, using the extended metaphor of a tolling bell, related to his Holy Sonnet 10 ("Death, be not proud"). The first meditation in his *Devotions* and the dedication of the volume are presented here. In them, Donne relates the spiritual crisis he suffered during a time of illness and describes himself as having been reborn for a third time, as the Father of "this Booke." [AM]

FROM *DEVOTIONS UPON EMERGENT OCCASIONS,* DEDICATION, FIRST *MEDITATION AND PRAYER,* NUMBER ONE
TO THE MOST EXCELLENT PRINCE, PRINCE CHARLES.

Most Excellent Prince,

I *Have had three* Births; *One,* Naturall, *when I came into the* World; *One* Supernatural, *when I entred into the* Ministery; *and now, a* preternaturall Birth, *in returning to* Life, *from this* Sicknes. *In my* second Birth, *your* Highnesse Royall Father *vouchsafed mee his Hand, not onely to sustaine mee* in it, *but to lead mee* to it. *In this* last Birth, *I my selfe am borne a* Father: *This* Child *of mine, this* Booke, *comes into the world,* from *mee, and* with *mee. And therefore, I presume (as I did the* Father *to the* Father) *to present the* Sonne *to the* Sonne; *This* Image *of my* Humiliation, *to the lively* Image *of his* Majesty, *your* Highnesse. *It might bee enough, that* God *hath seene my* Devotions: *But* Examples *of* Good Kings *are* Commandements; *And* Ezechiah *writt the* Meditations *of his* Sicknesse, *after his* Sicknesse. *Besides, as I have liv'd to see, (not as a* Witnesse *onely, but as a* Partaker) *the happinesses of a part of your* Royal *Fathers time, so shall I live,* (in my way) *to see the happinesses of the times of your* Highnesse *too, if this* Child *of mine, inanimated by your gracious Acceptation, may so long preserve alive the* Memory *of*

Your Highnesse
Humblest and
Devotedst
JOHN DONNE.

I. Insultus Morbi primus;
The first alteration, The first grudging of the sicknesse.
I. Meditation

Variable, and therfore miserable condition of Man; this minute I was well, and am ill, this minute. I am surpriz'd with a sodaine change, & alteration to worse, and can impute it to no cause, nor call it by any name. We study *Health*, and we deliberate upon our *meats*, and *drink*, and *Ayre*, and *exercises*, and we hew, and wee polish every stone, that goes to that building; and so our *Health* is a long & a regular work; But in a minute a Cannon batters all, overthrowes all, demolishes all; a *Sicknes* unprevented for all our diligence, unsuspected for all our curiositie; nay, undeserved, if we consider only *disorder*, summons us, seizes us, possesses us, destroyes us in an instant. O miserable condition of Man, which was not imprinted by *God*; who as hee is *immortall* himselfe, had put a *coale*, a *beame* of *Immortalitie* into us, which we might have blowen into a *flame*, but blew it out, by our first sinne; wee beggard our selves by hearkning after false riches, and infatuated our selves by hearkning after false knowledge. So that now, we doe not onely die, but die upon the Rack, die by the torment of sicknesse; nor that onely, but are preafflicted, super-afflicted with these jelousies and suspitions, and apprehensions of *Sicknes*, before we can cal it a sicknes; we are not sure we are ill; one hand askes the other by the pulse, and our eye askes our own urine, how we do. O multiplied misery! we die, and cannot enjoy death, because wee die in this torment of sicknes; we are tormented with sicknes, & cannot stay till the torment come, but pre-apprehensions and presages, prophecy those torments, which induce that *death* before either come; and our *dissolution* is conceived in these *first changes*, *quickned* in the *sicknes* it selfe, and *borne* in *death*, which beares date from these first changes. Is this the honour which Man hath by being a *little world*, That he hath these *earthquakes* in him selfe, sodaine shakings; these *lightnings*, sodaine flashes; these *thunders*, sodaine noises; these *Eclypses*, sodain offuscations, & darknings of his senses; these *blazing stars*, sodaine fiery exhalations; these *rivers of blood*, sodaine red waters? Is he a *world* to himselfe onely therefore, that he hath inough in himself, not only to destroy, and execute himselfe, but to presage that execution upon himselfe; to assist the sicknes, to antidate the sicknes, to make the sicknes the more irremediable, by sad apprehensions, and as if hee would make a fire the more vehement, by sprinkling water upon the coales, so to wrap a hote fever in cold Melancholy, least the fever alone shold not destroy fast enough, without this contribution, nor perfit the work (which is *destruction*) except we joynd an artificiall sicknes, of our owne *melancholy*, to our natural, our unnaturall fever. O perplex'd discomposition, O ridling distemper, O miserable condition of Man.

I. Expostulation

If I were but meere *dust* & *ashes*, I might speak unto the *Lord*, for the *Lordes* hand made me of this *dust*, and the *Lords* hand shall recollect these *ashes;* the *Lords* hand was the wheele, upon which this vessell of clay was framed, and the *Lordes* hand is the *Urne*, in which these *ashes* shall be preserv'd. I am the *dust*, & the *ashes* of the *Temple* of the *H. Ghost;* and what Marble is so precious? But I am more then *dust* & *ashes;* I am my best part, I am my *soule*. And being so, the *breath* of *God*, I may breath back these pious *expostulations* to my *God. My God, my God*, why is not my *soule*, as sensible as my *body?* Why hath not my *soule* these apprehensions, these presages, these changes, those antidates, those jealousies, those suspitions of a *sinne*, as well as my body of a *sicknes?* why is there not alwayes a *pulse* in my *Soule*, to beat at the approch of a *tentation* to sinne? Why are there not alwayes *waters* in mine eyes, to testifie my spiritual sicknes? I stand in the way of tentations, (naturally, necessarily, all men doe so: for there is a *Snake in every path*, tentations in every vocation) but I go, I run, I flie into the wayes of tentation, which I might shun; nay, I breake into houses, wher the plague is; I presse into places of tentation, and tempt the *devill* himselfe, and solicite & importune them, who had rather be left unsolicited by me. I fall sick of *Sin*, and am bedded and bedrid, buried and putrified in the practise of *Sin*, and all this while have no presage, no pulse, no sense of my *sicknesse;* O heighth, O depth of misery, where the first *Symptome* of the sicknes is Hell, & where I never see the fever of lust, of envy, of ambition, by any other light, then the darknesse and horror of *Hell* it selfe; & where the first Messenger that speaks to me doth not say, *Thou mayst die*, no, nor *Thou must die*, but *Thou art dead:* and where the first notice, that my *Soule* hath of her sicknes, is *irrecoverablenes, irremedia-blenes:* but, *O my God, Job did not charge thee foolishly*, in his temporall afflictions, nor may I in my spirituall. Thou hast imprinted a *pulse* in our *Soule*, but we do not examine it; a voice in our conscience, but wee doe not hearken unto it. We talk it out, we jest it out, we drinke it out, we sleepe it out; and when wee wake, we doe not say with *Jacob, Surely the Lord is in this place, and I knew it not:* but though we might know it, we do not, we wil not. But will *God* pretend to make a *Watch*, and leave out the *springe?* to make so many various wheels in the faculties of the Soule, and in the organs of the body, and leave out *Grace*, that should move them? or wil *God* make a *springe*, and not *wind* it up? Infuse his first *grace*, & not second it with more, without which, we can no more use his first *grace*, when we have it, then wee could dispose our selves by *Nature*, to have it? But alas, that is not our case; we are all *prodigall sonnes*, and not *disinherited;* wee have received our portion, and misspent it, not bin denied it. We are *Gods tenants* heere, and yet here, he, our *Land-lord* payes us *Rents;* not yearely, nor quarterly, but hourely, and quarterly; *Every minute he renewes his mercy*, but wee *will not understand, least that we should be converted, and he should heale us.*

I. Prayer

O eternall, and most gracious *God*, who considered in thy selfe, art a *Circle*, first and last, and altogether; but considered in thy working upon us, art a *direct line*, and leadest us from our *beginning*, through all our wayes, to our *end*, enable me by thy *grace*, to looke forward to mine end, and to looke backward to the considerations of thy mercies afforded mee from the beginning; that so by that practise of considering thy mercy, in my beginning in this world, when thou plantedst me in the *Christian Church*, and thy mercy in the beginning in the other world, when thou writest me in the *Booke of life*, in my *Election*, I may come to a holy consideration of thy *mercy*, in the beginning of all my actions here: That in all the beginnings, in all the accesses, and approches of spirituall sicknesses of *Sinn*, I may heare and hearken to that voice, *O thou Man of God, there is death in the pot*, and so refraine from that, which I was so hungerly, so greedily flying to. *A faithfull Ambassador is health*, says thy wise servant *Solomon*. Thy voice received, in the beginning of a sicknesse, of a sinne, is true health. If I can see that light betimes, and heare that voyce early, *Then shall my light breake forth as the morning, and my health shall spring foorth speedily.* Deliver mee therefore, O my God, from these vaine imaginations; that it is an overcurious thing, a dangerous thing, to come to that tendernesse, that rawnesse, that scrupulousnesse, to feare every *concupiscence*, every offer of *Sin*, that this suspicious, & jealous diligence will turne to an inordinate dejection of spirit, and a diffidence in thy care & providence; but keep me still establish'd, both in a constant assurance, that thou wilt speake to me at the beginning of every such sicknes, at the approach of every such *Sinne;* and that, if I take knowledg of that voice then, and flye to thee, thou wilt preserve mee from falling, or raise me againe, when by naturall infirmitie I am fallen: doe this, *O Lord,* for his sake, who knowes our naturall infirmities, for he had them; and knowes the weight of our sinns, for he paid a deare price for them, thy *Sonne,* our *Saviour, Chr: Jesus, Amen.*

BROTHER
LAWRENCE

[1 6 1 4 – 1 6 9 1]

My soul had found its center

and place of rest.

Brother Lawrence of the Resurrection was born Nicolas Herman, in 1614, in a small village near Lunéville in Lorraine, France. At the age of eighteen he experienced a profound spiritual crisis and, after serving in the Thirty Years' War, he finally adopted a hermit's life, entering the order of Discalced Carmelites at the age of twenty-six. Because he served as a lay brother engaged in manual labor, he has been referred to as the "kitchen saint." Brother Lawrence was cook for a community of one hundred brothers for a period of fifteen years, until sciatica forced him to retire to sandal making. By his own account, his emphasis on the awareness of the presence of God at all times brought him an ineffable peace that transformed the simplest of his daily activities into events of joy. His reputation for holiness grew rapidly during his lifetime and he received many eminent visitors. Among these were the Bishop of Paris and François Fénelon, whose interest in the interior life of prayer had made him, for a time, an adherent of Madame Guyon's "quietest" school. The selections that follow are passages taken from various letters of Brother Lawrence to fellow religious who had requested that he describe his experience for them.   [AM]

FROM *THE PRACTICE OF THE PRESENCE OF GOD*

Since I am not able to find my way of life described in books—although this does not really disturb me—I would, nonetheless, like to have the reassurance of knowing your thoughts on my present state.

Several days ago during a discussion with a pious person, I was told the spiritual life was a life of grace that begins with servile fear, that intensifies with the hope of eternal life, and that finds its consummation in pure love; and that there are various ways of ultimately arriving at this blessed consummation.

I haven't followed these methods at all; on the contrary, I don't know why they provoked such fear in me in the beginning. But for this reason, on my entrance into religious life I made the resolution to give myself entirely to God in atonement for my sins, and to renounce everything else for the sake of his love.

During the first years I ordinarily thought about death, judgment, hell, paradise, and my sins when I prayed. I continued in this fashion for a few years, carefully applying myself the rest of the day—even during my work —to the practice of the presence of God who was always near me, often in the very depths of my heart. This gave me a great reverence for God, and in this matter faith alone was my reassurance.

I gradually did the same thing during mental prayer, and this gave me great joy and consolation. This is how I began. I will admit that during the first ten years I suffered a great deal. The apprehension that I did not belong to God as I wished, my past sins always before my eyes, and the lavish graces God gave me, were the sum and substance of all my woes. During this period I fell often, but I got back up just as quickly. It seemed to me that all creatures, reason, and God himself were against me, and that faith alone was on my side. I was sometimes troubled by thoughts that this was the result of my presumption, in that I pretended to be all at once where others were able to arrive only with difficulty. Other times I thought I was willingly damning myself, that there was no salvation for me.

When I accepted the fact that I might spend my life suffering from these troubles and anxieties—which in no way diminished the trust I had in God and served only to increase my faith—I found myself changed all at once.

And my soul, until that time always in turmoil, experienced a deep inner peace as if it had found its center and place of rest.

Since that time I do my work in simple faith before God, humbly and lovingly, and I carefully apply myself to avoid doing, saying, or thinking anything that might displease him. I hope that, having done all that I can, he will do with me as he pleases.

I cannot express to you what is taking place in me at present. I feel neither concern nor doubt about my state since I have no will other than the will of God, which I try to carry out in all things and to which I am so surrendered that I would not so much as pick up a straw from the ground against his order, nor for any other reason than pure love.

I gave up all devotions and prayers that were not required and I devote myself exclusively to remaining always in his holy presence. I keep myself in his presence by simple attentiveness and a general loving awareness of God that I call "actual presence of God" or better, a quiet and secret conversation of the soul with God that is lasting. This sometimes results in interior, and often exterior, contentment and joys so great that I have to perform childish acts, appearing more like folly than devotion, to control them and keep them from showing outwardly.

Therefore . . . I cannot doubt at all that my soul has been with God for more than thirty years. I will omit a number of things so as not to bore you. I think, however, it would be appropriate to indicate the manner in which I see myself before God, whom I consider as my King.

I consider myself as the most miserable of all human beings, covered with sores, foul, and guilty of all sorts of crimes committed against my King; moved by sincere remorse I confess all my sins to him. I ask him pardon and abandon myself into his hands so he can do with me as he pleases. Far from chastising me, this King, full of goodness and mercy, lovingly embraces me, seats me at his table, waits on me himself, gives me the keys to his treasures, and treats me in all things as his favorite; he converses with me and takes delight in me in countless ways, without ever speaking of forgiveness or taking away my previous faults. Although I beg him to fashion me according to his heart, I see myself still weaker and miserable, yet ever more caressed by God. This is what I see from time to time while in his holy presence.

My most typical approach is this simple attentiveness and general loving awareness of God, from which I derive greater sweetness and satisfaction than an infant receives from his mother's breast. Therefore, if I may dare use the expression, I would gladly call this state the "breasts of God," because of the indescribable sweetness I taste and experience there.

If on occasion I turn away either because of necessity or weakness, inner movements so charming and delightful that I am embarrassed to talk about them, call me immediately back to him. I beg you, Reverend Father, to think about my great weaknesses, of which you are fully aware, rather than these great graces with which God favors my soul, unworthy and ignorant as I am.

Regarding the prescribed hours of prayer, they are nothing more than a continuation of this same exercise. Sometimes I think of myself as a piece of stone before a sculptor who desires to carve a statue; presenting myself in this way before God I ask him to fashion his perfect image in my soul, making me entirely like himself.

At other times, as soon as I apply myself I feel my whole mind and soul raised without trouble or effort, and it remains suspended and permanently rooted in God as in its center and place of rest.

I know that some would call this state idleness, self-deception, and self-love. I maintain that it is a holy idleness and a blessed self-love, should the soul in this state be capable of it. In fact, when the soul is in this state of rest its former acts do not trouble it; these acts were formerly its support but now they would do more harm than good.

I cannot agree to calling this self-deception, since the soul in this state desires God exclusively. If this is self-deception then it is up to God to correct it; may he do with me as he pleases, for I seek him alone and want to be entirely his.

THIS IS, IN MY OPINION, THE ESSENCE OF THE SPIRITUAL LIFE, AND it seems to me that by practicing it properly you become spiritual in no time.

I know that to do this your heart must be empty of all other things because God desires to possess it exclusively, and he cannot possess it exclusively without first emptying it of everything other than himself; neither can he act within it nor do there what he pleases.

There is no way of life in the world more agreeable or delightful than continual conversation with God; only those who practice and experience it can understand this. I do not suggest, however, that you do it for this reason. We must not seek consolations from this exercise, but must do it from a motive of love, and because God wants it.

If I were a preacher, I would preach nothing but the practice of the presence of God; and if I were a spiritual director, I would recommend it to everyone, for I believe there is nothing so necessary or so easy.

FINALLY . . . I DO NOT KNOW WHAT WILL BECOME OF ME. IT SEEMS to me that peace of mind and soul comes to me in my sleep. Even if I were capable of suffering, it would be from not having any suffering at all; and if God permitted it, purgatory, where I believe I could suffer in atonement for my sins, would be a consolation to me. I only know that God looks after me. My tranquility is so great that I fear nothing. What could I fear when I am with him? I cling to him with all my strength. May he be blessed by all. *Amen.*

I CANNOT UNDERSTAND HOW RELIGIOUS PEOPLE CAN REMAIN CON-tent without the practice of the presence of God. As for me, I keep myself recollected in him in the depth and center of my soul as much as possible, and when I am thus with him I fear nothing, though the least deviation is hell for me.

This exercise does not hurt the body. It is nonetheless appropriate to deprive it occasionally, and even with some frequency, of some innocent, permissible, little consolations. For God will not permit a soul desirous of being entirely his to find consolation other than with him, and that is more than reasonable!

I do not say we must put ourselves to a great deal of trouble to do this; no, we must serve God in holy freedom. We must work faithfully, without turmoil or anxiety, gently and peacefully bringing our minds back to God as often as we find ourselves distracted.

We must, however, place all our trust in God and let go of all our cares, including a multitude of private devotions, very good in themselves but often carried out for the wrong reason, for these devotions are nothing more than the means to arrive the end. If, then, we are with the one who is our end by this practice of the presence of God, it is certainly useless to return to the means. We can continue our loving exchange with him, remaining in his holy presence.

I WILL SHARE WITH YOU THE METHOD I HAVE USED TO ARRIVE AT this state of awareness of God's presence that Our Lord in his mercy has granted me, since you insist that I do so. I cannot hide the repugnance I feel in yielding to your request, even under the condition that you show my letter to no one. If I thought you would let someone see it, all the desire I have for your perfection could not make me comply. This is what I can tell you about it.

In several books I found different methods to approach God and various practices of the spiritual life that I feared would burden my mind rather than facilitate what I wanted and what I sought, namely, a means of being completely disposed to God. This led me to resolve to give all for all. Thus, after offering myself entirely to God in atonement for my sins, I renounced for the sake of his love everything other than God, and I began to live as if only he and I existed in the world. Sometimes I considered myself before him as a miserable criminal at his judge's feet, and at other times I regarded him in my heart as my Father, as my God. I adored him there as often as I could, keeping my mind in his holy presence, and recalling him as many times as I was distracted. I had some trouble doing this exercise, but contin- ued in spite of all the difficulties I encountered, without getting disturbed or anxious when I was involuntarily distracted. I was as faithful to this practice during my activities as I was during my periods of mental prayer, for at every moment, all the time, in the most intense periods of my work I banished and rid from my mind everything that was capable of taking the thought of God away from me.

This . . . is the devotion I have practiced since I entered religious life. Although I have practiced it feebly and imperfectly, I have nonetheless received many advantages from it. I certainly know this is due to the Lord's mercy and goodness—and this must be acknowledged—since we can do nothing without him, myself even less than others. But when we faithfully keep ourselves in his holy presence, seeing him always before us, not only avoiding offending or displeasing him—at least deliberately—but consider- ing him in this fashion, we take the liberty to ask him for the graces we need. So, by repeating these acts they become more familiar, and the practice of the presence of God becomes more natural. Join me in thanking him, please, for his great goodness to me, for I cannot esteem highly enough the great number of graces he bestows on me, a miserable sinner. May he be blessed by all. *Amen.*

SAINT MARGARET
MARY ALACOQUE

[1 6 4 7 – 1 6 9 0]

He is urging me to love Him

with a love of conformity to His

suffering life!

Born in Burgundy in 1647, Margaret Mary took a vow of chastity at the age of four. As a girl, she underwent mortifications and austerities in order to expel all human distractions. In 1671 she became a member of the Visitation order of nuns and was encouraged to practice discursive meditation, a systematic method of prayer recommended for novices in the spiritual life. She was temperamentally inclined to "passive prayer," however, during which, as she once put it, Christ himself came and communed with her. Like Brother Lawrence, she constantly felt the sensible presence of Jesus. Her experience also closely resembles the mystical revelations of Julian of Norwich in the intense empathy she felt toward the passion and suffering of Jesus. Also like Julian, Margaret Mary received three visions, during which Jesus revealed to her his Sacred Heart, pierced with thorns. According to her account, Jesus commissioned her to spread devotion to the Sacred Heart.

Her autobiography, dictated at the direction of her spiritual confessor, vividly details her early life as well as her later conversations with Jesus. Her letters, excerpts of which follow, also offer eloquent testimony to a life devoted to the pursuit of a single spiritual goal, to share in Christ's passion and suffering. [EP]

FROM HER LETTERS

TO MOTHER DE SAUMAISE, AT MOULINS

1682

Dearest Mother,

It would give me great satisfaction to be able to tell you my miseries, for they would make you understand better our sovereign Master's great mercies to me. One of the most precious and useful of these is my illness. Yes, I assure you the cross of infirmity and humiliation is so necessary for me that my Sovereign told me that without it I should not have been able to avoid another which, I think, would have been very dangerous. I need not think about myself any more, nor about what it may please my Savior to do concerning me or in me. He said He would never fail to take care of me except when I insisted on meddling in my own affairs. I have often found this out through my infidelity which has brought about the upsetting of my plans. All I wish to do now is what He has so often told me. "Let Me act," He said.

Moreover, He has turned loose in me three persecutors. They torment me continually. The first one calls up the other two. That first one is such a great desire to love Him that it seems everything I see ought to be changed into flames of pure love so that He may be loved in the Blessed Sacrament. It is a martyrdom to me to think He is so little loved there, and that there are so many hearts that reject His pure love, forget it, and spurn it. If only I myself at least would love Him my heart would be consoled with its sorrow. But I am the most ungrateful and faithless of creatures and lead a life wholly unmortified and filled with self-love.

I feel myself continually urged to suffer, but with what terrible repugnance on the part of my lower nature! This makes my crosses so heavy that I would be crushed many a time if the Heart of my adorable Jesus did not sustain me and assist me in all my needs. And all the while in the midst of my constant sufferings my heart continues to thirst after suffering. My soul suffers great agony at not yet being able to be separated from the body. I can think of no greater sacrifice than that of having to continue to live. Yet I would go on living from now till judgment day if God wanted me to, although the thought of being separated so long from my Lord would be harder for me to bear than a thousand deaths. Everything conspires to afflict and torment me because I cannot give my whole affection to my divine Love, Who favors me continually with His holy presence and Himself instructs me to describe it to you as follows:

Suppose that a powerful monarch, feeling urged to exercise his charity, should cast his eyes about over his subjects in order to select the poorest, most miserable and utterly destitute among them. Then, having found her, with overflowing liberality he poured out upon her his riches, of which the greatest would be that this great monarch would want so to humble himself as to walk constantly at the side of this poor outcast, carrying a torch and all gleaming in his royal purple. And, after allowing himself to be seen, he hid this light in the darkness of night, so as to give this poor outcast courage to approach him, and to listen to and speak to him with confidence, to receive his embraces and return them on her part. He always looked out for her needs and took care of everything that concerned her. But if, after all that, this person should come to withdraw herself from her benefactor and to be unfaithful to him, and if, to punish her, he did nothing else than let the light he had hidden shine forth, so that she could see what he is and what she is, he all resplendent with beauty, she all covered with dirt, wounds, and all sorts of filth . . . and if she saw at the same time the enormity of her malice and ingratitude, in contrast with the goodness of this Sovereign . . . I do not know whether I put it clearly enough to make you see what I mean.

This is something like the way in which my Sovereign has dealt with His unworthy slave. Indeed, this divine presence makes diverse impressions on me. Sometimes He raises me to the height of all bliss from which I draw inexpressible delight. Then all I can exclaim is: "My Life, my Love, and my All! You are all mine and I am all Yours!" At other times He plunges me into the depths of my own nothingness where I suffer inexplicable confusion at seeing this abyss of every misery close to the abyss of all perfection. At still other times He so enters into me that He seems to leave me with no other being or life than Himself. He does this in so painful a manner that I have to repeat incessantly: "I want to suffer everything without complaint, since my pure love prevents me from being afraid of anything."

But I would weary you if I recounted all these things in detail, for God is an unfathomable abyss of every good. All my glory ought to consist, as He has taught me, in considering myself but a plaything to give pleasure to His adorable Heart, which is my whole treasure. I must confess that I have nothing but my Savior Jesus Christ. He often says to me: "What would you do without Me? You would certainly be very poor!"

As for the other graces and gifts I receive from His bounty, I must confess that they are very great. But the *Giver* is more precious than all His gifts. My heart cannot love or be attached to anything but Him alone. All else is nothing and often serves only to contaminate pure love, and to separate the soul from its Well-Beloved, Who wants to be loved solely and without self-interest. I beg you to thank the Lord for His great mercies to me.

TO FATHER CROISET

From our Monastery,
November 3, 1689

. . . I must tell you, therefore, that my Lord, appearing one day to His unworthy slave, said to me:

"I am looking for a victim for My Heart, one who is willing to offer herself as a holocaust for the accomplishment of My designs."

Feeling myself altogether overcome by the splendor of this sovereign Majesty before Whom I had prostrated myself, I mentioned to Him several holy souls who would cooperate faithfully with His plans. But He said:

"I want you and no one else, and I want you to consent to My desire."

Quite overcome and in tears, I replied that He knew I was a criminal, that victims ought to be innocent, and that I would do only what my superior ordered. He agreed to this but kept on insisting, and I kept on resisting, because of the great fear that these extraordinary ways might withdraw me from the pure spirit of my vocation. I resisted Him in vain, however, for He gave me no rest until under obedience He made me immolate myself to all His desires. He wanted me to hand myself over as a victim sacrificed to every kind of suffering, humiliation, contradiction, pain, and contempt, with no other purpose than the accomplishment of His designs. I did so. He told me He knew my fears and promised, as I think I have already told you, to so accommodate His graces to the spirit of my rule, to the obedience due my superiors and to my own weakness and infirmity that there should be no conflict in anything.

After that He so showered His graces on me that I did not know myself any more. This only served to increase my fears and forced me to insist that He would never allow to appear in me outwardly anything but what would make me more vile, abject and contemptible in the eyes of men. He promised.

I made a retreat sometime afterwards, during which I received many graces from His wonderful liberality and mercy. Of these I need not speak. I shall say only that it was then His goodness showed me most of the graces He had determined to give me, especially those connected with His lovable Heart. Thereupon I prostrated myself and asked Him to be so good as to give these graces to some faithful soul who would know how to correspond with them. He knew well, I told Him, that I would only be an obstacle to His designs. But He gave me to understand that it was for that very reason He had chosen me, so that I might not be able to attribute anything to myself. He Himself would make up for what was wanting in me.

Once when this Sovereign of my soul favored me with a visit, He said: "I am going to show you how much you will suffer for My love and for the accomplishment of My designs." Then He showed me so vividly what I was going to be doing for the rest of my life that it was as though I was actually enduring all those sufferings at that very moment. He added that I need fear nothing and promised me one of the greatest graces He had ever given to any of His friends: to let me enjoy His actual and continual presence. Like a faithful and perfect friend, He takes delight in being with His unworthy slave, favoring her with His loving converse.

"And when you commit some fault, I shall purge it away with suffering if you do not do it yourself with penance. I shall never deprive you of My presence on that account, but I will make it so painful for you that it will take the place of every other torment."

At that very moment He began to fulfill His promise of always being present to me. I felt Him always near me, as one feels oneself near another at night without being able to see him because of the darkness. The penetrating eyes of love made me see and feel Him in a most loving and certain way, and under various aspects.

This divine presence evokes from me such great reverence that when I am alone it gives me no rest unless I am prostrate or on my knees, like a little bit of nothingness before this Omnipotent One. This infinite grandeur encompasses me with Its power and so takes possession of mine and of my whole body and soul that I think I can say that I no longer have any power over myself, for He acts in me independently of me. I am powerless to resist Him, although the fear of being deceived often makes me do all in my power to do so. It is all in vain. He leaves me no liberty at all whenever it so pleases Him. But He does give me profound peace, a joy, a satisfaction, an ardent desire to be conformed to the suffering, humble, hidden, and lowly life of my Savior. And that in such a way that contempt, poverty, sorrow, and humiliations are the delicious meat with which He continually nourishes my soul. It no longer has a taste for any other. All my pleasure in this land of exile is that of having every kind of suffering found on the cross, deprived of every other consolation except that of the Sacred Heart.

I tell you earnestly that this Sovereign of my soul has so taken possession of me that, if instead of Him it was an evil spirit, I shall certainly be condemned to the lowest pit of hell. I present all this to you as I see it. Alas, I do not know whether I am deceiving myself, having neither good judgment nor discernment in what pertains to myself. Tell me what you think about it.

But to return to what you want to know touching the Sacred Heart. The first special grace I think I received in this regard was on the feast of Saint John the Evangelist. Our Lord made me rest for several hours on His sacred breast and from this lovable Heart I received graces whose very memory carries me out of myself. I do not think it necessary to say what they are, although the remembrance of them and the impression they made will remain all my life.

After that I saw this divine Heart as on a throne of flames, more brilliant than the sun and transparent as crystal. It had Its adorable wound and was encircled with a crown of thorns, which signified the pricks our sins caused Him. It was surmounted by a cross which signified that, from the first moment of His Incarnation, that is, from the time this Sacred Heart was formed, the cross was planted in It; that It was filled, from the very first moment, with all the bitterness, humiliations, poverty, sorrow, and contempt His sacred humanity would have to suffer during the whole course of His life and during His holy Passion.

He made me understand that the ardent desire He had of being loved by men and of drawing them from the path of perdition into which Satan was hurrying them in great numbers, had caused Him to fix upon this plan of manifesting His Heart to men, together with all Its treasures of love, mercy, grace, sanctification and salvation. This He did in order that those who were willing to do all in their power to render and procure for Him honor, love, and glory might be enriched abundantly, even profusely, with these divine treasures of the Heart of God, which is their source. It must be honored under the symbol of this Heart of flesh, Whose image He wished to be publicly exposed.

He wanted me to carry it on my person, over my heart, that He might imprint His love there, fill my heart with all the gifts with which His own is filled, and destroy all inordinate affection. Wherever this sacred image would be exposed for veneration He would pour forth His graces and blessings. . . .

This Sovereign of my soul once ordered me to keep vigil for one hour with Him every night between Thursday and Friday, prostrate on the ground. He said He would tell me what He wanted of me, which was, in part, reparation for that hour in the Garden of Olives when He complained that His apostles could not watch one hour with Him.

Obedience having permitted me to do this, I cannot tell you how much I suffered. For it seemed to me this divine Heart poured into mine all Its bitterness, reducing my soul to such a state of agony and anguish that I sometimes thought I would die. It was during this time that He made me see that my life would be one of continual suffering. It would be spent on a cross made up of many different kinds of wood, because He wanted to establish His reign and the empire of His Sacred Heart upon the complete destruction of myself. And so it happened. I was not without suffering for a moment, and that almost always to the full extent of my powers of body and soul.

This is how He makes me suffer a continual martyrdom: One day He caused me to see in this adorable Heart two kinds of holiness, the holiness of love and the holiness of justice. With this latter He surrounds the impenitent sinner who has ignored all the means of salvation given him. This sanctity of justice thereupon rejects him from the Heart of Jesus Christ, abandoning him to himself and rendering him insensible to his own sad state. It is for this sanctity that He makes me suffer, especially when He wants to abandon some soul consecrated to Him. He makes me bear the weight of it in so painful a manner that there is no suffering in this life comparable to it. I should willingly cast myself into a red-hot furnace to avoid it. But it would take too long to tell you all I experience. Suffice it to say that this justice cannot suffer the least stain on a soul that is in intimate converse with God; it would annihilate the sinner a thousand times over if mercy did not intervene. But, in its own way, the sanctity of love is scarcely less painful. It suffers to make reparation to some extent for the ingratitude of so many hearts who make no return for the burning love of the Heart of Jesus Christ in the sacrament of His love. This sanctity of love causes one to suffer from not being able to suffer enough. It brings on such ardent desires to love God and make Him loved that there is no torture one would not be willing to undergo to bring this about.

He showed me, therefore, that these two sanctities would always be at work to make me suffer. Also that there is nothing better for me than to live and die on the cross, overwhelmed with every kind of suffering. It seems to me indeed that I could not live without suffering, though I should often succumb did He not sustain me with His powerful grace. This is one reason why He commanded me to receive Holy Communion every first Friday of the month. Or, rather, it was to make reparation for the outrages He received during the month in the Blessed Sacrament. But one of my greatest sufferings was caused by this divine Heart addressing to me these words: "I thirst with such a terrible thirst to be loved by men in the Blessed Sacrament that this thirst consumes Me. Yet I find no one trying to quench it according to My desire by some return of My love."

Sometimes this lovable Heart is like a sun shooting forth its rays in every direction and into every heart. But how different the response It receives! For reprobate souls are like mud that becomes yet more hard, while just souls are purified and sanctified.

I felt myself ever urged and importuned to make known this divine Heart, yet without being able to find means for doing so until Father de la Colombière was sent here. Then within the octave of Corpus Christi I could not resist any longer, I finally had to surrender. I had to tell him, in spite of myself, what I had always kept secret so carefully, because he was sent for the execution of this great design. I must confess that I neither know how nor am I able to express what He has made known to me about it, for it is a profound mystery. But I believe He knows enough about it and will supply what is wanting in me. If you but knew the terrible martyrdom I am suffering in writing this! But I must do it because you told me it was necessary for the glory of the Sacred Heart of my Sovereign Master, to Whom I am completely dedicated and sacrificed. Still, an express command under obedience was necessary to get me to do violence to myself and tell you all this as it seems to me to have taken place. Alas, I do not know whether I am being deceived. Perhaps my whole life is but an illusion. Tell me what you think. What consoles me in all this is that I shall at least always have the happiness of suffering in conformity with my crucified Spouse.

JEANNE-MARIE
DE LA
MOTTE GUYON

[1 6 4 8 – 1 7 1 7]

Thy love, O my God, burned

as a fire devouring all that was

left of self.

Madame Guyon, as she is generally referred to in pietist literature, practiced a form of quietism that emphasized contemplation, disinterested surrender to God, and exaltation of spirit. She might have remained in obscurity had she not been so engaging and her personal piety so attractive that her influence extended into the highest circles of the French court, including that of Madame de Maintenon, who had secretly married Louis XIV in 1684. Madame Guyon went on to stand at the center of one of the greatest controversies of the seventeenth century French church, concerning the permissible limits of mysticism. The quarrel, focused on a concept of love of God so disinterested *(pur amour)* that it even renounces a desire for salvation, engaged churchmen and other distinguished intellectuals in France. Among the figures who became attracted by Madame Guyon's views was François Fénelon, tutor to the heir-presumptive to the French throne, the Duke of Burgundy. Madame Guyon herself spent this period of controversy for the most part in prison.

From her autobiography emerges a

portrait of the brutalities and humiliations endured by even well-born women in an earlier age, but it also depicts a woman called upon to testify to holiness, whose devotional life was her main occupation. In the intensity of her focus, Madame Guyon resembles Carmelites like Teresa of Avila and John of the Cross, though her theological views are more akin to Puritans and Quakers in their emphasis on God's saving grace.   [EP]

FROM HER AUTOBIOGRAPHY

My near relations did not signify any eager desire for my return. The first thing they proposed to me, a month after my arrival at Gex, was not only to give up my guardianship, but to make over all my estate to my children and to reserve an annuity to myself. This proposition, coming from people who regarded nothing but their own interest, to some might have appeared very unpleasing; but it was in no wise so to me. I had not any friend to advise with. I knew not anyone whom I could consult about the manner of executing the thing, as I was quite free and willing to do it. It appeared to me that I had now the means of accomplishing the extreme desire I had of being conformable to Jesus Christ, poor, naked, and stripped of all. They sent me an article to execute, which had been drawn under their inspection, and I innocently signed it, not perceiving some clauses which were inserted therein. It expressed that, when my children should die, I should inherit nothing of my own estate, but that it should revolve to my kindred. There were many other things, which appeared to be equally to my disadvantage. Though what I had reserved to myself was sufficient to support me in this place; yet it was scarcely enough to do so in some other places. I then gave up my estate with more joy, for being thereby conformed to Jesus Christ, than they could have who asked it from me. It is what I have never repented of, nor had any uneasiness about. What pleasure to lose all for the Lord! The love of poverty, thus contracted, is the kingdom of tranquillity.

I forgot to mention that toward the end of my miserable state of privation, when just ready to enter into newness of life, our Lord illuminated me so clearly to see that the exterior crosses came from Him, that I could not harbor any resentment against the persons who procured me them. On the contrary, I felt the tenderness of compassion for them, and had more pain for those afflictions which I innocently caused to them, than for any which they had heaped upon me. I saw that these persons feared the Lord too much to oppress me as they did, had they known it. I saw His hand in it, and I felt the pain which they suffered, through the contrariety of their humors. It is hard to conceive the tenderness which the Lord gave me for them, and the desire which I have had, with the utmost sincerity, to procure them every sort of advantage. . . .

I fell sick even to extremity. This sickness proved a means to cover the great mysteries which it pleased God to operate in me. Scarce ever was a disorder more extraordinary, or of longer continuance in its excess. . . . During this extraordinary sickness, which continued more than six months, the Lord gradually taught me that there was another manner of conversing among souls wholly His, than by speech. Thou madest me conceive, O divine Word, that as Thou art ever speaking and operating in a soul, though therein thou appearest in profound silence; so there was also a way of communication in thy creatures, in an ineffable silence. I heard then a language which before had been unknown to me. I gradually perceived, when Father La Combe entered, that I could speak no more. There was formed in my soul the same kind of silence toward him, as was formed in it in regard to God. I comprehended that God was willing to show me that men might in this life learn the language of angels. I was gradually reduced to speak to him only in silence. It was then that we understood each other in God, after a manner unutterable and divine. Our hearts spoke to each other, communicating a grace which no words can express. It was like a new country, both for him and for me; but so divine, that I cannot describe it. At first this was done in a manner so perceptible, that is to say, God penetrated us with Himself in a manner so pure and so sweet, that we passed hours in this profound silence, always communicative, without being able to utter one word. It was in this that we learned, by our own experience, the operations of the heavenly Word to reduce souls into unity with itself, and what purity one may arrive at in this life. It was given me to communicate this way to other good souls, but with this difference: I did nothing but communicate to them the grace with which they were filled, while near me, in this sacred silence, which infused into them an extraordinary strength and grace; but I received nothing from them; whereas with Father La Combe there was a flow and return of communication of grace, which he received from me, and I from him, in the greatest purity.

In this long malady the love of God, and of Him alone, made up my whole occupation, I seemed so entirely lost to Him, as to have no sight of myself at all. It seemed as if my heart never came out of that divine ocean, having been drawn into it through deep humiliations. Oh, happy loss, which is the consummation of bliss, though operated through crosses and through deaths!

Jesus was then living in me and I lived no more. These words were imprinted in me, as a real state into which I must enter (Matt. 8:20), "The foxes have holes, and the birds of the air have nests, but the Son of man hath not where to lay his head." This I have since experienced in all its extent, having no sure abode, no refuge among friends, who were ashamed of me, and openly renounced me, when universally decried; nor among my relations, most of whom declared themselves my adversaries, and were my greatest persecutors; while others looked on me with contempt and indignation. I might as David say, "For thy sake I have borne reproach; shame hath covered my face; I am become a stranger to my brethren, and an alien unto my mother's children; a reproach to men, and despised of the people."

He showed me all the world in a rage against me, without anyone daring to appear for me and assured me in the ineffable silence of His eternal Word, that He would give me vast numbers of children, which I should bring forth by the cross. I left it to Him to do with me whatever He pleased, esteeming my whole and sole interest to be placed entirely in His divine will. He gave me to see how the Devil was going to stir up an outrageous persecution against prayer, yet it should prove the source of the same prayer, or rather the means which God would make use of to establish it. He gave me to see farther how He would guide me into the wilderness, where He would cause me to be nourished for a time. The wings, which were to bear me thither, were the resignation of my whole self to His holy will. I think I am at present in that wilderness, separated from the whole world in my imprisonment. I see already accomplished in part what was then shown me. Can I ever express the mercies which my God has bestowed on me? No; they must ever remain in Himself, being of a nature not to be described, by reason of their purity and immensity. . . .

What made me go by Grenoble was the desire I had to spend two or three days with a lady, an eminent servant of God, and one of my friends. When I was there Father La Combe and that lady spoke to me not to go any farther. God would glorify Himself in me and by me in that place. He returned to Verceil, and I left myself to be conducted as a child by Providence. This lady took me to the house of a good widow, there not being accommodations at the inn. As I was ordered to stop at Grenoble, at her house I resided. I placed my daughter in a convent, and resolved to employ all this time in resigning myself to be possessed in solitude by Him who is the absolute Sovereign of my soul. I made not any visit in this place; no more had I in any of the others where I had sojourned. I was greatly surprised when, a few days after my arrival, there came to see me several persons who made profession of a singular devotion to God. I perceived immediately a gift which He had given me, of administering to each that which suited their states. I felt myself invested, all of a sudden, with the apostolic state. I discerned the conditions of the souls of such persons as spoke to me, and that which so much facility, that they were surprised at it, and said one to another, that I gave every one of them "the very thing they had stood in need of." It was thou, O my God, who didst all these things; some of them sent others to me. It came to such excess, that, generally from six in the morning till eight in the evening, I was taken up in speaking of the Lord. People flocked on all sides, far and near, friars, priests, men of the world, maids, wives, widows, all came one after another. The Lord supplied me with what was pertinent and satisfactory to them all, after a wonderful manner, without any share of my study or meditation therein. Nothing was hid from me of their interior state, and of what passed within them. Here, O my God, Thou madest an infinite number of conquests known to Thyself only. They were instantly furnished with a wonderful facility of prayer. God conferred on them His grace plentifully, and wrought marvelous changes in them. The most advanced of these souls found, when with me, in silence, a grace communicated to them which they could neither comprehend, nor cease to admire. The others found an unction in my words, and that they operated in them what I said. Friars of different orders, and priests of merit, came to see me, to whom our Lord granted very great favors, as indeed He did to all, without exception, who came in sincerity.

One thing was surprising; I had not a syllable to say to such as came only to watch my words, and to criticize them. Even when I thought to try to speak to them, I felt that I could not, and that God would not have me do it. Some of them in return said, "The people are fools to go to see that lady. She cannot speak." Others of them treated me as if I were only a stupid simpleton. After they left me there came one and said, "I could not get hither soon enough to apprize you not to speak to those persons; they come from such and such, to try what they can catch from you to your disadvantage." I answered them, "Our Lord has prevented your charity; for I was not able to say one word to them."

I felt that what I spoke flowed from the fountain, and that I was only the instrument of Him who made me speak. Amid this general applause, our Lord made me comprehend what the apostolic state was, with which He had honored me; that to give one's self up to the help of souls, in the purity of His Spirit, was to expose one's self to the most cruel persecutions. These very words were imprinted on my heart: "To resign ourselves to serve our neighbor is to sacrifice ourselves to a gibbet. Such as now proclaim, 'Blessed is he who cometh in the name of the Lord,' will soon cry out, 'Away with him, crucify him.' " When one of my friends speaking of the general esteem the people had for me, I said to her, "Observe what I now tell you, that you will hear curses out of the same mouths which at present pronounce blessings." Our Lord made me comprehend that I must be conformable to Him in all His states; and that, if He had continued in a private life with His parents, He never had been crucified; that, when He would resign any of

His servants to crucifixion, He employed such in the ministry and service of their neighbors. It is certain that all the souls employed herein by apostolic destination from God, and who are truly in the apostolic state, are to suffer extremely. I speak not of those who put themselves into it, who, not being called of God in a singular manner, and having nothing of the grace of the apostleship, have none of its crosses; but of those only who surrender themselves to God without any reserve, and who are willing with their whole hearts to be exposed, for His sake, to sufferings without any mitigation.

FRANCIS
THOMPSON

[1 8 5 9 – 1 9 0 7]

Fear wist not to evade

as Love wist to pursue.

Francis Thompson was born in the industrial city of Manchester, England. Because of an early addiction to opium, Thompson led the life of a vagrant in London, coming to know intimately the condition of the poor and disenfranchised. Unlike Tolstoy or Huysmans, Thompson was never touched with the despair or skepticism that characterized many nineteenth-century intellectuals. He was a poet through and through, an inheritor of the British Romantic tradition of Wordsworth and Coleridge. Like other mystics presented here, his vision sought to penetrate beyond the material world.

Thompson believed that poets communicate an experience of life that testifies to the vital and dynamic connection between things seen and unseen. His difficult poems, which emphasize the mysterious and unseen hand of God guiding all men's actions, are best exemplified by his most famous one, "The Hound of Heaven." Sensual imagery, obscure vocabulary, and deeply contorted phrasing also characterize the works of Metaphysical poets like John Donne or Sor Juana Inés de la Cruz. [EP]

THE HOUND OF HEAVEN

I fled Him, down the nights and down the days;
  I fled Him, down the arches of the years;
I fled Him, down the labyrinthine ways
    Of my own mind; and in the mist of tears
I hid from Him, and under running laughter.
        Up vistaed hopes, I sped;
        And shot, precipitated,
Adown Titanic glooms of chasmèd fears,
   From those strong Feet that followed, followed after.
      But with unhurrying chase,
      And unperturbèd pace,
    Deliberate speed, majestic instancy,
      They beat—and a Voice beat
      More instant than the Feet—
"All things betray thee, who betrayest Me."

     I pleaded, outlaw-wise,
By many a hearted casement, curtained red,
  Trellised with intertwining charities;
(For, though I knew His love Who followed,
      Yet was I sore adread
Lest, having Him, I must have naught beside)
But, if one little casement parted wide,
  The gust of His approach would clash it to.
  Fear wist not to evade as Love wist to pursue.
Across the margent of the world I fled,
  And troubled the gold gateways of the stars,
  Smiting for shelter on their clangèd bars;
     Fretted to dulcet jars
And silvern chatter the pale ports o' the moon.
I said to dawn: Be sudden; to eve; Be soon—
  With thy young skyey blossoms heap me over
    From this tremendous Lover!
Float thy vague veil about me, lest He see!
  I tempted all His servitors, but to find
My own betrayal in their constancy,
In faith to Him their fickleness to me,
  Their traitorous trueness, and their loyal deceit.

To all swift things for swiftness did I sue;
  Clung to the whistling mane of every wind.
      But whether they swept, smoothly fleet,
    The long savannahs of the blue;
          Or whether, Thunder-driven,
        They clanged His chariot 'thwart a heaven,
Plashy with flying lightnings round the spurn o' their feet:—
  Fear wist not to evade as Love wist to pursue.
          Still with unhurrying chase,
          And unperturbèd pace,
      Deliberate speed, majestic instancy,
          Came on the following Feet,
          And a Voice above their beat—
    "Naught shelters thee, who wilt not shelter Me."

I sought no more that, after which I strayed,
        In face of man or maid;
But still within the little children's eyes
        Seems something, something that replies,
They, at least, are for me, surely for me!
I turned me to them very wistfully;
But just as their young eyes grew sudden fair
        With dawning answers there,
Their angel plucked them from me by the hair.
"Come then, ye other children, Nature's—share
With me" (said I) "your delicate fellowship;
        Let me greet you lip to lip,
        Let me twine with you caresses,
            Wantoning
        With our Lady-Mother's vagrant tresses,
            Banqueting
        With her in her wind-walled palace,
        Underneath her azured daïs,
        Quaffing, as your taintless way is,
            From a chalice
Lucent-weeping out of the dayspring."
        So it was done:
I, in their delicate fellowship was one—
Drew the bolt of Nature's secrecies.
        I knew all the swift importings
        On the wilful face of skies;
        I knew how the clouds arise,

Spumèd of the wild sea-snortings;
            All that's born or dies
        Rose and drooped with; made them shapers
Of mine own moods, or wailful or divine—
            With them joyed and was bereaven.
            I was heavy with the even,
        When she lit her glimmering tapers
        Round the day's dead sanctities.
            I laughed in the morning's eyes.
I triumphed and I saddened with all weather,
            Heaven and I wept together,
And its sweet tears were salt with mortal mine;
Against the red throb of its sunset-heart
            I laid my own to beat,
            And share commingling heat;
But not by that, by that, was eased my human smart.
In vain my tears were set on Heaven's grey cheek.
For ah! we know not what each other says,
            These things and I; in sound I speak—
Their sound is but their stir, they speak in silences.
Nature, poor stepdame, cannot slake my drought;
            Let her, if she would owe me,
Drop yon blue bosom-veil of sky, and show me
            The breasts o' her tenderness:
Never did any milk of hers once bless
            My thirsting mouth.
            Nigh and nigh, draws the chase,
            With unperturbèd pace,
        Deliberate speed, majestic instancy,
            And past those noisèd Feet
            A Voice comes yet more fleet—
        "Lo! naught contents thee, who content'st
not Me."

Naked I wait Thy love's uplifted stroke!
My harness piece by piece Thou hast hewn from me,
            And smitten me to my knee;
            I am defenceless utterly.
            I slept, methinks, and woke,
And, slowly gazing, find me stripped in sleep.
In the rash lustihead of my young powers,
            I shook the pillaring hours

And pulled my life upon me; grimed with smears,
I stand amid the dust o' the mounded years—
My mangled youth lies dead beneath the heap.
My days have crackled and gone up in smoke,
Have puffed and burst as sun-starts on a stream.
       Yea, faileth now even dream
The dreamer, and the lute the lutanist;
Even the linked fantasies, in whose blossomy twist
I swung the earth a trinket at my wrist,
Are yielding; cords of all too weak account
For earth, with heavy griefs so overplussed.
       Ah! is Thy love indeed
A weed, albeit an amaranthine weed,
Suffering no flowers except its own to mount?
       Ah! must—
       Designer infinite!—
Ah! must Thou char the wood ere Thou canst limn with it?
My freshness spent its wavering shower i' the dust;
And now my heart is as a broken fount,
Wherein tear-drippings stagnate, spilt down ever
       From the dank thoughts that shiver
Upon the sighful branches of my mind.
       Such is; what is to be?
The pulp so bitter, how shall taste the rind?
I dimly guess what Time in mists confounds;
Yet ever and anon a trumpet sounds
From the hid battlements of Eternity,
Those shaken mists a space unsettle, then
Round the half-glimpsèd turrets slowly wash again;
       But not ere Him Who summoneth
       I first have seen, enwound
With glooming robes purpureal, cypress-crowned;
His Name I know, and what His trumpet saith.
Whether man's heart or life it be which yields
       Thee harvest, must Thy harvest fields
       Be dunged with rotten death?

       Now of that long pursuit
       Comes on at hand the bruit;
That Voice is round me like a bursting sea:
       "And is thy earth so marred,
       Shattered in shard on shard?

Lo, all things fly thee, for thou fliest Me!
　　　　Strange, piteous, futile thing!
Wherefore should any set thee love apart?
Seeing none but I makes much of naught" (He said),
"And human love needs human meriting:
　　　　How hast thou merited—
Of all man's clotted clay the dingiest clot?
　　　　Alack, thou knowest not
How little worthy of any love thou art!
Whom wilt thou find to love ignoble thee,
　　　　Save Me, save only Me?
All which I took from thee I did but take,
　　　　Not for thy harms,
But just that thou might'st seek it in My arms.
　　　　All which thy child's mistake
Fancies as lost, I have stored for thee at home:
　　　　Rise, clasp My hand, and come."

　　　　Halts by me that footfall;
　　　　Is my gloom, after all,
Shade of His hand, outstretched caressingly?
　　　　"Ah, fondest, blindest, weakest,
　　　　I am He Whom thou seekest!
Thou dravest love from thee, who dravest Me."

HENRIETTA
GANT

[1 8 6 8 – ?]

You gotta pray for something to get

the spirit.

During the New Deal of the 1930s, a collection of interviews with African Americans, many of whom had been born into slavery, were conducted under the Federal Writer's Project. The narrative presented here, that of Henrietta Gant's experience upon baptism, is reproduced exactly as transcribed by the interviewer, who described Henrietta as follows: "small, rather stockily built, neatly dressed in black. She wore an old black coat, and carried an old figured knitted bag. She wears glasses and looks to be well in her seventies, although she says she is sixty-one."

Although differing from other accounts presented here in being an oral rather than a written narrative, Gant's spiritual autobiography places her among the great mystics of the Christian tradition.   [AM]

NARRATIVE OF HER BAPTISM

It took me a long time to get religion. Ah said when Ah got religion, Ah would be finished with the world, an' that there would be no backslidin'. Ahm 61. Ah made 61 on the 6th of last month, an' Ahse only bin a member of the church 22 years, but Ah ain't never fell away, an' Ah never bin called up to the Board, or sot back, since Ah bin a christian.

Ah was born an raised here, but Ah got religion on Bayou Lafourche. My husband was cuttin' cane in the field there, an' Ah went to Bayou Lafourche to him. When Ah was there, Ah started to pray for my religion. Ah went off my myself an' Ah jest talked to God by myself. It took me a long time to get religion but when He did give it to me, He did everything but kill me. Ah prayed about 3 weeks, but Ah was converted in one week. Ah wanted Him to come an' talk to me. Ah wanted Him to talk to me, to sit down an' talk like we's talkin'. He didn't do that, but He apeared to me. He came to me in a cloud, an' He jest kep bowin' to me an' welcomin' me. The clouds opened an' it was jest like a little ball about that big (extending her hand showing the size of the ball) appeared in the clouds. He was dressed in a little blue uniform with gold buttons, an' a blue girdle an' sash. He looked at me jest like Ahm lookin' at you. Ah was so frightened, Ah didn't know what to do. Did Ah cry? Ah wouldn't ask you those words—Then he appeared to me again in a chariot. He had on that same blue uniform an' He was in a gold chariot with diamonds in it. An' it was pulled by six white horses. It looked like He had wings on his back. He was sittin' on the edge of the chariot, an' He bowed an' beckoned to me, to make me understand it was Him, an' He was callin' me. He was welcomin' me home, an' you know with all that, Ah didn't believe Ah was converted. So Ah told the Lord, Ah sez, "If Ahm really a christian, make the sun shout to me 3 times."

Well, Ah was by myself, my husband was out in the field yet, an' Ah bin prayin' all day, an' it was about 6 o'clock in the evenin' an' the sun had gone behind the clouds. An' Ah said, "Father, let the sun come out, an' shout three times, an' shout three times, an' shout three times." Well, do you know somethin', that whole day sun jest ris outa those clouds, an' it shouted to me three times. It bowed to me, an' then it went back in the clouds. That didn't convert me.

Den after that, Ah asked Him what He will have me to do. Ah was sittin' down in the house jest like Ahm sittin' here, then Ah heard a knock at the door, an' Ah went out, an' there was a nurse standin' at the door, dressed like the ones at Tero. This lady come an' said, "Henrietta, you will have to come on duty, an' you'll have to be in uniform." An' Ah sez to her, "Ah can't go with you, 'cause where am Ah gonna get a uniform like you got?" She sez, "It's right here." Ah went in the back room, an' Ah looked in the mirror, an' Ah was all shrouded in white, shoes an' stockings an' everything, just like she has. She said, "Let's go," and we walked outa the house together an' we went to another house, an' there was a mother an' father in one bed, sick, an' the son and daughter in another bed, sick. She said, "Ah want you to heal these people, an' you got to stay here until you heals them. You gotta stay here an' heal them children in the bed." An when Ah turned around an' said, "With what?" she was gone. Ah didn't know what to do, 'cause Ah ain't never healed nobody in my life, so Ah jest rubbed them with my naked hands, an' they gotta outa bed an' walked. An' they said, "You got the most beautifullest talent that ever was seen."

That woman was my gospel-mother. Your gospel-mother is somebody God sends for you. Someone you travel with, in your visions. It's somebody in the church, but He sends them to you an' then they your gospel-mother. They pray with you an' take care of you. It took a long time for me to be converted, but Ah got it to stay, haven't Ah?

Well, when the Spirit really got on me, it was between half past 3 an' a quarter to 4 in the mornin'. Ah got up at 12 o'clock an' prayed an' Ah said to God, "Convert me." At 4 o'clock, the minister of the Baptist Church in the country on Bayou Lafourche, came to my door with the Late Mole, the deacon of the church. He worked in the field, he was an overseer. They stopped in from of my doah with a gray mare, an' the minister said, "Ah come to get you to baptise you," they carried me to the bayou an' back an' they put me under the water. No they didn't take me on the mare, they carried me in the buggy. The mare was hitched to the buggy. Ah screamed so, 'till Ah woke up the whole place. Ah woke up everybody in the quarters, even my husband. They didn't do nothing to me, they jest said, "She's got religion." Ah don't know how long the Spirit stayed on me, 'cause Ah never tried to minite myself, an' Ah jest don't know how long. When that Spirit hit me, Ah jest saw a light lit. You talk about shoutin'—when Ah told my conversion, that church really shouted for me. An' when they dipped me in that water, there was plenty more shoutin'.

Ah wasn't baptised in Bayou Lafourche, 'cause Ah told the Lord that whatever church Ah would be baptised in, Ah would join, an' Ahd stay with that church. An' Ah asked Him to show me, or to send someone to tell me, what church to jine. Well, it was one Sunday night in the month of December, an' it was cold. Ah was sittin' in the church an' Ah told the Lord, "If this is the church for me, take me outa my seat with your will power an' send me to the rostrum." You know what He did—He jest stood me up an' took me outa my seat, an' when Ah come to, Ah found myself standin' in the rostrum. They say that Ah shouted so much when the preacher was preachin' that Ah stopped the man from preachin'. Ah lost my handkerchief, an' haven't found it to this day. An' if my sister hadn't bin sittin' by me an' taken it for me, Ah wouldn't have it to this day. If you'd give me this world full of money to tell you where that handkerchief went that night, Ah wouldn't be able to tell you. Ah was baptised in St. John's Church on First between Ferret and Howard, an' Ah bin a member there since. An' that's 22 years ago. No, Ah never bin on no Board. Rev. Taylor, that's our pastor, always sez to me, "Ah don't see why you haven't bin on the Board." An' Ah sez, "Ah guards the meetin'." Ah don't wanta be on no Board, 'cause sometimes they provoke you so on those Boards, that they make you commit yourself. You got so much to contend with on the Board. Rev. Taylor is sho a good man. He's a wonderful minister. Ah says he's a child, 'cause Ahm so old, he's a child under me. You know he's good, 'cause we baptises every month in the year.

You gotta pray for something to get the spirit. An' when Ah prayed Ah wasn't near the church. You know the quarters on the plantation, well, the church is way aroun' on the front, an', of course, it was too far, an' Ah jest prayed in my house. Ah didn't sing no hymn when the Spirit hit me, Ah jest shouted. Ah screamed an' hollared, an' Ah sho' cried. You jest get so sorry you cry an' cry an' cry. The Spirit of God makes you jump benches, an' they never hurts themselves. Ah never jumps. Ah jest runs an' shouts an' hollars. But now, Ah stop runnin'.

Ah went to a white house on the hill an' the Host of Heaven sayin, "Why should we start an' fear to die?" The doors of that white house on the hill opened an' the Lord was standin' there. He laid me on a table, jest like a doctor. The Father, the Son and the Mother were there an' they was all dressed in white. Her hair, was so shinin' gold, that you couldn't look at her. An' She put her hand out, an' it glittered like diamonds. It glittered so you couldn't look at it. She was beautiful. He's got a different resemblance to anyone Ahve ever seen. Ah don't know how to tell you how He looks. The Father, Son and Mother didn't say a word to me. The Lord jest put me on that table an' operated on me. He took my heart out, scraped it, put it back, an' it dripped 3 drops of blood. The 3 drops was the healin' power. Then the Mother turned to me an' she said, "Why did you come?" Ah said, "Ah come to work." An' she said, "You could mind these little children, your work is finished. There is nothin' for you to do." She took me in another room an' it was filled with little children. They was all dressed in white with crowns on their heads. Dat was to show me that Ah was a teacher for Sabbath school. You see the Lord shows you what you cut out to be. Ah used to teach Sabbath school but Ah give it up since Ahm gettin' old. The only time Ah don't come to get my communion is when Ahm sick.

Ah bin sick since New Year's Eve night. Ah was comin' from work, Ah does washin' an' ironin' at 3018 Monroe Street, Ah was gettin' off the bus on Washington Ave. an' Ah was filled with bundles, an' somebody knocked me down an' took my purse. Ah had $25.19 in my purse an' $15.19 belonged to the church. An' Ah gotta put the money that belonged to the church back. That was the drive money, not Sunday School money. Ahm jest able to go out now an' do some work, an' all Ah make Ahm savin' to pay back for the church. Ah don't know who knocked me down but they took everythin' Ah had. Ah had to have the doctor, an' my sister thought Ah was gonna die. Ah still can't walk so good. The doctor said the reason Ah was so sick was Ah was sufferin' from shock, Ah was so nervous Sunday was the first time Ah took communion in the church since before the New Year's 'cause Ah bin too sick to go. Ah got well, 'cause Ah trust the Lord.

If you trust the Lord, for one thing, you trust Him for all. An' Ah really trust Him, Ah really does that. If you don't trust him you don't have Faith. An' there's nothin' in life if you don't have Faith. Ahm tellin' you religion is better felt than it ever was told. An' if you felt always like you does the day you baptise you would sho' die. When you baptise you jest sits and waits, an' when your time comes, they ties a band aroun' your haid an' they tie you up aroun' your legs. You sho' feels funny. Jest so happy you can't wait for your time to come. You feels like you could leap over walls an' run through troops. Ah don't remember nothin' when Ah was baptised. Ah don't know a thing. They tells me Ah shouted so when they dipped me, they could hardly hold me. It was on the 31 of December an ishickles was hangin' from the trees. An' Ah took my coat off an' Ah give it to my sister an' Ah walked home in that drippin' gown an' Ah never caught cold that Ah knows of. Ah didn't eat nothin' that whole day—Ah didn't even take coffee—an' Ahm crazy about coffee, coffee is my whiskey. An' that night when they welcomed you in the church, an' gives you the righthand fellowship, Ah shouted so that Ah had the whole church shoutin'. Ahm tellin' you religion is the most wonderfullest thin' in this world.

Wese havin' a revival at 12 o'clock every day to get souls for Easter. We sings in our church

He Will Understand

If when you give the best of your service
Telling the World that the Savior has gone
Be not desolate if men don't believe you
He will understand and say well done.

If when you give, then enter my journey
Wearied of night and the battle is won

Carry the staff and cross of redemption
He will understand and say well done.

Ah got to go out an' get me somethin' to eat before Ah go to the revival
so Ah can't talk to you any longer, but if you come back some other time Ahl
be glad to talk with you, 'cause Ah always like to talk about religion. Ah
never gets tired doin' that.

SAINT THÉRÈSE
DE LISIEUX

[1 8 7 3 – 1 8 9 7]

*I was resolved to remain in spirit
at the foot of the cross.*

Thérèse de Lisieux, known as the "Little Flower," was the youngest of four sisters who all became Carmelite nuns. Like Brother Lawrence, her sense of the continual presence of the supernatural in her world is expressed in a simple and childlike manner. She became a popular saint because of her emphasis, throughout her brief years, on simple progress in spiritual life, which she termed "the little way." Apparently eager to pursue a contemplative vocation from an early age, she successfully petitioned the Pope to allow her to enter the convent earlier than usual, at fifteen. In her *Story of a Soul,* excerpted here, Thérèse describes the years following the loss of her mother, and her adoption of her older sisters as surrogate "mamans." Her manuscript is addressed to many mothers under that title: her own deceased mother, her sisters, her mother superior, and her heavenly mother, Mary, the mother of Jesus.

Thérèse's awareness of her own weaknesses and inabilities prompted her pursuit of "the little way," service of God in small sacrifices and simple devotions, a spiritual course that found a tremendous popular response. In the announcement of her sanctification in 1925, Pope Pius XI observed that she had achieved sainthood "without going beyond the common order of things."   [AM]

FROM *THE STORY OF A SOUL*

In the story of my soul, up until my entrance into Carmel, I distinguish three separate periods. The first is not the least fruitful in memories in spite of its short duration. It extends from the dawn of my reason till our dear Mother's departure for Heaven.

God granted me the favor of opening my intelligence at an early age and of imprinting childhood recollections so deeply on my memory that it seems the things I'm about to recount happened only yesterday. Jesus in His love willed, perhaps, that I know the matchless Mother He had given me, but whom His hand hastened to crown in heaven.

God was pleased all through my life to surround me with *love,* and the first memories I have are stamped with smiles and the most tender caresses. But although He placed so much *love* near me, He also sent much love into my little heart, making it warm and affectionate. I loved Mama and Papa very much and showed my tenderness for them in a thousand ways, for I was very expressive. . . .

NOW I MUST SPEAK OF THE SORROWFUL TRIAL THAT BROKE LITTLE Thérèse's heart when Jesus took away her dear *Mama,* her tenderly loved *Pauline!*

I had said to Pauline, one day, that I would like to be a hermit and go away with her alone in a faraway desert place. She answered that my desire was also hers and that she *was waiting* for me to be big enough for her to leave. This was no doubt not said seriously, but little Thérèse had taken it seriously; and how she suffered when she heard her dear Pauline speaking one day to Marie about her coming entrance into Carmel. I didn't know what Carmel was, but I understood that Pauline was going to leave me to enter a convent. I understood, too, she *would not wait for me* and I was about to lose my second *Mother!* Ah! how can I express the anguish of my heart! In one instant, I understood what life was; until then, I had never seen it so sad; but it appeared to me in all its reality, and I saw it was nothing but a continual suffering and separation. I shed bitter tears because I did not yet understand the *joy* of sacrifice. I was *weak,* so *weak* that I consider it a great grace to have been able to support a trial that seemed to be far above my strength! If I had learned of my dear Pauline's departure very gently, I would not have suffered as much perhaps, but having heard about it by surprise, it was as if a sword were buried in my heart.

I shall always remember, dear Mother, with what tenderness you consoled me. Then you explained the life of Carmel to me and it seemed so beautiful! When thinking over all you had said, I felt that Carmel was the *desert* where God wanted me to go also to hide myself. I felt this with so much force that there wasn't the least doubt in my heart; it was not the dream of a child led astray but the *certitude* of a divine call; I wanted to go to Carmel not for *Pauline's sake* but for *Jesus alone.* I was thinking *very much* about things that words could not express but which left a great peace in my soul.

The next day, I confided my secret to Pauline; she considered my desires as the will of heaven and told me that soon I would go with her to see the Mother Prioress of the Carmel and that I must tell her what God was making me feel. A Sunday was chosen for this solemn visit, and my embarrassment was great when I learned that Marie Guérin was to stay with me since she was still small enough to see the Carmelites. I had to find a way, however, to remain alone with the Prioress and this is what entered my mind: I said to Marie that since we had the privilege of seeing Mother Prioress, we should be very nice and polite and to do this we would have to confide our *secrets* to her. Each one in turn was to leave the room and leave the other all alone for a moment. Marie took me on my word, and, in spite of her repugnance of confiding *secrets she didn't have,* we remaining alone, one after the other, with Mother Prioress. Having listened to my *great confidences,* Mother Marie de Gonzague believed I had a vocation, but she told me they didn't receive postulants at the age of *nine* and that I must wait till I was sixteen. I resigned myself in spite of my intense desire to enter as soon as possible and to make my First Communion the day Pauline received the Habit. It was on this day I received compliments for the second time. Sister Teresa of St. Augustine came to see me and did not hesitate to say that I was pretty. I had not counted on coming to Carmel to receive praises like this, and after the visit I did not cease repeating to God that it was for *Him alone* I wished to be a Carmelite.

THE "BEAUTIFUL DAY OF DAYS" FINALLY ARRIVED. THE *SMALLEST details* of that heavenly day have left unspeakable memories in my soul! The joyous awakening at dawn, the *respectful* embraces of the teachers and our older companions! The large room filled with *snow-white* dresses in which each child was to be clothed in her turn! Above all, the procession into the chapel and the singing of the *morning* hymn: "O altar of God, where the angels are hovering!"

I don't want to enter into detail here. There are certain things that lose their perfume as soon as they are exposed to the air; there are deep *spiritual thoughts* which cannot be expressed in human language without losing their intimate and heavenly meaning; they are similar to "*. . . the white stone I will give to him who conquers, with a name written on the stone which no one KNOWS except HIM who receives it.*"

Ah! how sweet was that first kiss of Jesus! It was a kiss of *love;* I *felt* that *I was loved,* and I said: "I love You, and I give myself to You forever!" There were no demands made, no struggles, no sacrifices; for a long time now Jesus and poor little Thérèse *looked at* and understood each other. That day, it was no longer simply a *look,* it was a fusion; they were no longer two, Thérèse had vanished as a drop of water is lost in the immensity of the ocean. Jesus alone remained; He was the Master, the King. Had not Thérèse asked Him to take away her *liberty,* for her *liberty* frightened her? She felt so feeble and fragile that she wanted to be united forever to the divine Strength! Her joy was too great, too deep for her to contain, and tears of consolation soon flowed, to the great consternation of her companions. They asked one another: "Why was she crying? Was there something bothering her?"—"No, it was because her mother was not there or her sister whom she loves so much, her sister the Carmelite." They did not understand that all the joy of Heaven [had] entered my heart. . . .

The day after my Communion, the words of Marie came to my mind. I felt born within my heart a *great desire* to suffer, and at the same time the interior assurance that Jesus reserved a great number of crosses for me. I felt myself flooded with consolations so *great* that I look upon them as one of the *greatest* graces of my life. Suffering became my attraction; it had charms about it which ravished me without my understanding them very well. Up until this time, I had suffered without *loving* suffering, but since this day I felt a real love for it. I also felt the desire of loving only God, of finding my joy only in Him. Often during my Communions, I repeated these words of the Imitation: "O Jesus, unspeakable *sweetness*, change all the consolations of this earth into *bitterness* for me." This prayer fell from my lips without effort, without constraint; it seemed I repeated it not with my will but like a child who repeats the words a person he loves has inspired in him. Later I will tell you, dear Mother, how Jesus was pleased to realize my desire, and how He was always my ineffable *sweetness*. Were I to speak of this right now, I would be anticipating the time of my life as a young girl, and there are many details about my life as a child that I have to give you.

. . .

ALTHOUGH GOD SHOWERED HIS GRACES UPON ME, IT WASN'T BE-
cause I merited them because I was still very imperfect. I had a great desire,
it is true, to practice virtue, but I went about it in a strange way. Being the
youngest in the family, I wasn't accustomed to doing things for myself.
Céline tidied up the room in which we slept, and I myself didn't do any
housework whatsoever. After Marie's entrance into Carmel, it sometimes
happened that I tried to make up the bed to please God, or else in the
evening, when Céline was away, I'd bring in her plants. But as I already said,
it was for *God alone* I was doing these things and should not have expected
any *thanks* from creatures. Alas, it was just the opposite. If Céline was unfortunate enough not to seem happy or surprised because of these little services,
I became unhappy and proved it by my tears.

I was really unbearable because of my extreme touchiness; if I happened
to cause anyone I loved some little trouble, even unwittingly, instead of
forgetting about it and not *crying,* which made matters worse, I *cried* like a
Magdalene and then when I began to cheer up, I'd begin *to cry again for
having cried.* All arguments were useless; I was quite unable to correct this
terrible fault. I really don't know how I could entertain the thought of
entering Carmel when I was still in the *swaddling clothes of a child!*

God would have to work a little miracle to make me *grow up* in an instant,
and this miracle He performed on that unforgettable Christmas day. On that
luminous *night* which sheds such light on the delights of the Holy Trinity,
Jesus, the gentle; *little* Child of only one hour, changed the night of my soul
into rays of light. On that *night* when He made Himself subject to *weakness*
and suffering for love of me, He made me *strong* and courageous, arming me
with His weapons. Since that night I have never been defeated in any
combat, but rather walked from victory to victory, beginning, so to speak, *"to
run as a giant"!* The source of my tears was dried up and has since reopened
rarely and with great difficulty. This justified what was often said to me:
"You cry so much during your childhood, you'll no longer have tears to shed
later on!"

It was December 25, 1886, that I received the grace of leaving my childhood, in a word, the grace of my complete conversion. We had come back
from Midnight Mass where I had the happiness of receiving the *strong* and
powerful God. Upon arriving at Les Buissonnets, I used to love to take my
shoes from the chimney corner and examine the presents in them; this old
custom had given us so much joy in our youth that Céline wanted to continue
treating me as a baby since I was the youngest in the family. Papa had always
loved to see my happiness and listen to my cries of delight as I drew each
surprise from the *magic shoes,* and my dear King's gaiety increased my own
happiness very much. However, Jesus desired to show me that I was to give

up the defects of my childhood and so He withdrew its innocent pleasures. He permitted Papa, tired out after the Midnight Mass, to experience annoyance when seeing my shoes at the fireplace, and that he speak those words which pierced my heart: "Well, fortunately, this will be the last year!" I was going upstairs, at the time, to remove my hat, and Céline, knowing how sensitive I was and seeing the tears already glistening in my eyes, wanted to cry too, for she loved me very much and understood my grief. She said, "Oh, Thérèse, don't go downstairs; it would cause you too much grief to look at your slippers right now!" But Thérèse was no longer the same; Jesus had changed her heart! Forcing back my tears, I descended the stairs rapidly; controlling the poundings of my heart, I took my slippers and placed them in front of Papa, and withdrew all the objects joyfully. I had the happy appearance of a Queen. Having regained his own cheerfulness, Papa was laughing; Céline believed it was all a *dream!* Fortunately, it was a sweet reality; Thérèse had discovered once again the strength of soul which she had lost at the age of four and a half, and she was to preserve it forever!

On that *night of light* began the third period of my life, the most beautiful and the most filled with graces from heaven. The work I had been unable to do in ten years was done by Jesus in one instant, contenting himself with my *good will* which was never lacking. I could say to Him like His apostles: "Master, I fished all night and caught nothing." More merciful to me than He was to His disciples, Jesus *took the net Himself*, cast it, and drew it in filled with fish. He made me a fisher of *souls*. I experienced a great desire to work for the conversion of sinners, a desire I hadn't felt so intensely before.

I felt *charity* enter into my soul, and the need to forget myself and to please others; since then I've been happy! One Sunday, looking at a picture of Our Lord on the Cross, I was struck by the blood flowing from one of the divine hands. I felt a great pang of sorrow when thinking this blood was falling to the ground without anyone's hastening to gather it up. I was resolved to remain in spirit at the foot of the Cross and to receive the divine dew. I understood I was then to pour it out upon souls. The cry of Jesus on the Cross sounded continually in my heart: "*I thirst!*" These words ignited within me an unknown and very living fire. I wanted to give my Beloved to drink and I felt myself consumed with a *thirst for souls*. As yet, it was not the souls of priests that attracted me, but those of *great sinners;* I *burned* with the desire to snatch them from the eternal flames.

AFTER RECEIVING PAPA'S PERMISSION, I BELIEVED I'D BE ABLE TO fly to Carmel without any fears, but painful trials were still to prove my vocation. It was with trembling I confided my resolution to Uncle. He showed me great tenderness but did not grant me his permission to leave. He forbade me to speak about my vocation to him until I was seventeen. It was contrary to human prudence, he said, to have a child of fifteen enter Carmel. This Carmelite life was, in the eyes of many, a life of mature reflection, and it would be doing a great wrong to the religious life to allow an inexperienced child to embrace it. Everybody would be talking about it, etc., etc. He even said that for him to decide to allow me to leave would require a *miracle*. I saw all reasoning with him was useless and so I left, my heart plunged into the most profound bitterness. My only consolation was prayer. I begged Jesus to perform the *miracle* demanded, since at this price only I'd be able to answer His call.

A long time passed by before I dared speak to him again. It was very difficult for me to go to his home, and he himself seemed to be no longer considering my vocation. I learned later on that my great sadness influenced him very much. Before allowing any ray of hope to shine in my soul, God willed to send me a painful martyrdom lasting *three days*. Oh! never had I understood so well as during this trial, the sorrow of Mary and Joseph during their three-day search for the divine Child Jesus. I was in a sad desert, or rather my soul was like a fragile boat delivered up to the mercy of the waves and having no pilot. I knew Jesus was there sleeping in my boat, but the night was so black it was impossible to see Him; nothing gave me any light, not a single flash came to break the dark clouds. No doubt, lightning is a dismal light, but at least if the storm had broken out in earnest I would have been able to see Jesus for one passing moment. But it was night! The dark night of the soul! I felt I was all alone in the garden of Gethsemane like Jesus, and I found no consolation on earth or from heaven; God Himself seemed to have abandoned me. Nature seemed to share in my bitter sadness, for during these three days the sun did not shine and the rain poured down in torrents. (I have noticed in all the serious circumstances of my life that nature always reflected the image of my soul. On days filled with tears the heavens cried along with me; on days of joy the sun sent forth its joyful rays in profusion and the blue skies were not obscured by a single cloud.)

Finally, on the fourth day, which happened to be a Saturday, the day consecrated to the sweet Queen of heaven, I went to see Uncle. What was my surprise when I saw him looking at me, and, without expressing any desire to speak to him, he had me come into his study! He began by making some gentle reproaches because I appeared to be afraid of him, and then he said it wasn't necessary to beg for a *miracle*, that he had only asked God to give him "a simple change of heart" and that he had been answered. Ah! I was not tempted to beg for a miracle because *the miracle had been granted;* Uncle was no longer the same. Without making any allusion whatsoever to "human prudence," he told me I was a *little flower God wanted to gather,* and he would no longer oppose it!

This definitive response was truly worthy of him. For the third time now, this Christian of another age allowed one of the adopted daughters of his heart to go bury herself far from the world. Aunt, too, was admirable in her tenderness and prudence. I don't remember her saying a single word during my trial that could have increased my sufferings. I understood she pitied her little Thérèse. But when Uncle gave his consent, she too gave hers, but at the same time she showed me in a thousand little ways the great sorrow my departure would be for her. Alas, our dear relatives were far from expecting the same sacrifice would be asked of them twice over. But when God stretches out His *hand* to ask, His hand is never *empty*, and His intimate friends can draw from Him the courage and strength they need.

My heart is carrying me far from my subject and so, regretfully, I return to it. After Uncle's response you can easily understand, dear Mother, how I took the road back to Les Buissonnets with happiness flooding my heart. It was under *"a beautiful* sky, from which all the clouds were dispersed"! In my soul, too, the night had come to an end. Awakening, Jesus brought back joy, the noise of the waves was abated, and in place of the wind of trial, a light breeze expanded my sail and I believed I'd reach the blessed *shore,* now seemingly so close! It was really very close to my boat, but *more than one storm* was still to arise. Hiding from me the view of the luminous beacon, these storms caused me to fear lest I should be driven far from the shore so ardently desired without any hope of return.

I obtained, then, Uncle's permission and a few days afterward went to see you, dear Mother. I told you of my joy at seeing that my trials were all over. What was my surprise and sadness when you told me that the Superior was not giving his consent to my entrance until I was twenty-one. No one had thought of this opposition, and it was the most insurmountable of all. Without giving up hope, however, I went myself with Papa and Céline to pay him a visit, trying to change his mind by showing I really had a Carmelite vocation.

He received us coldly; my *incomparable* little Father joined his insistence to mine but in vain. Nothing would change the Superior's attitude. He told me there wasn't any danger in staying at home, I could lead a Carmelite life there, and if I didn't take the discipline all was not lost, etc., etc. He ended by saying he was only the *Bishop's delegate,* and if the latter wished me to enter Carmel, he himself would have nothing to say.

I left the rectory in *tears,* and fortunately my umbrella was able to hide them as the *rain* was coming down in torrents. Papa was at a loss as to how to console me. He promised to accompany me to Bayeux the moment I expressed my desire to go there since I was determined *to do all within my power,* even saying I would go to the *Holy Father* if the Bishop did not want to allow me to enter at fifteen. . . .

October 31 was the day set for the trip to Bayeux. I left alone with Papa, my heart filled with hope, but also rather scared at the thought of meeting the Bishop. For the first time in my life, I was to make a visit unaccompanied by my sisters and this visit was to a *Bishop*. I had never had any reason to speak unless in answer to questions addressed to me, and now I had to explain the purpose of my visit, to develop the reasons that made me seek entrance into Carmel; in a word, I was to show the firmness of my vocation. Ah! what that trip cost me! God had to give me a very special grace to overcome my timidity. It's also very true that *"love never finds impossibilities, because it believes everything is possible, everything is permitted."* It was surely only love of Jesus that could help me surmount these difficulties and the ones that followed, for it pleased Him to have me buy my vocation with very great trials. . . .

It *was raining* in torrents when we arrived at Bayeux. Papa, unwilling to have his little Queen enter the Bishop's house with her *beautiful dress* soaking wet, made her get on a bus and brought her to the cathedral. There my miseries began. The Bishop and all the clergy were attending an important funeral. The cathedral was filled with ladies in mourning and, as a consequence, I was stared at by everybody, dressed as I was in a bright frock and white hat. I would have much preferred to go out of the church, but this was out of the question because of the rain. To humiliate me more, God permitted that Papa in his fatherly simplicity made me take a front seat in the cathedral. Not wishing to give him any trouble, I executed this with great grace and thus procured this distraction for the good inhabitants of Bayeux, whom I would have preferred never to have known.

Finally, I was able to breathe freely in a small chapel behind the main altar and stayed there a long time praying fervently and waiting for the rain to stop and allow us to leave. When we were leaving, Papa had me admire the beauty of the edifice which appeared much larger when empty, but one single thought occupied my mind and I was able to enjoy nothing. We went directly to Father Révérony's who was aware of our arrival as he himself had set the date of the trip, but he was absent; we had to wander through the streets which appeared *very sad* to me. Finally, we returned close to the Bishop's residence, and Papa brought me into a magnificent hotel where I did not do honors to the excellent cooking. Poor little Father's tenderness for me was incredible! He told me not to be sad, that certainly the Bishop would agree with me. After we had rested, we returned to Father Révérony's; a gentleman arrived at the same time, but the Vicar General politely asked him to wait and had us enter his study first (the poor man had time to be bored for the visit was long).

Father Révérony was very friendly, but I believe the reason for our trip took him by surprise. After looking at me with a smile and asking me a few simple questions, he said: "I am going to introduce you to the Bishop; will you kindly follow me?" Seeing the tears in my eyes, he added: "Ah! I see diamonds; you mustn't show them to the Bishop!" He had us traverse several huge rooms in which portraits of bishops were hanging on the walls. When I saw myself in these large rooms, I felt like a poor little ant, and I asked myself what I would dare say to the Bishop.

The Bishop was walking on the balcony with two priests. I saw Father Révérony say a few words to him and return with him to where we were waiting in his study. There, three enormous armchairs were set before the fireplace in which a bright fire was crackling away. When he saw his Excellency enter, Papa knelt down by my side to receive his blessing; the Bishop had Papa take one of the armchairs, and then he sat down facing him. Father Révérony wanted me to take the one in the middle; I excused myself politely, but he insisted, telling me to show if I knew how to obey. And so I took it without further reflection and was mortified to see him take a chair while I was buried in a huge armchair that could hold four like me comfortably (more comfortably, in fact, for I was far from being so!). I had hoped that Papa would speak; however, he told me to explain the object of our visit to the Bishop. I did so as *eloquently* as possible and his Excellency, accustomed to *eloquence*, did not appear touched by my reasons; in their stead a single word from the Father Superior would have been much better, but I didn't have it and this did not help me in any way.

The Bishop asked me if it had been a long time since I desired to enter Carmel. "Oh! yes, Bishop, a very long time." "Come, now," said Father Révérony with a smile, "you can't say it is fifteen *years* since you've had the desire." Smiling, I said: "That's true, but there aren't too many years to subtract because I wanted to be a religious since the dawn of my reason, and I wanted Carmel as soon as I knew about it. I find all the aspirations of my soul are fulfilled in this Order."

I don't know, dear Mother, if these are my exact words. I believe they were expressed more poorly, but they contain the substance.

The Bishop, believing he'd please Papa, tried to have me stay with him a few more years, and he was very much *surprised* and *edified* at seeing him take my part, interceding for me to obtain permission to fly away at fifteen. And still everything was futile. The Bishop said an interview with the *Superior of Carmel* was indispensable before making his decision. I couldn't possibly have heard anything that would cause me more pain than this because I was aware of his formal opposition. Without taking into account Father Révérony's advice, I did more than *show my diamonds* to the Bishop. I *gave* him some!

He was very much touched by this and putting his arm around my neck, he placed my head on his shoulder and caressed me as no one, it appears, was ever caressed by him before. He told me all was not lost, that he was very happy I was making the trip to Rome to strengthen my vocation, that instead of crying I should rejoice. He added that the following week, before going to Lisieux, he'd speak about me to the pastor of St. James and I would receive an answer from him in Italy. I understood it was useless to make further entreaties, and besides I had nothing to say, having exhausted all the resources of my *eloquence*.

The Bishop brought us out as far as the garden. Papa *amused him very much* by telling him that in order to appear older I had put up my hair. (This wasn't lost on the Bishop, for he never spoke about "his little daughter" without telling the story of the hair.) Father Révérony wanted to accompany us to the end of the garden, and he told Papa that never had the like been seen before: "A father as eager to give his child to God as this child was to offer herself to Him!"

Papa asked him for a few explanations about the pilgrimage, among them how one must dress to appear before the Holy Father. I still can see him turning around in front of Father Révérony saying: "Am I good enough as I am?" He had told the Bishop that if he didn't allow me to enter Carmel, I was going to ask the Sovereign Pontiff. Papa was very simple in his words and manners, but he was so *handsome*, and he had a natural dignity about him which must have pleased the Bishop, accustomed to see himself surrounded by people who knew all the rules of polite society; but the *King of France and Navarre* in person, along with his *little Queen*, was not one of these.

When in the street again my tears began to flow, not so much because of my sorrow but because of my little Father who had made a useless trip. He had his heart set on sending a telegram to the Carmel announcing a favorable answer from the Bishop and was obliged to return without any answer at all. Ah! how painful it was! It seemed my future was ruined forever. The more I approached the goal, the more I saw my affairs all mixed up. My soul was plunged into bitterness but into peace too, for I was seeking God's will.

SUNDAY, NOVEMBER 20, AFTER DRESSING UP ACCORDING TO VATICAN regulations, i.e., in black with a lace mantilla as headpiece, and decorated with a large medal of Leo XIII, tied with a blue and white ribbon, we entered the Vatican through the Sovereign Pontiff's chapel. At eight o'clock in the morning our emotion was profound when we saw him enter to celebrate Holy Mass. After blessing the numerous pilgrims gathered round him, he climbed the steps of the altar and showed us through his piety, worthy of the Vicar of Jesus, that he was truly "the *Holy* Father." My heart beat strongly and my prayers were fervent when Jesus descended into the hands of His

Pontiff. However, I was filled with confidence, for the Gospel of the day contained these beautiful words: "Fear not, little flock, for it is your Father's good pleasure to give you the kingdom." No, I did not fear, I hoped the kingdom of Carmel would soon belong to me; I was not thinking then of those other words of Jesus: "And I appoint to you a kingdom even as my Father has appointed to me . . ." In other words, I reserve crosses and trials for you, and it is thus you will be worthy of possessing this kingdom after which you long; since it was necessary that the Christ suffer and that He enter through it into His glory, if you desire to have a place by His side, then drink the chalice He has drunk! This chalice was presented to me by the Holy Father and my tears mingled with the bitter potion I was offered.

After the Mass of thanksgiving, following that of the Holy Father, the audience began. Leo XIII was seated on a large armchair; he was dressed simply in a white cassock, with a cape of the same color, and on his head was a little skullcap. Around him were cardinals, archbishops, and bishops, but I saw them only in general, being occupied solely with the Holy Father. We passed in front of him in procession; each pilgrim knelt in turn, kissed the foot and hand of Leo XIII, received his blessing, and two noble guards touched him as a sign to rise (touched the pilgrim, for I explain myself so badly one would think it was the Pope).

Before entering the pontifical apartment, I was really determined *to speak*, but I felt my courage weaken when I saw *Father Révérony* standing by the Holy Father's right side. Almost at the same instant, they told us on the Pope's *behalf* that *it was forbidden to speak*, as this would prolong the audience too much. I turned toward my dear Céline for advice: "Speak!" she said. A moment later I was at the Holy Father's feet. I kissed his slipper and he presented his hand, but instead of kissing it I joined my own and lifting tear-filled eyes to his face, I cried out: "Most Holy Father, I have a great favor to ask you!"

The Sovereign Pontiff lowered his head toward me in such a way that my face almost touched his, and I saw his *eyes, black and deep*, fixed on me and they seemed to penetrate to the depths of my soul. "Holy Father, in honor of your Jubilee, permit me to enter Carmel at the age of fifteen!"

Emotion undoubtedly made my voice tremble. He turned to Father Révérony who was staring at me with surprise and displeasure and said: "I don't understand very well." Now if God had permitted it, it would have been easy for Father Révérony to obtain what I desired, but it was the cross and not consolation God willed to give me.

"Most Holy Father," answered the Vicar General, "this is *a child* who wants to enter Carmel at the age of fifteen, but the Superiors are considering the matter at the moment." "Well, my child," the Holy Father replied, looking at me kindly, "do what the Superiors tell you!" Resting my hands on his knees, I made a final effort, saying in a suppliant voice: "Oh! Holy Father, if you say yes, everybody will agree!" He gazed at me steadily, speaking these words and stressing each syllable: "Go ... go ... *You will enter if God wills it!*" (His accent had something about it so penetrating and so convincing, it seems to me I still hear it.)

I was encouraged by the Holy Father's kindness and wanted to speak again, but the two guards *touched* me *politely* to make me rise. As this was not enough they took me by the arms and Father Révérony helped them lift me, for I stayed there with joined hands resting on the knees of Leo XIII. It was with *force* they dragged me from his feet. At the moment I was *thus lifted*, the Holy Father placed his hand on my lips, then raised it to bless me. Then my eyes filled with tears and Father Révérony was able to contemplate at least as many *diamonds* as he had seen at Bayeux. The two guards literally carried me to the door and there a third one gave me a medal of Leo XIII. ...

At the termination of the audience, my dear Father was grieved to find me in tears. He did his best to console me but without success. In the bottom of my heart I felt a great peace, since I had done everything in my power to answer what God was asking of me. This *peace*, however, was in the *depths* only; bitterness *filled* my soul, for Jesus was silent. He seemed to be absent, nothing served to reveal His presence. That day, too, the sun dared not shine and Italy's beautiful blue skies, covered with dark clouds, never stopped crying with me. Ah! it was all over; my trip no longer held any attraction for me since its purpose had failed. The final words of the Pontiff should have consoled me, for were they not a real prophecy? *In spite of* all obstacles, what *God willed* was really accomplished. *He did not allow* creatures to do what they willed but *what He willed*.

THE DAY CHOSEN FOR MY ENTRANCE INTO CARMEL WAS APRIL 9, 1888, the same day the community was celebrating the feast of the Annunciation, transferred because of Lent. The evening before, the whole family gathered round the table where I was to sit for the last time. Ah! how heartrending these family reunions can really be! When you would like to see yourself forgotten, the most tender caresses and words are showered upon you, making the sacrifice of separation felt all the more.

Papa was not saying very much, but his gaze was fixed upon me lovingly. Aunt cried from time to time and Uncle paid me many affectionate compliments. Jeanne and Marie gave me all sorts of little attentions, especially Marie, who, taking me aside, asked pardon for the troubles she thought she caused me. My dear little Léonie, who had returned from the Visitation a few months previously, kissed and embraced me often. There is only Céline, about whom I have not spoken, but you can well imagine, dear Mother, how we spent that last night together.

On the morning of the great day, casting a last look upon Les Buissonnets, that beautiful cradle of my childhood which I was never to see again, I left on my dear King's arm to climb Mount Carmel. As on the evening before, the whole family was reunited to hear Holy Mass and receive Communion. As soon as Jesus descended into the hearts of my relatives, I heard nothing around me but sobs. I was the only one who didn't shed any tears, but my heart was beating *so violently* it seemed impossible to walk when they signaled for me to come to the enclosure door. I advanced, however, asking myself whether I was going to die because of the beating of my heart! Ah! what a moment that was! One would have to experience it to know what it is.

My emotion was not noticed exteriorly. After embracing all the members of the family, I knelt down before my matchless Father for his blessing, and to give it to me he placed *himself on his knees* and blessed me, tears flowing down his cheeks. It was a spectacle to make the angels smile, this spectacle of an old man presenting his child, still in the springtime of life, to the Lord! A few moments later, the doors of the holy ark closed upon me, and there I was received by the *dear Sisters* who embraced me. They had acted as mothers to me and I was going to take them as models for my actions from now on. My desires were at last accomplished; my soul experienced a *PEACE* so sweet, so deep, it would be impossible to express it. For seven years and a half that inner peace has remained my lot, and has not abandoned me in the midst of the greatest trials.

I was led, as are all postulants, to the choir immediately after my entrance into the cloister. The choir was in darkness because the Blessed Sacrament was exposed and what struck me first were the eyes of our holy Mother Geneviève which were fixed on me. I remained kneeling for a moment at her feet, thanking God for the grace He gave me of knowing a saint, and then I followed Mother Marie de Gonzague into the different places of the community. Everything thrilled me; I felt as though I was transported into a desert; our little cell, above all, filled me with joy. But the joy I was experiencing was *calm*, the lightest breeze did not undulate the quiet waters upon which my little boat was floating and no cloud darkened my blue heaven. Ah! I was fully recompensed for all my trials. With what deep joy I repeated those words: "I am here forever and ever!"

ANNIE
DILLARD

[1 9 4 5 –]

I am light; I am prayer and I can

hardly see.

Acclaimed novelist and author of the Pulitzer Prize–winning *Pilgrim at Tinker Creek*, Annie Dillard continuously addresses spiritual matters in her work. She has received several honorary degrees and prizes, particularly for her study of literature, *Living by Fiction*, and for her autobiographical work, *An American Childhood. Holy the Firm*, which followed *Pilgrim at Tinker Creek*, is an anguished meditation on a near-fatal plane crash that has severely injured a seven-year-old child. In the last chapter, presented here, Dillard opens the metaphysical wound—the problem of how to reconcile faith in a loving God with the horrors of the natural world; how to understand the beauties of a natural world that is also "red in tooth and in claw." Her response is to cast herself and her faith into the breach, in the spirit of sacrificial love and ecstatic renunciation. [AM]

FROM *HOLY THE FIRM*

I know only enough of God to want to worship him, by any means ready to hand. There is an anomalous specificity to all our experience in space, a scandal of particularity, by which God burgeons up or showers down into the shabbiest of occasions, and leaves his creation's dealings with him in the hands of purblind and clumsy amateurs. This is all we are and all we ever were; God *kann nicht anders* [knows nothing else]. This process in time is history; in space, at such shocking random, it is mystery.

A blur of romance clings to our notions of "publicans," "sinners," "the poor," "the people in the marketplace," "our neighbors," as though of course God should reveal himself, if at all, to these simple people, these Sunday school watercolor figures, who are so purely themselves in their tattered robes, who are single in themselves, while we now are various, complex, and full at heart. We are busy. So, I see now, were they. Who shall ascend into the hill of the Lord? or who shall stand in his holy place? There is no one but us. There is no one to send, nor a clean hand, nor a pure heart on the face of the earth, nor in the earth, but only us, a generation comforting ourselves with the notion that we have come at an awkward time, that our innocent fathers are all dead—as if innocence had ever been—and our children busy and troubled, and we ourselves unfit, not yet ready, having each of us chosen wrongly, made a false start, failed, yielded to impulse and the tangled comfort of pleasures, and grown exhausted, unable to seek the thread, weak, and involved. But there is no one but us. There never has been. There have been generations which remembered, and generations which forgot; there has never been a generation of whole men and women who lived well for even one day. Yet some have imagined well, with honesty and art, the detail of such a life, and have described it with such grace, that we mistake vision for history, dream for description, and fancy that life has devolved. So. You learn this studying any history at all, especially the lives of artists and visionaries; you learn it from Emerson, who noticed that the meanness of our days is itself worth our thought; and you learn it, fitful in your pew, at church.

THERE IS ONE CHURCH HERE, SO I GO TO IT. ON SUNDAY MORNINGS I quit the house and wander down the hill to the white frame church in the firs. On a big Sunday there might be twenty of us there; often I am the only person under sixty, and feel as though I'm on an archaeological tour of Soviet Russia. The members are of mixed denominations; the minister is a Congregationalist, and wears a white shirt. The man knows God. Once, in the middle of the long pastoral prayer of intercession for the whole world— for the gift of wisdom to its leaders, for hope and mercy to the grieving and pained, succor to the oppressed, and God's grace to all—in the middle of this he stopped, and burst out, "Lord, we bring you these same petitions every week." After a shocked pause, he continued reading the prayer. Because of this, I like him very much. "Good morning!" he says after the first hymn and invocation, startling me witless every time, and we all shout back, "Good morning!"

The churchwomen all bring flowers for the altar; they haul in arrangements as big as hedges, of wayside herbs in season, and flowers from their gardens, huge bunches of foliage and blossoms as tall as I am, in vases the size of tubs, and the altar still looks empty, irredeemably linoleum, and beige. We had a wretched singer once, a guest from a Canadian congregation, a hulking blond girl with chopped hair and big shoulders, who wore tinted spectacles and a long lacy dress, and sang, grinning, to faltering accompaniment, an entirely secular song about mountains. Nothing could have been more apparent than that God loved this girl; nothing could more surely convince me of God's unending mercy than the continued existence on earth of the church.

The higher Christian churches—where, if anywhere, I belong—come at God with an unwarranted air of professionalism, with authority and pomp, as though they knew what they were doing, as though people in themselves were an appropriate set of creatures to have dealings with God. I often think of the set pieces of liturgy as certain words which people have successfully addressed to God without their getting killed. In the high churches they saunter through the liturgy like Mohawks along a strand of scaffolding who have long since forgotten their danger. If God were to blast such a service to bits, the congregation would be, I believe, genuinely shocked. But in the low churches you expect it any minute. This is the beginning of wisdom.

TODAY IS FRIDAY, NOVEMBER 20. JULIE NORWICH IS IN THE HOSPItal, burned; we can get no word of her condition. People released from burn wards, I read once, have a very high suicide rate. They had not realized, before they were burned, that life could include such suffering, nor that they personally could be permitted such pain. No drugs ease the pain of third-degree burns, because burns destroy skin: the drugs simply leak into the sheets. His disciples asked Christ about a roadside beggar who had been blind from birth, "Who did sin, this man or his parents, that he was born blind?" And Christ, who spat on the ground, made a mud of his spittle and clay, plastered the mud over the man's eyes, and gave him sight, answered, "Neither hath this man sinned, nor his parents: but that the works of God should be made manifest in him." Really? If we take this answer to refer to the affliction itself—and not the subsequent cure—as "God's works made manifest," then we have, along with "Not as the world gives do I give unto you," two meager, baffling, and infuriating answers to one of the few questions worth asking, to wit, What in the Sam Hill is going on here?

The works of God made manifest? Do we really need more victims to remind us that we're all victims? Is this some sort of parade for which a conquering army shines up its terrible guns and rolls them up and down the streets for the people to see? Do we need blind men stumbling about, and little flamefaced children, to remind us what God can—and will—do?

I am drinking boiled coffee and watching the bay from the window. Almost all of the people who reef net have hauled their gears for the winter; the salmon runs are over, days are short. Still, boats come and go on the water—tankers, tugs and barges, rowboats and sails. There are killer whales if you're lucky, rafts of harlequin ducks if you're lucky, and every day the scoter and the solitary grebes. How many tons of sky can I see from the window? It is morning: morning! and the water clobbered with light. Yes, in fact, we do. We do need reminding, not of what God can do, but of what he cannot do, or will not, which is to catch time in its free fall and stick a nickel's worth of sense into our days. And we need reminding of what time can do, must only do; churn out enormity at random and beat it, with God's blessing, into our heads: that we are created, *created*, sojourners in a land we did not make, a land with no meaning of itself and no meaning we can make for it alone. Who are we to demand explanations of God? (And what monsters of perfection should we be if we did not?) We forget ourselves, picnicking; we forget where we are. There is no such thing as a freak accident. "God is at home," says Meister Eckhart, "We are in the far country."

We are most deeply asleep at the switch when we fancy we control any switches at all. We sleep to time's hurdy-gurdy; we wake, if we ever wake, to the silence of God. And then, when we wake to the deep shores of light uncreated, then when the dazzling dark breaks over the far slopes of time, then it's time to toss things, like our reason, and our will; then it's time to break our necks for home.

THE RE ARE NO EVENTS BUT THOUGHTS AND THE HEART'S HARD turning, the heart's slow learning where to love and whom. The rest is merely gossip, and tales for other times. The god of today is a tree. He is a forest of trees or a desert, or a wedge from wideness down to a scatter of stars, stars like salt low and dumb and abiding. Today's god said: shed. He peels from eternity always, spread; he winds into time like a rind. I am or seem to be on a road walking. The hedges are just where they were. There is a corner, and a long hill, a glimpse of snow on the mountains, a slope planted in apple trees, and a store next to a pasture, where I am going to buy the communion wine.

How can I buy the communion wine? Who am I to buy the communion wine? Someone has to buy the communion wine. Having wine instead of grape juice was my idea, and of course I offered to buy it. Shouldn't I be wearing robes and, especially, a mask? Shouldn't I *make* the communion wine? Are there holy grapes, is there holy ground, is anything here holy? There are no holy grapes, there is no holy ground, nor is there anyone but us. I have an empty knapsack over my parka's shoulders; it is cold, and I'll want my hands in my pockets. According to the Rule of St. Benedict, I should say, Our hands in our pockets. "All things come of thee, O Lord, and of thine own have we given thee." There must be a rule for the purchase of communion wine. "Will that be cash, or charge?" All I know is that when I go to this store—to buy eggs, or sandpaper, broccoli, wood screws, milk—I like to tease a bit, if he'll let me, with the owners' son, two, whose name happens to be Chandler, and who himself likes to play in the big bins of nails.

And so, forgetting myself, thank God: Hullo. Hullo, short and relatively new. Welcome again to the land of the living, to time, this hill of beans. Chandler will have, as usual, none of it. He keeps his mysterious counsel. And I'm out on the road again walking, my right hand forgetting my left. I'm out on the road again walking, and toting a backload of God.

HERE IS A BOTTLE OF WINE WITH A LABEL, CHRIST WITH A CORK. I bear holiness splintered into a vessel, very God of very God, the sempiternal silence personal and brooding, bright on the back of my ribs. I start up the hill.

The world is changing. The landscape begins to respond as a current upwells. It is starting to clack with itself, though nothing moves in space and there's no wind. It is starting to utter its infinite particulars, each overlapping and lone, like a hundred hills of hounds all giving tongue. The hedgerows are blackberry brambles, white snowberries, red rose hips, gaunt and clattering broom. Their leafless stems are starting to live visibly deep in their centers, as hidden as banked fires live, and as clearly as recognition, mute, shines forth from eyes. Above me the mountains are raw nerves, sensible and exultant; the trees, the grass, and the asphalt below me are living petals of mind, each sharp and invisible, held in a greeting or glance full perfectly formed. There is something stretched or jostling about the sky which, when I study it, vanishes. Why are there all these apples in the world, and why so wet and transparent? Through all my clothing, through the pack on my back and through the bottle's glass I feel the wine. Walking faster and faster, weightless, I feel the wine. It sheds light in slats through my rib cage, and fills the buttressed vaults of my ribs with light pooled and buoyant. I am moth; I am light. I am prayer and I can hardly see.

Each thing in the world is translucent, even the cattle, and moving, cell by cell. I remember this reality. Where has it been? I sail to the crest of the hill as if blown up the slope of a swell. I see, blasted, the bay transfigured below me, the saltwater bay, far down the hill past the road to my house, past the firs and the church and the sheep in the pasture: the bay and the islands on fire and boundless beyond it, catching alight the unraveling sky. Pieces of the sky are falling down. Everything, everything, is whole, and a parcel of everything else. I myself am falling down, slowly, or slowly lifting up. On the bay's stone shore are people among whom I float, real people, gathering of an afternoon, in the cells of whose skin stream thin colored waters in pieces which give back the general flame.

Christ is being baptized. The one who is Christ is there, and the one who is John, and the dim other people standing on cobbles or sitting on beach logs back from the bay. These are ordinary people—if I am one now, if those are ordinary sheep singing a song in the pasture.

The two men are bare to the waist. The one walks him into the water, and holds him under. His hand is on his neck. Christ is coiled and white under the water, standing on stones.

He lifts from the water. Water beads on his shoulders. I see the water in balls as heavy as planets, a billion beads of water as weighty as worlds, and he lifts them up on his back as he rises. He stands wet in the water. Each one bead is transparent, and each has a world, or the same world, light and alive and apparent inside the drop: it is all there ever could be, moving at once, past and future, and all the people. I can look into any sphere and see people stream past me, and cool my eyes with colors and the sight of the world in spectacle perishing ever, and ever renewed. I do; I deepen into a drop and see all that time contains, all the faces and deeps of the worlds and all the earth's contents, every landscape and room, everything living or made or fashioned, all past and future stars, and especially faces, faces like the cells of everything, faces pouring past me talking, and going, and gone. And I am gone.

For outside it is bright. The surface of things outside the drops has fused. Christ himself and the others, and the brown warm wind, and hair, sky, the beach, the shattered water—all this has fused. It is the one glare of holiness; it is bare and unspeakable. There is no speech nor language; there is nothing, no one thing, nor motion, nor time. There is only this everything. There is only this, and its bright and multiple noise.

I SEEM TO BE ON A ROAD, STANDING STILL. IT IS THE TOP OF THE hill. The hedges are here, subsiding. My hands are in my pockets. There is a bottle of wine on my back, a California red. I see my feet. I move down the hill toward home.

YOU MUST REST NOW. I CANNOT REST YOU. FOR ME THERE IS, I AM trying to tell you, no time.

THERE ARE A THOUSAND NEW ISLANDS TODAY, UNCHARTED. THEY are salt stones on fire and dimming; I read by their light. Small the cat lies on my neck. In the bathroom the spider is working on yesterday's moth.

Esoteric Christianity, I read, posits a substance. It is a created substance, lower than metals and minerals on a "spiritual scale," and lower than salts and earths, occurring beneath salts and earths in the waxy deepness of planets, but never on the surface of planets where men could discern it; and it is in touch with the Absolute, at base. In touch with the Absolute! At base. The name of this substance is: Holy the Firm.

Holy the Firm: and is Holy the Firm in touch with metals and minerals? With salts and earths? Of course, and straight on up, till "up" ends by curving back. Does something that touched something that touched Holy the Firm in touch with the Absolute at base seep into ground water, into grain; are islands rooted in it, and trees? Of course.

Scholarship has long distinguished between two strains of thought which proceed in the West from human knowledge of God. In one, the ascetic's metaphysic, the world is far from God. Emanating from God, and linked to him by Christ, the world is yet infinitely other than God, furled away from him like the end of a long banner falling. This notion makes, to my mind, a vertical line of the world, a great chain of burning. The more accessible and universal view, held by Eckhart and by many peoples in various forms, is scarcely different from pantheism: that the world is immanation, that God is in the thing, and eternally present here, if nowhere else. By these lights the world is flattened on a horizontal plane, singular, all here, crammed with heaven, and alone. But I know that it is not alone, nor singular, nor all. The notion of immanence needs a handle, and the two ideas themselves need a link, so that life can mean aught to the one, and Christ to the other.

For to immanence, to the heart, Christ is redundant and all things are one. To emanance, to the mind, Christ touches only the top, skims off only the top, as it were, the souls of men, the wheat grains whole, and lets the chaff fall where? To the world flat and patently unredeemed; to the entire rest of the universe, which is irrelevant and nonparticipant; to time and matter unreal, and so unknowable, an illusory, absurd, accidental, and over-elaborate stage.

But if Holy the Firm is "underneath salts," if Holy the Firm is matter at its dullest, Aristotle's *materia prima*, absolute zero, and since Holy the Firm is in touch with the Absolute at base, then the circle is unbroken. And it is. Thought advances, and the world creates itself, by the gradual positing of, and belief in, a series of bright ideas. Time and space are in touch with the Absolute at base. Eternity sockets twice into time and space curves, bound and bound by idea. Matter and spirit are of a piece but distinguishable; God has a stake guaranteed in all the world. And the universe is real and not a dream, not a manufacture of the senses; subject may know object, knowledge may proceed, and Holy the Firm is in short the philosopher's stone.

THESE ARE ONLY IDEAS, BY THE SINGLE HANDFUL. LINES, LINES, AND their infinite points! Hold hands and crack the whip, and yank the Absolute out of there and into the light, God pale and astounded, spraying a spiral of salts and earths, God footloose and flung. And cry down the line to his passing white ear, "Old Sir! Do you hold space from buckling by a finger in its hole? O Old! Where is your other hand?" His right hand is clenching, calm, round the exploding left hand of Holy the Firm.

HOW CAN PEOPLE THINK THAT ARTISTS SEEK A NAME? A NAME, LIKE a face, is something you have when you're not alone. There is no such thing as an artist: there is only the world, lit or unlit as the light allows. When the candle is burning, who looks at the wick? When the candle is out, who needs it? But the world without light is wasteland and chaos, and a life without sacrifice is abomination.

What can any artist set on fire but his world? What can any people bring to the altar but all it has ever owned in the thin towns or over the desolate plains? What can an artist use but materials, such as they are? What can he light but the short string of his gut, and when that's burnt out, any muck ready to hand?

His face is flame like a seraph's, lighting the kingdom of God for the people to see; his life goes up in the works; his feet are waxen and salt. He is holy and he is firm, spanning all the long gap with the length of his love, in flawed imitation of Christ on the cross stretched both ways unbroken and thorned. So must the work be also, in touch with, in touch with, in touch with; spanning the gap, from here to eternity, home.

Hoopla! All that I see arches, and light arches around it. The air churns out forces and lashes the marveling land. A hundred times through the fields and along the deep roads I've cried Holy. I see a hundred insects moving across the air, rising and falling. Chipped notes of birdsong descend from the trees, tuneful and broken; the notes pile about me like leaves. Why do these molded clouds make themselves overhead innocently changing, trailing their flat blue shadows up and down everything, and passing, and gone? Ladies and gentlemen! You are given insects, and birdsong, and a replenishing series of clouds. The air is buoyant and wholly transparent, scoured by grasses. The earth stuck through it is noisome, lighted, and salt. Who shall ascend into the hill of the Lord? or who shall stand in his holy place? "Whom shall I send," heard the first Isaiah, "and who will go for us?" And poor Isaiah, who happened to be standing there—and there was no one else—burst out, "Here am I; send me."

There is Julie Norwich. Julie Norwich is salted with fire. She is preserved like a salted fillet from all evil, baptized at birth into time and now into eternity, into the bladelike arms of God. For who will love her now, without a face, when women with faces abound, and people are so? People are reasoned, while God is mad. They love only beauty; who knows what God loves? Happy birthday, little one and wise: you got there early, the easy way. The world knew you before you knew the world. The gods in their boyish, brutal games bore you like a torch, a firebrand, recklessly over the heavens, to the glance of the one God, fathomless and mild, dissolving you into the sheets.

You might as well be a nun. You might as well be God's chaste bride, chased by plunderers to the high caves of solitude, to the heartless rooms empty of voices, and of warm limbs hooking your heart to the world. Look how he loves you! Are you bandaged now, or loose in a sterilized room? Wait till they hand you a mirror, if you can hold one, and know what it means. That skinlessness, that black shroud of flesh in strips on your skull, is your veil. There are two kinds of nun, out of the cloister or in. You can serve or you can sing, and wreck your heart in prayer, working the world's hard work. Forget whistling: you have no lips for that, or for kissing the face of a man or a child. Learn Latin, and it please my Lord, learn the foolish downward look called Custody of the Eyes.

And learn power, however sweet they call you, learn power, the smash of the holy once more, and signed by its name. Be victim to abruptness and seizures, events intercalated, swellings of heart. You'll climb trees. You won't be able to sleep, or need to, for the joy of it. Mornings, when light spreads over the pastures like wings, and fans a secret color into everything, and beats the trees senseless with beauty, so that you can't tell whether the beauty is *in* the trees—dazzling in cells like yellow sparks or green flashing waters—or *on* them—a transfiguring silver air charged with the wings' invisible motion; mornings, you won't be able to walk for the power of it: earth's too round. And by long and waking day—Sext, None, Vespers—when the grasses, living or dead, drowse while the sun reels, or lash in any wind, when sparrows hush and tides slack at the ebb, or flood up the beaches and cliff-sides tangled with weed, and hay waits, and elsewhere people buy shoes— then you kneel, clattering with thoughts, ill, or some days erupting, some days holding the altar rail, gripping the brass-bolt altar rail, so you won't fly. Do you think I don't believe this? You have no idea, none. And nights? Nights after Compline under the ribs of Orion, nights in rooms at lamps or windows like moths? Nights you see Deneb, one-eyed over the trees; you vanish into the sheets, shrunken, your eyes bright as candles and as sightless, exhausted. Nights Murzim, Arcturus, Aldebaran in the Bull: You cry, My father, my father, the chariots of Israel, and the horsemen thereof! Held, held fast by love in the world like the moth in wax, your life a wick, your head on fire with prayer, held utterly, outside and in, you sleep alone, if you call that alone, you cry God.

Julie Norwich; I know. Surgeons will fix your face. This will all be a dream, an anecdote, something to tell your husband one night: I was burned. Or if you're scarred, you're scarred. People love the good not much less than the beautiful, and the happy as well, or even just the living, for the world of it all, and heart's home. You'll dress your own children, sticking their arms through the sleeves. Mornings you'll whistle, full of the pleasure of days, and afternoons this or that, and nights cry love. So live. I'll be the nun for you. I am now.

PART FOUR

PHILOSOPHERS
& SCHOLARS

"PHILOSOPHERS AND SCHOLARS" MAY SEEM AN AUSTERE HEAD-
ing for several of the writers represented in this section, especially for
those writers of idiosyncratic literary gifts like Gerard Manley Hopkins
and Flannery O'Connor, or for the Sufi mystic Abū Hāmid Muhammad
Ghazālī. In sharp contrast to the immediate, yielding response of a passionate mystic or pilgrim, these authors approach the supernatural with
intellectual certitude. For some of them this relationship is one that is
established with great difficulty, for others it is as unquestioning as a
physical reflex, but ultimately their reason tells them that the universe
reflects a coherent ordering. With this recognition comes acceptance of
the finiteness of human understanding as well as the purposefulness of
the individual life.

Two excellent illustrations are the narratives of Marcus Aurelius and
Benjamin Franklin, though in mood and tone the *Meditations* and *The
Autobiography* could hardly differ more. It is true that the former is at
times reminiscent of Ecclesiastes and the Book of Job in its author's
recognition of the seeming futility of human endeavor. As with the biblical Wisdom stories, the author stresses the smallness of even the greatest
of mortals in comparison with the immensity of the universe. Yet Marcus
Aurelius shares something important with Franklin's optimistic "project
for moral perfection": namely, the certainty that divine providence rules
an orderly world and that human beings, through exercise of their intellectual faculties, can define and live the good life.

Two authors more conventional in their religious outlook are John
Henry Newman and Flannery O'Connor. For both, history is a spectacle
of folly, of the success of evil, of suffering. Yet it is the contrast between
mankind's fallen state and an inner prompting to achieve a more transcendent and pure nature that confirms for both Newman and O'Connor
that the human condition is out of joint with the intentions of its creator.

Many of the authors in this section, quite a few of whom were indeed bona fide scholars or philosophers, resist (sometimes futilely, sometimes not) a commitment that would carry them beyond themselves and the limits of their own understanding. Trying to think their way to God, scholarly writers like T. S. Eliot, C. S. Lewis, or Sheldon Vanauken do not expect or even desire to make the leap of faith, but are unable to turn back. Others, like Petrarch or Sor Juana Inés de la Cruz, pursue through introspection and logic an analysis of their spiritual condition and reach an untenable position, finding themselves perched on a dizzying height and beholden to God for rescue. Others, like Simone Weil, end by refusing—despite the most compelling of spiritual experiences—the life of faith they are called to because of a philosophical principle they cannot relinquish. [EP]

For Socrates there existed a realm of eternal, immutable truths—justice, beauty, wisdom, and love—of which the visible world offered only a dim and imperfect reflection. It was through reason that each individual had a direct connection to that realm and thus a measure for assessing the rightness of his actions. This philosophy marked a radical departure from the materialism of Greek mythology, in which the gods were portrayed as having their favorites, whom they in turn rewarded for their prowess or beauty. Socrates challenged his contemporaries to abandon the search for worldly profit and renown. The purpose of life was instead to cultivate one's reason and ascend to the realm of spiritual truths. Nothing less than one's immortal soul was at stake, which for Socrates was more important than mortal life.

The personal consequences of such beliefs are spelled out in the following passage from *The Apology*. Besides being a record of the memorable trial at which Socrates was condemned to death, *The Apology* is historically interesting for its reproduction of his actual language. In defending himself against charges of "ir-

SOCRATES

[C A . 4 7 0 – 3 9 9 B . C .]

A man has . . . only to consider

whether he is doing right or wrong.

religion," Socrates describes how God has endowed him with an individual conscience, with the choice of obeying or disobeying the dictates of reason. Because humans are responsible for their actions, they must themselves determine the ethical and spiritual consequences of those actions. Such responsibility may lead to death, as in the case of Socrates, but it conveys a dignity that is absent from the unexamined life.   [EP]

FROM *THE APOLOGY*

Some one will say: And are you not ashamed, Socrates, of a course of life which is likely to bring you to an untimely end? To him I may fairly answer: There you are mistaken: a man who is good for anything ought not to calculate the chance of living or dying; he ought only to consider whether in doing anything he is doing right or wrong—acting the part of a good man or of a bad. Whereas, according to your view, the heroes who fell at Troy were not good for much, and the son of Thetis above all, who altogether despised danger in comparison with disgrace; and when his goddess mother said to him, in his eagerness to slay Hector, that if he avenged his companion Patroclus, and slew Hector, he would die himself—"Fate," as she said, "waits upon you next after Hector:" he, hearing this, utterly despised danger and death, and instead of fearing them, feared rather to live in dishonor, and not to avenge his friend. "Let me die next," he replies, "and be avenged of my enemy, rather than abide here by the beaked ships, a scorn and a burden of the earth." Had Achilles any thought of death and danger? For wherever a man's place is, whether the place which he has chosen or that in which he has been placed by a commander, there he ought to remain in the hour of danger; he should not think of death or of anything, but of disgrace. And this, O men of Athens, is a true saying.

   Strange, indeed, would be my conduct, O men of Athens, if I who, when I was ordered by the generals whom you chose to command me at Potidaea and Amphipolis and Delium, remained where they placed me, like any other man, facing death; if, I say, now, when, as I conceive and imagine, God orders me to fulfil the philosopher's mission of searching into myself and other men, I were to desert my post through fear of death, or any other fear; that would indeed be strange, and I might justly be arraigned in court for denying the existence of the gods, if I disobeyed the oracle because I was afraid of death: then I should be fancying that I was wise when I was not wise. For this fear of death is indeed the pretence of wisdom, and not real wisdom, being the appearance of knowing the unknown; since no one knows whether death, which they in their fear apprehend to be the greatest evil, may not be the greatest good. Is there not here conceit of knowledge, which is a disgraceful sort of ignorance? And this is the point in which, as I think, I am superior to men in general, and in which I might perhaps fancy myself wiser than other men,—that whereas I know but little of the world below, I do not suppose that I know: but I do know that injustice and disobedience to a better, whether God or man, is evil and dishonorable, and I will never fear or avoid a possible good rather than a certain evil. And therefore if you let me go now, and reject the counsels of Anytus, who said that if I were not put to death I ought not to have been prosecuted, and that if I escape now, your sons will all be utterly ruined by listening to my words—if you say to me, Socrates, this time we will not mind Anytus, and will let you off, but upon one condition, that you are not to inquire and speculate in this way any more, and that if you are caught doing this again you shall die;—if this was the condition on which you let me go, I should reply: Men of Athens, I honor and love you; but I shall obey God rather than you, and while I have life and strength I shall never cease from the practice and teaching of philosophy, exhorting any one whom I meet after my manner, and convincing him, saying: O my friend, why do you, who are a citizen of the great and mighty and wise city of Athens, care so much about laying up the greatest amount of money and honor and reputation, and so little about wisdom and truth and the greatest improvement of the soul, which you never regard or heed at all? Are you not ashamed of this? And if the person with whom I am arguing, says: Yes, but I do care; I do not depart or let him go at once; I interrogate and examine and cross-examine him, and if I think that he has no virtue, but only says that he has, I reproach him with undervaluing the greater, and overvaluing the less. And this I should say to every one whom I meet, young and old, citizen and alien, but especially to the citizens, inasmuch as they are my brethren. For this is the command to God, as I would have you know; and I believe that to this day no greater good has ever happened in the state than my service to the God. For I do nothing but go about persuading you all, old and young alike, not to take thought for your persons or your properties, but first and chiefly to care about the greatest improvement of the soul. I tell you that virtue is not given by money, but that from virtue come money and every other good of man, public as well as private. This is my teaching, and if this is the doctrine which corrupts the youth, my influence is ruinous indeed. But if any one says that this is not my teaching, he is speaking an untruth. Wherefore, O men of Athens, I say to you, do as Anytus bids or not as Anytus bids, and either acquit me or not; but whatever you do, know that I shall never alter my ways, not even if I have to die many times.

Men of Athens, do not interrupt, but hear me; there was an agreement between us that you should hear me out. And I think that what I am going to say will do you good: for I have something more to say, at which you may be inclined to cry out; but I beg that you will not do this. I would have you know, that if you kill such a one as I am, you will injure yourselves more than you will injure me. Meletus and Anytus will not injure me: they can not; for it is not in the nature of things that a bad man should injure a better than himself. I do not deny that he may, perhaps, kill him, or drive him into exile, or deprive him of civil rights; he may imagine, and others may imagine, that he is doing him a great injury: but in that I do not agree with him; for the evil of doing as Anytus is doing—of unjustly taking away another man's life—is greater far. And now, Athenians. I am not going to argue for my own sake, as you may think, but for yours, that you may not sin against the God, or lightly reject his boon by condemning me. For if you kill me you will not easily find another like me, who, if I may use such a ludicrous figure of speech, am a sort of gadfly, given to the state by the God; and the state is like a great and noble steed who is tardy in his motions owing to his very size, and requires to be stirred into life. I am that gadfly which God has given the state, and all day long and in all places am always fastening upon you, arousing and persuading and reproaching you. And as you will not easily find another like me, I would advise you to spare me. I dare say that you may feel irritated at being suddenly awakened when you are caught napping; and you may think if you were to strike me dead as Anytus advises, which you easily might, then you would sleep on for the remainder of your lives, unless God in his care of you gives you another gadfly. And that I am given to you by God is proved by this:—that if I had been like other men, I should not have neglected all my own concerns or patiently seen the neglect of them during all these years, and have been doing yours, coming to you individually like a father or elder brother, exhorting you to regard virtue; this, I say, would not be like human nature. And had I gained anything, or if my exhortations had been paid, there would have been some sense in that: but now, as you will perceive, not even the impudence of my accusers dares to say that I have ever exacted or sought pay of any one; they have no witness of that. And I have a witness of the truth of what I say; my poverty is a sufficient witness.

Some one may wonder why I go about in private giving advice and busying myself with the concerns of others, but do not venture to come forward in public and advise the state. I will tell you the reason of this. You have often heard me speak of an oracle or sign which comes to me, and is the divinity which Meletus ridicules in the indictment. This sign I have had ever since I was a child. The sign is a voice which comes to me and always forbids me to do something which I am going to do, but never commands me to do anything, and this is what stands in the way of my being a politician. And rightly, as I think. For I am certain, O men of Athens, that if I had engaged in politics, I should have perished long ago, and done no good either to you or to myself. And don't be offended at my telling you the truth: for the truth is, that no man who goes to war with you or any other multitude, honestly struggling against the commission of unrighteousness and wrong in the state, will save his life; he who will really fight for the right, if he would live even for a little while, must have a private station and not a public one.

I can give you as proofs of this, not words only, but deeds, which you value more than words. Let me tell you a passage of my own life which will prove to you that I should never have yielded to injustice from any fear of death, and that if I had not yielded I should have died at once. I will tell you a story—tasteless perhaps and commonplace, but nevertheless true. The only office of state which I ever held, O men of Athens, was that of senator: the tribe Antiochis, which is my tribe, had the presidency at the trial of the generals who had not taken up the bodies of the slain after the battle of Arginusae; and you proposed to try them all together, which was illegal, as you all thought afterwards; but at the time I was the only one of the Prytanes who was opposed to the illegality, and I gave my vote against you; and when the orators threatened to impeach and arrest me, and have me taken away, and you called and shouted, I made up my mind that I would run the risk, having law and justice with me, rather than take part in your injustice be-cause I feared imprisonment and death. This happened in the days of the democracy. But when the oligarchy of the Thirty was in power, they sent for me and four others into the rotunda, and bade us bring Leon the Salaminian from Salamis, as they wanted to execute him. This was a specimen of the sort of commands which they were always giving with the view of implicating as many as possible in their crimes; and then I showed, not in word only but in deed, that, if I may be allowed to use such an expression, I cared not a straw for death, and that my only fear was the fear of doing an unrighteous or unholy thing. For the strong arm of that oppressive power did not frighten me into doing wrong; and when we came out of the rotunda the other four went to Salamis and fetched Leon, but I went quietly home. For which I might have lost my life, had not the power of the Thirty shortly afterwards come to an end. And to this many will witness.

Now do you really imagine that I could have survived all these years, if I had led a public life, supposing that like a good man I had always supported the right and had made justice, as I ought, the first thing? No indeed, men of Athens, neither I nor any other. But I have been always the same in all my actions, public as well as private, and never have I yielded any base compliance to those who are slanderously termed my disciples, or to any other. For the truth is that I have no regular disciples: but if any one likes to come and hear me while I am pursuing my mission, whether he be young or old, he may freely come. Nor do I converse with those who pay only, and not with those who do not pay; but any one, whether he be rich or poor, may ask and answer me and listen to my words; and whether he turns out to be a bad man or a good one, that can not be justly laid to my charge, as I never taught him anything. And if any one says that he has ever learned or heard anything from me in private which all the world has not heard, I should like you to know that he is speaking an untruth.

FRIENDS, WHO WOULD HAVE ACQUITTED ME, I WOULD LIKE ALSO TO talk with you about this thing which has happened, while the magistrates are busy, and before I go to the place at which I must die. Stay then awhile, for we may as well talk with one another while there is time. You are my friends, and I should like to show you the meaning of this event which has happened to me. O my judges—for you I may truly call judges—I should like to tell you of a wonderful circumstance. Hitherto the familiar oracle within me has constantly been in the habit of opposing me even about trifles, if I was going to make a slip or error about anything; and now as you see there has come upon me that which may be thought, and is generally believed to be, the last and worst evil. But the oracle made no sign of opposition, either as I was leaving my house and going out in the morning, or when I was going up into this court, or while I was speaking, at anything which I was going to say; and yet I have often been stopped in the middle of a speech, but now in nothing I either said or did touching this matter has the oracle opposed me. What do I take to be the explanation of this? I will tell you. I regard this as a proof that what has happened to me is a good, and that those of us who think that death is an evil are in error. This is a great proof to me of what I am saying, for the customary sign would surely have opposed me had I been going to evil and not to good.

Let us reflect in another way, and we shall see that there is great reason to hope that death is a good, for one of two things:—either death is a state of nothingness and utter unconsciousness, or, as men say, there is a change and migration of the soul from this world to another. Now if you suppose that there is no consciousness, but a sleep like the sleep of him who is undisturbed even by the sight of dreams, death will be an unspeakable gain. For if a person were to select the night in which his sleep was undisturbed even by dreams, and were to compare with this the other days and nights of his life, and then were to tell us how many days and nights he had passed in the course of his life better and more pleasantly than this one, I think that any man, I will not say a private man, but even the great king will not find many such days or nights, when compared with the others. Now if death is like this, I say that to die is gain; for eternity is then only a single night. But if death is the journey to another place, and there, as men say, all the dead are, what good, O my friends and judges, can be greater than this? If indeed when the pilgrim arrives in the world below, he is delivered from the professors of justice in this world, and finds the true judges who are said to give judgment there, Minos and Rhadamanthus and Aeacus and Triptolemus, and other sons of God who were righteous in their own life, that pilgrimage will be worth making. What would not a man give if he might converse with Orpheus and Musaeus and Hesiod and Homer? Nay, if this be true, let me die again and again. I, too, shall have a wonderful interest in a place where I can converse with Palamedes, and Ajax the son of Telamon, and other heroes of old, who have suffered death through an unjust judgment; and there will be no small pleasure, as I think, in comparing my own sufferings with theirs. Above all, I shall be able to continue my search into true and false knowledge; as in this world, so also in that; I shall find out who is wise, and who pretends to be wise, and is not. What would not a man give, O judges, to be able to examine the leader of the great Trojan expedition; or Odysseus or Sisyphus, or numberless others, men and women too! What infinite delight would there be in conversing with them and asking them questions! For in that world they do not put a man to death for this; certainly not. For besides being happier in that world than in this, they will be immortal, if what is said is true.

Wherefore, O judges, be of good cheer about death, and know this of a truth—that no evil can happen to a good man, either in life or after death. He and his are not neglected by the gods; nor has my own approaching end happened by mere chance. But I see clearly that to die and be released was better for me; and therefore the oracle gave no sign. For which reason, also, I am not angry with my accusers or my condemners; they have done me no harm, although neither of them meant to do me any good; and for this I may gently blame them.

Still I have a favor to ask of them. When my sons are grown up, I would ask you, O my friends, to punish them; and I would have you trouble them, as I have troubled you, if they seem to care about riches, or anything, more than about virtue; or if they pretend to be something when they are really nothing,—then reprove them, as I have reproved you, for not caring about that for which they ought to care, and thinking that they are something when they are really nothing. And if you do this, I and my sons will have received justice at your hands.

The hour of departure has arrived, and we go our ways—I to die, and you to live. Which is better God only knows.

MARCUS
AURELIUS

[1 2 1 – 1 8 0]

Whatever I am, is flesh and vital
spirit and governing self.

Marcus Aurelius put into practice what Socrates preached. Besides being emperor of Rome, he was a serious student of philosophy. The philosophy of which he was an adherent, Stoicism, stressed the power of reason to lead humans to align their individual lives in accordance with a likewise rational universal order. Marcus's thoughts on this subject were recorded in his *Meditations*, a profound soliloquy regarding of his reflections on the moral life. Composed in 172, while he was on tours of duty in the Roman provinces, it ranges from short, almost aphoristic jottings to longer observations. This is the undisputed master of Rome and of the Roman world, talking to himself, during a period of unrest in the empire that included the refusal of Christians to offer sacrifice to the official state gods.

The first book of the *Meditations* is private in character, revealing Marcus's recognition of his uniqueness and his individuality. In naming the individuals who contributed to forming his personality, he also shows his sense of the interconnectedness of humans. This disclosure of his private self is abandoned in the remainder of the *Meditations*, which more reticently enumerates a series of thoughts and actions on the best way to live a virtuous life and to bring one's individual existence into conformity with the divine plan.   [EP]

FROM *MEDITATIONS*

1. FROM MY GRANDFATHER VERUS, a kindly disposition and sweetness of temper.

2. FROM WHAT I HEARD OF MY FATHER AND MY MEMORY OF HIM, modesty and manliness.

3. FROM MY MOTHER, the fear of God, and generosity; and abstention not only from doing ill but even from the very thought of doing it; and furthermore to live the simple life, far removed from the habits of the rich.

4. FROM MY GRANDFATHER'S FATHER, to dispense with attendance at public schools, and to enjoy good teachers at home, and to recognize that on such things money should be eagerly spent.

5. FROM MY TUTOR, not to side with the Green Jacket or the Blue at the races, or to back the Light-Shield Champion or the Heavy-Shield in the lists; not to shirk toil, and to have few wants, and to do my own work, and mind my own concerns; and to turn a deaf ear to slander.

6. FROM DIOGNETUS, not to be taken up with trifles; and not to give credence to the statements of miracle-mongers and wizards about incantations and the exorcizing of demons, and such-like marvels; and not to keep quails, nor to be excited about such things: not to resent plain speaking; and to become familiar with philosophy and be a hearer first of Baccheius, then of Tandasis and Marcianus; and to write dialogues as a boy; and to set my heart on a pallet-bed and a pelt and whatever else tallied with the Greek regimen.

7. FROM RUSTICUS, to become aware of the fact that I needed amendment and training for my character; and not to be led aside into an argumentative sophistry; nor compose treatises on speculative subjects, or deliver little homilies, or pose ostentatiously as the moral athlete or unselfish man; and to eschew rhetoric, poetry, and fine language; and not to go about the house in my robes, nor commit any such breach of good taste; and to write letters without affectation, like his own letter written to my mother from Sinuessa; to shew oneself ready to be reconciled to those who have lost their temper and trespassed against one, and ready to meet them halfway as soon as ever they seem to be willing to retrace their steps; to read with minute care and not to be content with a superficial bird's-eye view; nor to be too quick in

agreeing with every voluble talker; and to make the acquaintance of the *Memoirs of Epictetus*, which he supplied me with out of his own library.

8. FROM APOLLONIUS, self-reliance and an unequivocal determination not to leave anything to chance; and to look to nothing else even for a moment save Reason alone; and to remain ever the same, in the throes of pain, on the loss of a child, during a lingering illness; and to see plainly from a living example that one and the same man can be very vehement and yet gentle: not to be impatient in instructing others; and to see in him a man who obviously counted as the least among his gifts his practical experience and facility in imparting philosophic truths; and to learn in accepting seeming favours from friends not to give up our independence for such things nor take them callously as a matter of course.

9. FROM SEXTUS, kindliness, and the example of a household patriarchally governed; and the conception of life in accordance with Nature; and dignity without affectation; and an intuitive consideration for friends; and a toleration of the unlearned and the unreasoning.

And his tactful treatment of all his friends, so that simply to be with him was more delightful than any flattery, while at the same time those who enjoyed this privilege looked up to him with the utmost reverence; and the grasp and method which he shewed in discovering and marshalling the essential axioms of life.

And never to exhibit any symptom of anger or any other passion, but to be at the same time utterly impervious to all passions and full of natural affection; and to praise without noisy obtrusiveness, and to possess great learning but make no parade of it.

10. FROM ALEXANDER THE GRAMMARIAN, not to be captious; nor in a carping spirit find fault with those who import into their conversation any expression which is barbarous or ungrammatical or mispronounced, but tactfully to bring in the very expression, that ought to have been used, by way of answer, or as it were in joint support of the assertion, or as a joint consideration of the thing itself and not of the language, or by some such graceful reminder.

11. FROM FRONTO, to note the envy, the subtlety, and the dissimulation which are habitual to a tyrant; and that, as a general rule, those amongst us who rank as patricians are somewhat wanting in natural affection.

12. FROM ALEXANDER THE PLATONIST, not to say to anyone often or without necessity, nor write in a letter, *I am too busy*, nor in this fashion constantly plead urgent affairs as an excuse for evading the obligations entailed upon us by our relations towards those around us.

13. FROM CATULUS, not to disregard a friend's expostulation even when it is unreasonable, but to try to bring him back to his usual friendliness; and to speak with whole-hearted good-will of one's teachers as it is recorded that Domitius did of Athenodotus; and to be genuinely fond of one's children.

14. FROM MY "BROTHER" SEVERUS, love of family, love of truth, love of justice, and (thanks to him!) to know Thrasea, Helvidius, Cato, Dion, Brutus; and the conception of a state with one law for all, based upon individual equality and freedom of speech, and of a sovranty which prizes above all things the liberty of the subject; and furthermore from him also to set a well-balanced and unvarying value on philosophy; and readiness to do others a kindness, and eager generosity, and optimism, and confidence in the love of friends; and perfect openness in the case of those that came in for his censure; and the absence of any need for his friends to surmise what he did or did not wish, so plain was it.

15. FROM MAXIMUS, self-mastery and stability of purpose; and cheeriness in sickness as well as in all other circumstances; and a character justly proportioned of sweetness and gravity; and to perform without grumbling the task that lies to one's hand.

And the confidence of every one in him that what he said was also what he thought, and that what he did was done with no ill intent. And not to shew surprise, and not to be daunted; never to be hurried, or hold back, or be at a loss, or downcast, or smile a forced smile, or, again, be ill-tempered or suspicious.

And beneficence and placability and veracity; and to give the impression of a man who cannot deviate from the right way rather than of one who is kept in it; and that no one could have thought himself looked down upon by him, or could go so far as to imagine himself a better man than he; and to keep pleasantry within due bounds.

16. FROM MY FATHER, mildness, and an unshakable adherence to decisions deliberately come to; and no empty vanity in respect to so-called honours; and a love of work and thoroughness; and a readiness to hear any suggestions for the common good; and an inflexible determination to give every man his due; and to know by experience when is the time to insist and when to desist; and to suppress all passion for boys.

And his public spirit, and his not at all requiring his friends to sup with him or necessarily attend him abroad, and their always finding him the same when any urgent affairs had kept them away; and the spirit of thorough investigation which he shewed in the meetings of his Council and his perseverance; nay his never desisting prematurely from an enquiry on the strength of off-hand impressions; and his faculty for keeping his friends and never being bored with them or infatuated about them; and his self-reliance in every emergency, and his good humour; and his habit of looking ahead and making provision for the smallest details without any heroics.

And his restricting in his reign public acclamations and every sort of adulation; and his unsleeping attention to the needs of the empire, and his wise stewardship of its resources, and his patient tolerance of the censure that all this entailed; and his freedom from superstition with respect to the Gods and from hunting for popularity with respect to men by pandering to their desires or by courting the mob; yea his soberness in all things and stedfastness; and the absence in him of all vulgar tastes and any craze for novelty.

And the example that he gave of utilizing without pride, and at the same without any apology, all the lavish gifts of Fortune that contribute towards the comfort of life, so as to enjoy them when present as a matter of course, and, when absent, not to miss them: and no one could charge him with sophistry, flippancy, or pedantry; but he was a man mature, complete, deaf to flattery, able to preside over his own affairs and those of others.

Besides this also was his high appreciation of all true philosophers without any upbraiding of the others, and at the same time without any undue subservience to them; then again his easiness of access and his graciousness that yet had nothing fulsome about it; and his reasonable attention to his bodily requirements, not as one too fond of life, or vain of his outward appearance, nor yet as one who neglected it, but so as by his own carefulness to need but very seldom the skill of the leech or medicines and outward applications.

But most of all a readiness to acknowledge without jealousy the claims of those who were endowed with any especial gift, such as eloquence or knowledge of law or ethics or any other subject, and to give them active support, that each might gain the honour to which his individual eminence entitled him; and his loyalty to constitutional precedent without any parade of the fact that it was according to precedent.

Furthermore he was not prone to change or vacillation, but attached to the same places and the same things; and after his spasms of violent headache he would come back at once to his usual employments with renewed vigour; and his secrets were not many but very few and at very rare intervals, and then only political secrets; and he shewed good sense and moderation in his management of public spectacles, and in the construction of public works, and in congiaria and the like, as a man who had an eye to what had to be done and not to the credit to be gained thereby.

He did not bathe at all hours; he did not build for the love of building; he gave no thought to his food, or to the texture and colour of his clothes, or the comeliness of his slaves. His robe came up from Lorium, his country-seat in the plains, and Lanuvium supplied his wants for the most part. Think of how he dealt with the customs' officer at Tusculum when the latter apologized, and it was a type of his usual conduct.

There was nothing rude in him, nor yet overbearing or violent nor carried, as the phrase goes "to the sweating state"; but everything was considered separately, as by a man of ample leisure, calmly, methodically, manfully, consistently. One might apply to him what is told of Socrates, that he was able to abstain from or enjoy those things that many are not strong enough to refrain from and too much inclined to enjoy. But to have the strength to persist in the one case and be abstemious in the other is characteristic of a man who has a perfect and indomitable soul, as was seen in the illness of Maximus.

17. FROM THE GODS, to have good grandfathers, good parents, a good sister, good teachers, good companions, kinsmen, friends—nearly all of them; and that I fell into no trespass against any of them, and yet I had a disposition that way inclined, such as might have led me into something of the sort, had it so chanced; but by the grace of God there was no such coincidence of circumstances as was likely to put me to the test.

And that I was not brought up any longer with my grandfather's concubine, and that I kept unstained the flower of my youth; and that I did not make trial of my manhood before the due time, but even postponed it.

That I was subordinated to a ruler and a father capable of ridding me of all conceit, and of bringing me to recognize that it is possible to live in a Court and yet do without body-guards and gorgeous garments and linkmen and statues and the like pomp; and that it is in such a man's power to reduce himself very nearly to the condition of a private individual and yet not on this account to be more paltry or more remiss in dealing with what the interests of the state require to be done in imperial fashion.

That it was my lot to have such a brother, capable by his character of stimulating me to watchful care over myself, and at the same time delighting me by his deference and affection: that my children have not been devoid of intelligence nor physically deformed. That I did not make more progress in rhetoric and poetry and my other studies, in which I should perhaps have been engrossed, had I felt myself making good way in them. That I lost no time in promoting my tutors to such posts of honour as they seemed to desire, and that I did not put them off with the hope that I would do this later on since they were still young. That I got to know Apollonius, Rusticus, Maximus.

That I had clear and frequent conceptions as to the true meaning of a life according to Nature, so that as far as the Gods were concerned and their blessings and assistance and intention, there was nothing to prevent me from beginning at once to live in accordance with Nature, though I still come short of this ideal by my own fault, and by not attending to the reminders, nay, almost the instructions, of the Gods.

That my body holds out so long in such a life as mine; that I did not touch Benedicta or Theodotus, but that even afterwards, when I did give way to amatory passions, I was cured of them; that, though often offended with Rusticus, I never went so far as to do anything for which I should have been sorry; that my mother, though she was to die young, yet spent her last years with me.

That as often as I had the inclination to help anyone, who was in pecuniary distress or needing any other assistance, I was never told that there was no money available for the purpose; and that I was never under any similar need of accepting help from another. That I have been blessed with a wife so docile, so affectionate, so unaffected; that I had no lack of suitable tutors for my children.

That by the agency of dreams I was given antidotes both of other kinds and against the spitting of blood and vertigo; and there is that response also at Caieta, *"as thou shall use it."* And that, when I had set my heart on philosophy, I did not fall into the hands of a sophist, nor sat down at the author's desk, or became a solver of syllogisms, nor busied myself with physical phenomena. For all the above *the Gods as helpers and good fortune need.*

Algazali was born in a village in what is present-day northeastern Iran. At the age of thirty-six, while enjoying a distinguished academic position as a professor of philosophy, he underwent a spiritual crisis that led him to engage in a profound criticism of the rational certitudes of Islamic philosophers. Donning the coarse wool garment worn by Sufi mystics and adopting their ascetic practices, Algazali made solitary pilgrimages for ten years throughout the Islamic world. His polemical writings, including the autobiographical work excerpted here concerning his spiritual quests, affirm the heart's knowledge in apprehending the unity of God.

Because of his strong spiritual personality, Algazali is sometimes credited with making Islam a mystic faith. To be a Sufi, he wrote, "means to abide continuously in God and to live at peace with men." At the same time, Algazali contributed to the medieval flourishing of Islamic learning that occurred as Muslims sought to incorporate Greek philosophic and scientific traditions into their interpretation of the Koran, the Word of God as revealed to Muhammad. It was via Arabic transla-

ABŪ HĀMID MUHAMMAD GHAZĀLĪ (ALGAZALI)

[1 0 5 8 – 1 1 1 1]

I was on the brink of a crumbling bank of sand.

tions that much Greek learning was later transmitted to the Christian West.
[EP]

FROM *DELIVERANCE FROM ERROR*

When God by His grace and abundant generosity cured me of this disease
[skepticism], I came to regard the various seekers *(sc.* after truth) as compris-
ing four groups:—

(1) the *Theologians (mutakallimūn)*, who claim that they are the exponents
of thought and intellectual speculation;

(2) the *Bāṭinīyah*, who consider that they, as the party of "authoritative
instruction" *(ta'līm)*, alone derive truth from the infallible *imam;*

(3) the *Philosophers*, who regard themselves as the exponents of logic and
demonstration;

(4) the *Sufis or Mystics*, who claim that they alone enter into the "presence"
(sc. of God), and possess vision and intuitive understanding.

I said within myself: "The truth cannot lie outside these four classes.
These are the people who tread the paths of the quest for truth. If the truth
is not with them, no point remains in trying to apprehend the truth. There
is certainly no point in trying to return to the level of the naive and derivative
belief *(taqlīd)* once it has been left, since a condition of being at such a level
is that one should not know one is there; when a man comes to know that,
the glass of his naive beliefs is broken. This is a breakage which cannot be
mended, a breakage not to be repaired by patching or by assembling of
fragments. The glass must be melted once again in the furnace for a new
start, and out of it another fresh vessel formed."

I now hastened to follow out these four ways and investigate what these
groups had achieved, commencing with the science of theology and then
taking the way of philosophy, the "authoritative instruction" of the Bāṭinīyah,
and the way of mysticism, in that order. . . .

When I had finished with [the first three of] these sciences, I next turned
with set purpose to the method of mysticism (or Sufism). I knew that the
complete mystic "way" includes both intellectual belief and practical activity; the latter consists in getting rid of the obstacles in the self and in
stripping off its base characteristics and vicious morals, so that the heart may
attain to freedom from what is not God and to constant recollection of Him.

The intellectual belief was easier to me than the practical activity. I began
to acquaint myself with their belief by reading their books, such as *The Food
of the Hearts* by Abū Ṭālib al-Makkī (God have mercy upon him), the works

of al-Ḥārith al-Muḥāsibī, the various anecdotes about al-Junayd, ash-Shiblī and Abū Yazīd al-Bisṭāmī (may God sanctify their spirits), and other discourses of their leading men. I thus comprehended their fundamental teachings on the intellectual side, and progressed, as far as is possible by study and oral instruction, in the knowledge of mysticism. It became clear to me, however, that what is most distinctive of mysticism is something which cannot be apprehended by study, but only by immediate experience [*dhawq* —literally "tasting"], by ecstasy and by a moral change. What a difference there is between *knowing* the definition of health and satiety, together with their causes and presuppositions, and *being* healthy and satisfied! What a difference between being acquainted with the definition of drunkenness— namely, that it designates a state arising from the domination of the seat of the intellect by vapours arising from the stomach—and being drunk! Indeed, the drunken man while in that condition does not know the definition of drunkenness nor the scientific account of it; he has not the very least scientific knowledge of it. The sober man, on the other hand, knows the definition of drunkenness and its basis, yet he is not drunk in the very least. Again the doctor, when he is himself ill, knows the definition and causes of health and the remedies which restore it, and yet is lacking in health. Similarly there is a difference between knowing the true nature and causes and conditions of the ascetic life and actually leading such a life and forsaking the world.

I apprehended clearly that the mystics were men who had real experiences, not men of words, and that I had already progressed as far as was possible by way of intellectual apprehension. What remained for me was not to be attained by oral instruction and study but only by immediate experience and by walking in the mystic way.

Now from the sciences I had laboured at and the paths I had traversed in my investigation of the revelational and rational sciences [that is, presumably, theology and philosophy], there had come to me a sure faith in God most high, in prophethood [or revelation], and in the Last Day. These three credal principles were firmly rooted in my being, not through any carefully argued proofs, but by reason of various causes, coincidences and experiences which are not capable of being stated in detail.

It had already become clear to me that I had no hope of the bliss of the world to come save through a God-fearing life and the withdrawal of myself from vain desire. It was clear to me too that the key to all this was to sever the attachment of the heart to worldly things by leaving the mansion of deception and returning to that of eternity, and to advance towards God most high with all earnestness. It was also clear that this was only to be achieved by turning away from wealth and position and fleeing from all time-consuming entanglements.

Next I considered the circumstances of my life, and realized that I was caught in a veritable thicket of attachments. I also considered my activities, of which the best was my teaching and lecturing, and realized that in them I was dealing with sciences that were unimportant and contributed nothing to the attainment of eternal life.

After that I examined my motive in my work of teaching, and realized that it was not a pure desire for the things of God, but that the impulse moving me was the desire for an influential position and public recognition. I saw for certain that I was on the brink of a crumbling bank of sand and in imminent danger of hell-fire unless I set about to mend my ways.

I reflected on this continuously for a time, while the choice still remained open to me. One day I would form the resolution to quit Baghdad and get rid of these adverse circumstances; the next day I would abandon my resolution. I put one foot forward and drew the other back. If in the morning I had a genuine longing to seek eternal life, by the evening the attack of a whole host of desires had reduced it to impotence. Worldly desires were striving to keep me by their chains just where I was, while the voice of faith was calling, "To the road! to the road! What is left of life is but little and the journey before you is long. All that keeps you busy, both intellectually and practically, is but hypocrisy and delusion. If you do not prepare *now* for eternal life, when will you prepare? If you do not now sever these attachments, when will you sever them?" On hearing that, the impulse would be stirred and the resolution made to take to flight.

Soon, however, Satan would return. "This is a passing mood," he would say; "do not yield to it, for it will quickly disappear; if you comply with it and leave this influential position, these comfortable and dignified circumstances where you are free from troubles and disturbances, this state of safety and security where you are untouched by the contentions of your adversaries, then you will probably come to yourself again and will not find it easy to return to all this."

For nearly six months beginning with Rajab 488 A.H. [= July 1095 A.D.], I was continuously tossed about between the attractions of worldly desires and the impulses towards eternal life. In that month the matter ceased to be one of choice and became one of compulsion. God caused my tongue to dry up so that I was prevented from lecturing. One particular day I would make an effort to lecture in order to gratify the hearts of my following, but my tongue would not utter a single word nor could I accomplish anything at all.

This impediment in my speech produced grief in my heart, and at the same time my power to digest and assimilate food and drink was impaired; I could hardly swallow or digest a single mouthful of food. My powers became so weakened that the doctors gave up all hope of successful treatment. "This trouble arises from the heart," they said, "and from there it has spread through the constitution; the only method of treatment is that the anxiety which has come over the heart should be allayed."

Thereupon, perceiving my impotence and having altogether lost my power of choice, I sought refuge with God most high as one who is driven to Him, because he is without further resources of his own. He answered me, He who "answers him who is driven [to Him by affliction] when he calls upon Him" [Qur'an 27, 63]. He made it easy for my heart to turn away from position and wealth, from children and friends. I openly professed that I had resolved to set out for Mecca, while privately I made arrangements to travel to Syria. I took this precaution in case the Caliph and all my friends should oppose my resolve to make my residence in Syria. This stratagem for my departure from Baghdad I gracefully executed, and had it in my mind never to return there. There was much talk about me among all the religious leaders of Iraq, since none of them would allow that withdrawal from such a state of life as I was in could have a religious cause, for they looked upon that as the culmination of a religious career; that was the sum of their knowledge.

Much confusion now came into people's minds as they tried to account for my conduct. Those at a distance from Iraq supposed that it was due to some apprehension I had of action by the government. On the other hand those who were close to the governing circles and had witnessed how eagerly and assiduously they sought me and how I withdrew from them and showed no great regard for what they said, would say, "This is a supernatural affair; it must be an evil influence which has befallen the people of Islam and especially the circle of the learned."

I left Baghdad, then. I distributed what wealth I had, retaining only as much as would suffice myself and provide sustenance for my children. This I could easily manage, as the wealth of Iraq was available for good works, since it constitutes a trust fund for the benefit of the Muslims. Nowhere in the world have I seen better financial arrangements to assist a scholar to provide for his children.

In due course I entered Damascus, and there I remained for nearly two years with no other occupation than the cultivation of retirement and solitude, together with religious and ascetic exercises, as I busied myself purifying my soul, improving my character and cleansing my heart for the constant recollection of God most high, as I had learnt from my study of mysticism. I used to go into retreat for a period in the mosque of Damascus, going up the minaret of the mosque for the whole day and shutting myself in so as to be alone.

At length I made my way from Damascus to the Holy House (that is, Jerusalem). There I used to enter into the precinct of the Rock every day and shut myself in.

Next there arose in me a prompting to fulfil the duty of the Pilgrimage, gain the blessings of Mecca and Medina, and perform the visitation of the Messenger of God most high (peace be upon him), after first performing the visitation of al-Khalīl, the Friend of God (God bless him). I therefore made the journey to the Hijaz. Before long, however, various concerns, together with the entreaties of my children, drew me back to my home [country]; and so I came to it again, though at one time no one had seemed less likely than myself to return to it. Here, too, I sought retirement, still longing for solitude and the purification of the heart for the recollection [of God]. The events of the interval, the anxieties about my family, and the necessities of my livelihood altered the aspect of my purpose and impaired the quality of my solitude, for I experienced pure ecstasy only occasionally, although I did not cease to hope for that; obstacles would hold me back, yet I always returned to it.

I continued at this stage for the space of ten years, and during these periods of solitude there were revealed to me things innumerable and unfathomable. This much I shall say about that in order that others may be helped: I learnt with certainty that it is above all the mystics who walk on the road of God; their life is the best life, their method the soundest method, their character the purest character; indeed, were the intellect of the intellectuals and the learning of the learned and the scholarship of the scholars, who are versed in the profundities of revealed truth, brought together in the attempt to improve the life and character of the mystics, they would find no way of doing so; for to the mystics all movement and all rest, whether external or internal, brings illumination from the light of the lamp of prophetic revelation; and behind the light of prophetic revelation there is no other light on the face of the earth from which illumination may be received.

A leading proponent of Renaissance humanism, Petrarch was a renowned scholar, orator, and poet. Like his near-contemporary, Dante, he directed some of his greatest poetry (the *Canzonière*) to an idealized woman whose untimely death inspired his poetic reflections on mortality. Petrarch's accomplishments were imitated by a wide circle of epigones, a trend that began during Petrarch's lifetime and had spread throughout Europe by the sixteenth century, including such poets as Michelangelo, Tasso, Louise Labé, Gongora, and Shakespeare. Although he perpetuated the cult of courtly love, Petrarch also questioned the viability of a beloved female figure as an emblem of the transcendent; he challenged the spiritual nature of Dante's love for Beatrice on this score. His perception of the human impulse to reach for God was also revealingly staged as a psychic drama or dialogue in his other writings. His introspective works have an almost modern tone.

In 1341, Petrarch was crowned poet laureate in Rome and was lionized by the most prestigious and wealthy circles; as a

PETRARCH (FRANCESCO PETRARCA)

[1 3 0 4 – 1 3 7 4]

I turned my inner eye

towards myself.

result, he experienced intense conflict between the pleasures of worldly life and what he sensed to be a spiritual calling to withdraw from the world. He describes this struggle in three dialogues between himself and Saint Augustine, published as *My Secret*. His spiritual conflict was precipitated by his experiences while climbing Mont Ventoux in France. At the peak of this climb, he read Augustine's *Confessions* and experienced a spiritual awakening. The hours of intensive self-examination and spiritual questioning that followed are described in this letter to his spiritual father and confessor. [AM]

THE ASCENT  MONT VENTOUX

LETTER TO FRANCESCO DIONIGI DE'ROBERTI OF BORGO SAN SEPOLCRO, PROFESSOR OF THEOLOGY IN PARIS. MALAUCÈNE, APRIL 26, 1336. (*FAM.*, IV, I, IN *LE FAMILIARI*, ED. V. ROSSI, I, 153–61; *OPERA* [BASEL, 1581], PP. 624–27.)

To Dionigi da Borgo San Sepolcro, of the Order of Saint Augustine, Professor of Theology, about his own troubles

Today I ascended the highest mountain in this region, which, not without cause, they call the Windy Peak. Nothing but the desire to see its conspicuous height was the reason for this undertaking. For many years I have been intending to make this expedition. You know that since my early childhood, as fate tossed around human affairs, I have been tossed around in these parts, and this mountain, visible far and wide from everywhere, is always in your view. So I was at last seized by the impulse to accomplish what I had always wanted to do. It happened while I was reading Roman history again in Livy that I hit upon the passage where Philip, the king of Macedon—the Philip who waged war against the Roman people—"ascends Mount Haemus in Thessaly, since he believed the rumor that you can see two seas from its top: the Adriatic and the Black Sea." Whether he was right or wrong I cannot make out because the mountain is far from our region, and the disagreement among authors renders the matter uncertain. I do not intend to consult all of them: the cosmographer Pomponius Mela does not hesitate to report the fact as true; Livy supposes the rumor to be false. I would not leave it long in doubt if that mountain were as easy to explore as the one here. At any rate, I had better let it go, in order to come back to the mountain I mentioned at first. It seemed to me that a young man who holds no public office might be excused for doing what an old king is not blamed for.

I now began to think over whom to choose as a companion. It will sound strange to you that hardly a single one of all my friends seemed to me suitable in every respect, so rare a thing is absolute congeniality in every attitude and habit even among dear friends. One was too sluggish, the other too vivacious; one too slow, the other too quick; this one too gloomy of temper, that one too gay. One was duller, the other brighter than I should have liked. This man's taciturnity, that man's flippancy; the heavy weight and obesity of the next, the thinness and weakliness of still another were reasons to deter me. The cool lack of curiosity of one, like another's too eager interest, dissuaded me from choosing either. All such qualities, however difficult they are to bear, can be borne at home: loving friendship is able to endure everything; it refuses no burden. But on a journey they become intolerable. Thus my delicate mind, craving honest entertainment, looked about carefully, weighing every detail, with no offense to friendship. Tacitly it rejected whatever it could foresee would become troublesome on the projected excursion. What do you think I did? At last I applied for help at home and revealed my plan to my only brother, who is younger than I and whom you know well enough. He could hear of nothing he would have liked better and was happy to fill the place of friend as well as brother.

We left home on the appointed day and arrived at Malaucène at night. This is a place at the northern foot of the mountain. We spent a day there and began our ascent this morning, each of us accompanied by a single servant. From the start we encountered a good deal of trouble, for the mountain is a steep and almost inaccessible pile of rocky material. However, what the Poet says is appropriate: "Ruthless striving overcomes everything."

The day was long, the air was mild; this and vigorous minds, strong and supple bodies, and all the other conditions assisted us on our way. The only obstacle was the nature of the spot. We found an aged shepherd in the folds of the mountain who tried with many words to dissuade us from the ascent. He said he had been up to the highest summit in just such youthful fervor fifty years ago and had brought home nothing but regret and pains, and his body as well as his clothes torn by rocks and thorny underbrush. Never before and never since had the people there heard of any man who dared a similar feat. While he was shouting these words at us, our desire increased just because of his warnings; for young people's minds do not give credence to advisers. When the old man saw that he was exerting himself in vain, he went with us a little way forward through the rocks and pointed with his finger to a steep path. He gave us much good advice and repeated it again and again at our backs when we were already at quite a distance. We left with him whatever of our clothes and other belongings might encumber us, intent only on the ascent, and began to climb with merry alacrity. However, as almost always happens, the daring attempt was soon followed by quick fatigue.

Not far from our start we stopped at a rock. From there we went on again, proceeding at a slower pace, to be sure. I in particular made my way up with considerably more modest steps. My brother endeavored to reach the summit by the very ridge of the mountain on a short cut; I, being so much more of a weakling, was bending down toward the valley. When he called me back and showed me the better way, I answered that I hoped to find an easier access on the other side and was not afraid of a longer route on which I might proceed more smoothly. With such an excuse I tried to palliate my laziness, and, when the others had already reached the higher zones, I was still wandering through the valleys, where no more comfortable access was revealed, while the way became longer and longer and the vain fatigue grew heavier and heavier. At last I felt utterly disgusted, began to regret my perplexing error, and decided to attempt the heights with a wholehearted effort. Weary and exhausted, I reached my brother, who had been waiting for me and was refreshed by a good long rest. For a while we went on together at the same pace. However, hardly had we left that rock behind us when I forgot the detour I had made just a short while before and was once more drawing down the lower regions. Again I wandered through the valleys, looking for the longer and easier path and stumbling only into longer difficulties. Thus I indeed put off the disagreeable strain of climbing. But nature is not overcome by man's devices; a corporeal thing cannot reach the heights by descending. What shall I say? My brother laughed at me; I was indignant; this happened to me three times and more within a few hours. So often was I frustrated in my hopes that at last I sat down in a valley. There I leaped in my winged thoughts from things corporeal to what is incorporeal and addressed myself in words like these:

"What you have so often experienced today while climbing this mountain happens to you, you must know, and to many others who are making their way toward the blessed life. This is not easily understood by us men, because the motions of the body lie open, while those of the mind are invisible and hidden. The life we called blessed is located on a high peak. 'A narrow way,' they say, leads up to it. Many hilltops intervene, and we must proceed 'from virtue to virtue' with exalted steps. On the highest summit is set the end of all, the goal toward which our pilgrimage is directed. Every man wants to arrive there. However, as Naso says: 'Wanting is not enough; long and you attain it.' You certainly do not merely want; you have a longing, unless you are deceiving yourself in this respect as in so many others. What is it, then, that keeps you back? Evidently nothing but the smoother way that leads through the meanest earthly pleasures and looks easier at first sight. However, having strayed far in error, you must either ascend to the summit of the blessed life under the heavy burden of hard striving, ill deferred, or lie prostrate in your slothfulness in the valleys of your sins. If 'darkness and the shadow of death' find you there—I shudder while I pronounce these ominous words—you must pass the eternal night in incessant torments."

You cannot imagine how much comfort this thought brought my mind and body for what lay still ahead of me. Would that I might achieve with my mind the journey for which I am longing day and night as I achieved with the feet of my body my journey today after overcoming all obstacles. And I wonder whether it ought not to be much easier to accomplish what can be done by means of the agile and immortal mind without any local motion "in the twinkling of the trembling eye" than what is to be performed in the succession of time by the service of the frail body that is doomed to die and under the heavy load of the limbs.

There is a summit, higher than all the others. The people in the woods up there call it "Sonny," I do not know why. However, I suspect they use the word in a sense opposite to its meaning, as is done sometimes in other cases too. For it really looks like the father of all the surrounding mountains. On its top is a small level stretch. There at last we rested from our fatigue.

And now, my dear father, since you have heard what sorrows arose in my breast during my climb, listen also to what remains to be told. Devote, I beseech you, one of your hours to reading what I did during one of my days. At first I stood there almost benumbed, overwhelmed by a gale such as I had never felt before and by the unusually open and wide view. I looked around me: clouds were gathering below my feet, and Athos and Olympus grew less incredible, since I saw on a mountain of lesser fame what I had heard and read about them. From there I turned my eyes in the direction of Italy, for which my mind is so fervently yearning. The Alps were frozen stiff and covered with snow—those mountains through which that ferocious enemy of the

Roman name once passed, blasting his way through the rocks with vinegar if we may believe tradition. They looked as if they were quite near me, though they are far, far away. I was longing, I must confess, for Italian air, which appeared rather to my mind than my eyes. An incredibly strong desire seized me to see my friend and my native land again. At the same time I rebuked the weakness of a mind not yet grown to manhood, manifest in both these desires, although in both cases an excuse would not lack support from famous champions.

Then another thought took possession of my mind, leading it from the contemplation of space to that of time, and I said to myself: "This day marks the completion of the tenth year since you gave up the studies of your boyhood and left Bologna. O immortal God, O immutable Wisdom! How many and how great were the changes you have had to undergo in your moral habits since then." I will not speak of what is still left undone, for I am not yet in port that I might think in security of the storms I have had to endure. The time will perhaps come when I can review all this in the order in which it happened, using as a prologue that passage of your favorite Augustine: "Let me remember my past mean acts and the carnal corruption of my soul, not that I love them, but that I may love Thee, my God."

Many dubious and troublesome things are still in store for me. What I used to love, I love no longer. But I lie: I love it still, but less passionately. Again have I lied: I love it, but more timidly, more sadly. Now at last I have told the truth; for thus it is: I love, but what I should love not to love, what I should wish to hate. Nevertheless I love it, but against my will, under compulsion and in sorrow and mourning. To my own misfortune I experience in myself now the meaning of that most famous line: "Hate I shall, if I can; if I can't, I shall love though not willing." The third year has not yet elapsed since that perverted and malicious will, which had totally seized me and reigned in the court of my heart without an opponent, began to encounter a rebel offering resistance. A stubborn and still undecided battle has been long raging on the field of my thoughts for the supremacy of one of the two men within me.

Thus I revolved in my thoughts the history of the last decade. Then I dismissed my sorrow at the past and asked myself: "Suppose you succeed in protracting this rapidly fleeing life for another decade, and come as much nearer to virtue, in proportion to the span of time, as you have been freed from your former obstinacy during these last two years as a result of the struggle of the new and the old wills—would you then not be able—perhaps not with certainty but with reasonable hope at least—to meet death in your fortieth year with equal mind and cease to care for that remnant of life which descends into old age?"

These and like considerations rose in my breast again and again, dear father. I was glad of the progress I had made, but I wept over my imperfection and was grieved by the fickleness of all that men do. In this manner I seemed to have somehow forgotten the place I had come to and why, until I was warned to throw off such sorrows, for which another place would be more appropriate. I had better look around and see what I had intended to see in coming here. The time to leave was approaching, they said. The sun was already setting, and the shadow of the mountain was growing longer and longer. Like a man aroused from sleep, I turned back and looked toward the west. The boundary wall between France and Spain, the ridge of the Pyrenees, is not visible from there, though there is no obstacle of which I knew, and nothing but the weakness of the mortal eye is the cause. However, one could see most distinctly the mountains of the province of Lyons to the right and, to the left, the sea near Marseilles as well as the waves that break against Aigues Mortes, although it takes several days to travel to this city. The Rhone River was directly under our eyes.

I admired every detail, now relishing earthly enjoyment, now lifting up my mind to higher spheres after the example of my body, and I thought it fit to look into the volume of Augustine's *Confessions* which I owe to your loving kindness and preserve carefully, keeping it always in my hands, in remembrance of the author as well as the donor. It is a little book of smallest size but full of infinite sweetness. I opened it with the intention of reading whatever might occur to me first: nothing, indeed, but pious and devout sentences could come to hand. I happened to hit upon the tenth book of the work. My brother stood beside me, intently expecting to hear something from Augustine on my mouth. I ask God to be my witness and my brother who was with me: Where I fixed my eyes first, it was written: "And men go to admire the high mountains, the vast floods of the sea, the huge streams of the rivers, the circumference of the ocean, and the revolutions of the stars —and desert themselves." I was stunned, I confess. I bade my brother, who wanted to hear more, not to molest me, and closed the book, angry with myself that I still admired earthly things. Long since I ought to have learned, even from pagan philosophers, that "nothing is admirable besides the mind; compared to its greatness nothing is great."

I was completely satisfied with what I had seen of the mountain and turned my inner eye toward myself. From this hour nobody heard me say a word until we arrived at the bottom. These words occupied me sufficiently. I could not imagine that this had happened to me by chance: I was convinced that whatever I had read there was said to me and to nobody else. I remembered that Augustine once suspected the same regarding himself, when, while he was reading the Apostolic

Epistles, the first passage that occurred to him was, as he himself relates: "Not in banqueting and drunkenness, not in chambering and wantonness, not in strife and envying; but put ye on the Lord Jesus Christ, and make no provision for the flesh to fulfil your lusts." The same had happened before to Anthony: he heard the Gospel where it is written: "If thou wilt be perfect, go and sell that thou hast, and give to the poor, and come and follow me, and thou shalt have treasure in heaven." As his biographer Athanasius says, he applied the Lord's command to himself, just as if the Scripture had been recited for his sake. And as Anthony, having heard this, sought nothing else, and as Augustine, having read the other passage, proceeded not further, the end of all my reading was the few words I have already set down. Silently I thought over how greatly mortal men lack counsel who, neglecting the noblest part of themselves in empty parading, look without for what can be found within. I admired the nobility of the mind, had it not voluntarily degenerated and strayed from the primordial state of its origin, converting into disgrace what God had given to be its honor.

How often, do you think, did I turn back and look up to the summit of the mountain today while I was walking down? It seemed to me hardly higher than a cubit compared to the height of human contemplation, were the latter not plunged into the filth of earthly sordidness. This too occurred to me at every step: "If you do not regret undergoing so much sweat and hard labor to lift the body a bit nearer to heaven, ought any cross or jail or torture to frighten the mind that is trying to come nearer to God and set its feet upon the swollen summit of insolence and upon the fate of mortal men?" And this too: "How few will ever succeed in not diverging from this path because of fear of hardship or desire for smooth comfort? Too fortunate would be any man who accomplished such a feat—were there ever such anywhere. This would be him of whom I should judge the Poet was thinking when he wrote:

> *Happy the man who succeeded in baring the causes of things*
> *And who trod underfoot all fear, inexorable Fate and*
> *Greedy Acheron's uproar. . . .*

How intensely ought we to exert our strength to get under foot not a higher spot of earth but the passions which are puffed up by earthly instincts."

Such emotions were rousing a storm in my breast as, without perceiving the roughness of the path, I returned late at night to the little rustic inn from which I had set out before dawn. The moon was shining all night long and offered her friendly service to the wanderers. While the servants were busy preparing our meal, I withdrew quite alone into a remote part of the house to write this letter to you in all haste and on the spur of the moment. I was afraid the intention to write might evaporate, since the rapid change of scene was likely to cause a change of mood if I deferred it.

And thus, most loving father, gather from this letter how eager I am to leave nothing whatever in my heart hidden from your eyes. Not only do I lay my whole life open to you with the utmost care but every single thought of mine. Pray for these thoughts, I beseech you, that they may at last find stability. So long have they been idling about and, finding no firm stand, been uselessly driven through so many matters. May they now turn at last to the One, the Good, the True, the stably Abiding.

Farewell.

On the twenty-sixth day of April, at Malaucène.

SOR JUANA INÉS DE LA CRUZ

[1 6 5 1 – 1 6 9 5]

*In order to be the mistress
over the others, the Powerful,
Wise Hand,
not in vain, adorned. . . .*

The leading Baroque poet of Mexico during her lifetime, Sor Juana Inés de la Cruz was praised by her contemporaries as the "Tenth Muse" and the "Phoenix of Mexico." In part because of her illegitimate birth, and partly because of social and ecclesiastical restrictions upon women, Sor Juana was repeatedly called upon to defend her pursuit of higher learning and poetry. *A Spiritual Self-Defense* and her much-acclaimed *Response to the Most Illustrious Poetess Sor Filotea de la Cruz* are the first New World works defending the rights of women to participate fully in scholarship and the arts. A popular figure as a result of her intransigency, Sor Juana's portrait has been reproduced on Mexican currency, postage stamps, and murals, and in the popular arts.

Her poetic masterpiece, called alternately "First Dream" ("*Primero sueño,*" also known as "The Dream," or "*El sueño*"), is an account of the soul's journey through hierarchies of wisdom from the earth's mineral realms to celestial spheres. The poem culminates in a vision of the confounding darkness of confusion pierced by the sunrise. The dizzying imagery and complex language drenched with literary and philosophical allusions are typical of Baroque metaphysical poetry. [AM]

FIRST DREAM

A pyramidal, doleful shadow,
born of the earth, directed its proud point
of vain obelisks toward Heaven,
seeking to scale the Stars,
while their beautiful lights
—forever free, forever scintillating—
ridiculed from such great distance
the gloomy war intimated
by the frightening, fugitive shadow
with black vapors,
that its darkened scowl
did not even reach the convex surface
of the orb of the trebly-beautiful Goddess,
who manifests herself in three beautiful faces,
but only mastered
the air that it clouded
with the dense breath it was exhaling,
and in the contented quiet
of silent empire,
only permitted the submissive voices
of nocturnal birds,
so dark, so deep,
that the silence wasn't even interrupted.

*   This sorrowful, intermittent sound*
from the timid, shadowed crowd
solicited attention less
than it brought on sleep;
indeed, slowly,
its dull, deliberate consonance
induced the limbs
to calm and to rest
—silent Harpocrates, the night,
intimating silence to the living,

sealing dark lips of one and another
with his pointing finger,
his precept, imperious
although not harsh,
all obeyed—.
          The wind becalmed, the dog asleep,
the latter rests, the former
does not move its atoms,
fearing with light whisper
to make a sacrilegious, if small sound,
violator of the calm silence.
The sea, now undisturbed,
was not even rocking the unstable, cerulean cradle
where the Sun was sleeping.

          Sleep, at last, possessed everything;
everything, at last, was occupied by silence:
even the thief was sleeping;
even the lover was not awake.

          Suspended, then, from
external governance—occupied with which
material effort it brings forth the day
either well or badly—
the Soul, remote, but not separated
from everything, is only distributing
to the languid limbs, to peaceful bones,
oppressed by temporary death,
their wages in vegetative heat,
the body being, in calm tranquility,
a cadaver without soul,
dead to life and alive to death,
slow signs of the latter
provided by the vital balance wheel
of the human clock, which, if not by hand,
by arterial arrangement, pulsing,
slowly manifests some small signs
of its well-regulated movement.

This then, if not the forge of Vulcan,
the tempered blaze of human heat,
sent to the brain the vapors

of the four temperate humors,
humid, but so clear
that not only did it not obscure
with these the simulacra that reason
gave the imagination,
which, for safer custody,
were turned over in an even purer form
to memory, diligent and careful guard,
which tenaciously recorded them,
but they then provided fantasy
the means to form diverse images.
And just as
in the clear surface
of Pharaoh's crystalline marvel, rare sanctuary,
were seen at great distance
(without this being a hindrance)
the distant ships that cut through
almost the entire realm of Neptune
—being clearly seen
in its mercuried moon
the number, size, and fate
of all those risked upon
the unstable, transparent expanse,
while their frivolous sails and grave keels
were dividing waters and winds—
just so she [Fantasy], becalmed, was copying
the images of all things,
and her invisible brush was forming
of mental colors, lightless, although always brilliant,
the figures of not only
all sublunar creatures,
but also of those that are
bright, intellectual stars,
and however it is possible
to conceive of the invisible,
she skillfully represented them within herself
and showed them to the soul.
        Who, meanwhile, completely converted
to her immaterial being and beautiful essence,
contemplated that spark,
partaker of high Being,
and enjoyed the similitude within herself;

and judging herself almost divided
from that corporeal chain
that she, impeded, always carries,
which grossly obstructs and torpidly hinders
the flight of intellect with which she now measures
the immense quantity of the Sphere,
now considers the regular course
in which in the unequal
heavenly bodies turn
—an offense so grave, meriting punishment
for study vainly astrological
(rigorous distorter of tranquility)—
positioned, in her opinion, on the eminent
summit of a mountain that Atlas himself,
who presides over the rest
like a giant, obeyed like a dwarf,
and for which Olympus, whose tranquil facade
never consented to the violation
of an agitated breeze,
does not even deserve to be the skirt;
and even the clouds—which form an opaque crown
for the most elevated corporeality
of the most magnificent volcano on earth
that, gigantically arrogant, announces war against the sky—
are scarcely a dense zone
for its prideful eminence
or a crude sash
for its vast waist, which—poorly cinched—
either the wind undoes with tugging
or the nearby Sun finishes off with heat.
       To the first region of this height
(the lowest part, I mean, dividing
into thirds its continuous, horrific body)
the speedily swift flight
of the eagle—which challenges Heaven
and drinks in rays of the Sun, striving
to establish a nest among its lights—
could not reach, even though it forced
the impulse more than ever, now beating
its two feathered sails, now combing
the air with its claws as it attempted,
weaving stairs of the atoms,
to break through immunity with its two wings.

... *according to the judgement of Homer, I say,*
the Pyramids were only material
types, exterior signs
of the interior dimensions
which are species of intentions of the soul:
that just as the ambitious, ardent flame
rises to Heaven in a pyramidal point,
so the human mind
transcribes its shape
and always aspires to the First Cause
—central point to which a straight line
is drawn, if not the infinite circumference
that contains all essence—
                    These two artificial Mountains, then,
(whether they are marvelous or miracles),
and even that blasphemous, arrogant Tower
of which today the sad signs
—not in stone, but in unequal tongues,
since voracious time does not erase them—
are the diverse languages that reduce
peoples' social relations
(causing those that Nature made one
to appear different by the strangeness of their tongues alone),
if they were compared
to the elevated mental pyramid
where—without knowing how—
the Soul sees herself positioned,
they would be found so far below
that anyone would gauge
this summit to be the Sphere:
since her ambitious yearning,
making a summit of its own flight,
lifted her to the most eminent part of her own mind,
so far above herself, that she believed
that she was leaving herself behind
for a new and different region.

... *and [the understanding] by looking at everything, saw*
  nothing,
(the intellectual faculty dulled
by so many and such diffuse,
incomprehensible species, that it looked
from one axis in which

the rotating machinery of the Sphere freely rested,
to the opposing pole)
nor was it able
to discern the parts, not only
those that all consider
perfecting of the universe,
and those no more pertinent than its ornament,
but not even those that are integral
members of its dilated body,
proportionately competent.
        But just as one for whom
long-lasting darkness has usurped
the visible colors of objects,
if unexpected splendors assault her,
with the excess of light remains more blind
—since excess creates contrary effects
in the torpid faculty, which then
cannot admit the light of the sun,
not being accustomed to it—
and to the darkness itself, which earlier
was a murky impediment to sight,
she now appeals from the injuries of light,
and time and again hides with her hand
the vacillating rays
from her weak, bedazzled eyes,
the shadow serving now
—compassionate mediator—
as an instrument by which
by degrees they are restored
so that afterwards, more steadily,
they might exercise their operation with constancy. . . .

. . . in a not dissimilar fashion the Soul,
stunned by the sight of so many objects,
collected together the attention, which,
scattered into such diversity by the powerful shock
that had paralyzed its judgement, she was still unable
to call back within itself,
scarcely permitting her
the formless embryo
of a confused concept, which poorly formed,
portrayed the disordered chaos

of confused species she took in,
—without order collectively,
without order individually,
the more involved in combinations,
the more they dissolve disunited,
full of diversity—
violently confining the diffusion
of so many objects to such a small vessel,
constricted even for the lowest, even for the least.
        Its sails, in effect, furled,
which it had carelessly entrusted
to the traitor sea, to the ventilating wind
—distractedly seeking
fidelity in the sea, constancy in the wind—
the ship, against its will,
ran aground on
the mental shore,
shattered, with ruined rudder, broken mast,
fragment by fragment kissing, grain by grain,
the sand of the beach,
where—once recovered—
prudent reflection and restrained discretion
took advantage of the place for the repair of
its careless judgement,
which, restrained in its operation,
judged it more suitable
to restrict itself to a single matter
or to separately, one by one,
examine things,
which end up conforming to
the ten
artful categories:
metaphysical reduction
(conceiving general entities
only in some mental fantasies
where abstract reason
disdains matter)
that teaches how to form a science of universals,
correcting, with careful art,
the defect of not being able
to understand all creation
with an act of intuition,

instead of which, constructing a ladder,
it ascends from one concept
to another, rung by rung,
and the relative order of comprehension
follows, necessitated by the limited vigor
of the understanding, which entrusts
its progress to successive reasoning,
whose weakened forces doctrine
strengthens with learned nourishment,
and which the prolonged, if gentle, continuing
course of discipline instills
with robust courage,
with which it aspires
more spiritedly to the victory pennant
for its most arduous, arrogant ambition,
ascending the high steps
—developed now in one, now in
another faculty—until insensibly
it looks upon the honorable summit,
sweet terminus of its deep longing
(from bitter sowing, fruit pleasing to the taste,
cheap even after long labor)
and with courageous footstep
treads upon the peak of its arrogant facade.
            My intellect wanted to follow
the method of this series,
or from the lowest grade
of inanimate being
(less favored
if not more helpless,
produced by the second cause)
to pass to the more noble hierarchy
that, in vegetable vigor,
although coarse, is the firstborn
of Thetis—the first
that she, by virtue of attraction,
nourished at her fertile maternal breasts,
sweet springs
of terrestrial humor, which as natural
nourishment is sweetest food—
and, adorned with four operations
of contrary actions,

it now attracts, now diligently separates
that which it judges to be not suitable,
now it expels what is superfluous, and of the abundance
makes the most useful substance its own;
—and having investigated this—
to infuse a more beautiful form
(adorned with feeling,
and even more than feeling, with
the apprehending power of imagination),
which can occasion legitimate complaint
—even if it's not an affront—
from the inanimate Star that
sparkles most brightly:
although it radiates magnificent splendor
—even the least of creatures, even the lowest,
can surpass it, can cause envy
even among the superior Stars—
　　　　　and making of this corporeal knowledge
a foundation, however scant,
to pass to the supreme compound,
miraculous, tripartite,
ordered by three harmonious lines
and the mysterious compendium
of all the inferior forms:
connecting hinge
between that which pure Nature
raises up most enthroned
and the less noble creature, which
sees itself most beaten down:
adorned not only by the
five sensible faculties alone,
but ennobled by the interior ones,
which are three rectrices
—that in order to be the mistress
over the others, the Powerful, Wise Hand,
not in vain, adorned—
end of His works, Circle that closes
the Sphere with earth,
ultimate perfection of creation
and ultimate grace of its Eternal Author,
in whom His immense magnificence
rests with satisfied complacence:

marvelous fabric,
which the more proudly it touches Heaven,
dust seals its mouth
—for whom the sacred vision
that the Evangelist Eagle saw in Patmos,
which measured stars and earth with equal steps,
could be a mysterious image,
or the lofty statue
that revealed its rich, proud forehead
to be of the most precious metal,
and weakly made its foundation
of the most despised matter,
so that with a slight tremor it was destroyed—
Man, I say, in the end the greatest marvel
that human understanding ponders,
absolute compendium, who
resembles Angel, plant, animal;
in whose lofty lowness
all of Nature shares.
Why? Perhaps because more fortunate
than all he would be elevated
to the grace
of loving Union. Oh! although repeated,
never sufficiently recognized
grace, since it seems unknown,
little appreciated,
or poorly answered.
            These steps I wanted to examine
some times. But other times I desisted,
judging the examination of everything
excessive boldness
for she who didn't understand even the smallest,
even the simplest part
of manageable,
natural effects. . . .

. . . and feeling the lack of nourishment,
the weakened members,
tired of rest,
neither totally awakened nor asleep,
showed signs,
with slow stretches,

of desiring movement, extending
little by little their torpid nerves
and turning their tired bones
to the other side
(still not entirely at the will of their owner)—
sweetly impeded
by natural narcotic,
the senses began to recover
their operation, the eyes half-open.
                    And from the brain, now idle,
the phantasms fled,
and—as though fashioned of fragile vapor—
dissolved their shapes,
converted into facile smoke, into wind.
Just so a magic lantern
represents various painted figures,
simulated on a blank wall,
assisted no less by shadow
than by light: maintaining in its
flickering reflections the appropriate distance
of learned perspective,
its certain measurements
approved by various experiments;
and so the fugitive shadow, which vanishes
in the same radiance,
feigns a formed body,
adorned with every dimension,
when it is not even worthy to be a surface. . . .

            The Sun, in effect, arrived, closing its revolution
which it engraved in gold on blue sapphire:
a thousand golden streams of a thousand points,
multiplied a thousand times,
—lines, I say, of bright light—left
his luminous circumference,
lining the cerulian page of Heaven;
and, assembled, attacked her, who earlier
had been the mournful tyrant of his empire:
and she, quickly fleeing without plan
—stumbling over her own horrors—
treading on her own shadow,
tried to reach the West

with her (now without order) unruly
army of shadows, harassed by
the light that pursued her.
The fugitive flight attained
sight of the West, at last,
and—in her very rout recovered,
forcing courage from ruin—
in the half of the globe
the Sun left unprotected,
she rebelliously determines a second time
to see herself crowned;
meanwhile our Hemisphere was being illuminated
by the lovely, golden mane of the Sun,
which, with judicious light
of distributive order, was proportioning
their colors to things
and restoring
exterior senses to their full operation,
leaving the world illuminated
in a more certain
light, and me awake.

A philosophical and scientific genius, Pascal cherished a faith deeply connected to his understanding of higher mathematics and science. The inventor of the first calculator, he also contributed significantly to the development of differential calculus and the theory of probability. In the domain of physics, Pascal conducted experiments on barometric pressure and developed the hydraulic principle known as "Pascal's Law." In 1654, he experienced a dramatic spiritual moment that he wrote down and sewed to the lining of his jacket, where it was discovered after his death. The text of this "Memorial" is given here in its entirety.

Pascal was associated with the convent of Port-Royal, the center of Jansenism, a movement that emphasized the total depravity of humankind and the need for God's grace toward salvation. His unfinished reflections on faith and Christian doctrine appear in his posthumously published *Pensées*. Creating a foundation for much subsequent Christian apologetics, Pascal is known for his "Wager," a logical demonstration of the rational reasons to choose faith in Christ over atheism. [AM]

BLAISE PASCAL

[1 6 2 3 – 1 6 6 2]

Eternally in joy

for a day's training on earth . . .

THE MEMORIAL

In the year of Grace, 1654,
On Monday, 23rd of November, Feast of St. Clement, Pope and Martyrs and others in the Martyrology,
  Vigil of Saint Chrysogonus, Martyr, and others,
  From about half past ten in the evening until about half past twelve,

Fire

God of Abraham, God of Isaac, God of Jacob, not of the philosophers and scholars (Ex. 3:6; Matt. 22:32).
Certitude.
Certitude. Feeling. Joy. Peace.
God of Jesus Christ
Deum meum et Deum vestrum ("My God and your God," John 20:17).
Forgetfulness of the world and of everything except God.
  He is to be found only by the ways taught in the Gospel.
  Greatness of the human soul.
  "Righteous Father, the world hath not known Thee, but I have known Thee" (John 17:25).
  Joy, joy, joy, tears of joy.
  I have separated myself from Him
Derelinquerunt me fontem aquae vivae ("They have forsaken me, the fountain of living waters," Jer. 2:13).
  "My God, wilt Thou leave me?" (Matt. 27:46).
  Let me not be separated from Him eternally.
  "This is the eternal life, that they might know Thee, the only true God and the one whom Thou has sent, Jesus Christ" (John 17:3).
  Jesus Christ.
  Jesus Christ.
  I have separated myself from Him: I have fled from Him, denied Him, crucified Him.
  Let me never be separated from Him.
  We keep hold of Him only by the ways taught in the Gospel.
  Renunciation, total and sweet.
  Total submission to Jesus Christ and to my director.
  Eternally in joy for a day's training on earth.
  Non obliviscar sermones tuos ("I will not forget Thy words," Psalm 118:16).
Amen.

By the eighteenth century, both in Europe and America, the opportunity for self-reflection and self-cultivation that was once restricted to such intellectuals as Petrarch or Sor Juana had been extended to include individuals of more humble origins. Benjamin Franklin's *Autobiography*, the first part of which was written in 1771, when its author was sixty-five, describes the genesis of the legend Franklin had already become: an ordinary boy of humble Puritan origins, one of seventeen children of a Boston candlemaker, bent on self-improvement, who, through self-education and the pursuit of a life of industry, achieved eminence as a businessman, politician, diplomat, and inventor.

The Autobiography has been criticized for its neglect of the dark workings of the soul, indeed for its tendency to view the soul as an engine, yet it is clear that Franklin, who won the cause of American independence at the French court, was a powerful exponent of the new absolutism of personal experience and the belief in the power of individuals to control their own destinies.   [EP]

BENJAMIN FRANKLIN

[1 7 0 6 – 1 7 9 0]

I conceiv'd the bold and arduous

project of arriving at

moral perfection.

FROM *THE AUTOBIOGRAPHY*

It was about this time [ca. 1730] I conceiv'd the bold and arduous project of arriving at moral perfection. I wish'd to live without committing any fault at any time; I would conquer all that either natural inclination, custom, or company might lead me into. As I knew, or thought I knew, what was right and wrong, I did not see why I might not always do the one and avoid the other. But I soon found I had undertaken a task of more difficulty than I had imagined. While my care was employ'd in guarding against one fault, I was often surprised by another; habit took the advantage of inattention; inclination was sometimes too strong for reason. I concluded, at length, that the mere speculative conviction that it was our interest to be completely virtuous, was not sufficient to prevent our slipping; and that the contrary habits must be broken, and good ones acquired and established, before we can have any dependence on a steady, uniform rectitude of conduct. For this purpose I therefore contrived the following method.

In the various enumerations of the moral virtues I had met with in my reading, I found the catalogue more or less numerous, as different writers included more or fewer ideas under the same name. Temperance, for example, was by some confined to eating and drinking, while by others it was extended to mean the moderating every other pleasure, appetite, inclination, or passion, bodily or mental, even to our avarice and ambition. I propos'd to myself, for the sake of clearness, to use rather more names, with fewer ideas annex'd to each, than a few names with more ideas; and I included under thirteen names of virtues all that at that time occurr'd to me as necessary or desirable, and annexed to each a short precept, which fully express'd the extent I gave to its meaning.

These names of virtues, with their precepts, were:
1. TEMPERANCE.
Eat not to dullness; drink not to elevation.
2. SILENCE.
Speak not but what may benefit others or yourself; avoid trifling conversation.
3. ORDER.
Let all your things have their places; let each part of your business have its time.
4. RESOLUTION.
Resolve to perform what you ought; perform without fail what you resolve.
5. FRUGALITY.
Make no expense but to do good to others or yourself; *i.e.*, waste nothing.

6. INDUSTRY.

Lose no time; be always employ'd in something useful; cut off all unnecessary actions.

7. SINCERITY.

Use no hurtful deceit; think innocently and justly, and, if you speak, speak accordingly.

8. JUSTICE.

Wrong none by doing injuries, or omitting the benefits that are your duty.

9. MODERATION.

Avoid extreams; forbear resenting injuries so much as you think they deserve.

10. CLEANLINESS.

Tolerate no uncleanliness in body, cloaths, or habitation.

11. TRANQUILLITY.

Be not disturbed at trifles, or at accidents common or unavoidable.

12. CHASTITY.

Rarely use venery but for health or offspring, never to dulness, weakness, or the injury of your own or another's peace or reputation.

13. HUMILITY.

Imitate Jesus and Socrates.

My intention being to acquire the *habitude* of all these virtues, I judg'd it would be well not to distract my attention by attempting the whole at once, but to fix it on one of them at a time; and, when I should be master of that, then to proceed to another, and so on, till I should have gone thro' the thirteen; and, as the previous acquisition of some might facilitate the acquisition of certain others, I arrang'd them with that view, as they stand above. Temperance first, as it tends to procure that coolness and clearness of head, which is so necessary where constant vigilance was to be kept up, and guard maintained against the unremitting attraction of ancient habits, and the force of perpetual temptations. This being acquir'd and establish'd, Silence would be more easy; and my desire being to gain knowledge at the same time that I improv'd in virtue, and considering that in conversation it was obtain'd rather by the use of the ears than of the tongue, and therefore wishing to break a habit I was getting into of prattling, punning, and joking, which only made me acceptable to trifling company, I gave *Silence* the second place. This and the next, *Order*, I expected would allow me more time for attending to my project and my studies. *Resolution*, once become habitual, would keep me firm in my endeavors to obtain all the subsequent virtues; *Frugality* and Industry freeing me from my remaining debt, and producing affluence and independence, would make more easy the practice of Sincerity and Justice, etc., etc. Conceiving then, that, agreeably to the advice of Pythagoras in his Golden Verses, daily examination would be necessary, I contrived the following method for conducting that examination.

I made a little book, in which I allotted a page for each of the virtues. I rul'd each page with red ink, so as to have seven columns, one for each day of the week, marking each column with a letter for the day. I cross'd these columns with thirteen red lines, marking the beginning of each line with the first letter of one of the virtues, on which line, and in its proper column, I might mark, by a little black spot, every fault I found upon examination to have been committed respecting that virtue upon that day.

Form of the pages.

TEMPERANCE.						
EAT NOT TO DULNESS; DRINK NOT TO ELEVATION.						
	S.	M.	T.	W.	T.	F.	S.
T.							
S.	•	•		•		•	
O.	• •	•	•		•	•	•
R.			•			•	
F.		•			•		
I.			•				
S.							
J.							
M.							
C.							
T.							
C.							
H.							

I determined to give a week's strict attention to each of the virtues successively. Thus, in the first week, my great guard was to avoid every the least offence against *Temperance,* leaving the other virtues to their ordinary chance, only marking every evening the faults of the day. Thus, if in the first week I could keep my first line, marked T, clear of spots, I suppos'd the habit of that virtue so much strengthen'd, and its opposite weaken'd, that I might venture extending my attention to include the next, and for the following week keep both lines clear of spots. Proceeding thus to the last, I could go thro' a course compleat in thirteen weeks, and four courses in a year. And like him who, having a garden to weed, does not attempt to eradicate all the bad herbs at once, which would exceed his reach and his strength, but works on one of the beds at a time, and, having accomplish'd the first, proceeds to a second, so I should have, I hoped, the encouraging pleasure of seeing on my pages the progress I made in virtue, by clearing successively my lines of their spots, till in the end, by a number of courses, I should be happy in viewing a clean book, after a thirteen weeks' daily examination.

This my little book had for its motto these lines from Addison's *Cato*:

> *Here will I hold. If there's a power above us*
> *(And that there is, all nature cries aloud*
> *Thro' all her works), He must delight in virtue;*
> *And that which he delights in must be happy.*

Another from Cicero,

"O vitæ Philosophia dux! O virtutum indagatrix expultrixque vitiorum! Unus dies, bene et ex præceptis tuis actus, peccanti immortalitati est anteponendus."

Another from the Proverbs of Solomon, speaking of wisdom or virtue:

"Length of days is in her right hand, and in her left hand riches and honour. Her ways are ways of pleasantness, and all her paths are peace." iii. 16, 17.

And conceiving God to be the fountain of wisdom, I thought it right and necessary to solicit his assistance for obtaining it; to this end I formed the following little prayer, which was prefix'd to my tables of examination, for daily use.

"*O powerful Goodness! bountiful Father! merciful Guide! Increase in me that wisdom which discovers my truest interest. Strengthen my resolutions to perform what that wisdom dictates. Accept my kind offices to thy other children as the only return in my power for thy continual favors to me.*"

I used also sometimes a little prayer which I took from Thomson's Poems, viz.:

> *Father of light and life, thou Good Supreme!*
> *O teach me what is good; teach me Thyself!*
> *Save me from folly, vanity, and vice,*
> *From every low pursuit; and fill my soul*
> *With knowledge, conscious peace, and virtue pure;*
> *Sacred, substantial, never-fading bliss!*

The precept of *Order* requiring that *every part of my business should have its allotted time*, one page in my little book contain'd the following scheme of employment for the twenty-four hours of a natural day:

THE MORNING. *Question.* What good shall I do this day?	5 6 7	Rise, wash, and address *Powerful Goodness!* Contrive day's business, and take the resolution of the day; prosecute the present study, and breakfast.
	8 9 10 11	Work.
NOON.	12 1	Read, or overlook my accounts, and dine.
	2 3 4 5	Work.
EVENING. *Question.* What good have I done to-day?	6 7 8 9	Put things in their places. Supper. Music or diversion, or conversation. Examination of the day.
NIGHT.	10 11 12 1 2 3 4	Sleep.

I enter'd upon the execution of this plan for self-examination, and continu'd it with occasional intermissions for some time. I was surpris'd to find myself so much fuller of faults than I had imagined; but I had the satisfaction of seeing them diminish. To avoid the trouble of renewing now and then my little book, which, by scraping out the marks on the paper of old faults to make room for new ones in a new course, became full of holes, I transferr'd my tables and precepts to the ivory leaves of a memorandum book, on which the lines were drawn with red ink, that made a durable stain, and on those lines I mark'd my faults with a black-lead pencil, which marks I could easily wipe out with a wet sponge. After a while I went thro' one course only in a year, and afterward only one in several years, till at length I omitted them entirely, being employ'd in voyages and business abroad, with a multiplicity of affairs that interfered; but I always carried my little book with me.

My scheme of ORDER gave me the most trouble; and I found that, tho' it might be practicable where a man's business was such as to leave him the disposition of his time, that of a journeyman printer, for instance, it was not possible to be exactly observed by a master, who must mix with the world, and often receive people of business at their own hours. *Order*, too, with regard to places for things, papers, etc., I found extreamly difficult to acquire. I had not been early accustomed to it, and, having an exceeding good memory, I was not so sensible of the inconvenience attending want of method.

This article, therefore, cost me so much painful attention, and my faults in it vexed me so much, and I made so little progress in amendment, and had such frequent relapses, that I was almost ready to give up the attempt, and content myself with a faulty character in that respect, like the man who, in buying an ax of a smith, my neighbour, desired to have the whole of its surface as bright as the edge. The smith consented to grind it bright for him if he would turn the wheel; he turn'd, while the smith press'd the broad face of the ax hard and heavily on the stone, which made the turning of it very fatiguing. The man came every now and then from the wheel to see how the work went on, and at length would take his ax as it was, without farther grinding. "No," said the smith, "turn on, turn on; we shall have it bright by-and-by; as yet, it is only speckled." "Yes," said the man, *"but I think I like a speckled ax best."* And I believe this may have been the case with many, who, having, for want of some such means as I employ'd, found the difficulty of obtaining good and breaking bad habits in other points of vice and virtue, have given up the struggle, and concluded that *"a speckled ax was best"*; for something, that pretended to be reason, was every now and then suggesting to me that such extream nicety as I exacted of myself might be a kind of foppery in morals, which, if it were known, would make me ridiculous; that a perfect character might be attended with the inconvenience of being envied and hated; and that a benevolent man should allow a few faults in himself, to keep his friends in countenance.

In truth, I found myself incorrigible with respect to Order; and now I am grown old, and my memory bad, I feel very sensibly the want of it. But, on the whole, tho' I never arrived at the perfection I had been so ambitious of obtaining, but fell far short of it, yet I was, by the endeavour, a better and a happier man than I otherwise should have been if I had not attempted it; as those who aim at perfect writing by imitating the engraved copies, tho' they never reach the wish'd-for excellence of those copies, their hand is mended by the endeavor, and is tolerable while it continues fair and legible.

It may be well my posterity should be informed that to this little artifice, with the blessing of God, their ancestor ow'd the constant felicity of his life, down to his 79th year, in which this is written. What reverses may attend the remainder is in the hand of Providence; but, if they arrive, the reflection on past happiness enjoy'd ought to help his bearing them with more resignation. To Temperance he ascribes his long-continued health, and what is still left to him of a good constitution; to Industry and Frugality, the early easiness of his circumstances and acquisition of his fortune, with all that knowledge that enabled him to be a useful citizen, and obtained for him some degree of reputation among the learned; to Sincerity and Justice, the confidence of his country, and the honorable employs it conferred upon him; and to the joint influence of the whole mass of the virtues, even in the imperfect state he was able to acquire them, all that evenness of temper, and that cheerfulness in conversation, which makes his company still sought for, and agreeable even to his younger acquaintance. I hope, therefore, that some of my descendants may follow the example and reap the benefit.

It will be remark'd that, tho' my scheme was not wholly without religion, there was in it no mark of any of the distinguishing tenets of any particular sect. I had purposely avoided them; for, being fully persuaded of the utility and excellency of my method, and that it might be serviceable to people in all religions, and intending some time or other to publish it, I would not have any thing in it that should prejudice any one, of any sect, against it. I purposed writing a little comment on each virtue, in which I would have shown the advantages of possessing it, and the mischiefs attending its opposite vice; and I should have called my book The Art of Virtue because it would have shown the means and manner of obtaining virtue, which would have distinguished it from the mere exhortation to be good, that does not instruct and indicate the means, but is like the apostle's man of verbal charity, who only without showing to the naked and hungry how or where they might get clothes or victuals, exhorted them to be fed and clothed.— James ii. 15, 16.

But it so happened that my intention of writing and publishing this comment was never fulfilled. I did, indeed, from time to time, put down short hints of the sentiments, reasonings, etc., to be made use of in it, some of which I have still by me; but the necessary close attention to private business in the earlier part of my life, and public business since, have occasioned my postponing it; for, it being connected in my mind with *a great and extensive project*, that required the whole man to execute, and which an unforeseen succession of employs prevented my attending to, it has hitherto remain'd unfinish'd.

In this piece it was my design to explain and enforce this doctrine, that vicious actions are not hurtful because they are forbidden, but forbidden because they are hurtful, the nature of man alone considered; that it was, therefore, every one's interest to be virtuous who wish'd to be happy even in this world; and I should, from this circumstance (there being always in the world a number of rich merchants, nobility, states, and princes, who have need of honest instruments for the management of their affairs, and such being so rare), have endeavored to convince young persons that no qualities were so likely to make a poor man's fortune as those of probity and integrity.

My list of virtues contain'd at first but twelve; but a Quaker friend having kindly informed me that I was generally thought proud; that my pride show'd itself frequently in conversation; that I was not content with being in the right when discussing any point, but was overbearing, and rather insolent, of which he convinc'd me by mentioning several instances; I determined endeavouring to cure myself, if I could, of this vice or folly among the rest, and I added *Humility* to my list, giving an extensive meaning to the word.

I cannot boast of much success in acquiring the *reality* of this virtue, but I had a good deal with regard to the *appearance* of it. I made it a rule to forbear all direct contradiction to the sentiments of others, and all positive assertion of my own. I even forbid myself, agreeably to the old laws of our Junto, the use of every word or expression in the language that imported a fix'd opinion, such as *certainly, undoubtedly,* etc., and I adopted, instead of them, *I conceive, I apprehend,* or *I imagine* a thing to be so or so; or it *so appears to me at present.* When another asserted something that I thought an error, I deny'd myself the pleasure of contradicting him abruptly, and of showing immediately some absurdity in his proposition; and in answering I began by observing that in certain cases or circumstances his opinion would be right, but in the present case there *appear'd* or *seem'd* to me some difference, etc. I soon found the advantage of this change in my manner; the conversations I engag'd in went on more pleasantly. The modest way in which I propos'd my opinions pro-cur'd them a readier reception and less contradiction; I had less mortification when I was found to be in the wrong, and I more easily prevail'd with others to give up their mistakes and join with me when I happened to be in the right.

And this mode, which I at first put on with some violence to natural inclination, became at length so easy, and so habitual to me, that perhaps for these fifty years past no one has ever heard a dogmatical expression escape me. And to this habit (after my character of integrity) I think it principally owing that I had early so much weight with my fellow-citizens when I proposed new institutions, or alterations in the old, and so much influence in public councils when I became a member; for I was but a bad speaker, never eloquent, subject to much hesitation in my choice of words, hardly correct in language, and yet I generally carried my points.

In reality, there is, perhaps, no one of our natural passions so hard to subdue as *pride*. Disguise it, struggle with it, beat it down, stifle it, mortify it as much as one pleases, it is still alive, and will every now and then peep out and show itself; you will see it, perhaps, often in this history; for, even if I could conceive that I had compleatly overcome it, I should probably be proud of my humility.

SAMUEL JOHNSON

[1 7 0 9 – 1 7 8 4]

I have been slowly recovering . . . from the general disease of my life.

Like Benjamin Franklin, Samuel Johnson was a man of immense industry, one who made his own way. But he was also half blind and half deaf from infant tuberculosis, and in such bad health and often in such exigent circumstances that he once confessed to a friend that he had never known a day without physical distress. Despite these personal infirmities, the words of Johnson, as recorded by his great biographer, James Boswell, have delighted and consoled generations of readers. After Shakespeare, Johnson is the most quoted Englishman. His power comes from his ability to describe the true condition of the unadorned life: "When I was running about this town [of London] a very poor fellow, I was a great arguer for the advantages of poverty; but I was, at the same time, very sorry to be poor."

Johnson's prayers and meditations, grounded in confidence in a divine order, are nevertheless eloquent concerning the new existential uncertainty that many began to feel in the eighteenth century. The rational ordering of the universe that such figures as Socrates had intuited through reason was, in a sense, confirmed by the mathematical and scientific discoveries of figures like Pascal. These discoveries, however, made the universe more immense than previously imagined, while lessening the importance of the individual within this order of things. [EP]

PRAYERS AND MEDITATIONS

Before any new Study.

November [1752]

Almighty God, in whose hands are all the powers of man; who givest understanding, and takest it away; who, as it seemeth good unto Thee, enlightenest the thoughts of the simple, and darkenest the meditations of the wise, be present with me in my studies and enquiries.

Grant, O Lord, that I may not lavish away the life which Thou hast given me on useless trifles, nor waste it in vain searches after things which Thou hast hidden from me.

Enable me, by thy Holy Spirit, so to shun sloth and negligence, that every day may discharge part of the task which Thou hast allotted me; and so further with thy help that labour which, without thy help, must be ineffectual, that I may obtain, in all my undertakings, such success as will most promote thy glory, and the salvation of my own soul, for the sake of Jesus Christ. Amen.

Jan. 1, 1767, imâ mane scripsi.

Almighty and most merciful Father, in whose hand are life and death, as thou hast suffered me to see the beginning of another year, grant, I beseech thee, that another year may not be lost in Idleness, or squandered in unprofitable employment. Let not sin prevail on the remaining part of life, and take not from me thy Holy Spirit, but as every day brings me nearer to my end, let every day contribute to make my end holy and happy. Enable me O Lord, to use all enjoyments with due temperance, preserve me from unseasonable and immoderate sleep, and enable me to run with diligence the race that is set before me, that, after the troubles of this life, I may obtain everlasting happiness, through Jesus Christ our Lord. Amen.

1771, *September* 18, 9 at night.

I am now come to my sixty-third year. For the last year I have been slowly recovering both from the violence of my last illness, and, I think, from the general disease of my life. My Breath is less obstructed, and I am more capable of motion and exercise. My mind is less encumbered, and I am less interrupted in mental employment. Some advances I hope have been made towards regularity. I have missed Church since Easter only two Sundays, both which I hope I have endeavoured to supply by attendance on Divine Worship in the following week. Since Easter, my Evening devotions have been lengthened. But Indolence and indifference has been neither conquered nor opposed. No plan of Study has been pursued or formed, except that I have commonly read every week, if not on Sunday, a stated portion of the New Testament in greek. But what is most to be considered I have neither attempted nor formed any scheme of Life by which I may do good, and please God.

One great hindrance is want of rest, my nocturnal complaints grow less troublesome towards morning, and I am tempted [to] repair the deficiencies of the night. I think however to try to rise every day by eight, and to combat indolence as I shall obtain strength. Perhaps Providence has yet some use for the remnant of my life.

Almighty and everlasting God, whose mercy is over all thy works, and who hast no pleasure in the Death of a Sinner, look with pity upon me, succour and preserve me; enable me to conquer evil habits, and surmount temptations. Give me Grace so to use the degree of health which Thou hast restored to my Mind and Body, that I may perform the task thou shalt yet appoint me. Look down, O gracious Lord upon my remaining part of Life; grant, if it please thee, that the days few or many which thou shalt yet allow me, may pass in reasonable confidence, and holy tranquillity. Withhold not thy Holy Spirit from me, but strengthen all good purposes till they shall produce a life pleasing to Thee. And when thou shalt call me to another state, forgive me my sins, and receive me to Happiness, for the Sake of Jesus Christ our Lord. Amen.

Safely brought us, & c.

SATURDAY *APR.* 10 [1773], I DINED ON CAKES AND FOUND MYSELF filled and satisfied.

Saturday 10. Having offered my prayers to God, I will now review the last year.

Of the Spring and Summer, I remember that I was able in those seasons to examine and improve my dictionary, and was seldom withheld from the work but by my own unwillingness. Of my Nights I have no distinct remembrance but believe that as in many foregoing years they were painful and restless.

A little before Christmas I had caught cold, of which at first, as is my custom, I took little notice, but which harrassed me as it grew more violent, with a cough almost incessant, both night and day. I was let blood three times, and after about ten weeks, with the help of warm weather I recovered. From this time I have been much less troubled with nocturnal flatulencies, and have had some nights of that quiet and continual sleep, which I had wanted till I had almost forgotten it.

O God, grant that I may not mispend or lose the time which thou shalt yet allow me. For Jesus Christs sake have mercy upon me.

My purpose is to attain in the remaining part of the year as much knowledge as can easily be had of the Gospels and Pentateuch. Concerning the Hebrew I am in doubt. I hope likewise to enlarge my knowledge of Divinity, by reading at least once a week some sermon or small theological tract, or some portion of a larger work.

To this important and extensive study, my purpose is to appropriate (libere) part of every Sunday, Holyday, Wednesday, and Friday, and to begin with the Gospels. Perhaps I may not be able to study the Pentateuch before next year.

My general resolution to which I humbly implore the help of God is to methodise my life; to resist sloth. I hope from this time to keep a Journal.

N. B. On Friday I read the first of Mark, and Clarks sermon on Faith.

On Saturday I read little, but wrote the foregoing account, and the following prayer.

Almighty God, by whose mercy I am now about to commemorate the death of my Redeemer, grant that from this time I may so live as that his death may be efficacious to my eternal happiness. Enable me to conquer all evil customs. Deliver me from evil and vexatious thoughts. Grant me light to discover my duty, and Grace to perform it. As my life advances, let me become more pure, and more holy. Take not from me thy Holy Spirit, but grant that I may serve thee with diligence and confidence; and when thou shalt call me hence, receive me to everlasting happiness, for the sake of Jesus Christ our Lord. Amen.

Apr. 10, near midnight.

10° 30′ p.m. [Easter 1775]

When I look back upon resolutions of improvement and amendments, which have year after year been made and broken, either by negligence, forgetfulness, vicious idleness, casual interruption, or morbid infirmity, when I find that so much of my life has stolen unprofitably away, and that I can descry by retrospection scarcely a few single days properly and vigorously employed, why do I yet try to resolve again? I try because Reformation is necessary and despair is criminal. I try in humble hope of the help of God.

As my life has from my earliest years been wasted in a morning bed my purpose is from Easter day to rise early, not later than eight.

11° 15′ p.m. D.j.

1776, *Apr.* 7, Easter Day.

The time is again at which, since the death of my poor dear Tetty, on whom God have mercy, I have annually commemorated the mystery of Redemption, and annually purposed to amend my life. My reigning sin, to which perhaps many others are appendant, is waste of time, and general sluggishness, to which I was always inclined, and in part of my life have been almost compelled by morbid melancholy and disturbance of mind. Melancholy has had in me its paroxisms and remissions, but I have not improved the intervals, nor sufficiently resisted my natural inclination, or sickly habits. I will resolve henceforth to rise at eight in the morning, so far as resolution is proper, and will pray that God will strengthen me. I have begun this morning.

Though for the past week I have had an anxious design of communicating to-day, I performed no particular act of devotion, till on Friday I went to Church. My design was to pass part of the day in exercises of piety, but Mr. Boswel interrupted me: of him, however, I could have rid myself, but poor Thrale, orbus et exspes, came for comfort and sat till seven when we all went to Church.

In the morning I had at Church some radiations of comfort.

I fasted though less rigorously than at other times. I by negligence poured milk into the tea, and, in the afternoon drank one dish of coffee with Thrale;

yet at night, after a fit of drowsiness I felt myself very much disordered by emptiness, and called for tea with peevish and impatient eagerness. My distress was very great.

Yesterday I do not recollect that to go to Church came into my thoughts, but I sat in my chamber, preparing for preparation; interrupted, I know not how. I was near two hours at dinner.

I go now with hope

To rise in the morning at eight.

To use my remaining time with diligence.

To study more accurately the Christian Religion.

Almighty and most merciful Father, who hast preserved me by thy tender forbearance, once more to commemorate thy Love in the Redemption of the world, grant that I may so live the residue of my days, as to obtain thy mercy when thou shalt call me from the present state. Illuminate my thoughts with knowledge, and inflame my heart with holy desires. Grant me to resolve well, and keep my resolutions. Take not from me thy Holy Spirit, but in life and in death have mercy on me for Jesus Christs sake. Amen.

acts of forgiveness.

p.m. In the pew I read my prayer and commended my friends, and those that θ [i.e., died] this year. At the Altar I was generally attentive, some thoughts of vanity [idle or worthless thoughts] came into my mind while others were communicating, but I found when I considered them, that they did not tend to irreverence of God. At the altar I renewed my resolutions. When I received, some tender images struck me. I was so mollified by the concluding address to our Saviour that I could not utter it. The Communicants were mostly women. At intervals I read collects, and recollected, as I could, my prayer. Since my return I have said it. 2 p.m.

May 21.

These resolutions I have not practised nor recollected. O God grant me to begin now for Jesus Christ's Sake. Amen.

EASTER EVE, *April* 3, [1779], 11 p.m.

This is the time of my annual review, and annual resolution. The review is comfortless. Little done. Part of the life of Dryden and the Life of Milton have been written; but my mind has neither been improved nor enlarged. I have read little, almost nothing. And I am not conscious that I have gained any good, or quitted any evil habits.

Of resolutions I have made so many with so little effect, that I am almost weary, but, by the Help of God, am not yet hopeless. Good resolutions must be made and kept. I am almost seventy years old, and have no time to lose. The distressful restlessness of my nights, makes it difficult to settle the course of my days. Something however let me do.

Aug. 12,—84.

Against inquisitive and perplexing thoughts.

O Lord, my Maker and Protector, who hast graciously sent me into this world, to work out my salvation, enable me to drive from me all such unquiet and perplexing thoughts as may mislead or hinder me in the practice of those duties which thou hast required. When I behold the works of thy hands and consider the course of thy providence, give me Grace always to remember that thy thoughts are not my thoughts, nor thy ways my ways. And while it shall please Thee to continue me in this world where much is to be done and little to be known, teach me by thy Holy Spirit to withdraw my mind from unprofitable and dangerous enquiries, from difficulties vainly curious, and doubts impossible to be solved. Let me rejoice in the light which thou hast imparted, let me serve thee with active zeal, and humble confidence, and wait with patient expectation for the time in which the soul which Thou receivest, shall be satisfied with knowledge. Grant this, O Lord, for Jesus Christ's sake. Amen.

John Henry Newman, one of the great minds and most eloquent writers of the nineteenth century, redefined the role of the intellect as the basis of religious faith. He did this in a period that was perceived to be one of crisis: in England, the forces of scientific rationalism and secularism, along with the menace of parliamentary restrictions on the Anglican church, seemed to threaten the very existence of religious life.

Already at the age of fifteen, as the *Apologia pro vita sua* records, Newman had emerged from a spiritual crisis with a mistrust of material phenomena and a profound awareness of the presence of God. The *Apologia* is not a history of his spiritual struggles but, as the subtitle indicates, a "history of his religious opinions," specifically the way those opinions led Newman to Catholicism—and away from a prominent and secure position as an Anglican churchman and a leading figure at Oxford University. In his autobiography, we witness one of the most incisive intellects of the modern world offering an antidote to the corrosive power of reason to empty the world of the presence of God or of human meaning. [EP]

JOHN HENRY CARDINAL NEWMAN

[1 8 0 1 – 1 8 9 0]

If I looked into a mirror, and did

not see my face . . .

FROM *APOLOGIA PRO VITA SUA*

Starting then with the being of a God (which, as I have said, is as certain to me as the certainty of my own existence, though when I try to put the grounds of that certainty into logical shape I find a difficulty in doing so in mood and figure to my satisfaction), I look out of myself into the world of men, and there I see a sight which fills me with unspeakable distress. The world seems simply to give the lie to that great truth, of which my whole being is so full; and the effect upon me is, in consequence, as a matter of necessity, as confusing as if it denied that I am in existence myself. If I looked into a mirror, and did not see my face, I should have the sort of feeling which actually comes upon me, when I look into this living busy world, and see no reflexion of its Creator. This is, to me, one of the great difficulties of this absolute primary truth, to which I referred just now. Were it not for this voice, speaking so clearly in my conscience and my heart, I should be an atheist, or a pantheist, or a polytheist when I looked into the world. I am speaking for myself only; and I am far from denying the real force of the arguments in proof of a God, drawn from the general facts of human society, but these do not warm me or enlighten me; they do not take away the winter of my desolation, or make the buds unfold and the leaves grow within me, and my moral being rejoice. The sight of the world is nothing else than the prophet's scroll, full of "lamentations, and mourning, and woe."

To consider the world in its length and breadth, its various history, the many races of man, their starts, their fortunes, their mutual alienation, their conflicts; and then their ways, habits, governments, forms of worship; their enterprises, their aimless courses, their random achievements and acquirements, the impotent conclusion of long-standing facts, the tokens so faint and broken, of a superintending design, the blind evolution of what turn out to be great powers or truth, the progress of things, as if from unreasoning elements, not towards final causes, the greatness and littleness of man, his far-reaching aims, his short duration, the curtain hung over his futurity, the disappointments of life, the defeat of good, the success of evil, physical pain, mental anguish, the prevalence and intensity of sin, the pervading idolatries, the corruptions, the dreary hopeless irreligion, that condition of the whole race, so fearfully yet exactly described in the Apostle's words, "having no hope and without God in the world"—all this is a vision to dizzy and appal; and inflicts upon the mind the sense of a profound mystery, which is absolutely beyond human solution.

What shall be said to this heart-piercing, reason-bewildering fact? I can only answer, that either there is no Creator, or this living society of men is in a true sense discarded from His presence. Did I see a boy of good make and mind, with the tokens on him of a refined nature, cast upon the world without provision, unable to say whence he came, his birthplace or his family connections, I should conclude that there was some mystery connected with his history, and that he was one, of whom, from one cause or other, his parents were ashamed. Thus only should I be able to account for the contrast between the promise and condition of his being. And so I argue about the world;—*if* there be a God, *since* there is a God, the human race is implicated in some terrible aboriginal calamity. It is out of joint with the purposes of its Creator. This is a fact, a fact as true as the fact of its existence; and thus the doctrine of what is theologically called original sin becomes to me almost as certain as that the world exists, and as the existence of God.

And now, supposing it were the blessed and loving will of the Creator to interfere in this anarchical condition of things, what are we to suppose would be the methods which might be necessarily or naturally involved in His object of mercy? Since the world is in so abnormal a state, surely it would be no surprise to me, if the interposition were of necessity equally extraordinary —or what is called miraculous. But that subject does not directly come into the scope of my present remarks. Miracles as evidence, involve an argument; and of course I am thinking of some means which does not immediately run into argument. I am rather asking what must be the face-to-face antagonist, by which to withstand and baffle the fierce energy of passion and the all-corroding, all-dissolving scepticism of the intellect in religious inquiries? I have no intention at all to deny, that truth is the real object of our reason, and that, if it does not attain to truth, either the premiss or the process is in fault; but I am not speaking of right reason, but of reason as it acts in fact and concretely in fallen man. I know that even the unaided reason, when correctly exercised, leads to a belief in God, in the immortality of the soul, and in a future retribution; but I am considering it actually and historically; and in this point of view, I do not think I am wrong in saying that its tendency is towards a simple unbelief in matters of religion. No truth, however sacred, can stand against it, in the long run; and hence it is that in the pagan world, when our Lord came, the last traces of the religious knowledge of former times were all but disappearing from those portions of the world in which the intellect had been active and had had a career.

And in these latter days, in like manner, outside the Catholic Church things are tending, with far greater rapidity than in that old time from the circumstance of the age, to atheism in one shape or other. What a scene, what a prospect, does the whole of Europe present at this day! and not only Europe, but every government and every civilisation through the world, which is under the influence of the European mind! . . .

I am defending myself here from a plausible charge brought against Catholics . . . The charge is this:—that I, as a Catholic, not only make profession to hold doctrines which I cannot possibly believe in my heart, but that I also believe in the existence of a power on earth, which at its own will imposes upon men any new set of *credenda*, when it pleases, by a claim to infallibility; in consequence, that my own thoughts are not my own property; that I cannot tell that to-morrow I may not have to give up what I hold to-day, and that the necessary effect of such a condition of mind must be a degrading bondage, or a bitter inward rebellion relieving itself in secret infidelity, or the necessity of ignoring the whole subject of religion in a sort of disgust, and of mechanically saying everything that the Church says, and leaving to others the defence of it. . . .

And now, having thus described [the doctrine of infallibility], I profess my own absolute submission to its claim. I believe the whole revealed dogma as taught by the apostles, as committed by the apostles to the Church, and as declared by the Church to me. I receive it, as it is infallibly interpreted by the authority to whom it is thus committed, and (implicitly) as it shall be, in like manner, further interpreted by that same authority till the end of time. . . .

All this being considered to be a profession *ex animo*, as on my own part, so also on the part of the Catholic body, as far as I know it, it will at first sight be said that the restless intellect of our common humanity is utterly weighed down to the repression of all independent effort and action whatever, so that, if this is to be the mode of bringing it into order, it is brought into order only to be destroyed. But this is far from the result, far from what I conceive to be the intention of that high Providence who has provided a great remedy for a great evil—far from borne out by the history of the conflict between infallibility and reason in the past, and the prospect of it in the future. The energy of the human intellect "does from opposition grow;" it thrives and is joyous, with a tough elastic strength, under the terrible blows of the divinely-fashioned weapon, and is never so much itself as when it has lately been overthrown. It is the custom with Protestant writers to consider that, whereas there are two great principles in action in the history of religion, authority and private judgment, they have all the private judgment to themselves, and we have the full inheritance and the superincumbent oppression of authority. But this is not so; it is the vast Catholic body itself, and it only, which affords an arena for both combatants in that awful, never-dying duel. It is necessary for the very life of religion, viewed in its large operations and its history, that the warfare should be incessantly carried on. Every exercise of infallibility is brought out into act by an intense and varied operation of the reason, from within and without, and provokes again a reaction of reason against it; and, as in a civil polity the state exists and endures by means of the rivalry and collision, the encroachments and defeats of its constituent parts, so in like manner Catholic Christendom is no simple exhibition of religious absolutism, but it presents a continuous picture of authority and private judgment alternately advancing and retreating as the ebb and flow of the tide;—it is a vast assemblage of human beings with wilful intellects and wild passions, brought together into one by the beauty and the majesty of a superhuman power—into what may be called a large reformatory or training-school, not to be sent to bed, not to be buried alive, but for the melting, refining, and moulding, as in some moral factory, by an incessant noisy process (if I may proceed to another metaphor), of the raw material of human nature, so excellent, so dangerous, so capable of divine purposes.

St. Paul says in one place that his apostolical power is given him to edification, and not to destruction. There can be no better account of the infallibility of the Church. It is a supply for a need, and it does not go beyond that need. Its object is, and its effect also, not to enfeeble the freedom or vigour of human thought in religious speculation, but to resist and control its extravagance.

GERARD
MANLEY
HOPKINS

[1 8 4 4 – 1 8 8 9]

Soul, self: come poor Jackself.

Gerard Manley Hopkins was a poet of great complexity, both in his selection of themes and in terms of his radical innovations in prosodic form. During his lifetime he resisted publishing his poems, but after his death his poetry became widely read, influencing such leading figures as T. S. Eliot, W. H. Auden, and Dylan Thomas. Like many poets experimenting with verse form at that time, Hopkins created his own system of metrical versification, termed "sprung rhythm." He developed a unique form of prosodic stress, liberating the metrical foot from a fixed number of stressed and unstressed syllables. Hopkins's feet are tonic, bearing one stress to an unlimited number of unstressed syllables. His poetic lines are measured by the number of stresses rather than feet. His themes are likewise unbounded: the presence of God in nature, the power of God in words.

Hopkins was influenced by the artistic trends of the late nineteenth century, which emphasized intricacy, ornamentation, and medieval themes and coloration. The practices of the Pre-Raphaelite Brotherhood, the "aesthetes" and adherents of "art for art's sake," and the theories of John Ruskin and Walter Pater contributed to Hopkins's sensitivity to literary form.

As a student at Balliol College, Oxford, Hopkins came into contact with the Oxford Movement, a group of scholars and writers considering reuniting the Church of England with Rome. His own conversion to the Catholic Church cost Hopkins his family's approbation; his taking of holy orders put an end to his creative activity for some time, and he burned his own early verse.

After his ordination to the priesthood in 1877, Hopkins again began to write poetry, notably the "terrible sonnets," which express a very modern despair at God's apparent withdrawal from the world. Hopkins developed this spiritual struggle into a metaphysical principle that he termed "inscape." Basing his thought on the philosophy of the medieval Franciscan thinker Duns Scotus, Hopkins embraced the idea that every individual natural creature could possess its own unique quality, its "inscape." Many of Hopkins's most compelling natural images in his verse reflect this conviction of the spirituality of the material world, through which God's creative power is apprehended and diffused. At the same time, the profusion of gorgeous sound in his verse creates a linguistic mirror of the prolix beauties of creation.

The poems presented here were composed at different times of his life and were selected as those most reflective of his ongoing struggle with spiritual aridity and despair. His capacity to sing glorias into a whirling void lends his verse a very modern tenor, while his energetic exploration of the richness of language continues to seem new, even by contemporary standards. [AM]

SELECTED POEMS

16

Myself unholy, from myself unholy
To the sweet living of my friends I look—
Eye-greeting doves bright-counter to the rook,
Fresh brooks to salt sand-teasing waters shoaly:—

And they are purer, but alas! not solely
The unquestion'd readings of a blotless book.
And so my trust, confusèd, struck, and shook
Yields to the sultry siege of melancholy.
He has a sin of mine, he its near brother;
Knowing them well I can but see the fall.
This fault in one I found, that in another:
And so, though each have one while I have all,
No better *serves me now, save* best; *no other*
Save Christ: to Christ I look, on Christ I call.

17

See how Spring opens with disabling cold,
And hunting winds and the long-lying snow.
Is it a wonder if the buds are slow?
Or where is strength to make the leaf unfold?

Chilling remembrance of my days of old
Afflicts no less, what yet I hope may blow,
That seed which the good sower once did sow,
So loading with obstruction that threshold
Which should ere now have led my feet to the field.
It is the waste done in unreticent youth
Which makes so small the promise of that yield
That I may win with late-learnt skill uncouth
From furrows of the poor and stinting weald.
Therefore how bitter, and learnt how late, the truth!

18

My prayers must meet a brazen heaven
And fail or scatter all away.
Unclean and seeming unforgiven
My prayers I scarcely call to pray.
I cannot buoy my heart above;
Above it cannot entrance win.
I reckon precedents of love,
But feel the long success of sin.

My heaven is brass and iron my earth:
Yea iron is mingled with my clay,
So harden'd is it in this dearth
Which praying fails to do away.
Nor tears, nor tears this clay uncouth
Could mould, if any tears there were.

A warfare of my lips in truth,
Battling with God, is now my prayer.

22

The Habit of Perfection

Elected Silence, sing to me
And beat upon my whorlèd ear,
Pipe me to pastures still and be
The music that I care to hear.

Shape nothing, lips; be lovely-dumb:
It is the shut, the curfew sent
From there where all surrenders come
Which only makes you eloquent.

Be shellèd, eyes, with double dark
And find the uncreated light:
This ruck and reel which you remark
Coils, keeps, and teases simple sight.

Palate, the hutch of tasty lust,
Desire not to be rinsed with wine:
The can must be so sweet, the crust
So fresh that come in fasts divine!

Nostrils, your careless breath that spend
Upon the stir and keep of pride,
What relish shall the censers send
Along the sanctuary side!

O feel-of-primrose hands, O feet
That want the yield of plushy sward,
But you shall walk the golden street
And you unhouse and house the Lord.

And, Poverty, be thou the bride
And now the marriage feast begun,
And lily-coloured clothes provide
Your spouse not laboured-at nor spun.

23

Nondum
"Verily Thou art a God that hidest Thyself."
ISAIAH XIV. 15.

God, though to Thee our psalm we raise
No answering voice comes from the skies;
To Thee the trembling sinner prays
But no forgiving voice replies;
Our prayer seems lost in desert ways,
Our hymn in the vast silence dies.

We see the glories of the earth
But not the hand that wrought them all:
Night to a myriad worlds gives birth,
Yet like a lighted empty hall
Where stands no host at door or hearth
Vacant creation's lamps appal.

We guess; we clothe Thee, unseen King,
With attributes we deem are meet;
Each in his own imagining
Sets up a shadow in Thy seat;
Yet know not how our gifts to bring,
Where seek Thee with unsandalled feet.

And still th'unbroken silence broods
While ages and while aeons run,
As erst upon chaotic floods
The Spirit hovered ere the sun
Had called the seasons' changeful moods
And life's first germs from death had won.

And still th'abysses infinite
Surround the peak from which we gaze.
Deep calls to deep, and blackest night
Giddies the soul with blinding daze
That dares to cast its searching sight
On being's dread and vacant maze.

And Thou art silent, whilst Thy world
Contends about its many creeds
And hosts confront with flags unfurled
And zeal is flushed and pity bleeds
And truth is heard, with tears impearled,
A moaning voice among the reeds.

My hand upon my lips I lay;
The breast's desponding sob I quell;
I move along life's tomb-decked way

And listen to the passing bell
Summoning men from speechless day
To death's more silent darker spell.

Peace

When will you ever, Peace, wild wooddove, shy wings shut,
Your round me roaming end, and under be my boughs?
When, when, Peace, will you, Peace? I'll not play hypocrite

To own my heart: I yield you do come sometimes; but
That piecemeal peace is poor peace. What pure peace allows
Alarms of wars, the daunting wars, the death of it?

O surely, reaving Peace, my Lord should leave in lieu
Some good! And so he does leave Patience exquisite,
That plumes to Peace thereafter. And when Peace here does house
He comes with work to do, he does not come to coo,
               He comes to brood and sit.

65

No worst, there is none. Pitched past pitch of grief,
More pangs will, schooled at forepangs, wilder wring.
Comforter, where, where is your comforting?
Mary, mother of us, where is your relief?
My cries heave, herds-long; huddle in a main, a chief-
woe, world-sorrow; on an age-old anvil wince and sing—
Then lull, then leave off. Fury had shrieked 'No ling-
ering! Let me be fell: force I must be brief'.
O the mind, mind has mountains; cliffs of fall
Frightful, sheer, no-man-fathomed. Hold them cheap
May who ne'er hung there. Nor does long our small
Durance deal with that steep or deep. Here! creep,
Wretch, under a comfort serves in a whirlwind: all
Life death does end and each day dies with sleep.

66

To seem the stranger lies my lot, my life
Among strangers. Father and mother dear,
Brothers and sisters are in Christ not near
And he my peace, my parting, sword and strife.

England, whose honour O all my heart woos, wife
To my creating thought, would neither hear
Me, were I pleading, plead nor do I: I weary
of idle a being but by where wars are rife.

I am in Ireland now; now I am at a third
Remove. Not but in all removes I can
Kind love both give and get. Only what word

Wisest my heart breeds dark heaven's baffling ban
Bars or hell's spell thwarts. This to hoard unheard,
Heard unheeded, leaves me a lonely began.

67

I wake and feel the fell of dark, not day.
What hours, O what black hours we have spent
This night! what sights you, heart, saw; ways you went!
And more must, in yet longer light's delay.

With witness I speak this. But where I say
Hours I mean years, mean life. And my lament
Is cries countless, cries like dead letters sent
To dearest him that lives alas! away.

I am gall, I am heartburn. God's most deep decree
Bitter would have me taste: my taste was me;
Bones built in me, flesh filled, blood brimmed the curse.

Selfyeast of spirit a dull dough sours. I see
The lost are like this, and their scourge to be
As I am mine, their sweating selves; but worse.

68

Patience, hard thing! the hard thing but to pray,
But bid for, Patience is! Patience who asks
Wants war, wants wounds; weary his times, his tasks;
To do without, take tosses, and obey.

Rare patience roots in these, and, these away,
Nowhere. Natural heart's ivy, Patience masks
Our ruins of wrecked past purpose. There she basks
Purple eyes and seas of liquid leaves all day.

We hear our hearts grate on themselves: it kills
To bruise them dearer. Yet the rebellious wills
Of us we do bid God bend to him even so.

And where is he who more and more distills
Delicious kindness?—He is patient. Patience fills
His crisp combs, and that comes those ways we know.

69

My own heart let me more have pity on; let
Me live to my sad self hereafter kind,
Charitable; not live this tormented mind
With this tormented mind tormenting yet.

I cast for comfort I can no more get
By groping round my comfortless, than blind
Eyes in their dark can day or thirst can find
Thirst's all-in-all in all a world of wet.

Soul, self; come, poor Jackself, I do advise
You, jaded, let be; call off thoughts awhile
Elsewhere; leave comfort root-room; let joy size

At God knows when to God knows what; whose smile's
not wrung, see you; unforeseen times rather—as skies
Between mountains—lights a lovely mile.

75

The shepherd's brow, fronting forked lightning, owns
The horror and the havoc and the glory
Of it. Angels fall, they are towers, from heaven—a story
Of just, majestical, and giant groans.
But man—we, scaffold of score brittle bones;
Who breathe, from groundlong babyhood to hoary
Age gasp; whose breath is our memento mori—
What bass is our viol for tragic tones?
He! Hand to mouth he lives, and voids with shame;
And, blazoned in however bold the name,
Man Jack the man is, just; his mate a hussy.
And I that die these deaths, that feed this flame,
That . . . in smooth spoons spy life's masque mirrored: tame
My tempests there, my fire and fever fussy.

PAUL
CLAUDEL

[1 8 6 8 – 1 9 5 5]

Everyone who enjoyed any sort of

reputation . . . was irreligious.

aul Claudel's youthful literary tastes for Symbolism and Naturalism were part of the antireligious spirit of his time, tending at best toward a non-divine idealism. In the year 1886, Claudel encountered the poetry of Arthur Rimbaud. In this suffering poet, Claudel sensed an individual touched with divine grace. This perception may have led in the same year to Claudel's Christmas conversion, recorded below. In the years following this event, as his literary output increased, Claudel also entered the French ministry of foreign affairs. Diplomatic postings in the U.S., China, and Japan deepened his enormous store of cultural knowledge.

Like many who came of age in the nineteenth century, Claudel was appalled by the materialistic spirit of the world in which he lived, yet he was too close to God not to regard all events of life as part of a divine if apocalyptic plan and to view his own life and work within the framework of his interpretation of this plan. His dramas as well as his voluminous poetic output are characterized by lyric fervor, striking imagery, and religious emotion. A recurrent theme concerns the attempt to link grace and beauty in a world in which the two are nearly always separated. [EP]

MY CONVERSION

I was born on August 6th, 1868. My conversion took place on December 25th, 1886. I was thus eighteen when it happened, though at the time I was very advanced for my age. Although I was descended on both sides from Catholic families which had given several priests to the Church, my own family had grown indifferent to matters of religion, and after our arrival in Paris had definitely lapsed from the Faith. Earlier I had made a good first communion which, for me, as for most other boys of my age, was both the peak and end of my religious practice.

I was brought up, or rather instructed, first by a private tutor, then at provincial secular schools and finally at the Lycée Louis-le-Grand. As soon as I entered this establishment I lost the Faith which seemed to me to be irreconcilable with the Plurality of Worlds (! ! !). Renan's *Life of Jesus* furnished a fresh pretext for this change of ideas, and everything about me seemed to facilitate and encourage it. One must, of course, remember that this was during the eighteen-eighties, the period when the literature of naturalism was at its height. Never had the yoke of matter seemed firmer or better established. Everyone who enjoyed any sort of reputation in art or science or literature was irreligious, and all the so-called great men of the end of the century were noted for their hostility to the Church. Renan was king. He presided at my last prize-giving at the Lycée Louis-le-Grand, and I fancy that I actually received a prize from his own hands. Victor Hugo had just died in a sort of apotheosis.

At eighteen, then, I believed much the same as most of my contemporaries who were supposed to be cultured. The deep idea of the individual and of the concrete had become dimmed. I accepted the monist and mechanist hypothesis in the strictest sense and believed that everything was bound by "Laws," and I assumed that this world was an unchanging series of causes and effects for which science was about to provide a perfect explanation. It all seemed rather boring and depressing. Still, I never managed to swallow the Kantian theory of duty which my professor of philosophy, M. Burdeau, used to expound to us. What is more, I lived in a state of immorality and was gradually falling into a state of despair.

The death of my grandfather, who had been suffering from cancer of the stomach, filled me with terror and the thought of death haunted me. I had completely forgotten religion and as far as that was concerned I lived in the ignorance of a savage. The first glimpse of the truth came from an encounter with the works of a great poet to whom I am lastingly indebted as he played a decisive part in the formation of my mind—Arthur Rimbaud. The discovery of the *Illuminations* and then, a few months afterwards, of *Un Saison en Enfer* was an event of capital importance for me. For the first time these books made a crack in my materialist prison and gave me a vivid and almost physical sense of the supernatural. But my habitual state of apathy and despair did not change.

Such was the unhappy child who found his way to Notre-Dame of Paris on December 25th, 1886, to follow the Christmas offices. I was just beginning to write, and thought that Catholic ceremonies, if treated with a sort of superior dilletantism, would provide me with both stimulus and copy for a few decadent exercises in verse. It was in this mood, and jostled hither and thither by the crowd, that I attended High Mass and it provided only a doubtful pleasure. Then, having nothing better to do, I returned for Vespers. There were children from the choir-school dressed in white, and some students from the Petit Séminaire of St. Nicholas-du-Chardonnet were helping them to sing what I later discovered to be the *Magnificat*. I myself was standing in the crowd near the second pillar at the entrance to the choir on the right of the sacristy. It was then that the event took place which revolutionized my whole life. Suddenly my heart was touched and I BELIEVED. I believed with such power, with such force of my whole being, with a conviction that was so overwhelming and a certainty that shut out so completely any tiniest doubt—that nothing since, neither books nor reasoning nor the vicissitudes of an extremely varied life, has been able to shake or even to touch my faith. I was overcome with a sudden and overwhelming sense of the innocence and the eternal infancy of God—an inexpressible revelation.

When I have tried, as I often have, to reconstruct the minutes which followed this extraordinary moment, I have isolated the following elements which, however, simply formed a single flash of illumination, a single weapon which Divine Providence used in order to force an opening into the heart of a poor despairing child. "How happy the people are who can believe! Supposing it were true, though? It *is* true! God exists. He is there. It's someone. It's a Being as personal as myself. He loves me and calls me." Tears flowed and my sobs mingled with the singing of the *Adeste* which increased my emotion. It was a tender emotion, but an emotion not unmixed with fear and something very much resembling horror! For my philosophical opinions remained intact. God had contemptuously left them where they were. I could see nothing to change. The Catholic religion still seemed to me to be the same treasure-house of absurd fairy stories. Its priests and faithful filled me with exactly the same aversion as before—an aversion which was not far from disgust. The fabric of my opinions and knowledge remained standing and I could not see the slightest fault in it. And yet I had found the way out. A new person, making the most terrifying demands on the young man and the artist that I was, had revealed himself and refused to be reconciled with any of the things that surrounded me. I was like a man whose skin has been torn off with a single movement and who finds himself planted inside a strange body in the middle of an unknown world; that is the only comparison I can find to express my state of complete dereliction. Everything that was most repugnant to my opinions and tastes had turned out to be true, and I had to adapt myself to it whether I liked it or not.

Not, alas, without doing everything in my power to resist. My resistance lasted four years. I must say that I put up a very good defence and that the struggle was thorough and complete. Nothing was left out. I made use of every means of resistance but one after another I had to abandon these weapons which served no purpose. This was the great crisis of my life—the agony of mind of which Rimbaud has written: "The spiritual battle is just as brutal as the battle between men. Night of anguish! The dried-up blood smokes on my face."

All these young men who give up their faith easily do not know how much it costs to get it back again, with what anguish one must ransom it. The thought of hell, and the thought of all the joy and beauty which I imagined I should have to sacrifice by returning to the Truth, held me back.

Still, the very evening of that memorable day at Notre-Dame, when I had returned home through the wet and suddenly-strange streets, I read a German protestant Bible which a German friend had once given to my sister Camilla, and I listened for the first time to the sound of the Voice which is so gentle yet so inflexible and which has never ceased to echo in my heart. The story of Christ was known to me only from Renan's *Vie de Jésus,* and thanks to this impostor, I did not even know that Christ had ever claimed to be the Son of God. Every word and every line contradicted with its majestic simplicity the impudent assertions of the apostate and helped to open my eyes. It was true—I confessed it with the centurion—it was true that Jesus was the Son of God. It was I, Paul, whom he had singled out from all others to speak to and to promise his love to. But at the same time, if I didn't follow him, he left me no alternative but damnation. There was no need to explain what hell was: I had already done "time" there. For these few hours had been enough to show me that everywhere was hell where Christ was not. And what did I care for the rest of the world compared with this new and prodigious Being who had just been revealed to me? But though the new man in me spoke like this, the old man resisted with all his force and would not give up a jot of the life which was opening before him. Shall I admit that at bottom the thing that really prevented me from announcing my belief was human pride? The thought of telling everyone about my conversion, of telling my parents that I wanted to abstain on Fridays, to admit that I was one of these Catholics whom everyone jeered at, sent me into a cold sweat; and at times I actually became wildly indignant at the violence that had been done to me.

But I felt a firm hand resting on me. I did not know any priests and I hadn't a single Catholic friend. The study of religion became my chief interest. Another curious thing: the awakening of the soul and the poetic faculty took place in me at the same time and entirely removed my childish terrors and prejudices. It was about this time that I wrote the first version of my plays, *Tête d'Or* and *La ville*. Although I lived without the sacraments, I was already taking part in the life of the Church. At last I felt able to breathe and life flowed into me at every pore. The books that helped me most at this period were first and foremost Pascal's *Pensées*—a work of inestimable value to those in search of the Faith, though in other respects Pascal's influence has often been disastrous; Bossuet's *Elévations sur les Mystères* and the *Méditations sur les Evangiles* and his other philosophical works; Dante's poem and the admirable writings of Sister Emmerich. Aristotle's *Metaphysics* cleared my mind and introduced me into the realms of true reason. The *Imitation* belonged to a sphere that was too much above me and the first two books seemed terribly hard.

But the great Book which was open to me was the Church. Praised be for ever the great Mother, at whose knees I learnt everything. I spent every Sunday at Notre-Dame and went there as often as possible during the week. I was still as ignorant of my religion as I might have been of Buddhism; but there the sacred drama unfolded before me with a splendour which surpassed anything I had imagined—not in the poor language of devotional works, but in the deepest and most glorious poetry, the most solemn gestures that have ever been entrusted to human beings. I never tired of the spectacle of the mass, and every movement of the priest was deeply imprinted in my mind and heart. The reading of the offices of the dead and the offices of Christmas, the ceremonies of Holy Week, the sublime chant of the *Exultet* —beside which the loftiest and most ecstatic moments of Sophocles and Pindar seemed weak—overcame me with a sense of awe, joy, gratitude, repentance and adoration.

Little by little, slowly and painfully, the idea that art and poetry were divine things made its way into my heart; and also the idea that things of the flesh, far from being indispensable to them, were rather detrimental to them. How I envied the Christians whom I saw communicate! As for myself, I hardly dared to slip in among the throng who came every Good Friday to kiss the Crown of Thorns. Nevertheless, the years passed and my position gradually became intolerable. I prayed to God secretly with tears, and yet I dared not open my mouth. Each day my objections became feebler and the demands of God more imperious. I realized at this time how powerful His touch was. How did I find the courage to resist Him?

The third year I read Baudelaire's *Œuvres posthumes*, and I saw that the poet whom I preferred to all other French poets had found the Faith in his last years and had suffered the same anguish and the same remorse as myself: One afternoon I summoned up my courage and went into a confessional at St. Médard, my own parish. The minutes I waited for the priest are among the bitterest of my life. Finally, I found an old man who appeared to be unmoved by a story which seemed so interesting to me. He spoke to me about "memories of my first Communion" which irritated me profoundly, and bade me before receiving absolution announce my conversion to my family—a point on which I have to admit to-day that he was perfectly right. I left the confessional angry and humiliated and did not return until the next year, when I was absolutely at the end of my tether. In the very same church I found a young priest, M. l'Abbé Ménard, who was extremely sympathetic and brotherly, and who reconciled me; and later I found the saintly and venerable ecclesiastic, the Abbé Villaume, who became my director and well-beloved father in God and whose protection from heaven, where he now is, I have never ceased to feel. I made my second communion this same Christmas Day, December 25th, 1890, at Notre-Dame.

T. S. ELIOT

[1 8 8 8 – 1 9 6 5]

Although I do not hope to turn

again

Although I do not hope

Although I do not hope to turn

Thomas Stearns Eliot is generally recognized as the leading American poet of his time. His first volume of poetry, *Prufrock and Other Observations,* was published in 1917, and *The Waste Land,* which established his reputation, appeared in 1922. The author of numerous poetic dramas, the most famous being *Murder in the Cathedral,* Eliot is noted for the experimental quality of his verse and his habit of thick literary allusions. *Four Quartets* is usually considered his masterpiece; its publication garnered him the Nobel Prize for Literature.

A native of St. Louis, Missouri, Eliot was largely educated abroad and finally settled in London. His early years were shaped by the strong literary and academic background of his immediate family: his mother, Charlotte Champe Stearns, was a recognized poet of her day; his grandfather had been founder and chancellor of Washington University. After studying at Harvard with the eclectic philosopher and poet George Santayana, Eliot traveled to France, where he studied with the philosopher Henri Bergson and encountered the poet Ezra Pound.

During the interwar period, Eliot became a British citizen and a member of the Anglican Church. The latter step was motivated partly by an intellectual interest in Christian theology and doctrine that appears in *The Idea of a Christian Society*. Following the publication of this study, Eliot was forced to work his conversion through, spiritually and emotionally. The effort of this step, and its attendant sense of a bleak, philosophical despair, is expressed in the ruined landscapes and dismal meditations of the long poem *Ash-Wednesday*, presented here in its entirety.   [AM]

ASH-WEDNESDAY

I

Because I do not hope to turn again
Because I do not hope
Because I do not hope to turn
Desiring this man's gift and that man's scope
I no longer strive to strive towards such things
(Why should the agèd eagle stretch its wings?)
Why should I mourn
The vanished power of the usual reign?

Because I do not hope to know again
The infirm glory of the positive hour
Because I do not think
Because I know I shall not know
The one veritable transitory power
Because I cannot drink
There, where trees flower, and springs flow, for there is nothing
  again

Because I know that time is always time
And place is always and only place
And what is actual is actual only for one time
And only for one place
I rejoice that things are as they are and
I renounce the blessèd face
And renounce the voice
Because I cannot hope to turn again

Consequently I rejoice, having to construct something
Upon which to rejoice.

   And pray to God to have mercy upon us
And I pray that I may forget
These matters that with myself I too much discuss
Too much explain
Because I do not hope to turn again
Let these words answer
For what is done, not to be done again
May the judgement not be too heavy upon us

   Because these wings are no longer wings to fly
But merely vans to beat the air
The air which is now thoroughly small and dry
Smaller and dryer than the will
Teach us to care and not to care
Teach us to sit still.

   Pray for us sinners now and at the hour of our death
Pray for us now and at the hour of our death.

II

Lady, three white leopards sat under a juniper-tree
In the cool of the day, having fed to satiety
On my legs my heart my liver and that which had been contained
In the hollow round of my skull. And God said
Shall these bones live? shall these
Bones live? And that which had been contained
In the bones (which were already dry) said chirping:
Because of the goodness of this Lady
And because of her loveliness, and because
She honours the Virgin in meditation,
We shine with brightness. And I who am here dissembled
Proffer my deeds to oblivion, and my love
To the posterity of the desert and the fruit of the gourd.
It is this which recovers
My guts the strings of my eyes and the indigestible portions
Which the leopards reject. The Lady is withdrawn
In a white gown, to contemplation, in a white gown.
Let the whiteness of bones atone to forgetfulness.
There is no life in them. As I am forgotten
And would be forgotten, so I would forget

Thus devoted, concentrated in purpose. And God said
Prophesy to the wind, to the wind only for only
The wind will listen. And the bones sang chirping
With the burden of the grasshopper, saying

    Lady of silences
Calm and distressed
Torn and most whole
Rose of memory
Rose of forgetfulness
Exhausted and life-giving
Worried reposeful
The single Rose
Is now the Garden
Where all loves end
Terminate torment
Of love unsatisfied
The greater torment
Of love satisfied
End of the endless
Journey to no end
Conclusion of all that
Is inconclusible
Speech without word and
Word of no speech
Grace to the Mother
For the Garden
Where all love ends.

    Under a juniper-tree the bones sang, scattered and shining
We are glad to be scattered, we did little good to each other,
Under a tree in the cool of the day, with the blessing of sand,
Forgetting themselves and each other united
In the quiet of the desert. This is the land which ye
Shall divide by lot. And neither division nor unity
Matters. This is the land. We have our inheritance.

III

At the first turning of the second stair
I turned and saw below
The same shape twisted on the banister
Under the vapour in the fetid air

Struggling with the devil of the stairs who wears
The deceitful face of hope and of despair.

At the second turning of the second stair
left them twisting, turning below;
There were no more faces and the stair was dark,
Damp, jaggèd, like an old man's mouth drivelling, beyond repair,
Or the toothed gullet of an agèd shark.

At the first turning of the third stair
Was a slotted window bellied like the fig's fruit
And beyond the hawthorn blossom and a pasture scene
The broadbacked figure drest in blue and green
Enchanted the maytime with an antique flute.
Blown hair is sweet, brown hair over the mouth blown,
Lilac and brown hair;
Distraction, music of the flute, stops and steps of the mind over
  the third stair,
Fading, fading; strength beyond hope and despair
Climbing the third stair.

Lord, I am not worthy
Lord, I am not worthy
        but speak the word only.

IV

Who walked between the violet and the violet
Who walked between
The various ranks of varied green
Going in white and blue, in Mary's colour,
Talking of trivial things
In ignorance and in knowledge of eternal dolour
Who moved among the others as they walked,
Who then made strong the fountains and made fresh the springs

Made cool the dry rock and made firm the sand
In blue of larkspur, blue of Mary's colour,
Sovegna vos

Here are the years that walk between, bearing
Away the fiddles and the flutes, restoring
One who moves in the time between sleep and waking, wearing

White light folded, sheathed about her, folded.
The new years walk, restoring

Through a bright cloud of tears, the years, restoring
With a new verse the ancient rhyme. Redeem
The time. Redeem
The unread vision in the higher dream
While jewelled unicorns draw by the gilded hearse.

   The silent sister veiled in white and blue
Between the yews, behind the garden god,
Whose flute is breathless, bent her head and signed but spoke no
   word

   But the fountain sprang up and the bird sang down
Redeem the time, redeem the dream
The token of the word unheard, unspoken

   Till the wind shake a thousand whispers from the yew

   And after this our exile

V

If the lost word is lost, if the spent word is spent
If the unheard, unspoken
Word is unspoken, unheard;
Still is the unspoken word, the Word unheard,
The Word without a word, the Word within
The world and for the world;
And the light shone in darkness and
Against the Word the unstilled world still whirled
About the centre of the silent Word.

         O my people, what have I done unto thee.

   Where shall the word be found, where will the word
Resound? Not here, there is not enough silence
Not on the sea or on the islands, not
On the mainland, in the desert or the rain land,
For those who walk in darkness
Both in the day time and in the night time
The right time and the right place are not here
No place of grace for those who avoid the face
No time to rejoice for those who walk among noise and deny the
   voice

   Will the veiled sister pray for
Those who walk in darkness, who chose thee and oppose thee,

Those who are torn on the horn between season and season, time
  and time, between
Hour and hour, word and word, power and power, those who
  wait
In darkness? Will the veiled sister pray
For children at the gate
Who will not go away and cannot pray:
Pray for those who chose and oppose

      O my people, what have I done unto thee.

  Will the veiled sister between the slender
Yew trees pray for those who offend her
And are terrified and cannot surrender
And affirm before the world and deny between the rocks
In the last desert between the last blue rocks
The desert in the garden the garden in the desert
Of drouth, spitting from the mouth the withered apple-seed.

      O my people.

VI

Although I do not hope to turn again
Although I do not hope
Although I do not hope to turn

  Wavering between the profit and the loss
In this brief transit where the dreams cross
The dreamcrossed twilight between birth and dying
(Bless me father though I do not wish to wish these things
From the wide window towards the granite shore
The white sails still fly seaward, seaward flying
Unbroken wings

  And the lost heart stiffens and rejoices
In the lost lilac and the lost sea voices
And the weak spirit quickens to rebel
For the bent golden-rod and the lost sea smell
Quickens to recover
The cry of quail and the whirling plover
And the blind eye creates
The empty forms between the ivory gates
And smell renews the salt savour of the sandy earth

This is the time of tension between dying and birth
The place of solitude where three dreams cross
Between blue rocks
But when the voices shaken from the yew-tree drift away
Let the other yew be shaken and reply.

Blessèd sister, holy mother, spirit of the fountain, spirit of the
garden,
Suffer us not to mock ourselves with falsehood
Teach us to care and not to care
Teach us to sit still
Even among these rocks,
Our peace in His will
And even among these rocks
Sister, mother
And spirit of the river, spirit of the sea,
Suffer me not to be separated

And let my cry come unto Thee.

C. S. LEWIS

[1 8 9 8 – 1 9 6 3]

That which I greatly feared had at last come upon me.

One of the twentieth century's leading Christian apologists and essayists, C. S. Lewis was also the author of a science fiction trilogy (*Out of the Silent Planet*, *Perelandra*, and *That Hideous Strength*), and of the children's book series known as "The Chronicles of Narnia." A don at Oxford and later at Cambridge in the fields of English literature and philosophy, and the author of numerous scholarly works, C. S. Lewis was associated with the Inklings, a group of scholars who met to read aloud and discuss their writing. Among members of the Inklings were the authors J. R. R. Tolkien, Charles Williams, and Dorothy Sayers.

In his spiritual autobiography, *Surprised by Joy: The Shape of My Early Life*, Lewis recounts a persistent recurrence in his life of moments when a sense of joy stimulated in him an apprehension of the transcendent. Trying to re-create and understand this experience became the main goal of his life. As a scholar initially committed to atheism and then to a series of different philosophical positions, he finally and, by his own account, reluctantly turned to faith in God as the ulti-

mate author of joy and beauty. The passages presented here are those portions of *Surprised by Joy* that trace his experience and relate his discovery of
the transcendent and the spiritually transformative.   [AM]

FROM *SURPRISED BY JOY*

I was born in the winter of 1898 at Belfast, the son of a solicitor and of a
clergyman's daughter. My parents had only two children, both sons, and I
was the younger by about three years. Two very different strains had gone
to our making. My father belonged to the first generation of his family that
reached professional station. His grandfather had been a Welsh farmer; his
father, a self-made man, had begun life as a workman, emigrated to Ireland,
and ended as a partner in the firm of Macilwaine and Lewis, "Boiler-makers,
Engineers, and Iron Ship Builders." My mother was a Hamilton with many
generations of clergymen, lawyers, sailors, and the like behind her; on her
mother's side, through the Warrens, the blood went back to a Norman knight
whose bones lie at Battle Abbey. The two families from which I spring
were as different in temperament as in origin. My father's people were true
Welshmen, sentimental, passionate, and rhetorical, easily moved both to
anger and to tenderness; men who laughed and cried a great deal and who
had not much of the talent for happiness. The Hamiltons were a cooler race.
Their minds were critical and ironic and they had the talent for happiness in
a high degree—went straight for it as experienced travellers go for the best
seat in a train. From my earliest years I was aware of the vivid contrast
between my mother's cheerful and tranquil affection and the ups and downs
of my father's emotional life, and this bred in me long before I was old
enough to give it a name a certain distrust or dislike of emotion as something
uncomfortable and embarrassing and even dangerous.

Both my parents, by the standards of that time and place, were bookish
or "clever" people. My mother had been a promising mathematician in her
youth and a B.A. of Queen's College, Belfast, and before her death was able
to start me both in French and Latin. She was a voracious reader of good
novels, and I think the Merediths and Tolstoys which I have inherited were
bought for her. My father's tastes were quite different. He was fond of
oratory and had himself spoken on political platforms in England as a young
man; if he had had independent means he would certainly have aimed at a
political career. In this, unless his sense of honour, which was fine to the
point of being Quixotic, had made him unmanageable, he might well have
succeeded, for he had many of the gifts once needed by a Parliamentarian—

a fine presence, a resonant voice, great quickness of mind, eloquence, and memory. Trollope's political novels were very dear to him; in following the career of Phineas Finn he was, as I now suppose, vicariously gratifying his own desires. He was fond of poetry provided it had elements of rhetoric or pathos, or both; I think *Othello* was his favourite Shakespearian play. He greatly enjoyed nearly all humorous authors, from Dickens to W. W. Jacobs, and was himself, almost without rival, the best *raconteur* I have ever heard; the best, that is, of his own type, the type that acts all the characters in turn with a free use of grimace, gesture, and pantomime. He was never happier than when closeted for an hour or so with one or two of my uncles exchanging "wheezes" (as anecdotes were oddly called in our family). What neither he nor my mother had the least taste for was that kind of literature to which my allegiance was given the moment I could choose books for myself. Neither had ever listened for the horns of elfland. There was no copy either of Keats or Shelley in the house, and the copy of Coleridge was never (to my knowledge) opened. If I am a romantic my parents bear no responsibility for it. Tennyson, indeed, my father liked, but it was the Tennyson of *In Memoriam* and *Locksley Hall*. I never heard from him of the *Lotus Eaters* or the *Morte d' Arthur*. My mother, I have been told, cared for no poetry at all.

In addition to good parents, good food, and a garden (which then seemed large) to play in, I began life with two other blessings. One was our nurse, Lizzie Endicott, in whom even the exacting memory of childhood can discover no flaw—nothing but kindness, gaiety, and good sense. There was no nonsense about "lady nurses" in those days. Through Lizzie we struck our roots into the peasantry of County Down. We were thus free of two very different social worlds. To this I owe my lifelong immunity from the false identification which some people make of refinement with virtue. From before I can remember I had understood that certain jokes could be shared with Lizzie which were impossible in the drawing-room; and also that Lizzie was, as nearly as a human can be, simply good.

The other blessing was my brother. Though three years my senior, he never seemed to be an elder brother; we were allies, not to say confederates, from the first. Yet we were very different. Our earliest pictures (and I can remember no time when we were not incessantly drawing) reveal it. His were of ships and trains and battles; mine, when not imitated from his, were of what we both called "dressed animals"—the anthropomorphised beasts of nursery literature. His earliest story—as my elder he preceded me in the transition from drawing to writing—was called *The Young Rajah*. He had already made India "his country"; Animal-Land was mine. I do not think any of the surviving drawings date from the first six years of my life which I am now describing, but I have plenty of them that cannot be much later. From them it appears to me that I had the better talent. From a very early age I could draw movement—figures that looked as if they were really running or fighting—and the perspective is good. But nowhere, either in my brother's work or my own, is there a single line drawn in obedience to an idea, however crude, of beauty. There is action, comedy, invention; but there is not even the germ of a feeling for design, and there is a shocking ignorance of natural form. Trees appear as balls of cotton wool stuck on posts, and there is nothing to show that either of us knew the shape of any leaf in the garden where we played almost daily. This absence of beauty, now that I come to think of it, is characteristic of our childhood. No picture on the walls of my father's house ever attracted—and indeed none deserved—our attention. We never saw a beautiful building nor imagined that a building could be beautiful. My earliest aesthetic experiences, if indeed they were aesthetic, were not of that kind; they were already incurably romantic, not formal. Once in those very early days my brother brought into the nursery the lid of a biscuit tin which he had covered with moss and garnished with twigs and flowers so as to make it a toy garden or a toy forest. That was the first beauty I ever knew. What the real garden had failed to do, the toy garden did. It made me aware of nature—not, indeed, as a storehouse of forms and colours but as something cool, dewy, fresh, exuberant. I do not think the impression was very important at the moment, but it soon became important in memory. As long as I live my imagination of Paradise will retain something of my brother's toy garden. And every day there were what we called "the Green Hills"; that is, the low line of the Castlereagh Hills which we saw from the nursery windows. They were not very far off but they were, to children, quite unattainable. They taught me longing—*Sehnsucht;* made me for good or ill, and before I was six years old, a votary of the Blue Flower.

If aesthetic experiences were rare, religious experiences did not occur at all. Some people have got the impression from my books that I was brought up in strict and vivid Puritanism, but this is quite untrue. I was taught the usual things and made to say my prayers and in due time taken to church. I naturally accepted what I was told but I cannot remember feeling much interest in it. My father, far from being specially Puritanical, was, by nineteenth-century and Church of Ireland standards, rather "high," and his approach to religion, as to literature, was at the opposite pole from what later became my own. The charm of tradition and the verbal beauty of Bible and Prayer Book (all of them for me late and acquired tastes) were his natural delight, and it would have been hard to find an equally intelligent man who cared so little for metaphysics. Of my mother's religion I can say almost nothing from my own memory. My childhood, at all events, was not in the least other-worldly. Except for the toy garden and the Green Hills it was not even imaginative; it lives in my memory mainly as a period of humdrum, prosaic happiness and awakes none of the poignant nostalgia with which I look back on my much less happy boyhood. It is not settled happiness but momentary joy that glorifies the past.

IT WILL BE CLEAR THAT AT THIS TIME—AT THE AGE OF SIX, SEVEN, and eight—I was living almost entirely in my imagination; or at least that the imaginative experience of those years now seems to me more important than anything else. Thus I pass over a holiday in Normandy (of which, nevertheless, I retain very clear memories) as a thing of no account; if it could be cut out of my past I should still be almost exactly the man I am. But imagination is a vague word and I must make some distinctions. It may mean the world of reverie, day-dream, wish-fulfilling fantasy. Of that I knew more than enough. I often pictured myself cutting a fine figure. But I must insist that this was a totally different activity from the invention of Animal-Land. Animal-Land was not (in that sense) a fantasy at all. I was not one of the characters it contained. I was its creator, not a candidate for admission to it. Invention is essentially different from reverie; if some fail to recognise the difference that is because they have not themselves experienced both. Anyone who has will understand me. In my day-dreams I was training myself to be a fool; in mapping and chronicling Animal-Land I was training myself to be a novelist. Note well, a novelist; not a poet. My invented world was full (for me) of interest, bustle, humour, and character; but there was no poetry, even no romance, in it. It was almost astonishingly prosaic. Thus if we use the word imagination in a third sense, and the highest sense of all, this invented world was not imaginative. But certain other experiences were; and I will now try to record them. The thing has been much better done by Traherne and Wordsworth, but every man must tell his own tale.

The first is itself the memory of a memory. As I stood beside a flowering currant bush on a summer day there suddenly arose in me without warning, and as if from a depth not of years but of centuries, the memory of that earlier morning at the Old House when my brother had brought his toy garden into the nursery. It is difficult to find words strong enough for the sensation which came over me; Milton's "enormous bliss" of Eden (giving the full, ancient meaning to "enormous") comes somewhere near it. It was a sensation, of course, of desire; but desire for what? not, certainly, for a biscuit-tin filled with moss, nor even (though that came into it) for my own past. Ἰουλίαν ποθῶ [Oh, I desire too much]—and before I knew what I desired, the desire itself was gone, the whole glimpse withdrawn, the world turned commonplace again, or only stirred by a longing for the longing that had just ceased. It had taken only a moment of time; and in a certain sense everything else that had ever happened to me was insignificant in comparison.

The second glimpse came through *Squirrel Nutkin;* through it only, though I loved all the Beatrix Potter books. But the rest of them were merely entertaining; it administered the shock, it was a trouble. It troubled me with what I can only describe as the Idea of Autumn. It sounds fantastic to say that one can be enamoured of a season, but that is something like what happened; and, as before, the experience was one of intense desire. And one went back to the book, not to gratify the desire (that was impossible—how can one *possess* Autumn?) but to re-awake it. And in this experience also there was the same surprise and the same sense of incalculable importance. It was something quite different from ordinary life and even from ordinary pleasure; something, as they would now say, "in another dimension."

The third glimpse came through poetry. I had become fond of Longfellow's *Saga of King Olaf:* fond of it in a casual, shallow way for its story and its vigorous rhythms. But then, and quite different from such pleasures, and like a voice from far more distant regions, there came a moment when I idly turned the pages of the book and found the unrhymed translation of *Tegner's Drapa* and read

> *I heard a voice that cried,*
> *Balder the beautiful*
> *Is died, is dead*

I knew nothing about Balder; but instantly I was uplifted into huge regions of northern sky, I desired with almost sickening intensity something never to be described (except that it is cold, spacious, severe, pale, and remote) and then, as in the other examples, found myself at the very same moment already falling out of that desire and wishing I were back in it.

The reader who finds these three episodes of no interest need read this book no further, for in a sense the central story of my life is about nothing else. For those who are still disposed to proceed I will only underline the quality common to the three experiences; it is that of an unsatisfied desire which is itself more desirable than any other satisfaction. I call it Joy, which is here a technical term and must be sharply distinguished both from Happiness and from Pleasure. Joy (in my sense) has indeed one characteristic, and one only, in common with them; the fact that anyone who has experienced it will want it again. Apart from that, and considered only in its quality, it might almost equally well be called a particular kind of unhappiness or grief. But then it is a kind we want. I doubt whether anyone who has tasted it would ever, if both were in his power, exchange it for all the pleasures in the world. But then Joy is never in our power and pleasure often is.

I cannot be absolutely sure whether the things I have just been speaking of happened before or after the great loss which befell our family and to which I must now turn. There came a night when I was ill and crying both with headache and toothache and distressed because my mother did not come to me. That was because she was ill too; and what was odd was that there were several doctors in her room, and voices and comings and goings all over the house and doors shutting and opening. It seemed to last for hours. And then my father, in tears, came into my room and began to try to convey to my terrified mind things it had never conceived before. It was in fact cancer and followed the usual course; an operation (they operated in the patient's house in those days), an apparent convalescence, a return of the disease, increasing pain, and death. My father never fully recovered from this loss.

Children suffer not (I think) less than their elders, but differently. For us boys the real bereavement had happened before our mother died. We lost her gradually as she was gradually withdrawn from our life into the hands of nurses and delirium and morphia, and as our whole existence changed into something alien and menacing, as the house became full of strange smells and midnight noises and sinister whispered conversations. This had two further results, one very evil and one very good. It divided us from our father as well as our mother. They say that a shared sorrow draws people closer together; I can hardly believe that it often has that effect when those who share it are of widely different ages. If I may trust my own experience, the sight of adult misery and adult terror has an effect on children which is merely paralysing and alienating. Perhaps it was our fault. Perhaps if we had been better children we might have lightened our father's sufferings at this time. We certainly did not. His nerves had never been of the steadiest and his emotions had always been uncontrolled. Under the pressure of anxiety his temper became incalculable; he spoke wildly and acted unjustly. Thus by a peculiar cruelty of fate, during those months the unfortunate man, had he but known it, was really losing his sons as well as his wife. We were coming, my brother and I, to rely more and more exclusively on each other for all that made life bearable; to have confidence only in each other. I expect that we (or at any rate I) were already learning to lie to him. Everything that had made the house a home had failed us; everything except one another. We drew daily closer together (that was the good result)—two frightened urchins huddled for warmth in a bleak world.

Grief in childhood is complicated with many other miseries. I was taken into the bedroom where my mother lay dead; as they said, "to see her"; in reality, as I at once knew, "to see it." There was nothing that a grown-up would call disfigurement—except for that total disfigurement which is death itself. Grief was overwhelmed in terror. To this day I do not know what they mean when they call dead bodies beautiful. The ugliest man alive is an angel of beauty compared with the loveliest of the dead. Against all the subsequent paraphernalia of coffin, flowers, hearse, and funeral I reacted with horror. I even lectured one of my aunts on the absurdity of mourning clothes in a style which would have seemed to most adults both heartless and precocious; but this was our dear Aunt Annie, my maternal uncle's Canadian wife, a woman almost as sensible and sunny as my mother herself. To my hatred for what I already felt to be all the fuss and flummery of the funeral I may perhaps trace something in me which I now recognise as a defect but which I have never fully overcome—a distaste for all that is public, all that belongs to the collective; a boorish inaptitude for formality.

My mother's death was the occasion of what some (but not I) might regard as my first religious experience. When her case was pronounced hopeless I remembered what I had been taught; that prayers offered in faith would be granted. I accordingly set myself to produce by will-power a firm belief that my prayers for her recovery would be successful; and, as I thought, I achieved it. When nevertheless she died I shifted my ground and worked myself into a belief that there was to be a miracle. The interesting thing is that my disappointment produced no results beyond itself. The thing hadn't worked, but I was used to things not working, and I thought no more about it. I think the truth is that the belief into which I had hypnotised myself was itself too irreligious for its failure to cause any religious revolution. I had approached God, or my idea of God, without love, without awe, even without fear. He was, in my mental picture of this miracle, to appear neither as Saviour nor as Judge, but merely as a magician; and when He had done what was required of Him I supposed He would simply—well, go away. It never crossed my mind that the tremendous contact which I solicited should have any consequences beyond restoring the *status quo*. I imagine that a "faith" of this kind is often generated in children and that its disappointment is of no religious importance; just as the things believed in, if they could happen and be only as the child pictures them, would be of no religious importance either.

With my mother's death all settled happiness, all that was tranquil and reliable, disappeared from my life. There was to be much fun, many pleasures, many stabs of Joy; but no more of the old security. It was sea and islands now; the great continent had sunk like Atlantis.

... THE AUTHENTIC "JOY" (AS I TRIED TO DESCRIBE IT IN AN EARlier chapter) had vanished from my life: so completely that not even the memory or the desire of it remained. The reading of *Sohrab* had not given it to me. Joy is distinct not only from pleasure in general but even from aesthetic pleasure. It must have the stab, the pang, the inconsolable longing.

This long winter broke up in a single moment, fairly early in my time at

Chartres. Spring is the inevitable image, but this was not gradual like Nature's springs. It was as if the Arctic itself, all the deep layers of secular ice, should change not in a week nor in an hour, but instantly, into a landscape of grass and primroses and orchards in bloom, deafened with bird songs and astir with running water. I can lay my hand on the very moment; there is hardly any fact I know so well, though I cannot date it. Someone must have left in the schoolroom a literary periodical: *The Bookman*, perhaps, or the *Times Literary Supplement*. My eye fell upon a headline and a picture, carelessly, expecting nothing. A moment later, as the poet says, "The sky had turned round."

What I had read was the words *Siegfried and the Twilight of the Gods*. What I had seen was one of Arthur Rackham's illustrations to that volume. I had never heard of Wagner, nor of Siegfried. I thought the Twilight of the Gods meant the twilight in which the gods lived. How did I know, at once and beyond question, that this was no Celtic, or silvan, or terrestrial twilight? But so it was. Pure "Northernness" engulfed me: a vision of huge, clear spaces hanging above the Atlantic in the endless twilight of Northern summer, remoteness, severity . . . and almost at the same moment I knew that I had met this before, long, long ago (it hardly seems longer now) in *Tegner's Drapa*, that Siegfried (whatever it might be) belonged to the same world as Balder and the sunward-sailing cranes. And with that plunge back into my own past there arose at once, almost like heartbreak, the memory of Joy itself, the knowledge that I had once had what I had now lacked for years, that I was returning at last from exile and desert lands to my own country; and the distance of the Twilight of the Gods and the distance of my own past Joy, both unattainable, flowed together into a single, unendurable sense of desire and loss, which suddenly became one with the loss of the whole experience, which, as I now stared round that dusty schoolroom like a man recovering from unconsciousness, had already vanished, had eluded me at the very moment when I could first say *It is*. And at once I knew (with fatal knowledge) that to "have it again" was the supreme and only important object of desire.

After this everything played into my hands. One of my father's many presents to us boys had been a gramophone. Thus at the moment when my eyes fell on the words *Siegfried and the Twilight of the Gods*, gramophone catalogues were already one of my favourite forms of reading; but I had never remotely dreamed that the records from Grand Opera with their queer German or Italian names could have anything to do with me. Nor did I for a week or two think so now. But then I was assailed from a new quarter. A magazine called *The Soundbox* was doing synopses of great operas week by week, and it now did the whole *Ring*. I read in a rapture and discovered who Siegfried was and what was the "twilight" of the gods. I could contain myself no longer—I began a poem, a heroic poem on the Wagnerian version of the Niblung story. My only source was the abstracts in *The Soundbox*, and I was so ignorant that I made Alberich rhyme with *ditch* and Mime with *time*. My model was Pope's *Odyssey* and the poem began (with some mixture of mythologies)

> *Descend to earth, descend, celestial Nine*
> *And chant the ancient legends of the Rhine. . . .*

Since the fourth book had carried me only as far as the last scene of *The Rheingold*, the reader will not be surprised to hear that the poem was never finished. But it was not a waste of time and I can still see just what it did for me and where it began to do it. The first three books (I may, perhaps, at this distance of time, say it without vanity) are really not at all bad for a boy. At the beginning of the unfinished fourth it goes all to pieces; and that is exactly the point at which I really began to try to make poetry. Up to then, if my lines rhymed and scanned and got on with the story I asked no more. Now, at the beginning of the fourth, I began to try to convey some of the intense excitement I was feeling, to look for expressions which would not merely state but suggest. Of course I failed, lost my prosaic clarity, spluttered, gasped, and presently fell silent; but I had learned what writing means.

All this time I had still not heard a note of Wagner's music, though the very shape of the printed letters of his name had become to me a magical symbol. Next holidays, in the dark, crowded shop of T. Edens Osborne (on whom be peace), I first heard a record of the *Ride of the Valkyries*. They laugh at it nowadays, and, indeed, wrenched from its context to make a concert piece, it may be a poor thing. But I had this in common with Wagner, that I was thinking not of concert pieces but of heroic drama. To a boy already crazed with "the Northernness," whose highest musical experience had been Sullivan, the *Ride* came like a thunderbolt. From that moment Wagnerian records (principally from the *Ring*, but also from *Lohengrin* and *Parsifal*) became the chief drain on my pocket money and the presents I invariably asked for. My general appreciation of music was not, at first, much altered. "Music" was one thing, "Wagnerian music" quite another, and there was no common measure between them; it was not a new pleasure but a new kind of pleasure, if indeed "pleasure" is the right word, rather than trouble, ecstasy, astonishment, "a conflict of sensations without name."

That summer our cousin H. . . . asked us to spend some weeks with her on the outskirts of Dublin, in Dundrum. There, on her drawing-room table, I found the very book which had started the whole affair and which I had never dared to hope I should see, *Siegfried and the Twilight of the Gods* illustrated by Arthur Rackham. His pictures, which seemed to me then to be the very music made visible, plunged me a few fathoms deeper into my delight. I have seldom coveted anything as I coveted that book; and when I heard that there was a cheaper edition at fifteen shillings (though the sum was to me almost mythological) I knew I could never rest till it was mine. I got it in the end, largely because my brother went shares with me, purely through kindness, as I now see and then more than half suspected, for he was not enslaved by the Northernness. With a generosity which I was even then half ashamed to accept, he sank in what must have seemed to him a mere picture-book seven and sixpence for which he knew a dozen better uses.

Although this affair will already seem to some readers undeserving of the space I have given it, I cannot continue my story at all without noting some of its bearings on the rest of my life.

First, you will misunderstand everything unless you realise that, at the time, Asgard and the Valkyries seemed to me incomparably more important than anything else in my experience—than the Matron Miss C., or the dancing mistress, or my chances of a scholarship. More shockingly, they seemed much more important than my steadily growing doubts about Christianity. This may have been—in part, no doubt was—penal blindness; yet that might not be the whole story. If the Northernness seemed then a bigger thing than my religion, that may partly have been because my attitude towards it contained elements which my religion ought to have contained and did not. It was not itself a new religion, for it contained no trace of belief and imposed no duties. Yet unless I am greatly mistaken there was in it something very like adoration, some kind of quite disinterested self-abandonment to an object which securely claimed this by simply being the object it was. We are taught in the Prayer Book to "give thanks to God for His great glory," as if we owed Him more thanks for being what He necessarily is than for any particular benefit He confers upon us; and so indeed we do and to know God is to know this. But I had been far from any such experience; I came far nearer to feeling this about the Norse gods whom I disbelieved in than I had ever done about the true God while I believed. Sometimes I can almost think that I was sent back to the false gods there to acquire some capacity for worship against the day when the true God should recall me to Himself. Not that I might not have learned this sooner and more safely, in ways I shall now never know, without apostasy, but that Divine punishments are also mercies, and particular good is worked out of particular evil, and the penal blindness made sanative.

Secondly, this imaginative Renaissance almost at once produced a new appreciation of external nature. At first, I think, this was parasitic on the literary and musical experiences. On that holiday at Dundrum, cycling among the Wicklow mountains, I was always involuntarily looking for scenes that might belong to the Wagnerian world, here a steep hillside covered with firs where Mime might meet Sieglinde, there a sunny glade where Siegfried might listen to the bird, or presently a dry valley of rocks where the lithe scaly body of Fafner might emerge from its cave. But soon (I cannot say how soon) nature ceased to be a mere reminder of the books, became herself the medium of the real joy. I do not say she ceased to be a reminder. All Joy reminds. It is never a possession, always a desire for something longer ago or further away or still "about to be." But Nature and the books now became equal reminders, joint reminders, of—well, of whatever it is. I came no nearer to what some would regard as the only genuine love of nature, the studious love which will make a man a botanist or an ornithologist. It was the mood of a scene that mattered to me; and in tasting that mood my skin and nose were as busy as my eyes.

Thirdly, I passed on from Wagner to everything else I could get hold of about Norse mythology, *Myths of the Norsemen, Myths and Legends of the Teutonic Race*, Mallet's *Northern Antiquities*. I became knowledgeable. From these books again and again I received the stab of Joy. I did not yet notice that it was, very gradually, becoming rarer. I did not yet reflect on the difference between it and the merely intellectual satisfaction of getting to know the Eddaic universe. If I could at this time have found anyone to teach me Old Norse I believe I would have worked at it hard.

And finally, the change I had undergone introduces a new difficulty into the writing of this present book. From that first moment in the schoolroom at Chartres my secret, imaginative life began to be so important and so distinct from my outer life that I almost have to tell two separate stories. The two lives do not seem to influence each other at all. Where there are hungry wastes, starving for Joy, in the one, the other may be full of cheerful bustle and success; or again, where the outer life is miserable, the other may be brimming over with ecstasy. By the imaginative life I here mean only my life as concerned with Joy—including in the outer life much that would ordinarily be called imagination, as, for example, much of my reading, and all my erotic or ambitious fantasies; for these are self-regarding. Even Animal-Land and India belong to the "Outer."

THE HISTORY OF JOY, SINCE IT CAME RIDING BACK TO ME ON HUGE waves of Wagnerian music and Norse and Celtic mythology several chapters ago, must now be brought up to date.

I have already hinted how my first delight in Valhalla and Valkyries began to turn itself imperceptibly into a scholar's interest in them. I got about as far as a boy who knew no old Germanic language could get. I could have faced a pretty stiff examination in my subject. I would have laughed at popular bunglers who confused the late mythological Sagas with the classic Sagas, or the Prose with the Verse Edda, or even, more scandalously, Edda with Saga. I knew my way about the Eddaic cosmos, could locate each of the roots of the Ash and knew who ran up and down it. And only very gradually did I realise that all this was something quite different from the original Joy. And I went on adding detail to detail, progressing towards the moment when "I should know most and should least enjoy." Finally I woke from building the temple to find that the God had flown. Of course I did not put it that way. I would have said simply that I didn't get the old thrill. I was in the Wordsworthian predicament, lamenting that "a glory" had passed away.

Thence arose the fatal determination to recover the old thrill, and at last the moment when I was compelled to realise that all such efforts were failures. I had no lure to which the bird would come. And now, notice my blindness. At that very moment there arose the memory of a place and time at which I had tasted the lost Joy with unusual fullness. It had been a particular hill-walk on a morning of white mist. The other volumes of the *Ring* (*The Rheingold* and *The Valkyrie*) had just arrived as a Christmas present from my father, and the thought of all the reading before me, mixed with the coldness and loneliness of the hillside, the drops of moisture on every branch, and the distant murmur of the concealed town, had produced a longing (yet it was also fruition) which had flowed over from the mind and seemed to involve the whole body. That walk I now remembered. It seemed to me that I had tasted heaven then. If only such a moment could return! But what I never realised was that it had returned—that the remembering of that walk was itself a new experience of just the same kind. True, it was desire, not possession. But then what I had felt on the walk had also been desire, and only possession in so far as that kind of desire is itself desirable, is the fullest possession we can know on earth; or rather, because the very nature of Joy makes nonsense of our common distinction between having and wanting. There, to have is to want and to want is to have. Thus, the very moment when I longed to be so stabbed again, was itself again such a stabbing. The Desirable which had once alighted on Valhalla was now alighting on a particular moment of my own past; and I would not recognise him there because, being an idolater and a formalist, I insisted that he ought to appear in the temple I had built him; not knowing that he cares only for temples building and not at all for temples built. Wordsworth, I believe, made this mistake all his life. I am sure that all that sense of the loss of vanished vision which fills *The Prelude* was itself vision of the same kind, if only he could have believed it. . . .

Such, then, was the state of my imaginative life; over against it stood the life of my intellect. The two hemispheres of my mind were in the sharpest contrast. On the one side a many-islanded sea of poetry and myth; on the other a glib and shallow "rationalism." Nearly all that I loved I believed to be imaginary; nearly all that I believed to be real I thought grim and meaningless.

AND THEN . . . CAME THAT EVENT WHICH I HAVE ALREADY MORE THAN once attempted to describe in other books. I was in the habit of walking over to Leatherhead about once a week and sometimes taking the train back. In summer I did so chiefly because Leatherhead boasted a tiny swimming-bath; better than nothing to me who had learned to swim almost before I can remember and who, till middle age and rheumatism crept upon me, was passionately fond of being in water. But I went in winter, too, to look for books and to get my hair cut. The evening that I now speak of was in October. I and one porter had the long, timbered platform of Leatherhead station to ourselves. It was getting just dark enough for the smoke of an engine to glow red on the underside with the reflection of the furnace. The hills beyond the Dorking Valley were of a blue so intense as to be nearly violet and the sky was green with frost. My ears tingled with the cold. The glorious week-end of reading was before me. Turning to the bookstall, I picked out an Everyman in a dirty jacket, *Phantastes, a faerie Romance*, George MacDonald. Then the train came in. I can still remember the voice of the porter calling out the village names, Saxon and sweet as a nut—"Bookham, Effingham, Horsley train." That evening I began to read my new book.

The woodland journeyings in that story, the ghostly enemies, the ladies both good and evil, were close enough to my habitual imagery to lure me on without the perception of a change. It is as if I were carried sleeping across the frontier, or as if I had died in the old country and could never remember how I came alive in the new. For in one sense the new country was exactly like the old. I met there all that had already charmed me in Malory, Spenser, Morris, and Yeats. But in another sense all was changed. I did not yet know (and I was long in learning) the name of the new quality, the bright shadow, that rested on the travels of Anodos. I do now. It was Holiness. For the first time the song of the sirens sounded like the voice of my mother or my nurse. Here were old wives' tales; there was nothing to be proud of in enjoying them. It was as though the voice which had called to me from the world's end were now speaking at my side. It was with me in the room, or in my own body, or behind me. If it had once eluded me by its distance, it now eluded me by proximity—something too near to see, too plain to be understood, on this side of knowledge. It seemed to have been always with me; if I could ever have turned my head quick enough I should have seized it. Now for the first time I felt that it was out of reach not because of something I could not do but because of something I could not stop doing. If I could only leave off, let go, unmake myself, it would be there. Meanwhile, in this new region all the confusions that had hitherto perplexed my search for Joy were disarmed. There was no temptation to confuse the scenes of the tale with the light that rested upon them, or to suppose that they were put forward as realities, or even to dream that if they had been realities and I could reach the woods where Anodos journeyed I should thereby come a step nearer to my desire. Yet, at the same time, never had the wind of Joy blowing through any story been less separable from the story itself. Where the god and the *idolon* were most nearly one there was least danger of confounding them. Thus, when the great moments came I did not break away from the woods and cottages that I read of to seek some bodiless light shining beyond them, but gradually, with a swelling continuity (like the sun at mid-morning burning through a fog) I found the light shining on those woods and cottages, and then on my own past life, and on the quiet room where I sat and on my old teacher where he nodded above his little *Tacitus*. For I now perceived that while the air of the new region made all my erotic and magical perversions of Joy look like sordid trumpery, it had no such disenchanting power over the bread upon the table or the coals in the grate. That was the marvel. Up till now each visitation of Joy had left the common world momentarily a desert—"The first touch of the earth went nigh to kill." Even when real clouds or trees had been the material of the vision, they had been so only by reminding me of another world; and I did not like the return to ours. But now I saw the bright shadow coming out of the book into the real world and resting there, transforming all common things and yet itself unchanged. Or, more accurately, I saw the common things drawn into the bright shadow. *Unde hoc mihi?* In the depth of my disgraces, in the then invincible ignorance of my intellect, all this was given me without asking, even without consent. That night my imagination was, in a certain sense, baptised; the rest of me, not unnaturally, took longer.

IT SEEMED TO ME SELF-EVIDENT THAT ONE ESSENTIAL PROPERTY OF love, hate, fear, hope, or desire was attention to their object. To cease thinking about or attending to the woman is, so far, to cease loving; to cease thinking about or attending to the dreaded thing is, so far, to cease being afraid. But to attend to your own love or fear is to cease attending to the loved or dreaded object. In other words the enjoyment and the contemplation of our inner activities are incompatible. You cannot hope and also think about hoping at the same moment; for in hope we look to hope's object and we interrupt this by (so to speak) turning round to look at the hope itself. Of course the two activities can and do alternate with great rapidity; but they are distinct and incompatible. This was not merely a logical result of Alexander's analysis, but could be verified in daily and hourly experience. The surest means of disarming an anger or a lust was to turn your attention from the girl or the insult and start examining the passion itself. The surest way of spoiling a pleasure was to start examining your satisfaction. But if so, it followed that all introspection is in one respect misleading. In introspection we try to look "inside ourselves" and see what is going on. But nearly everything that was going on a moment before is stopped by the very act of our turning to look at it. Unfortunately this does not mean that introspection finds nothing. On the contrary, it finds precisely what is left behind by the suspension of all our normal activities; and what is left behind is mainly mental images and physical sensations. The great error is to mistake this mere sediment or track or by-product for the activities themselves. That is how men may come to believe that thought is only unspoken words, or the appreciation of poetry only a collection of mental pictures, when these in reality are what the thought or the appreciation, when interrupted, leave behind—like the swell at sea, working after the wind has dropped. Not, of course, that these activities, before we stopped them by introspection, were unconscious. We do not love, fear, or think without knowing it. Instead of the twofold division into Conscious and Unconscious, we need a three-fold division: the Unconscious, the Enjoyed, and the Contemplated.

This discovery flashed a new light back on my whole life. I saw that all my waitings and watchings for Joy, all my vain hopes to find some mental content on which I could, so to speak, lay my finger and say, "This is it," had been a futile attempt to contemplate the enjoyed. All that such watching and waiting ever *could* find would be either an image (Asgard, the Western Garden, or what not) or a quiver in the diaphragm. I should never have to bother again about these images or sensations. I knew now that they were merely the mental track left by the passage of Joy—not the wave but the wave's imprint on the sand. The inherent dialectic of desire itself had in a way already shown me this; for all images and sensations, if idolatrously mistaken for Joy itself, soon honestly confessed themselves inadequate. All said, in the last resort, "It is not I. I am only a reminder. Look! Look! What do I remind you of?"

So far, so good. But it is at the next step that awe overtakes me. There was no doubt that Joy was a desire (and, in so far as it was also simultaneously a good, it was also a kind of love). But a desire is turned not to itself but to its object. Not only that, but it owes all its character to its object. Erotic love is not like desire for food, nay, a love for one woman differs from a love for another woman in the very same way and the very same degree as the two women differ from one another. Even our desire for one wine differs in tone from our desire for another. Our intellectual desire (curiosity) to know the true answer to a question is quite different from our desire to find that one answer, rather than another, is true. The form of the desired is in the desire. It is the object which makes the desire harsh or sweet, coarse or choice, "high" or "low." It is the object that makes the desire itself desirable or hateful. I perceived (and this was a wonder of wonders) that just as I had been wrong in supposing that I really desired the Garden of the Hesperides, so also I had been equally wrong in supposing that I desired Joy itself. Joy itself, considered simply as an event in my own mind, turned out to be of no value at all. All the value lay in that of which Joy was the desiring. And that object, quite clearly, was no state of my own mind or body at all. In a way, I had proved this by elimination. I had tried everything in my own mind and body; as it were, asking myself, "Is it this you want? Is it this?" Last of all I had asked if Joy itself was what I wanted; and, labelling it "aesthetic experience," had pretended I could answer Yes. But that answer too had broken down. Inexorably Joy proclaimed, "You want—I myself am your want of— something other, outside, not you nor any state of you." I did not yet ask, Who is the desired? only What is it? But this brought me already into the region of awe, for I thus understood that in deepest solitude there is a road right out of the self, a commerce with something which, by refusing to identify itself with any object of the senses, or anything whereof we have biological or social need, or anything imagined, or any state of our own minds, proclaims itself sheerly objective. Far more objective than bodies, for it is not, like them, clothed in our senses; the naked Other, imageless (though our imagination salutes it with a hundred images), unknown, undefined, desired.

That was the second Move; equivalent, perhaps, to the loss of one's last remaining bishop. The third Move did not seem to me dangerous at the time. It consisted merely in linking up this new *éclaircissement* about Joy with my idealistic philosophy. I saw that Joy, as I now understood it, would fit in. We mortals, seen as the sciences see us and as we commonly see one another, are mere "appearances." But appearances of the Absolute. In so far as we really are at all (which isn't saying much) we have, so to speak, a root in the Absolute, which is the utter reality. And that is why we experience Joy: we yearn, rightly, for that unity which we can never reach except by ceasing to be the separate phenomenal beings called "we." Joy was not a deception. Its visitations were rather the moments of clearest consciousness we had, when we became aware of our fragmentary and phantasmal nature and ached for that impossible reunion which would annihilate us or that self-contradictory waking which would reveal, not that we had had, but that we *were*, a dream. This seemed quite satisfactory intellectually. Even emotionally too; for it matters more that Heaven should exist than that we should ever get there. What I did not notice was that I had passed an important milestone. Up till now my thoughts had been centrifugal; now the centripetal movement had begun. Considerations arising from quite different parts of my experience were beginning to come together with a click. This new dovetailing of my desire-life with my philosophy foreshadowed the day, now fast approaching, when I should be forced to take my "philosophy" more seriously than I ever intended. I did not foresee this. I was like a man who has lost "merely a pawn" and never dreams that this (in that state of the game) means mate in a few moves.

The fourth Move was more alarming. I was now teaching philosophy (I suspect very badly) as well as English. And my watered Hegelianism wouldn't serve for tutorial purposes. A tutor must make things clear. Now the Absolute cannot be made clear. Do you mean Nobody-knows-what, or do you mean a superhuman mind and therefore (we may as well admit) a Person? After all, did Hegel and Bradley and all the rest of them ever do more than add mystifications to the simple, workable, theistic idealism of Berkeley? I thought not. And didn't Berkeley's "God" do all the same work as the Absolute, with the added advantage that we had at least some notion of what we meant by Him? I thought He did. So I was driven back into something like Berkeleyanism; but Berkeleyanism with a few top-dressings of my own. I distinguished this philosophical "God" very sharply (or so I said) from "the God of popular religion." There was, I explained, no possibility of being in a personal relation with Him. For I thought He projected us as a dramatist projects his characters, and I could no more "meet" Him, than Hamlet could meet Shakespeare. I didn't call Him "God" either; I called Him "Spirit." One fights for one's remaining comforts.

Then I read Chesterton's *Everlasting Man* and for the first time saw the whole Christian outline of history set out in a form that seemed to me to make sense. Somehow I contrived not to be too badly shaken. You will remember that I already thought Chesterton the most sensible man alive "apart from his Christianity." Now, I veritably believe, I thought—I didn't of course *say;* words would have revealed the nonsense—that Christianity itself was very sensible "apart from its Christianity." But I hardly remember, for I had not long finished *The Everlasting Man* when something far more alarming happened to me. Early in 1926 the hardest boiled of all the atheists I ever knew sat in my room on the other side of the fire and remarked that the evidence for the historicity of the Gospels was really surprisingly good. "Rum thing," he went on. "All that stuff of Frazer's about the Dying God.

Rum thing. It almost looks as if it had really happened once." To understand the shattering impact of it, you would need to know the man (who has certainly never since shown any interest in Christianity). If he, the cynic of cynics, the toughest of the toughs, were not—as I would still have put it— "safe," where could I turn? Was there then no escape?

The odd thing was that before God closed in on me, I was in fact offered what now appears a moment of wholly free choice. In a sense. I was going up Headington Hill on the top of a bus. Without words and (I think) almost without images, a fact about myself was somehow presented to me. I became aware that I was holding something at bay, or shutting something out. Or, if you like, that I was wearing some stiff clothing, like corsets, or even a suit of armour, as if I were a lobster. I felt myself being, there and then, given a free choice. I could open the door or keep it shut; I could unbuckle the armour or keep it on. Neither choice was presented as a duty; no threat or promise was attached to either, though I knew that to open the door or to take off the corslet meant the incalculable. The choice appeared to be momentous but it was also strangely unemotional, I was moved by no desires or fears. In a sense I was not moved by anything. I chose to open, to unbuckle, to loosen the rein. I say, "I chose," yet it did not really seem possible to do the opposite. On the other hand, I was aware of no motives. You could argue that I was not a free agent, but I am more inclined to think that this came nearer to being a perfectly free act than most that I have ever done. Necessity may not be the opposite of freedom, and perhaps a man is most free when, instead of producing motives, he could only say, "I am what I do." Then came the repercussion on the imaginative level. I felt as if I were a man of snow at long last beginning to melt.' The melting was starting in my back— drip-drip and presently trickle-trickle. I rather disliked the feeling.

The fox had been dislodged from Hegelian Wood and was now running in the open, "with all the woe in the world," bedraggled and weary, hounds barely a field behind. And nearly everyone was now (one way or another) in the pack; Plato, Dante, MacDonald, Herbert, Barfield, Tolkien, Dyson, Joy itself. Everyone and everything had joined the other side. Even my own pupil Griffiths—now Dom Bede Griffiths—though not yet himself a be-liever, did his share. Once, when he and Barfield were lunching in my room, I happened to refer to philosophy as "a subject." "It wasn't a *subject* to Plato," said Barfield, "it was a way." The quiet but fervent agreement of Griffiths, and the quick glance of understanding between these two, revealed to me my own frivolity. Enough had been thought, and said, and felt, and imagined. It was about time that something should be done.

For of course there had long been an ethic (theoretically) attached to my Idealism. I thought the business of us finite and half-unreal souls was to multiply the consciousness of Spirit by seeing the world from different positions while yet remaining qualitatively the same as Spirit; to be tied to a particular time and place and set of circumstances, yet there to will and think as Spirit itself does. This was hard; for the very act whereby Spirit projected souls and a world gave those souls different and competitive interests, so that there was a temptation to selfishness. But I thought each of us had it in his power to discount the emotional perspective produced by his own particular selfhood, just as we discount the optical perspective produced by our position in space. To prefer my own happiness to my neighbour's was like thinking that the nearest telegraph post was really the largest. The way to recover, and act upon, this universal and objective vision was daily and hourly to remember our true nature, to reascend or return into that Spirit which, in so far as we really were at all, we still were. Yes; but I now felt I had better try to do it. I faced at last (in MacDonald's words) "something to be neither more nor less nor other than *done.*" An attempt at complete virtue must be made.

Really, a young Atheist cannot guard his faith too carefully. Dangers lie in wait for him on every side. You must not do, you must not even try to do, the will of the Father unless you are prepared to "know of the doctrine." All my acts, desires, and thoughts were to be brought into harmony with universal Spirit. For the first time I examined myself with a seriously practical purpose. And there I found what appalled me; a zoo of lusts, a bedlam of ambitions, a nursery of fears, a hareem of fondled hatreds. My name was legion. . . .

People who are naturally religious find difficulty in understanding the horror of such a revelation. Amiable agnostics will talk cheerfully about "man's search for God." To me, as I then was, they might as well have talked about the mouse's search for the cat. The best image of my predicament is the meeting of Mime and Wotan in the first act of *Siegfried; hier brauch' ich nicht Spärer noch Späher, Einsam will ich* . . . (I've no use for spies and snoopers. I would be private. . . .)

Remember, I had always wanted, above all things, not to be "interfered with." I had wanted (mad wish) "to call my soul my own." I had been far more anxious to avoid suffering than to achieve delight. I had always aimed at limited liabilities. The supernatural itself had been to me, first, an illicit dram, and then, as by a drunkard's reaction, nauseous. Even my recent attempt to live my philosophy had secretly (I now knew) been hedged round by all sorts of reservations. I had pretty well known that my ideal of virtue would never be allowed to lead me into anything intolerably painful; I would be "reasonable." But now what had been an ideal became a command; and what might not be expected of one? Doubtless, by definition, God was Reason itself. But would He also be "reasonable" in that other, more comfortable, sense? Not the slightest assurance on that score was offered me.

Total surrender, the absolute leap in the dark, were demanded. The reality with which no treaty can be made was upon me. The demand was not even "All or nothing." I think that stage had been passed, on the bus-top when I unbuckled my armour and the snow-man started to melt. Now, the demand was simply "All."

You must picture me alone in that room in Magdalen, night after night, feeling, whenever my mind lifted even for a second from my work, the steady, unrelenting approach of Him whom I so earnestly desired not to meet. That which I greatly feared had at last come upon me. In the Trinity Term of 1929 I gave in, and admitted that God was God, and knelt and prayed: perhaps, that night, the most dejected and reluctant convert in all England. I did not then see what is now the most shining and obvious thing; the Divine humility which will accept a convert even on such terms. The Prodigal Son at least walked home on his own feet. But who can duly adore that Love which will open the high gates to a prodigal who is brought in kicking, struggling, resentful, and darting his eyes in every direction for a chance of escape? The words *compelle intrare*, compel them to come in, have been so abused by wicked men that we shudder at them; but, properly understood, they plumb the depth of the Divine mercy. The hardness of God is kinder than the softness of men, and His compulsion is our liberation.

Written in 1945, "Experiences in a Concentration Camp" is a slender, elegant work detailing the struggle to live a life of human dignity amid the humiliation and brutality of the Nazi death camps. Its author, Viktor Frankl, was born in Vienna, the son of religiously observant middle-class Jews. After his medical training, he concentrated in the new discipline of psychotherapy. Before the war, his work with suicidal patients led him to the insights that he later developed as "logotherapy," or healing through reason. Unlike other schools of psychotherapy, this now-widespread therapeutic approach required patients to find fulfillment in life through connections with the outside world: through love or work or good deeds, or through dealing with adversity.

Frankl was soon required to practice such precepts. In 1942 he was deported with his parents and his wife. In the next three years, in four different camps, he helped to save other prisoners from despair. In the book that is best known as *Man's Search for Meaning* (of which "Experiences in a Concentration Camp" forms the first part), Frankl eloquently

VIKTOR E. FRANKL

[1 9 0 5 – 1 9 9 7]

The salvation of man is through love and in love.

writes of the inner spiritual richness that alone gives meaning to life. As in the work of Simone Weil, his spiritual concerns were not separated from the realm of ordinary human activity. [EP]

FROM EXPERIENCES IN A CONCENTRATION CAMP

Cold curiosity predominated even in Auschwitz, somehow detaching the mind from its surroundings, which came to be regarded with a kind of objectivity. At that time one cultivated this state of mind as a means of protection. We were anxious to know what would happen next; and what would be the consequence, for example, of our standing in the open air, in the chill of late autumn, stark naked, and still wet from the showers. In the next few days our curiosity evolved into surprise; surprise that we did not catch cold.

There were many similar surprises in store for new arrivals. The medical men among us learned first of all: "Textbooks tell lies!" Somewhere it is said that man cannot exist without sleep for more than a stated number of hours. Quite wrong! I had been convinced that there were certain things I just could not do: I could not sleep without this or I could not live with that or the other. The first night in Auschwitz we slept in beds which were constructed in tiers. On each tier (measuring about six-and-a-half to eight feet) slept nine men, directly on the boards. Two blankets were shared by each nine men. We could, of course, lie only on our sides, crowded and huddled against each other, which had some advantages because of the bitter cold. Though it was forbidden to take shoes up to the bunks, some people did use them secretly as pillows in spite of the fact that they were caked with mud. Otherwise one's head had to rest on the crook of an almost dislocated arm. And yet sleep came and brought oblivion and relief from pain for a few hours.

I would like to mention a few similar surprises on how much we could endure: we were unable to clean our teeth, and yet, in spite of that and a severe vitamin deficiency, we had healthier gums than ever before. We had to wear the same shirts for half a year, until they had lost all appearance of being shirts. For days we were unable to wash, even partially, because of frozen water-pipes, and yet the sores and abrasions on hands which were dirty from work in the soil did not suppurate (that is, unless there was frost-bite). Or for instance, a light sleeper, who used to be disturbed by the slightest noise in the next room, now found himself lying pressed against a comrade who snored loudly a few inches from his ear and yet slept quite soundly through the noise.

If someone now asked of us the truth of Dostoevski's statement that flatly defines man as a being who can get used to anything, we would reply, "Yes, a man can get used to anything, but do not ask us how." But our psychological investigations have not taken us that far yet; neither had we prisoners reached that point. We were still in the first phase of our psychological reactions.

APATHY, THE MAIN SYMPTOM OF THE SECOND PHASE, WAS A NECES-sary mechanism of self-defense. Reality dimmed, and all efforts and all emotions were centered on one task: preserving one's own life and that of the other fellow. It was typical to hear the prisoners, while they were being herded back to camp from their work sites in the evening, sigh with relief and say, "Well, another day is over."

It can be readily understood that such a state of strain, coupled with the constant necessity of concentrating on the task of staying alive, forced the prisoner's inner life down to a primitive level. Several of my colleagues in camp who were trained in psychoanalysis often spoke of a "regression" in the camp inmate—a retreat to a more primitive form of mental life. His wishes and desires became obvious in his dreams.

What did the prisoner dream about most frequently? Of bread, cake, cigarettes, and nice warm baths. The lack of having these simple desires satisfied led him to seek wish fulfillment in dreams. Whether these dreams did any good is another matter; the dreamer had to wake from them to the reality of camp life, and to the terrible contrast between that and his dream illusions.

I shall never forget how I was roused one night by the groans of a fellow prisoner, who threw himself about in his sleep, obviously having a horrible nightmare. Since I had always been especially sorry for people who suffered from fearful dreams or deliria, I wanted to wake the poor man. Suddenly I drew back the hand which was ready to shake him, frightened at the thing I was about to do. At that moment I became intensely conscious of the fact that no dream, no matter how horrible, could be as bad as the reality of the camp which surrounded us, and to which I was about to recall him.

IN SPITE OF ALL THE ENFORCED PHYSICAL AND MENTAL PRIMITIVE-ness of the life in a concentration camp, it was possible for spiritual life to deepen. Sensitive people who were used to a rich intellectual life may have suffered much pain (they were often of a delicate constitution), but the damage to their inner selves was less. They were able to retreat from their terrible surroundings to a life of inner riches and spiritual freedom. Only in this way can one explain the apparent paradox that some prisoners of a less hardy makeup often seemed to survive camp life better than did those of a robust nature. In order to make myself clear, I am forced to fall back on personal experience. Let me tell what happened on those early mornings when we had to march to our work site.

There were shouted commands: "Detachment, forward march! Left-2-3-4! Left-2-3-4! Left-2-3-4! Left-2-3-4! First man about, left and left and left and left! Caps off!" These words sound in my ears even now. At the order "Caps off!" we passed the gate of the camp, and searchlights were trained upon us. Whoever did not march smartly got a kick. And worse off was the man who, because of the cold, had pulled his cap back over his ears before permission was given.

We stumbled on in the darkness, over big stones and through large puddles, along the one road leading from the camp. The accompanying guards kept shouting at us and driving us with the butts of their rifles. Anyone with very sore feet supported himself on his neighbor's arm. Hardly a word was spoken; the icy wind did not encourage talk. Hiding his mouth behind his upturned collar, the man marching next to me whispered suddenly: "If our wives could see us now! I do hope they are better off in their camps and don't know what is happening to us."

That brought thoughts of my own wife to mind. And as we stumbled on for miles, slipping on icy spots, supporting each other time and again, dragging one another up and onward, nothing was said, but we both knew: each of us was thinking of his wife. Occasionally I looked at the sky, where the stars were fading and the pink light of the morning was beginning to spread behind a dark bank of clouds. But my mind clung to my wife's image, imagining it with an uncanny acuteness. I heard her answering me, saw her smile, her frank and encouraging look. Real or not, her look was then more luminous than the sun which was beginning to rise.

A thought transfixed me: for the first time in my life I saw the truth as it is set into song by so many poets, proclaimed as the final wisdom by so many thinkers. The truth—that love is the ultimate and the highest goal to which man can aspire. Then I grasped the meaning of the greatest secret that human poetry and human thought and belief have to impart: *The salvation of man is through love and in love.* I understood how a man who has nothing left in this world still may know bliss, be it only for a brief moment, in the contemplation of his beloved. In a position of utter desolation, when man cannot express himself in positive action, when his only achievement may consist in enduring his sufferings in the right way—an honorable way—in such a position man can, through loving contemplation of the image he carries of his beloved, achieve fulfillment. For the first time in my life I was able to understand the meaning of the words, "The angels are lost in perpetual contemplation of an infinite glory."

In front of me a man stumbled and those following him fell on top of him. The guard rushed over and used his whip on them all. Thus my thoughts were interrupted for a few minutes. But soon my soul found its way back from the prisoner's existence to another world, and I resumed talk with my loved one: I asked her questions, and she answered; she questioned me in return, and I answered.

"Stop!" We had arrived at our work site. Everybody rushed into the dark hut in the hope of getting a fairly decent tool. Each prisoner got a spade or a pickaxe.

"Can't you hurry up, you pigs?" Soon we had resumed the previous day's positions in the ditch. The frozen ground cracked under the point of the pickaxes, and sparks flew. The men were silent, their brains numb.

My mind still clung to the image of my wife. A thought crossed my mind: I didn't even know if she were still alive. I knew only one thing—which I have learned well by now: Love goes very far beyond the physical person of the beloved. It finds its deepest meaning in his spiritual being, his inner self. Whether or not he is actually present, whether or not he is still alive at all, ceases somehow to be of importance.

I did not know whether my wife was alive, and I had no means of finding out (during all my prison life there was no outgoing or incoming mail); but at that moment it ceased to matter. There was no need for me to know; nothing could touch the strength of my love, my thoughts, and the image of my beloved. Had I known then that my wife was dead, I think that I would still have given myself, undisturbed by that knowledge, to the contemplation of her image, and that my mental conversation with her would have been just as vivid and just as satisfying. "Set me like a seal upon thy heart, love is as strong as death."

LONG AFTER I HAD RESUMED NORMAL LIFE AGAIN (THAT MEANS A long time after my release from camp), somebody showed me an illustrated weekly with photographs of prisoners lying crowded on their bunks, staring dully at a visitor. "Isn't this terrible, the dreadful staring faces—everything about it."

"Why?" I asked, for I genuinely did not understand. For at that moment I saw it all again: at 5:00 A.M. it was still pitch dark outside. I was lying on the hard boards in an earthen hut where about seventy of us were "taken care of." We were sick and did not have to leave camp for work; we did not have to go on parade. We could lie all day in our little corner in the hut and doze and wait for the daily distribution of bread (which, of course, was reduced for the sick) and for the daily helping of soup (watered down and also decreased in quantity). But how content we were; happy in spite of everything. While we cowered against each other to avoid any unnecessary loss of warmth, and were too lazy and disinterested to move a finger unnecessarily, we heard shrill whistles and shouts from the square where the night shift had just returned and was assembling for roll call. The door was flung open, and the snowstorm blew into our hut. An exhausted comrade, covered with snow, stumbled inside to sit down for a few minutes. But the senior warden turned him out again. It was strictly forbidden to admit a stranger to a hut while a check-up on the men was in progress. How sorry I was for that fellow and how glad not to be in his skin at that moment, but instead to be sick and able to doze on in the sick quarters! What a lifesaver it was to have two days there, and perhaps even two extra days after those!

All this came to my mind when I saw the photographs in the magazine. When I explained, my listeners understood why I did not find the photograph so terrible: the people shown on it might not have been so unhappy after all.

ANY ATTEMPT AT FIGHTING THE CAMP'S PSYCHOPATHOLOGICAL IN-fluence on the prisoner by psychotherapeutic or psychohygienic methods had to aim at giving him inner strength by pointing out to him a future goal to which he could look forward. Instinctively some of the prisoners attempted to find one on their own. It is a peculiarity of man that he can only live by looking to the future—*sub specie aeternitatis*. And this is his salvation in the most difficult moments of his existence, although he sometimes has to force his mind to the task.

I remember a personal experience. Almost in tears from pain (I had terrible sores on my feet from wearing torn shoes), I limped a few kilometers with our long column of men from the camp to our work site. Very cold, bitter winds struck us. I kept thinking of the endless little problems of our miserable life. What would there be to eat tonight? If a piece of sausage came as extra ration, should I exchange it for a piece of bread? Should I trade my last cigarette, which was left from a bonus I received a fortnight ago, for a bowl of soup? How could I get a piece of wire to replace the fragment which served as one of my shoelaces? Would I get to our work site in time to join my usual working party or would I have to join another, which might have a brutal foreman? What could I do to get on good terms with the Capo, who could help me to obtain work in camp instead of undertaking this horribly long daily march?

I became disgusted with the state of affairs which compelled me, daily and hourly, to think of only such trivial things. I forced my thoughts to turn to another subject. Suddenly I saw myself standing on the platform of a well-lit, warm and pleasant lecture room. In front of me sat an attentive audience on comfortable upholstered seats. I was giving a lecture on the psychology of the concentration camp! All that oppressed me at that moment became objective, seen and described from the remote viewpoint of science. By this method I succeeded somehow in rising above the situation, above the sufferings of the moment, and I observed them as if they were already of the past. Both I and my troubles became the object of an interesting psychoscientific study undertaken by myself. What does Spinoza say in his *Ethics?*—"*Affectus, qui passio est, desinit esse passio simulatque eius claram et distinctam formamus ideam.*" Emotion, which is suffering, ceases to be suffering as soon as we form a clear and precise picture of it.

. . . AS WE SAID BEFORE, ANY ATTEMPT TO RESTORE A MAN'S INNER strength in the camp had first to succeed in showing him some future goal. Nietzsche's words, "He who has a *why* to live for can bear with almost any *how*," could be the guiding motto for all psychotherapeutic and psychohygienic efforts regarding prisoners. Whenever there was an opportunity for it, one had to give them a why—an aim—for their lives, in order to strengthen them to bear the terrible *how* of their existence. Woe to him who saw no more sense in his life, no aim, no purpose, and therefore no point in carrying on. He was soon lost. The typical reply with which such a man rejected all encouraging arguments was, "I have nothing to expect from life any more." What sort of answer can one give to that?

What was really needed was a fundamental change in our attitude toward life. We had to learn ourselves and, furthermore, we had to teach the despairing men, that *it did not really matter what we expected from life, but rather what life expected from us.* We needed to stop asking about the meaning of life, and instead to think of ourselves as those who were being questioned by life—daily and hourly. Our answer must consist, not in talk and meditation, but in right action and in right conduct. Life ultimately means taking the responsibility to find the right answer to its problems and to fulfill the tasks which it constantly sets for each individual.

These tasks, and therefore the meaning of life, differ from man to man, and from moment to moment. Thus it is impossible to define the meaning of life in a general way. Questions about the meaning of life can never be answered by sweeping statements. "Life" does not mean something vague, but something very real and concrete, just as life's tasks are also very real and concrete. They form man's destiny, which is different and unique for each individual. No man and no destiny can be compared with any other man or any other destiny. No situation repeats itself, and each situation calls for a different response. Sometimes the situation in which a man finds himself may require him to shape his own fate by action. At other times it is more advantageous for him to make use of an opportunity for contemplation and to realize assets in this way. Sometimes man may be required simply to accept fate, to bear his cross. Every situation is distinguished by its uniqueness, and there is always only one right answer to the problem posed by the situation at hand.

When a man finds that it is his destiny to suffer, he will have to accept his suffering as his task; his single and unique task. He will have to acknowledge the fact that even in suffering he is unique and alone in the universe. No one can relieve him of his suffering or suffer in his place. His unique opportunity lies in the way in which he bears his burden.

For us, as prisoners, these thoughts were not speculations far removed from reality. They were the only thoughts that could be of help to us. They kept us from despair, even when there seemed to be no chance of coming out of it alive. Long ago we had passed the stage of asking what was the meaning of life, a naive query which understands life as the attaining of some aim through the active creation of something of value. For us, the meaning of life embraced the wider cycles of life and death, of suffering and of dying.

Once the meaning of suffering had been revealed to us, we refused to minimize or alleviate the camp's tortures by ignoring them or harboring false illusions and entertaining artificial optimism. Suffering had become a task on which we did not want to turn our backs. We had realized its hidden opportunities for achievement, the opportunities which caused the poet Rilke to write, *"Wie viel ist aufzuleiden!"* (How much suffering there is to get through!) Rilke spoke of "getting through suffering" as others would talk of "getting through work." There was plenty of suffering for us to get through. Therefore, it was necessary to face up to the full amount of suffering, trying to keep moments of weakness and furtive tears to a minimum. But there was no need to be ashamed of tears, for tears bore witness that a man had the greatest of courage, the courage to suffer. Only very few realized that. Shamefacedly some confessed occasionally that they had wept, like the comrade who answered my question of how he had gotten over his edema, by confessing, "I have wept it out of my system."

. . . .

. . . A VERY STRICT CAMP RULING FORBADE ANY EFFORTS TO SAVE A man who attempted suicide. It was forbidden, for example, to cut down a man who was trying to hang himself. Therefore, it was all important to prevent these attempts from occurring.

I remember two cases of would-be suicide, which bore a striking similarity to each other. Both men had talked of their intentions to commit suicide. Both used the typical argument—they had nothing more to expect from life. In both cases it was a question of getting them to realize that life was still expecting something from them; something in the future was expected of them. We found, in fact, that for the one it was his child whom he adored and who was waiting for him in a foreign country. For the other it was a thing, not a person. This man was a scientist and had written a series of books which still needed to be finished. His work could not be done by anyone else, any more than another person could ever take the place of the father in his child's affections.

This uniqueness and singleness which distinguishes each individual and gives a meaning to his existence has a bearing on creative work as much as it does on human love. When the impossibility of replacing a person is realized, it allows the responsibility which a man has for his existence and its continuance to appear in all its magnitude. A man who becomes conscious of the responsibility he bears toward a human being who affectionately waits for him, or to an unfinished work, will never be able to throw away his life. He knows the "why" for his existence, and will be able to bear almost any "how."

AND NOW TO THE LAST CHAPTER IN THE PSYCHOLOGY OF A CONCEN-tration camp—the psychology of the prisoner who has been released. In describing the experiences of liberation, which naturally must be personal, we shall pick up the threads of that part of our narrative which told of the morning when the white flag was hoisted above the camp gates after days of high tension. This state of inner suspense was followed by total relaxation. But it would be quite wrong to think that we went mad with joy. What, then, did happen?

With tired steps we prisoners dragged ourselves to the camp gates. Tim-idly we looked around and glanced at each other questioningly. Then we ventured a few steps out of camp. This time no orders were shouted at us, nor was there any need to duck quickly to avoid a blow or kick. Oh no! This time the guards offered us cigarettes! We hardly recognized them at first;

they had hurriedly changed into civilian clothes. We walked slowly along the road leading from the camp. Soon our legs hurt and threatened to buckle. But we limped on; we wanted to see the camp's surroundings for the first time with the eyes of free men. "Freedom"—we repeated to ourselves, and yet we could not grasp it. We had said this word so often during all the years we dreamed about it, that it had lost its meaning. Its reality did not penetrate into our consciousness; we could not grasp the fact that freedom was ours.

We came to meadows full of flowers. We saw and realized that they were there, but we had no feelings about them. The first spark of joy came when we saw a rooster with a tail of multicolored feathers. But it remained only a spark; we did not yet belong to this world.

In the evening when we all met again in our hut, one said secretly to the other, "Tell me, were you pleased today?"

And the other replied, feeling ashamed as he did not know that we all felt similarly, "Truthfully, no!" We had literally lost the ability to feel pleased and had to relearn it slowly.

THE BODY HAS FEWER INHIBITIONS THAN THE MIND. IT MADE GOOD use of the new freedom from the first moment on. It began to eat ravenously, for hours and days, even half the night. It is amazing what quantities one can eat. And when one of the prisoners was invited out by a friendly farmer in the neighborhood, he ate and ate and then drank coffee, which loosened his tongue, and he then began to talk, often for hours. The pressure which had been on his mind for years was released at last. Hearing him talk, one got the impression that he had to talk, that his desire to speak was irresistible. I have known people who have been under heavy pressure only for a short time (for example, through a cross-examination by the Gestapo) to have similar reactions. Many days passed, until not only the tongue was loosened, but something within oneself as well; then feeling suddenly broke through the strange fetters which had restrained it.

ONE DAY, A FEW DAYS AFTER THE LIBERATION, I WALKED THROUGH the country past flowering meadows, for miles and miles, toward the market town near the camp. Larks rose to the sky and I could hear their joyous song. There was no one to be seen for miles around; there was nothing but the wide earth and sky and the larks' jubilation and the freedom of space. I stopped, looked around, and up to the sky—and then I went down on my knees. At that moment there was very little I knew of myself or of the world —I had but one sentence in mind—always the same: "I called to the Lord from my narrow prison and He answered me in the freedom of space."

How long I knelt there and repeated this sentence memory can no longer recall. But I know that on that day, in that hour, my new life started. Step for step I progressed, until I again became a human being.

SIMONE
WEIL

[1 9 0 9 – 1 9 4 3]

*When one hungers for bread
one does not receive stones.*

Simone Weil was born into an assimilated Jewish family in Paris. After studies at the Ecole Normale Supérieure in the 1920s, she worked for a time as a farm and factory hand and also participated in the Spanish Civil War. What distinguished her political engagement from that of her more radical contemporaries was its spiritual dimension.

While living in Marseille, where her family fled after the Nazi takeover of Paris, Weil wrote some of her most important essays. She was befriended there by a Catholic priest to whom the following spiritual autobiography was addressed. Though it reveals an intensely mystical side, it coolly enumerates all the concerns that consumed the intellectual and spiritual energies of her short, ascetic life: the tension between the individual and the collective, whether the state or the church; free will and choice, even the choice for damnation; and the cosmic and social insignificance of the individual. In Weil, one senses an intellect that has stretched itself to its limits, only to arrive at something very near the end of existence, if not nihilism.

Obsessed by the suffering of her

countrymen during World War II, she reduced her own diet to an extreme minimum. She was in England, hoping to participate in Resistance work, when she died in a nursing home in Kent. [EP]

A SPIRITUAL AUTOBIOGRAPHY

P.S. To Be Read First.

This letter is fearfully long—but as there is no question of an answer —especially as I shall doubtless have gone before it reaches you—you have years ahead of you in which to read it if you care to. Read it all the same, one day or another.

From Marseilles, about May 15

Father,

Before leaving I want to speak to you again, it may be the last time perhaps, for over there I shall probably send you only my news from time to time just so as to have yours.

I told you that I owed you an enormous debt. I want to try to tell you exactly what it consists of. I think that if you could really understand what my spiritual state is you would not be at all sorry that you did not lead me to baptism. But I do not know if it is possible for you to understand this.

You neither brought me the Christian inspiration nor did you bring me to Christ; for when I met you there was no longer any need; it had been done without the intervention of any human being. If it had been otherwise, if I had not already been won, not only implicitly but consciously, you would have given me nothing, because I should have received nothing from you. My friendship for you would have been a reason for me to refuse your message, for I should have been afraid of the possibilities of error and illusion which human influence in the divine order is likely to involve.

I may say that never at any moment in my life have I "sought for God." For this reason, which is probably too subjective, I do not like this expression and it strikes me as false. As soon as I reached adolescence, I saw the problem of God as a problem the data of which could not be obtained here below, and I decided that the only way of being sure not to reach a wrong solution, which seemed to me the greatest possible evil, was to leave it alone. So I left it alone. I neither affirmed nor denied anything. It seemed to me useless to solve the problem, for I thought that, being in this world, our business was to adopt the best attitude with regard to the problems of this world, and that such an attitude did not depend upon the solution of the problem of God.

This held good as far as I was concerned at any rate, for I never hesitated in my choice of an attitude; I always adopted the Christian attitude as the only possible one. I might say that I was born, I grew up, and I always remained within the Christian inspiration. While the very name of God had no part in my thoughts, with regard to the problems of this world and this life I shared the Christian conception in an explicit and rigorous manner, with the most specific notions it involves. Some of these notions have been part of my outlook for as far back as I can remember. With others I know the time and manner of their coming and the form under which they imposed themselves upon me.

For instance I never allowed myself to think of a future state, but I always believed that the instant of death is the center and object of life. I used to think that, for those who live as they should, it is the instant when, for an infinitesimal fraction of time, pure truth, naked, certain, and eternal enters the soul. I may say that I never desired any other good for myself. I thought that the life leading to this good is not only defined by a code of morals common to all, but that for each one it consists of a succession of acts and events strictly personal to him, and so essential that he who leaves them on one side never reaches the goal. The notion of vocation was like this for me. I saw that the carrying out of a vocation differed from the actions dictated by reason or inclination in that it was due to an impulse of an essentially and manifestly different order; and not to follow such an impulse when it made itself felt, even if it demanded impossibilities, seemed to me the greatest of all ills. Hence my conception of obedience; and I put this conception to the test when I entered the factory and stayed on there, even when I was in that state of intense and uninterrupted misery about which I recently told you. The most beautiful life possible has always seemed to me to be one where everything is determined, either by the pressure of circumstances or by impulses such as I have just mentioned and where there is never any room for choice.

At fourteen I fell into one of those fits of bottomless despair that come with adolescence, and I seriously thought of dying because of the mediocrity of my natural faculties. The exceptional gifts of my brother, who had a childhood and youth comparable to those of Pascal, brought my own inferiority home to me. I did not mind having no visible successes, but what did grieve me was the idea of being excluded from that transcendent kingdom to which only the truly great have access and wherein truth abides. I preferred to die rather than live without that truth. After months of inward darkness, I suddenly had the everlasting conviction that any human being, even though practically devoid of natural faculties, can penetrate to the kingdom of truth reserved for genius, if only he longs for truth and perpetually concentrates all his attention upon its attainment. He thus becomes a genius too, even though for lack of talent his genius cannot be visible from outside. Later on, when the strain of headaches caused the feeble faculties I possess to be invaded by a paralysis, which I was quick to imagine as probably incurable, the same conviction led me to persevere for ten years in an effort of concentrated attention that was practically unsupported by any hope of results.

Under the name of truth I also included beauty, virtue, and every kind of goodness, so that for me it was a question of a conception of the relationship between grace and desire. The conviction that had come to me was that when one hungers for bread one does not receive stones. But at that time I had not read the Gospel.

Just as I was certain that desire has in itself an efficacy in the realm of spiritual goodness whatever its form, I thought it was also possible that it might not be effective in any other realm.

As for the spirit of poverty, I do not remember any moment when it was not in me, although only to that unhappily small extent compatible with my imperfection. I fell in love with Saint Francis of Assisi as soon as I came to know about him. I always believed and hoped that one day Fate would force upon me the condition of a vagabond and a beggar which he embraced freely. Actually I felt the same way about prison.

From my earliest childhood I always had also the Christian idea of love for one's neighbor, to which I gave the name of justice—a name it bears in many passages of the Gospel and which is so beautiful. You know that on this point I have failed seriously several times.

The duty of acceptance in all that concerns the will of God, whatever it may be, was impressed upon my mind as the first and most necessary of all duties from the time when I found it set down in Marcus Aurelius under the form of the *amor fati* of the Stoics. I saw it as a duty we cannot fail in without dishonoring ourselves.

The idea of purity, with all that this word can imply for a Christian, took possession of me at the age of sixteen, after a period of several months during which I had been going through the emotional unrest natural in adolescence. This idea came to me when I was contemplating a mountain landscape and little by little it was imposed upon me in an irresistible manner.

Of course I knew quite well that my conception of life was Christian.

l:

That is why it never occurred to me that I could enter the Christian community. I had the idea that I was born inside. But to add dogma to this conception of life, without being forced to do so by indisputable evidence, would have seemed to me like a lack of honesty. I should even have thought I was lacking in honesty had I considered the question of the truth of dogma as a problem for myself or even had I simply desired to reach a conclusion on this subject. I have an extremely severe standard for intellectual honesty, so severe that I never met anyone who did not seem to fall short of it in more than one respect; and I am always afraid of failing in it myself.

Keeping away from dogma in this way, I was prevented by a sort of shame from going into churches, though all the same I like being in them. Nevertheless, I had three contacts with Catholicism that really counted.

After my year in the factory, before going back to teaching, I had been taken by my parents to Portugal, and while there I left them to go alone to a little village. I was, as it were, in pieces, soul and body. That contact with affliction had killed my youth. Until then I had not had any experience of affliction, unless we count my own, which, as it was my own, seemed to me, to have little importance, and which moreover was only a partial affliction, being biological and not social. I knew quite well that there was a great deal of affliction in the world, I was obsessed with the idea, but I had not had prolonged and first-hand experience of it. As I worked in the factory, indistinguishable to all eyes, including my own, from the anonymous mass, the affliction of others entered into my flesh and my soul. Nothing separated me from it, for I had really forgotten my past and I looked forward to no future, finding it difficult to imagine the possibility of surviving all the fatigue. What I went through there marked me in so lasting a manner that still today when any human being, whoever he may be and in whatever circumstances, speaks to me without brutality, I cannot help having the impression that there must be a mistake and that unfortunately the mistake will in all probability disappear. There I received forever the mark of a slave, like the branding of the red-hot iron the Romans put on the foreheads of their most despised slaves. Since then I have always regarded myself as a slave.

In this state of mind then, and in a wretched condition physically, I entered the little Portuguese village, which, alas, was very wretched too, on the very day of the festival of its patron saint. I was alone. It was the evening and there was a full moon over the sea. The wives of the fishermen were, in procession, making a tour of all the ships, carrying candles and singing what must certainly be very ancient hymns of a heart-rending sadness. Nothing can give any idea of it. I have never heard anything so poignant unless it were the song of the boatmen on the Volga. There the conviction was suddenly borne in upon me that Christianity is pre-eminently the religion of slaves, that slaves cannot help belonging to it, and I among others.

In 1937 I had two marvelous days at Assisi. There, alone in the little twelfth-century Romanesque chapel of Santa Maria degli Angeli, an incomparable marvel of purity where Saint Francis often used to pray, something stronger than I was compelled me for the first time in my life to go down on my knees.

In 1938 I spent ten days at Solesmes, from Palm Sunday to Easter Tuesday, following all the liturgical services. I was suffering from splitting headaches; each sound hurt me like a blow; by an extreme effort of concentration I was able to rise above this wretched flesh, to leave it to suffer by itself, heaped up in a corner, and to find a pure and perfect joy in the unimaginable beauty of the chanting and the words. This experience enabled me by analogy to get a better understanding of the possibility of loving divine love in the midst of affliction. It goes without saying that in the course of these services the thought of the Passion of Christ entered into my being once and for all.

There was a young English Catholic there from whom I gained my first idea of the supernatural power of the sacraments because of the truly angelic radiance with which he seemed to be clothed after going to communion. Chance—for I always prefer saying chance rather than Providence—made of him a messenger to me. For he told me of the existence of those English poets of the seventeenth century who are named metaphysical. In reading them later on, I discovered the poem [by George Herbert] of which I read you what is unfortunately a very inadequate translation. It is called "Love." I learned it by heart. Often, at the culminating point of a violent headache, I make myself say it over, concentrating all my attention upon it and clinging with all my soul to the tenderness it enshrines. I used to think I was merely reciting it as a beautiful poem, but without my knowing it the recitation had the virtue of a prayer. It was during one of these recitations that, as I told you, Christ himself came down and took possession of me.

In my arguments about the insolubility of the problem of God I had never foreseen the possibility of that, of a real contact, person to person, here below, between a human being and God. I had vaguely heard tell of things of this kind, but I had never believed in them. In the *Fioretti* the accounts of apparitions rather put me off if anything, like the miracles in the Gospel. Moreover, in this sudden possession of me by Christ, neither my senses nor my imagination had any part; I only felt in the midst of my suffering the presence of a love, like that which one can read in the smile on a beloved face.

I had never read any mystical works because I had never felt any call to read them. In reading as in other things I have always striven to practice obedience. There is nothing more favorable to intellectual progress, for as far as possible I only read what I am hungry for at the moment when I have an appetite for it, and then I do not read, I *eat*. God in his mercy had prevented me from reading the mystics, so that it should be evident to me that I had not invented this absolutely unexpected contact.

Yet I still half refused, not my love but my intelligence. For it seemed to me certain, and I still think so today, that one can never wrestle enough with God if one does so out of pure regard for the truth. Christ likes us to prefer truth to him because, before being Christ, he is truth. If one turns aside from him to go toward the truth, one will not go far before falling into his arms.

After this I came to feel that Plato was a mystic, that all the *Iliad* is bathed in Christian light, and that Dionysus and Osiris are in a certain sense Christ himself; and my love was thereby redoubled.

I never wondered whether Jesus was or was not the Incarnation of God; but in fact I was incapable of thinking of him without thinking of him as God.

In the spring of 1940 I read the *Bhagavad-Gita*. Strange to say it was in reading those marvelous words, words with such a Christian sound, put into the mouth of an incarnation of God, that I came to feel strongly that we owe an allegiance to religious truth which is quite different from the admiration we accord to a beautiful poem; it is something far more categorical.

Yet I did not believe it to be possible for me to consider the question of baptism. I felt that I could not honestly give up my opinions concerning the non-Christian religions and concerning Israel—and as a matter of fact time and meditation have only served to strengthen them—and I thought that this constituted an absolute obstacle. I did not imagine it as possible that a priest could even dream of granting me baptism. If I had not met you, I should never have considered the problem of baptism as a practical problem.

During all this time of spiritual progress I had never prayed. I was afraid of the power of suggestion that is in prayer—the very power for which Pascal recommends it. Pascal's method seems to me one of the worst for attaining faith.

Contact with you was not able to persuade me to pray. On the contrary I thought the danger was all the greater since I also had to beware of the power of suggestion in my friendship with you. At the same time I found it very difficult not to pray and not to tell you so. Moreover, I knew I could not tell you without completely misleading you about myself. At that time I should not have been able to make you understand.

Until last September I had never once prayed in all my life, at least not in the literal sense of the word. I had never said any words to God, either out loud or mentally. I had never pronounced a liturgical prayer. I had occasionally recited the *Salve Regina*, but only as a beautiful poem.

Last summer, doing Greek with T———, I went through the Our Father word for word in Greek. We promised each other to learn it by heart. I do not think he ever did so, but some weeks later, as I was turning over the pages of the Gospel, I said to myself that since I had promised to do this thing and it was good, I ought to do it. I did it. The infinite sweetness of this Greek text so took hold of me that for several days I could not stop myself from saying it over all the time. A week afterward I began the vine harvest. I recited the Our Father in Greek every day before work, and I repeated it very often in the vineyard.

Since that time I have made a practice of saying it through once each morning with absolute attention. If during the recitation my attention wanders or goes to sleep, in the minutest degree, I begin again until I have once succeeded in going through it with absolutely pure attention. Sometimes it comes about that I say it again out of sheer pleasure, but I only do it if I really feel the impulse.

The effect of this practice is extraordinary and surprises me every time, for, although I experience it each day, it exceeds my expectation at each repetition.

At times the very first words tear my thoughts from my body and transport it to a place outside space where there is neither perspective nor point of view. The infinity of the ordinary expanses of perception is replaced by an infinity to the second or sometimes the third degree. At the same time, filling every part of this infinity of infinity, there is silence, a silence which is not an absence of sound but which is the object of a positive sensation, more positive than that of sound. Noises, if there are any, only reach me after crossing this silence.

Sometimes, also, during this recitation or at other moments, Christ is present with me in person, but his presence is infinitely more real, more moving, more clear than on that first occasion when he took possession of me.

I should never have been able to take it upon myself to tell you all this had it not been for the fact that I am going away. And as I am going more or less with the idea of probable death, I do not believe that I have the right to keep it to myself. For after all, the whole of this matter is not a question concerning me myself. It concerns God. I am really nothing in it all. If one could imagine any possibility of error in God, I should think that it had all happened to me by mistake. But perhaps God likes to use castaway objects, waste, rejects. After all, should the bread of the host be moldy, it would become the Body of Christ just the same after the priest had consecrated it. Only it cannot refuse, while we can disobey. It sometimes seems to me that when I am treated in so merciful a way, every sin on my part must be a mortal sin. And I am constantly committing them.

I have told you that you are like a father and brother at the same time to me. But these words only express an analogy. Perhaps at bottom they only correspond to a feeling of affection, of gratitude and admiration. For as to the spiritual direction of my soul, I think that God himself has taken it in hand from the start and still looks after it.

That does not prevent me from owing you the greatest debt of gratitude that I could ever have incurred toward any human being. This is exactly what it consists of.

First you once said to me at the beginning of our relationship some words that went to the bottom of my soul. You said: "Be very careful, because if you should pass over something important through your own fault it would be a pity."

That made me see intellectual honesty in a new light. Till then I had only thought of it as opposed to faith; your words made me think that perhaps, without my knowing it, there were in me obstacles to the faith, impure obstacles, such as prejudices, habits. I felt that after having said to myself for so many years simply: "Perhaps all that is not true," I ought, without ceasing to say it—I still take care to say it very often now—to join it to the opposite formula, namely: "Perhaps all that is true," and to make them alternate.

At the same time, in making the problem of baptism a practical problem for me, you have forced me to face the whole question of the faith, dogma, and the sacraments, obliging me to consider them closely and at length with the fullest possible attention, making me see them as things toward which I have obligations that I have to discern and perform. I should never have done this otherwise and it is indispensable for me to do it.

But the greatest blessing you have brought me is of another order. In gaining my friendship by your charity (which I have never met anything to equal), you have provided me with a source of the most compelling and pure inspiration that is to be found among human things. For nothing among human things has such power to keep our gaze fixed ever more intensely upon God, than friendship for the friends of God.

Nothing better enables me to measure the breadth of your charity than the fact that you bore with me for so long and with such gentleness. I may seem to be joking, but that is not the case. It is true that you have not the same motives as I have myself (those about which I wrote to you the other day), for feeling hatred and repulsion toward me. But all the same I feel that your patience with me can only spring from a supernatural generosity.

I have not been able to avoid causing you the greatest disappointment it was in my power to cause you. But up to now, although I have often asked myself the question during prayer, during Mass, or in the light of the radiancy that remains in the soul after Mass, I have never once had, even for a moment, the feeling that God wants me to be in the Church. I have never even once had a feeling of uncertainty. I think that at the present time we can finally conclude that he does not want me in the Church. Do not have any regrets about it.

He does not want it so far at least. But unless I am mistaken I should say that it is his will that I should stay outside for the future too, except perhaps at the moment of death. Yet I am always ready to obey any order, whatever it may be. I should joyfully obey the order to go to the very center of hell and to remain there eternally. I do not mean, of course, that I have a preference for orders of this nature. I am not perverse like that.

Christianity should contain all vocations without exception since it is catholic. In consequence the Church should also. But in my eyes Christianity is catholic by right but not in fact. So many things are outside it, so many things that I love and do not want to give up, so many things that God loves, otherwise they would not be in existence. All the immense stretches of past centuries, except the last twenty are among them; all the countries inhabited by colored races; all secular life in the white peoples' countries; in the history of these countries, all the traditions banned as heretical, those of the Manicheans and Albigenses for instance; all those things resulting from the Renaissance, too often degraded but not quite without value.

Christianity being catholic by right but not in fact, I regard it as legitimate on my part to be a member of the Church by right but not in fact, not only for a time, but for my whole life if need be.

But it is not merely legitimate. So long as God does not give me the certainty that he is ordering me to do anything else, I think it is my duty.

I think, and so do you, that our obligation for the next two or three years, an obligation so strict that we can scarcely fail in it without treason, is to show the public the possibility of a truly incarnated Christianity. In all the history now known there has never been a period in which souls have been in such peril as they are today in every part of the globe. The bronze serpent must be lifted up again so that whoever raises his eyes to it may be saved.

But everything is so closely bound up together that Christianity cannot be really incarnated unless it is catholic in the sense that I have just defined. How could it circulate through the flesh of all the nations of Europe if it did not contain absolutely everything in itself? Except of course falsehood. But in everything that exists there is most of the time more truth than falsehood.

Having so intense and so painful a sense of this urgency, I should betray the truth, that is to say the aspect of truth that I see, if I left the point, where I have been since my birth, at the intersection of Christianity and everything that is not Christianity.

I have always remained at this exact point, on the threshold of the Church, without moving, quite still, ἐν ὑπομένῃ (it is so much more beautiful a word than *patientia!*); only now my heart has been transported, forever, I hope, into the Blessed Sacrament exposed on the altar.

You see that I am very far from the thoughts that H———, with the best of intentions, attributed to me. I am far also from being worried in any way.

If I am sad, it comes primarily from the permanent sadness that destiny has imprinted forever upon my emotions, where the greatest and purest joys can only be superimposed and that at the price of a great effort of attention. It comes also from my miserable and continual sins; and from all the calamities of our time and of all those of all the past centuries.

I think that you should understand why I have always resisted you, if in spite of being a priest you can admit that a genuine vocation might prevent anyone from entering the Church.

Otherwise a barrier of incomprehension will remain between us, whether the error is on my part or on yours. This would grieve me from the point of view of my friendship for you, because in that case the result of all these efforts and desires, called forth by your charity toward me, would be a disappointment for you. Moreover, although it is not my fault, I should not be able to help feeling guilty of ingratitude. For, I repeat, my debt to you is beyond all measure.

I should like to draw your attention to one point. It is that there is an absolutely insurmountable obstacle to the Incarnation of Christianity. It is the use of the two little words *anathema sit*. It is not their existence, but the way they have been employed up till now. It is that also which prevents me from crossing the threshold of the Church. I remain beside all those things that cannot enter the Church, the universal repository, on account of those two little words. I remain beside them all the more because my own intelligence is numbered among them.

The Incarnation of Christianity implies a harmonious solution of the problem of the relations between the individual and the collective. Harmony in the Pythagorean sense; the just balance of contraries. This solution is precisely what men are thirsting for today.

The position of the intelligence is the key to this harmony, because the intelligence is a specifically and rigorously individual thing. This harmony exists wherever the intelligence, remaining in its place, can be exercised without hindrance and can reach the complete fulfillment of its function. That is what Saint Thomas says admirably of all the parts of the soul of Christ, with reference to his sensitiveness to pain during the crucifixion.

The special function of the intelligence requires total liberty, implying the right to deny everything, and allowing of no domination. Wherever it usurps control there is an excess of individualism. Wherever it is hampered or uneasy there is an oppressive collectivism, or several of them.

The Church and the State should punish it, each one in its own way, when it advocates actions of which they disapprove. When it remains in the region of purely theoretical speculation they still have the duty, should occasion arise, to put the public on their guard, by every effective means, against the danger of the practical influence certain speculations might have upon the conduct of life. But whatever these theoretical speculations may be, the Church and the State have no right either to try to stifle them or to inflict any penalty material or moral upon their authors. Notably, they should not be deprived of the sacraments if they desire them. For, whatever they may have said, even if they have publicly denied the existence of God, they may not have committed any sin. In such a case the Church should declare that they are in error, but it should not demand of them anything whatever in the way of a disavowal of what they have said, nor should it deprive them of the Bread of Life.

A collective body is the guardian of dogma; and dogma is an object of contemplation for love, faith, and intelligence, three strictly individual faculties. Hence, almost since the beginning, the individual has been ill at ease in Christianity, and this uneasiness has been notably one of the intelligence. This cannot be denied.

Christ himself who is Truth itself, when he was speaking before an assembly such as a council, did not address it in the same language as he used in an intimate conversation with his well-beloved friend, and no doubt before the Pharisees he might easily have been accused of contradiction and error. For by one of those laws of nature, which God himself respects, since he has willed them from all eternity, there are two languages that are quite distinct although made up of the same words; there is the collective language and there is the individual one. The Comforter whom Christ sends us, the Spirit of truth, speaks one or other of these languages, whichever circumstances demand, and by a necessity of their nature there is not agreement between them.

When genuine friends of God—such as was Eckhart to my way of thinking—repeat words they have heard in secret amidst the silence of the union of love, and these words are in disagreement with the teaching of the Church, it is simply that the language of the market place is not that of the nuptial chamber.

Everybody knows that really intimate conversation is only possible between two or three. As soon as there are six or seven, collective language begins to dominate. That is why it is a complete misinterpretation to apply to the Church the words "Wheresoever two or three are gathered together in my name, there am I in the midst of them." Christ did not say two hundred, or fifty, or ten. He said two or three. He said precisely that he always forms the third in the intimacy of the tête-à-tête.

Christ made promises to the Church, but none of these promises has the force of the expression "Thy Father who seeth in secret." The word of God is the secret word. He who has not heard this word, even if he adheres to all the dogmas taught by the Church, has no contact with truth.

The function of the Church as the collective keeper of dogma is indispensable. She has the right and the duty to punish those who make a clear attack upon her within the specific range of this function, by depriving them of the sacraments.

Thus, although I know practically nothing of this business, I incline to think provisionally that she was right to punish Luther.

But she is guilty of an abuse of power when she claims to force love and intelligence to model their language upon her own. This abuse of power is not of God. It comes from the natural tendency of every form of collectivism, without exception, to abuse power.

The image of the Mystical Body of Christ is very attractive. But I consider the importance given to this image today as one of the most serious signs of our degeneration. For our true dignity is not to be parts of a body, even though it be a mystical one, even though it be that of

Christ. It consists in this, that in the state of perfection, which is the vocation of each one of us, we no longer live in ourselves, but Christ lives in us; so that through our perfection Christ in his integrity and in his indivisible unity, becomes in a sense each one of us, as he is completely in each host. The hosts are not a *part* of his body.

This present-day importance of the image of the Mystical Body shows how wretchedly susceptible Christians are to outside influences. Undoubtedly there is real intoxication in being a member of the Mystical Body of Christ. But today a great many other mystical bodies, which have not Christ for their head, produce an intoxication in their members that to my way of thinking is of the same order.

As long as it is through obedience, I find sweetness in my deprivation of the joy of membership in the Mystical Body of Christ. For if God is willing to help me, I may thus bear witness that without this joy one can nevertheless be faithful to Christ unto death. Social enthusiasms have such power today, they raise people so effectively to the supreme degree of heroism in suffering and death, that I think it is as well that a few sheep should remain outside the fold in order to bear witness that the love of Christ is essentially something different.

The Church today defends the cause of the indefeasible rights of the individual against collective oppression, of liberty of thought against tyranny. But these are causes readily embraced by those who find themselves momentarily to be the least strong. It is their only way of perhaps one day becoming the strongest. That is well known.

You may perhaps be offended by this idea. You are not the Church. During the periods of the most atrocious abuse of power committed by the Church, there must have been some priests like you among the others. Your good faith is not a guarantee, even were it shared by all your Order. You cannot foresee what turn things may take.

In order that the present attitude of the Church should be effective and that she should really penetrate like a wedge into social existence, she would have to say openly that she had changed or wished to change. Otherwise who could take her seriously when they remembered the Inquisition? My friendship for you, which I extend through you to all your Order, makes it very painful for me to bring this up. But it existed. After the fall of the Roman Empire, which had been totalitarian, it was the Church that was the first to establish a rough sort of totalitarianism in Europe in the thirteenth century, after the war with the Albigenses. This tree bore much fruit.

And the motive power of this totalitarianism was the use of those two little words: *anathema sit.*

It was moreover by a judicious transposition of this use that all the parties which in our own day have founded totalitarian regimes were shaped. This is a point of history I have specially studied.

I must give you the impression of a Luciferian pride in speaking thus of a great many matters that are too high for me and about which I have no right to understand anything. It is not my fault. Ideas come and settle in my mind by mistake, then, realizing their mistake, they absolutely insist on coming out. I do not know where they come from, or what they are worth, but, whatever the risk, I do not think I have the right to prevent this operation.

Good-by, I wish you all possible good things except the cross; for I do not love my neighbor as myself, you particularly, as you have noticed. But Christ granted to his well-beloved disciple, and probably to all that disciple's spiritual lineage, to come to him not through degradation, defilement, and distress, but in uninterrupted joy, purity, and sweetness. That is why I can allow myself to wish that even if one day you have the honor of dying a violent death for Our Lord, it may be with joy and without any anguish; also that only three of the beatitudes *(mites, mundo corde, pacifici)* will apply to you. All the others involve more or less of suffering.

This wish is not due only to the frailty of human friendship. For, with any human being taken individually, I always find reasons for concluding that sorrow and misfortune do not suit him, either because he seems too mediocre for anything so great or, on the contrary, too precious to be destroyed. One cannot fail more seriously in the second of the two essential commandments. And as to the first, I fail to observe that, in a still more horrible manner, for every time I think of the crucifixion of Christ I commit the sin of envy.

Believe more than ever and forever in my filial and tenderly grateful friendship.

Sheldon Vanauken lived in Lynchburg, Virginia, where he was a professor of literature at Virginia Polytechnic University. Author of novels *(Gateway to Heaven)* and histories *(The Glittering Illusion)*, he was recipient of the National Religious Book Award, the Gold Medallion Award, and the American Book Award, all for his autobiography, *A Severe Mercy*. In this work, Vanauken recounts the story of his courtship and marriage to his wife, Davy, and her tragic death within a few years of their becoming Christians. In the early days of their relationship, they had shared certain oaths meant to secure their love against the onslaughts of time and the world; they raised what they called the "Shining Barrier" and established the "Appeal to Love." The Shining Barrier was meant to block out any concerns, even children or career, that might affect their love for each other. Similarly, the Appeal to Love could be invoked to settle any differences. Neither of these promises would be sufficient against the transformation of their spiritual lives or in the face of death.

After spending the early years of their

SHELDON
VANAUKEN

[1 9 1 4 – 1 9 9 7]

I suspected that all the yearnings I

had ever felt . . . were for God.

marriage posted overseas during the Second World War and then in sailing desultorily aboard their boat, the *Grey Goose*, they traveled to Oxford for a course of study at the university. This excerpt is Vanauken's account of their time at Oxford, their friendship with C. S. Lewis, and their turn toward religious faith.   [AM]

FROM *A SEVERE MERCY*

We had come up to the university for Michaelmas Term in the previous autumn, and by now we were to be numbered for ever amongst the lovers of Oxford. And amongst the lovers of England, too, especially rural England. On our crossing of the Atlantic in the P. & O. Line's *Stratheden*, eating mighty Indian curries every day, talking to English people aboard, already beginning to think in pounds, shillings, and pence, we had wondered how it would be to come to the England that we knew so well in books and that I, at least, had known as a small child: would it be, essentially, a foreign country, or— well, not foreign? But by the time the ship was coasting along the white cliffs and then proceeding up the Thames, we had begun to think what we later found to be true: that coming to England was like coming home, coming to a home half-remembered—but home. . . .

We were welcomed to Oxford by one Lew Salter, whose kinswoman I had known in Virginia, and his pretty wife, Mary Ann. Lew, a brilliant theoretical physicist, was in my college, Jesus. He and Mary Ann were, also, we discovered later, keen Christians. Through them we met, almost at once, their English friends, Peter and Bee Campion—Bee, tall and swift, impatient of nonsense; Peter, just out of the Royal Navy, pipe-smoking, nice grin, bright blue eyes. Peter was a physicist, too, in Exeter College. At the same time, we met another friend of theirs, Thad Marsh of Worcester College, lanky, witty, intelligent, who was reading English. These were our first friends, close friends. More to the point, perhaps, all five were keen, deeply committed Christians. But we liked them so much that we forgave them for it. We began, hardly knowing we were doing it, to revise our opinions, not of Christianity but of Christians. Our fundamental assumption, which we had been pleased to regard as an intelligent insight, had been that all Christians were necessarily stuffy, hide-bound, or stupid—people to keep one's distance from. We had kept our distance so successfully, indeed, that we didn't know anything about Christians. Now that assumption soundlessly collapsed. The sheer quality of the Christians we met at Oxford shattered our stereotype, and thenceforward a reference in a book or conversation to someone's being a Christian called up an entirely new image. Moreover, the astonishing fact sank home: our own contemporaries could be at once highly intelligent, civilised, witty, fun to be with—and Christian.

If we had been asked at that time what we meant when we spoke of someone as a Christian, we should have said that we meant someone who called himself a Christian. If pressed, we should have added that he was someone who believed that Jesus was God or one with God, or, at least, said he believed that. But there are people who are so nice in their understanding of the word "Christian" that they don't use it at all. Who are we, they say, to pretend to know who is truly a Christian in God's eyes? This is, indeed, very true, very nice. But a word that cannot be used is not very useful. And we need—we *must* have—a word for believers; and we must, therefore, hold to the age-old, New-Testament use to designate a believer: someone who says he is a believer. Someone we believe when he says it. No doubt there are those well loved of God who are not Christians; no doubt there are false Christians in the churches; God can sort them out as He chooses. In the meantime, we must stick to the plain, definite, original meaning of the word: one who accepts the teachings of the Apostles, one who *believes*.

We, then, were not Christians. Our friends were. But we liked them anyhow.

We found digs in North Oxford and bought bicycles. The three-room flat on the Woodstock Road included a piano that Davy could play to me on. And that Lew Salter could play on: if he hadn't decided on physics, he could have been a concert pianist. He often played for us; and when he played, lost in his music, his sensitive face wore a look of pain that he was unaware of. They would drift in, any or all of the five of them. We would have tea and crumpets by the fire, and we would talk, always talk: talk about the University, talk about books, talk about our work—Peter and Lew explaining He-ions (and perhaps She-ions) in cloud chambers or Thad talking about Spenser. And talk about Christianity. We didn't mind *talking* about it: that's what Oxford is, a place to talk about everything. And there would be always music, since we had the piano. . . .

We explored Oxford's grey magic, Oxford "that sweet City with her dreaming spires." Oxford and all the country round, sometimes on our bikes, sometimes on foot. There was Marston Ferry—a penny trip across the river and a pub on the other side. And that other country pub, the Perch, with its pleasant garden in the minute village of Binsey, which was across Port Meadow and the humpbacked bridge. Beyond the village, hidden away down a long lane of venerable beeches—one of our earliest and most enchanting walks with a college friend, Edmund—was the ancient and tiny village church, St. Margaret's, with a wishing well beside it into which one cast a penny to make the wish come true. And of course that favourite place of all the university, the Trout, where one lunched and drank brown ale on the terrace and fed the Queen's swans; and then walked back to Oxford along the Isis, sometimes called the Thames by Londoners, watching the college eights flash by.

Coming back to Oxford, we were always, it seemed, greeted by the sound of bells: bells everywhere striking the hour or bells from some tower change-ringing, filling the air with a singing magic. We explored every cranny of this city of enchanting crannies and unexpected breathtaking views of towers and spires. We were conscious all the time of the strong intellectual life of a thousand years. Despite the modern laboratories, Oxford is still "breathing the last enchantments of the middle ages": this wall was part of a great abbey; the Benedictines built the long, lovely buildings that are part of one college quad; the narrow passage where we bought tea things has been called Friars Entry for centuries; the Colleges bear names like Christ Church and Mary Magdalen and Corpus Christi; and the bells with their lovely clamour have rung through the centuries.

Imperceptibly the ages of faith, when men really believed, when the soaring spires carried their eyes and thoughts up to God, became *real* to us, not something in a book. What was happening was that our mind's gaze, almost without our knowing it, was being directed towards the Christian faith that, at once, animated our living contemporary friends *and* had brought this university with its colleges and churches and chapels into being. It was not precisely that we were being called upon to accept that faith but that we were being called upon to acknowledge its existence as an ancient and living force. There was a terrible splendour in these churches with their glorious glowing glass and in the music of the plainsong and in the words of the liturgy. The splendour of course did not mean that the faith was true; but perhaps we felt vaguely that it *did* somehow hint at a validity.

Even as we talked and played with our friends and explored the city, I was discovering Jesus College, dining "on" hall two or three times a week, and making further friends in the Junior Common Room: Trevor and John and Alan, all reading "Greats" (or classics); Edmund Dews, tall and urbane, who had taken us on our first walk to Binsey; and John Dickey, who was reading law and concealed beneath an amiable, easy-going friendliness a mind like a razor. There were conversations with various dons about my work—the matter of choosing a subject for research—and a good deal of exploratory reading amidst the ancient grandeur of the Bodleian Library. Often as I, or Davy and I, pored over the books, there would be in the very background of awareness the persistent sound—almost monotonous and yet, after all, not monotonous, and cheerful, even gay—of change-ringing bells from one of the churches round about. Then, too, there were the college and university societies to look into, societies for every conceivable interest, serious and frivolous, including a yacht club through which we did a bit of sailing on the Isis. . . .

One afternoon, having strolled with a friend along the Isis, I was walking alone across Port Meadow into Oxford, hearing change-ringing bells in the distance. It may be that the bells led me to picture a church spire surmounted by a cross. Anyhow, into my mind came, as it had done every now and then through the years, . . . my resolve some day to have another look at the case for Christianity. Perhaps now was the time to do it? The idea seemed less revolting than at other times it had recurred. Of course Christianity couldn't possibly be *true*, a thought suggested. Still, another thought pointed out, there was that resolve; and one ought to be *fair*. As I made my way through the streets to Jesus to collect my bicycle, I happened to look up. There against the darkening grey sky was the tremendous soaring uprush of the spire of St. Mary the Virgin. My resolve came to the point: this *was* the time to do it. I swung about, nearly colliding with another Jesus man, and went into Blackwell's, the booksellers.

Somewhile later I arrived at the Woodstock flat with an armload of books on Christianity. Over tea I told Davy of my thoughts and the effect of that thirteenth-century spire of St. Mary's, quite possibly the loveliest spire in Christendom. Davy was pleased.

"I've been thinking that we ought to *know* more," she said. "Oh, good! I see you've got some C. S. Lewis. Thad and the others are always talking about him. Who is he, anyhow?"

"A don," I said. "He's a don in one of the colleges—Magdalen, it says on this book. Not theology, though. English lit. Very brilliant, I think. I read part of a debate he was having with some philosopher. I think I'll read this one first—*Miracles*."

"Okay," said Davy. "I'll read *Screwtape Letters*. Then we can trade. Mary Ann and Lew, everyone in fact, will be pleased, won't they?"

"They certainly will," I said. "But listen, Davy. We're just having a look, you know. Let's keep our heads. There are enormous arguments against Christianity."

"Oh, I know!" she said. "I don't see how it could be true. But—well, how would you feel if we decided that it *was* true?"

"Um," I said. "I'm not sure. One would know the meaning of things. That would be good. But we'd have to go to church and all that. And, well, pray. Still, it would be great to know meanings and, you know, the purpose of everything. But, dammit! it *couldn't* be true! How could Earth's religion— *one* of Earth's religions—be true for the whole galaxy—millions of planets, maybe? That's what rules it out right in the beginning. It's—it's too little!"

"I know," said Davy. "Look—these three are a sort of science-fiction trilogy: *Out of the Silent Planet, Perelandra,* and *That Hideous Strength.* Did you know that?"

"Good lord!" I said. "No. I'll read those first—unless you want to?"

"No," she said. "I want to read *Screwtape.* Thad says it's funny."

And that's how it all began. The encounter with Light. Only of course it *didn't* begin then. It began when we came to Oxford. Or it began with shadows of masts and trees. Or it began with our abandoning our childhood religion: To believe with certainty, somebody said, one has to begin by doubting. Wherever it began, what it *was* was a coming-together of disparate things—our love for each other and for beauty, our longing for unpressured time and the night of the cold sea-fire on *Grey Goose,* the quality of our Christian friends and the Oxford built by hands and the Oxford that I saw in the face of the Warden of All Souls. They came together into one, into focus, and the Light fell upon them.

There were half a hundred books that first autumn and winter in Oxford. We became interested, absorbed, in the study of Christianity right from the start—though, still, it was only a *study.* It was fortunate that I chose to read that C. S. Lewis science-fiction triology first, for, apart from being beautiful and enthralling, it made me conscious of an alliance with him: what he hated *(That Hideous Strength)* I hated and feared. Much more important, perhaps, the triology showed me that the Christian God might, after all, be quite big enough for the whole galaxy. Nothing was proved except that, quite reasonably, He might be big enough; but, in fact, an insuperable difficulty—that of Christianity's being only a *local* religion—was overcome. Apart from Lewis, we read G. K. Chesterton, who with wit presented in *The Everlasting Man* and other works a brilliant, reasoned case for the faith. And Charles Williams, theologian and novelist, who opened up realms of the spirit we didn't know existed, was tremendously important to us both. Graham Greene showed—terribly—what sin was, and what faith was—also terrible. Dorothy Sayers made Christianity dramatic and exciting, and attacked complacency and dullness like a scorpion. We had read T. S. Eliot for years, but now we began to see what he was really saying in *Ash-Wednesday* and the *Four Quartets*—and it scared us, rather. His description of the state of being a Christian lingered in our minds: "A condition of complete simplicity/(Costing not less than everything)." Everything! There were many other books, including Christian classics like St. Augustine, *The Imitations of Christ,* and the *Apologia Pro Vita Sua.* And we read the New Testament, of course, in numerous translations along with commentaries. But there is no doubt that C. S. Lewis was, first to last, overwhelmingly the most important reading for us both. Only someone who has faced the questions—is Christianity false? —can help someone else resolve the counter-question—is it true? We read everything he ever wrote, including *Great Divorce, Miracles, Problem of Pain,*

Pilgrim's Regress (which I found very meaningful), and much more, including his scholarly works, such as *The Allegory of Love*. The man's learning was immense, in English literature, in the classics, and, despite his disclaimers, in theology. His was perhaps the most brilliant and certainly the most lucid mind we ever knew: he wrote about Christianity in a style as clear as spring water without a hint of sanctimoniousness or vagueness or double-talk, never suggesting that anything be accepted on other than reasonable grounds. He gave us, simply, straightforward, telling argument laced with wit. And that incredible imagination.

As we read, we talked to our Christian friends, raising our questions and doubts. They answered us very patiently and thoughtfully. By now there were other Christian friends besides the original five, particularly a little Welshman in my college named Geraint Gruffydd, a poet and a reader of poetry. An important insight struck us—Davy and me—one day when we realised that our friends, though Anglican, Baptist, Roman Catholic, and Lutheran, were united by far more—mere Christianity, as Lewis would put it—than divided them. "And they're all so—so happy in their Christianity," said Davy. And I said, "Could it be—that happiness—what's called 'Christian joy,' do you think?" That night I wrote in our Journal:

> *The best argument for Christianity is Christians: their joy, their certainty, their completeness. But the strongest argument against Christianity is also Christians —when they are sombre and joyless, when they are self-righteous and smug in complacent consecration, when they are narrow and repressive, then Christianity dies a thousand deaths. But, though it is just to condemn some Christians for these things, perhaps, after all, it is not just, though very easy, to condemn Christianity itself for them. Indeed, there are impressive indications that the positive quality of joy is in Christianity—and possibly nowhere else. If that were certain, it would be proof of a very high order.*

If minds like St. Augustine's and Newman's and Lewis's could wrestle with Christianity and become fortresses of that faith, it had to be taken seriously. I writhed a bit at the thought of my easy know-nothing contempt of other years. Most of the people who reject Christianity know almost nothing of what they are rejecting: those who condemn what they do not understand are, surely, *little* men. Thank God, if there is a God, we said, that we are at least looking seriously and honestly at this thing. If our Christian friends—nuclear physicists, historians, and able scholars in other fields—can believe in Christ, if C. S. Lewis can believe in Christ, we must, at least, weigh it very seriously. . . .

And by now we knew that it was important. If true—and we admitted to each other the possibility that it was—it was, very simply, the only really important truth in the world. And if untrue, it was *false*. No halfway house. First or nothing. I wrote:

> *It is not possible to be "incidentally a Christian." The fact of Christianity must be overwhelmingly first or nothing. This suggests a reason for the dislike of Christians by nominal or non-Christians: their lives contain no overwhelming firsts but many balances.*

One December night, after Davy and I had been talking about the fact that Christianity claimed to be an *answer* to all the eternal questions—a *consistent* answer, our physicist friends kept murmuring—we admitted to each other that we did, quite desperately, want an answer. The only trouble, I added, was that we couldn't believe the Christian one. Then I suggested that we go out for a walk, but she said she was a bit headachey and wanted to go to bed. I told her to go on, then, and I should just walk up to the corner and back. While I was walking I thought what I should like to ask C. S. Lewis if only he were here. When I returned to the flat, I sat down, on an impulse, and wrote to Lewis, a busy man whom I had never so much as seen. He replied, straight to the point, immediately; and I wrote again.

The correspondence, two letters apiece, now follows with only the salutations and closings omitted:

To C. S. Lewis (I)

I write on an impulse—which in the morning may appear so immodest and presumptuous that I shall destroy this. But a few moments ago I felt that I was embarked for a voyage that would someday lead me to God. Even now, five minutes later, I'm inclined to add a qualifying "maybe." There is a leap I cannot make; it occurs to me that you, having made it, having linked certainty with Christianity, might, not do it for me, but give me a hint of how it's to be done. Having felt the aesthetic and historical appeal of Christianity, having begun to study it, I have come to awareness of the strength and "possibleness" of the Christian answer. I should like to believe it. I want to know God—if He is knowable. But I cannot pray with any conviction that Someone hears. I can't believe.

Very simply, it seems to me that some intelligent power made this universe and that all men must know it, axiomatically, and must feel awe at the power's infiniteness. It seems to me natural that men, knowing and feeling so, should attempt to elaborate on that simplicity—the prophets, the Prince Buddha, the Lord Jesus, Mohammed, the Brahmins—and so arose the world's religions. But how can just one of them be singled out as true? To an intelligent visitor from Mars, would not Christianity appear to be merely one of a host of religions?

I said at starting that I felt I was treading a long road that would one day lead me to Christianity; I must, then, believe after a fashion that it is the truth. Or is it only that I want to believe it? But at the same time, something else in me says: "Wanting to believe is the way to self-deception. Honesty is better than any easy comfort. Have the courage to face the fact that all men may be nothing to the Power that made the suns."

And yet I would like to believe that the Lord Jesus is in truth my merciful God. For the apostles who could talk to Jesus, it must have been easy. But I live in a "real world" of red buses and nylon stockings and atomic bombs; I have only the record of others' claimed experiences with deity. No angels, no voices, nothing. Or, yes, one thing: living Christians. Somehow you, in this very same world, with the same data as I, are more meaningful to me than the bishops of the faithful past. You accomplished the leap from agnosticism to faith: how? I don't quite know how I dare write this to you, a busy Oxford don, not a priest. Yet I do know: you serve God, not yourself; you must do, if you're a Christian. Perhaps, if I had the wit to see it, my answer lies in the fact that I did write.

From C. S. Lewis (I)

My own position at the threshold of Xtianity was exactly the opposite of yours. You wish it were true; I strongly hoped it was not. At least, that was my conscious wish: you may suspect that I had unconscious wishes of quite a different sort and that it was these which finally shoved me in. True: but then I may equally suspect that under your conscious wish that it were true, there lurks a strong unconscious wish that it were not. What this works out to is that all that modern stuff about concealed wishes and wishful thinking, however useful it may be for explaining the origin of an error which you already know to be an error, is perfectly useless in deciding which of two beliefs is the error and which is the truth. For (a.) One never knows all one's wishes, and (b.) In very big questions, such as this, even one's conscious wishes are nearly always engaged on both sides. What I think one can say with certainty is this: the notion that everyone would like Xtianity to be true, and that therefore all atheists are brave men who have accepted the defeat of all their deepest desires, is simply impudent nonsense. Do you think people like Stalin, Hitler, Haldane, Stapledon (a corking good writer, by the way) wd. be pleased on waking up one morning to find that they were not their own masters, that they had a Master and a Judge, that there was nothing even in the deepest recesses of their thoughts about which they cd. say to Him "Keep out! Private. This is my business?" Do you? Rats! Their first reaction wd. be (as mine was) rage and terror. And I v. much doubt whether even you wd. find it simply pleasant. Isn't the truth this: that it wd. gratify some of our desires (ones we feel in fact pretty seldom) and outrage a great many others? So let's wash out all the wish business. It never helped anyone to solve any problem yet.

I don't agree with your picture of the history of religion—Christ, Buddha,

Mohammed and others elaborating an original simplicity. I believe Buddhism to be a simplification of Hinduism and Islam to be a simplification of Xtianity. Clear, lucid, transparent, simple religion (Tao plus a shadowy, ethical god in the background) is a late development, usually arising among highly educated people in great cities. What you really start with is ritual, myth, and mystery, the death & return of Balder or Osiris, the dances, the initiations, the sacrifices, the divine kings. Over against that are the Philosophers, Aristotle or Confucious, hardly religious at all. The only two systems in which the mysteries and the philosophies come together are Hinduism & Xtianity: there you get both Metaphysics and Cult (continuous with the primeval cults). That is why my first step was to be sure that one or other of these had the answer. For the reality can't be one that appeals either *only to savages* or *only to high brows. Real things aren't like that (e.g.* matter *is the first most obvious thing you meet— milk, chocolates, apples, and also the object of quantum physics). There is no question of just a crowd of disconnected religions. The choice is between (a.) The materialist world picture: wh.* I *can't believe. (b.) The real archaic primitive religions: wh. are not moral enough. (c.) The (claimed) fulfilment of these in Hinduism. (d.) The claimed fulfilment of these in Xtianity. But the weakness of Hinduism is that it* doesn't *really join the two strands. Unredeemably savage religion goes on in the village; the Hermit philosophies in the forest: and neither really interferes with the other. It is only Xtianity wh. compels a high brow like me to partake in a ritual blood feast, and also compels a central African convert to attempt an enlightened universal code of ethics.*

Have you tried Chesterton's The Everlasting Man? *the best popular apologetic I know.*

Meanwhile, the attempt to practice the Tao *is certainly the right line. Have you read the* Analects *of Confucius? He ends up by saying "This is the Tao. I do not know if any one has ever kept it." That's significant: one can really go direct from there to the* Epistle to the Romans.

I don't know if any of this is the least use. Be sure to write again, or call, if you think I can be of any help.

To C. S. Lewis (II)

My fundamental dilemma is this: I can't believe in Christ unless I have faith, but I can't have faith unless I believe in Christ. This is "the leap." If to be a Christian *is to have faith (and clearly it is), I can put it thus: I must accept Christ to become a Christian, but I must* be *a Christian to accept Him. I don't have faith and I don't as yet believe; but everyone seems to say: "You must have faith to believe." Where do I get it? Or will you tell me something different? Is there a proof? Can Reason carry one over the gulf . . . without faith?*

Why does God expect so much of us? Why does He require this effort to believe? If He made it clear that He is—as clear as a sunrise or a rock or a baby's cry—wouldn't we be right joyous to choose Him and His Law? Why should the right exercise of our free will contain this fear of intellectual dishonesty?

I must write further on the subject of "wishing it were true"—although I do agree that I probably have wishes on both sides, and my wish does not help to solve any problem. Your point that Hitler and Stalin (and I) would be horrified at discovering a Master from whom nothing *could be withheld is very strong. Indeed, there is nothing in Christianity which is so repugnant to me as humility—the bent knee. If I knew beyond hope or despair that Christianity were true, my fight for ever after would have to be against the pride of "the spine may break but it never bends." And yet, Sir, would not I (and even Stalin) accept the humbling of the Master to escape the horror of ceasing to be, of* nothingness *at death? Moreover, the knowledge that Jesus was in truth Lord would* not *be merely pleasant news gratifying some of our rare desires. It would mean overwhelmingly: (a) that Materialism was Error as well as ugliness; (b) that the several beastly futures predicted by the Marxists, the Freudians, and the Sociologist manipulators would not be real (even if they came about); (c) that one's growth towards wisdom—soul-building—was not to be lost; and (d), above all, that the good and the beautiful would survive. And so I wish it were true and would accept any humbling, I think, for it to be true. The bad part of wishing it were true is that any impulse I feel towards belief is regarded with suspicion as stemming from the wish; the good part is that the wish leads on. And I shall go on; I must go on, as far as I can go.*

From C. S. Lewis (II)

The contradiction "we must have faith to believe and must believe to have faith" belongs to the same class as those by which the Elastic philosophers proved that motion was impossible. And there are many others. You can't swim unless you can support yourself in water & you can't support yourself in water unless you can swim. Or again, in an act of volition (e.g. getting up in the morning) is the very beginning of the act itself voluntary or involuntary? If voluntary then you must have willed it, ∴ you were willing already, ∴ it was not really the beginning. If involuntary, then the continuation of the act (being determined by the first moment) is involuntary too. But in spite of this we do swim, & we do get out of bed.

I do not think there is a demonstrative *proof (like Euclid) of Christianity, nor of the existence of matter, nor of the good will & honesty of my best & oldest friends. I think all three are (except perhaps the second) far more probable than the alternatives. The case for Xtianity in general is well given by Chesterton; and I tried to do something in my* Broadcast Talks. *As to why God doesn't make it demonstratively clear: are we sure that He is even interested in the kind* of Theism which wd. be a compelled logical assent to a conclusive argument? Are we interested in it in personal matters? I demand from my friend a trust in my good faith which is certain without demonstrative proof. It wouldn't be confidence at all if he waited for rigorous proof. Hang it all, the very fairy-tales embody the truth. Othello believed in Desdemona's innocence when it was proved: but that was too late. Lear believed in Cordelia's love when it was proved: but that was too late. "His praise is lost who stays till all commend." The magnanimity, the generosity wh. will trust on a reasonable probability, is required of us. But supposing one believed and was wrong after all? Why, then you wd. have paid the universe a compliment it doesn't deserve. Your error wd. even so be more interesting & important than the reality. And yet how cd. that be? How cd. an idiotic universe have produced creatures whose mere dreams are so much stronger, better, subtler than itself?

Note that life after death, which still seems to you the essential thing, was itself a late revelation. God trained the Hebrews for centuries to believe in Him without promising them an after-life, and, blessings on Him, he trained me in the same way for about a year. It is like the disguised prince in the fairy tale who wins the heroine's love before she knows he is anything more than a woodcutter. What wd. be a bribe if it came first had better come last.

It is quite clear from what you say that you have conscious wishes on both sides. And now, another point about wishes. A wish may lead to false beliefs, granted. But what does the existence of the wish suggest? At one time I was much impressed by Arnold's line "Nor does the being hungry prove that we have bread." But surely, tho' it doesn't prove that one particular man will get food, it does prove that there is such a thing as food! i.e. if we were a species that didn't normally eat, weren't designed to eat, wd. we feel hungry? You say the materialist universe is "ugly." I wonder how you discovered that! If you are really a product of a materialistic universe, how is it you don't feel at home there? Do fish complain of the sea for being wet? Or if they did, would that fact itself not strongly suggest that they had not always been, or wd. not always be, purely aquatic creatures? Notice how we are perpetually surprised at Time. ("How time flies! Fancy John being grown-up & married! I can hardly believe it!") In heaven's name, why? Unless, indeed, there is something in us which is not temporal.

Total Humility is not in the Tao because the Tao (as such) says nothing about the Object to which it wd. be the right response: just as there is no law about railways in the acts of Q. Elizabeth. But from the degree of respect wh. the Tao demands for ancestors, parents, elders, & teachers, it is quite clear what the Tao wd. prescribe towards an object such as God.

But I think you are already in the meshes of the net! The Holy Spirit is after you. I doubt if you'll get away!

Yours,
C. S. Lewis

These letters gave us much to think on, then and later. Seldom if ever have I encountered anybody who could say so much in so little. And the letters frightened us, or frightened me anyway—especially that shocking last paragraph. This was getting *serious*. Alarum bells sounded, but I couldn't decide where to run.

Intellectually, our positions here on the brink were the same. We had had that second look, and we had found—what had we found? Much more than we expected to find, certainly. Christianity now appeared intellectually stimulating and aesthetically exciting. The personality of Jesus emerged from the Gospels with astonishing consistency. Whenever they were written, they were written in the shadow of a personality so tremendous that Christians who may never have seen him knew him utterly: that strange mixture of unbearable sternness and heartbreaking tenderness. No longer did the Church appear only a disreputable congeries of quarrelling sects: now we saw the Church, splendid and terrible, sweeping down the centuries with anthems and shining crosses and steady-eyed saints. No longer was the Faith something for children: intelligent people held it strongly—and they walked to a secret singing that we could not hear. Or *did* we hear something: high and clear and unbearably sweet?

Christianity had come to seem to us *probable*. It all hinged on this Jesus. Was he, in fact, the Lord Messiah, the Holy One of Israel, the Christ? Was he, indeed, the incarnate God? Very God of very God? This was the heart of the matter. *Did* he rise from the dead? The Apostles, the Evangelists, Paul believed it with utter conviction. Could we believe on their belief? Believe in a miracle? The fact that we had never seen a miracle did not prove, or even imply, that there might not be miracles at the supreme occasion of history. There was absolutely no proof, no proof *possible*, that it didn't happen. No absolute proof that it did. It seemed to us probable. It had a sort of *feel* of truth. A ring of truth. But was that enough?

Emotionally, our positions were not the same. I was excited, enthralled even, by the intellectual challenge. I might not have admitted it, but I was coming to love the Jesus that emerged from the New Testament writings. I had impulses to fall on my knees and reach out to him. I suspected that all the yearnings for I knew not what that I had ever felt—when autumn leaves were burning in the twilight, when wild geese flew crying overhead, when I looked up at bare branches against the stars, when spring arrived on an April morning—were in truth yearnings for *him*. For God. I yearned towards him. But I didn't need him—not consciously.

But Davy's emotional position was not the same—there was need. What we talked about, mostly, were the intellectual things that can be put into words so much more easily than feelings, especially feelings that are not, perhaps, altogether known to oneself. But there were for Davy needs growing out of sin and pain. She had not forgotten of course that night when "all the world fell away"—the experience she painted in her "Sin Picture" with its prophetic shadow of the crucified Lord. Even then, intuitively, she had known what it all pointed to. That experience and the very different one of the evil man in the park—the frightful evil of the monstrous ego—had, I think, undermined her confidence in herself and even, perhaps, undermined her confidence in the beautiful "us-sufficiency" of our love. She didn't know it, nor did I, but the Shining Barrier was not *quite* invulnerable. Moreover, we were both a little worried about her health: nothing clearly wrong, but she didn't feel quite as chipper as she ought to have done. Finally, her mother was dying of cancer. Davy's sister, who was taking care of their mother, had practically commanded Davy to go on to England, partly because her not doing so would be a grief to her mother. But Davy was deeply aware of her mother's suffering. And then, two or three months after our arrival in England, her mother died. All of this I knew, sharing her feelings, but all at one remove. But for Davy, with a poignancy that could not be utterly shared, there was not only a shaken confidence but a vivid experiencing of sin, suffering, grief, and death.

Thus, though her mind, too, asked the intellectual questions—questions to which answers were flooding in through our books—Christianity was offering consolation and assurance and, even, absolution. It fell into her soul as the water of life. One evening, after a lively discussion of the faith with Lew and Mary Ann, I asked Davy if she felt that she was near to believing that Christ was God. She said, "Well, I think He might be." And I said that "thinking" he "might" be was not the same as believing. She put this exchange in the Journal; and then she wrote: "Underneath I kept wanting to say 'I do, I do believe in Jesus—Jesus the Son of God and divine.'" She added: "I owe this to C. S. Lewis who has impressed me deeply with the necessity of Jesus to any thinking about God."

She was on the brink, indeed—and then she leaped. Only two days later she wrote:

Today, crossing from one side of the room to the other, I lumped together all I am, all I fear, hate, love, hope; and, well, DID it. I committed my ways to God in Christ.

She was alone when she took that walk across the room, and she told me when I came in an hour later. I was neither shocked nor astonished. It was as though I had known she would do it. I felt a sort of gladness for her, and told her. I also felt a bit forlorn, and perhaps there was an unformulated thought, which would not have borne the light of day, that she shouldn't have done it without me. I did not think about the implications for our future that day. Did I sense that I should follow her?

A few nights later, after a rather gentle talk about Christianity, she went to bed, leaving me lying upon the sofa in front of the fire reading Lewis's *Miracles*. A half hour passed. I let the book fall and switched off the lamp. Gazing into the glowing coals, I wondered with a strange mixture of hope and fear whether Christ might be in very truth my God. Suddenly I became aware that Davy was praying beside me—she had stolen into the room in her nightgown and knelt down by the sofa. I looked at the quiet figure for a few moments. I had never seen her pray. Then she spoke.

"When I was in bed," she said very softly, "it seemed to me that God was telling me to come to you. I have prayed to God to fulfil your soul."

She paused a moment, and then she whispered: "Oh, my dearest—please believe!"

Moved almost to tears, I whispered back—a broken whisper, she wrote in the Journal—I whispered, "Oh, I do believe." I was shaken by the affirmation that swept over me. She wrote that in the firelight I looked "gentle and sweet like some medieval saint." And she wrote, "We held one another tightly."

"Hold to this moment," she murmured. "Hold to it when doubts come. This is the true—I know it is."

But I did not hold on to it. I wish I had, if only for her sake. But, indeed, it was love for her that made me say it, not belief in God. Or so I told myself next morning. Or perhaps it was the assent of the heart and not the mind. Anyhow, the joy we might have shared that Advent, going together, hand in hand, was—except for that one holy night—denied. And yet I did not forget that sudden sincerity of believing, the affirmation welling up. Maybe it wasn't just love for her.

Still, I was back in the camp of the non-believers. And now I began to resent *her* conversion. I did not, I thought, resent her being a Christian; I resented her acting like one. Going to church without me—practically unfaithfulness. Going with all the other Christians, leaving me alone. I even resented her little special goodnesses, even goodness to me. I suspected she was doing it for God. I wanted the old Davy back. I didn't want her to be where I couldn't—or wouldn't—go. I didn't like my new isolation. The fun of *our* looking into Christianity was gone. I felt sulky.

The Shining Barrier came into my mind, mostly as an awareness of danger ahead if we remained a house divided. I did not think of the Appeal to Love, for it was not relevant to the situation. I hadn't rejected Christianity; I merely hadn't decided yet. There was a tacit understanding that this period was a hiatus until I did decide. It did not occur to me that if she were now committed to Christ, her commitment to our love must be lesser, as indeed mine must be if I followed her. At all events, I shied away from thinking about the Shining Barrier. Until later.

Here, on the brink, I hung for two months and more. I continued to read and think. I knew of course that Davy was praying for me. All our Christian friends were praying for me. Perhaps their friends. Perhaps whole churches. I regarded this activity with suspicion. I felt they were all waiting for something to happen. They gave me pleasantly questioning looks when we met on the street.

I was also suspicious of my own upsurges of feeling about this Jesus. I warned myself about emotion. It seemed to me sometimes that *Jesus* was giving me friendly but questioning looks, and at other times, intolerably severe ones. At the same time, I recognised that there was a place for emotion as well as reason, and wrote in the Journal:

> *It would seem that Christianity requires both emotional and intellectual assent. If these is only emotion, the mind asks troubling questions that, if not answered, might lead to a falling away, for love cannot be sustained without understanding. On the other hand, there is a gap which must be bridged by emotion. If one is suspicious of the upsurge of feeling that may be incipient faith, how is one to cross the gap?*

Christianity—in a word, the divinity of Jesus—seemed probable to me. But there is a gap between the probable and proved. How was I to cross it? If I were to stake my whole life on the Risen Christ, I wanted proof. I wanted certainty. I wanted to see Him eat a bit of fish. I wanted letters of fire across the sky. I got none of these. And I continued to hang about on the edge of the gap.

Davy and I, sometimes with friends, sometimes alone, were reading Dorothy Sayers's tremendous series of short plays on the life of Jesus. In one of them, I was forcibly struck by the reply of a man to Jesus's inquiry about his faith: "Lord, I believe; help thou mine unbelief." Wasn't that just my position? Believing and not believing? A paradox, like that other paradox: one must have faith to believe but must believe in order to have faith. A paradox to unlock a paradox? I felt that it was.

One day later there came the second intellectual breakthrough: it was the rather chilling realisation that I *could not go back*. In my old easy-going theism, I had regarded Christianity as a sort of fairy tale; and I had neither accepted nor rejected Jesus, since I had never, in fact, encountered Him. Now I had. The position was not, as I had been comfortably thinking all these months, merely a question of whether I was to accept the Messiah or not. It was a question of whether I was to accept Him—or *reject* My God! There was a gap *behind me*, too. Perhaps the leap to acceptance was a horrifying gamble —but what of the leap to rejection? There might be no certainty that Christ was God—but, by God, there was no certainty that He was not. If I were to accept, I might and probably would face the thought through the years: "Perhaps, after all, it's a lie; I've been had!" But if I were to reject, I would certainly face the haunting, terrible thought: "Perhaps it's true—and I have *rejected my God!*"

This was not to be borne. I *could not* reject Jesus. There was only one thing to do, once I had seen the gap behind me. I turned away from it and flung myself over the gap *towards* Jesus.

Early on a damp English morning with spring in the air, I wrote in the Journal and to C. S. Lewis:

> *I choose to believe in the Father, Son, and Holy Ghost—in Christ, my lord and my God. Christianity has the ring, the* feel, *of unique truth. Of essential truth. By it, life is made full instead of empty, meaningful instead of meaning-less. Cosmos becomes beautiful at the* Centre, *instead of chillingly ugly beneath the lovely pathos of spring. But the emptiness, the meaninglessness, and the ugliness can only be seen, I think, when one has glimpsed the fullness, the meaning, and the beauty. It is when heaven and hell have* both *been glimpsed that going back is impossible. But to go on seemed impossible, also. A glimpse is not a vision. A choice was necessary: and there is no certainty. One can only choose a side. So I—I now choose my side: I choose beauty; I choose what I love. But choosing to believe is believing. It's all I can do: choose. I confess my doubts and ask my Lord Christ to enter my life. I do not* know *God is, I do but say: Be it unto me according to Thy will. I do not affirm that I am without doubt, I do but ask for help, having chosen, to overcome it. I do but say: Lord, I believe—help Thou mine unbelief.*

Davy sat beside me while I wrote, full of quiet joy. Of course I had told her first. Indeed, she had been in the room when the series of thoughts about the gap behind me had flashed through my mind. She had heard me mutter, "My God!" And then, as she looked up, I'd said, rather tensely, "Wait." A couple of minutes went by. Then I said: "Davy? . . . dearling . . . I have chosen—the Christ! I *choose* to believe." She looked at me with joy. Then she came over to me and knelt. I knelt, too, and committed my ways to my God. When we rose, we held each other a long moment. It is perhaps significant that we prayed first.

The sonnet I was to write about the choice was already taking shape in my mind:

The Gap

> *Did Jesus live? And did he really say*
> *The burning words that banish mortal fear?*

And are they true? Just this is central, here
The Church must stand or fall. It's Christ *we weigh.*

All else is off the point: the Flood, the Day
Of Eden, or the Virgin Birth—Have done!
The Question is, did God send us the Son
Incarnate crying Love! Love is the Way!

Between the probable and proved there yawns
A gap. Afraid to jump, we stand absurd,
Then see behind *us sink the ground and, worse,*
Our very standpoint crumbling. Desperate dawns
Our only hope: to leap into the Word
That opens up the shuttered universe.

Although born in England, where she grew up in Essex with a passion for things English, Denise Levertov always felt herself an outsider. As she wrote in an autobiographical essay in 1984, this sense of difference, signifying an artistic vocation she had since childhood, was nurtured in her rich family environment. Her father, of Hasidic ancestry, steeped in Jewish scholarship, became a convert to Christianity and an Anglican priest. Her Welsh mother taught her at home until she was twelve, and reading aloud was a regular part of life with her parents and older sister. It was in the U.S., however, where she lived from the late 1940s, that Levertov came into her own literarily. Indeed, before her death, she spoke of herself as an American poet. One critic described her work as "poetry of the immediate," while readers have especially responded to the love for nature expressed in her poems.

From an early age Levertov was immersed in what she called humanitarian politics, and many of her poetic subjects are political. Yet her art always transcends purely social themes. She spoke of poems coming into being through her

DENISE LEVERTOV

[1 9 2 3 – 1 9 9 7]

I know this happiness

is provisional.

deep involvement in all aspects of the life around her. In the following poems, the emphasis is on the poet as poet, her vocation and destiny, her discovery and re-creation of the order behind the seeming chaos of life. They also trace what Levertov called her slow movement from agnosticism to Christian faith.

[EP]

SELECTED POEMS

Illustrious Ancestors

The Rav
of Northern White Russia declined,
in his youth, to learn the
language of birds, because
the extraneous did not interest him; nevertheless
when he grew old it was found
he understood them anyway, having
listened well, and as it is said, 'prayed
            with the bench and the floor.' He used
what was at hand—as did
Angel Jones of Mold, whose meditations
were sewn into coats and britches.
            Well, I would like to make
thinking some line still taut between me and them,
poems direct as what the birds said,
hard as a floor, sound as a bench
mysterious as the silence when the tailor
would pause with his needle in the air.

Human Being

Human being—walking
in doubt from childhood on: walking

a ledge of slippery stone in the world's woods
deep-layered with wet leaves—rich or sad: on one
side of the path, ecstasy, on the other
dull grief.   *Walking*

the mind's imperial cities, roofed-over alleys,
                              thoroughfares, wide boulevards
that hold evening primrose of sky in steady calipers.

Always the mind
walking, working, stopping sometimes to kneel
in awe of beauty, sometimes leaping, filled with the energy
of delight, but never able to pass
the wall, the wall
of brick that crumbles and is replaced,
of twisted iron,
of rock,
the wall that speaks, saying monotonously:

    Children and animals
                        who cannot learn
    anything from suffering,
    suffer, are tortured, die
    in incomprehension.

This human being, each night nevertheless
summoning—with a breath blown at a flame,
                                    or hand's touch
on the lamp-switch—darkness,
            silently utters,
impelled as if by a need to cup the palms
and drink from a river,
            the words, 'Thanks.
Thanks for this day, a day of my life.'
                        And wonders.
Pulls up the blankets, looking
into nowhere, always in doubt.
And takes strange pleasure
in having repeated once more the childish formula,
a pleasure in what is seemly.
And drifts to sleep, downstream
on murmuring currents of doubt and praise,
the wall shadowy, that tomorrow
will cast its own familiar, chill, clear-cut shadow
into the day's brilliance.

Of Being

I know this happiness
is provisional:

   the looming presences—
   great suffering, great fear—

   withdraw only
   into peripheral vision:

but ineluctable this shimmering
of wind in the blue leaves:

this flood of stillness
widening the lake of sky:

this need to dance,
this need to kneel:
     this mystery:

Flickering Mind

Lord, not you,
it is I who am absent.
At first
belief was a joy I kept in secret,
stealing alone
into sacred places:
a quick glance, and away—and back,
circling.
I have long since uttered your name
but now
I elude your presence.
I stop
to think about you, and my mind
at once
like a minnow darts away,
darts
into the shadows, into gleams that fret
unceasing over
the river's purling and passing.
Not for one second
will my self hold still, but wanders

anywhere,
everywhere it can turn. Not you,
it is I am absent.
You are the stream, the fish, the light,
the pulsing shadow,
you the unchanging presence, in whom all
moves and changes.
How can I focus my flickering, perceive
at the fountain's heart
the sapphire I know is there?

Suspended

I had grasped God's garment in the void
but my hand slipped
on the rich silk of it.
The 'everlasting arms' my sister loved to remember
must have upheld my leaden weight
from falling, even so,
for though I claw at empty air and feel
nothing, no embrace,
I have not plummetted.

The Tide

Where is the Giver to whom my gratitude
rose? In this emptiness
there seems no Presence.

•

How confidently the desires
of God are spoken of!
Perhaps God wants
something quite different.
Or nothing, nothing at all.

•

Blue smoke from small
peaceable hearths ascending
without resistance in luminous
evening air.
Or eager mornings—waking
as if to a song's call.

Easily I can conjure
a myriad images
of faith.
Remote. They pass
as I turn a page.

                 •

        Outlying houses, and the train's rhythm
        slows, there's a signal box,
        people are taking their luggage
        down from the racks.
        Then you wake and discover
        you have not left
        to begin the journey.

                 •

Faith's a tide, it seems, ebbs and flows responsive
to action and inaction.
Remain in stasis, blown sand
stings your face, anemones
shrivel in rock pools no wave renews.
Clean the littered beach, clear
the lines of a forming poem,
the waters flood inward.
Dull stones again fulfill
their glowing destinies, and emptiness
is a cup, and holds
the ocean.

The Beginning of Wisdom
Proverbs 9.–10

You have brought me so far.
                 •
I know so much. Names, verbs, images. My mind
overflows, a drawer that can't close.

                 •

Unscathed among the tortured. Ignorant parchment
uninscribed, light strokes only, where a scribe
tried out a pen.

                 •

I am so small, a speck of dust
moving across the huge world. The world
a speck of dust in the universe.

                 •

Are you holding
the universe? You hold
onto my smallness. How do you grasp it,
how does it not
slip away?

•

I know so little.

•

You have brought me so far.

Primary Wonder

Days pass when I forget the mystery.
Problems insoluble and problems offering
their own ignored solutions
jostle for my attention, they crowd its antechamber
along with a host of diversions, my courtiers, wearing
their colored clothes; cap and bells.

And then

once more the quiet mystery
is present to me, the throng's clamor
recedes: the mystery
that there is anything, anything at all,
let alone cosmos, joy, memory, everything,
rather than void: and that, O Lord,
Creator, Hallowed One, You still,
hour by hour sustain it.

FLANNERY
O'CONNOR

[1 9 2 5 – 1 9 6 4]

The imagination of the prophet . . .

Flannery O'Connor's highly polished yet disturbing fiction, including her first novel, *Wise Blood* (1952), and her first collection of stories, *A Good Man Is Hard to Find* (1955), is peopled with characters out of joint with their time. They pursue highly individual redemptive visions that usually result in mayhem, for themselves and others.

The outsider status of Flannery O'Connor's fictional characters is reflected in her own position as a Catholic in the South. It was to her family home in Milledgeville, Georgia, that she returned in 1951 when she discovered she suffered from lupus, the disease that claimed her life in 1964, when she was thirty-nine. From this southern town, which was undergoing the wrenching changes of the civil rights era, she communicated with a wide variety of correspondents. As the following letters reveal, she is unflinchingly orthodox and remarkably clearheaded in her grasp of Catholic doctrine, though there is little of devotion or piety in her beliefs or practice. As in her fiction, she accepts the unfathomable workings of the human spirit, for both good and evil. [EP]

FROM HER LETTERS

TO CECIL DAWKINS

9 December 58

... Glibness is the great danger in answering people's questions about religion. I won't answer yours because you can answer them as well yourself but I will give you, for what it's worth, my own perspective on them. All your dissatisfaction with the Church seems to me to come from an incomplete understanding of sin. This will perhaps surprise you because you are very conscious of the sins of Catholics; however what you seem actually to demand is that the Church put the kingdom of heaven on earth right here now, that the Holy Ghost be translated at once into all flesh. The Holy Spirit very rarely shows Himself on the surface of anything. You are asking that man return at once to the state God created him in, you are leaving out the terrible radical human pride that causes death. Christ was crucified on earth and the Church is crucified in time, and the Church is crucified by all of us, by her members most particularly because she is a Church of sinners. Christ never said that the Church would be operated in a sinless or intelligent way, but that it would not teach error. This does not mean that each and every priest won't teach error but that the whole Church speaking through the Pope will not teach error in matters of faith. The Church is founded on Peter who denied Christ three times and couldn't walk on the water by himself. You are expecting his successors to walk on the water. All human nature vigorously resists grace because grace changes us and the change is painful. Priests resist it as well as others. To have the Church be what you want it to be would require the continuous miraculous meddling of God in human affairs, whereas it is our dignity that we are allowed more or less to get on with those graces that come through faith and the sacraments and which work through our human nature. God has chosen to operate in this manner. We can't understand this but we can't reject it without rejecting life.

Human nature is so faulty that it can resist any amount of grace and most of the time it does. The Church does well to hold her own; you are asking that she show a profit. When she shows a profit you have a saint, not necessarily a canonized one. I agree with you that you shouldn't have to go back centuries to find Catholic thought, and to be sure, you don't. But you are not going to find the highest principles of

Catholicism exemplified on the surface of life nor the highest Protestant principles either. It is easy for any child to pick out the faults in the sermon on his way home from Church every Sunday. It is impossible for him to find out the hidden love that makes a man, in spite of his intellectual limitations, his neuroticism, his own lack of strength, give up his life to the service of God's people, however bumblingly he may go about it . . .

It is what is invisible that God sees and that the Christian must look for. Because he knows the consequences of sin, he knows how deep in you have to go to find love. We have our own responsibility for not being "little ones" too long, for not being scandalized. By being scandalized too long, you will scandalize others and the guilt for that will belong to you. . . .

To expect too much is to have a sentimental view of life and this is a softness that ends in bitterness. Charity is hard and endures; I don't want to discourage you from reading St. Thomas but don't read him with the notion that he is going to clear anything up for you. That is done by study but more by prayer. What you want, you have to be not above asking for. But homiletics isn't in my line, particularly with a broken rib . . .

TO LOUISE ABBOT

[undated] Sat. 1959

I think there is no suffering greater than what is caused by the doubts of those who want to believe. I know what torment this is, but I can only see it, in myself anyway, as the process by which faith is deepened. A faith that just accepts is a child's faith and all right for children, but eventually you have to grow religiously as every other way, though some never do.

What people don't realize is how much religion costs. They think faith is a big electric blanket, when of course it is the cross. It is much harder to believe than not to believe. If you feel you can't believe, you must at least do this: keep an open mind. Keep it open toward faith, keep wanting it, keep asking for it, and leave the rest to God.

Penance rightly considered is not acts performed in order to attract God's attention or get credit for oneself. It is something natural that follows sorrow. If I were you, I'd forget about penance until I felt called to perform it. Don't anticipate too much. I have the feeling that you irritate your soul with a lot of things that it isn't time to irritate it with.

My reading of the priest's article on hell was that hell is what God's love becomes to those who reject it. Now no one has to reject it. God made us to love Him. It takes two to love. It takes liberty. It takes the right to reject. If there were no hell, we would be like the animals. No hell, no dignity. And remember the mercy of God. It is easy to put this down as a formula and hard to believe it, but try believing the opposite, and you will find it too easy. Life has no meaning that way ...

Whatever you do anyway, remember that these things are mysteries and that if they were such that we could understand them, they wouldn't be worth understanding. A God you understood would be less than yourself.

This letter is full of non-sequiturs (sp?). I don't set myself up to give spiritual advice but all I would like you to know is that I sympathize and I suffer this way myself. When we get our spiritual house in order, we'll be dead. This goes on. You arrive at enough certainty to be able to make your way, but it is making it in darkness. Don't expect faith to clear things up for you. It is trust, not certainty ...

Come to see us whenever you can. We are building two extra rooms and a bath onto the house—a back parlor. We will let you set in it. Cheers.

TO "A"

28 October 61

I don't know anything that could grieve us here like this news [that "A" was leaving the Church]. I know that what you do you do because you think it is right, and I don't think any the less of you outside the Church than in it, but what is painful is the realization that this means a narrowing of life for you and a lessening of the desire for life. Faith is a gift, but the will has a great deal to do with it. The loss of it is basically a failure of appetite, assisted by sterile intellect. Some people when they lose their faith in Christ, substitute a swollen faith in themselves. I think you are too honest for that, that you never had much faith in yourself in the first place and that now that you don't believe in Christ, you will believe even less in yourself; which in itself is regrettable. But let me tell you this: faith comes and goes. It rises and falls like the tides of an invisible ocean. If it is presumptuous to think that faith will stay with you forever, it is just as presumptuous to think that unbelief will. Leaving the Church is not the solution, but since you think it is, all I can suggest to you, as your one-time sponsor, is that if you find in yourself the least return of a desire for faith, to go back to the Church with a light heart and without the conscience-raking to which you are probably subject. Subtlety is the curse of man. It is not found in the deity.

TO ALFRED CORN

30 May 62

I think that this experience you are having of losing your faith, or as you think, of having lost it, is an experience that in the long run belongs to faith; or at least it can belong to faith if faith is still valuable to you, and it must be or you would not have written me about this.

I don't know how the kind of faith required of a Christian living in the 20th century can be at all if it is not grounded on this experience that you are having right now of unbelief. This may be the case always and not just in the 20th century. Peter said, "Lord, I believe. Help my unbelief." It is the most natural and most human and most agonizing prayer in the gospels, and I think it is the foundation prayer of faith.

As a freshman in college you are bombarded with new ideas, or rather pieces of ideas, new frames of reference, an activation of the intellectual life which is only beginning, but which is already running ahead of your lived experience. After a year of this, you think you cannot believe. You are just beginning to realize how difficult it is to have faith and the measure of a commitment to it, but you are too young to decide you don't have faith just because you feel you can't believe. About the only way we know whether we believe or not is by what we do, and I think from your letter that you will not take the path of least resistance in this matter and simply decide that you have lost your faith and that there is nothing you can do about it.

One result of the stimulation of your intellectual life that takes place in college is usually a shrinking of the imaginative life. This sounds like a paradox, but I have often found it to be true. Students get so bound up with difficulties such as reconciling the clashing of so many different faiths such as Buddhism, Mohammedanism, etc., that they cease to look for God in other ways. Bridges once wrote Gerard Manley Hopkins and asked him to tell him how he, Bridges, could believe. He must have expected from Hopkins a long philosophical answer. Hopkins wrote back, "Give alms." He was trying to say to Bridges that God is to be experienced in Charity (in the sense of love for the divine image in human beings). Don't get so entangled with intellectual difficulties that you fail to look for God in this way.

The intellectual difficulties have to be met, however, and you will be meeting them for the rest of your life. When you get a reasonable hold on one, another will come to take its place. At one time, the clash of the different world religions was a difficulty for me. Where you have absolute solutions, however, you have no need of faith. Faith is what you have in the absence of knowledge. The reason this clash doesn't bother me any longer is because I have got, over the years, a sense of the immense sweep of creation, of the evolutionary process in everything, of how incomprehensible God must necessarily be to be the God of heaven and earth. You can't fit the Almighty into your intellectual categories. I might suggest that you look into some of the works of Pierre Teilhard de Chardin (*The Phenomenon of Man* et al.). He was a paleontologist—helped to discover Peking man—and also a man of God. I don't suggest you go to him for answers but for different questions, for that stretching of the imagination that you need to make you a sceptic in the face of much that you are learning, much of which is new and shocking but which when boiled down becomes less so and takes its place in the general scheme of things. What kept me a sceptic in college was precisely my Christian faith. It always said: wait, don't bite on this, get a wider picture, continue to read.

If you want your faith, you have to work for it. It is a gift, but for very few is it a gift given without any demand for equal time devoted to its cultivation. For every book you read that is anti-Christian, make it your business to read one that presents the other side of the picture; if one isn't satisfactory read others. Don't think that you have to abandon reason to be a Christian. A book that might help you is *The Unity of Philosophical Experience* by Etienne Gilson. Another is Newman's *The Grammar of Assent*. To find out about faith, you have to go to the people who have it and you have to go to the most intelligent ones if you are going to stand up intellectually to agnostics and the general run of pagans that you are going to find in the majority of people around you. Much of the criticism of belief that you find today comes from people who are judging it from the standpoint of another and narrower discipline. The Biblical criticism of the 19th century, for instance, was the product of historical disciplines. It has been entirely revamped in the 20th century by applying broader criteria to it, and those people who lost their faith in the 19th century because of it, could better have hung on in blind trust.

Even in the life of a Christian, faith rises and falls like the tides of an invisible sea. It's there, even when he can't see it or feel it, if he wants it to be there. You realize, I think, that it is more valuable, more mysterious, altogether more immense than anything you can learn or decide upon in college. Learn what you can, but cultivate Christian scepticism. It will keep you free—not free to do anything you please, but free to be formed by something larger than your own intellect or the intellects of those around you.

I don't know if this is the kind of answer that can help you, but any time you care to write me, I can try to do better.